Lecture Notes in Computer Science 5682

Commenced Publication in 1973
Founding and Former Series Editors:
Gerhard Goos, Juris Hartmanis, and Jan van Leeuwen

Benyuan Li Azer Bestavros Ding-Zhu Du
Jie Wang (Eds.)

Wireless Algorithms, Systems, and Applications

4th International Conference, WASA 2009
Boston, MA, USA, August 16-18, 2009
Proceedings

Volume Editors

Benyuan Li
Jie Wang
University of Massachusetts at Lowell, Department of Computer Science
Lowell, MA 01854, USA
E-mail: {bliu, wang}@cs.uml.edu

Azer Bestavros
Boston University, Department of Computer Science
Boston, MA 02215, USA
E-mail: best@bu.edu

Ding-Zhu Du
University of Texas at Dallas, Department of Computer Science
Dallas, TX 75083, USA
E-mail: dzdu@utdallas.edu

Library of Congress Control Number: Applied for

CR Subject Classification (1998): C.2, D.2, C.4, F.1, F.2, H.4

LNCS Sublibrary: SL 1 – Theoretical Computer Science and General Issues

ISSN 0302-9743
ISBN-10 3-642-03416-0 Springer Berlin Heidelberg New York
ISBN-13 978-3-642-03416-9 Springer Berlin Heidelberg New York

springer.com

Printed in Germany

Typesetting: Camera-ready by author, data conversion by Scientific Publishing Services, Chennai, India
Printed on acid-free paper SPIN: 12728053 06/3180 5 4 3 2 1 0

Preface

Advances in wireless communication and computing technologies have proliferated ubiquitous infrastructure and ad hoc wireless networks, enabling a wide variety of applications ranging from environment monitoring to health care, from critical infrastructure protection to wireless security, to name just a few. The complexity and ramifications of the ever-growing number of mobile users and the variety of services intensify the interest in developing fundamental principles, novel algorithms, rigorous and repeatable design methodologies, and systematic evaluation frameworks for the next generation of wireless networks.

The annual International Conference on Wireless Algorithms, Systems, and Applications (WASA) provides a forum for researchers and practitioners worldwide to exchange ideas, share new findings, and discuss challenging issues for the current and next-generation wireless networks. Past WASA conferences were held in Xian (2006), Chicago (2007), and Dallas (2008).

WASA 2009, the 4th WASA conference, took place at the Hyatt Regency hotel in downtown Boston, MA, USA, during August 16-18, 2009. Each submission was reviewed by at least three Program Committee members, who in some cases were assisted by external referees. Following a rigorous review process, 35 papers were selected for presentations at the conference. The best paper awards were given to Donghua Deng and Qun Li for "Communication in Naturally Mobile Sensor Networks" and to Yanxiao Zhao, Min Song, Jun Wang, and Eun Park for "Throughput Measurement-Based Access Point Selection for Multi-rate Wireless LANs." Fifteen invited presentations are also included in this volume.

Recognizing the rapid development and practical importance of online social networks, WASA 2009 offered a special workshop on online "Social Networks, Applications, and Systems." The workshop consisted of seven papers selected by the Program Committee of the workshop, chaired by Guanling Chen and Wei Ding.

We thank the authors for submitting their papers to the conference. We thank the members of the Program Committee and external referees for their work within demanding time constraints. We thank the University of Massachusetts Lowell for providing administrative support, the National Science Foundation for providing a student travel grant, and the Local Organizing Committee for making all the Local Arrangements. Many people contributed to the success of WASA 2009, and although their names cannot be listed here because of space limitations, we owe them our gratitude.

August 2009

Benyuan Liu
Azer Bestavros
Ding-Zhu Du
Jie Wang

Organization

General Co-chairs

Ding-Zhu Du	University of Texas at Dallas, USA
Jie Wang	University of Massachusetts Lowell, USA

Program Committee Co-chairs

Azer Bestavros	Boston University, USA
Benyuan Liu	University of Massachusetts Lowell, USA

Steering Committee

Xiuzhen Susan Cheng	The George Washington University, USA
David Hung-Chang Du	University of Minnesota, USA
Ding-Zhu Du	University of Texas at Dallas, USA
Wei Li	Texas Southern University, USA
Eun K. Park	National Science Foundation, USA
Jie Wang	University of Massachusetts Lowell, USA
Jie Wu	Florida Atlantic University, USA
Wei Zhao	University of Macau, China
Ty Znati	National Science Foundation, USA

Publicity Chair

Jason O. Hallstrom	Clemson University, USA
Yan Huang	University of North Texas, USA

Workshop Chair

Guanling Chen	University of Massachusetts Lowell, USA

Local Arrangements Committee

Jie Wang (Chair), Cindy Chen, Guanling Chen, Sharon Quigley, Karen Volis
University of Massachusetts Lowell, USA

Program Committee

Stephano Basagni	Northeasten University, USA
Prithwish Basu	BBN Technologies, USA
Mihaela Cardei	Florida Atlantic University, USA
Damiano Carra	University of Verona, Italy
Surendar Chandra	University of Notre Dame, USA
Do Young Eun	North Carolina State University, USA
Victor Firoiu	BAE Systems, Alpha Tech, USA
Xinwen Fu	University of Massachusetts Lowell, USA
Hiroaki Fukuda	Keio University, Japan
Majid Ghaderi	University of Calgary, Canada
Mina Guirguis	Texas State University, USA
Sharad Jaiswal	Bell Labs Research, India
Zhen Jiang	West Chester University of Pennsylvania, USA
Shudong Jin	Case Western Reserve University, USA
Qun Li	College of William and Mary, USA
Yingshu Li	Georgia State University, USA
Wenjing Lou	Worcester Polytechnic Institute, USA
Liran Ma	Michigan Technology University, USA
Ibrahim Matta	Boston University, USA
Pietro Michiardi	Institut Eurecom, France
Dajia Qiao	Iowa State University, USA
Krishna M. Sivalingam	University of Maryland, Baltimore County, USA
Ashwin Sridharan	Sprint Labs, USA
David Starobinski	Boston University, USA
Jun Suzuki	University of Massachusetts Boston, USA
Shan Suthaharan	University of North Carolina at Greensboro, USA
Sudarshan Vasudevan	University of Massachusetts Amherst, USA
Pengjun Wan	Illinois Institute of Technology, USA
Bing Wang	University of Connecticut, USA
Jiangping Wang	City University of Hong Kong, China
Amy Yuexuan Wang	Tsinghua University, China
Yu Wang	University of North Carolina at Charlotte, USA
Cedric Westphal	DoCoMo Labs, USA
Kui Wu	University of Victoria, Canada
Hongyi Wu	University of Louisiana at Lafayette, USA
Alexander M. Wyglinski	Worcester Polytechnic Institute, USA
Guoliang Xing	Michigan State University, USA
Guoliang Xue	Arizona State University, USA
Wensheng Zhang	Iowa State University, USA
Michael Zink	University of Massachusetts Amherst, USA

Workshop Committee on Online Social Networks, Applications, and Systems

Aris Anagnostopoulos	Yahoo! Research, USA
Denise L. Anthony	Dartmouth College, USA
Farnoush Banaei-Kashani	University of Southern California, USA
Andrew Campbell	Dartmouth College, USA
Guanling Chen	University of Massachusetts Lowell, USA; Co-chair
Ping Chen	University of Houston, USA
Wei Ding	University of Massachusetts Boston, USA; Co-chair
Steve Gregory	University of Bristol, UK
Yan Huang	University of North Texas, USA
Akshay Java	Microsoft Live Labs, USA
Chengkai Li	University of Texas at Arlington, USA
Spiros Papadimitriou	IBM, USA
Apratim Purakayastha	IBM, USA
Elisabeth Sylvan	TERC, USA
Duc Tran	University of Massachusetts Boston, USA
Jin Soung Yoo	Indiana University - Purdue University Fort Wayne, USA
Lin Zhong	Rice University, USA

External Referees

Chunyu Ai
Konstantin Avrachenkov
Xian Chen
Haining Chen
Xiuzhen Cheng
Taiming Feng
Qijun Gu
Zheng Guo
Jun Huang
Haiyang Liu
Donggang Liu
Gang Lu
Soumendra Nanda
Giovanni Neglia
Rajesh Prasad
Hua Qin
Minho Shin
Min Song
Nalin Subramanian
Yun Wang
Chuang Wang
Jizhi Wang
Yanwei Wu
Yiwei Wu
Naixue Xiong
Yinying Yang
Xiaogang Yang
Honggang Zhang

Sponsor Institution

Department of Computer Science and Center for Network and Information Security, University of Massachusetts Lowell.

Table of Contents

Applications, Experimentation, Power Management

Coverage, Detection, and Topology Control

Routing, Querying, and Data Collection

Localization, Security, and Services

Scheduling and Resource Management

Online Social Networks, Applications, and Systems

Long-Term Animal Observation by Wireless Sensor Networks with Sound Recognition

Ning-Han Liu, Chen-An Wu, and Shu-Ju Hsieh

Department of Management Information Systems, National Pingtung University of Science & Technology, Taiwan, R.O.C.
gregliu@mail.npust.edu.tw

Abstract. Due to wireless sensor networks can transmit data wirelessly and can be disposed easily, they are used in the wild to monitor the change of environment. However, the lifetime of sensor is limited by the battery, especially when the monitored data type is audio, the lifetime is very short due to a huge amount of data transmission. By intuition, sensor mote analyzes the sensed data and decides not to deliver them to server that can reduce the expense of energy. Nevertheless, the ability of sensor mote is not powerful enough to work on complicated methods. Therefore, it is an urgent issue to design a method to keep analyzing speed and accuracy under the restricted memory and processor. This research proposed an embedded audio processing module in the sensor mote to extract and analyze audio features in advance. Then, through the estimation of likelihood of observed animal sound by the frequencies distribution, only the interesting audio data are sent back to server. The prototype of WSN system is built and examined in the wild to observe frogs. According to the results of experiments, the energy consumed by sensors through our method can be reduced effectively to prolong the observing time of animal detecting sensors.

Keywords: Wireless sensor networks, animal observation, energy consumption.

1 Introduction

In the rapid progress and maturation of wireless communication technology, small size and mobility have been the primary design criteria for electronic products. This has stimulated interest in Wireless Sensor Networks (WSN) [4] research and deployment. WSN are automated, self-configuring and wireless communication capable [1].The low cost of sensor hardware and the ability to self-configure when randomly deployed enables sensor nodes to be deployed in remote and dangerous places to collect and transmit data. For example, WSN have commonly been used to sense changes in the environment such as temperature changes. In addition, WSN can be easily deployed and has low maintenance and installation costs. However, WSN have a limited energy source, which imposes a challenge that needs to be addressed. The energy consumed by a sensor during transmission is thousands of times greater than that used in computation [9]. If a sensor transmits all sensed data back to the server, then its energy source will be depleted quickly.

B. Liu et al. (Eds.): WASA 2009, LNCS 5682, pp. 1–11, 2009.

At present, there is limited research work in the area of audio signal processing in WSN. The challenge in this area is that audio signal processing is resource intensive and requires a large amount of memory for performing computations accurately. This is difficult for resource-constrained sensor nodes [3]. For instance, if a simple processing technique is applied, although only a small amount of memory and system resources would be required, the result obtained would be less accurate.

Different families of living animals make different, unique sounds. The same is true for animals belonging to the same family but of a different species or genus. This research targets this unique characteristic of living animals. Specifically, we study the ten different frog species in Taiwan because: (1) there is little research done on studying animal sounds. Current research work focuses on sounds made by humans and; (2) there is a need to autonomously monitor the frog species that only appear at unconventional hours, i.e. during the wet season for mating or during nighttime.

In this research, the sound identification technique used is known as SMDF (Sum of Magnitude Difference Function) [6]. In this technique, the detected sounds are first processed at the sensor node to extract feature of the sound such as the fundamental frequency and compare against the frequencies distribution state. Then, the sensor determines whether to transmit the sound to the server for further analysis or removes it entirely. At the server, existing classification methods such as GMM (Gaussian Mixture Models) [8] are then used to determine the frog species that the sound has originated from. In essence, SMDF uses a simple frequencies distribution state comparison technique to correctly distinguish sounds, performing autonomous analysis and decision making to reduce sensor energy consumption and prolong sensor network lifetime. This in effect reduces the need for manual battery replacement.

This paper is organized as follows: Section 2 describes related work pertaining to WSN and audio processing techniques. Section 3 introduces our research and details the proposed technique. Section 4 describes our experiments and the results obtained. Lastly, section 5 discusses conclusions and future works.

2 Related Work

WSN [4] are network systems formed by a large number of sensors and mobile base stations. A sensor communicates wirelessly with its neighbors and base station [5][14]. The sensor collects information in the area it has been deployed and transmits the information to the base station, which subsequently transmits the processed information to a workstation or server.

The modus operandi of WSN is very similar to existing ad hoc networks. However, due to the large number of nodes typically deployed for WSN, the topology of a sensor network changes more easily due to sensor node failures. A sensor is also limited in its operational capabilities due to its limited energy resource and restricted by the fact that WSN do not support identification for shared IP addressing. As a result, current communication protocols for wireless networks and data processing techniques cannot be directly applied to WSN [10].

The main resource limitations of sensor hardware include communication capability, residual energy, computational capability and unstable sensing capability [14]. In order to prolong a sensor's lifetime when deployed in those areas and minimize the need for manual battery replacement, it is necessary to factor in energy consumption in a sensor's software design. Prolonging sensor lifetime has also been an important factor for sensor hardware design [14]. For example, the MICA sensor that operates on 2 AA batteries which provides it with 2000mAH of energy can operate for one year on idle mode but only lasts a week in the constant operation mode [3].

There has been a lot of research and advances in audio processing in the past decades and new applications have been developed. Currently, audio processing techniques include speech encoding, speech synthesis, speech recognition [11] and applications include language learning, noise filtering, voice matching, voice activated security systems [12], etc.

Sound produces a signal that varies with time and the changes in the profile of the sound can occur very rapidly. However, if the audio signal is observed at small time intervals, this change is less prominent and the signal is in fact very stable. Therefore, prior to audio processing, it is customary to divide an audio signal into small units known as audio frames to facilitate signal change detection [13]. The size of a frame normally would be sufficient to encompass several fundamental periods of the audio signal.

Typically, there are three methods for extracting frequency i.e. ACF (Autocorrelation Function), AMDF (Average Magnitude Difference Function) and SMDF [6]. The concepts behind these three methods are similar except for the fact that SMDF uses addition while ACF and AMDR involve multiplication and division respectively. These methods consume very little energy and hence, are suitable for use in low-level processors.

After feature extraction, the audio signal is further analyzed using a classification technique. Commonly used techniques include GMM [8], HMM (Hidden Markov Models) [7] and KNN (K-Nearest Neighbor) [2]. Compared to GMM, the calculation functions in HMM are more complicated and require more training data [8]. Therefore, GMM is more suitable for our work.

3 System Framework and Proposed Method

Consider a scenario where sensor nodes are deployed in an environment with some background noise, i.e. apart from sounds emitted by frogs, there is also low volume environmental sound from rain, wind, falling leaves etc. When a sensor detects a sound, the sensor first performs feature extraction of the sound and identify. Lastly, the difference in energy consumption between "Sensor receives sound and transmits to server" and "Sensor does not transmit to server after identification" is established.

As shown in Figure 1, before the WSN is set up, the Training Module is first created so that the sample to be identified is used as the feature to be extracted. In this research, this is the frequency calculated by SMDF, which is later passed to the Module Training to obtain the training model of the sound. The training model can then be used later as the basis for audio signal comparison.

After the sensor's analyses the audio signal through its identification modules, if the signal is identified to be a frog sound, the extracted features of the audio signal are passed to the server for further recognition. Otherwise, if the signal is not required by the system, it will be discarded and not transmitted to the server. This in effect reduces the number of data transmissions in-network and prolong network lifetime.

At the server, the identification modules can carry out more complex calculations with greater identification accuracy due to its faster processing speed and much higher memory capacity, relative to the sensor node. This research uses the GMM technique. After the frequency extracted by the sensor is received, it is compared with training data modules within the server.

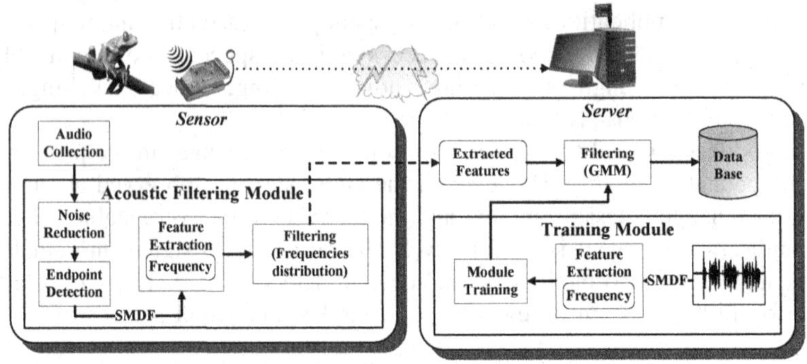

Fig. 1. Identification system framework

3.1 Feature Extraction from the Sound Profile

Before the audio signal feature is extracted, the whole audio segment is first divided into small units of audio frames, whereby neighboring audio frames are allowed to overlap.

Following this, in order to improve the continuity between two ends of the audio frame, the hamming window is applied on each audio frame. The calculation of the hamming window is shown in equation (1) where N is the frame length, W is the audio frame after the application of the hamming window and a is typically set as 0.46. The audio signal features are then extracted from these audio frames.

$$W(n,a) = (1-a) - a * \cos(\frac{2\pi n}{N-1}) \qquad 0 \le n \le N-1 \tag{1}$$

In our work, SMDF is used to detect fundamental frequency as its calculations do not consume a lot of resources. The calculation of the SMDF is shown in equation (2) where n is the distance by which the audio frame is right shifted, $x(p)$ is the amplitude of each point in the frame and M is the length of the frame.

$$D_m(n) = \sum_{p=0}^{M-1} |x_m(p) - x_m(p+n)| \qquad n = 0,1,2,3\,..... \tag{2}$$

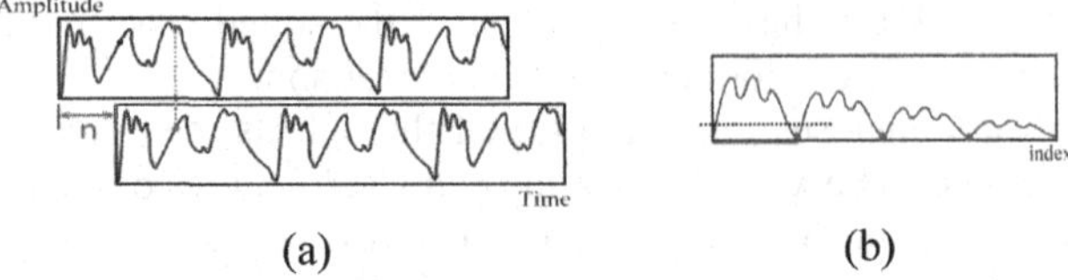

Fig. 2. SMDF calculation

As shown in Figure 2(a), the intention of using SMDF is to shift an audio frame right by n units and the overlapping segment with the original frame is mutually cancelled. After this, the absolute value is extracted, the combined sum is calculated and after repeating this process M times, the M inner product value is obtained. The final result obtained is shown in Figure 2(b). This figure shows the initial position as the minimum value of the SMDF with value zero. From this result, a threshold value can be set (dashed line) and the lowest point (dots) discovered to be lower than the threshold value but not be the zero starting point. Lastly, after the index values of these points are discovered, the smallest value is the frequency of the audio signal.

3.2 Training Module Set Up

In the sound recognition phase of the GMM, assume that every sound has its own model, its parameter set, also known as the basic density. The density of the Gaussian Mixture is the weighted sum of M basic density, calculated as equation (3):

$$p(x'|\lambda) = \sum_{i=1}^{M} w_i b_i(x') \quad (3)$$

Each λ involves three parameters: mean vector w_i, covariance matrix Σ_i and mixture weight u_i'. M is the integer value of the Gaussian distribution. In order to find the representative parameter combination for the sound features, the Maximum Likelihood is used in the calculation of the GMM. Let us assume that T trained feature parameter vectors are obtained after a trained audio sequence has undergone feature selection. The vector set is $X=\{x_1',x_2',....,x_T'\}$ and the GMM likelihood value is given in equation (4).

$$p(X|\lambda) = \prod_{t=1}^{T} p(x'_t|\lambda) \quad (4)$$

At the sensor's identification module, due to sensor computational limitation, this research statistically groups the frequency values obtained via SMDF and compares the difference in the group distribution for a simpler identification.

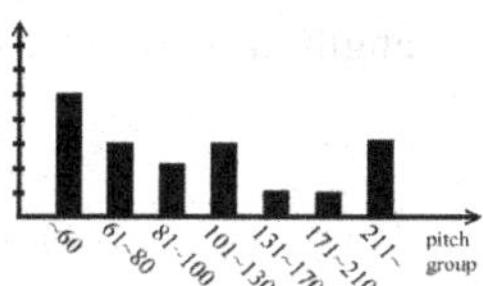

Fig. 3. Frequencies distribution chart

As a segment of detected sound is divided into dozens of frames, dozens of frequency values are obtained after SMDF calculations. If these dozens of frequency values were tabulated directly, it would be difficult to observe the differences between the sounds. Therefore, the frequency values first need to be grouped as shown in Figure 3. Our experimental trials maintain a group size lower than 10 for the purpose of minimizing the information processing load and at the same time, increasing the difference between frequencies groupings.

Under the same parameter setting, several samples of sound from a frog species are statistically analyzed to extract each group's count mean value. The frequency values distribution obtained is shown in Table 1. After the sound data has undergone feature extraction and module training, the parameter necessary for the identification array is obtained. This can be used as comparison to the frequency values array sensed by the sensor.

Table 1. Frequencies distribution of various animal sounds

Frequency / *sound*	*~60*	*61~80*	*81~100*	*101~130*	*131~170*	*171~210*	*211~*
Bull	7	6	5	4	0	2	1
Sheep	9	2	6	3	0	4	1
Dog	3	4	2	7	4	3	2
Horse	5	4	6	3	1	3	3
Chicken	7	5	2	1	6	0	4
Microhyla ornata	7	3	2	4	3	5	1
Buergeria japonica	5	4	5	3	5	2	1
Rana catesbeiana	8	3	4	0	5	3	2
Bufo melanostictus	6	7	3	4	2	2	1
Bufo bankorensis	7	5	3	4	0	3	3

3.3 Immediate Feature Extraction at the Sensor

After sound data has been collected at the sensor, the data needs to be normalized to avoid identification error due to volume differences with the sample. In normalization, sound volume is adjusted with respect to the primitive sound signal to allow the sample value to fall within the same range. The normalization function can be arbitrarily defined. This research uses equation (5) where $S(n)$ is the original audio sampling sequence, $S'(n)$ is the normalized sequence and S_{Max} is the highest value in $S(n)$.

$$S'(n) = \frac{S(n)}{S_{Max}} * 10 \tag{5}$$

In order to set the origin and destination point of the sound observed, it is first necessary to calculate the volume of each audio frame. In this research, basic functions are used in the calculation, i.e. at each audio frame, the sum of the absolute values are obtained, as shown in equation (6) where $x(k)$ is the amplitude of every point within the frame and L is the length of the frame.

$$E_m = \frac{1}{L}\sum_{k=0}^{L-1}|x_m(k)| \tag{6}$$

Therefore, when the audio frame's volume is greater than some threshold value and the volume persists for a period of time, we make the observation that there are animal sounds and hence, feature extraction can be performed on the current audio frame. When the origin and destination points of the sound data have been confirmed, features can then be extracted from the sound signal segment. The steps in this part are the same as the steps described in section 3.1.

3.4 Feature Comparison

When the sound data features have been extracted, the preliminary identification on the sensor is through the frequency comparison technique mentioned in section 3.2, i.e. when the frequencies distribution concentrates on certain groups or the group information is sparse, the possibility of a frog sound is high. At the start of the identification, the mean count value of frog sounds in each group is retrieved. Following this, the frequency values array computed through SMDF is compared with each frog species' frequency values array in Table 2 to determine the most probable frog species.

$$R_i = \begin{cases} 0, \; if \; |x_i - y_i| > 1 \\ 1, \quad otherwise \end{cases} \tag{7}$$

$$P = \sum_{i=1}^{N} R_i \tag{8}$$

x_i is the frequencies distribution number for unknown sounds, y_i is the frequencies distribution number for some frog species' sound. Equation (7) calculates the disparity between some category and other category of frog species while equation (8) then compares again to determine the categories with disparity less than 1 as being the probable frog species. However, if the number of categories with disparity less than 1 is less than 3, it is likely to be another sound. This is the basic identification carried out at the sensor node end.

After the frequency values are transmitted to the server, the sound model with the highest probability is derived from M GMMs. After the aforementioned feature extraction, a sequence of d dimensional test feature vectors $\{x_1, x_2, \ldots, x_t\}$ are obtained and the vectors are put into partial overlap segments according to the input unit length. Every segment is regarded as an independent test sentence and the unit length is T feature vectors, as illustrated below:

$$\overbrace{x_1, x_2, x_3, \ldots, x_T}^{Segment1}, x_{T+1}, x_{T+2}, \ldots, x_t$$

$$x_1, \overbrace{x_2, x_3, \ldots, x_T, x_{T+1}}^{Segment2}, x_{T+2}, \ldots, x_t$$

During identification, the system needs to consider all models to find the most likely sound model. In the mathematical sense, this identification process can be represented by the most likely model S', as shown in equation (9), where X is a segment.

$$S' = \arg \max_{1 \le k \le S} P(\lambda_k \mid X) \tag{9}$$

4 Experimental Results

4.1 Experimental Environment and Parameter Settings

This research uses sound with the following attributes: a sampling rate of 11025Hz, and single-channel wav profile. The experimental platform is a PC and the imote2 with battery pack developed by Crossbow Company (shown in Figure 4, imote2 with battery pack on the left and audio sensor board on the right). The sensor board is necessary because the imote2 has no audio sensing capability.

The experiment begins after a sensor collects sounds. Following this, feature extraction is performed on the sensor and the frequencies distribution is compared to determine if it is a frog sound. If it is a frog, the features are transmitted to the server to be further processed by the GMM. If the sensor identifies it as a non-frog sound, the sensor deletes the information. The experiments aim to study " the identification of frog sounds and other sounds", "the identification of various frog species' sounds " and compare energy consumption between "Sensor does not transmit to server after identification" (case 1) and "Sensor receives sound and transmits to server" (case 2).

Fig. 4. Imote2 by Crossbow Company with our sensor board

Prior to carrying out the experiment, we first determine the parameter settings for the identification experiments. Therefore, we first perform experiments targeting the parameters such as the audio frame length, audio frame overlap portion and SMDF frame shift degree. The results obtained show that an audio size of 256*ms*, overlap of 128*ms*, and SMDF shifting of 2 points can achieve the greatest contrast within the distribution. The obtained results are shown in Table 2. Other experimental settings include a threshold value of 80 for endpoint detection and that an observed sound would last for 0.3 seconds.

Table 2. Various frog sounds frequencies distribution table

frequency / *sound*	*~60*	*61~80*	*81~100*	*101~130*	*131~170*	*171~210*	*211~*
Microhyla ornata	7.1	3.7	2.9	4.8	3	5.8	1.2
Buergeria japonica	5.2	4	5.5	3.1	5.6	2.7	1
Rana catesbeiana	8.6	3.1	4.2	0.7	5.7	3	2.1
Bufo melanostictus	6.3	7.3	3.3	4.2	2.3	2.5	1.4
Bufo bankorensis	7.5	5.1	3.4	4	0.4	3.8	3
Hyla chinensis	6.8	8.2	2.6	1.8	2.1	3.3	2
Rana kuhlii	6.4	4.9	4.1	4.7	2.2	4.2	1.4
Rhacophorus taipeianus	8.1	7.1	3.5	1.2	1.9	4	1.3
Rana taipehensis	5.2	8.7	6.6	1.2	3	1.9	1.6
Micryletta steinegeri	4	6	5.2	2	4.1	2.9	2.8
Microhyla butleri	5.6	2.7	2	3.6	5.3	5.8	3.7
Rhacophorus aurantiventris	7.4	5.2	6.3	4.9	2	0.1	1
Rana limnocharis	7.1	3.9	6	3.7	1.4	2.1	3.6
Polypedates megacephalus	5.7	4.6	4.5	1.4	6.8	3	2
Rhacophorus prasinatus	6.1	4.3	6	2.1	3	3.4	1
Rana adenopleura	7.8	7.9	3.1	3.8	3.8	2.5	0.2
Chirixalus eiffingeri	4.2	3	6.8	5	1.6	3.2	3
Rhacophorus moltrechti	8.7	4.1	5.3	2.5	2.4	2	2.1
Rhacophorus arvalis	7.3	3.9	3.4	4.9	4	2.9	2
Rana psaltes	8	5.7	5	0.3	2.9	4	1.6

4.2 Audio Signal Identification Success Rate Experiments

The first part of our experiments targeted the identification of frog and non-frog sounds, as shown in Table 3. Our results show that a success rate of at least 70% is achieved during identification when 40 samples of frog sounds and 40 samples of non-frog sounds are used. Table 4 shows the results obtained from the second part of our experiments, which identifies sounds from various frog species. The accuracy is less than the first experiment at about 60%.

Table 3. Identification results for frog and non-frog species

Identified Sound	*Sample Size*	*Number correctly identified*	*Accuracy (%)*
Non frog	40	29	73
Frog	40	31	78

Table 4. Frog species identification results

Family	*Species*	*Sample Size*	*Number correctly identified*	*Accuracy (%)*
Bufonidae	Bufo melanostictus	12	7	58
	Bufo bankorensis	13	8	62
Hylidae	Hyla chinensis	13	7	54
Microhylidae	Microhyla butleri	13	8	62
	Micryletta steinegeri	14	7	50
	Microhyla ornata	13	7	54
Ranidae	Rana adenopleura	12	9	75
	Rana catesbeiana	13	7	54
	Rana kuhlii	13	8	62
	Rana limnocharis	13	9	69
	Rana psaltes	12	8	67
	Rana taipehensis	12	7	58
Rhacophoridae	Buergeria japonica	14	7	50
	Chirixalus eiffingeri	14	8	57
	Rhacophorus moltrechti	12	7	58
	Rhacophorus arvalis	14	6	43
	Polypedates megacephalus	13	7	54
	Rhacophorus prasinatus	12	7	58
	Rhacophorus urantiventris	12	6	50
	Rhacophorus taipeianus	13	8	62

4.3 Power Consumption Modeling Experiments

Lastly, we evaluate the relationship between a sensor's preliminary identification and the resultant energy consumed. The experimental setup is: the sensor performs sound detection for 2 hours. 50 sounds are received, 30 of which are frog sounds, and 3 brand new alkaline batteries are used. After 2 hours, the remaining voltage is measured. The results obtained are shown in Table 5. Evidently, a significant amount of energy is conserved when a sensor adopts the technique to first process the sound rather than to transmit all sounds to the server for processing. In other words, sensor lifetime is prolonged when identification is first performed at the sensor.

Table 5. Sensor's energy consumption comparison

	Number of received sounds	*Number of frog sounds*	*Remaining Energy*
Sensor with identification ability	50	30	88%
Sensor without identification ability	50	30	76%

5 Conclusions

In the past, animal habitats have been studied from historical records. However, due to the influence of modern-day humans on the environment, animals have moved to other locations for survival. This makes it inconvenient for biologists to study these animals. This research targets the unique sounds made by animals, combining audio signal processing research with WSN. Through the system we developed, biologists can monitor the presence of animals. The autonomous sound identification module on the sensor also reduces the energy consumed through directly transmissions to the server. Furthermore, it eliminates the labor-intensive task of manual identification and thus, improves the efficiency of biologists in conducting the research.

Due to the limited processing power of sensor nodes, this research uses a simple frequency extraction technique, SMDF, for feature extraction on the sensor device for identification. This is followed by a simple statistical method for classification. Although the success rate for frog and non-frog identification is moderate, the identification of various frog sounds can be improved. In the future, with progress in sensor processing capability, more intricate comparison would be possible on the sensor and it would be possible to increase the identification accuracy.

Acknowledgement

This work was supported by the NSC under contract numbers NSC97-2218-E-020-002 and NSC96-2218-E-020-004.

References

1. Akyildiz, I.F., Su, W., Sankarasubramaniam, Y., Cayirci, E.: A Survey on Sensor Networks. IEEE Communications Magazine 40(8), 102–114 (2002)
2. Gazor, S., Zhang, W.: Speech probability distribution. IEEE Signal Processing Letters 10(7), 204–207 (2003)
3. Hill, J., Culler, D.: A wireless embedded sensor architecture for system-level optimization. In: UC Berkeley Technical Report (2002)
4. Mainwaring, A., Polastre, J., Szewczyk, R., Culler, D., Anderson, J.: Wireless Sensor Networks for Habitat Monitoring. In: Proceedings of the 1st ACM International Workshop on Wireless Sensor Networks and Applications (2002)
5. Pottie, G.J.: Wireless sensor networks. In: IEEE Information Theory Workshop, pp. 139–140 (1998)
6. Quatieri, T.F.: Disctete-Time Speech Signal Processing. Prentice Hall, Inc., Englewood Cliffs (2002)
7. Rabiner, L.R.: A Tutorial on Hidden Markov Models and Selected Applications in Speech Recognition. IEEE Transactions on ASSP 77(2), 257–286 (1989)
8. Reynolds, D.A., Quatieri, T.F., Dunn, R.B.: Speaker Verification Using Adapted Gaussian Mixture Models. Digital Signal Processing 10, 19–41 (2000)
9. Tilak, S., Abu-Ghazaleh, N.B., Heinzelman, W.: A taxonomy of wireless micro-sensor network models. ACM SIGMOBILE Mobile Computing and Communications Review 6(2), 28–36 (2002)
10. Wang, A., Chandrakasan, A.: Energy-Efficient DSPs for Wireless Sensor Networks. IEEE Signal Processing Magazine 19(4), 68–78 (2002)
11. Wu, B.F., Wang, K.C.: A Robust Endpoint Detection Algorithm Based on the Adaptive Band-Partitioning Spectral Entropy in Adverse Environments. IEEE Transactions on Speech and Audio Processing 13(5), 762–775 (2005)

12. Wu, C.H., Chen, J.H.: Speech activated telephony email reader (SATER) based on speaker verification and text-to-speech conversion. IEEE Transactions On Consumer Electronics 43(3), 707–716 (1997)
13. Xing, B., et al.: Short-time Gaussianization for robust speaker verification. In: Proceedings of ICASSP, vol. 1, pp. 681–684 (2002)
14. Yao, Y., Gehrke, J.: Query processing for sensor networks. In: Proceedings of the CIDR, pp. 233–244 (2003)

Experimental Study on Mobile RFID Performance

Zhong Ren[1], Chiu C. Tan[2,*], Dong Wang[1], and Qun Li[2]

[1] Shanghai Jiao Tong University, China
renzhong@sjtu.edu.cn, wangdong@cs.sjtu.edu.cn
[2] College of William and Mary, Williamsburg, VA, USA
cct@cs.wm.edu, liqun@cs.wm.edu

Abstract. An increasing number of applications use RFID in their design, but there is a lack of understanding of how mobility affects RFID performance in these applications. Unlike static RFID experiments, mobile RFID studies require more expensive equipment that are unavailable to most researchers. In this paper, we conduct machine-aided experiments to study the effects of mobility on RFID. Our results show that up to 50 RFID tags moving at speeds up to 2 m/s can be reliably read.

Keywords: RFID, mobility, experimental study.

1 Introduction

The prevalent application of RFID lies in industrial applications such as logistics and supply chain management. However, there has been considerable recent interest in applying RFID technology to non-industrial areas such as medical applications [2] and physical world object location [8,12]. Many of these ubiquitous computing applications differ from traditional industrial applications in their *unpredictability*, having to contend with objects moving at different speeds and times, take unpredictable paths, and contain different number of tags per item. These unpredictable factors make designing such systems difficult.

Given the expanding role of RFID technology into new areas, a deeper understanding of the capabilities of RFID equipment is crucial in designing new RFID systems. While there has been prior research on RFID performance in static environments, where both the reader and tag are stationary, there are relatively few academic research on the effects of mobility on RFID performance. One reason is that experiments on mobility are difficult to conduct. Meaningful experiments require performing the same experiment multiple times at the same speed and conditions as far as possible. This rules out human based testing where a person with some RFID tags tries to walk pass an antenna at approximately the same speed over and over again.

In this paper, we conduct experiments using commercial RFID readers and EPC Class-1 Generation-2 RFID tags, together with machine-aided testing, to

* The first two authors are equal contributors of this paper.

B. Liu et al. (Eds.): WASA 2009, LNCS 5682, pp. 12–21, 2009.

examine the effects of mobility on RFID tags. As noted in [10] which used a robotic arm to perform extensive experiments on static tags, mechanical testing allows for tests that are otherwise impractical to conduct. Through this experimental study, we would like to show how a reader's reading behavior is like in a realistic mobile setting. We hope that this study could give researchers without access to the experimental equipment first hand experience and empirical understanding about the reading performance for mobile scenario.

Our main contributions in this paper are two fold. First, we conduct practical experiments to study the effects of mobility and RFID performance. As far as we know, most such experiments have been conducted by commercial vendors and the results are not widely available. Second, we plan to make publicly available all experimental data. This data will be useful for researchers interested in performing simulations for their own RFID projects. The rest of the paper is as follows. Section 2 reviews the related work. Section 3 explains our experimental setup, and Section 4 presents the results. Additional discussion of the findings are found in Section 5, and Section 6 concludes.

2 Related Work

Some earlier research efforts have focused on the RFID MAC layer. Work by [6] studied better techniques of selecting frame sizes to improve RFID reading performance, while [11] showed the effects of errors on reading performance. Other theoretical studies have looked at power modeling [9] for RFID systems.

Closer to our paper are real world RFID experimental studies. Fletcher et al. [5] examined the effects of different materials on RFID performance. Other work by [13,1] established performance benchmarks and performed speed and reliability experiments for static RFID tags. More recent work by [3] performed deeper analysis by utilizing specialized equipment to obtain physical layer RFID metrics such as error rates. Specific experimental studies on RFID and ubiquitous computing applications were done by [10,7]. In particular, [10] also used specialized equipment to perform extensive experiments that are difficult to perform. The main difference of our paper is that we focus extensively on *high speed, mobile* RFID experiments, while prior work focused mostly *static* experiments. The paper by [13] performed a limited experiment on a conveyor belt, but was limited to only 2 RFID tags. Extensive experiments utilizing a fast conveyor belt were performed by [14], but the experiments were limited to determine the best antenna placement position.

3 Experimental Setup

3.1 Hardware Used

All our experiments use the Alien-9800 reader and Alien-9610 linear antenna with a directional gain of 5.9dB. The 3dB beamwidth is 40 degrees. The RFID tags used are Alien 9540 general-purpose squiggle tags which support the EPC class 1 gen 2 standards [4].

The circular conveyor belt used to perform our experiments is approximately 18 meters long, with two parallel straight tracks each 4.4 meters long. The conveyor belt speed can be adjusted for speeds up to 2.0 m/s. A sketch diagram of the setup is shown in Fig. 1.

We mount the RFID tags on cardboard boxes, and placed the boxes on the conveyor belt track. This setup mimics a reader scanning a carton of items, where each item has an individual RFID tag. In all our experiments, we attached each RFID tag 4 cm away from each other. Each box is propped up so that the RFID tags are directly facing the antenna. We place each box on the conveyor belt at approximately equal distances from each other, making sure that at any one time, only one box is within the antenna's range. We use a total of 4 boxes, A B C D, in the experiments. The tag IDs for box A are labeled A1 to A10, IDs for box B as B1 to B10, and so on. Fig. 2 depicts our setup.

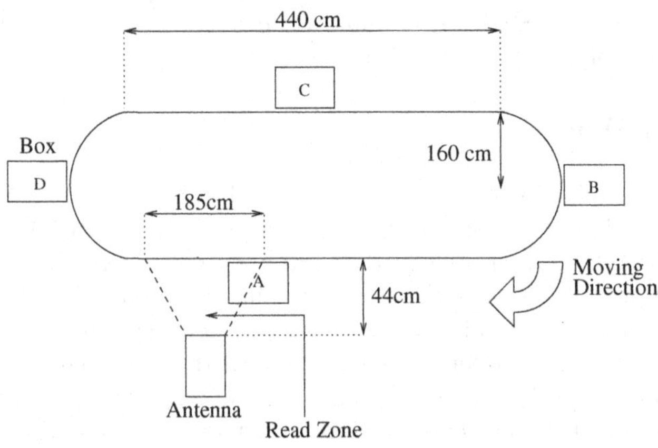

Fig. 1. Indoor conveyor belt

Fig. 2. Conveyor belt testbed. The picture on the left shows the entire route. The center photograph shows the position of antenna by the side of the track, and the rightmost photograph shows a box moving along the track.

3.2 Testbed Setup

One difficulty in setting up an RFID experiment lies in controlling the range of the antenna. To illustrate, we conduct a static experiment by placing some

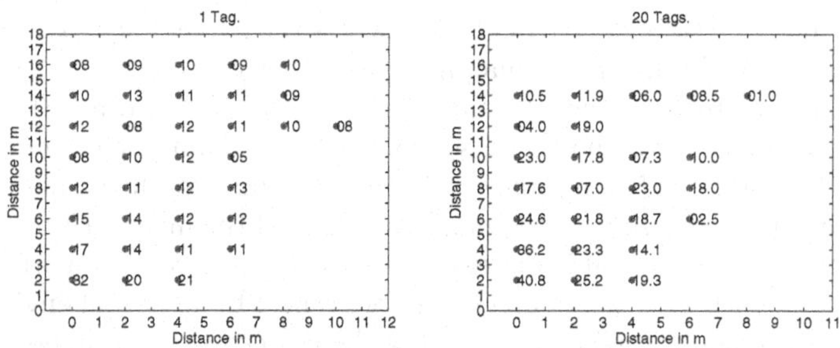

Fig. 3. Average number of times a tag is read at different locations

RFID tags in the middle of a large, empty room. We plotted a grid on the floor of the room, with each grid point two meters away from the other. We then place the antenna at each grid point, and set the reader to read for 30 seconds. Fig. 3 shows the results.

Each dot represents a grid location where at least one tag was read. The RFID tags at placed at position (0,0). The number corresponding to each dot is the average number of times an average tag is read at that location. We see that we can read some RFID tags even at distances of up to 14 meters away.

This large reading range makes it easy for accidental interference when conducting the experiments. We want to prevent the antenna from reading the boxes that are on the *opposite* track, i.e. preventing tags from box C from being read while box A is in front of the reader. We also want to prevent boxes that are along the curved portion of the track from being read as well.

Prior to an experiment, we first determine the reader's attenuation level. We position a box on the opposite track and reduce the attenuation of the antenna until the tags on the opposite track cannot be read. We determine that setting the reader attenuation at 15 dB is sufficient for our conveyor belt. Next we determine the extent of the reading zone by placing an RFID tag directly perpendicular to the antenna, and set the reader to read for 15 seconds, recording the number of times the tag is read. We then shift the tag to the next location several centimeters away, and performed the same test again until we reach a location where we get no tag reads.

3.3 Reader Settings

The RFID reader provides two methods for reading tags, *interactive* mode, and *autonomous* mode. In the interactive mode, a user will issue a command for the RFID reader to begin reading tags. Otherwise, the reader remains silent even if there are tags in the reading zone. In the autonomous mode, the reader is programmed to *constantly* try to read for tags. The reading process is triggered when a tag enters into the reading zone of an antenna. The advantage of using the autonomous mode is that it is easier to manage complex operations with multiple antennas since reads will automatically be performed when an object enters into the range of any antenna. We use the autonomous mode in our experiments to avoid manually triggering the read command.

We use the default setting for AcqG2Select where the reader issues a Select command once per cycle. From the manual, it appears that this command sets inventory flag of all tags to A at the beginning of the cycle. We also use the default AcqG2Session setting 1, which uses S1 session. In this session, each tag maintains its inventory flag between 500 ms and 5 s. In the experiments, the reader was able to read the tags fast enough that the persistent time of the inventory flag did not matter. However, we stress that in our experiments, the tags were always facing the reader's antenna with no other sources of interference. In an actual environment where it is more difficult to read the tags, the choice of session parameter may be important. The default modulation mode used by the reader is the Dense Reader Mode (DRM). This has a reader-to-tag data rate of 26.7kbps, and a tag-to-reader rate of 62.5kbps [3].

The reader has three parameters that will affect read performance, *cycle*, *round*, and *Q*. The *Q* parameter controls the frame size used to read the tags. In our experiments, the value of Q is 3. The *round* parameter determines the number of times we send send Q frames over to the tags, and the *cycle* parameter sets the number of times we execute the *round* parameter. In our experiments, the *round* parameter is set to 5, and the *cycle* parameter to 1. These are the default values for the reader.

4 Experimental Results

We ran read experiments using tag densities of 1 tag per box and 10 tags per box, and considered movement speeds of 0.5 m/s, 1.0 m/s, 1.5 m/s, and 2.0 m/s. We restrict the highest tested speed at 2.0 m/s due to the limitation of the conveyor belt. For instance, we tested the RFID performance at speed 2.0 m/s using 1 tag and 10 tags respectively.

For each experiment, we set the speed, and then turn on the conveyor belt. As the belt is moving, the RFID reader is set to continuously attempt to read. The

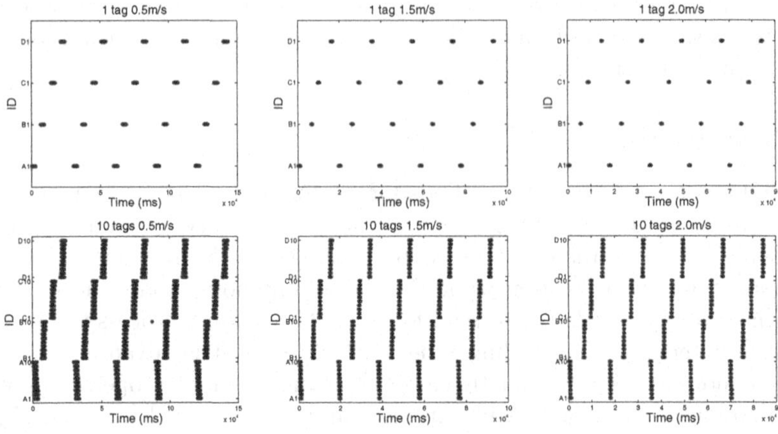

Fig. 4. Results for 1 tag and 10 tags for 5 rounds around the conveyor belt

boxes are left to run for 5 rounds, where each round is defined as all 4 boxes, A,B,C, and D have passed by the antenna once. We plot the time when each tag ID was read for all five rounds in Fig. 4. (The results for 1.0m/s are omitted due to space reasons). From the figure, we can clearly see the beginning and end of each round, and when each box enters and exits the reading zone. Fig. 5 shows a close up of one round.

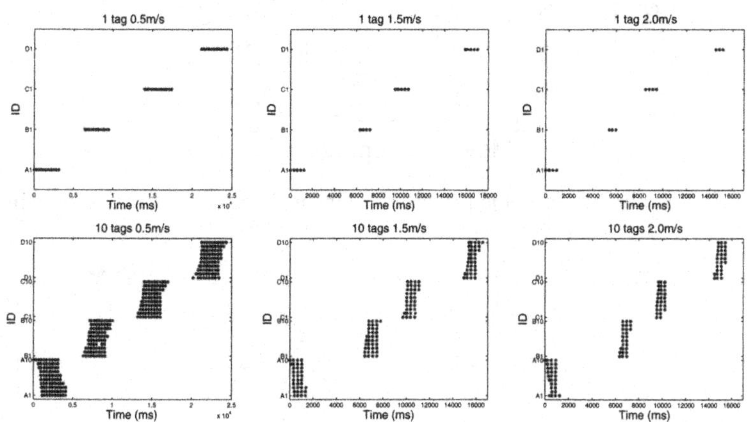

Fig. 5. Detailed results for one round around the conveyor belt. We can clearly see when each box enters and leaves the reading zone.

A popular metric for RFID performance is the number of reads performed per second. We can derive the reads per second for different speeds by

$$\text{Reads per second} = \frac{\text{Total number of reads}}{\text{Total reading time}}.$$

Unlike static experiments, we would like the total reading time to be the amount of time which the tags could *potentially* be read, rather than the total amount of time to complete the experiment. As seen in Fig. 5, there are gaps when a box has left a reading zone but another box has not entered the zone. We found that these gaps were unavoidable if we wanted to allow only one box in the reading zone at a time.

Instead, we define the total reading time as

$$\text{Total reading time} = B \cdot R \cdot T.$$

where B is the number of boxes used, R is the number of times a box passes the RFID reader, and T is the amount of time a box spends in the reader's reading zone. Since we know the length of the reading zone, and control the speed of the conveyor belt, we can determine the value of T any given speed. This total reading time is thus the amount of time in which tags could theoretically be read by the antenna. We plot the reads per second for various speeds in Fig. 6.

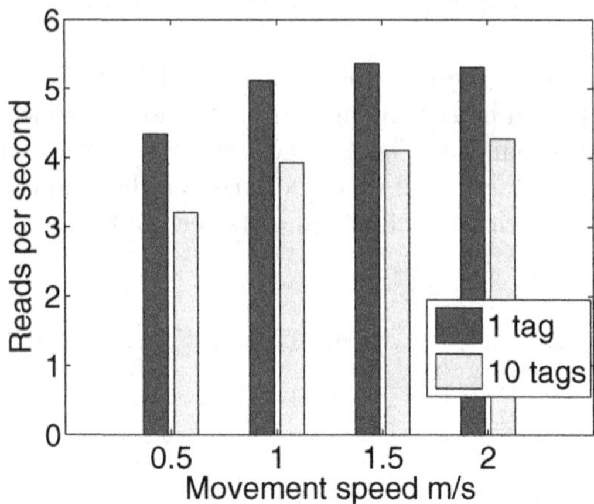

Fig. 6. Average number of reads per second for an average tag at different speeds

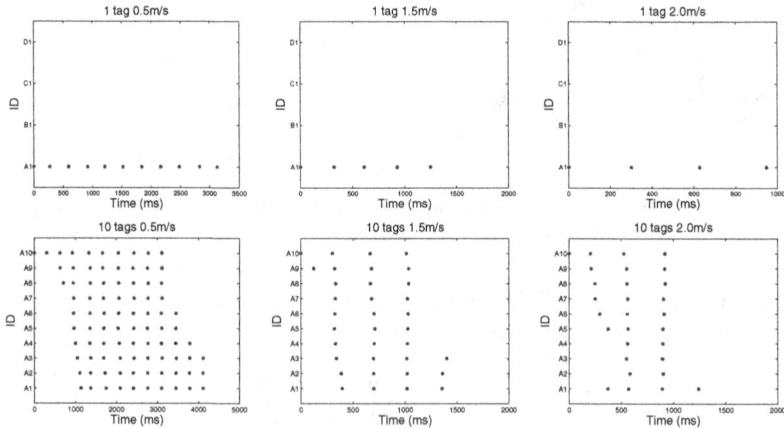

Fig. 7. One box entering and leaving the reading zone at different speeds

In the stationary case, the reads per second for a single tag and 10 tags is 3.11 and 1.716 respectively.

We see that as the speed increases, the reads per second increase as well. This is unexpected since the faster the tags move, the less time they spend in the reading zone, and thus should result in lesser number of reads.

To examine why faster speeds lead to more reads per second, we plot the results for one box with 10 tags entering and leaving the reading zone at different speeds in Fig. 7.

We see at time 0 ms, a tag enters the reading zone of the antenna, and the RFID reader begins reading for tags. Initially, there are fewer than 10 tags within the reading zone, thus there is only 1 tag being read. As the box moves further into the reading zone, more tags enter the reading range, and we begin to see all

10 tags being read. From the figure, we see that tags are read in orderly "groups" rather than individually tags randomly.

For instance, looking at the 1.5 m/s graph (center graph in Fig. 7), there are 6 distinct groups. The first group occurs at time 0 ms, and consists of only reading one tag, A10. The second group also consists of just a single tag, A9. In the third, fourth and fifth group, we see that all 10 tags are read. Finally in the sixth group, only three tags are read. We refer to one group as a single *read*. From the experimental data, we see that the time between two reads is approximately 300 ms regardless of the moving speed.

This partly explains why the reads per second increase as the moving speed increases. Looking at 1 tag moving at 0.5 m/s in Fig. 7, we see that in the first 1000 ms, the tag is read four times, and between 1000 ms and 2000 ms, the tag is read three times. We can compare this against the 1 tag moving at 2. 0m/s. In that experiments, the tag is also read four times in the first 1000 ms before leaving the reading zone. As a result, the reads per second for the 2.0 m/s is better than the 0.5m/s speed partly due to the wait in between two reads.

In the 10 tag experiments, we see that at slow speeds, the first few reads do not read all 10 tags, possible since the tags may not have entered the center of the reading zone where read performance is optimal. In the 10 tags 0.5 m/s results (left center graph in Fig. 7), the first three reads do not capture all the tags, where as in the 2.0 m/s results, we already capture all the tags within the first three reads.

5 Additional Discussion

Mobility Recommendations: The results shown above suggest that *continuous reading* tags may not be a good strategy due to the time lag in between reads. Instead ,the reader should try to estimate when the tags will be close to the center of the reader's antenna before attempting the next read. In Fig. 7, this occurs between the 1000 ms and 3000 ms when the speed is 0.5m/s. In the 1.5 m/s and 2.0 m/s speeds, the best opportunities to read lie between the 500 ms and 1000 ms mark. A careful issuing of read commands will also reduce overall interference since other readers in the vicinity cannot issue commands if the current reader is broadcasting. In addition, this information can be incorporated when cleaning the RFID data. Given an estimated movement speed, we can estimate which tag readings best represent the actual tags.

Detailed Look: Recall that we set the cycle parameter to one, the round parameter to five, and the Q value to three. Here, we wanted to see if we could determine how many tags were read in each round. The goal was to determine whether we could use a different round parameter to improve performance. We plot the data for a single read in Fig. 8. From the figure, we could not determine individual rounds from the data. We could only estimate that the time taken to read a tag is between 2 and 6 ms. There does not appear to be a pattern regarding the order of tag reads even though the plots depict the same box. This is probably due to the different random number used in each read.

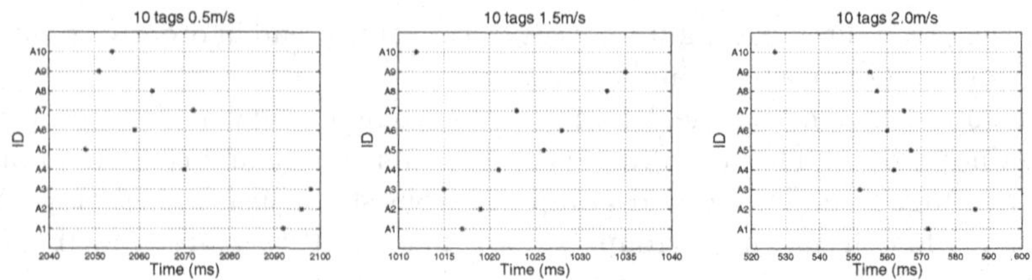

Fig. 8. One cycle at different speeds

Read Failures: One of the original goals of the experiment was to determine the reliability of reads at high speeds. Here we conduct an experiment with a denser number of tags. We place a total of 50 tags on a single box, and place the box on the conveyor belt to run for 5 rounds. The plot of when each tag is read is shown in Fig. 9.

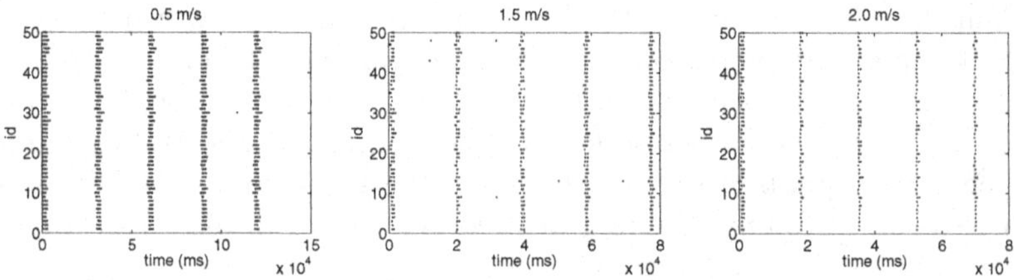

Fig. 9. 50 tags on a single box moving 5 rounds around the conveyor belt

We originally expected to be unable to read all the tags on a box at faster speeds because the box spends less amount of time within the reading zone. Also, faster movement might results in fading effects which will also impact performance. Unfortunately, as shown in the dense tag experiments, we were able to read all 50 tags traveling at the highest speed possible. One possible reason is that the reader's antenna is placed too close to the RFID tags (44 cm away) for noise resulting from fast movement to be a factor. Future experiments with greater distance between reader and tag are needed to examine this issue.

6 Conclusion

In this paper, we conducted experiments to determine the effects of mobility on RFID performance. We show that at a short reading range and a moving speed of 2.0 m/s, the reading capacity of 50 tags is achievable, showing that passive RFID tags can be used in pervasive computing applications for tracking people instead of more expensive sensor mote devices.

Acknowledgments

The authors would like to thank all the reviewers for their helpful comments. This project was supported in part by US National Science Foundation grants

CNS-0721443, CNS-0831904, CAREER Award CNS-0747108, and and the National High-Tech Research and Development Program of China (863) grants 2006AA04A114 and 2006AA04A105.

References

1. Aroor, S., Deavours, D.: Evaluation of the state of passive UHF RFID: An experimental approach. IEEE Systems Journal 1 (2007)
2. Arumugam, D.D., Gautham, A., Narayanaswamy, G., Engels, D.W.: Impacts of RF radiation on the human body in a passive wireless healthcare environment. In: IEEE Conference on Ambient Persuasion in Pervasive Healthcare (2008)
3. Buettner, M., Wetherall, D.: An empirical study of UHF RFID performance. In: MobiCom 2008 (2008)
4. EPCglobal. Class 1 generation 2 UHF air interface protocol standard version 1.0.9
5. Fletcher, R., Marti, U., Redemske, R.: Study of UHF RFID signal propagation through complex media. In: IEEE Antennas and Propagation Society International Symposium (2005)
6. Floerkemeier, C.: Transmission control scheme for fast RFID object identification. In: PercomW 2006 (2006)
7. Floerkemeier, C., Lampe, M.: Issues with RFID usage in ubiquitous computing applications. In: Ferscha, A., Mattern, F. (eds.) PERVASIVE 2004. LNCS, vol. 3001, pp. 188–193. Springer, Heidelberg (2004)
8. Guinard, D., Baecker, O., Michahelles, F.: Supporting a mobile lost and found community. In: MobileHCI 2008 (2008)
9. Hawrylak, P.J., Cain, J.T., Mickle, M.H.: Analytic modelling methodology for analysis of energy consumption for ISO 18000-7 RFID networks. In: IJRFITA 2007 (2007)
10. Hodges, S., Thorne, A., Mallinson, H., Floerkemeier, C.: Assessing and optimizing the range of UHF RFID to enable real-world pervasive computing applications. In: LaMarca, A., Langheinrich, M., Truong, K.N. (eds.) Pervasive 2007. LNCS, vol. 4480, pp. 280–297. Springer, Heidelberg (2007)
11. Kawakita, Y., Mitsugi, J.: Anti-collision performance of Gen2 air protocol in random error communication link. In: SAINTW 2006 (2006)
12. Nemmaluri, A., Corner, M., Shenoy, P.: Sherlock: Automatically locating objects for humans. In: Mobisys 2008 (2008)
13. Ramakrishnan, K., Deavours, D.: Performance benchmarks for passive UHF RFID tags. In: MMB 2006 (2006)
14. Wang, L., Norman, B., Rajgopal, J.: Optimizing the placement of multiple RFID reader antennas to maximize portal read-accuracy. In: Technical Report 07-01, Department of Industrial Engineering, University of Pittsburgh (2007)

Experimental Study on Secure Data Collection in Vehicular Sensor Networks

Harry Gao, Seth Utecht, Fengyuan Xu, Haodong Wang, and Qun Li

Department of Computer Science
College of William and Mary

Abstract. In this paper, we show through a simple secure symmetric key based protocol design and its implementation the feasibility of secure data collection in a vehicular sensor networks. We demonstrate that the protocol works in a realistic setting by collecting the real trace data through real implementation. Some of the key considerations are efficiency, deployability and security. The protocol does not safeguard against some of the techniques an adversary could deploy, such as jamming and deliberate battery-draining.

1 Introduction

We consider a simple vehicular network infrastructure composed of roadside sensors and the vehicles. Sensors are deployed to monitor road environment and the collected data can be collected by the vehicles passing by. In this network architecture, it is crucial to provide security support – only authorized vehicles can feed data into sensors and to obtain data from sensors. To block unauthorized and malicious vehicles, data collected by sensors must be encrypted. However, merely encrypting the data cannot prevent a malicious car to obtain the scrambled data. Although the encrypted data is of little use to the malicious vehicle, it is a serious problem when sensors expect vehicles to harvest all the data and carry them to a central station; a malicious vehicle can simply trap the data and leave a hole in the designated data repository. Therefore, authenticating a passing vehicle before transferring any data is indispensable.

A straightforward solution is to use a public-key based scheme, since some (e.g., the ECC) of the schemes can be implemented efficiently on sensor platforms. Taking a closer look at the problem in a real experimental study, we found that authentication takes about one to two seconds in many cases, which is non-negligible for a car traveling at tens meters a second. A car may rush out of a sensor's transmission range after the authentication is conducted. In this paper, we show our security solution to the vehicular sensor networks and give experimental results on a realistic deployment. We show through a simple secure protocol design and implementation the feasibility of secure data collection in a vehicular sensor networks. We deployed sensors along the road side to test the performance of the communication between the roadside sensors and the sensors in a moving vehicle. We demonstrate the protocol works in a realistic setting

B. Liu et al. (Eds.): WASA 2009, LNCS 5682, pp. 22–31, 2009.

by collecting the real trace data through real implementation. We hope this research shows valuable experience in deploying security support for this type of networks.

2 Related Work

A survey of the security of vehicular network can be found in [6]. There are many vulnerabilities for an unsecured network, such as jamming, forgery, impersonation, and in-transit traffic tampering [7]. Research shows that a symmetric key scheme is required [6]. A number of researching teams have put forth many solutions to group key and authentication problems [1] [2] [3] [8] [10]. Some of them utilize the Cabernet system where data is delivered opportunistically during travel. While less powerful, it does provide a quick solution that can be implemented without an overhaul [4] [5].

There have also been some research exploring the possibility of using a certifi cated-based protocol, such as the one proposed by Wang et al. [9]. It uses the short-range radio communication of motes to pass information from various roadside measuring devices to an information-gathering car mote, which then carries the information to a computer to process. However, it does not address some of the issues unveiled by Balfanz et al. [1].

3 Problem Setting

In this paper we assume the following environment and the availability of equipments:

- Many stationary sensors deployed on the side of the road that can detect, measure and record a certain aspect of the traffic pattern, such as the speed of vehicles in its range. Such motes are currently commercially available. It does not possess significant computational power, nor does it have much storage space.
- Another mote similar to the stationary ones placed in a car that can gather information from the stationary motes and then deliver it to a computer in the car. Its responsibility requires it to be able to securely communicate with other motes and with a computer.
- An upload server, which is to be located at the end of the road. It should be a computer with Wi-Fi capacity. It will obtain the relevant information from the computer in a car once in range. This upload server can be located in a toll gate, rest area, or any other similar structures. This server should have the ability to process and analyze the raw data, and notify relevant parties of its findings. As a computer, the upload server has much computational power. It is also assumed that its storage is virtually unlimited. This is justified by the fact it can communicate with external servers across the Internet. However, the upload server cannot communicate directly with the stationary motes.

- An authentication server, which is to be located at the beginning of the road. It should also be a computer with Wi-Fi capacity. It will permit the car mote to communicate with the stationary mote after the server verifies the car mote's identity. The exact protocol of authenticity between the car mote and authentication server is not discussed in this paper. This server, like the upload server, is assumed to have great computational power with virtually unlimited storage.

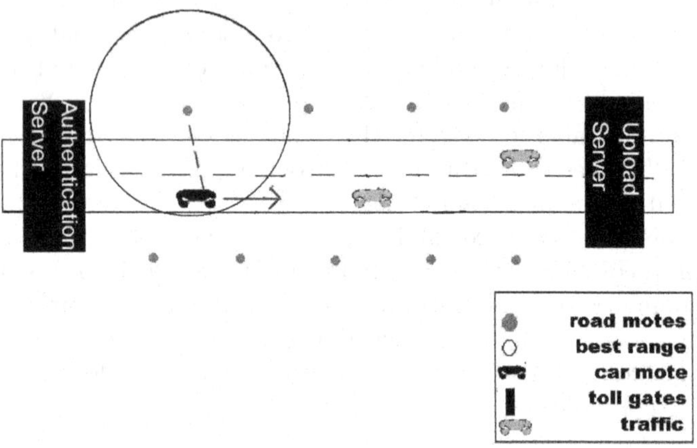

Fig. 1. A scenario of collecting data from roadside sensors in a vehicular networks

3.1 Adversary

Our goal is to design a protocol that is secure, reliable, and efficient. In the following we show our assumptions about the adversary.

The adversary is an unauthorized party that wishes to either obtain the secure information gathered by the roadside mote or at least block the car mote from gathering it. The adversary is assumed to have the ability unlimited access to any public information. It may try to impersonate the car mote so steal the data, or it may pretend to be a stationary roadside mote to provide the car mote with falsified data. Since the car mote is not a part of the infrastructure, it is even reasonable to assume that the car mote is malicious. However, this is not a major concern, since it is assumed that the authentication server will accurately identify any malicious parties before granting access. But in case the adversary successfully obtains the session key, it still cannot forge inaccurate data to the US, for it does not know the secret key.

The adversary is not expected to have the secret key, or know the hash function with which the secret message is encrypted. It is not able to physically damage any of the structures mentioned above, nor is it able to rewrite any pieces of software implemented on either the servers or the motes. That is, the adversary is an outside party without the knowledge of the inner workings of the system.

The adversary is also not expected to be able to crack the security via brute force. This assumption is reasonable since exemplary hashes are believed to be computationally infeasible to solve within any reasonable time frame [9].

4 Protocol

The following protocol is designed in order to balance security with efficiency. It provides a 3-key system that safeguards against various malicious parties, as well as a four-way handshake that allows the roadside mote and the info-gathering car mote to mutually authenticate. The symbols used in the protocol are summarized below:

Variable	**Symbol**
Car Mote	C
Roadside Mote	M
The secret massage	m
The authentication server	AS
The upload server	US
The session key generated by AS	k
Secret value known to M, AS and US	s
Randomly generated challenge value	r
Hash function of r and secret s	$hash(r,s)$
Random number used in the last step of verification	r_t

The first of the two servers provides car mote C with the necessary authentication information (denoted AS), while the second uploads and processes the data collected by C at the end of C's trip (denoted US. M wants to transfer data reliably to C as a car passes by. On the road, C will mutually authenticate with M and collect data encrypted with the secret key. At the end of the road, C will send all collected data to the upload server, which can use the secret key to decrypted the messages.

Pre-Distribution. The servers share the secret key s with M. No one else knows this key.

Communication between *AS* and *C*. To provide C the ability to access the information M holds, AS generates a random number R, and use this R to form a session key k:

$$k = hash(R, s) \tag{1}$$

AS performs this because it does not want C to know s, in order to prevent malicious C to forge fake sensors. After this process, AS gives k and R to C securely. C will now possess all the information it needs to collect data from M.

Communication between *C* and *M*. C broadcasts probe messages containing R on the road. When C and M are within the range of communication, M would receive the message and generate the session key k = hash(s,R), which is the same key known to C. M can then perform a 4-way handshake with C:

1. M generates a random challenge r, and send it back to C;
2. C generates another random number R_c; compute a temporary key;

$$TK = hash(k, r, R_c) \tag{2}$$

   then it generates a MAC for R_c by using this TK; then sends both of them back to M
3. M compute the TK in the same way and use the key to verify the MAC. M can then send back another random number r_t with the MAC generated by using this TK. After verification, C will confirm that M get the TK correctly.
4. After that, both motes are authenticated with each other. M sends a success message and both sides can then start encrypted data communication.

Communication between *C* and the *US*. Upon arriving in the range of the upload server *US*, *C* uploads all gathered data as well as the session key to it for processing. *US* should have the ability to decrypt the encrypted information with the secret key, and it can verify with the AS that the session key is indeed a valid one. Once uploaded, *C* has finished its mission and can now reset.

Summery of the Protocol. The following figure summarizes the protocol outlined above.

```
AS to C     : R, k = hash(R,s)
C to M      : R
M computes  : k = hash(R,s), generate r
M to C      : r
C computes  : generate another random number Rc
            : TK = hash(k,r,Rc)
            : generate a MAC for Rc using TK
C to M      : MAC, Rc
M computes  : TK in the same way; verify MAC, generate rt
M to C      : MAC, rt
C verifies  : MAC; handshake complete
```

5 Experimental Results

To evaluate the proposed protocol, we have implemented it on two TelosB motes, one of them is used as *M*, while the other *C*. TelosB is powered by the MSP430 microcontroller. MSP430 incorporates an 8MHz, 16-bit RISC CPU, 48K bytes flash memory (ROM) and 10K RAM. The RF transceiver on TelosB is IEEE 802.15.4/ZigBee compliant, and can have 250kbps data rate. While the hardware directly affects the RSSI and other aspects of the experimental results, TelosB is by no mean the sole platform for the protocol is practical.

5.1 Metrics and Methodology

In this implementation, we used the following three metrics to better evaluate our results: received/dropped packets, received signal strength indication (RSSI), and the displacement across which the packets are transferred. On an open stretch of road, we drove past the roadside mote M at different speeds with the car mote C on top of the car and connected to a laptop (via USB), which runs a Java program that reads, records and analyzes the data received. M continually sent out radio transmissions in an infinite loop. Upon entering M's range, C picked up the encrypted message *hash(r,s)*, decrypted it and responded, and finally obtained the message m.

5.2 Mote to Mote Communication

Three distinct tests prove conducted. C is driven by M at the constant speed of 30, 50, and 70 km/h. Three trials were conducted for each speed. In addition, stationary tests at fixed displacements before and after M along the road were conducted at the displacements of 25, 75, 125, 175 and 225 meters. A unique ID number was assigned to every packet received for easier identification. The ID, the RSSI as well as the packet's time of arrive (an offset from the start time) were recorded for each trial. Also recorded was C's approximate displacement from M. From this, it was possible to calculate when, where, how many, and at what speed packets were dropped. The location of C along the road is expressed in terms of its displacement from M, where a negative value X represents that

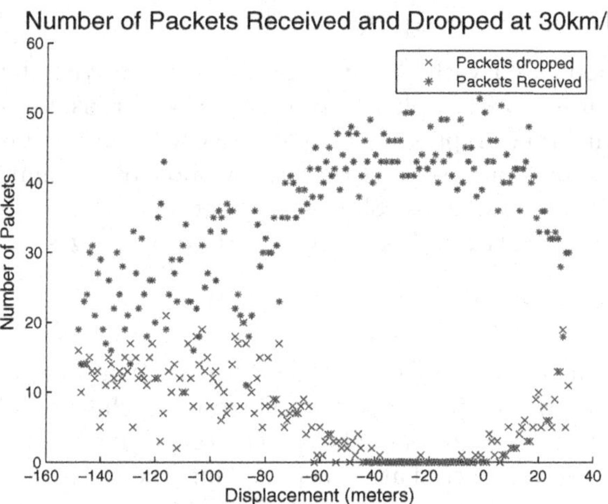

Fig. 2. This graph shows the number of packets received and dropped between the -150m and 50m, and it is the total of three separate trials. It shows that from about -40m to 0m, virtually all packets are successfully received for all three trials. It also shows that close to half of the packets are dropped near the ends of the graph.

C is X meters away from reaching the same point along the road as M, a value of 0 represent that it is at the exact same point along the road, and a positive value Y represent that C has passed M by Y meters.

In order to better analyze the relationship between possibility of dropping a package and the distance between the two motes, in figure 2, we graphed the total number of packets received/dropped for the three trials at 30km/h. From the graph, it is evident that at the possible range for C to receive packets from M is around between -150 meters and 50 meters. This represents a window of opportunity of about 200 meters, or about 24 seconds. However, significant number of packets was dropped from -155 meters to about -55 meters, and again resumes to drop significantly at around 25 meters. Therefore, the most reliable window of communication where very few packets (less than 5 percent) is around -55 meter to 25 meters. This 80 meter window represent about 10 seconds.

The data of 50 km/h and 70 km/h show a similar pattern. However, the optimal window of transmission is halved to just under 6 seconds. This could be too short to fully and securely transfer all data based on the currently protocol. The possible range of reception, optimal range of reception and approximate time frame to transfer data within the two ranges are summarized in the table below:

Analysis of Possible/Best Packet Transmission Frames

Car Speed	Possible Range	Optimal Range	Possible Duration	Optimal Duration
km/h	meters	meters	seconds	seconds
30	[-150, 50]	[-55, 25]	24	10
50	[-150, 50]	[-75, 5]	14	5.8
70	[-150, 50]	[-85, 25]	10	5.7

The table is populated with the average of the three trials for each speed. Possible range represents all displacement values where transmission is possible, whereas the optimal range represent the best range for transmission as discussed above. We can use our knowledge of the best window of communication to increase the reliability of our protocol. Possible/optimal duration represents the amount of time in seconds C will stay in the respective ranges.

5.3 RSSI

The signal strength (RSSI) is plotted against displacement in figure 3 to better analyze the relationship between the two. Three trials show an identical trend with slight horizontal displacement. The signal strength for the first trial peaked at about -13 meters, second trial at -5 meters, while the third one peaked at -26 meters. It is, however, clear from the graph that RSSI increases as the displacement narrows. The fact all three trials peaked at slightly negative displacement suggests that the radio signals are stronger before C passes M. However, there is little difference between about -175 meters and -75 meters in terms of RSSI, suggesting that the strength is not simply inversely proportional to the displacement. This information provides insight to the best timing of the handshake

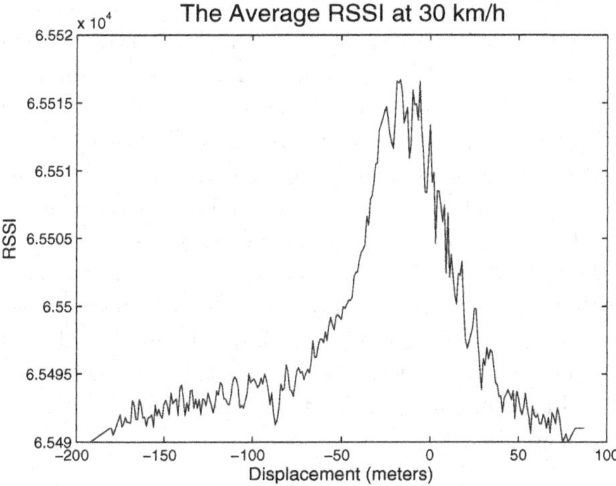

Fig. 3. The RSSI of the packets received within [-200m, 80m]. At about 50m away from the roadside mote the transmission becomes reliable, until it passes the roadside mote by about 25 meters. It peaks shortly before reaching 0m.

process, and we can use the RSSI as an indicator to show if the communication strength is high enough for the security protocol to start. At 50km/h and 70km/h, a similar pattern is shown. The results are summarized below:

Approx. Displacement of Best RSSI

Car Speed	Displacement	Time
30 km/h	-8 meters	-1.0 sec
50 km/h	-16 meters	-1.2 sec
70 km/h	-23 meters	-1.2 sec

The trend shows that as speed of the vehicle hosting C increases, the ideal displacement from M for packet transmission becomes increasingly negative. The ideal amount of time for packet transmission, on the other hand, seems to be about just more than 1.0 seconds regardless of the difference in speed.

5.4 Security

The amount of time authentication of this protocol takes is compared with other schemes in order to better analyze the efficiency and dependability of the protocol. In particular, the amount of time needed to encrypt the message with AES takes less than 1ms with 16 byte-long keys and random numbers. SHA-1 would take 4ms. The proposed protocol can use either one of those two. The speed of encryption/decryption is extremely important in the context. This is because the car mote only has about 6 seconds to communicate with a roadside mote at high speed, and we must ensure not only that we have enough time for the handshake, but also that the security part takes only a small fraction of the amount of time we have, and that sufficient amount of time is left for the actual data to pass through. On the same platform, we found that the ECC-based encryption needs 2 point multiplications, which takes roughly 3.1 seconds on the TelosB. Decryption will take one point multiplication, or about 1.55 seconds. This suggests that an asymmetric key scheme would take much longer to establish the secured connection and is not be suitable for a similar set up. Using the symmetric key protocol as proposed, the total amount of time needed for the motes to encrypt/decrypt is negligible. In addition to the calculation time, however, we also need to consider the amount of time it takes to actually transmit handshake messages. The protocol requires a 4-way handshake, 2 packets to be sent from the car mote to the roadside mote, and 2 more going the other way. At the experimental rate of 13 packets per second on average, the communication will take roughly 0.31s. Therefore, the total amount of time required for the authentication is about one third of a second, or less than 5 percent of the total amount of available time inside the optimal transmission range. This is very acceptable.

5.5 Further Observation

At high speed, there would be about 6.5 seconds left for the transferring of interesting data. The TelosB hardware has a maximum transfer rate of 250kbps (as declared on its specifications) and an experimental rate of 200kbps at 70km/h. This means that it will take about 6 cars to unload all 1024K bytes of data the hardware can hold at a time. However, in a realistic setting, we should extract the data long before the on board flash memory is full. The low percentage of communication time shows the protocol is useful in a realistic setting. In the experiment we did not try to tweak the packet size to maximize the amount of data transferred at a time; ideally, we should be able to reach the rate of 250kbps, and only five car motes need to drive by to collect all data resting on the roadside mote.

6 Conclusion

In this paper, we show our design of a secure data collection protocol for vehicular sensor networks. We conducted experimental study on this protocol. There are many interesting findings in this implementation. First of all, it shows that many of the goals of vehicular network communication can be easily achievable. At a speed as high as 70 km/h, the motes still have about 5.7 seconds of optimal transmission time, which should suffice under normal circumstances. Another interesting conclusion drawn from the data is that the signal strength is better when C is still some distance away from M than when the two are at the same point along the road. This is confirmed by the fact the optimal range of transmission is not centered at a displacement of 0 meters, but at around -30 to -15 meters.

Acknowledgments

This project was supported in part by US National Science Foundation grants CNS-0721443, CNS-0831904, CAREER Award CNS-0747108, and CSUMS grant DMS 0703532.

References

1. Balfanz, D., Durfee, G., Shankar, N., Smetters, D., Staddonand, J., Wong, H.C.: Secret handshakes from pairing-based key agreements. In: IEEE Symposium on Security and Privacy, pp. 180–196 (2003)
2. Chan, H., Perrig, A.: Pike: peer intermediaries for key establishment in sensor networks. In: INFOCOM, pp. 524–535 (2005)
3. Du, W., Han, Y.S., Chen, S., Varshney, P.K.: A key management scheme for wireless sensor networks using deployment knowledge. In: INFOCOM 2004. Twenty-third AnnualJoint Conference of the IEEE Computer and Communications Societies, pp. 586–597 (2004)
4. Eriksson, J., Balakrishnan, H., Madden, S.: Cabernet: vehicular content delivery using Wi-Fi. In: MOBICOM (2008)
5. David, H., Srinivasan, K., Tim, B., Shubham, A.: Vehicular opportunistic communication under the microscope. In: MobiSys 2007: Proceedings of the 5th international conference on Mobile systems, applications and services, New York, NY, USA, pp. 206–219 (2007)
6. Luo, J., Hubaux, J.-P.: A survey of inter-vehicle communication, epfl. Technical report (2004)
7. Raya, M., Papadimitratos, P., Hubaux, J.P.: Securing vehicular communications. In: IEEE Wireless Comm. (2006)
8. Vogt, H.: Exploring message authentication in sensor networks. In: Castelluccia, C., Hartenstein, H., Paar, C., Westhoff, D. (eds.) ESAS 2004. LNCS, vol. 3313, pp. 19–30. Springer, Heidelberg (2005)
9. Wang, H., Li, Q.: Distributed user access control in sensor networks. In: Gibbons, P.B., Abdelzaher, T., Aspnes, J., Rao, R. (eds.) DCOSS 2006. LNCS, vol. 4026, pp. 305–320. Springer, Heidelberg (2006)
10. Zhu, S., Setia, S., Jajodia, S.: An interleaved hop-by-hop authentication scheme for filtering of injected false data in sensor networks. In: IEEE Symposium on Security and Privacy, pp. 259–271 (2004)

Experimental Study of Independent and Dominating Sets in Wireless Sensor Networks Using Graph Coloring Algorithms

Dhia Mahjoub and David W. Matula

Lyle School of Engineering
Southern Methodist University
Dallas, TX 75275-0122, USA
dmahjoub@lyle.smu.edu, matula@lyle.smu.edu

Abstract. The domatic partition problem seeks to maximize the partitioning of the nodes of the network into disjoint dominating sets. These sets represent a series of virtual backbones for wireless sensor networks to be activated successively, resulting in more balanced energy consumption and increased network robustness. In this study, we address the domatic partition problem in random geometric graphs by investigating several vertex coloring algorithms both topology and geometry-aware, color-adaptive and randomized. Graph coloring produces color classes with each class representing an independent set of vertices. The disjoint maximal independent sets constitute a collection of disjoint dominating sets that offer good network coverage. Furthermore, if we relax the full domination constraint then we obtain a partitioning of the network into disjoint dominating and nearly-dominating sets of nearly equal size, providing better redundancy and a near-perfect node coverage yield. In addition, these independent sets can be the basis for clustering a very large sensor network with minimal overlap between the clusters leading to increased efficiency in routing, wireless transmission scheduling and data-aggregation. We also observe that in dense random deployments, certain coloring algorithms yield a packing of the nodes into independent sets each of which is relatively close to the perfect placement in the triangular lattice.

Keywords: Wireless Sensor Networks, random geometric graphs, independent sets, dominating sets, domatic partition problem, graph coloring, triangular lattice.

1 Introduction and Related Work

Connectivity and coverage are two fundamental quality of service objectives to optimize in Wireless Sensor Network (WSN) applications subject to the constraints that energy dissipation is reduced at the sensor level and the network lifetime is prolonged [9]. If we assume large-scale static Wireless Sensor Networks randomly deployed at a high density for applications like area-monitoring, then the area coverage can be approximated by the coverage of the sensor locations. In other words, owing to the large and dense sensor population, we can approximate the coverage of each point in the given area by covering each sensor location [4]. If we model the sensor network as a

B. Liu et al. (Eds.): WASA 2009, LNCS 5682, pp. 32–42, 2009.

geometric graph, then we can use strong concepts like coloring, independence, cover, and domination to solve the connected coverage problem. Extensive research has been carried out in the past years using the geometric graph model and the consensus has been to restructure or reorganize the network into a hierarchy so as to satisfy the connectivity and coverage objectives but also improve network capacity, reduce energy consumption and interference, and provide a robust, efficient infrastructure for routing and higher-level applications. The hierarchy restructuring can take two forms: build a collection of virtual backbones that are duty-cycled [4,9,16]; or cluster the network, where any node should have at least one cluster-head in its neighborhood [6,21]. The virtual backbone and cluster-heads should constitute a dominating set that covers all nodes in the network. Moreover, in the case of clustering, two cluster-heads should have minimum or no overlap, hence the independent set relevance. The partitioning of points into sets that are both dominating and independent is illustrated by considering the traditional cellular lattice. In this idealized case, large hexagonal regions of the triangular lattice are each partitioned into a fixed number k of smaller hexagons. The design effectively partitions the totality of small hexagons into k disjoint sets, where members of each disjoint set denote local regions which may broadcast with common frequencies sufficiently separated in distance not to interfere, but repetitively placed to broadcast to the whole geographic region. In the graph model, these k disjoint sets form a k-coloring of the implicit regular geometric graph with these sets being both independent and dominating, and all of the same size. On the other hand, constructing a virtual backbone can reduce to building a Minimum Dominating Set (MDS), itself approximable by building a Maximal Independent Set (MIS) [19]. The elements of the MDS play the role of coordinators for purposes of sensing coverage and/or network connectivity. A single MDS however puts heavy burden on its elements to sustain the network services. To maximize the lifetime of the network, the role of coordinators should be rotated among the nodes in the network, so that every node gets a chance to sleep and prolong its operational lifetime. Hence, the relevance of finding the maximum collection of disjoint dominating sets known as the Maximum Domatic Partition (MDP) problem [10], an NP-hard problem, as well as its variants: the k-domatic partition [17] and maximum disjoint set cover [4] problems. The MDP problem can address the area coverage; where it is known as the *Maximum Lifetime Target Coverage problem* [18], as well as the node coverage or clustering; where it's called the *Maximum Clustering Lifetime* problem [16]. In both cases, the MDP problem has useful applications in ensuring a sustained quality of coverage in area monitoring applications, as well maintaining the network connectivity at all times for the benefit of efficient routing while prolonging the network lifetime.

1.1 Contributions

Other than the application of one coloring algorithm in [5], we have not found, in the literature, any systematic investigation of various coloring algorithms to optimize the partitioning of nodes of a random geometric graph into disjoint sets that are both independent and dominating. Random geometric graphs (RGG) can closely represent the topological structure of sensor networks [9]. A random geometric graph, $G(n,r)$, is formed by placing n points uniformly at random in the unit square and connecting two points if their Euclidian distance is at most r. Another widely used communication model when all nodes have the same transmission range *r*, is the Unit Disk Graph (UDG) where the vertices of the graph are embedded in the plane and two vertices are adjacent if their Euclidian distance is less or equal to 1 (*r* is normalized to one unit). RGGs and UDGs are related in the sense that a random geometric graph simply induces a probability distribution on the unit disk graph. Both models assume a regular disk communication model. In practice, however, the communication range is non-isotropic and irregular: the radio signal is disrupted by large scale fading effects like reflection, diffraction and scattering; small scale fading effects such as interference, heterogeneous sending powers, and transmission errors [19]. Therefore, the quasi-UDG (qUDG) model was introduced in the literature to account for these irregularities [19]. In our work, we use the RGG model with the perfect disk range, and even though the disk model is oversimplified, we believe our results are still applicable in practice. For instance, when the communication range is irregular but has a lower bound, it can be regarded as a regular disk with radius equal to the lower bound [2]. With this approach, our results can provide conservative bounds on the properties we studied in RGGs using graph coloring.

In this work, our goal is to show that a large subset $V^* \subset V$ of a random geometric graph, e.g. over 80% of the vertices, can be partitioned by an appropriate coloring algorithm into disjoint fully and $(1\text{-}\varepsilon)$ dominating sets for ε quite small, e.g. $(1\text{-}\varepsilon)$>90%. For a random geometric graph in the unit square, there will be regions such as the four corners where the average degree is atypically low, and similarly there may be regions where the density of vertices is atypically high. If we can exclude a small portion of the vertices with atypically high or low degree, we are interested to find out if there is a subset of regularly distributed vertices $V^* \subset V$ containing most of V that can be covered by disjoint $(1\text{-}\varepsilon)$ dominating sets for ε quite small, e.g. $(1\text{-}\varepsilon)$>0.9.

In this paper, our contributions are two-fold. First, we present the results of an experimental investigation of the comparative performance of known and proposed coloring algorithms in random geometric graphs that are categorized as: topology-based, geometry-aware, randomized and color-adaptive. Graph coloring yields a partition into disjoint color classes of vertices where each color class forms an independent set of vertices. Our interest is not in minimizing the number of colors used but in evaluating the properties of the color classes produced. These properties are analyzed with particular regard for obtaining roughly equal sized independent sets that are also maximal independent, hence disjoint dominating. Certain coloring algorithms are shown to generate a collection of similar sized disjoint and verifiably dominating sets that have equally good performance in covering the network; hence these sets constitute good candidates for duty-cycled virtual backbones or minimal overlap clustering. Moreover, by relaxing the full domination constraint on the resulting disjoint independent sets, we are able to obtain a near-optimal node coverage yield with a much higher redundancy in the number of independent sets. For instance, using smallest-last (*SL*) coloring [15] on a random geometric graph *G(1600, 0.12)*, Table 1 shows that 25.9% of the network nodes can be packed in 7 independent sets (color classes) of average size 59.3 each covering on average 99.97% of the entire network. Furthermore, if we consider the first 14 colors, then 50.97% of the nodes partition into 14 sets, where each color of the second 7 colors covers on average 99.85% of the network. Similarly, the first 21 colors incorporate 73.83% of the nodes, where each one of the last 7 colors covers on average 99.30% of the network. We argue that by using selected coloring algorithms on random geometric graphs that model wireless sensor networks, we can incrementally pack a core portion of the network (25, 50 and 75%) into dominating and nearly-dominating independent sets of roughly equal size which offer a high node coverage yield. Our second contribution consists in observing that in very dense random geometric deployments of nodes, the packing of the nodes in the independent sets produced by our preferred colorings is nearly as regular and dense as the perfect packing in the triangular lattice. This property is somewhat remarkable, given the randomness of the deployment, and that some of the coloring algorithms are topology based without any reference to the geometrical positioning of the points.

Table 1. Coverage results obtained with SL coloring algorithm (10 case average)

Color groups	Cumulative number of vertices in color groups (%)	Average node coverage over 7 colors (%)	Average independent set size	Standard deviation on independent set size
1-7	25.9	99.97	59.3	0.92
8-14	50.97	99.85	57.21	1.54
15-21	73.83	99.30	52.25	2.22
22-28	91.59	94.82	40.58	5.85
29-35	99.41	60.69	17.85	8.03
36-42	100.00	6.05	1.35	1.61

1.2 Related Work

To ensure connected coverage of a sensing field, two main techniques are used: the first is to structure the network into a regular pattern close to the perfect triangular lattice, and the second is to use sleep scheduling where multiple subsets of the nodes constitute virtual backbones and are activated one at a time to provide a connected coverage [9]. Adopting the first technique, the ACE algorithm [6] distributively produces clusters with regular separation close to the hexagonal lattice. Layered Diffusion based Coverage Control Protocol (LDCC) [20] applies triangular tessellation to cover the sensor field with the minimum number of active nodes. GS^3 [21], is a location-aware scheme that produces an approximate hexagonal close packing of the sensors, and Optimal Geographical Density Control (OGDC) protocol [22] exploits nodes' location coordinates to create a triangle tessellation of the nodes to be active at a given time. Using the second approach, Cardei et al. [5] propose an original centralized algorithm, based on sequential vertex coloring, which maximizes the number of disjoint dominating sets for the purpose of increasing the network lifetime, whereas, Moscibroda and Wattenhofer [16] and Thai et al. [18] provide randomized distributed algorithms which approximate the optimal solution of the maximum domatic problem within $O(\log n)$.

The rest of the paper is organized as follows. Section 2 reviews the graph coloring algorithms employed and discusses the domatic partition problem. Section 3 provides bounds on the size of the maximal independent sets produced by the coloring algorithms in random geometric graphs. The experimental results are demonstrated in Section 4. Finally, Section 5 concludes the paper, and outlines our current and future work.

2 Background

2.1 Vertex Domination and Independence in Graphs

Dominating set: In a graph $G = (V, E)$, a dominating set $S \subseteq V$ of G is a subset of vertices such that every vertex of G is either in S or has at least one neighbor in S [19]. We define a $(1\text{-}\varepsilon)$ dominating set S as having at most $\varepsilon|V|$ vertices that are not adjacent to members of S, i.e. the $(1\text{-}\varepsilon)$ dominating set S covers nearly all vertices of G as $\varepsilon \to 0$.

Independent set: An independent set $S \subseteq V$ of a graph $G = (V, E)$ is a subset of vertices such that no two vertices $\forall u, v \in S$ are adjacent in G. S is a maximal independent set *(MIS)* if no vertex can be added to it without violating its independence, and equivalently if any vertex not in S has a neighbor in S, i.e., if S forms a dominating set.

Vertex coloring (independent set partition): Given an undirected graph $G = (V, E)$, a vertex coloring of G is a mapping $f: V \to \{1,\ldots,k\}$ such that $f(x) \neq f(y)$ if $(x,y) \in E$. The minimum number k to color G is called the chromatic number of G and denoted $\chi(G)$ [14]. Each set of vertices with the same color forms an independent set; hence a k coloring is a partition into k independent sets of the graph G.

Domatic partition: A domatic partition is a partition of the vertices so that each part is a dominating set of the graph. The *domatic number* of a graph G is the maximum number of dominating sets in a domatic partition of G, or equivalently, the maximum number of disjoint dominating sets [8]. The domatic number of a graph G, $D(G)$, is at most $\delta(G)+1$, where δ is the minimum degree, since every vertex can be dominated by at most $\delta(G)+1$ disjoint dominating sets.

2.2 Taxonomy of Vertex Coloring Algorithms

A sequential coloring algorithm of a graph G is an algorithm operating in the following two stages: (a) Determine a *vertex ordering* K (for sequential coloring) [13] of the vertices of G, and (b) Determine a *color selection strategy* to color the vertices in the ordering K.

a. Classification of vertex orderings

The coloring sequence or vertex ordering is the arrangement of the vertex set V into a specific sequence $K = (v1, v2,\ldots, vn)$ that will next be colored according to a specific color selection strategy. Table 2 summarizes the coloring sequences that we studied. For further details on existing orderings, we invite the reader to consult the references cited.

We also introduce geometry-aware vertex orderings which we briefly present below.

Center First method (CF): The vertices are sorted in non-decreasing order according to their Euclidian distance from the center c (0.5, 0.5) of the unit square.

Boundary First method (BF): The vertices are sorted in non-increasing order according to their distance from the center c of the unit square. This tends to build larger independent sets since we start from the boundary where vertices have lower degrees than in the interior of the unit square.

Spiral Center First method (SCF): This ordering is built by spiraling from the center out in a clockwise continuous sweep.

***Top Down Sweep method (TDS)*:** This ordering is built by sweeping the vertices in the unit square from left to right, top to bottom.

Table 2. Classification of vertex orderings from the literature

Coloring algorithm	Class	Vertex ordering characteristic
Identifier ordering	Labeling-based	Lexicographic order on identifier
Largest First (LF) [13]	Topology-based	Non-increasing order on degree
Smallest First (SF)	Topology-based	Non-decreasing order on degree
Smallest Last (SL) [14,15]	Topology-based	Recursive minimum degree last
Smallest First Recursive (SFR)	Topology-based	Recursive minimum degree first
Random Sequence (RS) [13]	Random	Uniform random order on vertex identifier
Saturation LF (SLF) or DSATUR [13]	Dynamic or color-adaptive	Dynamic ordering subject to degree of saturation of the vertex to color

b. Color selection strategy

Greedy-Color also known as First-Fit or Grundy function [13] is often used as the coloring strategy where to color a vertex v; we pick the smallest color not used by any adjacent vertex of v. With *Greedy-Color* the first color class is always a maximal independent set hence also a dominating set. Also, the vertices colored with the *ith* color dominate the induced subgraph determined by all vertices of color at least i.

3 Bounds on MIS Size in Random Geometric Graphs

Considering the unit square and as $n \to \infty$, we can provide an upper bound on the average number of nodes that can be packed in a maximal independent set *(MIS)*. We start from the fact that placing disks on the vertices of a triangular lattice (or equivalently, at the centers of regular hexagons in the dual lattice) is asymptotically optimal, in terms of the number of disks needed to achieve full coverage of a plane [4]. The nodes of a maximum size independent set are the centers of disks of radius r, where no two disks can mutually cover their respective centers (there is no edge between two disk centers). As $n \to \infty$, the coloring algorithm produces the pattern where three disk centers are close enough to form the vertices of an equilateral triangle, hence the relevance of the triangular lattice model. Based on the area of an equilateral triangle of side r, the unit square can pack on average $1/\frac{r^2\sqrt{3}}{4}$ triangles. Notice that a triangle is incident to 3 vertices and a vertex is incident to 6 triangles, therefore we can obtain essentially $1/\frac{r^2\sqrt{3}}{2}$ vertices in the unit square. Moreover, we can use the proof provided by J. Diaz et al. in [7] on the independence number $\beta_n(r)$ (size of the maximum independent set) in random geometric graphs. The authors prove that $\beta_n(r) \le (1+(1/r))^2$ which provides us with another absolute upper bound on the size of the maximal independent sets obtained by coloring random geometric graphs. Similarly, a lower bound on the size of the maximal independent set is obtained with $r' = r\sqrt{3}$ and the minimum size of the MIS which still covers all vertices is $1/\frac{r'^2\sqrt{3}}{2}$.

4 Experimental Results and Analysis

We experiment with a much broader choice of polynomial-time coloring algorithms than the related work in the literature [5]. We also consider much larger graph instances than [5] which allows us to bring far better properties, in terms of redundant coverage yield, of the maximal disjoint dominating and *(1-ε)* dominating sets in random geometric graphs. Our experiments consisted in running the collection of 11 coloring algorithms on a random geometric graph *G(n,r)* deployed in a unit square where *n=1600* and *r* belongs to *{0.06, 0.12. 0.18, 0.24, 0.3, 0.36}*, which yields average node degrees in {17, 65, 138, 232, 342, 463}. We run each coloring algorithm on 10 instances of the same graph *G(n,r)*. Given the random placement of the points in the plane, each graph instance is a different combinatorial instance of the same graph *G(n,r)*. Considering the unit square and normalizing the nominal transmission range *r* to the interval [0,1], we define the network density $\mu(r)$ as the number of nodes per nominal transmission area: $\mu(r)=n.\pi.r^2$, which also estimates the average node degree. Large scale and highly dense WSNs are prevalent in theory and practice. For instance, the ExScal project is the largest real life sensor network assembled to date [1] consisting of 10000 sensor devices placed in a tiered grid-like fashion on a 1.3km by 300m remote area in Florida. Although not randomly deployed, this initiative sets the ground for very large scale wireless sensor deployments. Moreover, the recent literature abounds with WSN experimental settings of uniform random deployments with high network sizes and densities. Table 3 shows a selection of references that we investigated. In practice, very dense networks suffer from interference and collision; therefore, as the network size grows, the nodes have to scale down their transmission range to keep the network density to a desirable level or a more involved MAC protocol becomes warranted to alleviate the increased channel contention. Our work applies to random geometric graphs in general, and to Wireless Sensor Networks in particular. Therefore, regardless of the application, we provide good experimental results on the asymptotic upper bounds of the properties that we have studied.

Table 3. Network sizes and densities from the literature

Paper	Deployment region	n	r	Avg. degree
Cardei et al. [3]	100x100	100	50	47.39
Chan et al. [6]	Unit square	2500		10,20,50,100
He et al. [11]	160x160	300	50	67.69
Iyengar et al. [12]	1000x1000	200-10000	100	5,14,28,57,114,172,287
Wang et al. [20]	Disk of radius 60	1200,1500	15,17	75,96
Zhou et al. [23]	400x400	1500	80	156

4.1 Nearly-Equal Sized Independent Sets

Figure 1 shows the cardinality of the color classes (independent sets size, 10 case average) for *n=1600* and *r=0.12*. *SL* and *DSATUR* produce the minimal coloring and tend to have roughly equal sized lower color classes. We verified that those color classes are also dominating sets of the whole graph. *SFR* and *BF* tend to use many more colors but build a few larger independent sets and show a sharper decrease in the independent sets sizes. For the same network instance, Figure 2 plots the node coverage of the individual color classes obtained with multiple colorings. We observe that nearly half the color classes have node coverage of more than 90%. We also notice that the size of the largest color class is nearly double the size of the smallest color class that still offers more than 90% node coverage. This corroborates the benefit of graph coloring in yielding a substantial collection of disjoint dominating and *(1-ε)* dominating sets with equal coverage that can be duty cycled. Notice that the points where *SFR* and *BF* intersect *SL* and *DSATUR* represent the number of disjoint dominating sets that we describe later.

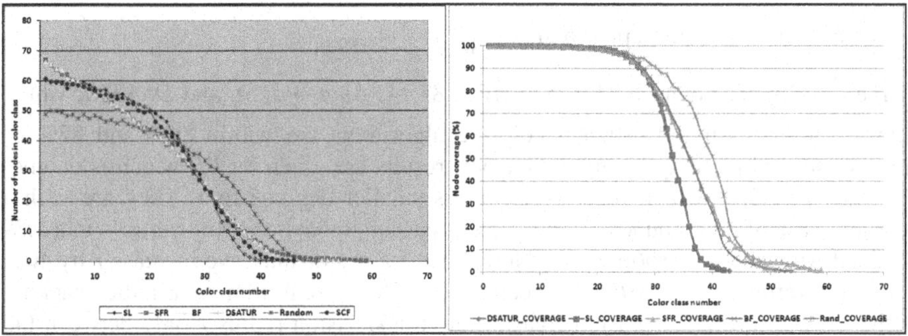

Fig. 1. Evolution of the color classes' sizes **Fig. 2.** Node coverage of the color classes

4.2 Collection of Disjoint Dominating Sets

Figure 3 shows the number of disjoint dominating sets (domatic number) obtained with 5 of the 11 coloring algorithms we experimented. For lack of space, we only present the most relevant results. Notice that *DSATUR* and *SL* offer similar performances. *SFR* and *BF* which consider low degree nodes first tend to build larger independent sets therefore they yield a much higher domatic partition size. *Random* which exploits no intelligence in the coloring produces the lowest results. In their seminal paper on domatic partitions [8], Feige et al. prove that every arbitrary graph with maximum degree Δ and minimum degree δ contains a domatic partition of size $((1-o(1))(\delta-1))/\ln \Delta$, where any $o(1)$ term denotes a function of Δ alone that goes to zero as Δ increases. They turn this proof into a polynomial time, centralized algorithm that produces a domatic partition of size $\Omega(\delta/\ln\Delta)$. In our experiments, notice that *lowerb* (i.e. lower bound) is the asymptotic bound of the domatic partition number obtained by the algorithm of [8]. *mindeg+1* is the upper bound of the domatic number. We are basically obtaining a much higher domatic partition size than [8] which is an approximation algorithm for arbitrary graphs. However, our coloring algorithms are applied on random geometric graphs which can explain the advantages taken from the geometry to produce better results.

4.3 Node Packing in the Independent Sets

We consider *r=0.12* with several n values as depicted in Table 4.

Table 4. Cardinality of the MIS obtained with different colorings

n	Avg. degree	SF	SL	SFR	Random	BF	DSATUR
400	16	52	49	56	46	55	50
800	32	57	57	61	50	61	56
1600	65	62	61	69	54	68	63
3200	128	63	65	71	54	71	67
6400	259	64	68	74	56	74	71
10000	405	65	71	77	57	77	72

The triangular packing upper bound is $1/\frac{(0.12)^2\sqrt{3}}{2}=80.18$.

The $\beta_n(r)$ upper bound is $(1+(1/0.12))^2 = 87.11$. As $n\rightarrow\infty$, *SL* and *DSATUR* which both are topology-based efficient coloring algorithms are within 89% and 82% of both bounds, which is quite good. Our best results are given by *BF* which is geometry-aware and *SFR* which recursively colors smaller degrees first. They are within 96% and 88% of both bounds. Figure 4 shows a sample layout of the vertices in a *MIS* obtained with *SL* on *G(1600, 0.12)*. Notice that for the display, we increase *r* by 40% to join the vertices of the *MIS* so we can observe the close to triangular lattice packing of the nodes. Furthermore, by increasing the transmission radius *r* only between the independent set vertices, we transform the independent set into a nearly-regular connected dominating set with full connected coverage.

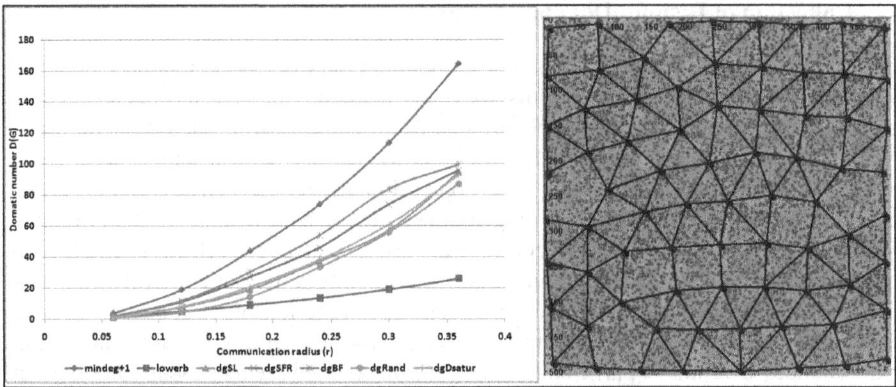

Fig. 3. Evolution of the domatic partition number

Fig. 4. MIS instance, size=75, r=0.12

5 Conclusion and Future Work

In this paper, we have given a comparative study of the performance of several graph coloring algorithms in addressing the domatic partition problem in random geometric graphs. We experimentally show good results on the node coverage yield of the disjoint fully dominating and *(1-ε)* dominating independent sets produced by the coloring algorithms. Owing to the large scale graphs and broad choice of coloring algorithms that we considered, we uncovered better properties on the graph models employed than in the literature [5] and revealed the quasi-triangular lattice of the placement of points in the maximal independent sets produced. Our future work is to study distributed graph coloring algorithms to address the domatic partition problem. Performance in a distributed setting is certainly not as good as in a centralized environment where the global topology of the network is available for study. However, Wireless Sensor Networks are often randomly deployed; therefore distributed and localized solutions have been the main focus of research in the recent years, since they offer better scalability and robustness. In fact, the work we presented in this paper constitutes a basis for comparison and evaluation of localized solutions and an upper bound on the cardinality of the domatic partition and packing of the nodes into maximal independent sets. These two properties are very useful in establishing redundant virtual backbones and regular clustering patterns for a better routing. We also intend to exploit the observed properties to design a holistic and robust routing approach that self-configures and adapts to the state of the environment in a hostile setting.

Acknowledgements

We thank both Dr. Mihaela Iridon and Dr. Saeed Abu-Nimeh for several valuable discussions and Ilteris Murat Derici for his initial work on the SL algorithm and RGG.

References

[1] Arora, A., et al.: ExScal: Elements of an Extreme Scale Wireless Sensor Network. In: Proc. of 11th IEEE RTCSA 2005 (2005)

[2] Bai, X., et al.: Deploying Wireless Sensors to Achieve Both Coverage and Connectivity. In: Proc. of 7th ACM MOBIHOC 2006, pp. 131–142 (2006)

[3] Cardei, M., et al.: Connected Domination in Multihop Ad Hoc Wireless Networks. In: Proc. of 6th Int. Conf. on Computer Science and Informatics (CS&I 2002), pp. 251–255 (2002)

[4] Cardei, M., Wu, J.: Energy-efficient coverage problems in wireless ad-hoc sensor networks. J. of Computer Communications 29(4), 413–420 (2006)

[5] Cardei, M., et al.: Wireless Sensor Networks with Energy Efficient Organization. J. of Interconnection Networks 3(3-4), 213–229 (2002)

[6] Chan, H., Perrig, A.: ACE: An Emergent Algorithm for Highly Uniform Cluster Formation. In: Karl, H., Wolisz, A., Willig, A. (eds.) EWSN 2004. LNCS, vol. 2920, pp. 154–171. Springer, Heidelberg (2004)

[7] Díaz, J., Petit, J., Serna, M.: Random geometric problems on $[0,1]^2$. In: Rolim, J.D.P., Serna, M., Luby, M. (eds.) RANDOM 1998. LNCS, vol. 1518, pp. 294–306. Springer, Heidelberg (1998)

[8] Feige, U., Halldórsson, M.M., Kortsarz, G., Srinivasan, A.: Approximating the domatic number. SIAM J. of Computing 32(1), 172–195 (2003)
[9] Ghosh, A., Das, S.K.: Coverage and connectivity issues in wireless sensor networks: A survey. J. of Pervasive and Mobile Computing 4(3), 303–334 (2008)
[10] Ha, R.W., et al.: Sleep scheduling for wireless sensor networks via network flow model. J. of Computer Communications 29(13-14), 2469–2481 (2006)
[11] He, Y., et al.: Energy Efficient Connectivity Maintenance in Wireless Sensor Networks. In: Proc. of International Conference on Intelligent Computing (ICIC 2006), pp. 95–105 (2006)
[12] Iyengar, R.: Low-coordination Topologies For Redundancy In Sensor Networks. In: Proc. of 6th ACM MOBIHOC 2005, pp. 332–342 (2005)
[13] Kubale, M.: Graph Colorings. American Mathematical Society (2004)
[14] Matula, D., Marble, G., Isaacson, J.D.: Graph Coloring Algorithms. In: Read, R. (ed.) Graph Theory and Computing, pp. 109–122. Academic Press, New York (1972)
[15] Matula, D., Beck, L.L.: Smallest-last ordering and clustering and graph coloring algorithms. J. of the ACM 30(3), 417–427 (1983)
[16] Moscibroda, T., Wattenhofer, R.: Maximizing the Lifetime of Dominating Sets. In: Proc. of 5th IEEE WMAN 2005 (2005)
[17] Pemmaraju, S.V., Pirwani, I.A.: Energy Conservation via Domatic Partitions. In: Proc. of 7th ACM MOBIHOC 2006, pp. 143–154 (2006)
[18] Thai, M.T., et al.: O(log n)-Localized Algorithms on the Coverage Problem in Heterogeneous Sensor Networks. In: Proc. of 26th IEEE IPCCC 2007, pp. 85–92 (2007)
[19] Wagner, D., Wattenhofer, R.: Algorithms for Sensor and Ad Hoc Networks, Advanced Lectures. Springer, Heidelberg (2007)
[20] Wang, B., Fu, C., Lim, H.B.: Layered Diffusion based Coverage Control in Wireless Sensor Networks. In: Proc. Of 32nd IEEE Conference on Local Computer Networks, pp. 504–511 (2007)
[21] Zhang, H., Arora, A.: GS^3: Scalable Self-configuration and Self-healing in Wireless Sensor Networks. J. of Computer Networks 43(4), 459–480 (2003)
[22] Zhang, H., Hou, J.C.: Maintaining Sensing Coverage and Connectivity in Large Sensor Networks. J. of Ad Hoc and Sensor Wireless Networks 1(1-2), 89–124 (2005)
[23] Zhou, Y., et al.: A Point-Distribution Index and Its Application to Sensor-Grouping in Wireless Sensor Networks. In: Proc. of IWCMC 2006, pp. 1171–1176 (2006)

A Comparison of Block-Based and Clip-Based Cooperative Caching Techniques for Streaming Media in Wireless Home Networks

Shahram Ghandeharizadeh and Shahin Shayandeh

Department of Computer Science, University of Southern California, CA 90089, USA
{shahram,shayande}@usc.edu

Abstract. Wireless home networks are widely deployed due to their low cost, ease of installation, and plug-and-play capabilities with consumer electronic devices. Participating devices may cache continuous media (audio and video clips) in order to reduce the demand for outside-the-home network resources and enhance the average delay incurred from when a user references a clip to the onset of its display (startup latency). In this paper, we focus on a home network consisting of a handful of devices configured with a mass storage device to cache data. A cooperative caching technique may manage the available cache space at the granularity of either a clip or individual blocks of a clip. The primary contribution of this paper is to evaluate these two alternatives using realistic specifications of a wireless home network, identifying factors that enable one to outperform the other.

1 Introduction

Wireless home networks are deployed widely due to their ease of installation and economical prices. A typical wireless home network may consist of a handful of devices such as PCs, laptops, TV set-top boxes such as Apple TV, and consumer electronic devices such as DVRs, audio tuners, video game consoles, and Plasma/LCD TVs. The latter is an interesting convergence of electronic devices with wireless technology to enable consumers to display digital content from Internet sites such as YouTube and Hulu to name a few.

With inexpensive mass storage devices (9 cents per gigabyte of magnetic disk storage), a device might be configured with substantial amount of storage to cache data. Algorithms that control the content of these caches are important for several reasons. First, they enhance startup latency as a key quality of service metric, defined as the delay incurred from when a user references a clip to the onset of its display. If the referenced content is cached on a device, the device may display this clip immediately, minimizing startup latency close to zero. Otherwise, the content must be delivered using the wireless network. With continuous media, audio and video clips, one may stream a clip and overlap its display at a device with its retrieval across the network. While streaming minimizes startup latency, it does not reduce it close to zero as with caching. Second,

B. Liu et al. (Eds.): WASA 2009, LNCS 5682, pp. 43–52, 2009.

servicing requests from a local cache minimizes the demand for the infrastructure (network bandwidth and remote servers) outside of the home, freeing these shared resources to service other requests.

The applications used by members of a household define the working set of the household, denoted WS. Examples include user visits to web pages specializing in their area of interest (such as financial) with the same advertisement clips, children shows watched by the younger members of the household over and over again, short video clips such as those found on YouTube and social networking sites, recent wedding and birthday clips watched repeatedly, and others[1].

In this study, we focus on Domical [1], a cooperative caching algorithm for wireless devices in a home network. Domical [1] abstracts the available storage space of a device into three parts named Private, Collaborative, and Elite. The content of the Private portion is dictated by either the user or an application. Domical will not manage or manipulate the Private content. The Collaborative and Elite portions of the storage space constitute the available cache space and are managed by Domical. Domical manages the Elite cache space with the objective to optimize a local metric such as cache hit rate. Candidate algorithms include LRU-K [2], GreedyDual-Size [3] or DYNSimple [4] to name a few. Domical renders the Collaborative cache space of different devices dependent on one another in order to enhance a global metric such as average startup latency. This dependence of collaborative caches does not compromise autonomy of different devices. In particular, if the content watched by the users of different devices is either non-overlapping or have very little overlap, the collaborative cache space of these devices behave as if they are not dependent on one another.

The parameter α [5,6] dictates what fraction of the available cache space is assigned to the Collaborative and Elite portions. Assuming S_{N_i} dictates the cache space of device N_i, the size of Elite space is $\alpha \times S_{N_i}$. The remainder, $(1-\alpha) \times S_{N_i}$, is the Collaborative space. In [1], we show Domical enhances the average startup latency significantly with $\alpha = 0$ when compared with $\alpha = 1$.

A key intuition behind the design of Domical is to minimize the likelihood of bottleneck links when the available bandwidth is asymmetric. This is applicable to both ad-hoc and infrastructure modes of communication as analyzed by a recent study of six wireless homes in United States and United Kingdom [7]. This study provides the following key insights. First, wireless links in a home are highly asymmetric and heavily influenced by precise node location, transmission power, and encoding rate, rather than physical distance between nodes. It showed many links were unable to utilize the maximum transmission rate of the deployed 802.11 technology. For example, with a US home network deployment operating at 30mW and 11 Mbps rate, all devices observed a bandwidth lower than 5 Mbps. While two devices numbered 5 and 6 could communicate, the bandwidth from device 6 to 5 was almost 3 Mbps while the reverse was 1 Mbps. This asymmetric bandwidth was exaggerated in a few instances where the reverse bandwidth was close to zero. Second, this study shows that coverage and

[1] While we focus on streaming media, our techniques apply to other large data items such as images.

performance is enhanced using a multi-hop topology instead of an infrastructure based deployment, motivating mesh capabilities for consumer electronics for seamless connectivity across the home. Without loss of generality, we assume Domical using a multi-hop, mesh deployment of wireless devices.

Different studies to date have focused on different design decisions for Domical, paying little attention to comparing the physical design and granularity of data placement. For example,the concept of urgency worthiness to manage placement of blocks with domical is studied in [8]. The main contribution of this study is to analyze Domical with two different granularities of data replacement: clip-based and block based. They are named Domical Clip-based Replacement (DCR) and Domical Block-based Replacement (DBR). We quantify their performance tradeoffs showing the following key lessons. First, when the total cache space in the home network is significantly smaller than the working set size of the clips referenced by the users of the home, caching at the granularity of a clip is a superior alternative because it minimizes the likelihood of bottleneck links in the home networks. The working set size is defined as the collection of clips that are repeatedly referenced by a household over a period of time, e.g., shows watched repeatedly by the children. With a small working set size and cooperative nodes (small α values), DBR with caching at the granularity of blocks enhances startup latency. If the members of a household do not watch the same content repeatedly or have different interests then the working set size is either very large or infinite, motivating the use of DCR with clips as the granularity of data placement. Second, with a small working set size and α values approximating 0 (cooperative caching), the system should use DBR and cache data at the granularity of a block. Third, we show these observations hold true with different access distributions to data and a variety of in-home network characteristics.

The rest of this paper is organized as follows. Section 2 surveys research related to our replacement techniques. In Section 3, we briefly describe the Domical clip replacement technique, DCR. Section 3.1 extends modifications to implement the DBR technique. We evaluate these alternatives and present our observations in Section 4. Brief conclusions and future research directions are presented in Section 5.

2 Related Work

Our proposed replacement techniques complement the vast body of work on proxy web servers for streaming media, see [9] for a survey. Below, we briefly compare our study with the cooperative replacement techniques found in the prior literature that strive to enhance average startup latency. This is a short comparison due to lack of space. A more detailed discussion can be found in [10].

A group of proxies may cooperate to increase the aggregate cache space, balance load, and improve system scalability [11,12,13,1]. Our study is novel because we quantify the tradeoffs associated with clip and block replacement techniques with Domical. In addition to above, Cooperative proxy caching for streaming media has been explored in overlay networks [14,15]. Our study is different because, in our architecture, the proxy and client caches are the same and one, while they are separate entities in the overlay networks. Finally, a cooperative replacement technique for home gateways in a neighborhood, named DCOORD, is detailed in [5]. In [6], we show Domical enhances startup latency for the home network when compared with DCOORD.

3 Domical Caching Framework

Domical [1] constructs dependencies between the caches of different devices with the objective to prevent the possibility of a wireless link from becoming a bottleneck. A device may contribute a fraction of its available cache space for cooperation with other devices. This is the collaborative space and data items occupying it might be either clips or blocks of different clips. To simplify the discussion and without loss of generality, in the following we assume the granularity of cached data is a clip. In Section 3.1, we describe modifications to support block caching.

The cache space of N_i is made dependent[2] on the state of caches managed by devices N_0, N_1, ..., N_{i-1}. This impacts how N_i victimizes clips as follows. N_i constructs a list of those clips with a replica in the cache space of N_0, N_1, ..., N_{i-1}. These are named common clips. The remaining clips are named rare clips. Domical victims the common clips with the lowest byte-hit rate first. If this does not release sufficient space for the incoming clip X and there are no common clips left, then Domical victimizes the rare clips starting with those that have the lowest byte-hit rate.

One may implement Domical in different ways. Assuming devices in the home network are single user devices with abundant amount of processing capability, a simple implementation would be as follows. When a clip X is admitted into the cache and Domical has insufficient space to store X, it victimizes existing clips as follows. First, it sorts[3] those clips occupying N_i's cache in descending order using their byte-hit rate, $\frac{f_j}{S_j}$, where f_j is the frequency of access to object j and S_j is the size of that object. Next, it marks the first k clips with a total size exceeding the size of the Elite space of the cache. These clips maximize the byte-hit rate of the Elite space. The remaining clips occupy the Collaborative space. Domical identifies the common and rare clips in the Collaborative space, removing as many common clips with a low byte-hit rate to provide space for the incoming clip X. Once common clips are exhausted, it deletes the rare clips starting with the ones that have the lowest byte-hit rate.

N_i may identify common and rare clips by listening on the traffic generated by different devices referencing different clips. Moreover, it may periodically exchange the identity of clips occupying its cache with other devices.

Domical computes dependencies between shared caches of different nodes using the bandwidth contention ratio metric [1]. This metric estimates the amount of imbalance across the network links when N_i streams a clip to every other node

[2] Towards the end of this section, we describe how Domical computes dependencies between different nodes.

[3] Sorting is not appropriate for devices with multiple simultaneous users due to its computational overhead.

in the network. Intuitively, the node with the smallest bandwidth contention value (N_{min}) results in the lowest imbalance, avoiding formation of hot spots and bottleneck links. N_{min} manages its entire cache space (both Elite and Collaborative) using a greedy caching technique. The state of Collaborative space of every other node in the cooperative group depends on N_{min}. Moreover, the remaining nodes are sorted in ascending order using their bandwidth contention ratio metric. The state of the Collaborative space of a node i is dependent on the cache of every other node (both Elite and Collaborative space) before it and N_{min}.

3.1 Domical Block-Based Replacement (DBR)

To change the granularity of data placement from a clip to a block, we modify the local replacement policy used by each device to manage its Elite and Collaborative cache space. Instead of byte hit rate, each device employs the urgency worthiness metric [8] to sort its list of blocks to choose victims. This metric is defined as $\frac{f_i}{B_{Display_i} \times d_{i,j}}$ where $B_{Display_i}$ is the bandwidth required to display clip i and $d_{i,j}$ denotes the display time of jth block of clip i relative to its start. The intuition behind this metric is to cache sufficient number of the first few of blocks of a clip (termed prefetch portion) to enable a client to display these blocks while streaming the remaining blocks of a clip without the client starving for data. This complements streaming to minimize observed startup latency close to zero, similar to a clip being cached in its entirety. The dependencies between Collaborative cache of different devices minimizes the likelihood of duplicate prefetch portions cached across multiple devices.

The use of frequency of access enables many (if not all) blocks of the most popular clip to evict the first few blocks of the least popular clips. This is shown in Section 4.2, see the discussion of Figure 1.

4 Comparison

In this section, we present the simulation model used to compare the alternative techniques. Subsequently, we present the key observations one at a time.

4.1 Simulation Model

We developed a simulation model to compare the alternative block-based and clip-based caching techniques. This model represents a device as a node. A node is configured with a fixed amount of storage and sets aside a portion of it as cache. Let S_T denote the sum of the size of Elite and Collaborative caches contributed by $\mathcal{N}$ nodes in a cooperative group, and S_{WS} to denote the size of the working set of our target application. A node may employ either DCR or DBR to manage the available cache space.

We assume a repository of constant bit rate (CBR) video clips. The display bandwidth requirement of each clip is 4 Mbps. We assume the working set (WS) consists of 864 clips. 864 is an arbitrary number of clips used to generate the test database. We have examined other values and have observed the results of Section 4.2 to hold true for different $\frac{S_T}{S_{WS}}$ values. We examined a variety of media and clip mixes that result in different bandwidth requirements. In all cases, We observed the same lessons. To simplify discussion and without loss of generality, for the rest of this section, we assume all clips have a display time of 30 minutes and each clip is 0.9 GB in size.

We use a Zipf-like distribution [16] with mean of μ to generate requests for different clips. Zipf has been used to model the distribution of web page requests [17,16,18], and sale of movie tickets[4] in the United States [19].

One node in the system is designated to admit requests in the network by reserving link bandwidth on behalf of a stream. This node, denoted N_{admit}, implements the Ford-Fulkerson algorithm [20] to reserve link bandwidths. When there are multiple paths available, N_{admit} chooses the path to minimize startup latency.

The simulator conducts ten thousand rounds. In each round, we select nodes one at a time in a round-robbin manner, ensuring that every node has a chance to be the first to stream a clip in the network. A node (say N_1) references a clip using a random number generator conditioned by the assumed Zipf-like distribution. With DCR, if this clip resides in N_1's local storage then its display incurs a zero startup latency. Otherwise, N_1 identifies those nodes containing its referenced clips, termed candidate servers. Next, it contacts N_{admit} to reserve a path from one of the candidate servers. N_{admit} provides N_1 with the amount of reserved bandwidth, the paths it must utilize, and how long it must wait prior to streaming the clip. This delay is the incurred startup latency.

With DBR, when N_1 references a clip X, the startup latency is zero if all blocks of X are in N_1's cache. Otherwise, N_1 identifies the missing blocks of X, identifies the candidate servers for each blocks, contacts N_{admit} to reserve a path from one of these servers for each block. N_{admit} provides N_1 with the amount of reserved bandwidth, the path it must utilize, and how long it must wait for each block. N_1 uses this information along with the identity of its cached blocks to compute the incurred startup latency.

In each iteration, we measure the following parameters local to a node: startup latency, byte-hit and cache hit rates. In addition, we measure the following global parameters: average startup latency, and average amount of bytes transmitted across the network. To minimize the impact of a cold-start on the observed parameters, the most popular clips are stored in the cache of every device at the start of each experiment. The number of such clips changes for different $\frac{S_T}{S_{WS}}$ values. Section 4.2 shows how this starting state evolves with DCR and DBR.

4.2 Performance Results

We focus on a realistic wireless home network corresponding to a deployment of six nodes employing 802.11a networking cards in a British household [7] with

[4] In [19], a Zipf-like distribution is defined as $\frac{\chi}{i^{(1-\omega)}}$ where ω is 0.27. In this paper, μ equals $1-\omega$. To be consistent with [19], we analyze 0.73 as a possible value for μ in Section 4.

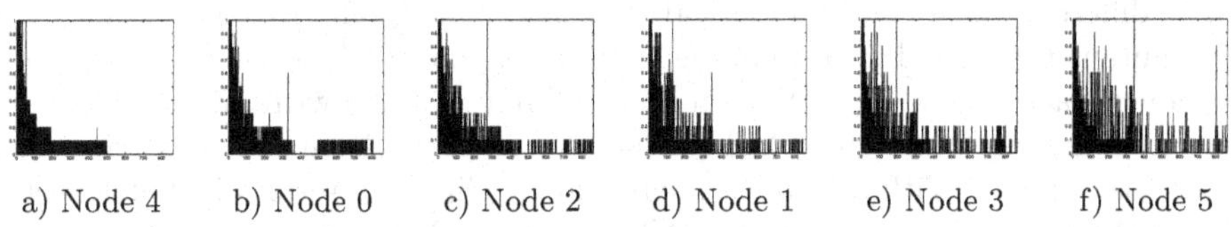

a) Node 4 b) Node 0 c) Node 2 d) Node 1 e) Node 3 f) Node 5

Fig. 1. Distribution of blocks across devices in the network, DBR, $\alpha = 0.7$, $\mu = 0.73$, $\frac{S_T}{S_{WS}} = 0.75$

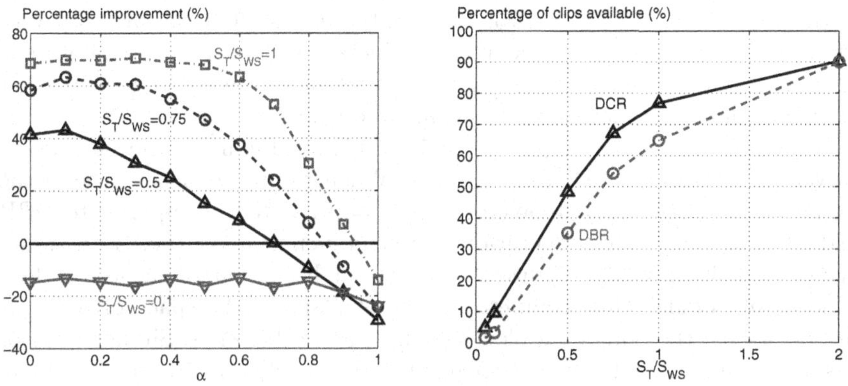

Fig. 2. DBR Vs. DCR, $\mu = 0.73$

Fig. 3. Data availability, $\mu = 0.73$

asymmetric link bandwidths. Domical constructs the same dependencies between the nodes with both DCR and DBR. Let d^i indicate the ith dependency group. Assignment of node N_j to d^i indicates that state of cache in N_j depends on the state of caches in dependency groups d^0 to d^{i-1}. Both DCR and DBR assign Node 4 to d^0. The remaining nodes are assigned as follows: Nodes 0, 2, 1, 3, and 5 to d^1, d^2, d^3, d^4, d^5, respectively. The key difference between the two techniques is the realized placement of data across devices.

Figure 2 shows the percentage improvement in average startup latency provided by DBR when compared with DCR for different α values and $\frac{S_T}{S_{WS}}$ ratios. Assuming δ is the average startup latency observed with each technique, percentage improvement is defined as $100 \times \frac{\delta(DCR)-\delta(DBR)}{\delta(DCR)}$. This is shown on the y-axis of Figure 2 as a function of different α values. This figure highlights two key trends. First, with high $\frac{S_T}{S_{WS}}$ values, small working set size, the percentage improvement observed by DBR when compared with DCR diminishes as α approaches 1. Second, the percentage improvement observed by DBR diminishes with lower $\frac{S_T}{S_{WS}}$ values. With $\frac{S_T}{S_{WS}} = 0.1$, DCR is superior to DBR. We explain each trend in turn.

With α=1, all cache space is Elite and DCR outperforms DBR with alternative $\frac{S_T}{S_{WS}}$ ratios. The explanation for this is as follows. With DBR, each node caches the first few blocks of the most popular clips, causing the placement of blocks across different nodes to be identical to Node 4 in Figure 1.a. The x-axis of this figure is the clip id in descending order of popularity. The y-axis shows the fraction of each cached clip. When a node references a clip with missing blocks, it must stream the remaining blocks of its referenced clip from the infrastructure outside the home. With all nodes referencing a clip, this results in bottleneck links and increased response time. DCR, on the other hand, caches the most popular clip in its entirety onto each node. Now, when a node observes a cache hit for its referenced clip, it services this clip from its local storage, freeing the home network to stream a clip for another node that may have observed a cache miss.

With $\alpha \leq 0.7$ and $\frac{S_T}{S_{WS}} \geq 0.75$, DBR outperforms DCR because different nodes in the network can cache the first few blocks of different clips, see Figure 1. This enables different nodes to act as servers for blocks referenced by another node enhancing startup latency when compared with DCR.

As we reduce the value of $\frac{S_T}{S_{WS}}$ from 1 to 0.1, see Figure 2, the percentage improvement observed by DBR diminishes. When the total cache space of the home network is 10% of the repository ($\frac{S_T}{S_{WS}} = 0.1$), DCR is superior to DBR regardless of the degree of cooperation between different nodes, i.e., all α values shown on the the x-axis of Figure 2. With a small amount of cache, the first few blocks of popular clips compete for the available cache space of different nodes, displacing the remaining blocks of these and other clips. Similar to prior discussion, DBR is now forced to stream the missing blocks of a referenced clip from the home gateway. When all nodes service their requests in this manner, this results in formation of hot spots and bottlenecks. While DCR must also stream a larger number of its requests using the home gateway, it benefits from having a clip in its entirety, enabling a device to observe a low response time every time it observes a cache hit.

With fully cooperative nodes ($\alpha = 0$) and small working set size ($\frac{S_T}{S_{WS}} \geq 0.5$), DBR outperforms DCR for three reasons. First, some devices contain the prefetch portion of a clip, enabling them to overlap the display of this portion with the retrieval of the rest of the clips, minimizing the incurred startup latency. Second, a device may retrieve the blocks of a clip in different order from different nodes, maximizing the utilization of network bandwidth. Third, block replacement has a higher percentage of the repository (as measured in blocks, see below for a discussion of unique clips) cached across devices; typically 10% higher. This enhances the ability of different nodes to stream blocks amongst each other, minimizing dependency of the network on the wireless connection of N_5 as the intermediatory to the home gateway and the outside infrastructure.

While the percentage of cached data is higher with DBR, a clip may not cache its entirety across the caches. These partially cached clips may not be displayed when the home network is disconnected from the outside infrastructure. Figure 3 shows the percentage of clips available with DCR and DBR. In general, DCR provides 10 to 15% higher clip availability when compared with DBR.

Same trends and observations hold true when we vary mean of the distribution of access and available bandwidth of the wireless network.

5 Conclusion and Future Research Directions

The primary contribution of this study is to analyze different granularity of data placement with the Domical cooperative caching technique in the context of a wireless home network. Block-based caching is appropriate when the working set size of an application is relatively small, enabling different devices to service blocks missing from each other's cache. If the working set size of an application is anticipated to be more than ten times the total cache size of the home network, caching at the granularity of a clip is a better alternative because it enhances the average startup latency.

We intend to extend this study in several ways. First, we plan to investigate impact of efficient data delivery algorithms such as patching [21,22] and stream merging [23] with the clip and block replacement techniques. Second, we are exploring a dynamic version of Domical that switches from one granularity of data placement (a block) to another (a clip) based on the observations reported in Section 4.2. To elaborate, these observations identify a few parameters such as the working set size and the available cache space as the basis for deciding the data caching granularity. Assuming a fixed physical block size, a device may switch to clip-based caching by managing its cache using a logical block size, and increasing the size of a logical block to equal the total size of the blocks that constitute a clip. A device may monitor the key parameters and use the average startup latency to decide the size of a logical block. Third, we will conduct a performance analysis of Domical under Dynamic network situations such as nodes joining and leaving the cooperative group due to either mobility or being turned off.

References

1. Ghandeharizadeh, S., Shayandeh, S.: Domical cooperative caching: A novel caching technique for streaming media in wireless home networks. In: Proceedings of the SEDE Conference, June 2008, pp. 274–279 (2008)
2. O'Neil, E.J., O'Neil, P.E., Weikum, G.: The LRU-K Page Replacement Algorithm for Database Disk Buffering. In: Proceedings of the ACM SIGMOD, pp. 413–417 (1993)
3. Jin, S., Bestavros, A.: Popularity-Aware GreedyDual-Size Web Proxy Caching Algorithms. In: Proceedings of the ICDCS, April 2000, pp. 254–261 (2000)
4. Ghandeharizadeh, S., Shayandeh, S.: Greedy cache management techniques for mobile devices. In: Proceedings of the IEEE ICDE, April 2007, pp. 39–48 (2007)
5. Bahn, H.: A Shared Cache Solution for the Home Internet Gateway. IEEE Transactions on Consumer Electronics 50(1), 168–172 (2004)
6. Ghandeharizadeh, S., Shayandeh, S.: An Analysis of Two Cooperative Caching Techniques for Streaming Media in Residential Neighborhoods. In: Submitted for consideration
7. Papagiannaki, K., Yarvis, M., Conner, W.S.: Experimental characterization of home wireless networks and design implications. In: Proceedings of the IEEE INFOCOM, April 2006, pp. 1–13 (2006)

8. Ghandeharizadeh, S., Shayandeh, S.: An evaluation of two domical block replacement techniques for streaming media in wireless home networks. In: Proceedings of the IEEE ISM, December 2008, pp. 372–377 (2008)
9. Liu, J., Xu, J.: Proxy caching for media streaming over the internet. IEEE Communications Magazine 42(8), 88–94 (2004)
10. Ghandeharizadeh, S., Shayandeh, S.: A Comparison of Block-based and Clip-based Cooperative Caching Techniques for Streaming Media in Wireless Home Networks. Technical Report 2009-01, USC Computer Science Department, Los Angeles, CA (2009)
11. Acharya, S., Smith, B.: MiddleMan: A Video Caching Proxy Server. In: Proceedings of the NOSSDAV, June 2000, pp. 162–172 (2000)
12. Chae, Y., Guo, K., Buddhikot, M., Suri, S., Zegura, E.: Silo, Rainbow, and Caching Token: Schemes for Scalable, Fault Tolerant Stream Caching. IEEE Journal on Selected Areas in Communications 20(7), 1328–1344 (2002)
13. Ghandeharizadeh, S., Shayandeh, S.: Cooperative caching techniques for continuous media in wireless home networks. In: Proceedings of the Ambi-Sys, ICST, February 2008, pp. 1–8 (2008)
14. Ip, A.T.S., Liu, J., Lui, J.C.S.: COPACC: An Architecture of Cooperative Proxy-Client Caching System for On-Demand Media Streaming. IEEE Trans. Parallel Distrib. Syst. 18(1), 70–83 (2007)
15. Tran, M., Tavanapong, W., Putthividhya, W.: Ocs: An effective caching scheme for video streaming on overlay networks. Multimedia Tools Appl. 34(1), 25–56 (2007)
16. Breslau, L., Cao, P., Fan, L., Phillips, G., Shenker, S.: Web Caching and Zipf-like Distributions: Evidence and Implications. In: Proceedings of the IEEE INFOCOM, pp. 126–134 (1999)
17. Glassman, S.: A caching relay for the world wide web. Computer Networks and ISDN Systems 27(2), 165–173 (1994)
18. Wolman, A., Voelker, M., Sharma, N., Cardwell, N., Karlin, A., Levy, H.M.: On the Scale and Performance of Cooperative Web Proxy Caching. SIGOPS Opereting Systems Review 33(5), 16–31 (1999)
19. Dan, A., Sitaram, D., Shahabuddin, P.: Scheduling Policies for an On-Demand Video Server with Batching. In: Proceedings of the ACM Multimedia Conference, October 1994, pp. 15–23 (1994)
20. Cormen, T., Leiserson, C., Rivest, R., Stein, C. (eds.): 26.2. In: Introduction to Algorithms. MIT Press, Cambridge (2001)
21. Hua, K., Cai, Y., Sheu, S.: Patching: A Multicast Technique for True Video-on-Demand Services. In: Proceedings of the ACM Multimedia Conference, September 1998, pp. 191–200 (1998)
22. Chen, S., Shen, B., Yan, Y., Zhang, X.: Buffer Sharing for Proxy Caching of Streaming Sessions. In: Proceedings of the WWW Conference (May 2003)
23. Eager, D., Vernon, M., Zahorjan, J.: Optimal and Efficient Merging Schedules for Video-on-Demand Servers. In: Proceedings of the ACM Multimedia Conference, October 1999, pp. 199–202 (1999)

Dynamic Power Management for Sensor Node in WSN Using Average Reward MDP

Somayeh Kianpisheh and Nasrolah Moghadam Charkari

School of Electrical and Computer Engineering
Tarbiat Modares University, Tehran, Iran
{s_kianpisheh,moghadam}@modares.ac.ir

Abstract. Reducing energy consumption is one of the key challenges in sensor networks. One technique to reduce energy consumption is dynamic power management. In this paper we model power management problem in a sensor node as an average reward Markov Decision Process and solve it using dynamic programming. We achieve an optimal policy that maximizes long-term average of utility per energy consumption. Simulation results show our approach has the ability of reaching to the same amount of utility as always on policy while consuming less energy than always on policy.

Keywords: Wireless sensor network, Power management, Average reward Markov Decision Process, Dynamic programming.

1 Introduction

Wireless sensor networks have different applications in medical care, military and environment monitoring. Because of energy constraints in sensor nodes, lots of researches have been done to reduce energy consumption. One technique to reduce energy consumption and extend network lifetime is dynamic power management (DPM). DPM is an effective tool in reducing system power consumption without significantly degrading performance. The basic idea is to shut down devices when not needed and wake them up when necessary [1]. Although lots of researches have been done for power management in sensor networks, most of proposed mechanisms take advantage of the energy saving feature of the deep sleep mode. [2] Reviews some of these works. There exist other modes for sensor nodes that exploiting them can effectively reduce energy consumption. Four major modes for a sensor node have been defined. On-Duty, Sensing Unit On-Duty, Transceiver On-Duty and Off-Duty [2]. In On-Duty all the components in the node including sensing unit, transceiver and processor are turned on. In Sensing Unit On-Duty, sensing unit and the processor are turned on but the transceiver is turned off. In Transceiver On-Duty, the transceiver and the processor are turned on but all the sensing units are turned off. In Off-Duty or sleep mode, the processor is turned off but a timer or some other triggering mechanism may be running to wake up the node. Four different sleep modes can be defined: Monitor, Observe, Listen and Deep Sleep [2]. The processor is turned off in all sleep modes. However, in the Monitor mode, both the sensing unit and the transceiver are left on. In the Observe mode, only the sensing unit is on. In Listen

B. Liu et al. (Eds.): WASA 2009, LNCS 5682, pp. 53–61, 2009.

mode, only the transceiver is turned on. Finally in the Deep Sleep mode, neither the sensing unit nor the transceiver is turned on [2].

There are some works that exploit different power modes of a sensor node. A dynamic power management for sensor networks has been proposed in [1] with five power modes for a sensor node. Using the fact that transition from active mode to a sleep mode and vice versa has the overhead of latency and energy, it computes a threshold for each sleep mode. When the node becomes idle it switches to the lowest possible power mode that the probability of event occurrence during its corresponding threshold is negligible. [3] makes the computing of thresholds used in [1] more precisely by considering additional energy consumption due to awakening the sensor node back to active state. [4] also modifies the protocol of [1] in such a way that coverage is supported. [5] proposes an algorithm based on wavelet neural network for DPM in sensor networks [5].

[1, 3, 4] Do not exploit some possible modes like Transceiver On-Duty and Listen mode. Exploiting these modes will reduce total energy consumption. They also do not deal with a generic system architecture which supports buffering of received packets or events. In this paper in addition to power modes used in [1, 3, 4] we utilize Transceiver On-Duty and Listen mode, and also buffering technique. We model power management problem in sensor networks as an average reward MDP. The goal is to find an optimal policy that maximizes long-term average of utility per energy consumption. The rest of paper is as follows. Section 2 briefly discusses on average reward MDP and dynamic programming. Proposed solution is described in section 3. Section 4 shows the results and finally section 5 contains conclusion and future works.

2 Markov Decision Process and Dynamic Programming

An MDP is defined as a $(\boldsymbol{S}, \boldsymbol{A}, \boldsymbol{P}, \boldsymbol{R})$ tuple, here $\boldsymbol{S}$ is the state space, $\boldsymbol{A}$ is the set of all possible actions at each state, $\boldsymbol{P}$ is transition function $\boldsymbol{S} \times \boldsymbol{A} \times \boldsymbol{S} \to [0, 1]$ and $\boldsymbol{R}$ is reward function $\boldsymbol{S} \times \boldsymbol{A} \to \mathbb{R}$. The transition function shows a probability distribution over the next state as a function of the current state and agent's action. According to this definition $P_{xy}(a)$ shows the probability of transitioning from state $x \in \boldsymbol{S}$ to state $y \in \boldsymbol{S}$ by doing action $a \in \boldsymbol{A}$ and $R_{xy}(a)$ shows the reward achieved in this transition. The Average reward MDP's solution consists of finding the optimal policy π^* that maximizes the average reward per stage [6]. The average reward of state x under policy π is defined as formula 1:

$$\rho^{\pi}(x) = \lim_{N \to \infty} \frac{E(\sum_{t=0}^{N-1} R_t^{\pi}(x))}{N} \tag{1}$$

Where $\rho^{\pi}(x)$ shows the average reward of state x under policy π, $R_t^{\pi}(x)$ is the reward received at time t and E(.) denotes the expected value. A *gain optimal* policy π^* is defined as one that maximizes the average reward over all states. In *average reward* frameworks the policy chain structure plays a critical role in average reward methods [7]. A key observation is that for unichain MDP's, the average reward of any policy is state independent and further more for any MDP that is either unichain or communicating there exists a value function V^* and a scalar ρ^* satisfying the bellman equation:

$$V^*(x) + \rho^* = \max_{a \in A(x)} (r(x,a) + \sum_y P_{xy}(a)\ V^*(y)) \tag{2}$$

Where $V^*(x)$ is optimal bias value for state x and ρ^* is the optimal average reward and $r(x,a)$ shows the expected reward achieved by doing action a in state x. Greedy policy resulting from V^* achieves the optimal average reward. One of the approaches for solving bellman equation is Dynamic programming methods. *Unichain policy iteration* is a dynamic programming method for computing optimal policy in an average reward MDP. If the MDP is unichain this algorithm surely converges to gain optimal policy [7]. As we will discuss in section 3 the MDP of power management problem is communicating but multichain. Although there are algorithms for computing gain optimal policy in communicating or even multichain MDPs like [8, 9], for simplicity with one assumption we simplify the problem to be unichain and use unichain policy iteration to compute optimal policy.

Table 1. Power modes for a sensor node (tx = transmit, rx = receive)

State	Processor	Sensing unit	Radio	utility	Power(mw)
On-Duty (S0)	active	sense	tx/rx	$n_s + n_r + n_t$	$P_0 = 1040$
Transceiver On-Duty (S1)	active	off	tx/rx	$n_r + n_t$	$P_1 = 980$
Monitor (S2)	sleep	sense	rx	$n_s + n_r$	$P_2 = 270$
Listen (S3)	sleep	off	rx	n_r	$P_3 = 210$
Observe (S4)	sleep	sense	off	n_s	$P_4 = 200$
Deep Sleep (S5)	Sleep	off	off	Small value	$P_5 = 10$

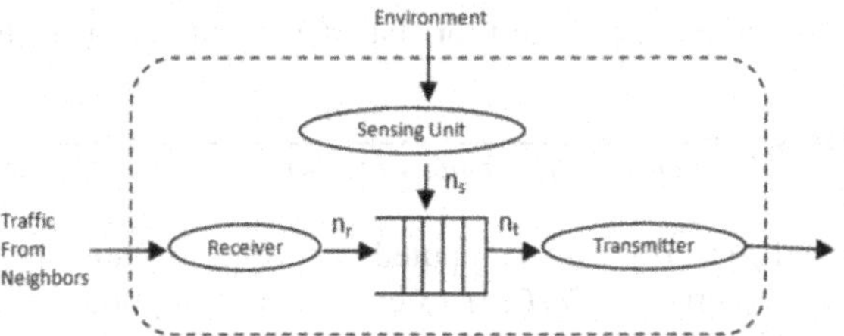

Fig. 1. Assumed architecture for a sensor node

3 Power Management in Sensor Node

A sensor node has several major components: processor, memory, A/D converter, sensing unit and radio. Each node sleep mode corresponds to a particular combination of component power modes. In general, if there are N components labeled *(*1,2, . . ., *N)* each with k_i sleep modes, the total number of node sleep modes is $\prod_{i=1}^{N} K_i$. However, from a practical point of view not all sleep modes are useful [3]. Table 1 shows the useful sleep modes in a sensor node. We assume that time is divided into time slices. The time slice is chosen in such a way that transitions to power modes satisfy the *minimum break-even time* introduced in [10] for every possible transition.

At the beginning of each time slice, the node has to decide in which power mode it operates. It decides in such a way that expected long-term average of utility per energy consumption be maximized. We define a utility for each power mode. To clarify how we define the utility and how we model the problem, figure 1 shows our assumed abstract architecture of a sensor node. We assume that sensing unit senses the environment and if any event detected packets containing required features are put into the buffer for transmission. Similarly, when receiver receives some packets from any neighbor it puts them into the buffer and transmitter removes packets from buffer for transmission. We define n_s as number of packets put into the buffer by sensing unit during a time slice. n_r shows number of packets put into the buffer by receiver during a time slice and finally n_t shows number of packets transmitted by transmitter during a time slice. Using n_s, n_r, n_t we define a utility for each of power modes (Table 1). In fact utility shows the throughput of the components which are on during a time slice. The goal is to maximize utility while minimize energy consumption. For achieving this goal, we define the objective function as long-term average of utility per total consumed energy. We want to find the optimal policy that maximizes this objective function. According to this optimal policy, at the beginning of each time slice the node chooses the best possible power mode.

3.1 Finding Power Management Policy Using Average Reward MDP

In this section we model power management problem as an average reward Markov Decision Process. The elements of MDP are as following:

State space: We model the states with number of packets in the buffer. In a formal way: $S = \{i \mid i \in \mathbb{N} \cup \{0\},\ 0 \le i \le \max\ buffer\ size\}$
Action space: power modes form the action space. $A = \{S0, S1, S2, S3, S4, S5\}$
Reward function: We define the reward for state n and action S_i as formula 3.

$$reward(n, S_i) = \frac{utility(S_i)}{(power(S_i) * time\ slice\ duration) + bufferCost(n')} \quad (3)$$

Where *utility(S_i)* and *power(S_i)* are computed according to table 1. To avoid buffer overflow, we added function *bufferCost* to energy consumption which shows buffer processing cost. *bufferCost* is a function of number of packets in the buffer. In simulations we used a linear function. That is $bufferCost(n') = an' + b$. Here n' denotes the next state. At the beginning of each time slice, sensor node selects a power mode according to number of packets in the buffer and the optimal policy computed.

We use dynamic programming to compute the optimal policy. As dynamic programming methods are model based, we need knowledge about the probability of transition between states. We model packet arrival from sensing unit and receiver with poisson distribution with mean packet arrival rate λ_s and λ_r respectively. So, the probability of receiving x packets from sensing unit and receiver during a time slice is computed by formula 4 and 5, respectively, where T denotes time slice duration.

$$P_{n_s}(x) = \frac{e^{-T\lambda_s} \times (T\lambda_s)^x}{x!} \quad (4)$$

$$P_{n_r}(x) = \frac{e^{-T\lambda_r} \times (T\lambda_r)^x}{x!} \tag{5}$$

Denoting the number of packet arrivals during a time slice, as $n_a = 0, 1 \ldots$ we define transition between states and corresponding probabilities as table 2. In this table, n_t shows the number of packets which can be transmitted by transmitter during a time slice. For simplicity, we assume that communication is reliable and n_t has a fixed value. These probabilities are computed by the fact that in each power mode sensing unit and receiver can be on or off. If the component is on some packets may come from it, otherwise it does not generate any packet. Now, we can use dynamic programming methods to find the optimal policy. In the next section, we discuss on properties of the MDP.

Table 2. Transition characteristics of power management problem. $n_a = 0, 1, 2 \ldots$

<Current State, action>	Transition Probability	Next State
$<n, S_0>$	$\sum_{x=0 \ldots n_a} P_{n_s}(x) \times P_{n_r}(n_a - x)$	$n + n_a - n_t$
$<n, S_1>$	$P_{n_r}(n_a)$	$n + n_a - n_t$
$<n, S_2>$	$\sum_{x=0 \ldots n_a} P_{n_s}(x) \times P_{n_r}(n_a - x)$	$n + n_a$
$<n, S_3>$	$P_{n_r}(n_a)$	$n + n_a$
$<n, S_4>$	$P_{n_s}(n_a)$	$n + n_a$
$<n, S_5>$	1	n

3.2 Discussion on MDP Structure

The MDP of power management problem *is multichain*. The reason is that there are some deterministic policies which generate more than one recurrent class. For example policy π which selects S_5 in every state generates (*max buffer size* + 1) recurrent classes. The MDP is *communicating*. The reason is that, we can reach from every state to other state with *positive probability* by combination of actions S_0, S_1, S_2, S_3, *and S4* through one or more transitions. Although there are algorithms for computing gain optimal policy in communicating or even multichain MDPs like [8, 9] for simplicity in the simulation we omit S_5 from action space. With this assumption the MDP becomes unichain. Thus, we can use a simple method like *unichain policy iteration* [7] to compute optimal policy.

If we omit S_5 from action space the MDP will be unichain. In general, the problem of detecting whether a finite state and action MDP is unichain under all deterministic policies, is NP-hard [11]. Some polynomial cases of the unichain classification problem for MDPs have been proposed in [12]. We use one of these cases to prove that the MDP with the assumption of omitting S_5 from action space is unichain. [12] Proposes a polynomial algorithm that detects whether a particular state *i* is recurrent and if it is recurrent, whether the MDP is unichain. Using this algorithm we prove that *buffer full state* is recurrent under all deterministic policies and use condition specified in [12] to conclude that MDP is unichain.

The set $Y \sqsubset S$ is called avoidable from state i, if there exists a deterministic policy φ such that $P_i^{\varphi}(x_t \epsilon Y) = 0$ for all t = 0, 1 … where $P_i^{\varphi}(x_t \epsilon Y)$ shows the probability of reaching from state i to state x_t under policy φ. $Z^A(Y)$ Denotes the set of $i \in S$ from which Y is avoidable. According to algorithm described in [12], if $Z^A(i) = \emptyset$, the state i is recurrent and the MDP is unichain. We show that $Z^A(buffer\ full\ state) = \emptyset$ and thus we conclude that *buffer full state* is recurrent and the MDP is unichain.

Figure 2 shows the algorithm proposed in [12] for computing $Z^A(Y)$. Starting from $Z := Y$, in step 2, this algorithm tries to expand Z with states ($\tilde{Z}$) which *under every deterministic policy, the process reaches from them to any member in Z.* In this step, $p(l|j,a)$ denotes the probability of transition from state j to state l by doing action a. In step 3, any state that is not a member of Z, is regarded as states that Y is avoidable from them.

Now, using this algorithm, we show that $Z^A(buffer\ full\ state) = \emptyset$. In the power management MDP (with omitted S_5 from action space), from any arbitrary state like $j \in \{0, 1, \dots\ max\ buffer\ size - 1\}$ under every deterministic policy, the probability of transitioning to buffer full state is positive. The reason is that in each state five actions are possible (S_0, S_1, S_2, S_3, S_4). Choosing action S_0 or S_1 in state j causes transition to some states like (j + n_a - n_t). when $n_a = \max buffer\ size - j + n_t > 0$, a transition to buffer full state occurs with a positive transition probability defined for actions S_0 or S_1 respectively in table 2. Similarly, choosing action S_2 or S_3 or S_4 in state j, causes transition to some states like j + n_a. In this case, when $n_a = \max buffer\ size - j$ a transition to buffer full state happens, with a transition probability defined for actions S_2 or S_3 or S_4, respectively in table 2. We conclude that all states reach to buffer full state under every deterministic policy and thus running algorithm proposed in [12] for our MDP, causes every state $j \in \{0, 1, \dots\ max\ buffer\ size - 1\}$ be added to Z = { $buffer\ full\ state$} and thus $Z^A(buffer\ full\ state) = \emptyset$. According to [12], we conclude that buffer full state is recurrent and the MDP is unichain.

1. Set $Z := Y, \tilde{Z} := Y$.
2. Do while $\tilde{Z} \neq \emptyset$: for $j \in S \setminus Z$ set

$$A(j) := A(j) \setminus \left\{ a \in A(j) | \sum_{l \in \tilde{Z}} p(l|j,a) > 0 \right\},$$

set $\tilde{Z} := \{j \in S \setminus Z : A(j) = \emptyset\}$, and set $Z := Z \cup \tilde{Z}$; end do.
3. Set $Z^A(Y) := S \setminus Z$. Stop.

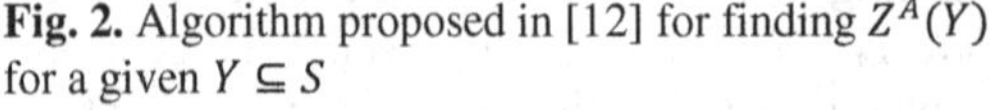

Fig. 2. Algorithm proposed in [12] for finding $Z^A(Y)$ for a given $Y \subseteq S$

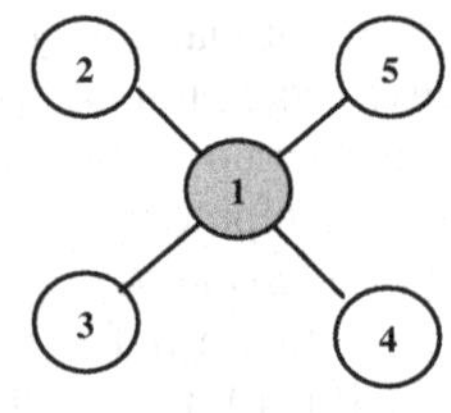

Fig. 3. Star topology used in simulation

4 Results

We did simulation in a star topology shown in figure 3. Nodes 2,3,4,5 send packets to node 1 with a poisson distribution with rates varies from 0.1 to 1 packet/second. Sensing unit generates no traffic. We control the power for node 1 in three ways:

Our approach (AR-MDP): It finds the policy that maximizes long-term average of utility per energy consumption.

Always on policy: this is a simple policy that always selects power mode S_0.

Random policy: This policy selects power modes randomly.

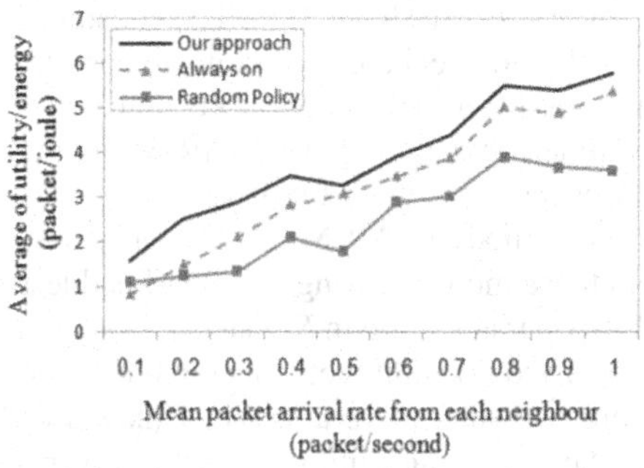

Fig. 4. Average of utility/energy consump-tion versus packet arrival rate in star topology

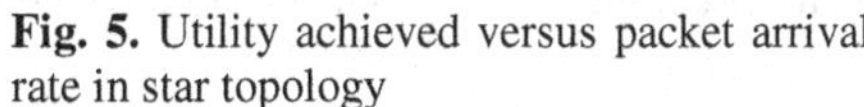

Fig. 5. Utility achieved versus packet arrival rate in star topology

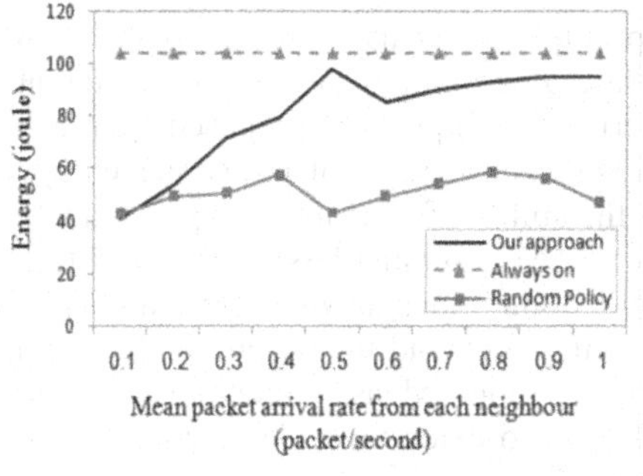

Fig. 6. Energy consumption versus packet arrival rate in star topology

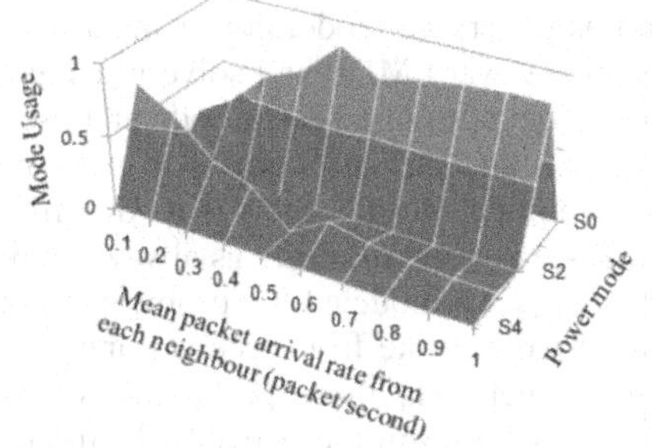

Fig. 7. Power mode usage for our approach (AR-MDP) in star topology

In our simulation we used a buffer with size 20 and time slice equal to 2 second. Figure 4 shows the average of utility per energy consumption versus packet arrival rate. As shown in this figure, average of utility per energy consumption increases when traffic load increases. The reason is that in larger packet arrival rates, more utility is achieved. As expected our approach has achieved higher average of utility per energy consumption than always on and random policy. As traffic load increases the distance between AR-MDP and always on policy decreases. The reason is that in high rates AR-MDP selects S_1 more than other power modes and the difference between power used in modes S_1 and S_0 which is used by always on policy is little. As expected Random policy has the lowest average of utility per energy.

Figure 5 shows sum of utility achieved during time slices. Our approach approximately achieves the same utility as always on policy. The reason is that AR-MDP tries not to miss utility if energy consumed for achieving that utility is acceptable and causes increase in objective function as a whole. Notice that always on policy achieves the maximum possible amount of utility. Random policy achieves the least amount of utility because it chooses power modes randomly.

Figure 6 illustrates the total energy consumed during time slices. Always on policy permanently operates in mode S_0 so it consumes more energy than two other policies. Our approach outperforms always on policy. In low traffic load AR-MDP consumes less energy than always on. In high traffic loads the difference between always on and our approach decreases because in high rates AR-MDP selects S_1 more than other power modes. Although random policy consumes less energy than AR-MDP but clearly it is not a good approach because it misses large amount of utility.

Figure 7 shows amount of usage for each power mode in AR-MDP. The only used power modes are S_1 and S_3. The reason is that in these modes sensing unit is off and less energy is consumed. In low traffic load AR-MDP operates more in S_3 than S_1. In fact, it prefers to buffer little amount of packets it receives and transmit them in a burst manner. In high traffic load it uses more S_1 because from one side, more utility is achieved by receiving and transmitting packets and from other side transmitting packets prevents buffer processing cost reduces average of reward in high traffic loads.

5 Conclusion

In this paper, we model power management problem in a sensor node in WSN as an average reward MDP and solve it using dynamic programming. We exploit different possible modes of a sensor node and use buffering technique. The proposed approach achieves an optimal policy that maximizes long-term average of utility per energy consumption. Results show that AR-MDP has the ability of reaching to approximately the same amount of utility as always on policy while consuming less energy than it. In this paper we modeled the problem using some assumptions about the probability of packet arrival rate from receiver and sensing unit. To extend the proposed algorithm for the network, these probabilities have to be computed as a function of event occurrence rate in the network. In future, we want to extend the idea for a network and complete our simulations for multi hop scenario.

References

[1] Sinha, A., Chandrakasan, A.: Dynamic Power Management in Wireless Sensor Networks. IEEE Design & Test of Computers 18, 62–74 (2001)

[2] Wang, L., Xiao, Y.: A Survey of Energy-Efficient Scheduling Mechanisms in Sensor Networks. Mobile Networks and Applications 11, 723–740 (2006)

[3] Lin, C., Xiong, N., Park, J.H., Kim, T.-H.: Dynamic power management in new architecture of wireless sensor networks. International Journal of Communication Systems (2008)

[4] Luo, R.C., Tu, L.C., Chen, O.: An Efficient Dynamic Power Management Policy on Sensor Network. In: Proceedings of the 19th International Conference on Advanced Information Networking and Applications (2005)
[5] Shen, Y., Guo, B.: Dynamic Power Management based on Wavelet Neural Network in Wireless Sensor Networks. In: International Conference on Network and Parallel Computing, pp. 431–436 (2007)
[6] Bertsekas, D.: Dynamic Programming and Optimal Control, 2nd edn., vol. 1 and 2. Athena Scientific, Belmont (2000)
[7] Mahadevan, S.: Average Reward Reinforcement Learning: Foundation, Algorithms, and Empirical Results. Machine Learning 22, 159–196 (1996)
[8] Haviv, M., Puterman, M.L.: An Improved Algorithm For Solving Communicating Average Reward Markov Decision Processes. Annals of Operations Research 28, 229–242 (1991)
[9] White, D.: Dynamic programming, markov chains, and the method of successive approximations. Journal of Mathematical Analysis and Applications 6, 373–376 (1963)
[10] Chiasserini, C.-F., Rao, R.R.: Improving Energy Saving in Wireless Systems by Using Dynamic Power Management. IEEE Transactions on WIRELESS COMMUNICATIONS 2, 1090–1100 (2003)
[11] Tsitsiklis, J.N.: NP-hardness of checking the unichain condition in average cost MDPs. Oper. Res. Lett. 35, 319–323 (2007)
[12] Feinberg, E.A., Yang, F.: On polynomial cases of the unichain classification problem for Markov Decision Processes. Operations Research Letters 36, 527–530 (2008)

Energy Consumption of Fair-Access in Sensor Networks with Linear and Selected Grid Topologies

Miao Peng and Yang Xiao*

Department of Computer Science,
The University of Alabama
101 Houser Hall, Box 870290
Tuscaloosa, AL 35487-0290 USA
mpeng@cs.ua.edu, yangxiao@ieee.org

Abstract. In this paper, we investigate energy consumption of medium access control (MAC) for multi-hop sensor networks. In a wireless sensor network, one of the primary tasks of sensor nodes is to gather data and give an accurate measurement of the sensing environment. Thus, obtaining a fair amount of data from each sensor node plays a key role to achieve this objective. In this scenario, we adopt the model of a fair-access criterion which requires that sensor nodes have an equal rate of frame delivery to the base station. Then we derive tight lower bounds on network energy consumption in a cycle during which the base station successfully receives at least one original data frame from each sensor node. The unique aspect of this study is that the lower bounds on energy consumption hold for any MAC protocol. Furthermore, we prove that these bounds are tight.

Keywords: MAC protocol.

1 Introduction

A wireless sensor network is composed of a great number of low-cost, multifunctional battery-operated sensor nodes. Distributed sensor nodes can perform many tasks such as military monitoring, pollution detection, and smart spaces [1]. Thus, the technology of wireless sensor networks has attracted significant research interest in recent years.

A sensor node is a microelectronic device and equipped by limited power battery. It is often difficult to change or recharge batteries for sensor nodes in many applications. For example, sensor nodes can be deployed in hostile field and some rough environments such as mountains and forests. Thus, energy efficiency is an important issue when designing MAC protocols. To analyze and evaluate the energy efficiency of MAC protocols, the sources of energy waste need analysis [2-3] and include idle listening, message collision, overhearing, control-packet overhead, and overemitting (i.e., after a source's transmission, the destination is still not ready for receiving). Many researchers have done research work in designed energy efficiency MAC protocols. The authors in [4] proposed an energy-efficient S-MAC protocol for

* Corresponding author.

B. Liu et al. (Eds.): WASA 2009, LNCS 5682, pp. 62–69, 2009.

a wireless sensor network [4]. In this protocol [4], nodes periodically sleep and neighboring nodes form virtual clusters to auto-synchronize on sleep schedules. Furthermore, S-MAC sets the radio to sleep during transmissions of other nodes to save energy. Recently, the authors in [5] proposed a fair-access criterion for MAC protocols which has many applications in an underwater sensor network [5]. In [5], the authors derived the tight upper bounds on network utilization for linear and two-row gird topologies (illustrated in Fig.1 and Fig.2). We further explored the issue of optimal utilization for more complicated topologies in [6] (illustrated in Fig.3 and Fig.4). The significance of their work is that those upper bounds on network utilization derived in [5-6] hold for any MAC protocol employing fair-access criterion. However, energy consumption is not considered in [5-6].

The main contribution of our work is explained as follows. We derive the tight lower bounds on energy consumption and these bounds hold for any MAC protocol employing the fair-access criterion no matter whether the protocol is a contention-free protocol or a contention-based protocol. Furthermore, these lower bounds can be reached by a version of TDMA protocol. Thus, these bounds are necessary to decide whether a designed MAC protocol is appropriate or not.

This paper is organized as follows. In Section 2, we first review the model of the wireless sensor network employing a fair-access criterion MAC protocol and then review the minimum cycle time derived in [5-6]. In Section 3, the tight lower bounds on energy consumption in each cycle are derived for linear, two-row, three-row and four-row grid topologies. In Section 4, we evaluate the energy consumption in a cycle. Finally, we conclude the paper in Section 5.

2 Review of Network with Fair-Access Criterion

2.1 Fair-Access Criterion

In this subsection, we review the model of the wireless sensor network which employs a fair-access MAC protocol. Based on [5-6], the definition of the wireless sensor network which employs a fair-access MAC protocol is given as follows. A wireless sensor network is composed of a base station (BS) and n sensor nodes which are denoted as O_i; $i = 1, 2, \dots n$. Sensor nodes generate data frames and send them to BS. Some sensor nodes not only generate sensor data frames but also forward/route frames to BS, i.e., a frame may need to be relayed by several nodes to reach BS. Let $U(n)$ denote the utilization of the above sensor network i.e., the fraction of time that the BS receives data frames. Let G_i denote the contribution of (i.e., data generated by) sensor O_i to the total utilization. The following holds: $U(n) = \sum_{i=1}^{n} G_i$. A fair-access criterion MAC protocol in a wireless sensor network requires sensor nodes contribute equally to the network utilization, i.e., the following condition holds: $G_1 = G_2 = \dots = G_i$.

2.2 Minimum Cycle Time

In this subsection, we review the minimum cycle time of fair-access with four specific topologies, linear, 2-row grid, 3-row gird and 4-row gird [5-6]. Firstly, we describe these four topologies. Then we review seven claims about minimum cycle time proposed in [5-6]. For convenience to state the claim, here we introduce some notations. Let x denote the cycle time for the network under the fair-access criteria. During the cycle time, the BS either be busy or be idle. Therefore, we have $x = b + y$, where b denote the busy time in a cycle and y denote the idle time in a cycle. Moreover, during the period x, the BS successfully receives at least one original data frame from each sensor node in the network. For example, in a wireless sensor network with n sensor nodes, during the time x the BS may receive more than n frames, but only n different original sources frame can be counted in the utilization under the fair-access criterion. In addition, let T denote the transmission time of one data frame.

The four topologies are reviewed in this section [5-6].

Linear Topology: The topology is illustrated in Fig. 1. There are n sensor nodes and a base station (BS) in a linear fashion. The transmission range of each node is one hop and the interference range is less than two hops. In other words, only neighboring nodes can hear each other. As illustrated in Fig. 1, O_i generates its own data frames and sends the frames to O_{i+1}. O_i also relays data frames received from O_{i-1} to O_{i+1}. Finally, O_n forwards data to the BS, which collects all the data frames.

2-Row Grid Topology: The topology is illustrated in Fig. 2.There are $2n$ sensor nodes and a base station (BS) in 2-row grid fashion. The transmission range of each node is one hop; namely only horizontal or vertical neighbors can hear each other but two diagonal neighbors cannot. Two routing patterns are considered: (i) the two rows forward data frames independently, as illustrated in Fig. 2a. (ii) the bottom sensor nodes forward data frames to the top row first, as illustrated in Fig. 2b.

3-Row Grid Topology: The topology is illustrated in Fig. 3.There are $3n$ sensor nodes and a base station (BS) in 3-row grid fashion. The transmission range of each node is one hop. In other words, only horizontal or vertical neighbors can hear each other but two diagonal neighbors can not. Two routing patterns are considered: (i) the three rows forward data frames independently, as illustrated in Fig. 3a. (ii) the top and bottom sensor nodes first forward data frame to the middle row as illustrated in Fig. 3b.

4-Row Grid Topology: The 4-row grid topology is illustrated in Fig. 4. Same as 3-row grid topology, the transmission range of each node is just one hop so that only horizontal or vertical neighbors can hear each other but two diagonal neighbors cannot. Likewise, two routing patterns illustrated in Fig. 4a and Fig. 4b are considered, respectively.

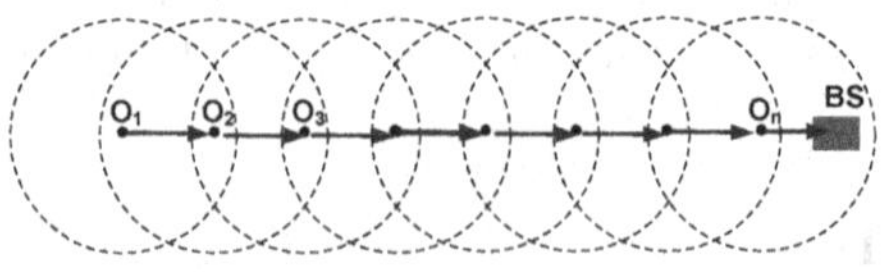

Fig. 1. Linear topology

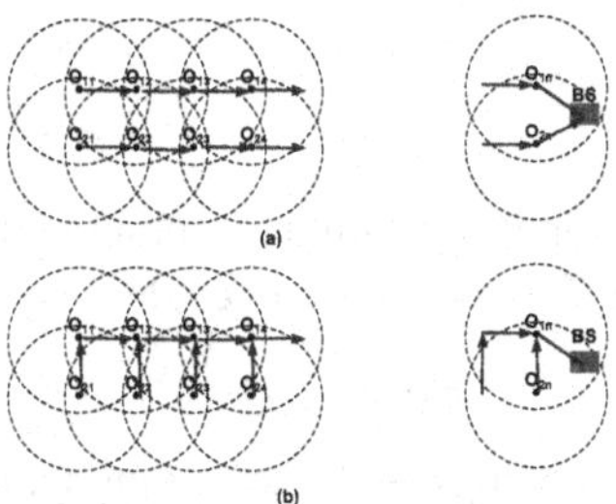

Fig. 2. Grid topology with two rows of sensor nodes

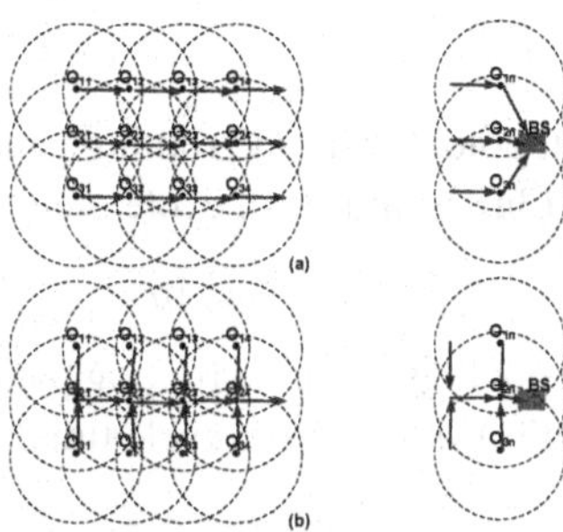

Fig. 3. Grid topology with three rows of sensor nodes

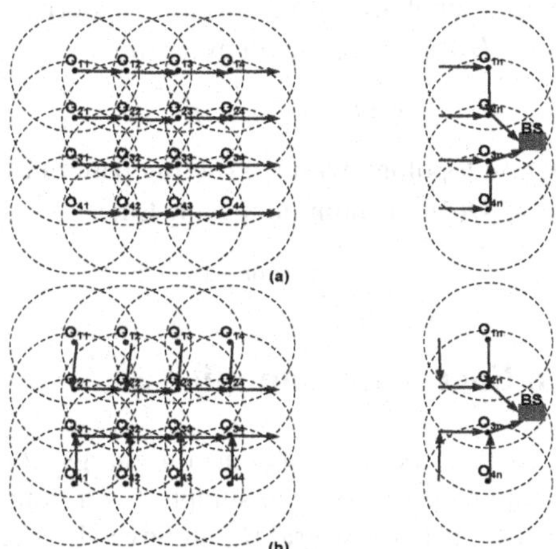

Fig. 4. Grid topology with four rows of sensor nodes

For network with these four specific topologies, the authors in [5] and [6] present the lower bounds on cycle time. We list seven claims about minimum cycle time proposed in [5-6] in the following:

Claim 1: For the linear topology under fair-access criterion, $D(n)$ is minimum cycle time:

$$X \geq D(n) = \begin{cases} 3(n-1)T & n \geq 2 \\ T & n = 1 \end{cases}$$

Claim 2: For the 2-row grid topology with the routing pattern as illustrated in Fig.2a, under fair-access criterion, $D(2n)$ is minimum cycle time:

$$X \geq D(2n) = (3n-1)T$$

Claim 3: For the 2-row grid topology with the routing pattern as illustrated in Fig.2b, under fair-access criterion, $D(2n)$ is minimum cycle time:

$$X \geq D(2n) = \begin{cases} (6n-5)T & n \geq 2 \\ 3T & n = 1 \end{cases}$$

Claim 4: For the 3-row grid topology with the routing pattern as illustrated in Fig.3a, under fair-access criterion, $D(3n)$ is minimum cycle time:

$$X \geq D(3n) = (4n-1)T$$

Claim 5: For the 3-row grid topology with the routing pattern as illustrated in Fig.3b, under fair-access criterion, $D(3n)$ is minimum cycle time:

$$X \geq D(3n) = \begin{cases} (9n-7)T & n \geq 2 \\ 5T & n = 1 \end{cases}$$

Claim 6: For the 4-row grid topology with the routing pattern as illustrated in Fig.4a, under fair-access criterion, $D(4n)$ is minimum cycle time:

$$X \geq D(4n) = (6n-1)T$$

Claim 7: For the 4-row grid topology with the routing pattern as illustrated in Fig.4b, under fair-access criterion, $D(4n)$ is minimum cycle time:

$$X \geq D(4n) = (6n-1)T$$

3 Lower Bound on Energy Consumption

In this section, we investigate the lower bound on energy consumption. The tight lower bound on sensor network energy consumption for four specific topologies, linear, 2-row grid [5], 3-row grid, 4-row grid [6] are given by analytical method based on the knowledge of TDMA scheduling algorithm stated in above section. Our method is independent of the MAC protocol. No matter which MAC protocol is used, as long as the protocol conforms to the fair-access criterion, the low bounds on energy consumption hold.

Before showing the proofs, Let us provide some notations using in the proofs. Let B_T denote the energy consumption per unit time when a node transmits or relays frame. Let B_R denote the energy consumption per unit time when a node receives frame and let B_L denote the energy consumption per unit time when a node listens the channel. As we know, when a sensor node in listening mode consumes more energy than when the sensor node in sleeping node. Thus, how to schedule sensor node sleeping to save energy is a hot research issue in wireless sensor networks. In this paper, we have proved that a version of TDMA algorithm can achieve the tight lower bound on cycle time. In these algorithms, each node in network knows clearly when it will receive a frame from upstream neighbor node. Thus, a sensor node can set itself in sleeping mode when it is idle and being active when it is the time to receive upstream frames. In this paper, we assume that when the sensor node is idle, it still in the listening mode. However, if we want to save more energy, the sensor node can change from the listening mode to the sleeping mode. In general, we have $B_T > B_R \geq B_L$.

3.1 Linear Topology

For simplicity to express, Let $E_i(n)$ denote the node O_i's energy consumption in a cycle. Note that due to the limited space in this conference paper, all proofs are omitted and will be included in a journal version of this paper.

Theorem 1: *For the linear topology illustrated in Fig. 1, under fair-access,* $E(n)$ *is lower bounded by the minimum energy consumption,* $E_{opt}(n)$*:*

$$E_{opt}(n) = \sum_{i=1}^{n} (B_T iT + B_R (i-1)T + B_L (3n-2i-2)T)$$

3.2 2-Row Topology

For simplicity of proof, let $E(2n)$ denote the energy consumption for Fig. 2 topology under fair-access in a cycle. Let $E_1(n)$ denote total energy consumption of the first row sensor nodes in a cycle, let $E_2(n)$ denote total energy consumption of the second row sensor nodes in a cycle. Let $E_{1i}(n)$ denote the first row node O_{1i}'s energy consumption in a cycle. Let $E_{2i}(n)$ denote the second row node O_{2i}'s energy consumption in a cycle.

Theorem 2: *For the Grid topology with two rows of sensor nodes in Fig. 2a, under fair-access,* $E(2n)$ *is lower bounded by the minimum energy consumption,* $E_{opt}(2n)$*:*

$$E_{opt}(2n) = 2\sum_{i=1}^{n} (B_T iT + B_R (i-1)T + B_L (3n-2i)T)$$

Theorem 3: *For the Grid topology with two rows of sensor nodes in Fig. 2b, under fair-access,* $E(2n)$ *is lower bounded by the minimum energy consumption,* $E_{opt}(2n)$*:*

$$E_{opt}(2n) = \sum_{i=1}^{n} (B_T (2i+1)T + B_R (2i-1)T + B_L (12n-4i-10)T)$$

3.3 3-Row Topology

For simplicity, let $E(3n)$ denote the energy consumption for Fig. 3 topology under fair-access in a cycle. Let $E_1(n)$ denote the energy consumption of the first row sensor nodes in a cycle. Let $E_2(n)$ denote the energy consumption of the second row sensor nodes in a cycle and let $E_3(n)$ denote the energy consumption of the third row sensor nodes in a cycle. Let $E_{1i}(n)$ denote the first row node O_{1i}'s energy consumption in a cycle. Let $E_{2i}(n)$ denote the second row node O_{2i}'s energy consumption in a cycle. Let $E_{3i}(n)$ denote the third row node O_{3i}'s energy consumption in a cycle.

Theorem 4: *For the Grid topology with three rows of sensor nodes in Fig. 3a, under fair-access,* $E(3n)$ *is lower bounded by the minimum energy consumption,* $E_{opt}(3n)$*:*

$$E_{opt}(3n) = 3\sum_{i=1}^{n}(B_T iT + B_R(i-1)T + B_L(4n-2i)T)$$

Theorem 5: *For the Grid topology with three rows of sensor nodes in Fig. 3b, under fair-access,* $E(3n)$ *is lower bounded by the minimum energy consumption,* $E_{opt}(3n)$*:*

$$E_{opt}(3n) = \sum_{i=1}^{n}(B_T(3i+2)T + B_R(3i-1)T + B_L(27n-6i-22)T)$$

3.4 4-Row Topology

For simplicity, let $E(4n)$ denote the energy consumption for Fig. 4 topology under fair-access in a cycle. Let $E_1(n)$ denote the energy consumption of the first row sensor nodes in a cycle. Let $E_2(n)$ denote the energy consumption of the second row sensor nodes in a cycle. Let $E_3(n)$ denote the energy consumption of the third row sensor nodes in a cycle. Let $E_4(n)$ denote the energy consumption of the fourth row sensor nodes in a cycle Let $E_{1i}(n)$ denote the first row node O_{1i}'s energy consumption in a cycle. Let $E_{2i}(n)$ denote the second row node O_{2i}'s energy consumption in a cycle. Let $E_{3i}(n)$ denote the third row node O_{3i}'s energy consumption in a cycle. Let $E_{4i}(n)$ denote the fourth row node O_{4i}'s energy consumption in a cycle.

Theorem 6: *For the Grid topology with four rows of sensor nodes in Fig. 4 a, under fair-access,* $E(4n)$ *is lower bounded by the minimum energy consumption,* $E_{opt}(4n)$*:*

$$E_{opt}(4n) = 4\sum_{i=1}^{n-1}(B_T iT + B_R(i-1)T + B_L(6n-2i)T) + 2(3B_T nT + B_R(3n-2)T + 6B_L nT)$$

Theorem 7: *For the Grid topology with four rows of sensor nodes in Fig. 4b, under fair-access,* $E(4n)$ *is lower bounded by the minimum energy consumption,* $E_{opt}(4n)$*:*

$$E_{opt}(4n) = 2\sum_{i=1}^{n}(B_T(2i+1)T + B_R(2i-1)T + B_L(12n-4i-2)T)$$

3.5 Tight Lower Bound on Energy Consumption

Theorem 8: *For the sensor networks with topologies illustrated in Fig.1, Fig.2, Fig.3 and Fig.4, under fair-access, the lower bounds on energy consumption per cycle can be achieved by a version of TDMA algorithm.*

4 Energy Consumption Evaluation

The evaluation is omitted to the limited space and will be included in the journal version of this paper.

5 Conclusion

In this paper, we present the tight lower bounds on network energy consumption for linear, two-row, three-row and four-row grid topologies. These bounds hold for any MAC protocol employing the fair-access criterion. In the future work, we will study more complicated topology.

Acknowledgments

This work is supported in part by the US National Science Foundation (NSF) under the grant numbers CCF-0829827, CNS-0716211, and CNS-0737325.

References

1. Akyildiz, I.F., Su, W., Sankarasubramaniam, Y., Cayirci, E.: A survey on sensor networks. IEEE Communications Magazine 40(8), 102–114 (2002)
2. Kulkarni, S.S., Arumugam, M.: TDMA service for sensor networks. In: Proceedings of the 24th International Conference on Distributed Computing Systems Workshops, Washington, D.C., pp. 604–609 (2004)
3. Demirkol, I., Ersoy, C., Alagoz, F.: MAC protocols for wireless sensor networks: a survey. IEEE Communications Magazine 44(4), 115–121 (2006)
4. Ye, W., Heidemann, J., Estrin, D.: An Energy-Efficient MAC protocol for wireless sensor networks. In: Proceedings of IEEE INFOCOM (2002)
5. Gibson, J., Xie, G.G., Xiao, Y.: Performance Limits of Fair-Access in Sensor Networks with Linear and Selected Grid Topologies. In: Proceedings of GLOBECOM Ad Hoc and Sensor Networking Symposium, Washington DC (2007)
6. Miao, P., Xiao, Y.: Upper Bound on Network Utilization under Fair-Access in Multi-Hop Wireless Grid Sensor Networks with 3-4 Rows. submitted to a conference (MSN 09)

Lookahead Expansion Algorithm for Minimum Power Multicasting in Wireless Ad Hoc Networks*

Manki Min and Austin F. O'Brien

South Dakota State University, Brookings, SD 57006, USA
manki.min@sdstate.edu, afobrien@jacks.sdstate.edu

Abstract. In this paper, we present a lookahead expansion algorithm (named as Shrinking and Lookahead Expansion, SLE for short) for minimum power multicast tree problem in wireless ad hoc networks. SLE adopts the powerful shrinking process from our previous work, SOR (Shrinking Overlapped Range) algorithm, and adds an intelligent lookahead process to further improve the solution quality. The lookahead process (called as lookahead expansion) expands the intermediate tree to a feasible tree by adding transmissions with minimum power, one by one. The algorithm maintains the found feasible tree with the minimum power sum in addition to the intermediate tree which is not feasible until the end. This lookahead process generates the effective diversification of the solution search space. The computational results strongly support the solid and outstanding performance of SLE owing to the lookahead process.

1 Introduction

Wireless ad hoc networking is beneficial in various situations such as rapid ad hoc deployment in hostile environments. The autonomous nature of the ad hoc networking does not require any infrastructure and the devices in such an ad hoc network tend to communicate with other devices more frequently for both data and control. In such a setting, use of the battery at each device makes the conservation of the battery power an essential and critical problem in order to prolong the whole network lifetime. In case of multicast, which has multiple destinations, the power consumption of a multicast tree is not the sum of power of each individual edge. Instead, it's the sum of the power of each individual transmission, where the power of each transmission is the power to reach the farthest device in its transmission range. As a result the more transmission power is used, the more devices can be reached by the transmission. This property is well described by WMA (wireless multicast advantage [13]). In other words, WMA is the overlapping property of wireless transmissions.

This interesting property WMA makes the minimum energy multicast tree problem challenging and most studies are under two main approaches; heuristic

* Research is supported by NSF Award CCF-0729182.

B. Liu et al. (Eds.): WASA 2009, LNCS 5682, pp. 70–79, 2009.

algorithm approach [1,2,6,7,8,9,11,12,13] and IP (integer programming)-based optimization approach [3,5,14,10]. The heuristic algorithm approach is to develop heuristics that efficiently compute good (but not optimal in most cases) solutions mostly based on the WMA property and the optimization approach is to develop mathematical (IP) formulations to compute the optimal solutions. Optimization approach is guaranteed to generate an optimal solution but is inherently time inefficient which hinders the scalability of the approach. One good way for the optimization approach is to use a good heuristic algorithm to generate a solid bound of the solution quality by which more search space is cut-off. In [5], we used our efficient heuristic SOR [6] in our iterated algorithm to find the optimal solutions. The positive balance of running time and solution quality of the heuristic algorithm allows significant cut-offs of the search space and dramatically reduces the running time of the iterated algorithm. A better way for the optimization approach can be found in [5]; during each iteration, we used a relaxed mathematical formulation to find an infeasible solution and added necessary constraints to make the solution feasible. The observation from our previous work is two-fold: 1) the combination of heuristic algorithm approach and optimization approach is promising and 2) intelligent diversification of search space greatly improves the solution quality. The work presented in this paper follows the second track, namely performance improvement through the intelligent diversification.

In this paper, we study the diversification of the search space by the help of lookahead process and present the SLE (Shrinking and Lookahead Expansion) algorithm. The computational results are compared with algorithms in the literature (MIP [13], EWMA [1], OMEGa [7], SOR [6], MIPF [12], and PSOR [9]) and an iterated version of SOR (ISOR [8]). The comparison is made mainly on the perspective of the quality of the solution which is represented by the sum of the transmission powers of the tree. Running time issues are partly discussed for the comparison of SLE with ISOR and PSOR. The computational results show the significant improvement on the solution quality.

Our contribution in this work is theoretical rather than practical. Even though the running time is still not practical, the solution quality improvement per increase of running time is better than other algorithms. And this result suggests possible relation of the lookahead scheme with the properties of the optimal solutions. We are hoping to be able to use the found result to identify the useful properties of the optimal solutions.

The rest of this paper consists as follows. In section 2, the minimum power multicast tree problem is defined and related work including heuristic algorithms and IP (integer programming)-based optimizations in the literature are reviewed. Section 3 presents our algorithm SLE. The computational results are discussed in section 4 and section 5 concludes this paper.

2 The Problem and Related Work

In this section, we describe the minimum power multicast tree problem and briefly review related work on the minimum energy multicast tree problem in wireless ad hoc networks. The literature study presented in this paper is mainly in two directions: heuristic algorithms and IP (integer programming)-based optimizations.

In wireless networks, the transmission power p_{ij} required for a link from node i to node j, separated by a distance r, is proportional to r^α. Ignoring the constant coefficient, we can model as $p_{ij} = r^\alpha$. For the experimental computations, we used 2 as the value of α. For multicasting communication, there exists a source node and a set of destination nodes (multicast group) consisting of some nodes other than the source node. In our work we assume that for any multicast request there is only one source node. The solution of the problem is a multicast tree rooted at the source node. In a multicast tree, there must be at least one path from the root to any node in the multicast group, and the sum of the transmission power of the tree should be minimized. Cagalj et al [1] showed that the minimum power broadcast tree problem is NP-hard by reduction from the Planar 3-SAT problem [4]. The multicast tree with the minimum transmission power will consume minimum energy and hence the minimum energy multicast tree problem in wireless ad hoc networks belongs to NP-hard.

Wieselthier et al presented the well known BIP (Broadcast Incremental Power algorithm) [13]. BIP is based on Prim's algorithm with iterative modifications of the link costs (incremental power of the transmission). The link costs are updated at each step as follows:

$$p'_{ij} = p_{ij} - P(i) \tag{1}$$

where $P(i)$ is the power level at which node i is already transmitting. Most incremental heuristics use this concept of additional transmission power (Eq. 1) as the metric for the transmission selection to increment the tree [1,2,7,6,11,12,13].

In [1], another heuristic algorithm based on WMA, EWMA (Embedded Wireless Multicast Advantage), is presented. EWMA starts from a feasible solution such as an MST (minimum spanning tree) and iteratively modify the tree by excluding some transmitting nodes so that the total power decreases.

Wan et al [12] proposed MIPF (Minimum Incremental Path First) for minimum power multicast tree problem. Instead of pruning branches in the broadcast tree, MIPF iteratively add paths from the source node to the required destinations by collapsing the current tree into a single virtual source node.

IP has been used in [3,14] as an optimization technique to solve the minimum energy broadcast tree problem. Five different IP formulations are proposed in [3,14]. The main difficulty of the problem comes from the constraints of connectivity, or cycle prevention. The IP formulation should represent the constraints which ensure the existence of a path from the root to any node in the tree, which increases the complexity of the problem.

Our previous computational results in [5] show that all those formulations in [3,14] find the optimal solutions very slowly even for small-sized problems with 10 or 20 nodes. Our results show that power assignment by finding direct transmission destination and cycle prevention by using flow constraints gives the fastest solution. This finding suggests a strong connection between the optimal solution structure and the discrete power assignments. However, when the number of nodes increases, the computation time is exponentially slow and it is practically not feasible to use the IP to solve the problem. Two interesting and important points about IP formulations are that the power assignment by finding direct transmission destination gives tighter LP relaxation value and that flow constraints use less memory and converge faster. In addition to the IP formulations, we presented two iterated algorithms which make use of relaxed IP subformulations which describes the problem without the connectivity constraints. We showed that our IP formulation finishes the computation significantly faster than any other formulations and our iterated algorithm dramatically reduces running time compared to our efficient IP formulation.

Our previous work presents a series of heuristic algorithms: OMEGa [7], SOR [6], PSOR [9]. OMEGa incrementally adds a transmission with the minimum value of estimation of energy gain when the transmission is added to the intermediate tree. In the case of multicasting, OMEGa allows a node not in the multicast group to be added with a low probability. After a broadcast tree is obtained, OMEGa prunes unnecessary transmissions, i.e., the transmissions of nodes that do not reach any node in the multicast group. SOR tries to change the current tree structure at the point when new nodes are added to the tree. The tree structure is changed by shrinking the overlapped transmission range based on WMA property. SOR also works for multicasting by means of the penalty function which ensures the node not in the multicast group can be selected as a relaying node only if it has a very close neighbor which is in the multicast group. The computational results showed that SOR outperforms other algorithms in the literature for the broadcast tree problem. The results presented in [6] showed that SOR did not produce the best solution for the multicast tree problem; however, recently we found that SOR actually outperforms other algorithms in multicasting as well [9]. PSOR is based on the SOR algorithm and it tries to change the shrinking process more aggressive. Instead of allowing the shrinking only when it does not hurt make a partition, PSOR allows aggressive shrinking and tries to recover from the resulting partitions.

In our previous work [8], we presented an iterated algorithm framework that works with any minimum energy multicast tree algorithms and the computational results show that most algorithms' performances can be significantly improved. However due to the increased search space, the running time also significantly increased and there was a tradeoff between quality improvement and time increase.

3 Shrinking and Lookahead Expansion

In this section, we describe the SLE algorithm.

The key concept in SOR (shrinking process) has been shown to successfully improve the solution quality through series of computational experiments [6,8,9]. SLE inherits the powerful shrinking process from SOR for better results. PSOR [9] adopts the modified penalty function which tries to estimate the potential cost

Initialization
1. Set $V' := \{s\}$ and $U' := M \setminus V'$, where s is the source node and M is the set of destination nodes.
2. Set $T := (V', \emptyset)$ without any link.

Iteration Do the following while $U' \neq \emptyset$:
3. For each transmission (v, u) for $v \in V', u \in V$ such that (v, u) covers all the nodes in W' and $W' \cap U' \neq \emptyset$,
3-i. Change the parent of $w \in W'$ to v for all w which is not an ancestor of v and shrink the overalapped range, and add the modified penalty calculated by Eq. 2 to compute the shrunk power sum of the intermediate tree $T_{v,u}$.
3-ii. Expand the tree $T_{v,u}$ into $T^E_{v,u}$ by adding transmissions of minimum transmission power from a node in the intermediate tree to a node which is in M and not in the tree and shrinking the overalapped range, one by one in an arbitrary order.
3-iii. Sum up the transmission powers in $T^E_{v,u}$ and keep the expanded tree T^E with the minimum power sum. Goto step 3.
4. Find the transmission (v, u) with the minimum shrunk power sum of $T_{v,u}$.
5. Update V', U' and T by doing the following:
$U' := U' \setminus W'$ and $V' := V' \cup W'$ and $T := T_{v,u}$.

Termination Output the tree with the smaller power sum among the two trees T and T^E.

Fig. 1. SLE algorithm

of one more hop increase of the intermediate tree as in Equation (2). The computational results show better performance by PSOR than SOR and this result supports the effectiveness of the modified penalty function. SLE adopts the same penalty function that is used in PSOR. In addition, SLE has the lookahead expansion process which significantly diversifies the solution search space for better performance. The lookahead expansion process expands the intermediate tree in each iteration into a feasible multicast tree by adding transmissions of minimum transmission power, one by one in arbitrary order. The benefit from this approach is that we can quickly get a feasible solution which works as an upper bound and moreover, the feasible solution obtained from the diversified solution space often outperforms the solutions from the other algorithms. SLE maintains the feasible multicast tree with the minimum power sum as well as the intermediate multicast tree which becomes feasible at the end of the algorithm execution. At the end, SLE outputs the multicast tree with the smaller power sum.

$$F_{vu} = \begin{cases} \min\{P_{xw} | x \in T_{v,u}, w \in M \setminus T_{v,u}\} & \text{if } u \notin M \\ 0 & \text{otherwise} \end{cases} \quad (2)$$

The shrinking process [6] works as in Fig 2. T is the intermediate tree at the beginning of an iteration as in (a). If we add the transmission (v, u) then it will cover w as well which was covered by x in T as in (b). As long as v is not an ancestor of w, we can change the parent of w from x to v and by doing so we may

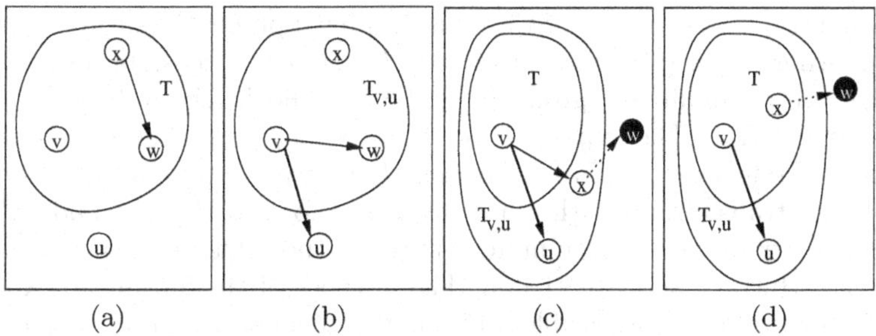

Fig. 2. Shrinking process and penalty function

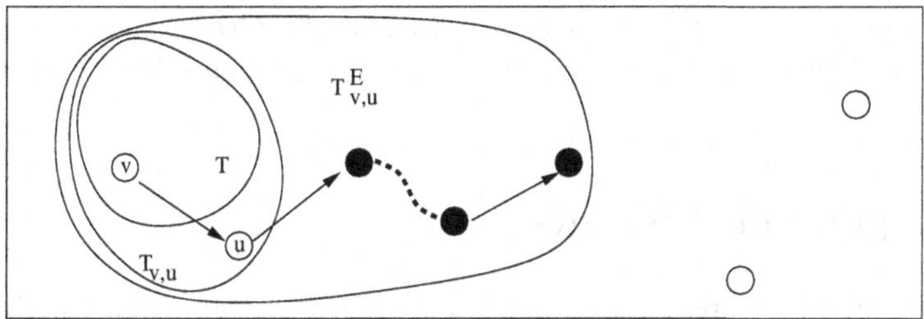

Fig. 3. Lookahead expansion

have an effect of reducing the transmission power of x. Note that SOR allows the consideration of a transmission inside the tree as long as it covers at least one node not in the tree. The transmission inside the tree results in significant tree structure change and helps the diversification of the solution space to a degree.

The penalty function [9] computes the minimum incremental power to grow the intermediate tree so that at least one new destination node is included in the resulting tree. The calculation of the penalty function can be considered as a two-hop transmission selection and contributes to a more precise selection of a transmission. In Figure 2, compare (c) and (d). The node w is in the multicast group (meaning it's one of the destination nodes) and denoted by a solid black circle. Since node u or x is not in the multicast group (more precisely the transmission (v, u) does not cover any node in the multicast group which is not yet in the tree), if we choose the selection (v, u) then the constructed tree $T_{v,u}$ may not be included in the final solution since it's not a feasible intermediate solution. However, if we add the penalty for one more hop transmission (x, w) and still the power sum is the minimum, then we found a potentially feasible intermediate solution $T_{v,u}$. Here, the transmission (v, u) is used only to convert an infeasible intermediate solution into a feasible one and is not included in the intermediate solution. Note that x can be any node in $T_{v,u}$, even a node in T as in (d). The penalty function helps to improve the solution quality while maintaining the feasibility of the intermediate solution.

The key concept of SLE is the lookahead expansion process which is described in Fig 3. T is the intermediate tree at the beginning of an iteration and we consider the transmission (v, u). SLE finds $T_{v,u}$ by applying the shrinking process and computing penalty function. However $T_{v,u}$ is not a feasible solution since some nodes in the multicast group (denoted by solid black circles) are not yet included in the tree. The expansion of the tree $T_{v,u}$ grows the tree by adding transmissions one by one. To accomplish that in a simple and effective way, SLE adds the transmission with minimum power for an arbitrary node which is not yet in the tree but is in the multicast group and adds another transmission for another arbitrary node and so on. The purpose of the lookahead expansion process is not for finding a feasible solution with the performance comparable to other algorithms at once. Rather, the process targets more diversification of the solution space and this arbitrary order of multicast group node fits our purpose due to the different tree structures of $T_{v,u}$. The algorithm is given in Figure 1.

The running time of SLE is evidently bounded by $O(n^5)$. However, the empirical data shows that the running time of SLE is comparable to SOR in most cases.

4 Computational Results

In this section, we compare the computational results of our proposed algorithm with other algorithms: MIP, EWMA, OMEGa, SOR, MIPF, PSOR (normal algorithms) and ISOR (iterative version of SOR). We only consider a static network configuration.

We generate 100 nodes located randomly in a 100×100 area with identical maximum transmission range of 142. In this way, every node can communicate directly with any other node by adjusting its transmission power appropriately. The first generated node is set as the source node and the multicast group is determined randomly. For each node placement, four different multicast groups are generated: 25 %, 50 %, 75 %, and 100 %(broadcast). The power sum is normalized so that the minimum heuristic solution has the normalized value 1. All the results presented here are averaged numbers over 100 sets.

Fig 4 summarizes the computational results. It shows the power sum which is our main performance metric of all the algorithms in four different multicasting settings. As seen from the graph, SLE outperforms other normal algorithms (every algorithm except ISOR) and performs competitively with ISOR.

Similarly we compared the performance of three algorithms ISOR, PSOR, and SLE that showed the best performance among all the algorithms used in the computational experiment (Fig. 5). In this case, still SLE outperforms PSOR but is slightly dragging behind ISOR except for the small-sized multicast (25 %) as in (a). However on average, SLE performs competitively with ISOR and the study in terms of trade-off between the solution quality improvement and the running time increase supports this claim.

Figure 6 compares SLE with ISOR and PSOR, all of which are based on SOR. (a) shows the solution quality improvement of the three algorithms against SOR. ISOR improves better than PSOR or SLE which is a natural result evident from (b) that shows more time consumption of ISOR than PSOR or SLE.

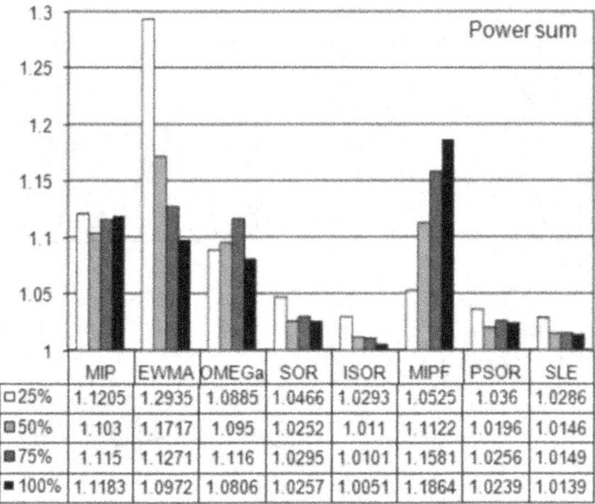

	MIP	EWMA	OMEGa	SOR	ISOR	MIPF	PSOR	SLE
25%	1.1205	1.2935	1.0885	1.0466	1.0293	1.0525	1.036	1.0286
50%	1.103	1.1717	1.095	1.0252	1.011	1.1122	1.0196	1.0146
75%	1.115	1.1271	1.116	1.0295	1.0101	1.1581	1.0256	1.0149
100%	1.1183	1.0972	1.0806	1.0257	1.0051	1.1864	1.0239	1.0139

Fig. 4. Comparison of all algorithms: MIP, EWMA, OMEGa, SOR, ISOR, MIPF, PSOR, and SLE

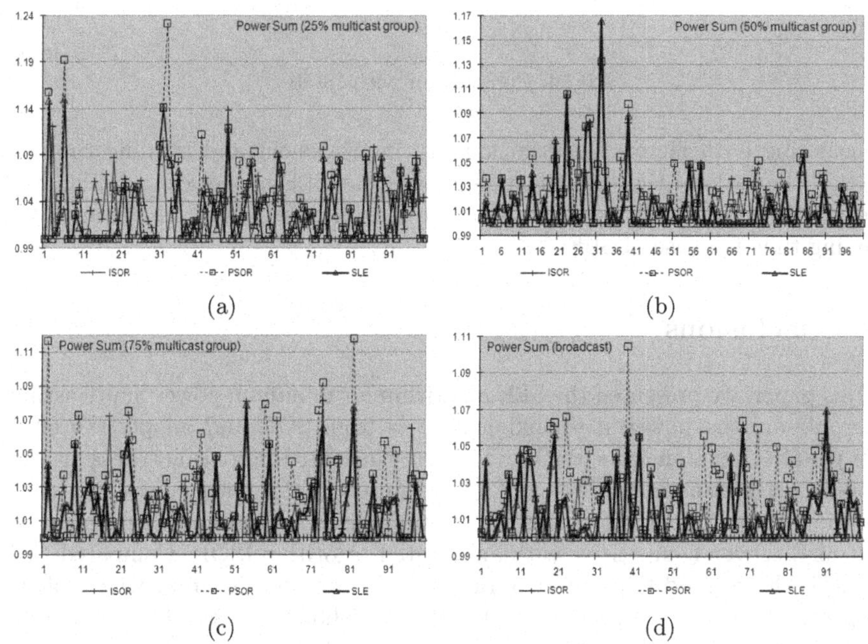

Fig. 5. Runs of the best three among all the algorithms

ISOR requires 36∼96 times more computation time than SOR while PSOR requires 9∼10 times more computation time. Meanwhile, SLE requires about 3 times more computation time than SOR. In addition, the running time increases of PSOR and SLE are stable, in contrast to the dynamic variations in ISOR.

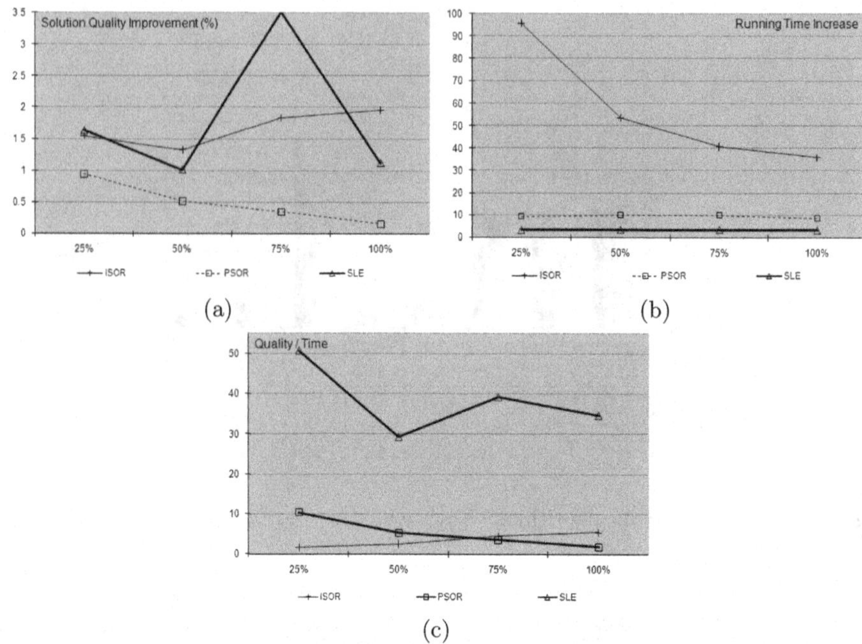

(a) (b) (c)

Fig. 6. Comparison with ISOR

Considering both factors (solution quality improvement and running time increase), the ratio of those two factors shows that SLE outperforms both ISOR and PSOR as in (c). The result is mainly due to the stable and small amount of running time increase of SLE.

5 Conclusions

In this paper, we presented the SLE algorithm for minimum power multicasting. SLE inherits the powerful shrinking process from SOR and adopts the effective penalty function from PSOR. The key concept, the lookahead expansions process, plays an important role in further improving the performance. The computational experiment shows that SLE outperforms any normal algorithms and that SLE is even competitive with an iterated algorithm ISOR. Compared with ISOR, it shows good solution/time ratio which supports the effectiveness of the proposed algorithm SLE. Similar to PSOR, SLE shows predictable running time for different multicasting settings, which is not observed from the iterated algorithm ISOR. The predictable running time suggests a careful theoretic study of the running time of SLE as one of our future works. Our future works also include a study of a tighter theoretical bound of the performance ratio. Based on the success of lookahead approach in this work, different types of lookahead are to be studied in our future works.

References

Cagalj, M., Hubaux, J.-P., Enz, C.: Minimum-Energy Broadcast in All-Wireless Networks: NP-Completeness and Distribution Issues. In: Proceedings of the international conference on Mobile computing and networking, pp. 172–182 (2002)

Cheng, M.X., Sun, J., Min, M., Du, D.-Z.: Energy-Efficient Broadcast and Multicast Routing in Ad Hoc Wireless Networks. In: Proceedings of the IEEE International Conference on Performance, Computing, and Communications Conference, pp. 87–94 (2003)

Das, A.K., Marks, R.J., El-Sharkawi, M., Arabshahi, P., Gray, A.: Minimum Power Broadcast Trees for Wireless Networks: Integer Programming Formulations. In: Proceedings of INFOCOM, vol. 2, pp. 1001–1010 (2003)

Garey, M.R., Johnson, D.S.: Computers and Intractibility: A Guide to the Theory of NP-completeness. W. H. Freeman, San Francisco (1979)

Min, M., Prokopyev, O., Pardalos, P.M.: Optimal Solutions to Minimum Total Energy Broadcasting Problem in Wireless Ad Hoc Networks. Journal of Combinatorial Optimization, Special Issue on Wireless Network Applications 11, 59–69 (2006)

Min, M., Pardalos, P.M.: Total Energy Optimal Multicasting in Wireless Ad Hoc Networks. Journal of Combinatorial Optimizations 13, 365–378 (2006)

Min, M., Pardalos, P.M.: OMEGa: an Optimistic Most Energy Gain Method for Minimum Energy Multicasting in Wireless Ad Hoc Networks. Journal of Combinatorial Optimization 16, 81–95 (2008)

Min, M.: Comparison of Iterated Algorithms for the Minimum Energy Multicast Tree Problem in Wireless Ad Hoc Networks. In: Proceedings of International Conference on Wireless Networks, pp. 215–221 (2008)

Min, M., O'Brien, A.F., Shin, S.Y.: Partitioning-Based SOR for Minimum Energy Multicast Tree Problem in Wireless Ad Hoc Networks. Technical Report, Dept. of EECS, South Dakota State University (August 2008)

Montemanni, R., Gambardella, L.M.: Minimum Power Symmetric Connectivity Problem in Wireless Networks: A New Approach. Mobile and Wireless Communication Networks 162, 497–508 (2005)

Wan, P.-J., Calinescu, G., Li, X.-Y., Frieder, O.: Minimum-Energy Broadcasting in Static Ad Hoc Wireless Networks. Wireless Networks 8, 607–617 (2002)

Wan, P.-J., Calinescu, G., Yi, C.-W.: Minimum-Power Multicast Routing in Static Ad Hoc Wireless Networks. IEEE/ACM Transactions on Networking 12, 507–514 (2004)

Wieselthier, J.E., Nguyen, G.D., Ephremides, A.: Energy-Efficient Broadcast and Multicast Trees in Wireless Networks. Mobile Networks and Applications 7, 481–492 (2002)

Yuan, D.: Computing Optimal or Near-Optimal Trees for Minimum-Energy Broadcasting in Wireless Networks. In: Proceedings of International symposyum on Modeling and Optimization in Mobile, Ad Hoc, and Wireless Networks, pp. 323–331 (2005)

RE^2-CD: Robust and Energy Efficient Cut Detection in Wireless Sensor Networks

Myounggyu Won, Stephen M. George, and Radu Stoleru

Department of Computer Science and Engineering
Texas A&M University
{mgwon,mikegeorge,stoleru}@cse.tamu.edu

Abstract. Reliable network connectivity in wireless sensor networks (WSN) is difficult to achieve. Harsh, unattended, low-security environments and resource-constrained nodes exacerbate the problem. An ability to detect connectivity disruptions, due to either security or environmental problems, allows WSN to conserve power and memory while reducing network congestion. We propose RE^2-CD, an integrated solution incorporating both robustness to attack and energy-efficiency. To enhance security, a robust outlier detection algorithm assists nodes in detecting a specific threat in their environment. To improve energy-efficiency, a cluster-based cut detection algorithm recognizes and reacts to disrupted connectivity. Extensive simulations across a range of network sizes and densities indicate that energy-efficiency can be improved by an order of magnitude in denser networks while malicious nodes are detected at deviations of 1% from expected behavior.

1 Introduction

Wireless sensor networks (WSN), composed of numerous sensor nodes with small, low-power, inexpensive radios, have attracted a large amount of research that has led to interesting and innovative applications. However, challenging problems still exist. One of the most challenging problems in WSN is maintaining network connectivity to reliably deliver data to a specified point, or sink, in an energy-efficient manner. Disrupted connectivity, known as a "cut", can lead to skewed data, ill-informed decisions and even entire network outages. It can also lead to memory and power exhaustion in disconnected nodes and network congestion in disconnected segments. Such data loss and wasted resources can be avoided if a node can independently determine if a cut exists in the network.

Cut detection algorithms attempt to recognize and locate cuts. Using a state-based convergence mechanism, the current state-of-the-art cut detection algorithm, Distributed Source Separation Detection (DSSD) [1], reliably detects arbitrarily-shaped cuts and allows individual nodes to perform cut detection autonomously. However, the algorithm suffers from a number of problems. First, DSSD fails to address security, a critical component of sensor deployments in unattended environments. Second, the algorithm requires a lengthy, iterative convergence process. Finally, all nodes participate in the frequent broadcasts

B. Liu et al. (Eds.): WASA 2009, LNCS 5682, pp. 80–93, 2009.

required to achieve convergence. This is cost-prohibitive with regards to power, especially in denser networks.

In light of these problems, we propose an algorithm with two principal components. Outlier detection, a statistical data analysis technique, resolves the security threat where a malicious node injects erroneous data into the cut detection process. Using data analysis, outlier detection identifies malicious source data and provides a light-weight, energy-efficient mechanism to validate neighbor data. Additionally, we propose an improved cut detection algorithm called *robust cluster-based cut detection.* This algorithm divides the network into a set of location-based clusters. Cluster leaders form a virtual grid network and the cut detection algorithm runs on this high-level network. As the algorithm executes, leaders converge to some state. A leader finding inconsistency in its expected state informs its neighbors and the sink that a cut has happened.

The contributions of this paper are:

- A method for identifying and recovering from changes caused by certain types of malicious nodes.
- An improved cut detection algorithm that converges faster while using less energy.
- Increased energy efficiency through more rapid detection of disrupted connectivity.

The paper is organized as follows. Section 2 discusses related work about cut detection and outlier detection algorithms in WSN. We introduce the robust cluster-based cut detection algorithm in Section 3. Our implementation is addressed in Section 4 which is followed by experimental results in Section 5. We offer conclusions and ideas for future work in Section 6.

2 Related Work

Outlier detection is a statistical analysis tool often used to identify problems in data sets like measurement error or abnormal data distribution. Outlier detection can be categorized into largely two mainstreams: a parametric approach, which assumes a priori known distribution of the data, and a non-parametric approach that does not rely on a specific distribution. With known data distribution, the parametric approach detects outliers with very high precision. However, in many cases, finding a matching distribution is very hard. Probabilistic models that infer distribution based on sample data compensate for this difficulty but often show high false positive rates [2]. Non-parametric approaches using distance-based and density-based methods attempt to overcome this limitation. Knorr and Ng [3] proposed the first distance-based algorithm, where a point is regarded as an outlier if its distance to a kth nearest neighbor point is greater than a certain threshold. One disadvantage is that the threshold must be defined. Ramaswamy et al. [4] studied distance-based detection, where a point is said to be an outlier if the distance to k^{th} nearest neighbor is greater than that of $n-1$ other points. Recently, Zhang et al [5] introduced an algorithm for finding an outlier based on the sum of distances to the point's k nearest neighbors. However, all distance-based solutions fail to detect outliers in clustered data. Density-based outlier detection schemes [6][7] gracefully solve this problem. Each data point is given a score called Local Outlier Factor (LOF) based on its local density, which is bounded by a specific value MinPts. In [6], an outlier is determined by score. In [7], the bounding value MinPts is determined autonomously using statistical values such as inter-cluster distances and cluster diameters.

Research in the area of cut detection has emphasized the importance of the network partition monitoring problem [8]. For example, Chong et al [9] mentioned the problem from a security perspective arguing that nodes deployed in a hostile environment must be able to detect tampering. In [10], Cerpa and Estrin stressed the importance of the network cut detection problem in their self-configuring topology scheme but left it as a future work. However, little progress has been made to resolve the problem. An early paper by Kleinberg, et al. [11] considered the problem in a wired network. Their main argument is to select good "agents" to monitor the partition and accurately detect separation events. Much like the "agent" node, Ritter et al. [12] defined "border" nodes responsible for the detection of network partition. Recently, Shrivasta et al. [13] proposed a deterministic algorithm to detect network separation using a set of sentinel nodes to monitor the linear-cut of a network. The most recent cut detection algorithm is proposed by Barooah, et. al. [1]. Their algorithm can not only detect an arbitrary shape of cut, but also enables every node in the network to autonomously detect a cut by maintaining state.

3 Robust and Energy Efficient Cut Detection

In this section, we present the theoretical foundations of cut detection and propose algorithms to enhance robustness and improve energy efficiency.

3.1 Preliminaries

We model our network as an undirected, connected graph $G = (V, E)$, where the set of vertices $V = \{v_1, v_2, ..., v_m\}$ is the set of m nodes in the network and the set of edges $E = \{(v_i, v_j)|v_i, v_j \in V\}$ represents radio connectivity among nodes in the network. We denote by $N_i = \{v_j|(v_i, v_j) \in E\}$ the set of *neighbors* of a node v_i, and by $|N_i|$ the *degree* of node v_i.

Time is denoted as a discrete counter $k = 0, 1, 2, ...$ Each node v_i maintains a positive real value $x_i(k)$ which is called the state. The state is initialized to zero, i.e., $x_i(0) = 0$ at time $k = 0$. One node in the network is designated as the *source node*. Although the *source node* may be selected arbitrarily, by convention we select the sink to be the source in WSN. For simplicity, we assume that v_1 is the *source node*.

At every iteration k, each node v_i updates its state $x_i(k)$ and broadcasts it. All nodes except the *source node* update their states using the following equation:

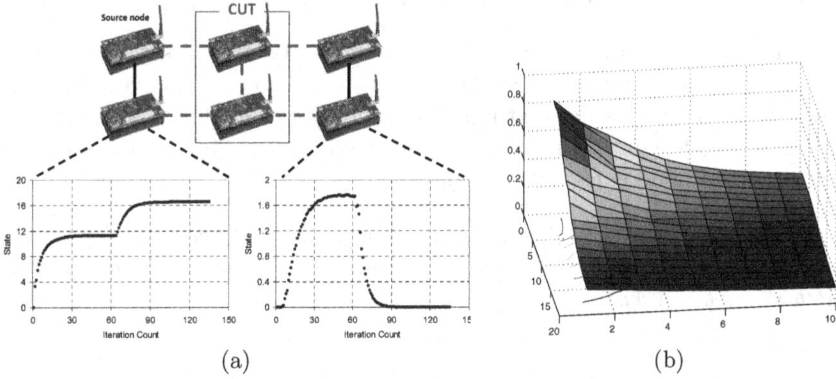

Fig. 1. (a) A cut occurs in a connected network of six nodes. The graph depicts the scalar states of two nodes, one in G_{source} and one $\notin G_{source}$. (b) The distribution of node states in a 20 grid network, with a source node at (0,0).

$$x_i(k+1) = \frac{1}{|N_i|+1} \sum_{j \in N_i(k)} x_j(k) \tag{1}$$

The *source node* v_1 uses a slightly different state update equation:

$$x_1(k+1) = \frac{1}{|N_1|+1} \left(\sum_{j \in N_1(k)} x_j(k) + s \right), \tag{2}$$

where s, called the *source strength*, is a user specified scalar. Previously it was proved that the state of each node converges, after a number of iterations, to a positive value [1].

We define a "cut" as a network partition, in which the graph G is separated into n disjoint connected components $G_{source}, G_2, ..., G_n$, where $G_{source} = (V_{source}, E_{source})$ is a graph which contains the *source node*. When a "cut" occurs, the state of each node $v \notin V_{source}$ converges to 0 [1].

The convergence of a node's state is illustrated in Figure 1(a). Around iteration 40, the scalar state of nodes in the network converges. Shortly after iteration 60, a cut occurs in the network when the two nodes in the middle fail. After the cut, the state of a node on the right side rapidly decays to 0 while the state of a node on the left side converges to a new higher state. A critical observation is that the states of all nodes converge to new values, hence *all nodes* have the ability to detect a cut in the network.

One troublesome aspect of cut detection using this distributed algorithm is that it is susceptible to attacks. A malicious node located in the disconnected part of the network can imitate a source node, and hence affect the state value that each node computes. In the following section we analyze the impact of such malicious nodes and propose an algorithm to detect and recover from malicious behavior.

3.2 Robust Cut Detection Algorithm

Temporary variations of a node's state, often caused by packet loss, can be tolerated by a system implementing cut detection as described above. The states of nodes in the network will eventually converge. However, this is not true when a non-source node continuously injects a constant state to the system. This malicious source node is formally defined as:

Definition 1. *A node $v_i \in G$ is a* malicious *node M_i if it acts as a source node in the network, i.e., it updates its state according to equation 2 with an arbitrary strength s', as given by:*

$$x_i(k+1) = \frac{1}{|N_i|+1}\left(\sum_{j \in N_i(k)} x_j(k) + s'\right). \tag{3}$$

In the following theorem, we prove the damaging impact of a malicious source node in the source-disconnected segment of the network:

Theorem 1. *If there exists a malicious node M_i in the disconnected region of the network, the nodes in that region cannot detect a cut using the state update equation (1).*

Proof. We can rewrite equations 1 and 2 together in a matrix representation, as follows:

$$X(k+1) = (D(k)+I)^{-1}(A(k)X(k) + se_1), \tag{4}$$

where D is the diagonal matrix of node degrees and A is the adjacency matrix of G. Note that equation 4 is an iteration based on the Jacobi method to solve:

$$LX = se_1, \textit{ where } L = D - A + I. \tag{5}$$

Now assume that a cut partitions the network G into $G_{source}, G_2, \ldots, G_n$ and that there is a malicious source M_k with strength s' in a partitioned network G_j. It is clear that A, D, and I can also be partitioned such that $A = A_1 + A_2 + \ldots + A_n$, $D = D_1 + D_2 + \ldots + D_n$, and $I = I_1 + I_2 + \ldots + I_n$. Thus:

$$\begin{aligned} L &= \sum_{i=1}^{n} D_i - \sum_{i=1}^{n} A_i + \sum_{i=1}^{n} I_i \\ &= \sum_{i=1}^{n}(D_i - A_i + I_i) \\ &= L_1 + L_2 + \ldots + L_3, \end{aligned}$$

which gives $(L_1 + L_2 + \ldots + L_n)X = se_1 + s'e_k$. Accordingly, the disconnected part of the network, which has a malicious node, is actually another system with M_k such that:

$$L_j X = s'e_k \tag{6}$$

Note that $L_j = D_j - A_j + I_j$ is the Dirichlet Laplacian and it is invertible if its graph is connected. Therefore, there exists a unique solution X where each node in the disconnected region G_j will converge to some positive value. □

Corollary 1. *If there exists more than one malicious node in the source-disconnected region of the network, nodes in that region cannot detect a cut.*

Proof. Assume that there is more than one malicious node $M_1, M_2, \ldots, M_n$ with corresponding source strength $s'_1, s'_2, \ldots, s'_n$ in the disconnected region G_j of the network. From (6) we have,

$$L_j X = \sum_{i=1}^{n} s'_i e_i \tag{7}$$

It is clear that a unique solution of X still exists as the right side of the equation does not affect the invertibility of L_j. □

Our proposed robust cut detection algorithm is based on the observation that the states of nodes in close proximity are similar. As shown in Figure 1(b), which depicts the distribution of state values for a sample 10×20 network, state values are inversely related to distance from the source node. One might observe that there is no significant state difference between nearby nodes and be tempted to directly use the states of neighbor nodes as samples to construct a distribution for outlier detection. However, this naive approach is insufficient. In fact, it is hard to assume a certain distribution based on samples of received states from neighbors, because: i) the sample size of states is irregular and small for some nodes; ii) states in close proximity are not always similar, i.e., regional variations exist for some nodes, especially nodes close to the source; iii) the range of the state value is relatively large. Hence, a straightforward outlier rejection algorithm might fail.

Our main idea is to derive new samples from the states of neighbor nodes in the way that the new samples are not susceptible to the aforementioned problems. We denote the set of received states of a node v as $S = \{s_1, s_2, \ldots, s_n\}$ and also denote the newly derived set of samples as S^N. The algorithm for converting S to S^N and finding a distribution of S^N is presented in Algorithm 1. For each neighbor state of a node v, i.e., $s_i \in S$, the algorithm selects p nearest neighbor states $s_l \in S$, and computes the distances: $d_{il} = |s_i - s_l|$, for $i \neq l$. We denote these distances as $\{d_{i1}, d_{i2}, \ldots, d_{i(p-1)}\}$. Then S^N is the set described by:

$$S^N = \left\{ \sum_{j=1}^{p-1} d_{1j}, \sum_{j=1}^{p-1} d_{2j}, \ldots \sum_{j=1}^{p-1} d_{nj} \right\} \tag{8}$$

Once the mean μ and variance σ to approximate the distribution of S^N are computed, the node v invokes, as shown in Algorithm 2, the extreme studentized deviate test (ESD) which performs well in detecting outliers in a random normal sample. In the ESD test, maximum deviation from the mean is calculated and compared with a tabled value. If the maximum deviation is greater than the

Algorithm 1. Compute Distribution

```
Input: S, p
Output: μ, σ
  S_i^N ← ∅, min_dist ← 0, min_idx ← 0
  for i = 0 to |S| do
    for k = 0 to p do
      for j = 0 to |S| do
        if i ≠ j and s_j ≠ −1 then
          dist ← |s_i − s_j|
          if dist < min_dist then
            min_dist ← dist
            min_idx ← j
          end if
        end if
      end for
      s_min_idx ← −1
      s_i^N ← s_i^N + min_dist
    end for
  end for
  μ ← Σ_i s_i^N / |S|
  σ ← sqrt( Σ_i (s_i^N − μ)^2 / (|S| − 1) )
```

Algorithm 2. Outlier Detection

```
Input: s_i^N
Output: True, or False
  if |s_i^N − μ| / σ > t_table[|S|] then
    return True
  end if
  return False
```

tabled value, then an outlier is identified. Since our algorithm is based on taking a difference between closest states, we can not only cancel out the regional variations in states, but also make the range of sample much smaller, which leads us to get a better sampling even for small data set.

3.3 Energy Efficient Cut Detection

The proposed robust cut detection algorithm (section 3.1), as well as other state of art algorithms [1], suffers from relatively high energy consumption, since all nodes participate in the execution of the algorithm. To address this problem, we propose to execute the robust cut detection algorithm on a small subset of nodes. The main idea is to partition the network into a grid of clusters as depicted in Figure 2(a). The nodes in each cluster elect a leader who executes the robust cut detection algorithm by exchanging state values only with leaders in adjacent clusters.

An interesting byproduct of clustering is that the grid topology formed by leaders in the network allows leaders to easily compute the expected convergence value of their states. This is possible because the grid structure bounds degree of each leader; therefore by knowing its position within the grid of leaders, an individual leader can easily compute the adjacency matrix and diagonal matrix of node degrees without additional message overheads. An additional benefit is that the degree of leaders in our clustered environment is much smaller, normally no larger than 4, than would be typical of a network where all nodes participate. Since the convergence is determined by the spectral gap (i.e., the smallest non-trivial eigenvalue of the graph Laplacian), convergence speed rapidly grows with increasing spectral gap [1]. Therefore, maintaining a small spectral gap is important for energy constrained WSN.

More formally, if the system parameters a and b are known to leaders (see upper left corner of Figure 2(a)), they can easily construct the adjacency matrix A and the diagonal matrix D of node degrees. The equations 1 and 2 can be rewritten in matrix representation:

$$X(k+1) = (D(k) + I)^{-1}(A(k)X(k) + se_1) \tag{9}$$

Consequently, by simple matrix multiplication, each leader can exactly compute the next state of itself and its neighbors (note that since $D + I$ is a diagonal matrix, its inverse is simply a diagonal matrix containing the inverse of each element of $D + I$). When a cut occurs, a leader can accurately detect it by checking if its state is different from the expected value. Similarly, a leader can detect a malicious source node in the network by comparing the received state from the malicious node to the expected state.

Details of the energy efficient cut detection protocol are further described below.

Network Initialization. The sensor network starts as a set of localized nodes distributed uniformly in a rectangular area of size $A \times B$. Nodes obtain their locations using any existing node localization protocol [14]. The network is divided into a set of rectangular clusters of size $a \times b$ (a and b are system parameters), as shown in Figure 2(a). Based on location, a node becomes a member of a particular cluster, e.g., a node located at (x, y) will become a member of cluster $G(i, j)$ if $x \in [i \cdot a, (i+1) \cdot a]$ and $y \in [j \cdot b, (j+1) \cdot b]$, where $0 \leq i \leq \lceil \frac{A}{a} \rceil$ and $0 \leq j \leq \lceil \frac{B}{b} \rceil$.

Next, in each cluster $G(i, j)$ a leader $L(i, j)$ is elected [15]. At the end of the leader election phase, all nodes in a cluster know the ID and location of their leader. As a byproduct, the leader also knows the total numbers of nodes participating in the election. Elected leaders in the network form a *the Virtual Grid Network*, denoted by $G_{grid} = (V_{grid}, E_{grid})$, where V_{grid} is a set of all $L(i, j)$'s and E_{grid} is a set of all undirected virtual links connecting $L(i, j)$ and $L(i \pm 1, j \pm 1)$, where $0 \leq i-1$, $i+1 \leq \lceil \frac{A}{a} \rceil$, $0 \leq j-1$, $j+1 \leq \lceil \frac{B}{b} \rceil$.

Cut Detection in the Virtual Grid Network. Once the network initialization phase is complete, the robust cut detection algorithm begins to execute on

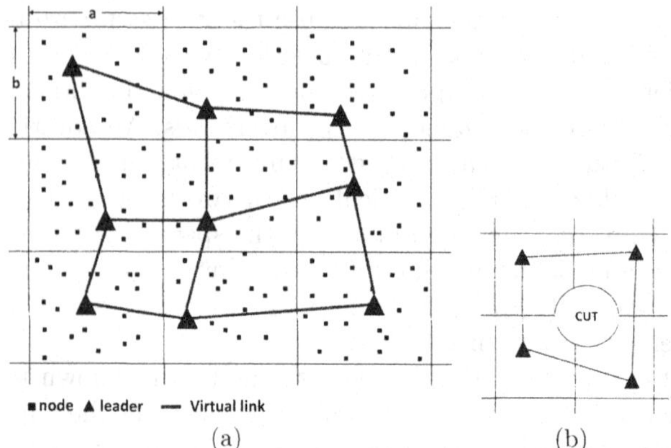

(a) (b)

Fig. 2. (a) A Virtual Grid Network obtained from leaders elected in their respective clusters. (b) The occurrence of a "local cut" that does not trigger a network partition.

G_{grid}. Each leader sends a "STATE_UPDATE" message containing the leader's current state value and location to leaders of adjacent clusters. Routing between leaders is handled with a variant of GPSR [16]. Since a leader, e.g., $L(i, j)$ does not know the ID or location of adjacent leaders, e.g., $L(i+1, j)$ it initially sends messages to a fictitious destination in the middle of cluster $G(i+1, j)$. When the messages reaches cluster $G(i+1, j)$, the first node that sees a "STATE_UPDATE" packet destined for a non-leader location updates the destination with the correct location and ID of the cluster's leader.

The execution of the cut detection in the virtual grid is complicated by a scenario in which a "local cut" does not include any leaders, as shown in Figure 2(b). This problem is overcome during a periodic leader rotation phase. Due to space constraints, we limit our description of the solution to the fact that, as part of leader rotation, the current leader node queries other nodes in the cluster about their energy level. If the leader detects that fewer than expected nodes responded, it may infer that a local cut has occurred. While leader rotation still occurs, the new leader is informed that a local cut may have occurred. The new leader executes a local cut detection algorithm in coordination with adjacent cluster leaders.

Since the cut detection algorithm iteratively executes in the the entire network, it is easy to observe that our proposed cluster-based cut detection algorithm consumes much less energy (since it performs only on the nodes in G_{grid}, which are significantly fewer). In addition, each leader in the virtual grid can detect erroneous state from a malicious attacker because it knows the expected states from its neighbors. Simple arithmetic comparison suffices as a defense algorithm against a malicious node.

4 Implementation

The proposed algorithms for robust and energy efficient cut detection were implemented in nesC for the TinyOS operating system [17] and executed in the

TOSSIM simulator. We assume that nodes in the network obtain their locations through other means and that a loose time synchronization protocol is present.

The complete system executes in two phases. In the "Network Initialization" phase, each node in the network broadcasts a beacon message every 5 sec. Using the beacon messages from neighbors, nodes build neighbor tables and measure link quality by computing the Packet Reception Ratio (PRR), defined as the ratio of successfully received beacons to the total number of beacons sent by a neighbor. The neighbor table and the link measurement is used to find a GPSR routing path [16]. Each node joins a cluster and the cluster elects a leader in a multihop, distributed manner [15]. At the end of this phase, each node knows the locations of its neighbors and the cluster's leader.

In the second phase, the RE^2-CD algorithm executes. Source strength is specified as $s = 100$ and the iteration period is set to 5 seconds. Each leader transmits its state to leaders in adjacent clusters using GPSR routing and the leader location discovery mechanism explained previously. After receiving state from an adjacent leader, a leader checks the sanity of the state by running the outlier detection algorithm. If the state is not an outlier, it is saved in the state table. The state is also stored in flash memory for future post-deployment analysis. When the iteration period expires, each node updates its state according to equation 1 and repeats the above procedure.

To ensure a lock-step execution of the algorithm, all motes are instructed to begin the first phase at roughly the same time via a "system start" message initiated by a designated node and forwarded by each node at most once.

5 Performance Evaluation

In order to evaluate the performance, we conducted simulations using TOSSIM [18] on a set of 264 uniformly deployed nodes in networks of sizes $320 \times 320\ m^2$, $560 \times 560\ m^2$ and $640 \times 640\ m^2$. The radio communication radius of a node was set to $50m$.

5.1 Convergence Speed

Convergence occurs when nodes participating in the cut detection algorithm achieve a steady state. This may be measured in iterations of the algorithm or in the amount of time required.

Cut-detection convergence latency measured in iterations is depicted in Figure 3(a). The number of iterations required for convergence depends on the average degree of a node [1]. Since the degree of a node is at most 4 in our virtual grid scheme, convergence is guaranteed to occur in a bounded number of iterations. Simulations show that convergence is obtained in RE^2-CD in an average of 34 iterations regardless of the number of clusters. In contrast, DSSD shows the number of iterations that rapidly increases as the degree of the network increases.

Figure 3(b) shows convergence latency measured in time, specifically in a "time unit" of packet transmission delay. To measure the convergence latency

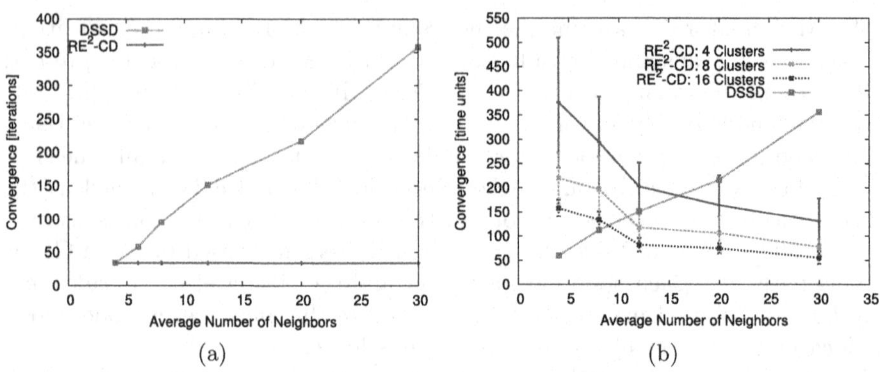

Fig. 3. (a) Convergence speed measured in number of iterations (b) Convergence speed measured in amount of time

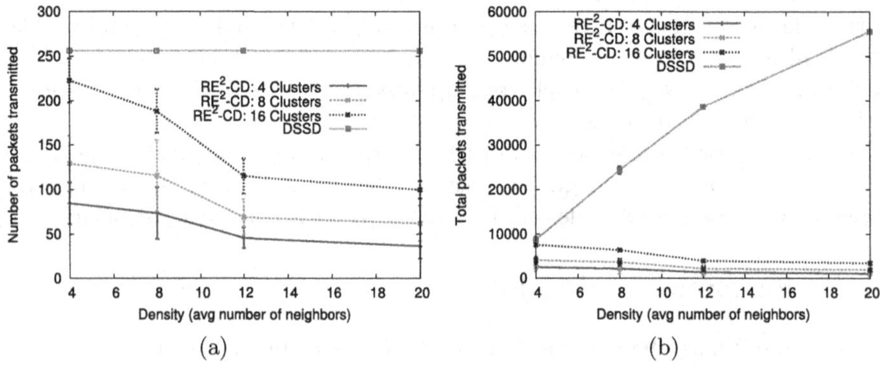

Fig. 4. (a) Number of packets transmitted per single iteration (b) Number of packets required to converge

in time unit, average hop count between leaders are considered. In DSSD, since a node communicates only with the neighbors within one hop distance, the hop count at each iteration is always 1, which means that convergence time depends only on the number of iterations. In RE^2-CD, however, increased density leads to decreased average hop count between leaders, because packets can be routed more directly. Since the number of iterations for convergence is almost constant in RE^2-CD, the convergence time depends on the average hop count; therefore, as the network density increases, the convergence latency in time unit decreases.

5.2 Protocol Overhead

Protocol overhead was calculated by measuring the number of algorithm-related packet transmissions in the entire network for single iteration of both DSSD and RE^2-CD cut detection algorithms using varied network density and cluster size.

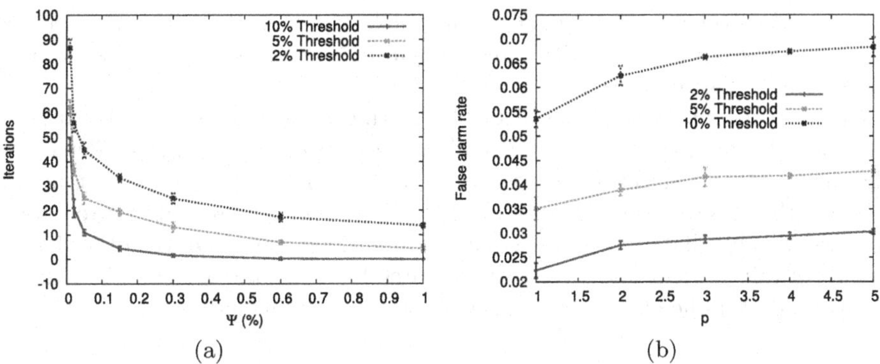

Fig. 5. (a) Number of iterations required to detect a malicious source (b) False alarm rate

The first step of this experiment was to randomly select a leader from each cluster. This was followed by the execution of one iteration of the cut detection algorithm on the virtual grid network of leaders (RE^2-CD) and, separately, on the entire network (DSSD). Each data point represents 50 iterations of this experiment.

Figure 4(a) depicts the results. As network density increased, the number of packet transmissions decreased when using RE^2-CD. This is primarily due to a reduction in the average number of hops in the GPSR routing path between pairs of leaders as the number of neighbors increased. For DSSD, the number of transmitted packets for each iteration remained constant at 264 because every node broadcasts once per iteration regardless of network density. Also note that larger cluster sizes yield lower packet overhead because leaders in larger clusters have more neighbors that can route packets more efficiently.

Figure 4(b) shows the total number of packet transmissions required for convergence. This is based on multiplication of total iterations to convergence by the number of packet transmissions for a single iteration. The two algorithms display significant differences in message overhead.

5.3 Robustness

Detection latency describes the number of iterations required to detect a malicious source. For this experiment, a cut was made by turning off some nodes at iteration k, after the network had converged, e.g., $k = 34$ for RE^2-CD. At iteration $k + 1$, a malicious source node began to inject false state into the network from a location in the disconnected segment. Elapsed time between malicious source injection and detection by a leader node was measured. For different thresholds, the experiment was repeated using different Ψ values, a representation of how much the state of a malicious source deviates from the average state of its neighbors in percentage.

Fig. 5(a) plots the result. In terms of detection accuracy, RE^2-CD detects a malicious source that deviates only 1% from the average state of neighbors. Higher thresholds allow faster detection but, as Fig 5(b) notes, they cause false alarms and cause correct states to be dropped. Although high false alarm rates cause unstable convergence with some fluctuations, rates less than 30% still allow the system to converge [19].

Figure 5(b) explores the problem of selecting p parameter. This parameter indicates the number of nearest neighbor states used in the outlier detection algorithm and its selection represents a tradeoff. Larger values of p tend to increase the false alarm rate but enhance detection of malicious source node clusters, which collaborate to inject similar malicious states. On the other hand, smaller p-values yield lower false alarm rates but may impact the algorithm's ability to detect the cluster of malicious sources injecting similar states.

6 Conclusions

We proposed a robust, energy-efficient algorithm to enhance the detection of disrupted network connectivity in harsh, unattended low-security environments using network of resource-constrained nodes. Our algorithm enhances security by enabling detection of malicious source nodes, even at very low thresholds. Simultaneously, through adoption of a clustered, leader-based convergence algorithm, we greatly reduced the energy required to detect a cut. Parameters including cluster size, node density, and deviation thresholds offer opportunities to trade off energy use and malicious source detection speed for optimal results in arbitrary networks.

Current work in progress includes deployment of a cut-detection enabled sensor network in an outdoor setting. Future work will address tradeoffs between security and energy efficiency and investigate the impact of modifying iteration length in response to changes in the local threat level. Longer breaks between iterations are likely to improve energy efficiency. Independent leader elections are another enhancement that promises to increase network lifespan. Instead of having leaders rotate in lock step, clusters internally determine when to elect a new leader based on local network activity and conditions. Other open questions include finding out other types of possible malicious behaviors critical to the operation of our cut detection algorithm and developing mechanisms to defend against the attacks.

References

1. Barooah, P.: Distributed cut detection in sensor networks. In: Proc of IEEE Conf. on Decision and Control (2008)
2. Mahoney, M.V., Chan, P.K.: Learning nonstationary models of normal network traffic for detecting novel attacks. In: Proc. of Conf. on Knowledge discovery and data mining (2002)
3. Knorr, E., Ng, R., Tucakov, V.: Distance-based outliers: algorithms and applications. VLDB Jrnl (2000)
4. Ramaswamy, S., Rastogi, R., Shim, K.: Efficient algorithms for mining outliers from large data sets. In: Proc. of Conf. on Management of data (2000)

5. Zhang, J., Wang, H.: Detecting outlying subspaces for high-dimensional data: the new task, algorithms, and performance. Knowledge and Information Systems (2006)
6. Breunig, M., Kriegel, H., Ng, R., Sander, J.: LOF: identifying density-based local outliers. In: SIGMOD (2000)
7. Papadimitriou, S., Kitagawa, H., Gibbons, P., Faloutsos, C.: LOCI: Fast outlier detection using the local correlation integral. In: Proc. of Conf. on Data Engineering (2003)
8. Park, V., Corson, M.: A highly adaptive distributed routing algorithm for mobile wireless networks. In: INFOCOM 1997. Sixteenth Annual Joint Conf. of the IEEE Computer and Communications Societies. Proceedings IEEE, vol. 3, pp. 1405–1413 (1997)
9. Chong, C.Y., Kumar, S.: Sensor networks: evolution, opportunities, and challenges. Proc. of the IEEE (2003)
10. Cerpa, A., Estrin, D.: ASCENT: Adaptive self-configuring sensor networks topologies. IEEE Trans. on Mobile Computing (2004)
11. Kleinberg, J.: Detecting a network failure. Internet Mathematics (2004)
12. Ritter, H., Winter, R., Schiller, J.: A partition detection system for mobile ad-hoc networks. In: Proc. of IEEE Conf. on Sensor and Ad Hoc Communications and Networks (SECON) (2004)
13. Shrivastava, N., Suri, S., Tóth, C.: Detecting cuts in sensor networks. ACM Trans. on Sensor Netwks (2008)
14. Stoleru, R., He, T., Stankovic, J.A.: Range-free localization. Secure Localization and Time Synchronization for Wireless Sensor and Ad Hoc Networks 30 (2007)
15. Malpani, N., Welch, J.L., Vaidya, N.: Leader election algorithms for mobile ad hoc networks. In: Proc. of Workshop on Discrete algorithms and methods for mobile computing and communications (2000)
16. Karp, B., Kung, H.T.: GPSR: Greedy perimeter stateless routing for wireless networks. In: Proc. of Conf. on Mobile Computing and Networking (MobiCom) (2000)
17. Hill, J., Szewczyk, R., Woo, A., Hollar, S., Culler, D., Pister, K.: System architecture directions for networked sensors. In: Proc. of Conf. on Architectural support for programming languages and operating systems (2000)
18. Levis, P., Lee, N., Welsh, M., Culler, D.: Tossim: accurate and scalable simulation of entire tinyos applications. In: SenSys 2003: Proc. of the 1st Int. Conf. on Embedded networked sensor systems, pp. 126–137. ACM, New York (2003)
19. Lamport, L., Shostak, R., Pease, M.: The byzantine generals problem. ACM Trans. Program. Lang. Syst. 4, 382–401 (1982)

Energy-Efficient Composite Event Detection in Wireless Sensor Networks

Mirela Marta, Yinying Yang, and Mihaela Cardei*

Department of Computer Science and Engineering
Florida Atlantic University
Boca Raton, FL 33431, U.S.A.
{mmarta,yyang4}@fau.edu, mihaela@cse.fau.edu

Abstract. Wireless sensor networks are deployed to monitor and control the physical environment. Sensors can be equipped with one or more sensing components, such as temperature, light, humidity, etc. An atomic event can be detected using one sensing component. A composite event is the combination of several atomic events. We consider a wireless sensor network densely deployed in a monitored area for reliable detection of a predefined composite event. In this paper, we study the energy-efficient k-watching composite event detection problem, concerned with designing a sensor scheduling mechanism that increases network lifetime, when the set of active sensor nodes are connected and collectively k-watch the composite event at all times. We propose a localized connected dominating set based approach and analyze its performance by simulations.

Keywords: Wireless sensor networks, composite event detection, energy efficiency, sensor scheduling, reliability.

1 Introduction

Sensors are used to monitor and control the physical environment. A Wireless Sensor Network (WSN) is composed of a large number of sensor nodes that are densely deployed either inside the phenomenon or very close to it [1], [3]. Sensor nodes measure various parameters of the environment and transmit data collected to one or more sinks. Once a sink receives sensed data, it processes and forwards it to the users.

A WSN can detect single (or *atomic*) events or *composite* events [9]. Considering the sensors manufactured by Crossbow Technology, Inc. [10] as an example, a sensor equipped with MTS400 multi sensor board can sense temperature, humidity, barometric pressure, and ambient light. Thus it can detect multiple atomic events.

Let us consider a single sensing component, for example the temperature. If the sensed temperature value rises above a predefined threshold, then we say that an *atomic* event has occurred. A *composite* event is the combination of several *atomic* events. For example, the composite event fire may be defined as the combination of events temperature and light. The *composite* event fire occurs only when both the temperature and the light rise above some predefined thresholds.

* This work was supported in part by NSF grant CCF 0545488.

B. Liu et al. (Eds.): WASA 2009, LNCS 5682, pp. 94–103, 2009.

In this paper, we consider a heterogeneous WSN deployed to reliably detect a predefined composite event. For a reliable detection, each atomic event part of the composite event has to be k-watched, that means k sensor nodes equipped with the corresponding sensing component have to be active.

A large number of sensors can be distributed in mass by scattering them from airplanes, rockets, or missiles [1]. Generally, more sensors are deployed than the minimum required to perform the proposed task. This compensates for the lack of exact positioning and improves fault tolerance. An important issue in WSNs is power scarcity, driven in part by battery size and weight limitations. One power saving technique that highly improves network lifetime is to schedule sensor nodes to alternate between active and sleep mode. The active nodes are then in charge with sensing and data gathering tasks.

We propose the energy-efficient k-watching composite event detection (k-ECED) problem. Given the initial deployment of a power-constrained heterogeneous WSNs containing sensors with different sensing capabilities, our objective is to design a sensor scheduling mechanism that maximizes network lifetime. The active sensor set must k-watch the composite event and must be connected. Providing a connected topology is an important property needed for event and data reporting. We propose a localized connected dominating set based approach for designing the sensor scheduling mechanism and we analyze its performance through simulations.

2 Related Work

Sensor nodes have limited power supply and therefore they can work a limited amount of time before they deplete their energy resources and become unfunctional. Many routing algorithms introduced in literature try to minimize sensor energy consumption using different approaches. One such method is sensor scheduling using Connected Dominated Set (CDS). Here, the nodes are either in the dominated set or at most one hop away from the CDS. In this way, all the nodes can communicate with the nodes in the CDS and can transmit their readings to the sink. The problem of routing in ad hoc networks using the CDS approach is described in [11]. The authors propose a three step algorithm for data delivery starting at the source gateways, forwarding the messages through the induced graph, and ending with the destination gateways.

Adjusting the transmission range represents another approach for saving energy in WSNs. Messages sent to a shorter distance will consume less energy than messages transmitted over a larger distance, but they might require multiple retransmissions.

Periodic data reporting and event detection are two main applications of WSNs. Periodic data reporting involves sensor nodes sending their sensed data to a sink periodically. The latter approach implies sending a message each time an event occurs. In [5], authors introduce a framework that deals with event detection in a distributed way by using nodes collaboration. Their goal is to have a distributed system that is resilient to nodes failures and low energy of nodes. The two protocols introduced here are simple event detection and composite event detection. Both build a tree using a communication model based on the Publish-Subscriber paradigm. They work in two phases: initialization phase and collection phase. In the first phase, the application advertises events of interest in the network, together with the region in the network (in terms of start and

Table 1. Notations

M	The number of atomic events which form the composite event
N	The number of sensor nodes
R_c	Sensor communication range
A	Deployment area
x_j	Sensing component which detects atomic event j
k	Fault tolerance level
E	Initial energy of each sensor
h	The number of hops in the local topology

end coordinates) where the event/events are desired to be detected. Based on this, an *Event-Based-Tree* (EBT) is constructed and is used to propagate the information from the source to the destination. In the collection phase, results are collected after an event happened and relied to the sink. In order to save energy, the results are collected using aggregation.

In [9], the authors introduce the *k-watching Event Detection Problem.* The goal is to have an area being k-watched, which means that there must be at least k sensor nodes in the respective area that have together at least k sensing units for each atomic event of interest. A topology and routing supported algorithm is introduced to compute the maximum number of detection sets such that each detection set ensures the k-watching property. The detection sets (or data collection trees) are constructed using the Breadth First Search algorithm starting from a gateway, which can be any sensor node with richer energy resources. One drawback of the proposed approach is the global knowledge required by the algorithm constructing the detection sets. The sets are computed by the gateway node and the decision if an event, simple or composite, occurs is also made by the gateway node. In this paper we proposed a localized approach for constructing detection sets, which is more scalable and thus more appropriate for large scale WSNs.

3 Problem Definition and Network Model

3.1 Problem Definition

Sensors can have single or multiple sensing components, such as the temperature, humidity, barometric pressure, and ambient light. In [9], authors introduce the definitions of an *atomic event* and a *composite event.* When we consider a single sensing component, for example, the temperature, if the temperature rises above some predefined threshold, an *atomic event* is detected. A *composite event* is the combination of several *atomic events.*

For example, consider a fire-detection application using sensors to measure various parameters of the environment. A *composite event* fire might be defined as the combination of the *atomic events* temperature $> th_1$, light $> th_2$, and smoke $> th_3$, where "th" denotes a threshold for the corresponding attribute. That is $fire = (temperature > th_1) \wedge (light > th_2) \wedge (smoke > th_3)$. It is more accurate to report the fire when all these atomic events occur, instead of the case when only one attribute is above the threshold.

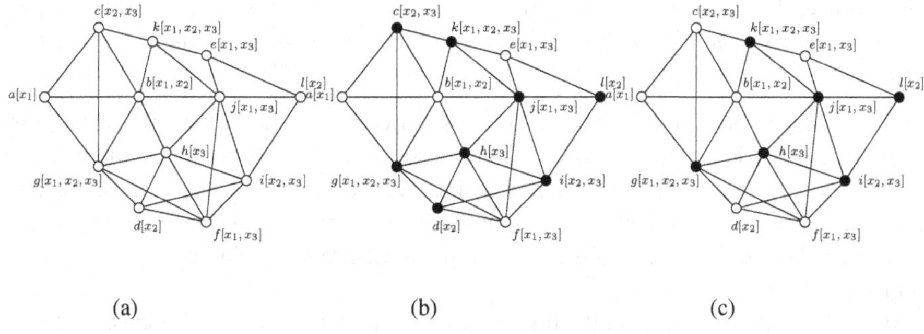

Fig. 1. CDS-LocalRule example (a) WSN topology, (b) CDS-LocalRule for $h = 1$, and (c) CDS-LocalRule for $h = 2$

The main notations used in this section are introduced in Table 1. We denote by M the total number of sensing components, $x_1, x_2, ..., x_M$. Sensors are equipped with single or multiple sensing components. The number and types of sensing components may be different among the sensors in the network. For each sensing component type, a sensor node can be equipped with at most one such sensing component. All of a sensor's sensing components turn on or off simultaneously.

There are several reasons why sensor nodes could have different sets of sensing components [5]:

- The deployed sensors might be manufactured with different sensing capabilities.
- Some sensing capabilities might fail over time.
- Some sensor nodes might have purposefully stopped some sensing components due to energy constraints.
- A sensor node might be unable to use some of its sensor data due to the lack of memory for storing data.

We consider a WSN deployed to detect a predetermined *composite event*, which is a combination of M atomic events $x_1 > th_1, x_2 > th_2, ..., x_M > th_M$. Sensor nodes are equipped with one or more sensing components and they cooperate to detect the composite event. Each sensor node is equipped with a subset of the sensing components set $\{x_1, x_2, ..., x_M\}$. Only when information about the occurrence of all the M atomic events is collected, the occurrence of the composite event is concluded.

Fig. 1a shows an example of a network with $N = 12$ sensor nodes equipped with one or more sensing components. There are three sensing components ($M = 3$) x_1, x_2, x_3 whose measurements have to be used to detect the composite event.

To achieve a reliable surveillance, an event must be observed by more than one sensor. We adopt the k-watched atomic/composite event definitions from [9]:

Definition 1. (k-watched atomic event) *An atomic event is k-watched by a set of sensors if at any time this event occurs at any point within the interested area, at least k sensors in the network can detect this occurrence.*

Definition 2. (k-watched composite event) *A composite event is k-watched by a set of sensors if every atomic event part of the composite event is k-watched by the set of sensors.*

In this paper, the objective is that the composite event is k-watched by the sensors in the area. A WSN is densely deployed, so more sensors are deployed than the number required to provide k-watching of a composite event. In order to prolong network lifetime, one solution is to schedule sensor activity to alternate between sleep and active mode, with the requirement that the active sensors ensure k-watching of the composite event.

Another important step is collecting of sensed data from the active nodes, to determine if the composite event has occurred. For this, the set of active nodes must provide a connected topology. The problem definition is presented next.

Definition 3. (Energy-efficient k-watching Composite Event Detection) *k-ECED Given a set of N sensors with different sensing capabilities, a monitored area A, a composite event which is a combination of M atomic events involving sensing components x_1, x_2, ..., x_M, and the energy constraint of each sensor E_{init}, design a sensor scheduling mechanism such that:*

1. *the composite event is k-watched in the area A*
2. *the set of active sensor nodes is connected*
3. *network lifetime is maximized.*

3.2 Network Model

In this paper we consider a heterogeneous WSN consisting of sensor nodes with different sensing capabilities and a sink, deployed to reliably detect when a predefined composite event takes place. The main objective of the *k-ECED* problem is to prolong network lifetime while ensuring that the composite event under consideration is k-watched and that the set of active nodes are connected.

In order to prolong network lifetime, we propose to use a sensor scheduling mechanism. Network activity is organized in rounds. Each round consists of two phases: *initialization phase* and *event detection phase*.

In the initialization phase, sensor nodes decide if they will be active or if they go to sleep during the next round. The active sensor set must provide a connected topology and must ensure k-watching property across the deployment area.

In this paper, we are not concerned with a specific location for the sink, but we assume that the sink is located within communication range of at least one active node. The sink could be static or it can move in the deployment area. If the sink is mobile, then flooding the alerts (when a composite event is detected) in the network will reach the sink. If the sink is static or moving at a slow speed, the sink could form a data collection tree rooted at the sink, as follows. At the beginning of each round, after the sensor initialization phase, the sink is flooding a query message in the network. Sensors will forward the first copy of the message received and set-up reverse links. When a composite event is detected, the alert is sent to the sink along the reverse links.

The decision of whether to use data collection trees depends on the application. If the composite event detection is expected to be very rare (e.g. forest fire detection), then sending an alert using flooding could be more efficient. If more event detections and reporting are expected in each round, then using a data collection tree could be more energy efficient.

We consider that all rounds take the same time. Network lifetime is measured as the number of rounds until no more detection sets can be formed due to the energy constraints. We consider a similar energy model as that presented in LEACH [4]. The energy used to transmit a l-bit message over a distance d is: $E_{Tx}(l, d) = E_{elec} * l + \varepsilon_{amp} * l * d^2$, and the energy consumed to receive a l-bit message is: $E_{Rx}(l) = E_{elec} * l$, where E_{elec} = 50 nJ/bit and ε_{amp} = 100 pJ/bit/m^2. We assume that the packet size of the $Hello$ messages is much smaller than the size of data messages.

Network topology is modeled as an undirected graph $G = (V, E)$, where the set of vertices V has one vertex for each sensor node. An edge is added between two vertices u and v if the Euclidean distance between nodes is less than or equal to the communication range R_c. We define the h-hop neighborhood of a node u as $N_h(u) = \{v|distance(u, v) \leq h\ hops\}$.

A subset of vertices C form a Connected Dominating Set (CDS) if the subgraph induced by C is connected and for any node $v \in V$, either $v \in C$ or v has a neighbor in C.

4 CDS-Approach to the k-ECED Problem

Our solution addresses the *initialization phase*, the decision mechanism used by a node with sufficient energy resources to decide whether it will be an active or sleeping during the next round.

The decision mechanism that we propose is a local algorithm, where each node relies only on local information from its h-hop neighborhood, where h is a given parameter. A local solution is more scalable, but may obtain sub-optimal solutions compared to a global solution.

The CDS-based local algorithm decides the sensor scheduling at the beginning of each round. Let us assume that each node has the h-hop neighborhood information which can be obtained by having nodes exchange Hello messages. For constructing h-hop neighborhood, each node s broadcasts h Hello messages. First Hello message contains only the node s's ID. Then the ith Hello message ($i = 2, ..., h$) contains s's $(i-1)$-hop neighborhood. We also consider that each node u has a priority $p(u)$ which is totally ordered within the network. The priority is defined as a 2-tuple $p(u) = (E(u), ID(u))$, where $E(u)$ is the node u's residual energy and ID(u) is the node u's ID. A node with higher residual energy has a higher priority. If two nodes have the same residual energy, then the node with higher ID has higher priority.

At the beginning of the initialization phase, all the nodes are active. For a node u, we define $N'_h(u)$ to be the set of nodes within the h-hop neighborhood which have priority higher than u's priority: $N'_h(u) = \{v \in N_h(u)|p(v) > p(u)\}$. Each node decides whether it will go to sleep during the current round based on the following rule:

CDS-LocalRule. *The default status of a sensor node is active. A sensor u is in sleep mode if the following two conditions hold:*

1. *(k-watching property) the set of nodes $N'_h(u)$ provides the k-watching of each of u's sensing components.*
2. *(Connectivity property) any two of u's neighbors in $N_1(u)$, w and v, are connected by a path with all intermediate nodes in $N'_h(u)$.*

The intuition behind this rule is that a sensor u can go to sleep if the nodes with higher priority in its h-hop neighborhood can provide the k-watching property and the connectivity property on behalf of u. Note that a node with higher priority can also go to sleep if the rule holds true in its h-hop neighborhood. To avoid inconsistencies, a mechanism that assigns global priorities to the nodes is used. If a node u has only one neighbor, then the connectivity requirement is fulfilled and u goes to sleep if the k-watching property holds.

h represents the number of hops in the local topology and is a given parameter which usually takes small values, e. g. $h \leq 3$. There is a trade-off in choosing h. When h is larger, more Hello messages are exchanged, resulting in a higher possibility of collisions and a higher overhead in collecting local information. But more nodes are expected to go to sleep since the local neighborhood $N'_h(u)$ has a larger cardinality, see Fig. 3. Let S be the set of sleeping sensors, $V' = V - S$, and let G' be the subgraph induced by V'.

Theorem. *Assume that the WSN $G(V, E)$ provides the composite event k-watching property and forms a connected topology. Let S be the set of sleeping sensor nodes after applying the CDS-LocalRule. Then the following properties hold:*

- *Each sensor in S has a neighbor in V'*
- *Sensors in V' are connected*
- *Sensors in V' provide the k-watching property.*

Proof: The first two properties ensure that the set of active sensor nodes V' forms a CDS. Let us take any sensor node a in the network, $a \in V$. We will show that any other node in the network is connected to a through a path with nodes in V'.

Let X be the set of nodes which is not connected to a by a path of active nodes and let Y be the set of sleeping neighbors of the set X which are connected to a. The set $Y \neq 0$ since the nodes in X are connected to a in the original graph G. Let y be the node with the highest priority in Y. Then the node y has two neighbors, one neighbor $b \in X$ and one neighbor $c \in V - X - Y$. Since node y is sleeping, then according to the *CDS-LocalRule*, any two neighbors b and c must be connected through a path with intermediate nodes of higher priority. Such a path must contain at least one node in Y, let us denote it y'. It follows that $p(y') > p(y)$ which contradicts the assumption that y has the highest priority in Y.

Let us show now that nodes V' provide the k-watching property. Assume by contradiction that V' does not provide the k-watching property for a sensing component x_i. Let v be the sleeping node in $V - V'$ with the highest priority which is equipped with sensing component x_i. Then, according to the CDS-LocalRule k-watching property, v went to sleep if all its components are k-watched by nodes in $N'_h(u)$. It follows that the nodes in $N'_h(u)$ have k components x_i. Also these components didn't go to sleep since the nodes in $N'_h(u)$ have higher priority than u. This contradicts our assumption and as a result the nodes in V' provide the k-watching property. ■

Let us consider an example of a WSN with 12 sensor nodes, deployed as illustrated in Fig. 1a. The composite event consists of three sensing components $\{x_1, x_2, x_3\}$, and each sensor is equipped with one or more sensing components. The fault tolerance level is $k = 2$. We consider the nodes priority in alphabetical order, that is $p(a) < p(b) < \ldots < p(l)$. Fig. 1b shows the active nodes after applying *CDS-LocalRule* for $h = 1$. The blackened nodes are the active nodes.

Let us consider node b for example. $N_1'(b) = \{c, k, j, h, g\}$ and this set provides 2-watching for x_1, x_2 and x_3. Also, taken any two neighbors (e.g. a and h) they are connected through a path with all intermediate nodes in $N_1'(b)$. Thus, node b goes to sleep. For node c, $N_1'(c) = \{g, k\}$. The 2-watching property holds, but the connectivity property does not. The neighbors g and k are not connected through a path with intermediate nodes in $N_1'(c)$. Thus node c does not go to sleep.

Fig. 1c shows the active nodes after applying *CDS-LocalRule* for $h = 2$. As h increases, more sensor nodes are expected to go to sleep. Let us consider node c with $N_2'(c) = \{g, k, h, d, f, j, e\}$. In this case both the 2-watching property and the connectivity property hold, thus node c goes to sleep.

5 Simulation

5.1 Simulation Environment and Settings

Metrics in the simulations include the network lifetime, the average number of active sensors, and the overhead. In each round, we choose one set of active sensors and only active sensors report data to the sink. The network lifetime is computed as the number of rounds where both the k-watching and connectivity requirements are met. The average number of active sensors is computed as $\frac{numActiveSensor}{numRound}$, where $numActiveSensor$ is the total number of active sensors during network lifetime and $numRound$ is the network lifetime in terms of the number of rounds. The overhead is the number of Hello messages sent and received for choosing the set of active sensors.

In the simulation, the monitored area is 100×100 units. The communication range of sensors is 15 units. We consider the composite event is a combination of three sensing components $M = 3$ and $k = 3$. The energy consumed for sending and receiving a data message is 60 units and 40 units respectively. The energy consumed for sending and receiving a Hello message is 3 and 2 units respectively. The sink is located at the center of the monitored area.

In each round during the network lifetime, active sensors form a data delivery tree initiated by the sink and each sensor generates 10 data messages. The data delivery tree is formed using controlled flooding. The sink broadcasts a message containing the number of hops, which is forwarded by active nodes which also keep a reference to the parent from which the message was received. We assume that each active sensor applies a data aggregation algorithm. The packet size that an active sensor reports is computed as $\lceil \alpha \cdot (msgReceived + 1) \rceil$, where α is the aggregation factor and we assume $\alpha = 0.5$, and $msgReceived$ is the total packet size it receives from its children in the data delivery tree. We conduct the simulations on a custom discrete event simulator, which generates a random initial sensor deployment. All the tests are repeated 50 times and the results are averaged.

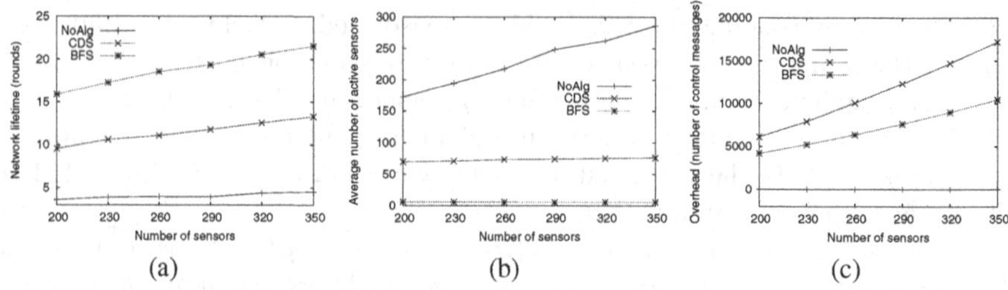

Fig. 2. Comparison among 3 cases. (a) Network lifetime. (b) The average number of active sensors. (c) Overhead.

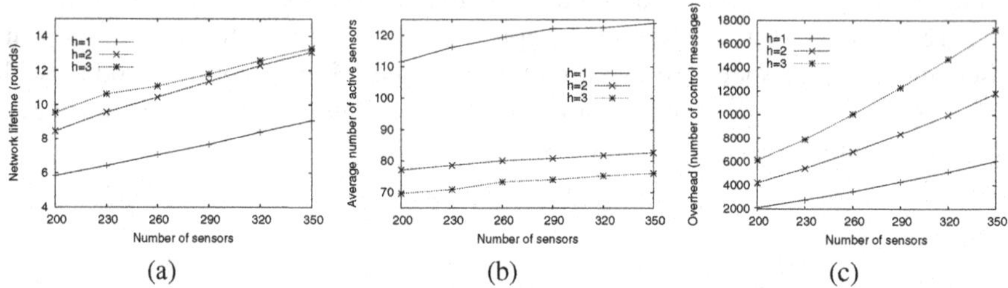

Fig. 3. Comparison among different h values for CDS algorithm. (a) Network lifetime. (b) The average number of active sensors. (c) Overhead.

5.2 Simulation Results

Fig. 2 compares three cases. $NoAlg$ is the case when no scheduling algorithm is applied and no sensor goes to sleep. CDS is our localized CDS-LocalRule approach. BFS is the centralized algorithm proposed in [9]. In Fig. 2b, BFS has the smallest average number of active sensors, while $NoAlg$ has the largest. Consequently, BFS has the longest network lifetime and $NoAlg$ has the shortest, see Fig. 2a. The overhead for choosing the set of active sensors are compared in Fig. 2c. Since BFS is centralized and all computations are done by the sink, each sensor first needs to report to the sink its location and other information and after the sink decides the set of active sensors, it sends back the scheduling plan to the sensors. In the CDS approach, sensors exchange information for h-hop neighborhood information. In $NoAlg$, no overhead is involved.

Fig. 3 compares the performance of the CDS algorithm for different values of h. When h is 3, the smallest number of sensors are chosen to be active and therefore, it has the longest network lifetime. When $h = 1$, it has the largest number of active sensors and the shortest network lifetime. That is because when checking the connectivity condition, when h is larger, the sensor has more neighborhood information and has more chances to find a path connecting pairs of two neighbors, thus the sensor has higher probability to go to sleep. As a trade-off, Fig. 3c shows that compared with the cases $h = 2$ and $h = 1$, the case $h = 3$ involves higher overhead to get more neighbor information.

6 Conclusions

In this paper, we focus on the energy efficient k-watching composite event detection problem. Given a WSN deployed for watching a composite event, our goal is to design a sensor scheduling mechanism such that the monitored area is k-watched, the connectivity condition is met and the lifetime is maximized. One localized CDS-based algorithm is proposed. Simulation results show that our method has low overhead and is effective in prolonging network lifetime.

References

1. Akyildiz, I., Su, W., Sankarasubramaniam, Y., Cayirci, E.: Wireless sensor networks: a survey. Computer Networks 38(4), 393–422 (2002)
2. Cheng, X., Thaeler, A., Xue, G., Chen, D.: TPS: A time-based positioning scheme for outdoor wireless sensor networks. In: IEEE INFOCOM (2004)
3. Culler, D., Estrin, D., Srivastava, M.: Overview of sensor networks. IEEE Computer 37(8), 41–49 (2004)
4. Heinzelman, W., Chandrakasan, A., Balakrishnan, H.: Energy-efficient communication protocol for wireless microsensor networks. In: Hawaii Intlernational Conference on System Sciences (HICSS) (2000)
5. Kumar, A.V.U.P., Reddy, A.M., Janakiram, V.D.: Distributed collaboration for event detection in wireless sensor networks. In: MPAC 2005 (2005)
6. Marta, M., Cardei, M.: Using sink mobility to increase wireless sensor networks lifetime. In: IEEE WoWMoM 2008 (2008)
7. Romer, K., Mattern, F.: Event based systems for detecting real-world states with sensor networks: a critical analysis. In: DEST Workshop on Signal Processing in Sensor Networks at ISSNIP, December 2004, pp. 389–395 (2004)
8. Stojmenovic, I., Lin, X.: Power-aware routing in ad hoc wireless networks. IEEE Transaction on Parallel and Distributed Systems (2001)
9. Vu, C.T., Beyah, R.A., Li, Y.: Composite event detection in wireless sensor networks. In: IEEE International Performance, Computing, and Communications Conference (2007)
10. `http://www.xbow.com/Home/HomePage.aspx`
11. Wu, J., Li, H.: An extended localized algorithm for connected dominating set formation in ad hoc wireless networks. In: IEEE Transactions on Parallel and Distributed Systems, October 2004, pp. 908–920 (2004)
12. Xu, Y., Heidemann, J., Estring, D.: Geography-informed energy conservation for ad hoc routing. In: ACM/IEEE International Conference on Mobile Computing and Networking (July 2001)

ε-Net Approach to Sensor k-Coverage

Giordano Fusco and Himanshu Gupta

Computer Science Department
Stony Brook University
Stony Brook, NY 11790
{fusco,hgupta}@cs.sunysb.edu

Abstract. Wireless sensors rely on battery power, and in many applications it is difficult or prohibitive to replace them. Hence, in order to prolongate the system's lifetime, some sensors can be kept inactive while others perform all the tasks. In this paper, we study the k-coverage problem of activating the minimum number of sensors to ensure that every point in the area is covered by at least k sensors. This ensures higher fault tolerance, robustness, and improves many operations, among which position detection and intrusion detection.

The k-coverage problem is trivially NP-complete, and hence we can only provide approximation algorithms. In this paper, we present an algorithm based on an extension of the classical ε-net technique. This method gives a $O(\log M)$-approximation, where M is the number of sensors in an optimal solution. We do not make any particular assumption on the shape of the areas covered by each sensor, besides that they must be closed, connected and without holes.

1 Introduction

Coverage problems have been extensively studied in the context of sensor networks (see for example [1,2,3,4]). The objective of sensor coverage problems is to minimize the number of active sensors, to conserve energy usage, while ensuring that the required region is sufficiently monitored by the active sensors. In an over-deployed network we can also seek k-coverage, in which every point in the area is covered by at least k sensors. This ensures higher fault tolerance, robustness, and improves many operations, among which position detection and intrusion detection.

The k-coverage problem is trivially NP-complete, and hence we focus on designing approximation algorithms. In this paper, we extend the well-known ε-net technique to our problem, and present an $O(\log M)$-factor approximation algorithm, where M is the size of the optimal solution. The classical greedy algorithm for set cover [5], when applied to k-coverage, delivers a $O(k \log n)$-approximation solution, where n is the number of *target points* to be covered. Our approximation algorithm is an improvement over the greedy algorithm, since our approximation factor of $O(\log M)$ is independent of k and of the number of target points.

Instead of solving the sensor's k-coverage problem directly, we consider a dual problem, the k-hitting set. In the k-hitting set problem, we are given sets and

B. Liu et al. (Eds.): WASA 2009, LNCS 5682, pp. 104–114, 2009.

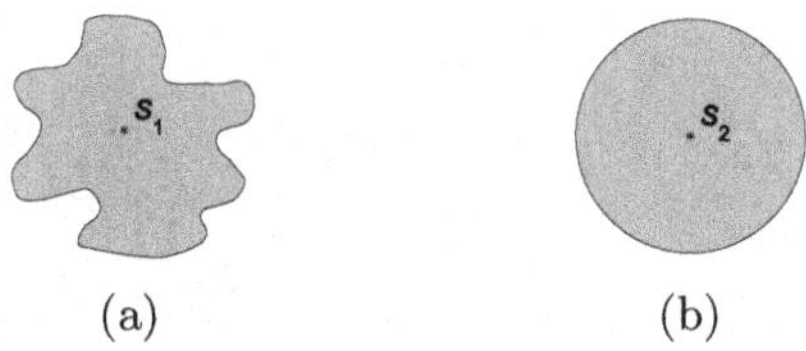

(a) (b)

Fig. 1. Sensing regions associated with a sensor: (a) a general shape that is closed, connected, and without holes, and (b) a disk

points, and we look for the minimum number of points that "hit" each set at least k times (a set is hit by a point if it contains it). Brönnimann and Goodrich were the first [6] to solve the hitting set using the ε-net technique [7]. In this paper, we introduce a generalization of ε-nets, which we call (k, ε)-nets. Using (k, ε)-nets with the Brönnimann and Goodrich algorithm's [6], we can solve the k-hitting set, and hence the sensor's k-coverage problem. Our main contribution is a way of constructing (k, ε)-nets by random sampling. A recent Infocom paper [8] uses ε-nets to solve the k-coverage problem. However we believe that their result is fundamentally flawed (see Section 2.1 for more details). So, to the best of our knowledge, we are the first to give a correct extension of ε-nets for the k-coverage problem.

2 Problem Formulation and Related Work

We start by defining the sensing region and then we will define the k-coverage problem with sensors. In the literature, sensing regions have been often modeled as disks. In this paper, we consider sensing regions of general shape, because this reflects a more realistic scenario.

Definition 1 (Sensing Region). *The sensing region of a sensor is the area "covered" by a sensor. Sensing regions can have any shape that is closed, connected, and without holes, as in Fig. 1(a). Often, sensing regions are modeled as disks as in Fig. 1(b), but we consider more general shapes.*

Definition 2 (Target Points). Target points *are the given points in the 2D plane that we wish to cover using the sensors.*

k-SC Problem. Given a set of sensors with fixed positions and a set of target points, select the minimum number of sensors, such that each target point is covered (is contained in the selected sensing region) by at least k of the selected sensors.

For simplicity, we have defined the above k-SC problem's objective as coverage of a set of given target *points*. However, as discussed later, our algorithms and techniques easily generalize to the problem of covering a given area.

Example 1. Suppose we are given 4 sensors and 20 points as in Fig. 2(a), and we want to select the minimum number of sensors to 2-cover all points. In this particular example, 2 sensors are not enough to 2-cover all points. Instead, 3 sensors suffices, as shown in Fig. 2(b).

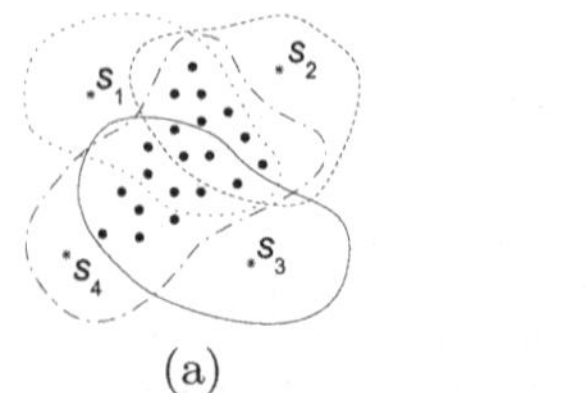

(a)

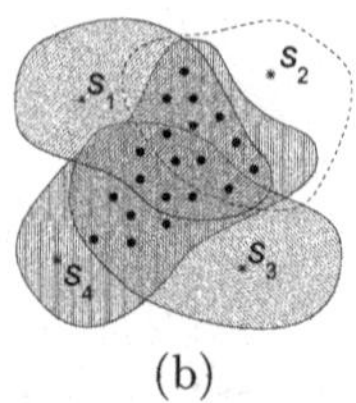

(b)

Fig. 2. Illustrating k-SC problem. Suppose we are given 4 sensors of centers $s_1, \ldots, s_4$ and 20 points as in (a). The problem is to select the minimum number of sensors to k-cover all points. A possible solution for $k = 2$ is shown in (b), where 3 sensors suffice to 2-cover all points.

2.1 Related Work

In recent years, there has been a lot of research done [2,3,9,1] to address the coverage problem in sensor networks. In particular, Slijepcevic and Potkonjak [3] design a centralized heuristic to select mutually exclusive sensor covers that independently cover the network region. In [2], Charkrabarty et al. investigate linear programming techniques to optimally place a set of sensors on a sensor field for a complete coverage of the field. In [10], Shakkottai et al. consider an unreliable sensor network, and derive necessary and sufficient conditions for the coverage of the region and connectivity of the network with high probability. In one of our prior works [1], we designed a greedy approximation algorithm that delivers a connected sensor-cover within a logarithmic factor of the optimal solution; this work was later generalized to k-coverage in [11].

Recently, Hefeeda and Bagheri [8] used the well-known ε-net technique to solve the problem of k-covering the sensor's *locations*. However, we strongly believe that their result is fundamentally flawed.[1] In this article we present a correct extension of the ε-net technique for k-coverage problem in sensor networks.

Two closely related problems to the sensor-coverage problem are set cover and hitting set problems. The area covered by a sensor can be thought as a set, which contains the points covered by that sensor. The hitting set problem is a "dual" of the set cover problem. In both set cover and hitting set problems, we are given sets and elements. While in set cover the goal is to select the minimum number of sets to cover all elements/points, in hitting set the goal is to select a subset of elements/points such that each set is hit. The classical result for set cover [5] gives a $O(\log n)$-approximation algorithm, where n is the number of *target points* to be covered. The same greedy algorithm also delivers a $O(k \log n)$-approximation solution for the k-SC problem. In contrast, the result in this article yields an $O(\log M)$-approximation algorithm for the k-SC problem,

[1] Essentially, they select a set of *subsets* of size k (called k-flowers) represented by the center of their locations. However, their result is based on the following incorrect claim that if the centers of a set of k-flowers 1-covers a set of points N, then the set of sensors associated with the k-flowers will k-cover N. In addition, in their analysis, they implicitly assume that an optimal solution can be represented as a disjoint union of k-flowers, which is incorrect.

where M is the optimal size (i.e., minimum number of *sensors* needed to provide k-coverage of the given target points). Note that our approximation factor is independent of k and of the number of target points.

Brönnimann and Goodrich [6] were the first to use the ε-net technique [7] to solve the hitting set problem and hence the set cover with an $O(\log M)$-approximation, where M is the size of the optimal solution. In this article, we extend their ε-net technique to k-coverage. It is interesting to observe that our extension is independent of k and it gives a $O(\log M)$-approximation also for k-coverage. For the particular case of 1-coverage with disks, it is possible to build "small" ε-nets using the method of Matoušek, Seidel and Welzl [12], and obtain a constant-factor approximation for the 1-hitting set problem. Their method [12] can be easily extended to k-hitting set, and this would give a constant-factor approximation for the k-SC problem when the sensing regions are disks. However, in this paper we focus on sensing regions of arbitrary shapes and sizes, as long as they are closed, connected, and without holes.

Another related problem is the art gallery problem (see [13] for a survey) which is to *place* a minimum number of guards in a polygon so that each point in the polygon is visible from at least one of the guards. Guards may be looked upon as sensors with infinite range. However, in this paper, we focus on *selecting* already deployed sensor.

3 The ε-Net Based Approach

In this section, we present an algorithm based on the classical ε-net technique, to solve the k-coverage problem. The classical ε-net technique is used to solve the hitting set problem, which is the dual of the set cover problem. The k-SC problem is essentially a generalization of the set cover problem – thus, we will extend the ε-net technique to solve the corresponding generalization of the hitting set problem.

3.1 Hitting Set Problem and the ε-Net Technique

We start by describing the use of classical ε-net technique to solve the traditional hitting set problem. We begin with a couple of formal definitions.

Set Cover (SC); Hitting Set (HS). Given a set of points X and a collection of sets $\mathcal{C}$, the *set cover* (SC) problem is to select the minimum number of sets from $\mathcal{C}$ whose union contains (covers) all points in X. The *hitting set* (HS) problem is to select the minimum number of points from X such that all sets in $\mathcal{C}$ are "hit" (a set is considered hit, if one of its points has been selected).

Note that HS is a *dual* of SC, and hence solving HS is sufficient to solve SC.

We now define ε-nets. Intuitively, an ε-net is a set of points that hits all *large* sets (but may not hit the smaller ones). For the overall scheme, we will assign weights to points, and use a generalized concept of weighted ε-nets that must hit all large-weighted sets.

Definition 3 (ε-Net; Weighted ε-Net). *Given a set system $(X, \mathcal{C})$, where X is a set of points and $\mathcal{C}$ is a collection of sets, a subset $H \in X$ is an* ε-net *if for every set S in $\mathcal{C}$ s.t. $|S| \geq \varepsilon|X|$, we have that $H \cap S \neq \emptyset$.*

Given a set system $(X, \mathcal{C})$, and a weight function $w : X \rightarrow Z^+$, define $w(S) = \sum_{x \in S} w(x)$ for $S \subseteq X$. A subset $H \subseteq X$ is a weighted ε-net *for $(X, \mathcal{C}, w)$ if for every set S in $\mathcal{C}$ s.t. $w(S) \geq \varepsilon \cdot w(X)$, we have that $H \cap S \neq \emptyset$.*

Using ε-Nets to Solve the Hitting Set Problem. The original algorithm for solving hitting set problem using ε-net was invented by Brönnimann and Goodrich [6]. Below, we give a high-level description of their overall approach (referred to as the BG algorithm), because it will help understand our own extension. We begin by showing how ε-nets are related to hitting sets, and then, show how to use ε-nets to actually compute hitting sets.

Let's assume that we have a black-box to compute weighted ε-nets, and that we know the optimal hitting set H^* which is of size M. Now, define a weight function w^* as $w^*(x) = 1$ if $x \in H^*$ and $w^*(x) = 0$ otherwise. Then, set $\varepsilon = 1/M$, and use the black-box to compute a weighted ε-net for $(X, \mathcal{C}, w^*)$. It is easy to see that this weighted ε-net is actually a hitting set for $(X, \mathcal{C})$, since $w^*(S) \geq \varepsilon w^*(X)$ for *all* sets $S \in \mathcal{C}$. There are known techniques [7] to compute weighted ε-nets of size $O((1/\varepsilon)\log(1/\varepsilon))$ for set systems with a constant VC-dimension (defined later); thus, the above gives us a $O(\log M)$-approximate solution. For the particular case of disks, it is possible to construct ε-nets of size $O(1/\varepsilon)$ [12], and hence obtain a constant-factor approximation.

However, in reality, we do not know the optimal hitting set. So, we iteratively guess its size M, starting with $M = 1$ and progressively doubling M until we obtain a hitting set solution (using the above approach). Also, to "converge" close to the w^* above, we use the following scheme. We start with all weights set to 1. If the computed weighted ε-net is not a hitting set, then we pick one set in $\mathcal{C}$ that is not hit by it and double the weights of all points that it contains. Then, we iterate with the new weights. It can be shown that if the estimate of M is correct and using $\epsilon = 1/(2M)$, then we are *guaranteed* to find a hitting set using the above approach after a certain number of iterations. Thus, if we don't find a hitting set after enough iterations, we double the estimate of M and try again. It can be shown [6] that the above approach finds an $O(\log M)$-approximate hitting set in polynomial time for set systems with constant VC-dimension (defined below), where M is the size of the optimal hitting set.

VC Dimension. We end the description of the BG algorithm, with the definition of Vapnik-Červonenkis (VC) dimension of set systems. Informally, the VC-dimension of a set system $(X, \mathcal{C})$ is a mathematical way of characterizing the "regularity" of the sets in $\mathcal{C}$ (with respect to the points X) in the system. A bounded VC-dimension allows the construction of an ε-net through random sampling of large enough size. The VC-dimension is formally defined in terms of set shattering, as follows.

Definition 4 (VC-Dimension). *A set S is considered to be* shattered *by a collection of sets $\mathcal{C}$ if for each $S' \subseteq S$, there exists a set $C \in \mathcal{C}$ such that*

$S \cap C = S'$. *The* VC-dimension *of a set system* $(X, \mathcal{C})$ *is the cardinality of the largest set of points in* X *that can be shattered by* $\mathcal{C}$.

In our case, the VC dimension is at most 23 as given by the following theorem by Valtr [14].

Theorem 1. *If* $X \subset \mathbb{R}^2$ *is compact and simply connected, then VC-dimension of the set system* $(X, \mathcal{C})$, *where* X *is a set of points and* $\mathcal{C}$ *is a collection of sets, is at most 23.*

Note that for a finite collection of sensors, whose covering regions are compact and simply connected, the dual is compact and simply connected too.

3.2 k-Hitting Set Problem and the (k, ε)-Net Technique

We now formulate the k-hitting set (k-HS) problem, which is a generalization of the hitting set problem, viz., we want each set in the system to be hit by k selected points.

Definition 5 (k-Hitting Set (k-HS)). *Given a set system* $(X, \mathcal{C})$, *the* k-hitting set (k-HS) *problem is to find the smallest subset of points* $H \subseteq X$ *with* at most one *point for each sibling-set such that* H *hits every set in* $\mathcal{C}$ *at least* k *times.*

Connection Between k-HS and k-SC Problem. Note that the above k-HS problem is the (generalized) dual of our sensor k-coverage problem (k-SC problem). Essentially, each point in the k-HS problem corresponds to a sensing region of a sensor, and each set in the k-HS problem corresponds to a target point. Below, we describe how to solve the k-HS problem, which essentially solves our k-SC problem. To solve the k-HS, we need to define and use a generalized notion of ε-net.

Definition 6 (Weighted (k, ε)-Net). *Suppose* $(X, \mathcal{C})$ *is a sibling-set system, and* $w : X \to Z^+$ *is a weight function. Define* $w(S) = \sum_{x \in S} w(x)$ *for* $S \subseteq X$. *A set* $N \subseteq X$ *is a* weighted (k, ε)-net *for* $(X, \mathcal{C}, w)$ *if* $|N \cap S| \geq k$, *whenever* $S \in \mathcal{C}$ *and* $w(S) \geq \varepsilon \cdot w(X)$.

Using (k, ε)-Nets to Solve k-HS. We can solve the k-HS problem using the BG algorithm [6], without much modification. However, we need an algorithm compute weighted (k, ε)-nets. The below theorem states that an appropriate random sampling of about $O(k/\varepsilon \log k/\varepsilon)$ points from X gives a (k, ε)-net with high probability, if the set system $(X, \mathcal{C})$ has a bounded VC-dimension. For the sake of clarity, we defer the proof of the following theorem.

Theorem 2. *Let* $(X, \mathcal{C}, w)$ *be a weighted set system. For a given number* m, *let* $N(m)$ *be a subset of points of size* m *picked randomly from* X *with probability proportional to the total weight of the points in such subset. Then, for*

$$m \geq \max\left(\frac{2}{\varepsilon}\log_2\frac{2}{\delta}, \frac{K}{\varepsilon}\log_2\frac{K}{\varepsilon}\right) \qquad (1)$$

the subset $N(m)$ is a weighted (k, ε)-sibling-net with probability at least $1 - \delta$, where $K = 4(d + 2k - 2)$, and d is the VC-dimension of the set system. □

Now, based on the above theorem, we can use the BG algorithm with some modifications to solve the k-HS problem. Essentially, we estimate the size M of an optimal k-HS (starting with 1 and iteratively doubling it), set $\varepsilon = k/(2M)$, and use Theorem 2 to compute[2] a (k, ε)-net N of size m. If N is indeed a k-hitting set, we stop; else, we pick a set in the system $\mathcal{C}$ that is not k-hit and double the weight of all the points it contains. With the new weights, we iterate the process. It can be shown[3] that within $(4/k)M \log_2(n/M)$ iterations of weight-doubling, we are guaranteed to get a k-HS solution if the optimal size of a k-HS is indeed M. Thus, after $(4/k)M \log_2(n/M)$ iterations, if we haven't found a k-HS, we can double our current estimate of M, and iterate. See Algorithm 1. The below theorem shows that the above algorithm gives an $O(\log M)$-approximate solution in polynomial time with high probability for general sets. The proof of the following theorem is again similar to that for the BG algorithm [6].

Theorem 3. *The algorithm described above (Algorithm 1) runs in time $O((|\mathcal{C}| + |X|)\,|X| \log |X|)$ and gives a $O(\log M)$-approximate solution for the k-HS problem for a general set systems $(X, \mathcal{C})$ of constant VC-dimension, where M is the optimal size of a k-HS.*

Proof. The outer `for` loop, where M is doubled each time, is run at most $O(\log |X|)$ times. The inner `for` loop, where the weights are doubled for a set, is executed at most $\frac{4}{k} M \log_2 \frac{|X|}{M} = O(|X|/k)$ times. Computing a (k, ε)-net using Theorem 2 takes at most $O(|X|)$ time, while the doubling-weight process may take up to $O(|\mathcal{C}|)$ time.

We now prove the approximation factor. An optimal algorithm would find a k-hitting set of size M. If the VC-dimension is a constant, the k-HS method of Theorem 2 finds a (k, ε)-net of size $O(\frac{k}{\varepsilon} \log \frac{k}{\varepsilon})$. So if $\varepsilon = \frac{k}{2M}$, the size of the k-hitting set is $O(M \log M)$, which is a $O(\log M)$-approximation. □

Outline of Proof of Theorem 2. There are two challenges in generalizing the random-sampling technique of [7], viz., (i) sampling with replacement cannot be used, and (ii) weights must be part of the sampling process.

Challenges in Extending the Technique of [7] to k-hitting set. The classical method [7] of constructing an ε-net consists of randomly picking a set N of at least m points, for a certain m, where each point is picked *independently* and randomly from the given set of points. This way of constructing an ε-net may result in duplicate points in N, but *the presence of duplicates does not cause a problem in the analysis.* Thus, we can also construct weighted ε-net easily by emulating weights using duplicated copies of the same point. The above described

[2] Theorem 2 gives a (k, ε)-net with high probability. It is possible to check efficiently if the obtained set is indeed a (k, ε)-net. If it is not, we can try again until we get one. On average, a small number of trials are sufficient to obtain a (k, ε)-net.

[3] See [15] for the proof, which is similar to the one for BG in [6].

Algorithm 1. Solving k-HS Problem using (k, ε)-nets.
Since k-HS is the dual of k-SC, this algorithm also solves k-SC
(in k-SC, X corresponds to the set of sensors, and $\mathcal{C}$ to the set of target points).

Given a set system $(X, \mathcal{C})$.
for $(M = 1;\ \ M <= |X|;\ \ M *= 2)$
  $\varepsilon = k/(2\,M)$;
  reset the weights of all points in X to 1;
  for $(i = 0;\ \ i < (4/k)M\log_2(|X|/M);\ \ i++)$
    Compute a (k, ε)-net N of size m using Theorem 2;
    if each set in $\mathcal{C}$ is k-hit by N, **return** N;
    select a set in $\mathcal{C}$ that is not k-hit, and double the weight of all the points in the set;

approach works well for 1-hitting set, partly because we do not count the number of times each set is hit. However, for the case of k-hitting set, when constructing a (k, ε)-net, we need to ensure that the number of *distinct* points that hit each set is at least k. Thus, constructing a (k, ε)-net by picking points independently at random (with duplicates) does not lead to correct analysis. Instead, we suggest a novel method to construct a weighted (k, ε)-net N by: (i) selecting a random subset of points (without duplicates) at once, and (ii) including the weights directly in the above sampling process. To the best of our knowledge, we are the first one to propose this extension.[4]

Proof Sketch of Theorem 2. Let m be as given by equation (1), and N be the subset of points randomly picked from X as described in Theorem 2. After picking N, pick another set T (for the purposes of the below analysis) in the same way as N. We now define two events

$$\begin{aligned} E_1 &= \{\exists A \in \mathcal{C} \text{ s.t. } |A \cap N| < k,\ w(A) \geq \varepsilon\, w(X)\} \\ E_2 &= \{\exists A \in \mathcal{C} \text{ s.t. } |A \cap N| < k,\ w(A) \geq \varepsilon\, w(X),\ |A \cap Z| \geq \varepsilon m\} \end{aligned}$$

where $Z = N \cup T$ and $\varepsilon m \leq \mathrm{E}[\,|A \cap Z|\,]/2$. The proof consists of 3 major steps:

1. First, we show that $\Pr[E_1] \leq 2\Pr[E_2]$.
2. Then, it's easier to bound the probability of E_2

$$\Pr[E_2] \ \leq\ (2m)^{d+2k-2}\, 2^{-\varepsilon m}$$

3. Finally, we have that m verifies $2(2m)^{d+2k-2}\, 2^{-\varepsilon m} \ \leq\ \delta$

The outline of each step follows:

1. From the definition of conditional probability

$$\Pr[E_2 \mid E_1] \ =\ \Pr[E_2 \cap E_1]/\Pr[E_1] \ =\ \Pr[E_2]/\Pr[E_1]$$

[4] As discussed before, [8] uses ε-nets to solve sensor's k-coverage, but their method is flawed (see Footnote 1 for more details).

So we just need to show that $\Pr[E_2 \mid E_1] \geq 1/2$. Let $Z = \{y_1, \dots, y_{2m}\}$ (where y_i's *are* pairwise different). Define the random variable

$$Y_i = \begin{cases} 1 & \text{if } y_i \in A \\ 0 & \text{o.w.} \end{cases}$$

Set $Y = \sum_{i=1}^{2m} Y_i$, and we have $Y = |A \cap Z|$. It is possible to show that $\mathrm{E}[Y] = \mu \geq 2\varepsilon m$, and $\mathrm{Var}[Y] \leq \mu$. Applying Chebyshev's inequality

$$\Pr[Y < \frac{\mu}{2}] \leq \Pr[|Y - \mathrm{E}[Y]| > \frac{\mu}{2}] \leq \frac{4}{\mu^2}\,\mathrm{Var}[Y] \leq \frac{1}{2}$$

and the result follows.

2. We use an alternate view. Instead of picking N and then T, pick $Z \subseteq X$ of size $2m$, then pick $N \subseteq Z$ and set $T = Z \setminus N$. It can be shown that the two views are equivalent. Now, define

$$E_A = \{|A \cap N| < k,\ |A \cap Z| \geq \varepsilon m\}$$

Since N and T are disjoint $|A \cap Z| = |A \cap N| + |A \cap T|$ and then $|A \cap N| < k$ iff $|A \cap Z| < k + |A \cap T|$. So we have that E_A happens only if $\varepsilon m \leq |A \cap Z| \leq m + k - 1$. By counting the number of ways of choosing N s.t. $|A \cap N| < k$, we can bound $\Pr[E_A]$

$$\begin{aligned}\Pr[E_A] &= \Pr[|A \cap N| < k,\ |A \cap Z| \geq \varepsilon m] \\ &\leq \Pr[|A \cap N| < k \mid \varepsilon m \leq |A \cap Z| \leq m + k - 1] \\ &\leq (2m)^{2k-2}\binom{2m-\varepsilon m}{m}\Big/\binom{2m}{m} \leq (2m)^{2k-2}\,2^{-\varepsilon m}\end{aligned}$$

Since E_A depends only on the intersection $A \cap Z$

$$\Pr[E_2] \leq \bigcup_{A \mid A \cap Z \text{ is unique}} \Pr[E_A] \leq |\mathcal{C}_{|Z}|\,(2m)^{2k-2}\,2^{-\varepsilon m}$$

3. Similar to [7]. □

Please, refer to [15] for the detailed proof, which is omitted here due to lack of space.

Remark. Note that the approximation factor of Theorem 3 could be improved, if we could design an algorithm to construct smaller (k, ε)-nets. For instance, if we could construct a (k, ε)-net of size $O(k/\varepsilon)$, then we would have a constant-factor approximation for the k-HS problem. For the particular case of disks, it is easy to extend[5] the method in [12] to build a (k, ε)-net of size $O(k/\varepsilon)$ (see [15] for more details).

[5] Essentially, it is enough to replace $\delta = \varepsilon/6$ with $\delta = \varepsilon/(6k)$ and the proof follows through. Also note that the dual of disks and points is also composed by disks and points.

3.3 Distributed ε-Net Approach

Distributed implementation of the ε-net algorithm requires addressing the following main challenges.

1. We need to construct a (k, ε)-net, through some sort of distributed randomized selection.
2. For each constructed (k, ε)-net N, we need to verify in a distributed manner whether N is indeed a k-coverage set (k-hitting set in the dual).
3. If N is not a k-coverage set, then we need to select *one* target point (a set in the dual) that is not k-covered by N and double the weights of all the sensing regions covering it.

We address the above challenges in the following manner. First, we execute the distributed algorithm in *rounds*, where a round corresponds to one execution of the inner `for` loop of Algorithm 1 (i.e., execution of the sampling algorithm for a particular set of weights and a particular estimate of M). We implement rounds in a weakly synchronized manner using internal clocks. Now, for each of the above challenges, we use the following solutions.

1. Each sensor keeps an estimate of the total weight of the system, and computes m independently. To select m sensors, each sensor decides to select itself independently with a probability $p = m * own\_weight/total\_weight$, resulting in selection of m sensors (in expectation). Each selected sensor picks an orientation (sensing-region) of highest weight.
2. Locally, verify k-coverage of the owned target points, by exchanging messages with near-by (that cover a common target point) sensors. If a target point owned by a sensor D and its near-by sensors are all k-covered for a certain number of rounds (for example 10), then D exits the algorithm.
3. Each sensor decides to select one of the owned target points with a probability of $q = 1/((1 - \varepsilon)\, n)$, which ensures that the expected number of selected target point is 1.

3.4 Generalizations to k-Coverage of an Area

The ε-net approach can also be used to k-cover a given area, rather than a given set of target points (as required by the formulation of k-SC problem). Essentially, coverage of an area requires dividing the given area into "subregions" as in our previous work [1]; a subregion is defined as a set of points in the plane that are covered by the *same* set of sensing regions. The number of such subregions can be shown to be polynomial in the total number of sensing regions in the system. The algorithm described here can then be used without any other modification, and the performance guarantees still hold.

4 Conclusions

In this paper, we studied the k-coverage problem with sensors, which is to select the minimum number of sensors so that each target point is covered by at least

k of them. We provided a $O(\log M)$-approximation, where M is the number of sensors in an optimal solution. We introduced a generalization of the classical ε-net technique, which we called (k, ε)-net. We gave a method to build (k, ε)-nets based on random sampling. We showed how to solve the sensor's k-coverage problem with the Brönnimann and Goodrich algorithm [6] together with our (k, ε)-nets. We believe to be the first one to propose this extension.

As a future work, we would like to extend this technique to *directional sensors.* A directional sensor is a sensor that has associated multiple sensing regions, and its *orientation* determines its actual sensing region. The k-coverage problem with directional sensors is NP-complete and in [16] we proposed a greedy approximation algorithm. We believe that using (k, ε)-nets can give better approximation factor for this problem.

References

1. Gupta, H., Zhou, Z., Das, S., Gu, Q.: Connected sensor cover: Self-organization of sensor networks for efficient query execution. TON 14(1) (2006)
2. Charkrabarty, K., Iyengar, S., Qi, H., Cho, E.: Grid coverage for surveillance and target location in distributed sensor networks. Transaction on Computers (2002)
3. Slijepcevic, S., Potkonjak, M.: Power efficient organization of wireless sensor ad-hoc networks. In: ICC (2001)
4. Meguerdichian, S., Koushanfar, F., Qu, G., Potkonjak, M.: Exposure in wireless ad-hoc sensor networks. In: MobiCom (2001)
5. Cormen, T.H., Leiserson, C.E., Rivest, R.L., Stein, C.: Introduction to algorithms, 2nd edn. MIT Press/ McGraw-Hill, Cambridge (2001)
6. Brönnimann, H., Goodrich, M.T.: Almost optimal set covers in finite vc-dimension. Discrete & Computational Geometry 14(4), 463–479 (1995)
7. Haussler, D., Welzl, E.: Epsilon-nets and simplex range queries. Discrete & Computational Geometry 2, 127–151 (1987)
8. Hefeeda, M., Bagheri, M.: Randomized k-coverage algorithms for dense sensor networks. In: INFOCOM, pp. 2376–2380 (2007)
9. Ye, F., Zhong, G., Lu, S., Zhang, L.: Peas: A robust energy conserving protocol for long-lived sensor networks. In: ICDCS (2003)
10. Shakkottai, S., Srikant, R., Shroff, N.: Unreliable sensor grids: Coverage, connectivity and diameter. In: INFOCOM (2003)
11. Zhou, Z., Das, S.R., Gupta, H.: Connected k-coverage problem in sensor networks. In: ICCCN, pp. 373–378 (2004)
12. Matoušek, J., Seidel, R., Welzl, E.: How to net a lot with little: Small ε-nets for disks and halfspaces. In: SCG, pp. 16–22 (1990)
13. O'Rourke, J.: Art Gallery Theorems and Algorithms, vol. 3. Oxford University Press, New York (1987)
14. Valtr, P.: Guarding galleries where no point sees a small area. Israel Journal of Mathematics 104, 1–16 (1998)
15. Fusco, G., Gupta, H.: ϵ-net approach to sensor k-coverage. Technical report, Stony Brook University (2009), `http://www.cs.sunysb.edu/~fusco/publications.html`
16. Fusco, G., Gupta, H.: Selection and orientation of directional sensors for coverage maximization. In: SECON (2009)

Biologically-Inspired Target Recognition in Radar Sensor Networks

Qilian Liang

Department of Electrical Engineering
University of Texas at Arlington
Arlington, TX 76019-0016, USA
liang@uta.edu
http://www3.uta.edu/faculty/liang

Abstract. Inspired by biological systems' (such as human's) innate ability to process and integrate information from disparate, network-based sources, we apply biologically-inspired information integration mechanisms to target detection in cognitive radar sensor network. Humans' information integration mechanisms have been modelled using maximum-likelihood estimation (MLE) or soft-max approaches. In this paper, we apply these two algorithms to radar sensor networks target detection. Discrete-cosine-transform (DCT) is used to process the integrated data from MLE or soft-max. We apply fuzzy logic system (FLS) to automatic target detection based on the AC power values from DCT. Simulation results show that our MLE-DCT-FLS and soft-max-DCT-FLS approaches perform very well in the radar sensor network target detection, whereas the existing 2-D construction algorithm doesn't work in this study.

1 Introduction and Motivation

A radar sensor network consists of multiple networked radar sensors and radar sensors sense and communicate with each other collaboratively to complete a mission. In real world, radar sensor network information integration is necessary in different applications. For example, in an emergency natural disaster scenario, such as Utah Mine Collapse in August 2007 or West Virginia Sago mine disaster in January 2006, radar sensor network-based information integration for first responders is critical for search and rescue. Danger may appear anywhere at any time, therefore, first responders must monitor a large area continuously in order to identify potential danger and take actions. Due to the dynamic and complex nature of natural disaster, some buried/foleage victims may not be found with image/video sensors, and UWB radar sensors are needed for penetrating the ground or sense-through-wall. Unfortunately, the radar data acquired are often limited and noisy. Unlike medical imaging or synthetic aperture radar imaging where abundance of data is generally available through multiple looks and where processing time may not be crucial, practical radar sensor networks are typically the opposite: availability of data is limited and required processing time is short. This need is also motivated by the fact that biological systems

B. Liu et al. (Eds.): WASA 2009, LNCS 5682, pp. 115–124, 2009.

such as humans display a remarkable capability to quickly perform target recognition despite noisy sensory signals and conflicting inputs. Humans are adept at network visualization, and at understanding subtle implications among the network connections. To date, however, human's innate ability to process and integrate information from disparate, network-based sources for situational understanding has not translated well to automated systems. In this paper, we apply biologically-inspired information integration mechanisms to information fusion in radar sensor network.

2 Sense-through-Foliage Radar Sensor Networks Data Measurement and Collection

Our work is based on the sense-through-foliage UWB radar sensor networks. The foliage experiment was constructed on a seven-ton man lift, which had a total lifting capacity of 450 kg. The limit of the lifting capacity was reached during the experiment as essentially the entire measuring apparatus was placed on the lift. The principle pieces of equipment secured on the lift are: Barth pulser, Tektronix model 7704 B oscilloscope, dual antenna mounting stand, two antennas, rack system, IBM laptop, HP signal Generator, Custom RF switch and power supply and Weather shield (small hut). The target is a trihedral reflector (as shown in Fig. 1). Throughout this work, a Barth pulse source (Barth Electronics, Inc. model 732 GL) was used. The pulse generator uses a coaxial reed switch to discharge a charge line for a very fast rise time pulse outputs. The model 732 pulse generator provides pulses of less than 50 picoseconds (ps) rise time, with amplitude from 150 V to greater than 2 KV into any load impedance through a 50 ohm coaxial line. The generator is capable of producing pulses with a minimum width of 750 ps and a maximum of 1 microsecond. This output pulse width is determined by charge line length for rectangular pulses, or by capacitors for 1/e decay pulses.

For the data we used in this paper, each sample is spaced at 50 picosecond interval, and 16,000 samples were collected for each collection for a total time duration of 0.8 microseconds at a rate of approximately 20 Hz. We plot the transmitted pulse (one realization) in Fig. 2a) and the received echos in one collection in Fig. 2b (averaged over 35 pulses).

3 Human Information Integration Mechanisms

Recently, a maximum-likelihood estimation (MLE) approach was proposed for multi-sensory data fusion in human [4]. In the MLE approach [4], sensory estimates of an environmental property can be represented by $\hat{S}_j = f_i(S)$ where S is the physical property being estimated, f is the operation the nervous system performs to derive the estimate, and $\hat{S}$ is the perceptual estimate. Sensory estimates are subject to two types of error: random measurement error and bias. Thus, estimates of the same object property from different cues usually differ. To

Fig. 1. The target (a trihedral reflector) is shown on the stand at 300 feet from the lift

reconcile the discrepancy, the nervous system must either combine estimates or choose one, thereby ignoring the other cues. Assuming that each single-cue estimate is unbiased but corrupted by independent Gaussian noise, the statistically optimal strategy for cue combination is a weighted average [4]

$$\hat{S}_c = \sum_{i=1}^{M} w_i \hat{S}_i \tag{1}$$

where $w_i = \frac{1/\sigma_i^2}{\sum_j 1/\sigma_j^2}$ and is the weight given to the ith single-cue estimate, σ_i^2 is that estimates variance, and M is the total number of cues. Combining estimates by this MLE rule yields the least variable estimate of S and thus more precise estimates of object properties.

Besides, some other summation rules have been proposed in perception and cognition such as soft-max rule: $y = (\sum_{i=1}^{M} x_i^n)^{\frac{1}{n}}$ [3] where x_i denotes the input from an input source i, and M is the total number of sources. In this paper, we will apply MLE and soft-max human brain information integration mechanisms to cognitive radar sensor network information integration.

4 Human-Inspired Sense-through-Foliage Target Detection

In Figs. 3a and 3b, we plot two collections of UWB radars. Fig. 3a has no target on range, and Fig. 3b has target at samples around 13,900. We plot the echo differences between Figs. 3a and 3b in Fig. 3c. However, it is impossible to identify whether there is any target and where there is target based on Fig. 3c. Since significant pulse-to-pulse variability exists in the echos, this motivate us to explore the spatial and time diversity using Radar Sensor Networks (RSN).

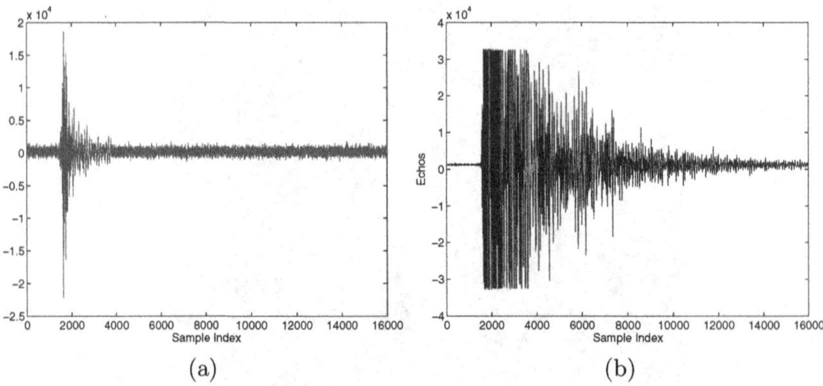

Fig. 2. Transmitted pulse and received echos in one experiment. (a) Transmitted pulse. (b) Received echos.

In RSN, each radar can provide their pulse parameters such as timing to their clusterhead radar, and the clusterhead radar can combine the echos (RF returns) from the target and clutter. In this paper, we propose a RAKE structure for combining echos, as illustrated by Fig. 4. The integration means time-average for a sample duration T and it's for general case when the echos are not in discrete values. It is quite often assumed that the radar sensor platform will have access to Global Positioning Service (GPS) and Inertial Navigation Unit (INU) timing and navigation data [1]. In this paper, we assume the radar sensors are synchronized in RSN. In Fig. 4, the echo, i.e., RF response by the pulse of each cluster-member sensor, will be combined by the clusterhead using a weighted average, and the weight w_i is determined by the two human-inspired mechanisms.

We applied the human-inspired MLE algorithm to combine the sensed echo collection from $M = 30$ UWB radars, and then the combined data are processed using discrete-cosine transform (DCT) to obtain the AC values. Based on our experiences, echo with a target generally has high and nonfluctuating AC values and the AC values can be obtained using DCT. We plot the power of AC values in Figs. 5a and 5b using MLE and DCT algorithms for the two cases (with target and without target) respectively. Observe that in Fig. 5b, the power of AC values (around sample 13,900) where the target is located is non-fluctuating (somehow monotonically increase then decrease). Although some other samples also have very high AC power values, it is very clear that they are quite fluctuating and the power of AC values behaves like random noise because generally the clutter has Gaussian distribution in the frequency domain.

Similarly, we applied the soft-max algorithm ($n = 2$) to combine the sensed echo collection from $M = 30$ UWB radars, and then used DCT to obtain the AC values. We plot the power of AC values in Figs. 5a and 5b using soft-max and DCT algorithms for the two cases (with target and without target) respectively. Observe that in Fig. 6b, the power of AC values (around sample 13,900) where the target is located is non-fluctuating (somehow monotonically increase then decrease).

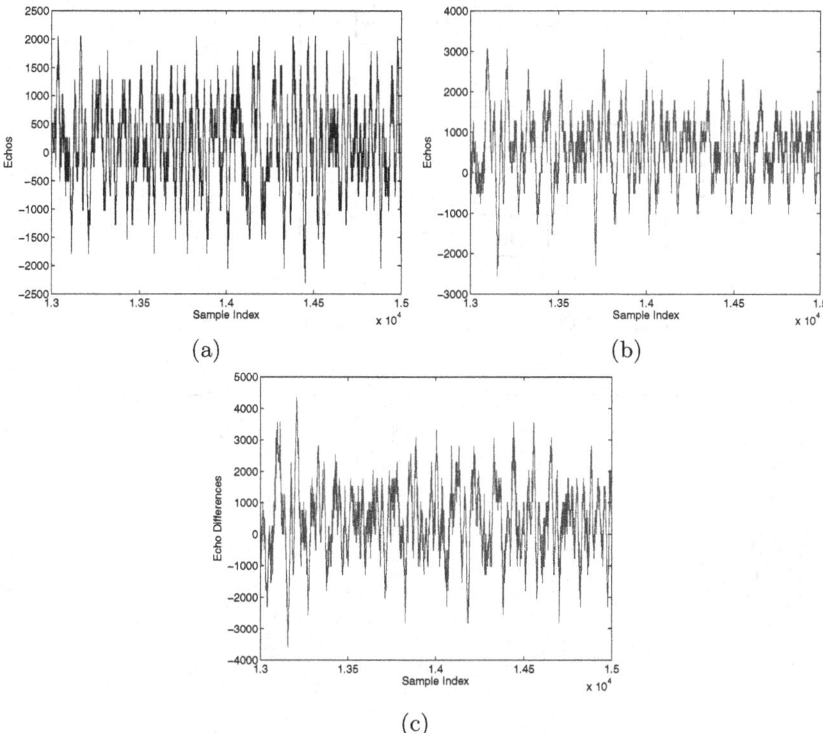

Fig. 3. Measurement with poor signal quality and 35 pulses average. (a) Expanded view of traces (no target) from sample 13,001 to 15,000. (b) Expanded view of traces (with target) from samples 13,001 to 15,000. (c) The differences between (a) and (b).

We made the above observations. However, in real world application, automatic target detection is necessary to ensure that our algorithms could be performed in real time. In Section 5, we apply fuzzy logic systems to automatic target detection based on the power of AC values (obtained via MLE-DCT or soft-max-DCT).

We compared our approaches to the scheme proposed in [6]. In [6], 2-D image was created via adding voltages with the appropriate time offset. In Figs. 7a and 7b, we plot the 2-D image created based on the above two data sets (from samples 13,800 to 14,200). The sensed data from 30 radars are averaged first, then plotted in 2-D [6]. However, it's not clear which image shows there is target on range.

5 Fuzzy Logic System for Automatic Target Detection

5.1 Overview of Fuzzy Logic Systems

Figure 8 shows the structure of a fuzzy logic system (FLS) [5]. When an input is applied to a FLS, the inference engine computes the output set corresponding

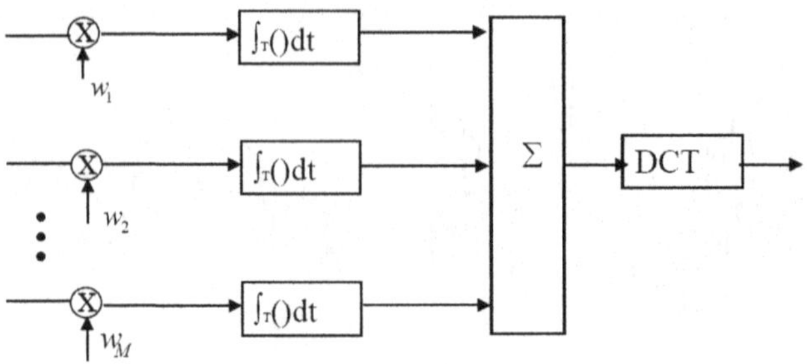

Fig. 4. Echo combining by clusterhead in RSN

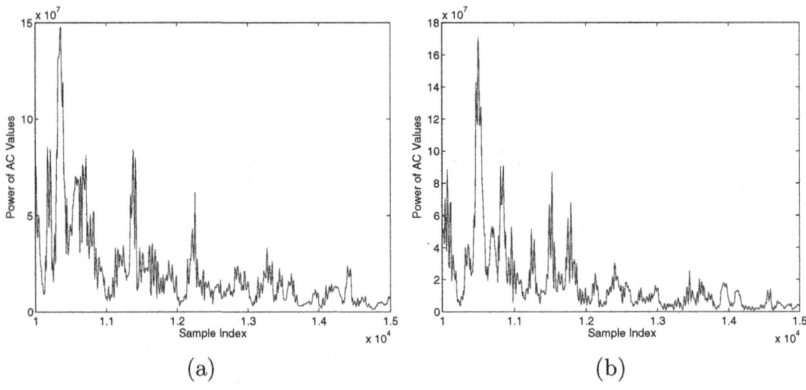

Fig. 5. Power of AC values using MLE-based information integration and DCT. (a) No target (b) With target in the field.

to each rule. The defuzzifer then computes a crisp output from these rule output sets. Consider a p-input 1-output FLS, using singleton fuzzification, *center-of-sets* defuzzification [5] and "IF-THEN" rules of the form

$$R^l : \text{IF } x_1 \text{ is } \mathrm{F}_1^l \text{ and } x_2 \text{ is } \mathrm{F}_2^l \text{ and } \cdots \text{ and } x_p \text{ is } \mathrm{F}_p^l, \text{ THEN } y \text{ is } \mathrm{G}^l.$$

Assuming singleton fuzzification, when an input $\mathbf{x}' = \{x_1', \ldots, x_p'\}$ is applied, the degree of firing corresponding to the lth rule is computed as

$$\mu_{\mathrm{F}_1^l}(x_1') \star \mu_{\mathrm{F}_2^l}(x_2') \star \cdots \star \mu_{\mathrm{F}_p^l}(x_p') = \mathcal{T}_{i=1}^{p} \mu_{\mathrm{F}_i^l}(x_i') \tag{2}$$

where $\star$ and $\mathcal{T}$ both indicate the chosen t-norm. There are many kinds of defuzzifiers. In this paper, we focus, for illustrative purposes, on the center-of-sets defuzzifier [5]. It computes a crisp output for the FLS by first computing the centroid, c_{G^l}, of every consequent set G^l, and, then computing a weighted average of these centroids. The weight corresponding to the lth rule consequent centroid is the degree of firing associated with the lth rule, $\mathcal{T}_{i=1}^{p} \mu_{\mathrm{F}_i^l}(x_i')$, so that

$$y_{cos}(\mathbf{x}') = \frac{\sum_{l=1}^{M} c_{\mathrm{G}^l} \mathcal{T}_{i=1}^{p} \mu_{\mathrm{F}_i^l}(x_i')}{\sum_{l=1}^{M} \mathcal{T}_{i=1}^{p} \mu_{\mathrm{F}_i^l}(x_i')} \tag{3}$$

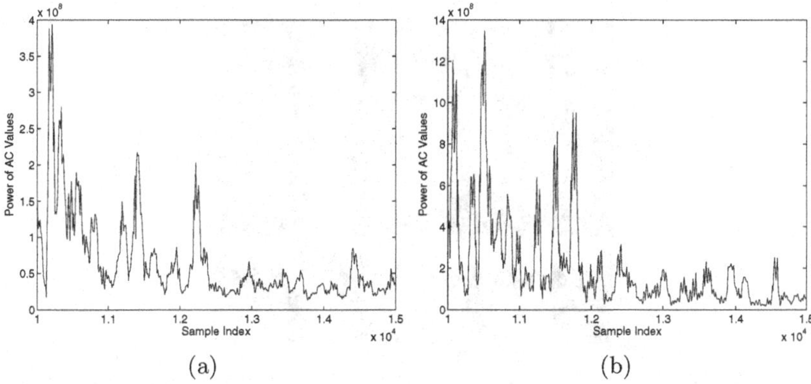

Fig. 6. Power of AC values using soft-max based information integration and DCT. (a) No target (b) With target in the field.

where M is the number of rules in the FLS. In this paper, we design a FLS for automatic target recognition based on the AC values obtained using MLE-DCT or soft-max-DCT.

5.2 FLS for Automatic Target Detection

Observe that in Figs. 5 and 6, the power of AC values are quite fluctuating and have lots of uncertainties. FLS is well known to handle the uncertainties. For convenience in describing the FLS design for Automatic Target Detection (ATD), we first give the definition of *footprint of uncertainty* of AC power values and *region of interest* in the footprint of uncertainty.

Definition 1 (Footprint of Uncertainty). *Uncertainty in the AC power values and time index consists of a bounded region, that we call the* footprint of uncertainty *of AC power values. It is the union of all AC power values.*

Definition 2 (Region of Interest (RoI)). *An RoI in the footprint of uncertainty is a contour consisting of a large number (greater than 50) of AC power values where AC power values increase then decrease.*

Definition 3 (Fluctuating Point in RoI). *$P(i)$ is called a* fluctuating point *in the RoI if $P(i-1), P(i), P(i+1)$ are non-monotonically increasing or decreasing.*

Our FLS for automatic target detection will classify each ROI (with target or no target) based on two antecedents: *the centroid of the ROI* and *the number of fluctuating points in the ROI.* The linguistic variables used to represent these two antecedents were divided into three levels: *low*, *moderate*, and *high.* The consequent – the possibility that there is a target at this RoI – was divided into 5 levels, *Very Strong, Strong, Medium, Weak, Very Weak.* We used trapezoidal membership functions (MFs) to represent *low*, *high*, *very strong*, and *very weak*;

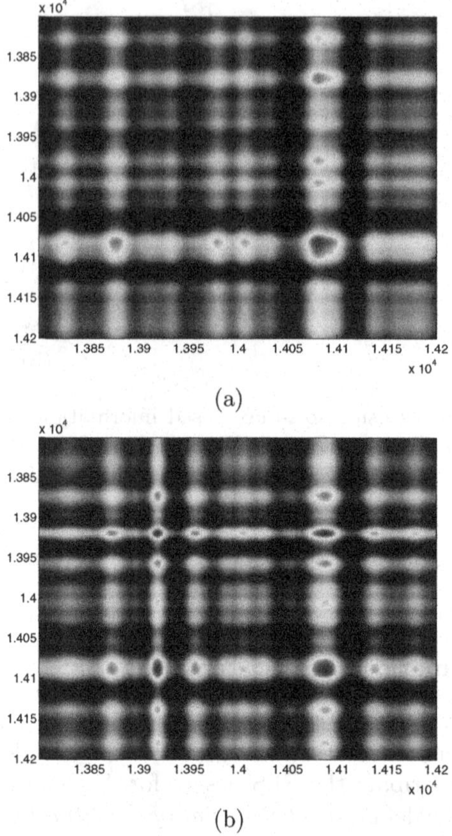

Fig. 7. 2-D image created via adding voltages with the appropriate time offset. (a) No target (b) With target in the field.

and triangle MFs to represent *moderate*, *strong*, *medium*, and *weak*. All inputs to the antecedents are normalized to 0–10.

Based on the fact the AC power value of target is non-fluctuating (somehow monotonically increase then decrease), and the AC power value of clutter behaves like random noise because generally the clutter has Gaussian distribution in the frequency domain, we design a fuzzy logic system using rules such as:

R^l : IF *centroid of a RoI* (x_1) is F_l^1, and *the number of fluctuating points in the ROI* (x_2) is F_l^2, THEN the possibility that there is a target at this RoI (y) is G^l.

where $l = 1, \ldots, 9$. We summarize all the rules in Table 1. For every input (x_1, x_2), the output is computed using

$$y(x_1, x_2) = \frac{\sum_{l=1}^{9} \mu_{\mathrm{F}_l^1}(x_1)\mu_{\mathrm{F}_l^2}(x_2)c_{avg}^l}{\sum_{l=1}^{9} \mu_{\mathrm{F}_l^1}(x_1)\mu_{\mathrm{F}_l^2}(x_2)} \tag{4}$$

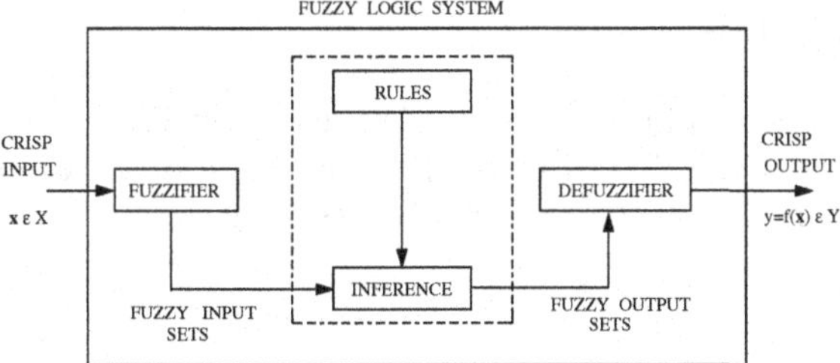

Fig. 8. The structure of a fuzzy logic system

We ran simulations to 1000 collections in the real world sense-through-foliage experiment, and found that our FLS performs very well in the automatic target detection based on the AC power values obtained from MLE-DCT or soft-max-DCT, and achieve probability of detection $p_d = 100\%$ and false alarm rate $p_{fa} = 0$.

Table 1. The rules for target detection. Antecedent 1 is *centroid of a RoI*, Antecedent 2 is *the number of fluctuating points in the ROI*, and Consequent is *the possibility that there is a target at this RoI.*

Rule #	Antecedent 1	Antecedent 2	Consequent
1	low	low	medium
2	low	moderate	weak
3	low	high	very weak
4	moderate	low	strong
5	moderate	moderate	medium
6	moderate	high	weak
7	high	low	very strong
8	high	moderate	strong
9	high	high	medium

6 Conclusions

Inspired by biological systems' (such as humans) innate ability to process and integrate information from disparate, network-based sources, we applied biologically-inspired information integration mechanisms to target detection in radar sensor network. Humans' information integration mechanisms have been modelled using maximum-likelihood estimation (MLE) or soft-max approaches. In this paper, we applied these two algorithms to cognitive radar sensor networks target detection. Discrete-cosine-transform (DCT) was used to process the integrated data from MLE or soft-max. We applied fuzzy logic system (FLS) to automatic target detection based on the AC power values from DCT. Simulation results showed that our MLE-DCT-FLS and soft-max-DCT-FLS approaches performed very well in the radar sensor network target detection, whereas the existing 2-D construction algorithm couldn't work in this study.

Acknowledgement

This work was supported in part by U.S. Office of Naval Research (ONR) under Grant N00014-07-1-0395, N00014-07-1-1024, and National Science Foundation (NSF) under Grant CNS-0721515 and CNS-0831902.

References

1. ONR BAA 07-017, NET-SENTRIC Surveillance, `http://www.onr.navy.mil`
2. Barton, D.K.: Radar System Analysis and Modeling. Artech House, Boston (2006)
3. Graham, N.V.S.: Visual pattern analyzers, pp. xvi, 646. Oxford University Press, New York (1989)
4. Hillis, J.M., Ernst, M.O., Banks, M.S., Landy, M.S.: Combining sensory information: Mandatory fusion within, but not between, senses. Science 298(5598), 1627–1630 (2002)
5. Mendel, J.M.: Uncertain Rule-Based Fuzzy Logic Systems. Prentice-Hall, Upper Saddle River (2001)
6. Withington, P., Fluhler, H., Nag, S.: Enhancing homeland security with advanced UWB sensors. IEEE Microwave Magazine (September 2003)

Stochastic k-Coverage in Wireless Sensor Networks

Habib M. Ammari

Wireless Sensor and Mobile Ad-hoc Networks (WiSeMAN) Research Lab
Department of Computer Science, Hofstra University
Hempstead, NY 11549, USA
Habib.M.Ammari@Hofstra.edu

Abstract. *Sensor scheduling* is a critical issue in the design of *wireless sensor networks* (WSNs) with a goal to achieve certain coverage degree of a field. In this paper, we focus on the sensor scheduling problem to guarantee *sensing k-coverage*, where each point in a field is *covered* by at least *k* sensors, while maintaining *network connectivity*. Precisely, we propose a global framework that considers both *deterministic* and *stochastic sensing* models of the sensors. For each of these sensing models, we decompose the sensor scheduling problem for *k*-coverage in WSNs into two sub-problems: *k-coverage characterization problem* and *k-coverage-preserving scheduling problem*. Our solution to the first problem is based on *Helly's Theorem* and the analysis of a geometric structure, called *Reuleaux triangle*. To solve the second problem, we propose a distributed approach that enables each sensor to run a *k-coverage candidacy algorithm* to check whether it is eligible to turn itself *on*. We find a perfect match between our simulation and analytical results.

Keywords: Wireless sensor networks, Stochastic coverage, Scheduling.

1 Introduction

One of the important research problems in WSNs is *sensor scheduling* with a goal to achieve *coverage* of a field. Indeed, there are several applications, such as intruder detection and tracking, which require that each location in a field be sensed by at least one sensor. Particularly, *k*-coverage is an appealing solution demanding that each point in a field be sensed by at least *k* sensors. One related problem is the *art gallery* (or *museum*) problem, which is a visibility problem that is well-studied in computational geometry. This problem is to find a minimum number of observers (or security cameras) that is required to guard a polygon field. A solution to this problem exists if for any point in the polygon field, there is at least one observer such that the line segment connecting the point and the observer lies entirely within the polygon field.

The problem of coverage has been well-studied in the literature [6]. Also, the problem of coverage-preserving scheduling (or duty-cycling) has gained considerable attention. Several existing works on *k*-coverage in WSNs assumed a perfect sensing model (also known as *deterministic sensing model*), where a point in a field is guaranteed to be covered by a sensor provided that this point is within the sensor's sensing range. A few works considered a more realistic sensing model, called *stochastic sensing model*, in the design of sensor scheduling protocols while preserving either

B. Liu et al. (Eds.): WASA 2009, LNCS 5682, pp. 125–134, 2009.

coverage [9] (respectively, k-coverage of a field [11], [12]), where a point is covered (or *sensed*) by a sensor (respectively, k sensors) with some probability. While some approaches focused on coverage only [6], others considered coverage and connectivity in an integrated framework [12].

1.1 Problem Statement

In this paper, we consider both deterministic and stochastic sensing models of the sensors, and focus on the problem of *sensor scheduling for k-coverage* in WSNs, where $k \geq 3$. More specifically, we decompose this problem into two sub-problems: *k-coverage characterization* and *k-coverage-preserving scheduling*, which can be formulated as follows depending on the sensing model being considered:

Sensor scheduling for deterministic (*stochastic*, respectively) *k-coverage:*

– *k-coverage characterization sub-problem:* Find a tight sufficient condition so that every point in the field is *deterministically* (*probabilistically*, respectively) covered by at least k sensors (with a probability no less than p_{th}, called *threshold probability*, respectively) and compute the corresponding minimum number of sensors.

– *k-coverage preserving scheduling sub-problem:* Show how to select and schedule the sensors while guaranteeing *deterministic* (providing *stochastic*, respectively) k-coverage of the field as well as connectivity between the selected sensors.

1.2 Contributions

In this paper, we make the following contributions: We propose a global framework for k-coverage in WSNs that considers both deterministic and stochastic sensing models. Precisely, we solve the sensor scheduling problem for k-coverage under the deterministic sensing model. Then, we adapt the results of this sensing model to solve the sensor scheduling problem for stochastic k-coverage under a probabilistic sensing model. As mentioned earlier, we split the sensor scheduling problem for k-coverage into two sub-problems: k-coverage characterization and k-coverage-preserving scheduling. To solve the first problem, we propose the *Reuleaux triangle* model to compute the minimum number of sensors to fully k-cover a field while ensuring connectivity between them, and determine their preferred locations. To solve the second problem, we propose a distributed approach where each sensor runs a *k-coverage candidacy algorithm* to check whether it is eligible to turn itself *on*. We find a good match between our theoretical and simulation results.

Organization. The remainder of this paper is organized as follows. Section 2 presents the network model and Section 3 reviews related work. Section 4 solves the k-coverage characterization problem for both sensing models, as well as the k-coverage-preserving scheduling problem for both sensing models. Section 5 presents simulation results of our proposed protocols. Section 6 concludes the paper.

2 Network Model

In this section, we present some key assumptions and introduce both of *deterministic sensing model* and a more realistic one, called *stochastic sensing model*.

2.1 Assumptions and Motivations

All the sensors and the sink are static and aware of their locations via a localization technique [3]. Also, all the sensors are randomly and uniformly deployed in a planar field. Moreover, we assume that all the sensors are *homogeneous* and have nominal sensing (or detection) and communication ranges of radii r and R, respectively. Moreover, we consider both *deterministic* and *stochastic* sensing models in our analysis of k-coverage. In the former, a point ξ in a field is covered by a sensor s_i based on the Euclidean distance $\delta(\xi,s_i)$ between ξ and s_i. This model considers the sensing range of a sensor as a *disk*, and hence all sensor readings are precise and have no uncertainty. However, given the signal attenuation and the presence of noise associated with sensor readings, it is necessary to consider a more realistic sensing model by defining the coverage $Cov(\xi,s_i)$ of a point ξ by s_i using some probability function. Thus, in our *stochastic sensing model*, the coverage $Cov(\xi,s_i)$ is defined as the *probability of detection* $p(\xi,s_i)$ of an event at ξ by s_i as follows:

$$p(\xi,s_i) = \begin{cases} e^{-\beta\,\delta(\xi,s_i)^{\alpha}} & \text{if } \delta(\xi,s_i) \le r \\ 0 & \text{otherwise} \end{cases} \quad (1)$$

where β represents the physical characteristic of the sensors' sensing units and $2 \le \alpha \le 4$ is the path-loss exponent. Our stochastic sensing model is motivated by the one introduced by Elfes [4], where the sensing capability of a sonar sensor is modeled by a Gaussian probability density function. Another probabilistic sensing model for coverage and target localization in WSNs considers $\delta(\xi,s_i) - (r - r_e)$, where $r_e < r$ is a measure of detection uncertainty [15].

2.2 Definitions

The *sensing neighbor set* of a sensor s_i consists of all sensors in the sensing range of s_i. The *communication neighbor set* of a sensor s_i includes all sensors located in the communication range of s_i. From now on, the location of s_i in a field is denoted by ξ_i.

Under the deterministic sensing model, a point ξ in a field is said to be *k-covered* if it belongs to the intersection of the sensing disks of at least k sensors. Under the stochastic sensing model, a point ξ in a field is said to be *probabilistically k-covered* if the detection probability of an event occurring at ξ by at least k sensors is at least equal to some *threshold probability* $0 < p_{th} < 1$. For both sensing models, A region A is said to be *k-covered* if every point $\xi \in A$ is *k-covered.*

The *width* of closed convex area is the maximum of the distances between any pair of parallel lines that bound it.

3 Related Work

In this section, we review a sample approaches for stochastic coverage in WSNs under stochastic sensing models.

In [6], it was showed that the minimum number of sensors needed to achieve k-coverage with high probability is approximately the same regardless of whether the sensors are deployed deterministically or randomly, if the sensors fail or sleep independently with equal probability. The coverage problem in heterogeneous WSNs was formulated in [7] as a set intersection problem and analytical expressions, which quantify the coverage achieved by stochastic coverage, were derived. Necessary and sufficient conditions for covered connected wireless sensor grid network were given and a variety of algorithms have been proposed to maintain connectivity and coverage in large WSNs [10]. The exposure in WSNs, which is related to the quality of coverage provided by WSNs, was studied in [9] based on a general sensing model, where the sensing signal of a sensor at an arbitrary point by a function that is inversely proportional to the distance between the sensor and point.

A joint scheduling scheme based on a randomized algorithm for providing statistical sensing coverage and guaranteed network connectivity was presented in [8]. This scheme works without the availability of per-node location information. A distributed approach for the selection of active sensors to fully cover a field based on the concept of connected dominating set was proposed in [14]. This approach is based on a probabilistic sensing model, where the probability of the existence of a target is defined by an exponential function that represents the confidence level of the received sensing signal.

Solutions to the k-coverage problem using both deterministic and probabilistic sensing models were proposed in [11]. These solutions compute the minimum number of sensors required to k-cover a field as well as their locations, and schedule the sensors to move to these locations. The CCP protocol [12] was extended to provide probabilistic coverage guarantee based on a probabilistic coverage model, where the sensors may have non-uniform and irregular communication and sensing regions. According to this model, a point in a convex coverage area is guaranteed to be k-covered with a probability no lower than β. CCP provides probabilistic coverage via a mapping of the (k,β)-coverage requirement to a *pseudo coverage degree* k', which is computed analytically.

Although the proposed approach in [12] is elegant and considers deterministic and probabilistic sensing models, it does not provide any proof on whether its k-coverage eligibility algorithm would yield a minimum number of selected sensors to k-cover a field. Similarly, our approach consider a global framework for deterministic and stochastic k-coverage in WSNs, where $k \geq 3$. Moreover, it uses a geometric model based on the Reuleaux triangle to prove that k-coverage is achieved with a minimum number of sensors in both deterministic and stochastic models.

4 Stochastic *k*-Coverage Characterization and Scheduling

In this section, we analyze the k-coverage problem in WSNs using the deterministic sensor model. Then, we adapt this analysis to our stochastic sensing model.

4.1 Deterministic Sensing Model

In order to characterize k-coverage, we need to compute the maximum size of an area (*not* a field) that is surely k-covered with exactly k sensors. To this end, we present a fundamental result of convexity theory, known as *Helly's Theorem* [2], which characterizes the intersection of convex sets. We will exploit this theorem to characterize k-coverage using a nice geometric structure, called *Reuleaux triangle* [1]. Then, we compute the minimum number of sensor required for k-coverage.

Helly's Theorem [2]. Let E be a family of convex sets in R^n such that for $m \geq n+1$ any m members of E have a non-empty intersection. Then, the intersection of all members of E is non-empty. ■

Lemma 1 is an instance of Helly's Theorem [2] in a two-dimensional space that characterizes the intersection of k sensing disks.

Lemma 1. Let $k \geq 3$. The intersection of k sensing disks is not empty if and only if the intersection of any three of those k sensing disks is not empty. ■

Based on Lemma 1, Lemma 2 gives a *sufficient condition* for k-coverage of a field [1]. For the sake of completeness, we also give the proof of Lemma 2.

Lemma 2 [1]. Let $k \geq 3$. A field is k-covered if any *Reuleaux triangle* region of width r (or simply *slice*) in the field contains at least k active sensors. ■

It is worth noting that *tiling* a field by Reuleaux triangles is impossible unless we allow overlap between them. It is easy to check that the sensing disk of a sensor can be covered by six Reuleaux triangles of width r with a minimum overlap when two sides of the triangles associated with two slices are totally coinciding with each other. Thus, the minimum overlap area of two adjacent slices forms a *lens* (Figure 1). Lemma 3 characterizes k-coverage based this notion of lens.

Lemma 3. k active sensors located in the lens of two adjacent slices in a field can k-cover both slices.

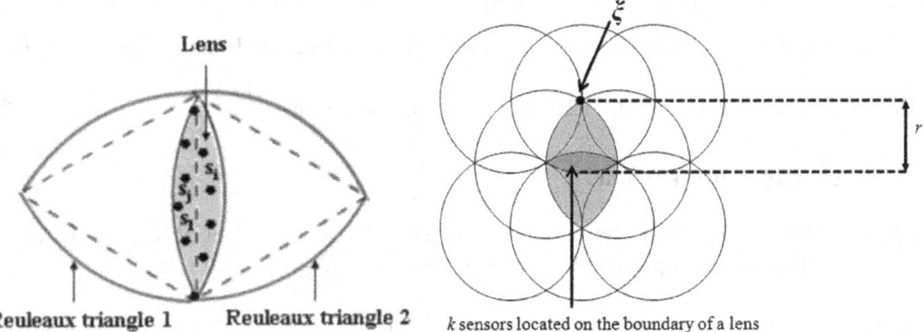

Fig. 1. Lens of two adjacent slices

Fig. 2. Least k-covered point

Proof. The proof is verbatim: the distance between any of these k sensors located in the lens and any point in the area of the union of both slices is at most equal to r. ■

Based on Lemma 3, Theorem 1 states a *tighter sufficient condition* for k-coverage.

Theorem 1. Let $k \geq 3$. A field is k-covered if for any slice of width r in the field there is an adjacent slice of width r such that their *lens* contains at least k active sensors, where r is the radius of the sensing disks of the sensors.

Proof. Assume that a field is decomposed into slices, where for any slice in the field there exists an adjacent slice such that their *lens* contains at least k active sensors. Given that the width of a slice is constant and equal to r, it is always true that the maximum distance between any of these k sensors and any point in both adjacent slices cannot exceed r. Thus, any point in the union of these two adjacent slices is k-covered. Since this applies to any slice in the field, the field is also k-covered. ■

Theorem 2 computes the minimum number of sensors to k-cover a field of area F.

Theorem 2. Let r be the radius of the sensors' sensing disks and $k \geq 3$. The minimum number of sensors $n(r,k)$ to k-cover a field of area F is given by

$$n(r,k) = \frac{6\,k\,F}{(4\pi - 3\sqrt{3})\,r^2}$$

Proof. Consider a field that is divided into adjacent slices. It is easy to check that the area $\|Area(r)\|$ of two adjacent slices (Figure 1) is equal to

$$\| Area(r) \| = 2\,A_1 + 4\,A_2 = (4\pi - 3\sqrt{3})\; r^2/6$$

where $A_1 = \sqrt{3}\,r^2/4$ is the area of the central triangle of side r and $A_2 = (\pi/6 - \sqrt{3}/4)\,r^2$ is the area of the curved region. By Theorem 1, k sensors should be deployed in the lens of two adjacent slices to k-cover them. Thus, the *minimum number of sensors* to k-cover a field of area F is

$$n(r,k) = (k/\| Area(r) \|) \times F = 6\,k\,F/(4\pi - 3\sqrt{3})\,r^2$$ ■

Theorem 3 states that k-coverage implies connectivity when $R \geq \sqrt{3}r$. Indeed, the maximum distance between an pair of sensors in two adjacent slides is equal to $\sqrt{3}r$.

Theorem 3. Let $k \geq 3$. A k-covered WSN is connected if $R \geq \sqrt{3}r$. ■

4.2 Stochastic Sensing Model

In this section, we exploit the results of Section 4.1 to characterize probabilistic k-coverage. Theorem 4 computes the *minimum k-coverage probability* $p_{k,min}$.

Theorem 4. Let r be the radius of the nominal sensing range of the sensors and $k \geq 3$. The minimum k-coverage probability so that each point in a field is probabilistically k-covered by at least k sensors under our stochastic sensing model in (1) is given by

$$p_{k,\min} = 1 - \left(1 - e^{-\beta\, r^{\alpha}}\right)^{k} \tag{2}$$

Proof. First, we identify the least k-covered point in a field so we can compute $p_{k,\min}$. By Theorem 1, k sensors should be deployed in the lens of two adjacent slices of a field to achieve k-coverage with a minimum number of sensors. By looking at the lens in Figure 2 and using the result of Theorem 1, it is easy to check that the point ξ is the least k-covered point when all deployed k sensors are located on the bottom boundary (or arc) of the lens. Indeed, ξ is the farthest point from the bottom arc of the lens. Moreover, ξ is equidistant from the k sensors $(s_1,..,s_k)$ located on the bottom arc of the lens as shown in Figure 2. Hence, the distance between ξ and each of these k sensors is equal to r. Thus, the *minimum k-coverage probability* for the least k-covered point ξ by k sensors under the stochastic sensing model in **(1)** is given by

$$p_{k,\min} = 1 - \prod_{i=1}^{k} (1 - p(\xi, s_i)) = 1 - \left(1 - e^{-\beta r^{\alpha}}\right)^{k}$$ ■

The stochastic k-coverage problem is to select a minimum subset $S_{min} \subseteq S$ of sensors such that each point in a field is k-covered by at least k sensors and that the minimum k-coverage probability of each point is at least equal to some given threshold probability p_{th}, where $0 < p_{th} < 1$. This helps us compute the stochastic sensing range r_s, which provides probabilistic k-coverage of a field with a probability no less than p_{th}. Lemma 4 computes the value of r_s.

Lemma 4. Let $k \geq 3$ and $2 \leq \alpha \leq 4$. The stochastic sensing range r_s of the sensors that is necessary to probabilistically k-cover a field with a minimum number of sensors and with a probability no lower than $0 < p_{th} < 1$ is given by

$$r_s = \left(-\frac{1}{\beta} \log\left(1 - (1 - p_{th})^{1/k}\right) \right)^{1/\alpha} \tag{3}$$

where β represents the physical characteristic of the sensors' sensing units.

Proof. $p_{k,\min} \geq p_{th} \Rightarrow r_s \leq \left(-\frac{1}{\beta} \log\left(1 - (1 - p_{th})^{1/k}\right) \right)^{1/\alpha}$ ■

The upper bound on the stochastic sensing range r_s of the sensors computed in Equation (3) will be used as one of the input parameters to the *k-coverage candidacy* algorithm [1], which will be briefly described in Section 4.3.

Similarly to Lemma 2 and Theorems 1, while Lemma 5 states a sufficient condition for probabilistic k-coverage, Theorem 5 states a tighter sufficient condition for probabilistic k-coverage based on our stochastic sensing model, p_{th}, and k.

Lemma 5. Let $k \geq 3$. A field is probabilistically k-covered with a probability no lower than $0 < p_{th} < 1$ if any slice of width r_s in the field contains at least k active sensors. ■

Theorem 5. Let $k \geq 3$. A field is probabilistically k-covered with a probability no lower than $0 < p_{th} < 1$ if for any slice of width r_s in the field there exists an adjacent slice of width r_s such that their *lens* contains at least k active sensors, where r_s is the stochastic sensing range of the sensors. ■

Lemma 6 states a sufficient condition for connectivity between sensors under our stochastic sensing model.

Lemma 6. Let $k \geq 3$. The sensors that are selected to k-cover a field with a probability no less than $0 \leq p_{th} \leq 1$ under the stochastic sensing model defined in Equation (1) are connected if the radius of their communication range is at least equal to $\sqrt{3}\, r_s$, where r_s is the stochastic sensing range of the sensors. ■

4.3 Stochastic *k*-Coverage-Preserving Scheduling

In our distributed sleep-wakeup scheduling protocol for stochastic k-coverage (SCP_k) of a field, a sensor turns active if its sensing disk is not k-covered. Based on Theorem 5, a sensor randomly decomposes its sensing range into six slices of width r_s (Lemma 4) and checks whether the lens of each of the three pairs of adjacent slices contains at least k active sensing neighbors. If any of the three lenses does not have k active sensors, a sensor checks whether each slice of width r_s contains at least k active sensors based on Lemma 5. Otherwise, it is a candidate to become active. We use the same state transition diagram given in [1].

5 Simulation Results

In this section, we present the simulation results of SCP_k using a high-level simulator written in the C language. We consider a square field of side length 1000m. We use the energy model given in [13], where the sensor energy consumption in transmission, reception, idle, and sleep modes are 60 mW, 12 mW, 12 mW, and 0.03 mW, respectively. The energy required for a sensor to stay idle for 1 second is equivalent to *one unit of energy*. We assume that the initial energy of each sensor is 60 Joules enabling a sensor to operate about 5000 seconds in reception/idle modes [13]. All simulations are repeated 20 times and the results are averaged.

In Figure 3, we plot the sensor spatial density as a function of the degree of coverage k for different values of the threshold probability p_{th} and path-loss exponent α. As expected, the density increases with p_{th} and α. Indeed, as we increase p_{th}, more sensors would be needed to achieve the same degree of coverage k. On the other hand, the sensor spatial density required to provide full k-coverage of a field is inversely proportional to the area of this Reuleaux triangle as stated in Lemma 4.

Figure 4 plots the achieved degree of coverage k versus the total number of deployed sensors. Moreover, we vary both p_{th} and α. Definitely, higher number of deployed sensors would yield higher coverage degree. Here also, any increase in p_{th} and α would require a larger number of sensors to provide the same coverage degree. Both experiments show a good match between simulation and analytical results.

Figure 5 shows that the number of active sensors required to provide 3-coverage increases with the characteristic of the sensors β used in the definition of our stochastic sensing model in Section 2.1. This result is expected given the definition of the sensing range of the sensors given in Equation (3).

Figure 6 shows the impact of p_{th} on the network lifetime to provide 3-coverage. As mentioned earlier, higher values of p_{th} require larger numbers of active sensors, and hence more energy consumption.

Observation. The CCP protocol described in [12] is the only one on probabilistic k-coverage. However, the probabilistic sensing model used by the CCP protocol is totally different from ours. While our stochastic sensing model quantifies the detection probability of a sensor by an exponential function, the one in [12] only assigns it a constant value. Therefore, it is impossible to provide a fair quantitative comparison between SCP_k and CCP [12].

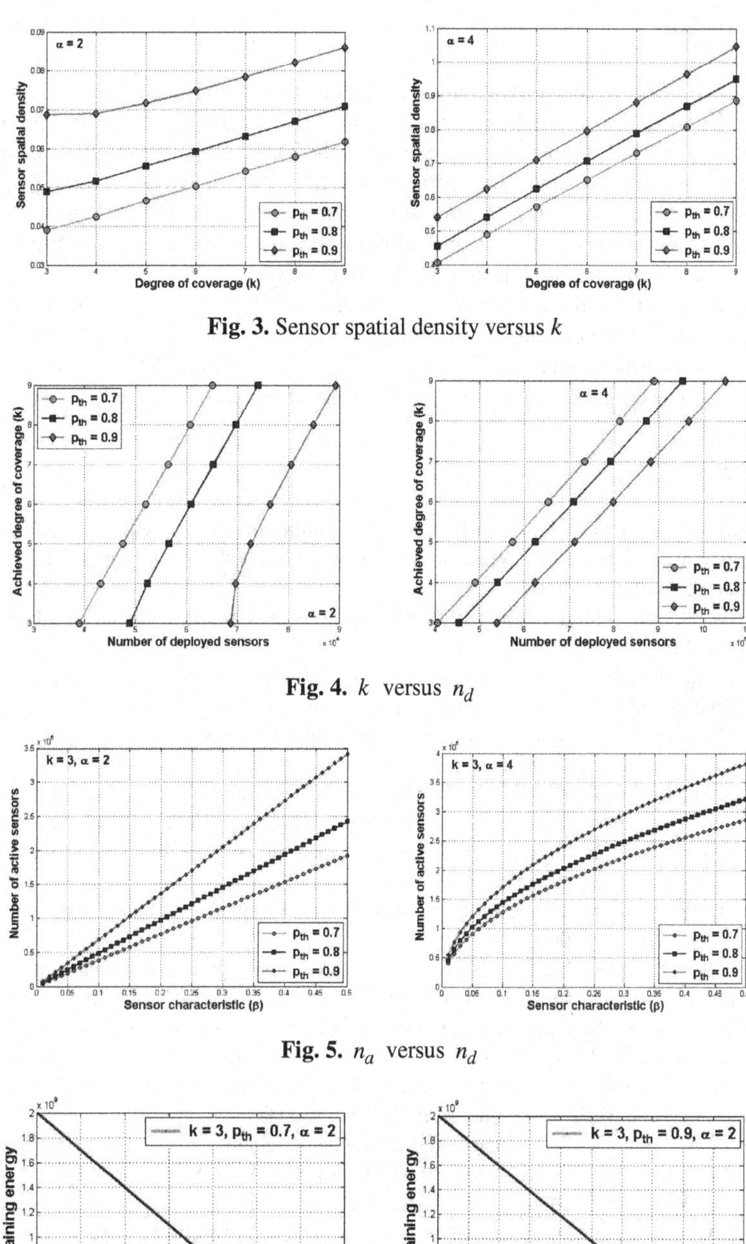

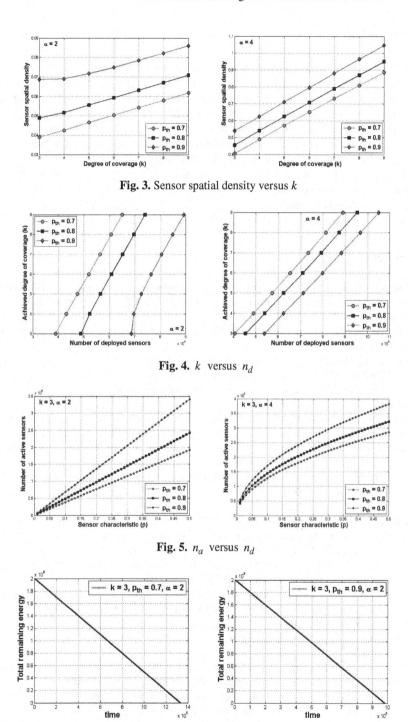

Fig. 3. Sensor spatial density versus k

Fig. 4. k versus n_d

Fig. 5. n_a versus n_d

Fig. 6. Total remaining energy versus time

6 Conclusion

In this paper, we proposed a distributed approach for sensor scheduling in stochastic k-covered WSNs. To gain more insight into the problem, we considered the deterministic sensing model and then extended the analysis to our stochastic sensing model. First, we characterized k-coverage in WSNs and provided a tight sufficient condition for k-coverage with a minimum number of sensors. Then, we presented our k-coverage preserving scheduling protocol based on this characterization. We found a good match between our simulation and analytical results.

Our future work is three-fold. First, we are working on the problem of joint stochastic k-coverage and data forwarding in WSNs. Second, we plan to extend this analysis to three-dimensional WSNs (3D), such as underwater WSNs, which are 3D in nature. Third, we plan to implement SCP_k using a real sensor testbed.

References

1. Ammari, H.M., Das, S.K.: Clustering-based minimum energy m-connected$k$-covered wireless sensor networks. In: Verdone, R. (ed.) EWSN 2008. LNCS, vol. 4913, pp. 1–16. Springer, Heidelberg (2008)
2. Bollobás, B.: The art of mathematics: Coffee time in Memphis. Cambridge University Press, Cambridge (2006)
3. Bulusu, N., Heidemann, J., Estrin, D.: GPS-less low cost outdoor localization for very small devices. IEEE Personal Communications Magazine 7(5), 28–34 (2000)
4. Elfes, A.: Using occupancy grids for mobile robot perception and navigation. IEEE Computer 22(6), 46–57 (1989)
5. Koushanfar, F., Meguerdichian, S., Potkonjak, M., Srivastava, M.: Coverage problems in wireless ad-hoc sensor networks. In: IEEE Proc. Infocom, pp. 1380–1387 (2001)
6. Kumar, S., Lai, T., Balogh, J.: On k-coverage in a mostly sleeping sensor network. In: Proc. ACM MobiCom, pp. 144–158 (2004)
7. Lazos, L., Poovendran, R.: Stochastic coverage in heterogeneous sensor networks. ACM TOSN 2(3), 325–358 (2006)
8. Liu, C., Wu, K., Xiao, Y., Sun, B.: Random coverage with guaranteed connectivity: Joint scheduling for wireless sensor networks. IEEE TPDS 17(6), 562–575 (2006)
9. Meguerdichian, S., Koushanfar, F., Potkonjak, M., Srivastava, M.: Exposure in wireless ad-hoc sensor networks. In: ACM MobiCom, pp. 139–150 (2001)
10. Shakkottai, S., Srikant, R., Shroff, N.: Unreliable sensor grids: Coverage, connectivity and diameter. In: Proc. IEEE Infocom, pp. 1073–1083 (2003)
11. Wang, Y.-C., Tseng, Y.-C.: Distributed deployment schemes for mobile wireless sensor networks to ensure multi-level coverage. IEEE TPDS 19(9), 1280–1294 (2008)
12. Xing, G., Wang, X., Zhang, Y., Lu, C., Pless, R., Gill, C.: Integrated coverage and connectivity configuration for energy conservation in sensor networks. ACM TOSN 1(1), 36–72 (2005)
13. Ye, F., Zhong, G., Cheng, J., Lu, S., Zhang, L.: PEAS: A robust energy conserving protocol for long-lived sensor networks. In: Proc. ICDCS, pp. 1–10 (2003)
14. Zou, Y., Chakrabarty, K.: A distributed coverage- and connectivity-centric technique for selecting active nodes in wireless sensor networks. IEEE TC 54(8), 978–991 (2005)
15. Zou, Y., Chakrabarty, K.: Sensor deployment and target localization in distributed sensor networks. ACM TOSN 3(2), 61–91 (2004)

Herd-Based Target Tracking Protocol in Wireless Sensor Networks

Xiaofei Xing[1], Guojun Wang[1,2,*], and Jie Wu[2]

[1] School of Information Science and Engineering, Central South University, Changsha 410083, China

[2] Department of Computer Science and Engineering, Florida Atlantic University, Boca Raton, FL 33431, USA

csgjwang@mail.csu.edu.cn

Abstract. Target tracking is a killer application in wireless sensor networks (WSNs). Energy efficiency is one of the most important design goals for target tracking. In this paper, we propose a herd-based target tracking protocol (HTTP) with the notions of *node state transition* and *herd-based node group* for target tracking. A sensor node has three states, namely, sleeping state, sensing state, and tracking state. Each sensor node is associated with a weight to be used to make a state transition among the three states. When a target moves into a monitoring area, a cluster node is selected as the herd head that is responsible for reporting the target information to the sink in the network. The sensor node can adjust the frequency of data reporting according to the velocity of the target. Simulation results show that HTTP not only improves the energy efficiency, but also enhances the tracking accuracy.

Keywords: Wireless sensor networks, target tracking, energy efficiency, node state transition, herd-based node group.

1 Introduction

Wireless sensor networks (WSNs) [1], [2] consist of a set of sensor nodes, each of which is a self-contained unit with a low-speed processor, one or multiple sensors, a radio module, and a battery module. The sensors in a WSN system are deployed over an area in an attempt to sense and monitor interesting events or to track the mobile targets or people as they move through the area. So it is widely used in military battlefields, environmental monitoring, traffic transportation, medical diagnosis, and many other fields. Target tracking is one of the killer applications in WSNs. Because of the uncertain movement of the target, it becomes a challenging issue to position and track the moving target effectively and efficiently.

WSNs have the advantage in high accuracy, real-time, and low cost in tracking the target by using random and uniform distribution and mutual cooperation of sensor nodes. Because of energy constraints of sensor nodes, which are closely

* Corresponding author.

B. Liu et al. (Eds.): WASA 2009, LNCS 5682, pp. 135–148, 2009.

related to the lifetime of the network, the designed target tracking protocol should be able to track the target accurately with low energy consumption. This study can be applied to many target tracking scenarios, such as military tank movement, vehicle movement, wild animal environments, and so on.

We study the issue of tracking mobile targets using wireless sensor networks. The whole tracking process is divided into the positioning stage and the tracking stage. In the process of target tracking, a lot of factors [3] affect energy consumption, which includes the number of moving targets, the speed of moving targets, data reporting frequency, tracking data accuracy, data collection frequency, and so on. Obviously, as design goals, the sensor nodes surrounding the moving target should be able to promptly provide reliable status information about the moving target and the area around it in an energy efficient way, and the sensor nodes should report this information to the sink in a fast and energy efficient way.

In this paper, we propose a herd-based target tracking protocol (HTTP) for single-target tracking in WSNs. In summary, the key contributions of this paper are as follows.

- The herd-based node group which consists of sensor nodes in the tracking state can track the target dynamically by using the node state transition mechanism and weight calculation mechanism.
- An appropriate threshold can be obtained to decide whether the sensor nodes should participate in tracking target or not.
- The data reporting frequency can be adjusted according to the velocity of the target to reduce unnecessary data transmission and improve the energy efficiency.

The rest of the paper is organized as follows: Section 2 summarizes some existing target tracking protocols in WSNs. Section 3 discusses the basic ideas behind the proposed HTTP protocol, including node state transition, node weight calculation, and the initialization and reconstruction of the herd-based node group. An extended HTTP is discussed in Section 4. We simulate and evaluate the proposed HTTP protocol in Section 5. Section 6 concludes the paper.

2 Related Work

Target tracking in wireless sensor networks has been investigated extensively. As one of the fundamental problems with target tracking, energy efficiency has been researched from different aspects. Lee et al [4], Niyogi et al [5], and Wang et al [6] propose prediction mechanisms to restrict the amount of transmitted messages and to select the nodes that participate in target tracking. A dual-prediction-based data aggregation scheme to decrease the communication overhead is proposed in [7]. Considering the tradeoff between tracking quality and energy efficiency and guaranteeing an acceptable tracking quality, some strategies are proposed in [8], [9] to keep the sensor nodes in sleeping state as long as possible.

Guo et al [10] propose a target tracking protocol based on energy efficiency which includes two energy efficient algorithms, i.e., RARE-Area and RARE-Node algorithms. The RARE-Area algorithm reduces the emergence of low quality data and the amount of involved tracking sensors. So only sensor nodes that can generate high quality data are permitted to track the target. The RARE-Node algorithm considers the spatial relationship among sensors in order to determine whether the data generated by a node is redundant or not.

He et al [11] present the design of an analysis of VigilNet, a large-scale outdoor WSN which detects, classifies, and tracks a target in a timely and efficient manner. Through simulation and experiments, the authors demonstrate that their system can meet the real-time requirement and their tradeoffs are validated. On the basis of the deadline partition method and theoretical derivations to guarantee each sub-deadline, they make a guided engineering decision to meet the end-to-end tracking deadline.

Lee et al [12] propose a distributed energy-efficient target positioning and tracking algorithm, and study the RVI positioning issue based on distance ratio. Moreover, they propose a scheme that dynamically adjusts the lead nodes' reporting frequency, so that the amount of the status information of the target and energy consumption can be reduced.

A dynamic convoy tree-based collaboration scheme is introduced in [13], [14]. The moving target can be tracked effectively by the reconfiguration convoy tree and node expansion and pruning. However, it incurs a significant amount of processing data and system overhead. Our work is most closely related to this work but our proposed scheme drastically decreases the overhead, while still keeping a good accuracy for tracking.

3 Basic HTTP (B-HTTP)

In this section, a basic herd-based target tracking protocol (B-HTTP) is proposed, including node state transition, node weight calculation, and the initial construction and reconstruction of the herd-based node group.

3.1 Basic Ideas

In B-HTTP, each sensor node has three states, namely, sleeping state, sensing state, and tracking state. We set a weight for each sensor node. The node calculates its weight to decide whether it should participate in target tracking or not according to the target's situation. When a target moves into a monitoring area, sensor nodes that are awake and closer to the target can detect the target. There will be more sensor nodes being transformed into the tracking state. Thus, these sensor nodes construct a dynamic tracking group surrounding the target. We call this dynamic tracking group a *herd-based node group*. One of the cluster heads is selected as a *herd head*, which is responsible for data reporting and also for managing the membership of the herd-based node group. At the same time, we select another cluster head in the herd-based node group to be a

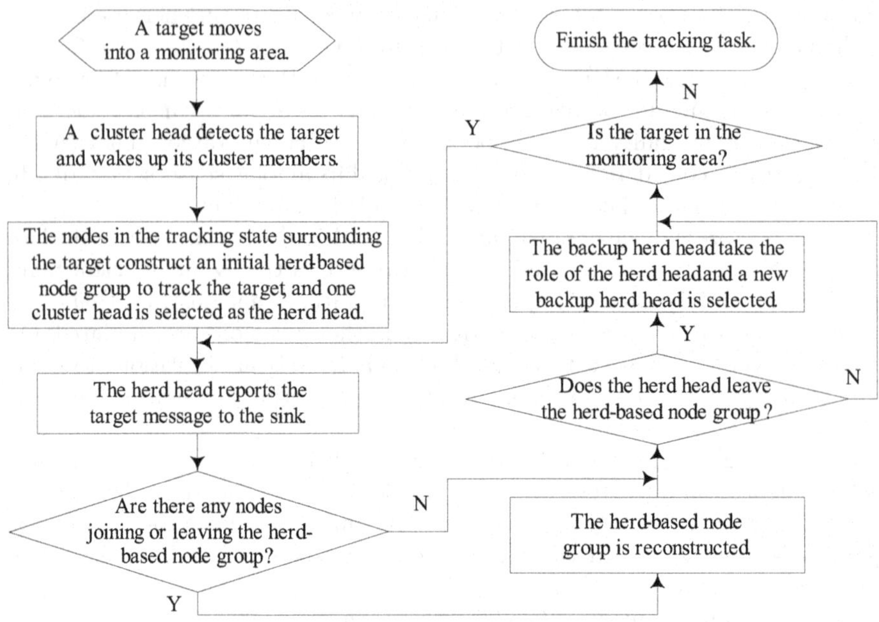

Fig. 1. Basic procedure of B-HTTP

backup herd head. Both the herd head and the backup herd head store the same information, such as membership information. The difference between them is that the backup herd head needs not to report the target information to the sink. The herd head sends the information to the backup herd head periodically. When the herd head can not take its role for the herd-based node group for some reason, for example if it runs out of energy, the backup herd head can change to take the role of the herd head by also reporting the data to the sink, that is, the backup herd head becomes the herd head. At the same time, a new backup herd head needs to be selected.

In this scheme, the membership of the herd-based node group is dynamic. With the moving of the target, some new nodes join this to track the target and some nodes leave as the target is not within their sensing range. The member nodes of the herd-based herd group send the target information to the herd head with a fixed frequency. Then the herd head is responsible for reporting the target information to the sink. In Section 3.5 and Section 3.6, we will discuss how to construct and maintain the herd-based node group. The basic procedure of B-HTTP is shown in Fig. 1.

3.2 Assumptions

We know that the large part of sensor node energy is dissipated on sensing module, processing module, and wireless communication module. With advances in integrated circuit technology, energy consumption on sensing module and

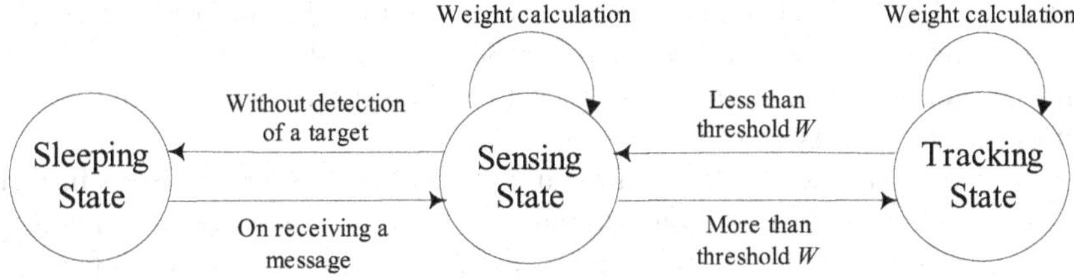

Fig. 2. Node state transition diagram

processing module become very low. Most of energy is dissipated on the wireless communication module [16]. So we mainly consider energy consumption dissipated on the communication module in this paper.

We adapt a wireless communication model proposed in [17] to calculate node energy consumption. To transmit and receive a k-bit message at distance d, the communication expenditure can be calculated as follows:

$$E_{T(k,d)} = E_{T-elec}k + \varepsilon_{amp}d^2k \tag{1}$$

$$E_R(k) = E_{R-elec}k \tag{2}$$

Where E_{T-elec} and E_{R-elec} denote energy consumption in the transmitter and receiver circuitry respectively, and ε_{amp} is the transmit amplifier. We assume $E_{T-elec} = E_{R-elec} = 50nJ/bit$, $\varepsilon_{amp} = 100pJ/bit/m^2$.

In this paper, we assume that wireless sensor nodes are homogeneous, that is, all the sensor nodes have the same sensing radius and communicating radius. Each sensor node has a unique *id*. Each node is aware of its own geographic location by using the global positioning system (GPS) or trilateration [18]. Here, three range measurements are required to locate the target. The distance information can be obtained from the received signal intensity measurements. A sensor node can get its geographic location information by using the two or more distance measurements which come from its neighbor nodes.

The sensor nodes are deployed densely over an area of interest. Based on a clustering algorithm called geographical adaptive fidelity (GAF) [15], the monitoring area is divided into some virtual *grids*. We call each virtual grid a *cluster*. Each node is assigned to a corresponding grid according to its geographic location. One node is selected periodically as a *cluster head* in each grid. The cluster head can manage its cluster member nodes.

3.3 Node State Transition

Each sensor node has three states, namely, sleeping state, sensing state, and tracking state. In the sleeping state, the communication module of the node is closed to preserve energy. The sensing state means that the node can monitor the surrounding environment, detect whether a target appears or not, and calculate the distance to the target. But the sensor nodes do not send data packets to the cluster head in this state. The most energy is dissipated when the nodes are in the tracking state because they not only monitor the surrounding setting, such as the target moving in or out, and collecting target information, but also transmitting or forwarding the data packets to the herd head. The node state transition mechanism is shown in Fig. 2.

From Fig. 2, we can see that the node in the sleeping state transforms into the sensing state when it receives a beacon message from its cluster head or neighbor nodes. The sensor node in the sensing state calculates its weight periodically. If a node's weight is larger than the threshold after the calculation of weight, it transforms into the tracking state automatically. Otherwise, the node transforms into the sleeping state when there is no target to appear. The node in the tracking state periodically calculates its own weight. If the weight of the node in the tracking state is less than the threshold W, it transforms into the sensing state automatically. The nodes in the tracking state can communicate with other nodes. In addition, the node state can not be transformed directly between the tracking state and sleeping state because we consider some other situations, for example when the target soon moves in the node sensing range again after it leaves.

3.4 Node Weight Calculation

We know that the further away a sensor node is from a target, the weaker the received signal intensity is. Therefore, the nodes near the target have a high qualification to participate in target tracking compared to those far away. So we can use the distance as its weight indicator. In order to reduce low quality redundant data, we should decrease the number of nodes that participate in target tracking when guaranteeing tracking quality. Each node that is not in the sleeping state can calculate its own weight according to the moving target information. Because of the noise signal interference, the effective sensing radius of the node ranges from 0 to $1.2R_s$, where R_s denotes the node's sensing radius. We use W_d and W_{dir} to denote distance weight and direction weight, respectively. The allocated weights for the sensor node are listed in Table 1.

The total weight of node W_{tol} can be calculated below:

$$W_{tol} = W_d + W_{dir} \tag{3}$$

Table 1. The weight allocation for a sensor node

Weight	Description	Value
W_d	d $\leq 1/3R_s$	4
	$1/3R_s < d \leq 2/3R_s$	3
	$2/3R_s < d \leq R_s$	2
	d $> R_s$	1
W_{dir}	Target moves towards sensor	1
	Target is stationary	0
	Target moves away from sensor	-1

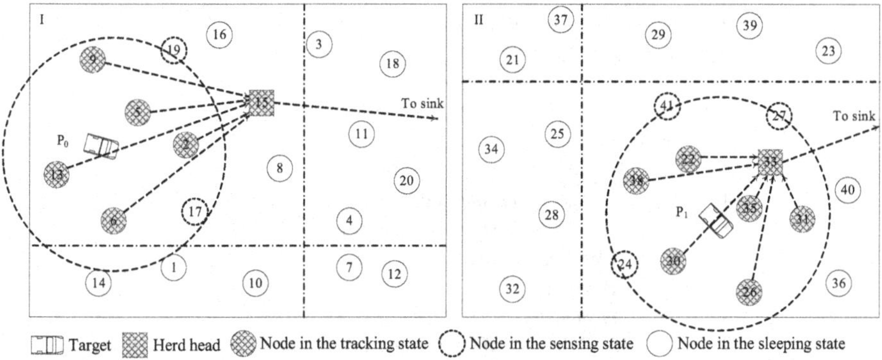

Fig. 3. An illustration of the target moving from P_0 to P_1 in the monitoring area

Obtained from equation (3) and Table 1, we can get a maximal weight value of 5 for the sensor node when the target moves towards the sensor and the distance between the target and the node is less than $1/3R_s$. It means the node owns an optimal sensing capacity. Also, a node would not keep tracking the moving target when its weight is 0. A node can participate in tracking the target when its weight value is more than the threshold. Setting a high threshold decreases positioning accuracy of the target. A greater node threshold means fewer nodes are involved in tracking.

3.5 Initial Construction of the Herd-Based Node Group

When a target moves into a monitoring area, the cluster heads that are awake and closer to the target first detect the target. Then the cluster head sends a beacon message to wake up the cluster member and its neighbor cluster heads. The nodes in the sleeping state transform into the sensing state and calculate their weights according to the target information. When their weight is larger than the threshold, the nodes transform into the tracking state. These sensor nodes in the tracking state form an initial herd-based node group. The cluster member can communicate with the cluster head directly. The amount of clusters that participate in target tracking is only determined by the grid size. For example, there are at least 4 clusters which can detect the target simultaneously if the size of a cluster equals to $\frac{\sqrt{2}}{2}R_s$. As shown in Fig. 3 (left), after the target moves into the monitoring area from grid I, some nodes are woken up by cluster head *node* 15. *Nodes* 9, 5, 2, 15, 6, 13 form an initial herd-based node group and cluster head *node* 15 of grid I is selected as the *herd head* because it first detects the target.

The nodes in the sensing or the tracking state calculate their own weight according to the collected information of the target. When their weights are larger than the threshold, the nodes transform into the tracking state automatically to track the moving target. The nodes report the target information to the herd

```
/* Algorithm 1: Node state transition */
W_thr: the threshold value.

If (Target moves into a monitoring area) {
Switch (Node state) {
   Case (Sleeping state) {
         If (Receive cluster head's message)
               Transform into sensing state;
         Else Keep sleeping state;
         Break; }
   Case (Sensing state) {
        If (W>W_thr) Transform into tracking state;
         Else If (No target appear || W≤W_thr)
                 Transform into sleeping state;
         Else Keep sensing state;
         Break; }.
   Case (Tracking state) {
         If ( W>W_thr) Keep tracking state;
          Else Transform into sensing state;
          Break; }
   }
}
```

Fig. 4. Node state transition algorithm

head. The information, including timestamp, node *id*, and the distance d to the target etc, is sent to its cluster head. Then, the cluster heads (excluding the herd head) send the collected target information to the herd head. The herd head reports the target information to the sink after data aggregation processing.

3.6 Reconstruction of the Herd-Based Node Group

In order to track the target effectively, the dynamic herd-based node group needs to be reconstructed dynamically. It mainly includes the herd membership management and the herd head selection mechanism.

We use the node state transition mechanism to decide whether a node should join or leave the herd-based node group. The sensor nodes in the tracking and the sensing states calculate their own weight periodically. When the target moves to a new grid, the nodes in the tracking state are divided into two kinds: some nodes transform into the sensing state when their weight is less than the threshold, and the others still stay in the tracking state to track the moving target. The node state transition is shown in Algorithm 1 (Fig. 4).

The nodes in the sensing state have two types. The first type is then the nodes cannot detect the moving target because the distance between the nodes and the target is beyond the nodes' sensing range. Therefore, these nodes transform into the sleeping state automatically. The second type is that the nodes transform into the tracking state as the nodes' weights are larger than the threshold.

When the target moves into a new grid, the cluster head wakes up its cluster member to track the target. The nodes that just detect the target transform into the tracking state and join the herd-based node group. Other cluster members whose weights are less than the threshold, will leave the herd-based node group. The herd head calculates its weight. It will keep on tracking if the weight is larger than the threshold. When the herd head can not take its role for the herd-based node group for some reasons, the backup herd head can change to take the role of the herd head by also reporting the data to the sink. Due to the reconfiguration cost, the herd-based node group should be reconfigured based on the distance between the herd head and the current location of the target. If this distance is larger than a certain threshold, the herd-based node group should be reconfigured. In order to decrease the overhead on calculations, we specify the cluster head that lastly joins the herd-based node group to act as the backup herd head. So this herd-based node group is reconstructed according to the target information. As shown in Fig. 3 (right), we can see that *nodes* 38, 22, 33, 35, 31, 30, 26 reconstruct a new herd-based node group and *node* 33 is selected as a new herd head when the target moves from P_0 to P_1.

4 Extended HTTP (E-HTTP)

In the last section, we designed the basic HTTP protocol by which the target information can be sent to the sink. In order to get a better performance for the proposed HTTP, we further design an extended HTTP (E-HTTP) to decrease energy consumption which can adjust the frequency of data reporting dynamically.

The frequency of the nodes reporting the target information to the sink can be determined by specific applications. The nodes periodically report about the moving target information regarding the reporting sensor node's *id*, tracking time, target's location and velocity, moving direction, and so on. As we do not know what speed the moving target is, it would bring some drawbacks as follows if the node adapts a fixed frequency for sending the data to the sink.

- Positioning accuracy decreases when the speed of moving target increases;
- Sensor nodes consume more energy if they report the target information to the sink with a high frequency while the target moves at a low speed;
- Sensor nodes run out of energy prematurely. If the moving target keeps stationary for a long time in the monitoring area, the node's energy would be exhausted as the node keeps tracking the target. Thus, it may cause the monitoring area to not be fully covered by the sensor nodes and the lifetime of the network to be shortened.

Therefore, if the frequency of data reporting can be adjusted according to the target situation, it can improve energy efficiency and data accuracy.

Before the backup herd head takes the role of the herd head, the herd head sends the location L_{pre} of the target at a previous time T_{pre} to the backup herd head. When the backup herd head takes the role of the herd head, we can get a new location L_{cur} of the target at current time T_{cur} using the positioning algorithm [18]. Thus, we get an average velocity of the target from T_{pre} to T_{cur}.

$$\overline{v} = \frac{|L_{cur} - L_{pre}|}{T_{cur} - T_{pre}} \tag{4}$$

Then we can get the frequency of the data reporting sent by the sensor node.

$$f = \lfloor \overline{v}/D_{th} \rfloor + 1 \tag{5}$$

Where D_{th} is a distance threshold for data reporting.

From Lee et al [12] we can get a formula as below.

$$D_{th} \leq 2R_{\max} - R_s - \frac{D_{\text{inter}-sensor}}{\sqrt{2}} - 2E_{\max} \tag{6}$$

Where R_{max} is the maximal communication radius of sensor node, R_s is the sensing radius of sensor node, and $D_{inter-sensor}$ is the pre-determined average inter-sensor distance. Suppose that R_{max}=R_s=40m (worst case), $D_{inter-sensor}$ =10m, and E_{max}=5m. Then, approximately, D_{th} is 12.9m or less. It denotes that the frequency of sending message to the sink is $f = \overline{v}/12 + 1$.

5 Performance Evaluation

5.1 Simulation Model

In order to test and evaluate the performance of the proposed HTTP protocol, we set up the simulation in a 600×600m^2 area based on the OMNET++[19] experimental platform.

In our simulation, the communication radius of a sensor node is 40m, and the monitoring area is divided into 14×14m^2 virtual grids, which can guarantee that one cluster head can communicate with 8 neighbor cluster heads directly. In each experiment, 1,000 or 5,000 sensor nodes are deployed randomly and uniformly to simulate a sparse setting or a dense setting, respectively. The parameters in our simulation are listed in Table 2.

Table 2. Simulation parameters

Parameter	Description	Value
l	Field size(m)	600×600
N	Number of nodes	1,000(sparse setting) or 5,000(dense setting)
R_c	Communication radius(m)	40.0
R_s	Sensing radius(m)	40.0
V	Speed of a moving target(m/s)	5.0-25.0
S_m	Size of message(bit)	1,000

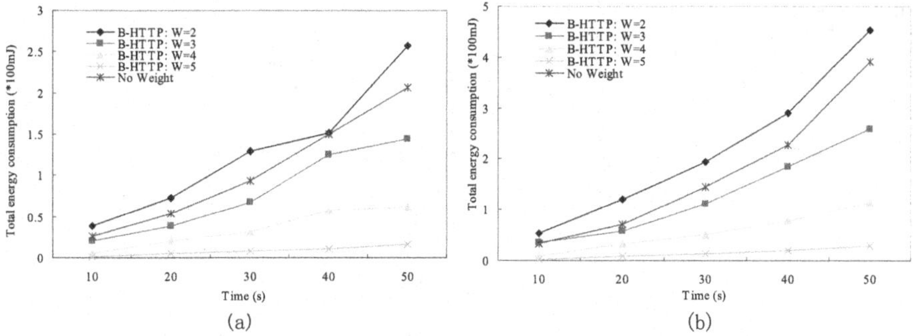

Fig. 5. Total energy consumption comparison of B-HTTP under different weights. (a) Sparse setting; (b) Dense setting.

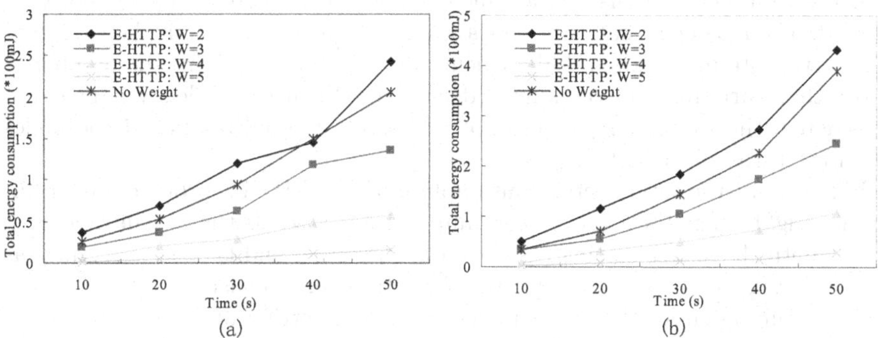

Fig. 6. Total energy consumption comparison of E-HTTP under different weights. (a) Sparse setting; (b) Dense setting.

5.2 Simulation Results

Fig. 5 describes the total energy consumption of the B-HTTP protocol under different weights. The two figures clearly show that the weight affects the total energy consumption of sensor nodes. The total energy consumption decreases as the weight increases. It is due to a fact that the larger the weight is, the smaller the amount of the nodes participating in tracking is. We can also see that a large energy consumption gap exists under different weights.

In order to demonstrate the advantage of the proposed B-HTTP protocol on the total energy consumption, we compare the total energy consumption under the sparse setting (as shown in Fig. 5(a)) and the dense setting (as shown in Fig. 5(b)). From the two figures, we can see that the total energy consumption under the dense setting is significantly larger than that under the sparse setting. It is because there are more sensor nodes participating in target tracking. The total energy consumption of the nodes under the dense setting is approximately twice as much as that under the sparse setting. At the same time, we can see

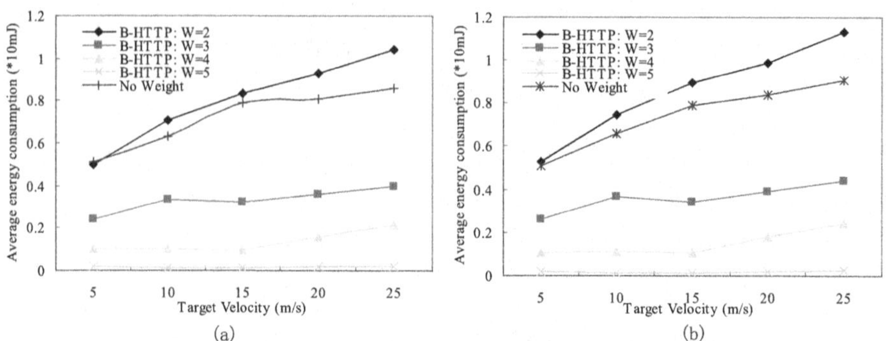

Fig. 7. The average energy consumption under different velocity of the target. (a) Sparse setting; (b) Dense setting.

that the total energy consumption increases when the node weight is not considered. The reason is that only nodes whose weight is more than the threshold can participate in tracking. So by calculating the node's weight, the number of nodes that participate in tracking is decreased. When the node's weight is not considered, the total energy consumption is almost equal to that of the nodes when the threshold W=2.

Fig. 6 shows the total energy consumption of the E-HTTP protocol under different weights. The total energy consumption decreases as the weight increases. Under both the sparse setting (as shown in Fig. 6(a)) and the dense setting (as shown in Fig. 6(b)), we can see that the total energy consumption under the dense setting is larger than that under the sparse setting and the total energy consumption increases when the node weight is not considered. By Comparing B-HTTP (as shown in Fig. 5), the saved total energy consumption of E-HTTP protocol is more than 5%.

We compare the average energy consumption under the sparse setting (as shown in Fig. 7(a)) and the dense setting (as shown in Fig. 7(b)). The average energy consumption increases as the velocity of the target increases. When the velocity increases, there are more nodes joining the herd-based node group under different weights, which consumes more energy. However, the amount of energy consumption is not so large. When the velocity of the target increases from $5m/s$ to $25m/s$, its range increases by 4 times, yet the average energy consumption only increases by 2 times. So the average energy consumption in the network increases with the velocity increment of the target, but the increasing rate is low. When the node's weight is not considered, we can see that the average energy consumption is only less than that of the nodes when the threshold W=2. Therefore, HTTP protocol has a distinct advantage in terms of energy consumption. When compared with the sparse setting, the average energy consumption under the dense setting increases slightly. Furthermore, we can see that the gap of the average energy consumption under different weights is relatively large. In summary, HTTP protocol shows an excellent performance on energy consumption.

6 Conclusion

In this paper, we proposed a protocol named HTTP, which can be used to detect and track a moving target in wireless sensor networks efficiently and effectively. The nodes in the tracking state can construct a herd-based node group to track the target dynamically. By setting the weight for each sensor node in the sensing and tracking state, the nodes can calculate their weight to determine whether they should join or leave the herd-based node group. Then the herd head adjusts the data reporting frequency according to the target's situation. We believe this work opens a new area of research in the near future. The optimization of the tracking group and evaluation of data accuracy will be further investigated in our future work.

Acknowledgement

This work is supported by the Hunan Provincial Natural Science Foundation of China for Distinguished Young Scholars under Grant No. 07JJ1010, the National Natural Science Foundation of China for Major Research Plan under Grant No. 90718034, and the Program for New Century Excellent Talents in University under Grant No. NCET-06-0686.

References

1. Akyildiz, I.F., Su, W., Sankarasubramaniam, Y., Cayirci, E.: Wireless Sensor Networks: A Survey. Computer Networks 38(4), 393–422 (2002)
2. Culler, D., Hong, W.: Wireless Sensor Networks. Communications of the ACM 47(6), 30–33 (2004)
3. Xu, Y., Winter, J., Lee, W.: Prediction-Based Strategies for Energy Saving in Object Tracking Sensor Networks. In: Proceedings of the 2004 IEEE International Conference on Mobile Data Management, pp. 346–357 (2004)
4. Lee, W.C., Xu, Y.: On Localized Prediction for Power Efficient Object Tracking in Sensor Networks. In: Proceedings of the 23rd International Conference on Distributed Computers Systems Workshops, pp. 434–439 (2003)
5. Niyogi, K., Mehrotra, S., Venkatasubramanian, N., Yu, X.: Adaptive Target Tracking in Sensor Networks. In: Proceedings of the 2004 Communication Networks and Distributed Systems Modeling and Simulation Conference, pp. 253–258 (2004)
6. Wang, G., Bhuiyan, M., Zhang, L.: Two-Level Cooperative and Energy-Efficient Tracking Algorithm in Wireless Sensor Networks. To appear in Wiley's Concurrency and Computation: Practice and Experience (2009)
7. Wang, G., Wang, H., Cao, J., Guo, M.: Energy-Efficient Dual Prediction-Based Data Gathering for Environmental Monitoring Applications. In: Proceedings of the 2007 IEEE Wireless Communications and Networking Conference (WCNC 2007), pp. 3516–3521 (2007)
8. Xu, Y., Heidemann, J., Estrin, D.: Geography Informed Energy Conservation for Ad Hoc Routing. In: Proceedings of ACM Mobile Computing and Networking, pp. 70–84 (2001)

9. Gui, C., Mohapatra, P.: Power Conservation and Quality of Surveillance in Target Tracking Sensor Networks. In: Proceedings of the Annual International Conference on Mobile Computing and Networking, pp. 129–143 (2004)
10. Guo, M., Olule, E., Wang, G., Guo, S.: Designing Energy Efficient Target Tracking Protocol with Quality Monitoring in Wireless Sensor Networks. The Journal of Supercomputing (2009), doi:10.1007/s11227-009-0278-5
11. He, T., Vicaire, P.A., Yan, T., et al.: Achieving Real-Time Target Tracking Using Wireless Sensor Nnetworks. In: Proceedings of the Twelfth IEEE Real-Time and Embedded Technology and Applications Symposium, pp. 37–48 (2006)
12. Lee, J., Cho, K., Lee, S.: Distributed and Energy-Efficient Target Localization and Tracking in Wireless Sensor Networks. Computer Communications 29, 2494–2505 (2006)
13. Zhang, W., Cao, G.: DCTC: Dynamic Convey Tree-Based Collaboration for Target Tracking in Sensor Networks. IEEE Transactions on Wireless Communication 11(5), 1689–1701 (2004)
14. Zhang, W., Cao, G.: Optimizing Tree Reconfiguration for Mobile Target Tracking in Sensor Networks. In: Proceedings of IEEE InfoCom, pp. 434–2445 (2004)
15. Xu, Y., Heidemann, J., Estrin, D.: Geography Informed Energy Conservation for Ad-hoc Routing. In: Proceedings of ACM Mobile Computing and Networking, pp. 70–84 (2001)
16. Sun, L., Li, J., Chen, Y., et al.: Wireless sensor networks (in Chinese). Tsinghua University Press, Beijing (2005)
17. Heinzelman, W., Chandrakasan, A., Balakrishnan, H.: Energy Efficient Communication Protocol for Wireless Microsensor Networks. In: Proceedings of the 33rd Hawaii International Conference on System Sciences, pp. 3005–3014 (2000)
18. Niculescu, D., Nath, B.: Ad Hoc Positioning System (APS). In: Proceedings of the 2001 IEEE Global Telecommunications Conference (GLOBECOM 2001), pp. 2926–2931 (2001)
19. Varga, A.: The OMNeT++ Discrete Event Simulation System. In: Proceedings of the European Simulation Multiconference (ESM 2001), pp. 319–324 (2001)

Minimum Interference Planar Geometric Topology in Wireless Sensor Networks

Trac N. Nguyen and Dung T. Huynh

Department of Computer Science
University of Texas at Dallas
Richardson, Texas 75083-0688
nguyentn@utdallas.edu, huynh@utdallas.edu

Abstract. The approach of using topology control to reduce interference in wireless sensor networks has attracted attention of several researchers. There are at least two definitions of interference in the literature. In a wireless sensor network the interference at a node may be caused by an edge that is transmitting data [15], or it occurs because the node itself is within the transmission range of another [3], [1], [6]. In this paper we show that the problem of assigning power to nodes in the plane to yield a planar geometric graph whose nodes have bounded interference is NP-complete under both interference definitions. Our results provide a rigorous proof for a theorem in [15] whose proof is unconvincing. They also address one of the open issues raised in [6] where Halldórsson and Tokuyama were concerned with the receiver model of node interference, and derived an $O(\sqrt{\Delta})$ upper bound for the maximum node interference of a wireless ad hoc network in the plane (Δ is the maximum interference of the so-called uniform radius network). The question as to whether this problem is NP-complete in the 2-dimensional case was left open.

Keywords: Wireless sensor networks, interference, NP-completeness, planar topology, geometric graphs.

1 Introduction

Wireless sensor networks (WSNs) have been widely used in military and civilian applications in the last two decades. Due to the wide applications of WSNs and the emergence of new technology, WSNs are now a very active research area. One of the core issues concerning WSNs is energy consumption since each node is equipped with a small limited battery. Another primary issue is interference which occurs when communication between a pair of nodes is affected by another node that is transmitting data. One of the well known approaches to reduce interference is to use topology control by reducing the power usage of certain nodes thereby establishing a simple connected network with low interference.

The approach of using topology control to reduce interference was first discussed in a number of papers including [3] and [12]. The authors in [3] defined the notion of interference load of an edge in a network, and showed an interesting result that certain sparse networks may not have low interference. This

B. Liu et al. (Eds.): WASA 2009, LNCS 5682, pp. 149–158, 2009.

paper argued that most of the known topology control algorithms perform worse than algorithms that simply minimize interference. Following the work in [3], the authors in [12] introduced a notion of node interference that is caused by surrounding nodes whose transmission range includes the given node. They analyzed the special case of the exponential 1-dimensional node chain which is also called the *highway* model. They showed that this sparse network has $\Omega(\sqrt{n})$ interference, where n is the number of nodes in the network . The authors described an algorithm that can achieve an $O(\sqrt[4]{\delta})$ approximation of the optimal connectivity preserving topology in the highway model where δ is the maximum node degree. Similarity, the papers [15],[11], and [8] focused on the notion of interference that is based on edges of the network. [8] gave a distributed algorithm called Average Path Interference that tries to preserve the spanner property of the original graph while reducing the interference in the network at the same time. [11] showed that the relative neighborhood graph and local spanning tree algorithms have a constant bounded average interferences ratio.

The NP completeness of both types of interference are discussed in [15], [1] and [2]. [15] extended the work of [3] with an NP-completeness proof for minimizing edge-based interference for general graphs along with a couple of heuristics, and [2] provided an NP-completeness proof for finding a spanning tree with minimum node interference for grid graphs. For the receiver-based interference model, in [1] the authors showed among other results that the problem of minimizing the maximum node interference is hard to approximate. On the other hand, [6] showed that for a set of n points in the plane a network with $O(\sqrt{\Delta})$ interference can be constructed using computational geometric tools (Δ is the maximum interference in the uniform-radius network). They left open the question whether this problem is NP-hard. In fact, the same question for the 1-dimensional case is also open.

In this paper, we study the problem of assigning power to sensor nodes in the plane to form a connected graph such that the interference load of each node is bounded. Specifically, we prove that the problem of assigning power to a set of nodes in the plane to yield a connected planar geometric graph whose nodes have bounded interference is NP-complete. Our result is significant as it provides an answer to one of the open issues in [6] and [1]. Moreover, it provides a rigorous proof for a theorem stated in [15] whose proof is unconvincing. We also point out that our result holds for the planar geometric graphs which are among the simplest models of WSNs.

The rest of this paper is organized as follows. Section II provides the definitions and explanations used in this paper. Section III is devoted to the NP-completeness proofs, and Section IV contains some concluding remarks.

2 Preliminaries

2.1 Network Model

Consider a set V of transceivers (nodes) in the plane. Each node u is assigned a power level denoted by $p(u)$. The signal transmitted by node u can only received by a node v if the distance between u and v, denoted by $d(u,v)$, is $\leq p(u)$. We only consider the bidirectional case in which a communication edge exists between two nodes u and v, (u,v), if both power levels $p(u) \geq d(u,v)$ and $p(v) \geq d(u,v)$. Thus, the set V of nodes in the plane together with the power levels assigned to the nodes define a *geometric* (also known as intersection) graph $G = (V,E)$. A geometric graph is said to be *planar* of no edge crosses another.

2.2 Interference Model

There are several definitions of the notion of interference in the literature. In this paper we consider two definitions of node interference, one described in [15] and the other described in [3], [12], [1] and [6]. Assuming that there is no obstacle blocking the broadcasting range, the two definitions of the node interference load are as follows.

Let $D(u,r)$ be the broadcasting disk of node u with radius r. For node interference load, the definition in [15] is based on the Euclidean distance, and is formally defined as follow:

$$NI(x) := |\{(u,v) \in E | x \notin \{u,v\} \ and \ x \in D(u,d(u,v)) \ or \ x \in D(v,d(v,u))\}|$$

and for a geometric graph $G = (V,E)$

$$NI(G) := max_{x \in V}\{NI(x)\} \qquad (1)$$

The node power levels are used in the definition of node interference load in the receiver interference model in [12], [6] and [1]:

$$RI(v) = |\{w \in (V - \{v\}) | v \in D(w,p(w))\}| \qquad (2)$$

and for a geometric graph $G = (V,E)$

$$RI(G = (V,E)) := max_{v \in V}\{RI(v)\}$$

3 The NP-Completeness of Minimum Interference in Planar Geometric Graphs

In this section, we first prove the NP-completeness of the problem of assigning power levels to nodes in the plane to produce a planar geometric graph G with bounded node interference load $NI(G)$. As a corollary we then show that the problem of assigning power to nodes to produce a planar geometric graph G with bounded $RI(G)$ is also NP-complete.

MINIMUM NI INTERFERENCE IN PLANAR GEOMETRIC GRAPHS

Instance: *Given a set of N nodes $V = \{v_1, v_2, ..., v_N\}$ in the plane, a set of M power levels $P = \{p_1, p_2, .., p_M\}$ that a node can transmit, and a positive number R.*

Question: *Is there a power assignment to all nodes so that it induces a connected planar geometric graph G(V,E) such that the interference $NI(v)$ of each node $v \in V$ is $\leq R$?*

The Minimum RI Interference in Planar Geometric Graphs problem is defined similarly. In the following we show that Minimum NI Interference in Planar Geometric Graphs is NP-complete.

Theorem 1. Minimum NI Interference is NP-complete for planar geometric graphs.

Proof of Theorem 1. Minimum NI Interference for Planar Geometric Graphs (MNIPG) is obviously in NP. Given a set V of nodes in the plane, a set P of power levels and a positive integer R, we can nondeterministically assign power levels to the nodes, and verify in polynomial time that (1) the power assignment yields a planar geometric graph $G(V, E)$, (2) the node interference $NI(v)$ of each node $v \in V$ is $\leq R$.

To prove the NP-harness of Minimum NI Interference in Planar Geometric Graphs, we construct a polynomial time reduction from the planar 3-SAT problem (P3SAT) which was proven NP-complete in [9]. Consider an instance ϕ of P3SAT, and the planar instance graph G of ϕ, where $G = (X \cup C, E \cup E')$ with edge sets $E = \{\{x, c\} | x \in C \vee \neg x \in C\}$ and $E' = \{\{x_i, x_{i+1}\} | 1 \leq i \leq n-1\}$.

To construct an instance $< V, P, R >$ of MNIPG, we first create a gadget for each variable of ϕ. As shown in Figure 1, the gadget for variable x contains 4 nodes, which are 2 pairs of x and $\neg x$. These nodes are connected through the *straight* and *curved* edges. To have sufficient nodes for x so that we can connect x to some clause nodes, we replace a variable node x in G by a chain of the above gadgets in such a way that every second gadget has its nodes and edges rearranged (see Figure 2). Note that consecutive gadgets are connected by two parallel *straight* edges. If the degree of node x is d, the number of $x's$ gadgets

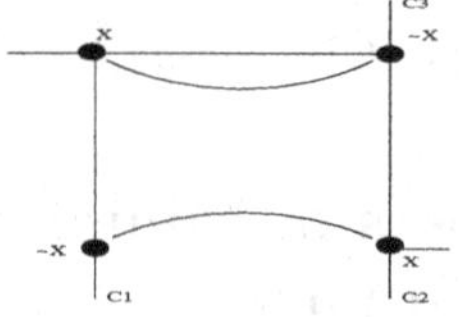

Fig. 1. A single gadget representing a variable x in a P3SAT instance

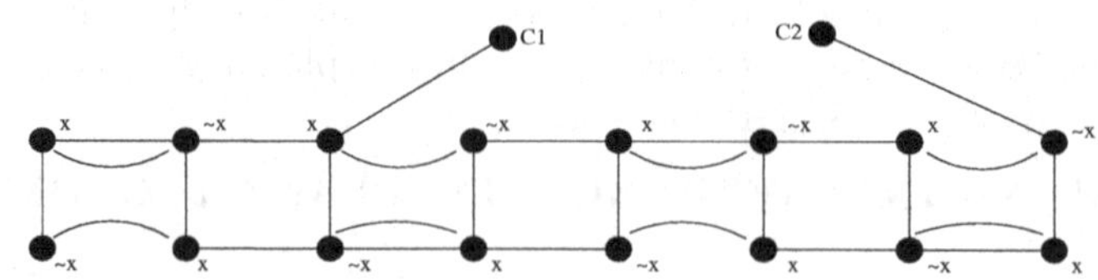

Fig. 2. A series of gadgets representing a variable x of a P3SAT instance

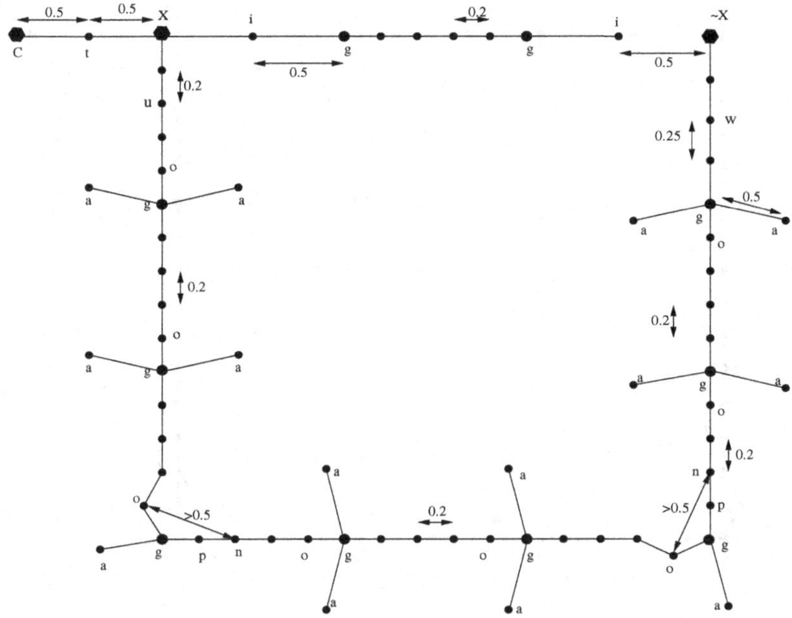

Fig. 3. Nodes added on the line segments replacing an edge of the embedded graph G

in this chain is $2 * d$ (see Figure 2 for the case x has degree 2). From each chain of gadgets representing a variable node in G, we only use the nodes with degree 3, to connect to a clause node. Furthermore, the variable link that connects all variables should enter each chain of gadgets via a degree 3 node at one end and exits via another degree 3 node at the other end. Thus, the new graph (also denoted G in the following for convenience) obtained from the original graph G has a maximum degree of 4 while the planarity of the graph is still preserved.

Next, we use Valiant's result [13] to embed the graph G with maximum degree 4 into the Euclidean plane:

> *A planar graph with maximum degree 4 can be embedded in the plane using $O(|V|)$ area in such a way that its verticies are at integer coordinates and its edges are drawn so that they are made up of line segments of form $x = i$ or $y = j$, for integers i and j.*

Moreover, this embedding process can easily be designed to satisfy the additional requirement that each line segment drawn to connect two original vertices of the graph G must be of length at least 2, and any two parallel line segments in the embedded graph are at least 2 units apart.

We define two radii r_1 and r_2 as follows: $r_1 := 1/4$ and $r_2 := 1/2$. For the sake of convenience let us call the variable and clause nodes of the P3SAT instance G embedded in the plane the *variable* and *clause* nodes, respectively. The line segments in the embedded graph G are further modified by placing additional

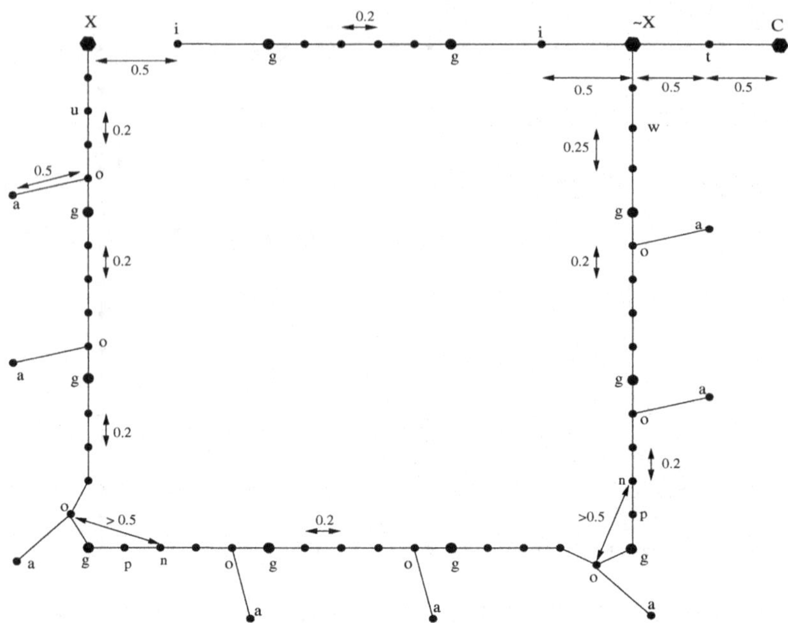

Fig. 4. Nodes added on the line segments replacing an edge of the embedded graph G

new nodes, called *intermediate* nodes, to create the instance $< V, P, R >$ of MNIPG as follows:

1. At each grid point on a line segment, add a new node called *grid* node.
2. Add new nodes, called *intermediate* nodes, on every straight line (which is a sequence of line segments after the embedding) connecting a variable node x and its negated node $\neg x$ in a chain of gadgets by the following steps starting from node $\neg x$:
   - On the unit segment (of length 1) that is adjacent to node $\neg x$, we add 3 *intermediate* nodes to divide this unit into 4 smaller pieces of length 1/4 each.
   - On the subsequent unit segments, we add 4 new *intermediate* nodes to divide each unit into 5 smaller pieces of length 1/5 each. If the current unit segment is perpendicular to the previous one, then pick the *intermediate* node next to the grid node and move this node 1/10 away from the line segment (see Figure 3). This ensures that the Euclidean distance from this (moved) *intermediate* node to the intermediate node on the previous unit segment (this node is denoted n in Figure 3) that is two hops away from the grid node is greater than 1/2.
   - Now, on the straight line (which is a sequence of line segments) connecting a variable node and its negated node we add several nodes as follows. Starting from the negated variable node $\neg x$ we add for each grid node and the next intermediate node two *auxiliary* nodes (see Figure 3) in

such a way that the distance from an *auxiliary* node to the closest *grid* node and the closest *intermediate* node is 1/2. If the grid node is adjacent to two perpendicular line segments, then only one *auxiliary* node is added in such a way that its distance to other *intermediate* nodes is $> 1/2$.

3. Add 4 *intermediate* nodes on each unit segment of the line segments representing the curved line connecting a variable and its negated node in G except the two units at the two ends. For each unit at the end of this line segment, place one node at the middle so that its distance to *(negated) variable* node and to the *grid* node is 1/2. These nodes are called *interfacing* nodes.
4. On each variable link in G connecting a chain of gadgets (representing a variable) to the next chain of gadgets (representing another variable), add 3 *intermediate* node that divides each unit into 4 pieces each of which is of length 1/4.
5. Add 1 *intermediate* node at the middle of each unit of the line segments connecting a *literal* node (x or $\neg x$) with a *clause* node.

As shown in Figure 3, nodes g's denote the *grid* nodes. x and $\neg x$ are *variable* nodes representing x and its negation $\neg x$ in G. C is a *clause* node, and a's denote *auxiliary* nodes. Nodes o's are the *intermediate* nodes sharing the *auxiliary* nodes with their neighboring *grid* nodes. p's denote the *intermediate* nodes that are on a unit perpendicular with a unit containing o's. t is the single *intermediate* node on the first unit of the line segments connecting a *clause* node with a *variable* node and i's are *interfacing* nodes.

The numbers of nodes added are as follows:

$$I_s = \sum_{(x,\neg x)\in E} ((4 * (l_{(x,\neg x)} - 1) + 3) + (l_{(x,\neg x)} - 1) + (2 * (l_{(x,\neg x)} - 1) - T_{(x,\neg x)}));$$

$$I_c = \sum_{(x,\neg x)\in E} ((4 * (l_{(x,\neg x)} - 2) + 2) + (l_{(x,\neg x)} - 1));$$

$$I_{xc} = \sum_{(x,C)\in E} (l_{(x,C)} + (l_{(x,C)} - 1)); \quad I_l = \sum_{(x,y)\in E} (3 * l_{(x,y)} + (l_{(x,y)} - 1));$$

where I_s is the number of *intermediate* nodes, *grid* nodes and *auxiliary* nodes added on the line segments representing the straight edges, and $T_{(x,\neg x)}$ is the number of turns from a variable to its negation on this line segments. I_c is the number of *intermediate* nodes, *interfacing* nodes and *grid* nodes for the curved edges connecting a variable and its negation in G. I_{xC} is the number of *intermediate* nodes and *grid* nodes added on the line segments representing an edge from variable node x to a clause node C. (The number $I_{\neg xC}$ is computed similarly.) The number of *intermediate* and *grid* nodes added on the line segments representing a variable link is I_l.

Let $P := \{0, r_1, r_2\}$ and $R := 4$. To show the correctness of the above polynomial reduction we prove that the instance ϕ of P3SAT is satisfiable if and only if the MNIPG instance $< V', P, R >$ has a power assignment that yields a planar geometric graph such that the interference load $NI(v)$ of each node v is $\leq R$.

For the "only-if" direction, suppose that ϕ has a satisfying Boolean assignment. We assign power levels to nodes in V as follows:

1. Assign the power level r_2 to *variable* node $x \in V'$ if variable $x \in \phi$ has the value *true*; otherwise, assign the power level r_1 to *variable* node x.
2. Assign the power level r_2 to all *intermediate*, *grid* and *clause* nodes on the line segments connecting a *variable* node and a *clause* node.
3. Assign the power level r_2 to two *interfacing* and its adjacent *grid* nodes on each of the line segments representing a curved edge connecting a variable node and its negation in G. Assign the power level r_1 to the rest of nodes on this line segment.
4. Assign the power level r_2 to all *auxiliary* nodes.
5. If the variable x has value *true*, assign the power r_2 to each *grid* node that is at the distance r_2 to its neighboring *auxiliary* node on the line segments representing a straight edge connecting the variable node x and its negation $\neg x$ in G; otherwise, assign the power r_2 to each *intermediate* nodes o that is at the distance r_2 to its neighboring *auxiliary* node. Assign the power r_1 to the rest of the *intermediate* and *grid* nodes on these line segments.

Clearly, this power assignment produces a planar geometric graph. The interference load NI(v) of each node v is contributed by its adjacent neighbors and the nearby neighbor with the power r_2. With this power assignment, it is straightforward to verify that the interference load $NI(v)$ of each node V is $\leq R = 4$.

For the "If" direction, suppose the instance $< V', P, R >$ has a power assignment that yields a connected planar geometric graph $G'(V', E')$ in which each node v has an interference load $NI(v) \leq R = 4$, we construct a satisfying Boolean assignment for the P3SAT instance ϕ based on the following observations:

1. Consider the line segments representing the curved edge connecting a variable node x and its negation $\neg x$ in G'. In order for G to be connected, either the *variable* node x is assigned the power level r_2 to connect to its neighboring *interfacing* node, or its negation $\neg x$ is assigned the power level r_2.
2. Consider the line segments representing the straight edge connecting a variable and its negation in G'. We argue that exactly one of the variable node or its negation is assigned the power level r_2, and the other is assigned the power level r_1. Suppose without loss of generality that the variable node x is assigned the power level r_2 and consider the *intermediate* node u that is at distance $2 \times 1/5$ from node x. Since the three edges adjacent to x contribute to the interference load of u, the intermediate node o close by must have the power level r_1; otherwise o and the two auxiliary nodes would produce two edges that contribute to the interference load of u which would be > 4. Consequently, the grid node close by must have the power level r_2 to connect to the pair of auxiliary nodes. Using similar argument we have that the remaining grid nodes on these line segments must have the power level

r_2. Now consider the middle intermediate node w on the last unit segment adjacent to $\neg x$. Since $NI(w) \leq 4$, it follows that $\neg x$ must have the power level r_1.

3. Since G is connected at least one *variable* node must be connected to a *clause* node C, and has a power level r_2 for the *clause* node C to be connected to the graph.

From the above observations, we can construct the Boolean assignment for the P3SAT instance ϕ using the following rules:

- If a *variable* node in G' has the power level r_2, then assign the value *true* to that variable in ϕ. Otherwise, if a *variable* node in G' representing a variable node in G having the power level r_1, assign the value $false$ to that variable in ϕ.

From Observation 3 it follows that each clause in ϕ is satisfied by at least 1 literal having the value *true*. Moreover, from Observations 1 and 2, the Boolean assignment for ϕ is consistent. This concludes the proof of Theorem 1.

Finally we show that the Minimum RI Interference in Planar Geometric Graphs problem is also NP-complete settling an issue left open in [6] and [1].

Theorem 2. Minimum RI Interference in Planar Geometric Graphs is NP-complete.

Proof of Theorem 2. The proof of Theorem 2 is similar to the proof of Theorem 1. We only need to make the following minor changes to the polynomial time reduction from P3SAT:

1. Only one *auxiliary* node is added between a *intermediate* node and its adjacent *grid* node on the line segments representing a straight edge in G to connect a variable and its negation (see Figure 4).
2. $R := 3$.

The correctness of the reduction can be proved in a similar way as in the proof of Theorem 1.

4 Conclusions

In this paper we have shown that the problems of minimizing NI or RI interference are both NP-complete for planar geometric graphs. This provides an answer to an issue left open in [6] and [1]. In fact, while Halldórsson and Tokuyama [6] focused on constructing 2-dimensional networks with $O(\sqrt{\Delta})$ RI interference, where Δ is the maximum interference of the uniform-radius network, Bilò and Proietti [1] showed that the problem is hard to approximate for general graphs. The question as to whether the problem of minimizing (NI or RI) interference for 2-dimensional geometric graphs is hard to approximate remains open. It is worth noting that there are some known results concerning the dominating set, independent set and vertex cover problems. While there are polynomial-time approximation schemes for the independent set and vertex cover problems (cf. [4], [7], [14]), it has been shown that the dominating set problem is hard to approximate for certain classes of intersection graphs, and it has polynomial-time constant-factor approximation algorithms for others (cf. [5] and [10]).

References

1. Bilò, D., Proietti, G.: On the Complexity of Minimizing Interference in Ad-Hoc and Sensor Networks. Theorectical Computer Science 402, 43–55 (2008)
2. Buchin, K.: Minimizing the Maximum Interference is Hard (2008), `http://arxiv.org/abs/0802.2134`
3. Burkhart, M., von Rickenbach, P., Wattenhofer, R., Zollinger, A.: Does Topology Control Reduce Interference? In: MOBIHOC 2004, pp. 9–19 (2004)
4. Erlebach, T., Jansen, K., Seidel, E.: Polynomial-time Approximation Schemes for Geometric Intersection Graphs. SIAM J. Comput. 6(34), 1302–1323 (2005)
5. Erlebach, T., van Leeuwen, E.J.: Domination in Geometric Intersection Graphs. In: Laber, E.S., Bornstein, C., Nogueira, L.T., Faria, L. (eds.) LATIN 2008. LNCS, vol. 4957, pp. 747–758. Springer, Heidelberg (2008)
6. Halldórsson, M.M., Tokuyama, T.: Minimizing Interference of a Wireless Ad-Hoc Network in a Plane. In: Nikoletseas, S.E., Rolim, J.D.P. (eds.) ALGOSENSORS 2006. LNCS, vol. 4240, pp. 71–82. Springer, Heidelberg (2006)
7. Hunt III, D.B., Marathe, M.V., Radhakrishnan, V., Ravi, S.S., Rosenkrantz, D.J., Stearns, R.E.: NC- Approximation Schemes for NP- and PSPACE-Hard Problems for Geometric Graphs. Journal Algorithms 2(26), 238–274 (1998)
8. Johansson, T., Carr-Motyckovaá, L.: Reducing Interference in Ad Hoc Networks Through Topology Control. In: DIALM-POMC 2005, pp. 17–23 (2005)
9. Lichtenstein, D.: Planar Formulae And Their Uses. SIAM J. of Compt. 11(23) (1982)
10. Marx, D.: Parameterized Complexity of Independence and Domination on Geometric Graphs. In: Bodlaender, H.L., Langston, M.A. (eds.) IWPEC 2006. LNCS, vol. 4169, pp. 154–165. Springer, Heidelberg (2006)
11. Moaveni-Nejad, K., Li, X.-Y.: Low-Interference Topology Control for Wireless Ad Hoc Networks. Ad Hoc and Wireless Sensor Networks 1, 41–64 (2005)
12. Rickenbach, P.V., Schmid, S., Wattenhofer, R., Zollinger, A.: A Roburst Interference Model for Wireless Ad-Hoc Networks. In: Proc. 19th IEEE Int. Par. and Dist. (2005)
13. Valiant, L.: Universality Considerations in VLSI Circuits. IEEE Trans. on Compupters C-30, 135–140 (1981)
14. van Leeuwen, E.J.: Better Approximation Schemes for Disk Graphs. In: Arge, L., Freivalds, R. (eds.) SWAT 2006. LNCS, vol. 4059, pp. 316–327. Springer, Heidelberg (2006)
15. Wu, K.-D., Liao, W.: On Constructing Low Interference Topology in Multihop Wireless Networks. Int. J. of Sensor Networks 2, 321–330 (2007)

Topology Inference in Wireless Mesh Networks*

Kai Xing[1], Xiuzhen Cheng[1], Dechang Chen[2], and David Hung-Chang Du[3]

[1] Department of Computer Science, The George Washington University, Washington DC 20052, USA
[2] Department of Preventive Medicine and Biometrics, Uniformed Services University of the Health Sciences Bethesda, MD 20814, USA
[3] Department of Computer Science and Engineering, University of Minnesota, Minneapolis, MN 55455, USA

Abstract. In this paper, we tackle the problem of topology inference in wireless mesh networks and present a novel approach to reconstructing the logical network topology. Our approach is based on the social fingerprint, a short bit pattern computed for each node to characterize the link status of the local neighborhood of the node. To conserve the communication resource, social fingerprints are piggybacked to the gateway with a small probability. Based on the information embedded in the social fingerprints, the gateway first estimates the set of parameters defining a Hidden Markov Model (HMM) that models the logical network topology, then infers the evolutions of the local and global network topologies. We have conducted extensive simulation to verify the performance of our approach in terms of "completeness" and "accuracy". The results indicate that our approach is very effective in topology inference.

1 Introduction

Recent research on topology discovery/inference focuses on the Internet [1,2] or Internet-based wired networks [3,4,5]. By exploring the information/metrics provided by the underlying network management protocols such as BGP or SNMP, the state of the network could be obtained [1, 2, 3, 4, 5]. However, the underlying wired network architecture, model, assumptions, and management functions, are fundamentally different from those in wireless mesh networks. Therefore the techniques designed for wired networks are not applicable to WMNs.

There exist topology learning techniques for sensor networks [6, 7, 8, 9, 10]. In static topology learning [6, 7, 8], the static topology could be derived based on the spacial correlations of the sensor nodes. In on-demand logical topology learning [9, 10], topology information is collected all over the network whenever needed. These topology learning approaches require the availability of robots traversing or queries flooding through the network for information collection.

In this paper, we propose a novel topology inference scheme for WMNs. In our approach, topology information collection is done via the *social fingerprint*,

* This research is partially supported by the US National Science Foundation under grants CNS-0831852 and CNS-0831939.

B. Liu et al. (Eds.): WASA 2009, LNCS 5682, pp. 159–168, 2009.

a short binary bit string summarizing the *social neighborhood* (a local neighborhood) of a node. Each social fingerprint embeds the partial local topology information in the subnetwork. A social fingerprint is recomputed whenever a link in the social neighborhood is activated or deactivated. The social fingerprint is piggybacked to the gateway with a small probability. After collecting the partial topology information from social fingerprints, the gateway first estimates the parameters defining a Hidden Markov Model (HMM) that models the network topology, then infers the evolution of the local network topology based on the Viterbi algorithm. Finally it computes the global logical topology evolution from the inferred local topologies.

2 Network Model and Preliminaries

2.1 Network Model

We consider a mesh network with stationary and time-synchronized mesh routers. The physical network topology or the network is represented by an undirected graph $G(V, E)$, where V is the set of nodes, and E is the set of physical links. Edge $e(u, v)$ is a logical link if and only if it is active, i.e., it is carrying some amount of traffic. Let N_r be the number of radios equipped with each node. Therefore, each node can have at most N_r logical or active links at any instant of time. Let $N(u)$ be the set of neighbors of u. Note that $u \notin N(u)$ and $N(u)$ could include all nodes in a general local neighborhood (e.g. two-hop neighborhood) of u. For simplicity, we assume $N(u) = N_1(u)$ in this paper, where $N_1(u)$ is the set of one-hop neighbors of u.

Given $G(V, E)$, the *social neighborhood* of any node $u \in V$ is defined to be the set of nodes in $N(N(u))$. The *social network* of $u \in V$ is the subgraph of G induced by all active links that are either incident on u or any node in $N(u)$. Therefore u's social network changes whenever a link incident on u or any node in $N(u)$ is activated or deactivated.

We assume that there exists a gateway that connects to the Internet. We further assume that with a small probability a mesh router u sends a message piggy-backed with its most recent social fingerprint to the gateway (via multi hop). Therefore the gateway has only partial information about the logical topology at any instant of time. Nevertheless, the gateway is aware of the global physical topology of the network. Note that we can treat this gateway as a virtual gateway representing multiple gateways, as long as all the gateways share their observations of the network instantly.

2.2 Hidden Markov Model

A (first order) hidden Markov model (HMM) models a system statistically by a Markov process with unknown parameters. A HMM consists of the following basic elements. First, the modeled system involves a finite set of states $S = \{S_1, S_2, \cdots, S_M\}$ that are not directly observed by the observer. Transitions among states are made according to the transition probability matrix $A = \{a_{ij}\}$ with

$$a_{ij} = P(q(t+1) = S_j | q(t) = S_i), 1 \leq i, j \leq M,$$

where $q(t)$ denotes the state at time t. It is seen that a_{ij} is the transition probability that at time $(t+1)$ the state is S_j, given that it is S_i at time t. Clearly, $\sum_{j=1}^{M} a_{ij} = 1$ for any i. When the state S_i is visited, an observation, visible to the observer, is generated from a fixed alphabet $R = \{r_1, r_2, \cdots, r_N\}$ in terms of the probability distribution $b_i(1), b_i(2), \cdots, b_i(N)$, with

$$b_i(k) = P(O(t) = r_k | q(t) = S_i),$$

where $O(t)$ is the observation at time t. It is seen that $\sum_{k=1}^{N} b_i(k) = 1$ for any i. A HMM also involves an initial state distribution $\pi = \{\pi_i\}$ with

$$\pi_i = P(q(1) = S_i).$$

Let B denote the $M \times N$ matrix $\{b_i(k)\}$. Then the set (A, B, π) represents the full set of parameters and can be used to denote a HMM. There are three basic assumptions made in the theory of above HMMs: (i) a next state only depends on the current state (memoryless property); (ii) transition probabilities are independent of the time t (time homogeneity property); and (iii) the current observation is independent of the previous observations. The first two assumptions are actually used in defining the transition probability matrix.

HMMs can be used to find effective solutions to typical questions regarding sequences of observations, sequences of states, and parameters. In this paper, we are interested in the following two problems. The first one seeks the estimates of the parameters of a HMM, given the observations, namely, finding $\theta = (A, B, \pi)$ that maximize $P(O_{1\to T}|\theta)$, where $O_{1\to T}$ is the sequence of observations $O(1), O(2), \cdots, O(T)$. The second one looks for the sequence of states $q(1)$, $q(2)$, $\cdots$, $q(T)$ that is most likely to have occurred, given the parameters and observations, namely, finding

$$\text{argmax} P(q(1), q(2), \cdots, q(T) | \theta, O_{1\to T}).$$

The estimation of θ is done via the expectation-maximization (EM) algorithm [11], which estimates the model parameters according to the Baum-Welch formulas at each iteration:

$$\hat{a}_{ij}^{(n+1)} = \frac{\sum_{t=2}^{T} P(q(t-1) = S_i, q(t) = S_j | O_{1\to T}, \hat{\theta}_n)}{\sum_{t=2}^{T} P(q(t-1) = S_i | O_{1\to T}, \hat{\theta}_n)} \tag{1}$$

$$\hat{b}_j(k)^{(n+1)} = \frac{\sum_{t=1}^{T} P(q(t) = S_j, O(t) = r_k | O_{1\to T}, \hat{\theta}_n)}{\sum_{t=1}^{T} P(q(t) = S_j | O_{1\to T}, \hat{\theta}_n)}, \tag{2}$$

where the probabilities in Eqs. (1) and (2) are conditioned on the observations $O_{1\to T}$ and on the current estimates of θ, i.e. $\hat{a}_{i,j}^{(n)}$ and $\hat{b}_j(k)^{(n)}$. The Baum-Welch formulas can be efficiently computed using the forward-backward procedure [11,12].

Given θ and the observation sequence $O_{1\to T}$, the best possible state sequence can be computed by the Viterbi algorithm [11,13], which is a dynamic programming method that computes two $M \times T$ matrices $\Delta = \{\delta_i(t)\}$ and $\Psi = \{\psi_i(t)\}$, where $\delta_i(t)$ is the most likely state sequence ending at state S_i at time t, and $\psi_i(t)$ keeps track of the state that maximize $\delta_i(t)$ at time $t-1$. Initially, $\delta_i(1) = \pi_i b_i(O(1))$ and $\psi_i(1) = 0$. At the tth iteration, where $t = 2, \cdots, T$,

$$\delta_j(t) = \max_i \delta_i(t-1)a_{ij} \cdot b_j(O(t)) \quad (3)$$

$$\psi_j(t) = \arg\max_i \delta_i(t-1)a_{ij} \quad (4)$$

At termination, $q^*(T) = \arg\max_i \delta_i(T)$. The state sequence can be backtracked by $q^*(t) = \psi_{q^*(t+1)}(t+1)$ for $t = T-1, T-2, \cdots, 1$.

3 Logical Topology Inference

3.1 Logical Topology Modeling

At time t, the logical topology of the network is determined by the actual active links. We denote by $q(t)$ the state of the topology at time t. Clearly, there are a finite number of such states, denoted by $S = \{S_1, S_2, \cdots, S_M\}$. Note that in wireless mesh networks, at any time t only a subset of nodes in the network send messages to the gateway, so that the gateway only has a partial information of the network topology. Therefore the actual network topology state $q(t)$ is not directly observable. For transitions among states, we realize that, given the current state, future states are independent of the past states. This is because the future link status of the entire network is mainly dependent on (changes from) the current status. For simplicity, we also assume that the network topology state transition probabilities are independent of the actual time at which the transitions occur. Therefore as in Section 2.2, the transition probability matrix $A = \{a_{ij}\}$ for the network topology can be well defined.

Though the states are not directly visible, there might be some observed information at time t, denoted by $O(t)$. In this paper the observation $O(t)$ consists of time stamps and social fingerprints (see Section 3.2). Due to the nature of their generation, social fingerprints collected at any specific time t are dependent only on the topology state $q(t)$. They are independent of any earlier collected fingerprints. Let $R = \{r_1, r_2, \cdots, r_N\}$ denote the fixed alphabet representing all possible observations. Then as in Section 2.2, we can compute the matrix $B = \{b_i(k)\}$ with $b_i(k)$ representing the probability that the state S_i 'generates' the observation $O(t) = r_k$. If letting $\pi = \{\pi_i\}$ denote an initial state distribution, then the above shows that the network topology can be modeled by the HMM with the parameters (A, B, π). We note that data $O_{1\to T} = O(1), O(2), \cdots, O(T)$ are incomplete, since the collected social fingerprints represent only a portion of the topology information.

We now have justified why we model the network logical topology by a HMM with a set of parameters $\theta = \{A, B, \pi\}$. Ideally, we would like to estimate θ first and then infer the evolution of the network logical topology. However, a direct estimation of θ is computationally intensive since the total number of possible topology states is $O(2^{|E|})$, where $|E|$ is the total number of edges in the physical network. Therefore we decide to cut the search space by considering local topology inference for each node first. Let $\theta_u = \{A_u, B_u, \pi_u\}$ be the

HMM parameters characterizing the social network of u. The observation sequence $O^u_{1\to T} = O_u(t_1), O_u(t_2), \cdots, O_u(t_T)$ contains the social fingerprints and the corresponding time stamps piggy-backed to the gateway as described in the following section.

3.2 Social Fingerprint Computation

As indicated in Subsection 2.1, a social fingerprint of node u encodes u's social activities (active links) with its social neighborhood. Therefore to compute the social fingerprint, u's neighbors in $N(u)$ should report active incident links to u. This can be done by beacon messages, which could be broadcasted periodically or only when an incident link is activated/deactivated.

At any instant of time, all the active links in the social neighborhood of u defines a local logical *topology state* of u. The union of all the states is the *social logical topology state space* of u, denoted by S^u. Note that the size of S^u is constrained by N_r, the number of radios per node. If we use '1' and '0' to encode the active and inactive status of an edge, a binary code encoding the statuses of all links in the social neighborhood of u represents a valid state of u if and only if it satisfies the radio constraints: each node can have at most N_r active links at any instant of time.

Let $S^u = \{S^u_1, S^u_2, \cdots, S^u_i, \cdots, S^u_{M_u}\}$ be the (lexicographically) ordered list of all the states in the local logical topology space of u, where M_u is the total number of states for u's social network. Let S^u_i denote the current topology state of u. Then a simple social fingerprint could be the binary representation of i, which signals the position of S^u_i in S^u. Denote this fingerprint by FP_u. Whenever u generates a new message to the gateway (GW), it "signs" the message with its fingerprint FP_u:

$$u \to GW : \{ID_u, FP_u, content, T_{stamp}(u)\}$$

where $T_{stamp}(u)$ denotes the time stamp of the most recent topology change in $N(u)$ at which time the fingerprint FP_u is computed.

Here we have a problem: the fingerprint FP_u defined above may have a variable length for different node u. To overcome this problem, we employ a simple hash function (e.g., MOD operation) to map the topology space into a smaller space $H^u = \{H^u_1, \cdots, H^u_j, \cdots, H^u_{L_u}\}$, where L_u is the number of states in H^u. Let $H^u_j = Hash(S^u_i)$. Then the binary representation of j will serve as the social fingerprint for u.

Note that the gateway knows the global physical topology and therefor it can compute the state space S^u and H^u easily. FP_u contains the partial logical topology information of v, where $v \in N(N(u))$. This partial information will be exploited for the logical topology inference at the gateway.

3.3 Local Logical Topology Characterization and Reconstruction

Suppose the states of the local topology of u, characterized by $\theta_u = \{A_u, B_u, \pi_u\}$, change at times $t_1, t_2, \cdots$. For any $v \in \{u \bigcup N(N(u))\}$, let $o_v(t_i)$ denote the observation $\{FP_v, t_i\}$ sent by v, where FP_v is generated at time t_i. Let $O_u(t_i)$ denote the observations from the social network of u which consists of all possible $o_v(t_i)$, and let $\theta_u(t_i)$ denote the estimation of the parameters θ_u after receiving $o_v(t_i)$. Let $\Theta_u^K = \{\theta_u(t_1), \theta_u(t_2), \cdots, \theta_u(t_K)\}$ be the ordered list of the K most recent estimations of θ_u with $t_1 < t_2 \cdots < t_K$. Correspondingly, we define the list $\mathcal{O}_u^K = \{O_u(t_1), O_u(t_2), \cdots, O_u(t_K)\}$. Whenever a new observation $o_v(t_i)$ is available, where $v \in \{u \cup N(N(u))\}$ and $t_i \geq t_1$, Θ_u^K will be updated based on Eqs. (1) and (2).

Note that K can be treated as a window size with the window containing the K most recent estimates of θ_u and O_u. When all nodes are time-synchronized and messages to the gateway are uniformly generated, a smaller K suffices. For example, in our simulation study, $K = 8$ works perfect for all the scenarios. We choose $K > 1$ because the time stamp (the time when the topology changes, which is the time when the fingerprint is computed) for observation O_1 may be earlier than that of O_2 that is received earlier than O_1. By maintaining $K > 1$ estimates, we can characterize and reconstruct the local logical topology at a higher accuracy.

This procedure needs an initial estimate of $\theta_u(0)$. According to [12,11], the initial estimation of θ does not affect the convergence of the EM method. Therefore we randomly choose a topology state S_i as our initial topology state. Define

$$a_{i,j}^{t=0} = \frac{1}{|M_u|} \tag{5}$$

$$b_j^{t=0}(k) = \frac{1}{L_u} \tag{6}$$

$$\pi_i^{t=0} = \frac{1}{|M_u|} \tag{7}$$

where $|M_u|$ is the total number of states of the social network of u, and L_u is the size of the harsh space given in the fingerprint computation.

Note that the whole observation sequence $O_{1\to T}^u$ for the node u needs to be kept during the computation of θ_u. Given θ_u and $O_{1\to T}^u$, the evolution of the local logical topology of u can be reconstructed based on the Viterbi algorithm elaborated in Section 2.2.

3.4 Global Topology Reconstruction

We reconstruct the global topology through the status estimation of each link. Given a link $e(u,v)$, let S^u and S^v denote the local topology state space for u and v, respectively, and S_i^u and S_j^v denote the i-th and the j-th local topology state in S^u and S^v, respectively. Let $Stat_{e(u,v)}(S_i^u)$ denote the status of link $e(u,v)$ in the local topology state S_i^u. Given $q_u(t)$ and $q_v(t)$ estimated by the procedure proposed in Section 3.3, the status of $e(u,v)$ at time t is estimated as follows,

- If $Stat_{e(u,v)}(q_u(t)) = Stat_{e(u,v)}(q_v(t))$,
  we have $Stat_{e(u,v)}(q_u(t))$ as the status of link $e(u,v)$ at time t;

– If $Stat_{e(u,v)}(q_u(t)) \neq Stat_{e(u,v)}(q_v(t))$,
we first define a boolean variable

$$B_{e(u,v)}(q_u(t), S_i^u) = \begin{cases} 1, \text{if } Stat_{e(u,v)}(q_u(t)) = \\ \quad Stat_{e(u,v)}(S_i^u) \\ 0, \text{if } Stat_{e(u,v)}(q_u(t)) \neq \\ \quad Stat_{e(u,v)}(S_i^u) \end{cases}$$

Then we compute $C_u = \Sigma_{S_i^u \in S^u} \delta_{S_i^u}(t) \cdot B_{e(u,v)}(q_u(t), S_i^u)$ and $C_v = \Sigma_{S_j^v \in S^v} \delta_{S_j^v}(t) \cdot B_{e(u,v)}(q_v(t), S_j^v)$, which denote u and v's confidence to support their decisions on the link status estimations $Stat_{e(u,v)}(q_u(t))$ and $Stat_{e(u,v)}(q_v(t))$, respectively.

If $C_u \geq C_v$, u has a higher confidence to make the right estimation on the status of $e(u,v)$ than v. Therefore, we employ u's estimation $q_u(t)$ to estimate the link status of $e(u,v)$, namely

$$Stat_{e(u,v)} = Stat_{e(u,v)}(q_u(t))$$

Otherwise, we employ v's estimation, that is

$$Stat_{e(u,v)} = Stat_{e(u,v)}(q_v(t))$$

4 Performance Evaluation

We implement all the algorithms in Matlab. Let N be the total number of physical links in the network G. Denote by '0' the inactive link status and '1' the active link status. At any instant of time t, define $N_1(t)$ and $N_0(t)$ be the number of active (logical) and inactive links at time t, respectively. We have $N_1(t) + N_0(t) = N$. Similarly, we define $N_1'(t)$ and $N_0'(t)$ be the number of inferred active and inactive links at time t, respectively. Let $N_{ij}(t)$ be the number of links that are actually in status i but the inferred link status by our approach is j, where $i, j = \{0, 1\}$.

We utilize the following two metrics to evaluate the performance of our approach. The first one is *Completeness*, which is defined to be $\frac{N_0'(t)+N_1'(t)}{N}$. Completeness tells us the percentage of links, active or inactive, that can be inferred by our approach. It indicates the capability of our algorithms to capture the status of all links. The second metric is *precision*, which represents how good in topology inference our algorithms are. We define two related parameters: *Accuracy* and *False Rate*, where Accuracy is defined to be $\frac{N_{11}}{N_1}$ and False Rate is defined to be $\frac{N_{01}}{N_0}$. Note that after computing the Accuracy and False Rate, other information such as $\frac{N_{10}}{N_1}$ and $\frac{N_{00}}{N_0}$ can be derived easily.

In our simulation we have considered an area of 100×100 square units with 100 randomly deployed nodes. The simulation settings are listed as follows:

– The simulation results are based on random network deployment: the placement of mesh nodes follows random distribution.

- The number of radios equipped by each node is set to 2. At the beginning of each simulation, we initialize the active links in the network as follows: each node u takes itself as a sender and establishes a (sender, receiver) pair as an active link. The receiver is randomly chosen from u's one-hop neighbors and must satisfy the radio constraint (the receiver should have at least one radio available/unoccupied for that active link). If none of u's neighbors have available radios (due to radio constraint), u has no active links and keeps silence at the beginning of the simulation.
- At each time t, there are p percent of nodes in the network that send messages as well as their fingerprints (FPs) to the gateway, where $p \in \{1\%, 5\%, 10\%\}$.
- At each time t, 5 logical links change their status to inactive. And 5 different inactive links also change their status to active. During this status transformation, the radio constraint of each node is preserved.
- The simulation time is set to $[1, 100]$. Within this amount of time, the local topology of each node will change multiple times.
- The results of each simulation setting are averaged over 20 rounds

In the following two subsections, we report our simulation results in terms of Completeness, Accuracy, and False Rate. Note that we choose not to evaluate the estimation of θ, the HMM model parameter, because the optimal value of θ_{opt} is unknown. Actually it is difficult to directly evaluate the goodness of the model parameter θ estimated by our algorithms. However, the evaluation of the accuracy and false rate of our algorithms in topology inference indirectly reflects the effectiveness of θ estimation.

4.1 Completeness

Fig. 1 reports our simulation results on evaluating the Completeness, denoted by $P_{inferred}$, of our algorithms.

In Fig. 1, the larger the $|N(u)|$, the more the network topology information that can be inferred when the percentage of traffics carrying fingerprints to the gateway (p) is fixed. When $|N(u)|$ is fixed, the larger the p, the more the network topology information can be inferred. It is also desirable to observe in Fig. 1 that even with a low percentage of nodes in the network that report to the gateway per unit time (e.g., $p = 1\%$), and a small size of neighbor set (e.g., $|N(u)| = 5$), a large amount of network topology information can still be inferred.

4.2 Accuracy

In this simulation, we fix the average node degree to 5. Fig. 2 reports the Accuracy and the False Rate of the estimated global logical topology q_{net} during the simulation time $[1, 100]$. We notice from Fig. 2(a) that the higher the p, the more fingerprint information (namely the partial local topology information) the gateway can obtain, then the higher the accuracy of our topology inference algorithms, and the lower the false rate, as shown in Fig. 2(b). Even under an extremely smaller p (i.e. $p = 1\%$), our algorithms can still achieve a relatively

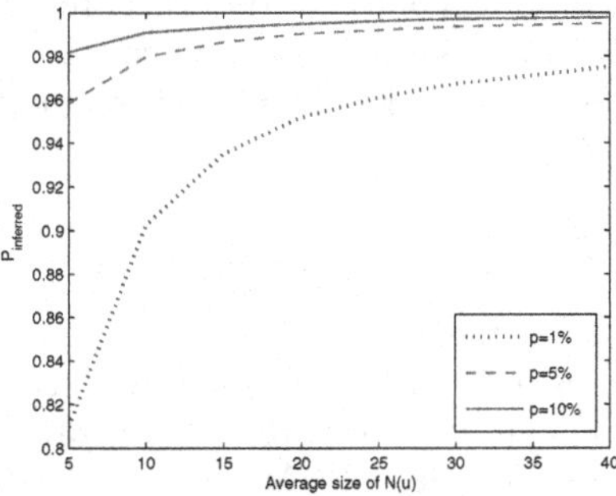

Fig. 1. The percentage of the network topology (including both active and inactive links) that can be inferred by our algorithms, denoted by $P_{inferred}$, *v.s.* the average size of the neighbor set, $|N(u)|$, for different p, the percentage of traffics carrying the social fingerprint to the gateway

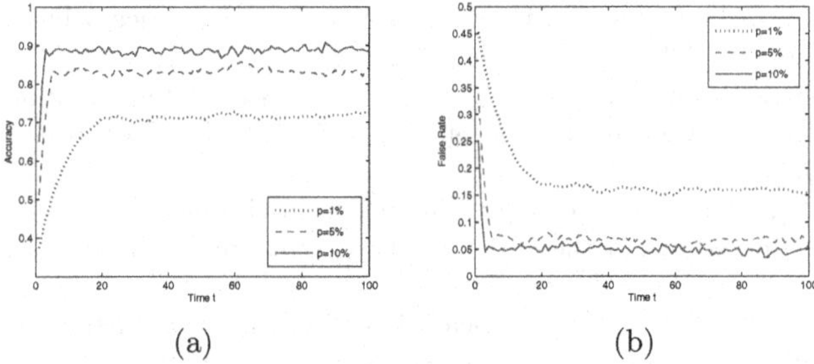

Fig. 2. Accuracy and False Rate of the inferred global topology q_{net} during the simulation time $[1, 100]$

high accuracy (70%) and a low false rate (15%). From Fig. 2, we further notice that the higher the p, the faster the curves become stable, which indicates that the topology information is collected at the gateway at a faster speed.

5 Conclusion

In this paper, we have proposed an approach for topology characterization and inference based on HMMs and social fingerprints. The social fingerprint encodes the activities in the social neighborhood of a node into a short bit string. It contains partial local topology information for the nodes in the nearby neighborhood and serves as the observation to the social network of the nodes. All observations to the social network of a node are employed to estimate the HMM model parameters of the node's social neighborhood. Given the model parameters and the observation sequence, the corresponding evolution of the local logical topology can be inferred based on the Viterbi algorithm. The evaluation results indicate the effectiveness of our approach.

Note that the proposed approach does not pose any special assumptions on the network configurations and settings (e.g., communication patterns). Therefore it is applicable to a wide range of networks. As a future research, we will investigate the realtime topology inference.

References

1. Lowekamp, B., O'Hallaron, D., Gross, T.: Topology discovery for large ethernet networks. SIGCOMM Comput. Commun. Rev. 31(4), 237–248 (2001)
2. Breitbart, Y., Garofalakis, M., Jai, B., Martin, C., Rastogi, R., Silberschatz, A.: Topology discovery in heterogeneous ip networks: the netinventory system. IEEE/ACM Trans. Netw. 12(3), 401–414 (2004)
3. Coates, M., Castro, R., Nowak, R., Gadhiok, M., King, R., Tsang, Y.: Maximum likelihood network topology identification from edge-based unicast measurements. SIGMETRICS Perform. Eval. Rev. 30(1), 11–20 (2002)
4. Rabbat, M., Nowak, R., Coates, M.: Multiple source, multiple destination network tomography. In: IEEE INFOCOM, vol. 3, pp. 1628–1639 (2004)
5. Fragouli, C., Markopoulou, A., Diggavi, S.: Topology inference using network coding techniques. In: Allerton Conference (2006)
6. Marinakis, D., Dudek, G., Fleet, D.: Learning sensor network topology through monte carlo expectation maximization. In: IEEE Intl. Conf. on Robotics and Automation (2005)
7. Marinakis, D., Dudek, G.: Topology inference for a vision-based sensor network. In: CRV 2005: Proceedings of the 2nd Canadian conference on Computer and Robot Vision (2005)
8. Marinakis, D., Dudek, G.: A practical algorithm for network topology inference. In: IEEE Intl. Conf. on Robotics and Automation (2006)
9. Deb, B., Bhatangar, S., Nath, B.: A topology discovery algorithm for sensor networks with applications to network management. In: IEEE CAS Workshop on Wireless Communications and Networking (2002)
10. Khedr, A.M., Osamy, W.: A topology discovery algorithm for sensor network using smart antennas. Computer Communications 29(12), 2261–2268 (2006)
11. Rabiner, L.R.: A tutorial on hidden markov models and selected applications in speech recognition. Readings in speech recognition, 267–296 (1990)
12. Bilmes, J.: A gentle tutorial on the em algorithm and its application to parameter estimation for gaussian mixture and hidden markov models. In: Technical Report, University of Berkeley, ICSI-TR-97-021 (1997)
13. Viterbi, A.: Error bounds for convolutional codes and an asymptotically optimum decoding algorithm. IEEE Transactions on Information Theory 13(2), 260–269 (1967)

Maximum Independent Set of Links under Physical Interference Model*

Peng-Jun Wan[1], Xiaohua Jia[2], and Frances Yao[2]

[1] Illinois Institute of Technology, Chicago IL 60616, USA
[2] City Univesrsity of Hong Kong, Kowloon, Hong Kong

Abstract. This paper addresses the following optimization problem in a plane multihop wireless networks under the physical interference model: From a given a set of communication links whose senders transmit at a fixed uniform power level, select a maximum set of independent links. This problem is known to be NP-hard. The existing approximation algorithms which were claimed to have constant approximation bounds are either valid only in the absence of background noise or simply incorrect in the presence of background noise. In this paper, we develop a new approximation algorithm with constant approximation bound regardless of the value of the background noise. In addition, our approximation bound valid in general is significantly smaller than all the known bounds which are only valid under certain special assumptions.

1 Introduction

This paper studies how to select a maximum number of interference-free links from a given set of communication links subject to the physical interference constraint. We adopt the following model of the multihop wireless networks. All the networking nodes V lie in plane and transmit at a fixed power P. The Euclidean distance between any pair of nodes is denoted by $\|uv\|$. By proper scaling, we assume that the Euclidean distance of a closest pair of the nodes in V is one. The path loss model is then determined by a positive reference loss parameter $\eta < 1$, and the path-loss exponent κ, which is a constant greater than 2 but less than 6 typically. Specifically, when a node u transmits a signal at power P, the power of this signal captured by another node v is $\eta P \|uv\|^{-\kappa}$. The signal quality perceived by a receiver is measured by the *signal to interference and noise ratio* (*SINR*), which is the quotient between the power of the wanted signal and the total power of unwanted signals and the ambient–both internal and external–noise. In order to correctly interpret the wanted signal, the SINR must be no less than certain threshold σ. Formally, consider a link (u, v) and a set W of nodes other than u and transmitting simultaneously with u. Let ξ be the noise power. The SINR of the link (u, v) with respect to W is given by

* This work was supported in part by NSF of USA under grant CNS-0831831, by the RGC of Hong Kong under Project No. 122807, and by the National Basic Research Program of China Grant 2007CB807900, 2007CB807901.

B. Liu et al. (Eds.): WASA 2009, LNCS 5682, pp. 169–178, 2009.

$$\frac{\eta P \|uv\|^{-\kappa}}{\xi + \sum_{w \in W} \eta P \|wv\|^{-\kappa}}.$$

If W is empty (i.e., the interference is absent), the SINR reduces to *signal to noise ratio (SNR)* given by $\eta P \|uv\|^{-\kappa} / \xi$. Let $R = \left(\frac{\eta P}{\sigma \xi}\right)^{1/\kappa}$. Then, a pair of nodes u and v can communicate with each other in the absence of interference if and only if $\|uv\| \leq R$. The value R is thus referred to as the *maximum transmission radius.*

A set $I = \{(u_i, v_i) : 1 \leq i \leq k\}$ of links are said to be *independent* if

1. all links in I are disjoint, i.e., the $2k$ nodes u_i for $1 \leq i \leq k$ and v_i for $1 \leq i \leq k$ are distinct;
2. for each $1 \leq i \leq k$, the SINR of the link (u_i, v_i) with respect to $\{u_j : 1 \leq j \leq k, j \neq i\}$ is at least σ.

The problem **Maximum Independent Set of Links** (**MISL**) seeks a largest number of independent links from a given set A of links. This optimization problem is NP-hard [3]. The first non-trivial approximation algorithm was proposed in [3], with approximation bound $O\left(\log \frac{\max_{a \in A} \|a\|}{\min_{a \in A} \|a\|}\right)$. We remark that the constant hidden inside this bound is very large, and this bound can be arbitrarily large in general. Recently, Goussevskaia et al. [4] made the first effort on developing a constant approximation. However, as observed in [6], the claimed constant approximation bound and its proof (Lemma 4.5 in [4]) are valid only when the noise $\xi = 0$. Indeed, we can construct counter-example to show that the approximation bound can be arbitrarily large in general. Xu and Tang [6] then made an attempt to fix this flaw. The partition the links into two groups: the short group consists of all links of length at most $R/3^{1/\kappa}$, and the long group consists of the rest links. They select the first set of independent links from the short group by simply applying the algorithm developed in [4], and also select the second set of independent links from the long group by a new algorithm. The larger one of these two sets is their output. Unfortunately, their new algorithm for selecting independent links from the long group is incorrect as the selected links may be not independent (Lemma 2 in [6] and its proof are false). Therefore, despite of these efforts, the existence of a constant approximation algorithm for **MISL** remains open.

In this paper, we develop an approximation algorithm for **MISL** which not only has a constant approximation bound regardless of the value of the noise and the lengths of the communication links, but also has a significantly smaller approximation bound. For example, consider the scenario with $\kappa = 4$ and $\sigma = 16$. The approximation bounds obtained in [4] (in the absence of noise) and in [6] (restricted to short links) are huge constants at least 138135 and 137890 respectively. In contrast, our approximation bound is at most 272, which is more than 500 times smaller than these two known bounds and is independent of the noise value and link lengths.

The remaining of this paper is organized as follows. Section 2 introduces a new concept of relative interference and its fundamental properties. Section 3 presents the design and analysis of our approximation algorithm. Finally, Section 4 discusses some generalizations and future works.

2 Relative Interference

Consider a link $a = (u, v)$ and a set W of "interfering" nodes other than u. In the presence of the interference from W, the SINR of a is

$$\frac{\eta P \|uv\|^{-\kappa}}{\xi + \sum_{w \in W} \eta P \|wv\|^{-\kappa}} = \frac{1}{\frac{\xi}{\eta P} \|uv\|^{\kappa} + \sum_{w \in W} (\|uv\| / \|wv\|)^{\kappa}}$$
$$= \frac{1}{\frac{1}{\sigma} (\|uv\| / R)^{\kappa} + \sum_{w \in W} (\|uv\| / \|wv\|)^{\kappa}}.$$

It's straightforward to verify that such SINR is at least σ if and only if

$$\sigma \frac{\sum_{w \in W} (\|uv\| / \|wv\|)^{\kappa}}{1 - (\|uv\| / R)^{\kappa}} \leq 1.$$

Motivated by this charaterization, we define the *relative interference* of node w other than u to the link a as

$$RI(w; a) = \sigma \frac{(\|uv\| / \|wv\|)^{\kappa}}{1 - (\|uv\| / R)^{\kappa}},$$

and define the *relative interference* of a set W of nodes other than u to a as

$$RI(W; a) = \sum_{w \in W} RI(w; a).$$

Then, in the presence of the interference from W, the link (u, v) succeeds if and only if the relative interference of W to the link (u, v) is at most one. We would like to remark that the relative interference defined in this paper is different from the one defined in [4]. In [4], the relative interference of node w other than u to the link a was defined to be $(\|uv\| / \|wv\|)^{\kappa}$, and the relative interference of a set W of nodes other than u to a was defined to be $\sum_{w \in W} (\|uv\| / \|wv\|)^{\kappa}$.

Now, we present a some simple sufficient condition for $RI(W; a)$ to be less than some given value $\phi \in (0, 1]$. Our condition will utilize the Riemann zeta function in the following form: $\zeta(x) = \sum_{j=1}^{\infty} j^{-x}$. Note $\zeta(1) = \infty$, and for any $x > 1$, $\zeta(x) < x/(x-1)$. The values of $\zeta(x)$ for small values of x are

$$\zeta(1.5) = 2.612, \zeta(2) = \frac{\pi^2}{6}, \zeta(2.5) = 1.341, \zeta(3) = 1.202,$$
$$\zeta(3.5) = 1.127, \zeta(4) = \frac{\pi^4}{90}, \zeta(5) = 1.041, \zeta(6) = \frac{\pi^6}{945} = 1.017.$$

Lemma 1. *Consider a link $a = (u, v)$ and a set W of nodes other than u. Suppose that $0 < \phi \leq 1$ and*

$$\rho = 1 + \left(\frac{\sigma \left(16\zeta \left(\kappa - 1 \right) + 8\zeta \left(\kappa \right) - 6 \right)}{\phi \left(1 - \left(\left\| a \right\| / R \right)^{\kappa} \right)} \right)^{1/\kappa}.$$

If all the nodes in $W \cup \{u\}$ *have mutual distances at least* $\rho \|uv\|$, *then* $RI(W; a) < \phi$.

Proof. For each $j \geq 1$, define

$$W_j = \{ w \in W : j\rho r \leq \|uw\| < (j+1) \rho r \},$$

Then, $W_1, W_2, \cdots$ form a partition of W. By a classic result due to Bateman and Erdös [2], $|W_1| \leq 18$. For $j \geq 2$, using the folklore area argument we have $|W_j| \leq 8(2j+1)$. In addition, for each $w \in W_j$ with $j \geq 1$, we have

$$\|wv\| \geq \|wu\| - \|uv\| \geq j\rho r - r \geq j(\rho - 1) r.$$

So,

$$\begin{aligned}
\sigma \sum_{w \in W} \left(\frac{\|uv\|}{\|wv\|} \right)^{\kappa} &= \sigma \sum_{j=1}^{\infty} \sum_{w \in W_j} \left(\frac{\|uv\|}{\|wv\|} \right)^{\kappa} \leq \sigma \sum_{j=1}^{\infty} \frac{|W_j|}{(j(\rho - 1))^{\kappa}} \\
&= \sigma (\rho - 1)^{-\kappa} \left(|W_1| + \sum_{j=2}^{\infty} \frac{|W_j|}{j^{\kappa}} \right) < \sigma (\rho - 1)^{-\kappa} \left(18 + 8 \sum_{j=2}^{\infty} \frac{2j+1}{j^{\kappa}} \right) \\
&\leq \sigma (\rho - 1)^{-\kappa} \left(16\zeta(\kappa - 1) + 8\zeta(\kappa) - 6 \right) = \phi \left(1 - \left(\frac{\|uv\|}{R} \right)^{\kappa} \right).
\end{aligned}$$

Thus, the lemma follows.

Next, we present a necessary condition for $RI(W; a) \leq 1$.

Lemma 2. *Consider a link* $a = (u, v)$ *and a set* W *of nodes other than* u *whose distances from* u *is at most* $\rho \|uv\|$. *If* $RI(W; a) \leq 1$, *then*

$$|W| \leq \frac{(\rho + 1)^{\kappa}}{\sigma} \left(1 - \left(\frac{\|uv\|}{R} \right)^{\kappa} \right).$$

Proof. Assume to the contrary that

$$|W| > \frac{(\rho + 1)^{\kappa}}{\sigma} \left(1 - \left(\frac{\|uv\|}{R} \right)^{\kappa} \right).$$

For any $w \in W$,

$$\|wv\| \leq \|wu\| + \|uv\| \leq (\rho + 1) \|uv\|.$$

Thus,

$$\sigma \sum_{w \in W} \left(\frac{\|uv\|}{\|wv\|} \right)^{\kappa} \geq \frac{\sigma |W|}{(\rho + 1)^{\kappa}} > \left(1 - \left(\frac{\|uv\|}{R} \right)^{\kappa} \right).$$

Hence, $RI(W; a) > 1$, which is a contradiction. So, the lemma holds.

3 Algorithm Design and Analysis

Our approximation algorithm for **MISL** is outlined in Table 1. The algorithm is associated with a parameter $\phi \in (0,1]$, whose value will be determined later on. Let A be the set of given communication links of length at most R. Three variables are maintained by the algorithm. S is the sequence–sorted in the increasing order of length–of links which haven't been selected or discarded, I stores the set of selected independent links, and U stores the senders of the links in I. The algorithm is iterative. In each iteration, the first link a in S is moved from S to I, and its sender is added to U. Then, some links from S are discarded in two steps. The first step discards all links in S whose senders are close to the sender of a. A parameter ρ is used to guide such discarding in the first step. The value of ρ is specified in the algorithm. It decreases with ϕ and but increases with the length of a. After the computation of ρ, all links in S whose senders lie in the disk of radius $\rho \|a\|$ centered at the sender of a are removed from S. The second step removes all links remaining in S to which the relative interference of U exceed $1-\phi$. Such iteration is then repeated until S is empty.

Table 1. The description of the approximation algorithm for **MISL**

Approximation Algorithm for MISL:
$S \leftarrow$ sequence of links in A in the increasing order of length;
$I \leftarrow \emptyset$, $U \leftarrow \emptyset$;
While $S \neq \emptyset$
  $a = (u,v) \leftarrow$ the first link in S;
  $S \leftarrow S \setminus \{a\}$, $I \leftarrow I \cup \{a\}$, $U \leftarrow U \cup \{u\}$;
  $\rho \leftarrow 1 + \left(\frac{\sigma(16\zeta(\kappa-1)+8\zeta(\kappa)-6)}{\phi(1-(\|uv\|/R)^\kappa)}\right)^{1/\kappa}$;
  $S' \leftarrow \{(u',v') \in S : \|u'u\| < \rho \|uv\|\}$;
  $S \leftarrow S \setminus S'$;
  $S'' \leftarrow \{a'' \in S : RI(U,a'') > 1-\phi\}$;
  $S \leftarrow S \setminus S''$;
Output I.

Next, we prove the correctness of the algorithm and derive its approximation bound. We introduce the following notations. Suppose that the algorithm runs in k iterations, and $a_i = (u_i, v_i)$ is the link selected in the i-th iteration for each $1 \leq i \leq k$. Then, the output I consists of $a_1, a_2, \cdots, a_k$. Let

$$U_0 = \emptyset,$$

$$\rho_0 = 1 + \left(\frac{\sigma(16\zeta(\kappa-1)+8\zeta(\kappa)-6)}{\phi}\right)^{1/\kappa},$$

and for each $1 \leq i \leq k$, let U_i and ρ_i be the set U and the parameter ρ respectively at the end of the i-th iteration. Then, for each $1 \leq i \leq k$,

$$U_i = \{u_j : 1 \leq j \leq i\},$$

$$\rho_i = 1 + \left(\frac{\sigma \left(16\zeta\left(\kappa - 1\right) + 8\zeta\left(\kappa\right) - 6\right)}{\phi\left(1 - \left(\|a_i\| / R\right)^{\kappa}\right)} \right)^{1/\kappa}.$$

It's easy to verify that for each $1 \leq i \leq k$,

$$\rho_i = 1 + \frac{\rho_0 - 1}{\left(1 - \left(\|a_i\| / R\right)^{\kappa}\right)^{1/\kappa}}$$

and $\rho_0 \leq \rho_1 \leq \rho_2 \leq \cdots \leq \rho_k$.

The theorem below asserts the correctness of our algorithm.

Theorem 1. *The output set I is independent.*

Proof. It's sufficient to show that for any $1 \leq i \leq k$, $RI\left(U \setminus \{u_i\}; a_i\right) \leq 1$. Fix an integer i between 1 and k. Since a_i is not discarded, $RI\left(U_{i-1}; a_i\right) \leq 1 - \phi$. Since none of $a_i, a_{i+1}, \cdots, a_k$ is discarded, for each $i \leq j < j' \leq k$, we have $\|u_j u_{j'}\| \geq \rho_j \|a_j\| \geq \rho_i \|a_i\|$. So, the mutual distances of the nodes $U \setminus U_{i-1}$ are at least $\rho_i \|a_i\|$. By Lemma 1, $RI\left(U \setminus U_i; a_i\right) \leq \phi$. Therefore,

$$RI\left(U \setminus \{u_i\}; a_i\right) = RI\left(U_{i-1}; a_i\right) + RI\left(U \setminus U_i; a_i\right) \leq 1.$$

So, the theorem holds.

Let

$$\mu_1 = \left\lfloor \frac{2\pi}{\sqrt{3}} \left(\frac{\rho_0}{\sigma^{1/\kappa} - 1} \right)^2 + \pi \frac{\rho_0}{\sigma^{1/\kappa} - 1} \right\rfloor + 1,$$

$$\mu_2 = 5 \left\lceil \left((1 - \phi)^{-\frac{1}{\kappa}} + 2\sigma^{-\frac{1}{\kappa}} \right)^{\kappa} \right\rceil.$$

The theorem below presents an approximation bound of our algorithm.

Theorem 2. *I is an $(1 + \mu_1 + \mu_2)$-approximation.*

We give a brief overview on the proof. For each $1 \leq j \leq k$, S'_j and S''_j be the sets S' and S'' respectively discarded from S in the j-th iteration. Let $A' = S'_1 \cup S'_2 \cup \cdots \cup S'_k$ and $A'' = S''_1 \cup S''_2 \cup \cdots \cup S''_k$. Then, I, S' and S'' form a partition of A. Consider an optimal solution OPT. We will prove in Lemma 3 that for each $1 \leq i \leq k$, $|OPT \cap S'_i| \leq \mu_1$, and in Lemma 4 that $|OPT \cap A''| \leq \mu_2 k$. Then,

$$|OPT \cap A'| = \sum_{j=1}^{k} |OPT \cap S'_i| \leq \mu_1 k.$$

So,

$$|OPT| = |OPT \cap I| + |OPT \cap A'| + |OPT \cap A''| \leq (1 + \mu_1 + \mu_2)\, k,$$

and Theorem 2 follows.

Lemma 3. *For each* $1 \leq i \leq k$, $|OPT \cap S'_i| \leq \mu_1$.

Proof. We first show that for any pair of links (u, v) and (u', v') in $OPT \cap S'_i$,

$$\frac{\|u'u\|}{\|a_i\|} \geq \frac{\sigma^{1/\kappa}}{(1-(\|a_i\|/R)^\kappa)^{1/\kappa}} - 1.$$

Since

$$\sigma\left(\frac{\|uv\|}{\|u'v\|}\right)^\kappa \leq 1 - \left(\frac{\|uv\|}{R}\right)^\kappa,$$

we have

$$\frac{\|u'v\|}{\|uv\|} \geq \frac{\sigma^{1/\kappa}}{(1-(\|uv\|/R)^\kappa)^{1/\kappa}} \geq \frac{\sigma^{1/\kappa}}{(1-(\|a_i\|/R)^\kappa)^{1/\kappa}}.$$

Thus,

$$\frac{\|u'u\|}{\|a_i\|} \geq \frac{\|u'v\| - \|uv\|}{\|uv\|} = \frac{\|u'v\|}{\|uv\|} - 1 \geq \frac{\sigma^{1/\kappa}}{(1-(\|a_i\|/R)^\kappa)^{1/\kappa}} - 1.$$

Now, we show that

$$\frac{\rho_i}{\frac{\sigma^{1/\kappa}}{(1-(\|a_i\|/R)^\kappa)^{1/\kappa}} - 1} < \frac{\rho}{\sigma^{1/\kappa} - 1}.$$

Since

$$\rho_i = 1 + \frac{\rho - 1}{(1-(\|a_i\|/R)^\kappa)^{1/\kappa}},$$

we have

$$\frac{\rho_i}{\frac{\sigma^{1/\kappa}}{(1-(\|a_i\|/R)^\kappa)^{1/\kappa}} - 1} = \frac{1 + \frac{\rho-1}{(1-(\|a_i\|/R)^\kappa)^{1/\kappa}}}{\frac{\sigma^{1/\kappa}}{(1-(\|a_i\|/R)^\kappa)^{1/\kappa}} - 1} = \frac{(1-(\|a_i\|/R)^\kappa)^{1/\kappa} + \rho - 1}{\sigma^{1/\kappa} - (1-(\|a_i\|/R)^\kappa)^{1/\kappa}}$$
$$< \frac{1 + \rho - 1}{\sigma^{1/\kappa} - 1} = \frac{\rho}{\sigma^{1/\kappa} - 1}.$$

Finally, we show that $|OPT \cap S'_i| \leq \mu_1$. Note that the senders of all links in $OPT \cap S'_i$ lie in the disk of radius $\rho_i \|a_i\|$ centered at u_i and their mutual distances are at least

$$\left(\frac{\sigma^{1/\kappa}}{(1-(\|a_i\|/R)^\kappa)^{1/\kappa}} - 1\right)\|a_i\|.$$

By Groemer's Inequality [5] on disk packing,

$$|OPT \cap S'_i| \leq \frac{2\pi}{\sqrt{3}}\left(\frac{\rho_i}{\frac{\sigma^{1/\kappa}}{(1-(\|a_i\|/R)^\kappa)^{1/\kappa}} - 1}\right)^2 + \pi\frac{\rho_i}{\frac{\sigma^{1/\kappa}}{(1-(\|a_i\|/R)^\kappa)^{1/\kappa}} - 1} + 1$$
$$< \frac{2\pi}{\sqrt{3}}\left(\frac{\rho}{\sigma^{1/\kappa} - 1}\right)^2 + \pi\frac{\rho}{\sigma^{1/\kappa} - 1} + 1.$$

Since $|OPT \cap S'_i|$ is an integer, we have

$$|OPT \cap S'_i| \leq \left\lfloor \frac{2\pi}{\sqrt{3}} \left(\frac{\rho}{\sigma^{1/\kappa} - 1} \right)^2 + \pi \frac{\rho}{\sigma^{1/\kappa} - 1} \right\rfloor + 1 = \mu_1.$$

So, the lemma holds.

Lemma 4. $|OPT \cap S''| \leq \mu_2 k$.

Proof. We prove the lemma by contradiction. Assume to the contrary that $|OPT \cap S''| > \mu_2 k$. Clearly, all links in $OPT \cap S''$ are disjoint. In addition, all links in $(OPT \cap S'') \cup S$ are also disjoint. Let W denote the set of senders of the links in $|OPT \cap S''|$, and let $l = \left\lceil \left((1-\phi)^{-\frac{1}{\kappa}} + 2\sigma^{-\frac{1}{\kappa}} \right)^{\kappa} \right\rceil$. We iteratively construct kl disjoint subsets W_{ij} for $1 \leq i \leq k$ and $1 \leq j \leq l$ as follows. Initialize W' to W and each W_{ij} to be the empty set. Repeat the following iterations for each $i = 1$ to k and for each $j = 1$ to q. Let w be a node in W' which is closest to u_i. Draw six (closed) 60°-sectors originating at u_i such that one of six boundary rays goes through w. Add w to W_{ij}. For each of these four sectors not containing w, if it contains at least one node in W', we choose a node among these nodes in W' and in this sector which is nearest to u_i and add it to W_{ij}. After that we remove W_{ij} from W' and repeat the iterations.

By the construction, each W_{ij} contains at most 5 nodes. Hence,

$$\sum_{i=1}^{k} \sum_{j=1}^{l} |W_{ij}| \leq 5kl = \mu_2 k.$$

Thus, the set $W \setminus \bigcup_{i=1}^{k} \bigcup_{j=1}^{q} W_{ij}$ is non-empty. Pick an arbitrary node u in this set and suppose that (u, v) is the link in $OPT \cap S''$. For each $1 \leq i \leq k$ and $1 \leq j \leq l$, there is a node $w_{ij} \in W_{ij}$ such that $\|u_i w_{ij}\| \leq \|u_i u\|$ and the angle $\angle w u_i u \leq 60^o$ by the construction of W_{ij}. Let L_i denote the lune of u_i and u, which is the intersection of the two disks of radius $\|u_i u\|$ centered at u_i and u respectively. Then, each w_{ij} lies in L_i. Thus each L_i contains at least l nodes in W. Let $\rho' = 1 + \left(\frac{\sigma}{1-\phi} \right)^{\frac{1}{\kappa}}$. By Lemma 2,

$$\frac{(\|u_i u\| / \|uv\| + 1)^{\kappa}}{\sigma} > l = \left\lceil \left((1-\phi)^{-\frac{1}{\kappa}} + 2\sigma^{-\frac{1}{\kappa}} \right)^{\kappa} \right\rceil = \left\lceil \frac{(\rho'+1)^{\kappa}}{\sigma} \right\rceil \geq \frac{(\rho'+1)^{\kappa}}{\sigma},$$

and hence $\|u_i u\| / \|uv\| > \rho'$.

We claim that

$$\left(\frac{\|uv\|}{\|u_i v\|} \right)^{\kappa} \leq (1-\phi) \sum_{j=1}^{l} \left(\frac{\|uv\|}{\|w_{ij} v\|} \right)^{\kappa}.$$

Indeed, for each $1 \leq j \leq l$,

$$\frac{\|u_i v\|}{\|w_{ij} v\|} \geq \frac{\|u_i u\| - \|uv\|}{\|w_{ij} u\| + \|uv\|} \geq \frac{\|u_i u\| - \|uv\|}{\|u_i u\| + \|uv\|} = \frac{\|u_i u\| / \|uv\| - 1}{\|u_i u\| / \|uv\| + 1}$$
$$= 1 - \frac{2}{\|u_i u\| / \|uv\| + 1} \geq 1 - \frac{2}{\rho' + 1} = \frac{\rho' - 1}{\rho' + 1}.$$

Hence,

$$\frac{\sum_{j=1}^{l} \left(\frac{\|uv\|}{\|w_{ij} v\|}\right)^{\kappa}}{\left(\frac{\|uv\|}{\|u_i v\|}\right)^{\kappa}} = \sum_{j=1}^{l} \left(\frac{\|u_i v\|}{\|w_{ij} v\|}\right)^{\kappa} \geq l \left(\frac{\rho' - 1}{\rho' + 1}\right)^{\kappa}$$
$$\geq \frac{(\rho' + 1)^{\kappa}}{\sigma} \left(\frac{\rho' - 1}{\rho' + 1}\right)^{\kappa} = \frac{(\rho' - 1)^{\kappa}}{\sigma} = \frac{1}{1 - \phi}.$$

So, the claim holds.

By the above claim, we have

$$\sigma \sum_{i=1}^{k} \left(\frac{\|uv\|}{\|u_i v\|}\right)^{\kappa} \leq (1 - \phi)\, \sigma \sum_{i=1}^{k} \sum_{j=1}^{l} \left(\frac{\|uv\|}{\|w_{ij} v\|}\right)^{\kappa} \leq (1 - \phi) \left(1 - \left(\frac{\|uv\|}{R}\right)^{\kappa}\right).$$

Therefore, the relative interference of $\{u_i : 1 \leq i \leq k\}$ to the link (u, v) is at most $1 - \phi$. This means (u, v) shouldn't have been removed, which is a contradiction. So, the lemma holds.

Finally, we choose the appropriate value of ϕ so that the overall approximation bound $\mu_1 + \mu_2 + 1$ is as small as possible. Clearly, μ_1 decreases with ϕ, and μ_2 increases with ϕ. So, it's not apparent where $\mu_1 + \mu_2 + 1$ can achieve its minimum. We will exploit the convexity to quickly find a suboptimal value of ϕ. Note that for $\kappa > 2$, both x^{κ} and $x^{-1/\kappa}$ are convex function of x on $(0, \infty)$. Using the fact the composite of two convex functions is also convex, we can assert the convexity of the next two functions in $(0, 1)$:

$$f_1(\phi) = \frac{2\pi}{\sqrt{3}} \left(\frac{\rho_0}{\sigma^{1/\kappa} - 1}\right)^2 + \pi \frac{\rho_0}{\sigma^{1/\kappa} - 1} + 1,$$
$$f_2(\phi) = 5 \left((1 - \phi)^{-\frac{1}{\kappa}} + 2\sigma^{-\frac{1}{\kappa}}\right)^{\kappa}.$$

By using standard binary search, we can obtain a short sub-interval of $(0, 1)$ containing the value of ϕ minimizing $f_1(\phi) + f_2(\phi)$. Then, we take a small number of samples of ϕ in this sub-interval. Among these samples, the one corresponding to the smallest value of $\mu_1 + \mu_2 + 1$ is then chosen as the value of ϕ.

For example, consider a scenario with $\kappa = 4$ and $\sigma = 16$. An appropriate choice of ϕ is 0.5. For such choice, $\rho = 6.145$, $\mu_1 = 156$, and $\mu_2 = 115$. So, the approximation bound of our algorithm is 272. In contrast, the approximation bounds obtained in [4] (in the absence of noise) and in [6] (restricted to short links) are

$$1+\left(2\left(2^5 3^2 \sigma \frac{\kappa-1}{\kappa-2}\right)^{1/\kappa}+1\right)^{\kappa}+5\cdot 3^{\kappa+1}$$

and

$$1+\left(2\left(2^5 3^2 \sigma \frac{\kappa-1}{\kappa-2}\right)^{1/\kappa}+1\right)^{\kappa}+5\cdot 2^{\kappa+1}\left(\left\lceil 3^{\kappa}\right\rceil/\sigma+1\right)$$

respectively. When $\kappa = 4$ and $\sigma = 16$, these two approximation bounds are at least 138135 and 137890 respectively, both of which are more than 500 times the approximation bound 272 of our algorithm.

4 Discussions

In this paper, we developed a constant-approximation algorithm for **MISL** under the assumption that the uniform transmission power by all nodes. Such assumption can be slightly relaxed to that all nodes transmit at different but fixed power levels and either the ratio of the maximum power level to the minimum power level or the number of power levels is bounded by a constant. It is also straightforward to extend our algorithm design and analysis to the case that the neworking nodes are located in a three-dimensional space.

There are two challenging variants of **MISL**. In the weighted variant of **MISL**, all input links are associated with some weights, and we would like to seek an independent set of input links whose total weight is maximized. In the power-adjustable variant, all nodes can freely adjust their transmission powers and the selection of the power levels is part of the problem. This variant is also NP-hard [1]. Neither of these two variants is known to have an logarithmic-approximation algorithm, let alone a constant-approximation algorithm. Any progress on these two variants towards constant-approximations would be significant.

References

1. Andrews, M., Dinitz, M.: Maximizing Capacity in Arbitrary Wireless Networks in the SINR Model: Complexity and Game Theory. In: Proc. of the 28th IEEE INFOCOM (April 2009)
2. Bateman, P., Erdös, P.: Geometrical extrema suggested by a lemma of besicovitch. The American Mathematical Monthly, 306–314 (May 1951)
3. Goussevskaia, O., Oswald, Y.A., Wattenhofer, R.: Complexity in geometric SINR. In: Proc. of the 8th ACM MOBIHOC, September 2007, pp. 100–109 (2007)
4. Goussevskaia, O., Halldorsson, M., Wattenhofer, R., Welzl, E.: Capacity of Arbitrary Wireless Networks. In: Proc. of the 28th IEEE INFOCOM (April 2009)
5. Groemer, H.: Über die Einlagerung von Kreisen in einen konvexen Bereich. Math. Zeitschrift. 73, 285–294 (1960)
6. Xu, X.-H., Tang, S.-J.: A Constant Approximation Algorithm for Link Scheduling in Arbitrary Networks under Physical Interference Model. In: The Second ACM International Workshop on Foundations of Wireless Ad Hoc and Sensor Networking and Computing (May 2009)

CSR: Constrained Selfish Routing in Ad-Hoc Networks

Christine Bassem and Azer Bestavros

Computer Science Department, Boston University, Boston MA 02215, USA

Abstract. Routing protocols for ad-hoc networks assume that the nodes forming the network are either under a single authority, or else that they would be altruistically forwarding data for other nodes with no expectation of a return. These assumptions are unrealistic since in ad-hoc networks, nodes are likely to be autonomous and rational (selfish), and thus unwilling to help unless they have an incentive to do so. Providing such incentives is an important aspect that should be considered when designing ad-hoc routing protocols. In this paper, we propose a dynamic, decentralized routing protocol for ad-hoc networks that provides incentives in the form of payments to intermediate nodes used to forward data for others. In our Constrained Selfish Routing (CSR) protocol, game-theoretic approaches are used to calculate payments (incentives) that ensure both the truthfulness of participating nodes and the fairness of the CSR protocol. We show through simulations that CSR is an energy efficient protocol and that it provides lower communication overhead in the best and average cases compared to existing approaches.

1 Introduction

Motivation: The design and implementation of practical routing protocols for ad-hoc networks is still an open and challenging problem, whose solution is critical for the widespread deployment of the many distributed applications envisioned for ad-hoc networks.

Most of the ad-hoc routing protocols proposed in the current literature presume that nodes are cooperative and are always willing to contribute their own resources (*e.g.*, power, bandwidth, storage) in support of routing processes. In such settings, nodes are assumed to be truthful in the sense that intermediate nodes do not alter the content of forwarded packets and do not mischaracterize routing parameters so as to gain an advantage with respect to routing. However, in real settings, nodes of an ad-hoc network are under the control of individuals, who may not necessarily be cooperative. Indeed, such individuals are likely to be rational, selfish, or even malicious. Malicious nodes are those bent on disrupting the network functionality, whereas rational, selfish nodes are those that do not aim to disrupt the network, but are simply interested in maximizing the utility they beget from the network, even if doing so requires them to be untruthful.

Besides cooperative routing protocols, there have been several proposed routing protocols that provide incentives for nodes to help out in carrying the network

B. Liu et al. (Eds.): WASA 2009, LNCS 5682, pp. 179–189, 2009.

load. Such incentives can be in the form of payment for cooperation [1,2,3,4,5] or in the form of punishment (disincentives) for non-cooperation [6,7]. In this paper, we focus on payment-based models, where nodes are rewarded for their help. In these models as well as in ours, a node would be willing to inform other nodes of its private (secret) costs for providing help in order to get paid, and a node would be willing to lie about its (or others') costs if this might lead to a higher payment.

Related Work: Routing protocols for ad-hoc networks vary greatly in design and in the assumptions they make about the network. Several protocols assume that the nodes in the network are selfless (altruistic) and are willing to help other nodes when such help is needed [8,9,10,11].

The Ad-hoc On-demand Distance Vector (AODV) protocol [8] and the Dynamic Source Routing protocol [9] are both reactive protocols, wherein routes are established on demand, thus reducing the communication overhead. In DSR, all the route information is kept in the control packets. This means that control packets grow larger as the route grows longer. This is in contrast to AODV where all route information is stored locally at the nodes and the control packet sizes remain constant. Therefore, AODV is largely considered a faster and less power-consuming protocol than DSR [10,11].

As we alluded earlier, in realistic settings, nodes are expected to be selfish, and thus would not help unless incentivised to do so (through the use of reward or punishment mechanisms). Example mechanisms that punish non-cooperative nodes through the use of reputation-based protocols include the works described in [6,7]. Example mechanisms that reward cooperative nodes include the works described in [1,2,5,3,4]. In [2] the intermediate nodes are paid with a virtual currency called NUGLETS. In [5], Sprite is proposed which provides incentive – in a game theoretic sense – for mobile nodes to cooperate and report actions honestly.

In Ad-hoc VCG [1], the route discovery process is based on the DSR [9] protocol where the source node floods a request packet to all of its neighbors looking for a path to the destination. Each intermediate node appends to the request packet its own costs to send data. This information is forwarded to its neighbors and so on until the request reaches the destination node. The destination node collects all the requests flooded through the network and integrates them to build a complete logical view of the network. Using this information, the destination chooses the most cost-efficient path and uses a variation of the VCG model (named after Vickrey [12], Clarke [13] and Groves [14]) to calculate the payments to be given to each intermediate node in that path. Using the VCG payment model, the destination node calculates for each intermediate node (i) in the most cost efficient path (SP) the cost of the second most-cost-efficient path without that node (SP^{-i}). As the intermediate node cooperates in delivering data from the source to the destination, it receives a payment to cover its costs plus a premium to ensure that the nodes would not lie about their secret costs. This premium is the difference between the costs of SP and SP^{-i}.

Paper Contributions and Organization: As mentioned above, the main disadvantage of DSR when compared to AODV is the increased communication overhead. In contrast, the Constrained Selfish Routing (CSR) protocol that we propose in this paper uses the Ad-hoc On demand Distance Vector (AODV) protocol [8] to decrease the communication overhead thus decreasing the power consumption at the nodes. In that respect, we design a mechanism that provides the most cost efficient path between a pair nodes in the network. It is a power efficient protocol that ensures the truthfulness of the nodes participating in it. We describe the system model in section 2, followed by a detailed description of the proposed Constrained Selfish Routing protocol in section 3. In section 4, we analyze the protocol's truthfulness properties and its overhead. In section 5, we evaluate the protocol's performance through simulations and provide results that support in an empirical setting the analytical results presented in section 4. Finally in section 6, we conclude the paper with a summary of our contributions.

2 System Model and Assumptions

We augment the model used by Anderegg and Eidenberz in [1] where the network is represented as a graph $G = (V, E, w)$ with the set of vertices V that represent the mobile nodes in the network and the set of directed edges E which represents the unidirectional links between the nodes in the network. The weight function $w : E- > R$ for each edge (i, j) represents the weight of the link between the node i and the node j, which is the cost of transmitting a packet from i to j.

Each node has a unique identifier i and has an individual cost of energy parameter c_i. The cost of energy c_i of a node i is its private type, *i.e.*, only i knows its true value, which is a measure of the level of inconvenience the node faces when asked to forward a packet. One of the factors affecting this measure is the level of difficulty the node faces in order to recharge its power. The payment that a node receives for helping others is proportional to its cost of energy c_i; therefore, a node might lie about its true value of c_i if such a lie would increase its payment.

All nodes use omni-directional antennas for communication, *i.e.*, when a node sends a signal carrying a packet, all neighboring nodes in its transmission range receive that packet. We assume that nodes can control their signal emission power; as the node increases its emission power, its transmission range increases, and as a result more neighboring nodes receive the packets sent and vice versa. When a node i uses an emission power P_i^{emit} to send a packet, the node j at distance d from i receives the signal with power given by

$$P_{i,j}^{rec} = K \times \frac{P_i^{emit}}{d^\alpha} \tag{1}$$

where K is a constant and α is the distance power gradient, another constant that ranges between 2 and 6 depending on the network conditions. A node successfully receives a signal if the power of the received signal is above a certain acceptance threshold. While the acceptance threshold might differ from one node to another in the network, for simplicity, we assume that all nodes in the network agree on the same value for the acceptance threshold P^{rec}_{min}. If the power of the signal received exceeds P^{rec}_{min}, then j successfully receives the packet carried by the signal. However, the original emission power used by node i (P^{emit}_i) might be *overvalued* and less emission power could have been used to successfully send a packet to j. Node j can calculate the minimum emission power that the node i would need to use to send a packet successfully to j using the following formula,

$$P^{min}_{i,j} = \frac{P^{emit}_i . P^{rec}_{min}}{P^{rec}_{i,j}} \tag{2}$$

Once calculated, this value is sent back to i and later, i uses this value as its default emission power – if it needs to transmit a packet to j in the future.

The total weight of a link (i, j) is the product of the cost of energy c_i and the minimum emission power that i uses to send a packet to j.

$$w(i, j) = c_i \times P^{min}_{i,j} \tag{3}$$

As previously mentioned, in the proposed protocol nodes will be paid to forward data for others. In [1], the authors propose two payment models; either the source node is responsible for paying all intermediate nodes or some central authority – a "bank" – holds accounts for all nodes in the network and is responsible for all transactions performed on them. Any node can communicate with the bank if it is in its communication range. If the bank is inaccessible, a node is allowed to store the transaction information locally. This information is relayed to the bank as soon as the bank becomes accessible again in the future. In Ad-Hoc VCG, the authors assume that the bank will deduct the payments given to cooperating nodes from the accounts of all the nodes in the network. In this paper, we assume that the destination node is responsible for calculating the payments for each of the helping nodes and it sends the payment information to the bank. The bank credits the accounts of all the intermediate nodes and debits the accounts of the source and/or destination nodes.

3 Constrained Selfish Routing Protocol

The Constrained Selfish Routing protocol is an on-demand routing protocol for ad-hoc networks. The VCG payment model is used to provide incentives for nodes to help out other nodes in the network as used in [1].

3.1 Overview

CSR consists of three components: route discovery, data transmission and route recovery. When a node S needs to sends data to D but D is not in the transmission range of S, route discovery begins. In route discovery, S floods the network with a request to find a path to D and payments for the intermediate nodes are calculated. The route discovery phase will be explained in more details later in this section.

During data transmission, after the path from S to D is known, the data is sent between them and intermediate nodes get paid for forwarding the data. Whenever the destination node successfully receives a data packet, it keeps track of how much it should pay each intermediate node and when possible it notifies the bank of the payments.

Route recovery is activated when links between nodes are broken during data transmission. If the next hop node is not available for any reason (such as node failures, link failures, or node mobility), the node that detects the failure sends an ERROR packet back to the source node. Upon receipt of such an error report, the source node starts the route discovery all over again.

3.2 Route Discovery

The route discovery in CSR is adapted from the AODV routing protocol, which is an on demand ad-hoc routing protocol proposed by Perkins and Royer in [8]. AODV provides several advantages in ad-hoc networks such as low communication overhead and less power consumption. In CSR, the route discovery phase is divided into two separate phases: the first phase is the actual discovery phase when the most cost-efficient path between the source and destination is found. The second phase is when the payment calculation occurs. Nodes do not have to wait for the termination of this phase to start data transmission as it can start on the completion of the first phase. The second phase can be performed offline and at any time after the first phase is completed or during data transmission.

Phase 1: Finding a route. The first phase is similar to the route discovery phase in AODV [8] where a source node S floods the network with its request to a destination node D. Then S has to wait for D to send out a reply with the most cost efficient path between them to start data transmission.

Packets Used: Two types of packets are used in this phase; the REQUEST and the REPLY packets.

The REQUEST packet is the packet that floods the network. In addition to the typical ID and addressing fields that constitute the *Packet header*, this packet contains a *Cost of Energy* field and an *Emission Power* field which indicates the cost of energy and emission power of the inner source when sending the current instance of the packet and a *Total Weight* field which represents the total weight of the path from the source node to the inner source node.

The REPLY packet is sent out by D and it contains information about the most cost-efficient path between S and D. It is only forwarded by the nodes in the best path between S and D. It contains the Packet Header, the original Request ID and the List of Costs, a list that includes the ID, cost of energy and the minimum power of each intermediate node along the chosen path.

Data Structures Used: During route discovery, each node maintains two data structures to help out in the route discovery phase. The *Best Route Cache* is used to store the best REQUEST packet received for a specific request between a pair of nodes and the *Neighbor Cache* is used to keep track of which of the nodes neighbors can provide a path to the source node.

Details of Phase 1: When a source node S wishes to find a path to a destination D, it prepares the initial REQUEST packet with its cost of energy and emission power and floods it to its neighbors.

When a node j receives a REQUEST packet from neighbor i it follows Algorithm 1 to decide whether to drop the packet or forward it. The weight in the packet is updated and forwarded if the packet carries a better weight than the best weight stored in the Best Route Cache. When the destination node receives the first REQUEST from the source node, it follows the same algorithm but without forwarding the packet with the best weight, and keeps listening for other route REQUEST packets in case a better REQUEST is received from the same source node. If a better REQUEST is received, the corresponding entry in the best route cache is updated. After a timeout period expires, the destination extracts the best REQUEST it received from neighbor i from the Best Route Cache and sends out a REPLY packet with $\{c(i), Pmin(i, D)\}$ to the source node through i.

Algorithm 1. Actions performed by a node j upon receiving a REQUEST packet from node i.

```
if REQUEST has no new information then
    drop REQUEST
else
    Add neighbor i to the Neighbor Cache
    Calculate Pmin(i,j) = Pemit(i) * Prec(min) / Prec(i,j)
    Calculate w = total weight of path from S to j through i
    best = total weight of the best REQUEST stored in the Best Route Cache
    if best is null then
        Replace Pemit(i) with Pmin(i,j) in REQUEST
        Add REQUEST to the Best Route Cache
        Forward REQUEST packet with c(j) and Pemit(j)
    else
        if w < best then
            Replace Pemit(i) with Pmin(i,j) in REQUEST
            Replace entry in the Best Route Cache with the current REQUEST
            Forward REQUEST packet with c(j) and Pemit(j)
        end
    end
end
```

Each intermediate node i receiving the REPLY packet from node j will extract the corresponding best REQUEST packet from the the Best Route Cache and extract the inner source node k from that packet. Then j will add $\{c(k), Pmin(k, i)\}$ to the list of costs in the original REPLY packet and forward it to k.

Once the source node receives the REPLY packet, it can enter the data transmission phase and does not have to wait for the second phase to end.

Phase 2: Payments Calculation. While route discovery allows the destination D to identify the best (most cost-effective) path, D is unable to calculate the payments to the intermediate nodes along that path. As we indicated earlier, in CSR these payments are based on a VCG model, requiring the calculation of the second-best path when each node on the best path is excluded. This process is carried out in Phase 2 of the CSR protocol. This phase is similar to the route discovery performed in phase 1, except that it is done in the opposite direction (from D to S) and the request packets have constraints to not include certain nodes in the discovery.

To start phase 2, S sends to D information about the intermediate nodes in the best path between them. This is done by piggy-backing a CONFIRM packet to the first DATA packet send to D.[1]

Packets Used: We introduce 3 types of packets in this phase, namely, the CONFIRM, FIND and FOUND packets. The CONFIRM packet is piggy-backed with the first DATA packet sent by the source node S. It is used to inform the destination node D about the details of the intermediate nodes in the chosen shortest path (SP) between S and D. There is only one field in the CONFIRM packet; the list of costs that were obtained from the REPLY packet in phase 1. When sending a DATA packet, the source node S signs and appends this list to the packet.

The FIND packet is used to discover whether a path between two nodes without a certain intermediate node. Its fields are the *Packet Header* with multiple inner destinations, the *Excluded Node*, the original *Request ID* and the *Hop Count* which is used to calculate the time out period the node will spend before sending the FOUND packet.

The reply to the FIND packet is the FOUND packet which is used by nodes in the second phase to notify the originator of the FIND packet that a path is indeed found excluding a specific node and it also carries the total weight of that found path. Its fields are the *Packet Header* with multiple inner destinations, the *Excluded Node*, original *Request ID*, *Total Weight* of the path and the *Cost of Energy* and *Emission Power* of the node sending the FOUND packet.

Data Structures Used: During phase 2, each node maintains similar data structures as those kept in phase 1 but for the FIND and FOUND packets.

The first data structure is the *Find Neighbor Cache* which is used to track which neighbors sent similar FIND packets to the node. It is used to keep track of which neighbors have previously sent a FIND packet, to guarantee that only one FIND and one FOUND packets are sent for each request. The second data structure is the *Best Found Cache* which is used to store the best FOUND packet received so far for each corresponding FIND packet.

Details of Phase: Once the destination node D receives the CONFIRM packet, it extracts the list of intermediate nodes in the shortest path between the source and the destination (SP). For each intermediate node i, D will search for a best path from S to D without that intermediate node (SP^{-i}).

---

[1] As mentioned above, this phase can be performed offline and data transmission does not depend on it.

The destination extracts from its Neighbor Cache the set of neighbors N that have paths to the source node and for each intermediate node i obtained from the CONFIRM packet, D will send a FIND packet with Hop Count of 1 excluding i to be sent to all the nodes in the set $N - i$. Then D starts a timer to indicate the end of phase 2.

When an intermediate node i receives a FIND packet from j, it drops the packet if it had been received before. Otherwise, it forwards the packet with an incremented Hop Count to all the nodes in the set of neighbors obtained from the Neighbor Cache except the excluded node. Then,node i starts a timer with a value inversely proportional to the Hop Count in the FIND packet.

When the source node receives a FIND packet with itself in the Destination field, it will send a FOUND packet to the Inner source of the FIND packet.

During the timeout period, when a node j (including the destination node D) receives a FOUND packet from node i, it updates the total weight of the packet and then decides to store the packet in the Best Found Cache if it's the first FOUND packet received for a corresponding FIND or it's the FOUND packet with the better total weight received so far.

When the timer at node i stops, i will extract the best FOUND packet received from the Best Found Cache and extract the set of neighbors from the Find Neighbor Cache. Then the node updates the fields in the FOUND packet and sends it to all the neighbors in list extracted from the Find Neighbor Cache and clears its caches.

When the D finishes its timeout period, it takes the information in the Best Found Cache and calculates the payments that should be made to each intermediate node using the following formula:

$$M(i) = |SP^{-i}| - |SP| + c_i * P_{i,j}^{min} \tag{4}$$

The value $|SP^{-i}|$ is obtained from the FOUND packets in the Best Found Cache and the values $|SP|$, c_i and $P_{i,j}^{min}$ are obtained from the CONFIRM packet received at the beginning of the phase.

4 Analysis

In CSR, since nodes only forward requests with better total weights, we guarantee that the most cost efficient route is always chosen in phase 1 in the route discovery. As for the incentives provided to the nodes in the network, our VCG-based payment model guarantees the truthfulness of all the nodes in the network.

Theorem 1. *CSR guarantees the truthfulness of all the nodes in the network.*

Proof. The payment of each node i is $M(i) = |SP^{-i}| - |SP| + c_i * P_{i,j}^{min}$ which is its utility. As mentioned before, node i may be untruthful (*i.e.*, lie about its type) in order to increase its utility. Let us consider the various possible ways that an intermediate node may be untruthful.

1. The node may lie about the true value of c_i or P_i^{emit} in phases 1 or 2.
2. The node may lie about the computed value $P_{i,j}^{min}$ in phases 1 or 2.

3. The node may change any entry in any packet when forwarding it in phases 1 or 2.

We prove that in CSR, intermediate nodes will be truthful in all of the previously mentioned cases. The complete proof can be found in [15].

A very important aspect of an ad-hoc routing protocol is its communication overhead because it affects the performance of the network and the power consumption at the nodes. We prove that CSR has a linear lower bound on the number packets sent and that the (worst-case) upper bound on the number of overhead packets is equal to that of the Ad-Hoc VCG protocol [1]. The detailed proofs of the theorems below can be found in [15].

Theorem 2. *The lower bound on the overhead of CSR in terms of the number of packets sent is $O(n)$.*

Theorem 3. *An upper bound on the overhead of CSR in terms of the number of packets sent is $O(n^4)$.*

5 Simulation Results

An event-based simulator was designed to simulate ad-hoc networks and to test the performance of various routing protocols. Using this simulator, the performance of CSR is compared to Ad-Hoc VCG [1]. The simulations were run in a closed environment in which any number of simulated nodes move freely.

The mobility model used in the simulator is adopted from the Random Walk model [16]. Initially, each node picks a random direction (Θ) taken from a uniform distribution on the interval $[0, 2\Pi]$. The node moves in the chosen direction for a fixed period (default is 4 seconds) and then pauses for another fixed period of time (a control variable). Next, the node picks a new random direction (Θ') taken from a uniform distribution on the interval $[\Theta - 20, \Theta + 20]$ and repeats the same process. The reason for choosing the interval $[\Theta - 20, \Theta + 20]$ when deciding Θ' is to simulate a realistic motion.

Applications on the simulated wireless nodes are designed to send data to random destinations (picked uniformly at random) at random times, with inter-messaging time picked from an exponential distribution with a mean of 10. Once a destination is chosen, the route discovery of the simulated protocol starts.

Four sets of simulations were performed to measure the efficiency of CSR in various conditions. In all simulations, the environment is $500m \times 500m$ in size, the nodes' transmission range is $100m$ and the total simulation time is $100sec$. The measured performance parameters are the *Communication overhead* which is represented in two forms: the total number of packets sent out during the route discovery phase, the total number of bytes sent out during the route discovery phase, and the *Power consumption rate* which measures the average rate of power consumed by the nodes during the whole simulation.

In the first set of simulations, the number of nodes in the network is varied from 8 to 12 devices, the pause time of each node is 6 sec and the total number of

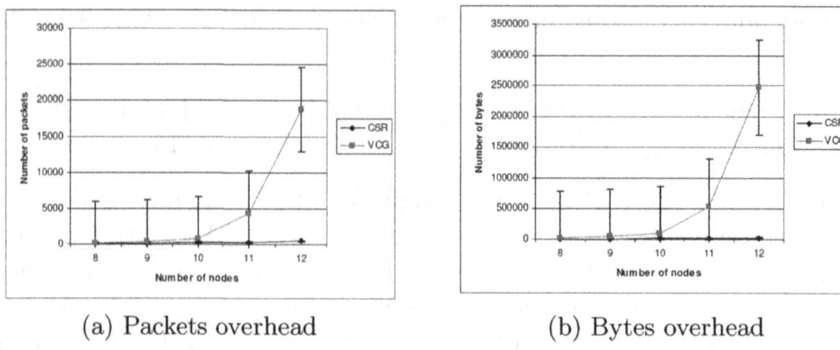

(a) Packets overhead (b) Bytes overhead

Fig. 1. Communication overhead as the network size increases. CSR shows an improved performance over Ad-Hoc VCG.

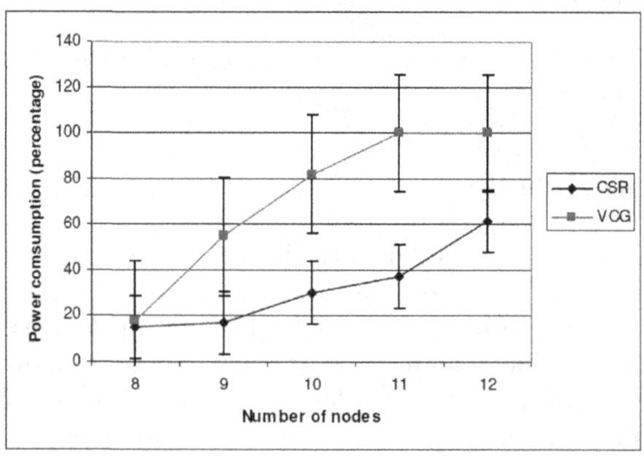

Fig. 2. Power consumption rate as the network size grows larger. CSR is more power efficient that Ad-Hoc VCG.

requests made in each simulations is 5 requests. The performance evaluation of the protocols is shown in Figure 1, Figure 2 . Each value in the graph represent an average of 5 simulation runs with different seeds within a 90th-percentile confidence interval.

The results show that as the network size grows larger, the communication overhead in CSR exhibits a nearly linear growth while Ad-Hoc VCG shows a super-linear growth. This is anticipated from the analytical results (see Theorem 2): CSR has a nearly linear communication overhead in the average case. Moreover, the results prove that CSR is more power efficient than Ad-Hoc VCG because of the less communication overhead of CSR.

The results of the other sets of simulations could be found in [15].

6 Conclusion

The CSR protocol is an incentive-based routing protocol which provides incentives for selfish nodes in the network in a game theoretic setting. In this paper, we have shown CSR to induce thruthful node behavior through the use of a VCG-based model for calculation of payments to intermediate nodes. With truthfulness guaranteed, CSR provides the most cost efficient path between any pair of nodes in an ad-hoc network with a linear lower bound of $O(n)$ on the communication overhead, where n is the number of nodes in the network. The lower communication overhead also guarantees lower power consumption.

Acknowledgment. We would like to acknowledge Professor Nancy Lynch (MIT, CSAIL) for her input and feedback on the work presented in this paper. This work was supported partially by NSF Awards #0820138, #0720604, #0735974, #0524477, and #0520166.

References

1. Anderegg, L., Eidenbenz, S.: Ad hoc-vcg: a truthful and cost-efficient routing protocol for mobile ad hoc networks with selfish agents. In: MobiCom 2003, pp. 245–259 (2003)
2. Buttyan, L., Hubaux, J.: Nuglets: a virtual currency to stimulate cooperation in self-organized ad hoc networks. Technical Report DSC/2001 (2001)
3. Feigenbaum, J., Papadimitriou, C., Sami, R., Shenker, S.: A bgp-based mechanism for lowest-cost routing. Distrib. Comput. 18(1), 61–72 (2005)
4. Zhong, S., Li, L.E., Liu, Y.G., Yang, Y.R.: On designing incentive-compatible routing and forwarding protocols in wireless ad-hoc networks: an integrated approach using game theoretic and cryptographic techniques. Wirel. Netw. 13(6), 799–816 (2007)
5. Zhong, S.: Sprite: A simple, cheat-proof, credit-based system for mobile ad-hoc networks. In: Proceedings of IEEE INFOCOM, pp. 1987–1997 (2003)
6. Buchegger, S., Le Boudec, J.Y.: Performance analysis of the confidant protocol. In: MobiHoc 2002, pp. 226–236 (2002)
7. Buchegger, S., Boudec, J.Y.L.: Nodes bearing grudges: towards routing security, fairness, and robustness in mobile ad hoc networks. In: Proceedings 10th Euromicro Workshop on Parallel, Distributed and Network-based Processing (2002)
8. Perkins, C.E., Royer, E.M.: Ad-hoc on-demand distance vector routing. In: Proceedings of the 2nd IEEE Workshop on Mobile Computing Systems and Applications, pp. 90–100 (1999)
9. Johnson, D.B., Maltz, D.A.: Dynamic source routing in ad hoc wireless networks. In: Mobile Computing, pp. 153–181. Kluwer Academic Publishers, Dordrecht (1996)
10. Misra, P.: Routing protocols for ad hoc mobile wireless networks. Technical report, Ohio State University (1999)
11. Hong, X., Xu, K., Gerla, M.: Scalable routing protocols for mobile ad hoc networks. IEEE Network 16(4), 11–21 (2002)
12. Vickrey, W.: The Journal of Finance (1), 8–37
13. Clarke, E.H.: Multipart pricing of public goods. Public Choice 11(1), 17–33 (1971)
14. Groves, T.: Incentives in teams. Econometrica 41(4), 617–631 (1973)
15. Bassem, C., Bestavros, A.: Csr: Constrained selfish routing in ad-hoc networks. Technical report, Computer Science Department, Boston University (2009)
16. Camp, T., Boleng, J., Davies, V.: A survey of mobility models for ad hoc network research. Wireless Communications & Mobile Computing (WCMC): Special issue on Mobile Ad Hoc Networking: Research, Trends and Applications 2, 483–502 (2002)

Multicast Extensions to the Location-Prediction Based Routing Protocol for Mobile Ad Hoc Networks

Natarajan Meghanathan

Jackson State University,
Jackson, MS 39217, USA
nmeghanathan@jsums.edu

Abstract. We propose multicast extensions to the location prediction-based routing protocol (NR-MLPBR and R-MLPBR) for mobile ad hoc networks to simultaneously reduce the number of tree discoveries, number of links and the hop count per path from the source to the multicast group. The multicast extensions work as follows: Upon failure of a path to the source, a receiver node attempts to locally construct a global topology using the location and mobility information collected during the latest global broadcast tree discovery. NR-MLPBR predicts a path that has the minimum number of hops to the source and R-MLPBR predicts a path to the source that has the minimum number of non-receiver nodes. If the predicted path exists in reality, the source accommodates the path as part of the multicast tree and continues to send the multicast packets in the modified tree. Otherwise, the source initiates another global broadcast tree discovery.

Keywords: Multicast Routing, Mobile Ad hoc Networks, Link Efficiency, Hop Count, Simulation.

1 Introduction

A mobile ad hoc network (MANET) is a dynamic distributed system of wireless nodes that move independent of each other in an autonomous fashion. Due to node mobility, routes between any pair of nodes frequently change and need to be reconfigured. As a result, on-demand route discovery is often preferred over periodic route discovery and maintenance, as the latter strategy will incur significant overhead due to the frequent exchange of control information among the nodes [1]. Multicasting is the process of sending a stream of data from one source node to multiple recipients by establishing a routing tree, which is an acyclic connected subgraph containing all the nodes in the network. The set of receiver nodes form the multicast group. The data gets duplicated, only when necessary, as it propagates down the tree. This is better than multiple unicast transmissions. Multicasting in ad hoc wireless networks has numerous applications, e.g., distributed computing applications like civilian operations, emergency search and rescue, warfare situations and etc.

In an earlier work [2], we developed a location prediction based routing (LPBR) protocol for unicast routing in MANETs. The specialty of LPBR is that it attempts to simultaneously reduce the number of global broadcast route discoveries as well as the

B. Liu et al. (Eds.): WASA 2009, LNCS 5682, pp. 190–199, 2009.

hop count of the paths for a source-destination session. LPBR works as follows: During a regular flooding-based route discovery, LPBR collects the location and mobility information of the nodes in the network and stores the collected information at the destination node of the route search process. When the minimum-hop route discovered through the flooding-based route discovery fails, the destination node attempts to predict the current location of each node using the location and mobility information collected during the latest flooding-based route discovery. A minimum hop path Dijkstra algorithm [3] is run on the locally predicted global topology. If the predicted minimum hop route exists in reality, no expensive flooding-based route discovery is needed and the source continues to send data packets on the discovered route; otherwise, the source initiates another flooding-based route discovery.

In this paper, we propose two multicast extensions to LPBR, referred to as NR-MLPBR and R-MLPBR. Both the multicast extensions are aimed at minimizing the number of global broadcast tree discoveries as well as the hop count per source-receiver path of the multicast tree. They use a similar idea of letting the receiver nodes to predict a new path based on the locally constructed global topology obtained from the location and mobility information of the nodes learnt through the latest broadcast tree discovery. Receiver nodes running NR-MLPBR (Non-Receiver aware Multicast extensions of LPBR) are not aware of the receivers of the multicast group, whereas each receiver node running R-MLPBR (Receiver-aware Multicast Extension of LPBR) is aware of the identity of the other receivers of the multicast group. NR-MLPBR attempts to predict a minimum hop path to the source, whereas R-MLPBR attempts to predict a path to the source that has the minimum number of non-receiver nodes. If more than one path has the same minimum number of non-receiver nodes, then R-MLPBR breaks the tie among such paths by choosing the path with the minimum number of hops to the source. Thus, R-MLPBR is also designed to reduce the number of links in the multicast tree, in addition to the average hop count per source-receiver path and the number of global broadcast tree discoveries.

The rest of the paper is organized as follows: Section 2 provides the detailed design of the two multicast extensions. Section 3 explains the simulation environment and illustrates the simulation results with respect to different performance metrics. Section 4 concludes the paper.

2 Multicast Extensions to LPBR

We assume periodic exchange of beacons in the neighborhood. We also assume that a multicast group comprises basically of receiver nodes that wish to receive data packets from an arbitrary source, which is not part of the multicast group.

2.1 Broadcast of Multicast Tree Request Messages

Whenever a source node has data packets to send to a multicast group and is not aware of a multicast tree to the group, the source initiates a broadcast tree discovery procedure by broadcasting a Multicast Tree Request Message (MTRM) to its neighbors. Each node, including the receiver nodes of the multicast group, on receiving the first MTRM of the current broadcast process (i.e., a MTRM with a sequence number greater than those seen before), includes its Location Update Vector, LUV in the MTRM packet. The LUV of a node comprises the following: node ID, X, Y co-ordinate information, Is Receiver flag, Current velocity and Angle of movement with respect to the X-axis. The *Is Receiver* flag in the LUV, if set, indicates that the node is a receiving node of the multicast group. The node ID is also appended on the "Route record" field of the MTRM packet. The structure of the LUV and the MTRM is shown in Figures 1 and 2 respectively.

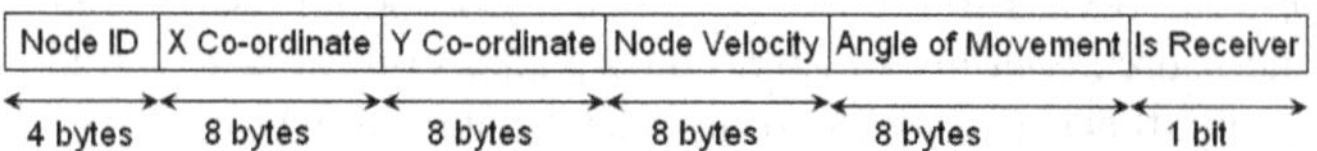

Fig. 1. Location Update Vector (LUV) per Node

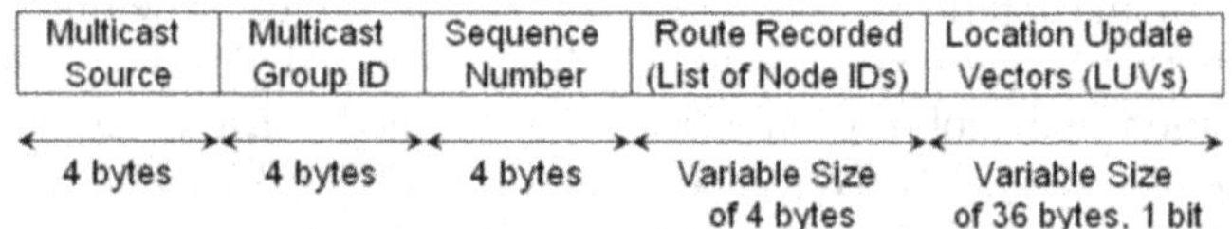

Fig. 2. Structure of the Multicast Tree Request Message

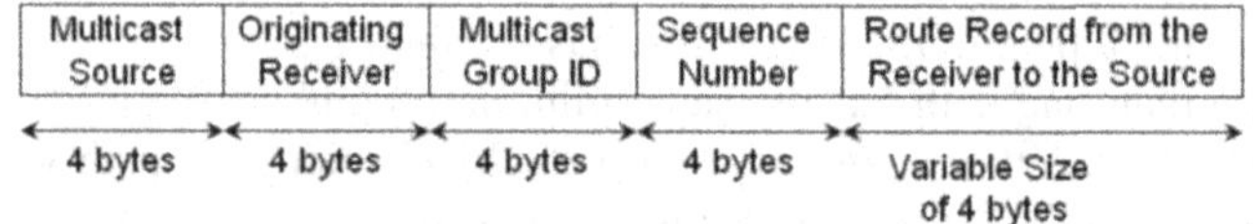

Fig. 3. Structure of Multicast Tree Establishment Message

2.2 Construction of the Multicast Tree

Paths constituting the multicast tree are independently chosen at each receiver node. A receiver node gathers several MTRMs obtained across different paths and selects the minimum hop path among them by looking at the "Route Record" field in these MTRMs. A Multicast Tree Establishment Message (MTEM) is sent on the discovered minimum hop route to the source. The MTEM originating from a receiver node has the list of node IDs corresponding to the nodes that are on the minimum hop path from the receiver node to the source (which is basically the reverse of the route recorded in the MTRM). The structure of the MTEM packet is shown in Figure 3.

An intermediate node upon receiving the MTEM packet checks its multicast routing table whether there exist an entry for the <Multicast Source, Multicast Group ID> in the table. If an entry exists, the intermediate node merely adds the tuple <One-hop sender of the MTEM, Originating Receiver node of the MTEM> to the list of <Downstream node, Receiver node> tuples for the multicast tree entry and does not forward the MTEM further. The set of downstream nodes are part of the multicast tree rooted at the source node for the multicast group. If a <Multicast Source, Multicast Group ID> entry does not exist in the multicast routing table, the intermediate node creates an entry and initializes it with the <One-hop sender of the MTEM, Originating

Receiver node of the MTEM> tuple. For each MTEM received, the source adds the neighbor node that sent the MTEM and the corresponding Originating Receiver node to the list of <Downstream node, Receiver node> tuples for the multicast group.

2.3 Multicast Tree Acquisition and Data Transmission

After receiving the MTEMs from all the receivers within the Tree Acquisition Time (*TAT*), the source starts sending the data packets on the multicast tree. The *TAT* is based on the maximum possible diameter of the network (an input parameter in our simulations). The diameter of a network is the maximum of the hop count of the minimum hop paths between any two nodes in the network. The *TAT* is dynamically set at a node based on the time it took to receive the first MTEM for a broadcast tree discovery procedure. The structure of the header of the multicast data packet is shown in Figure 4. In addition to the regular fields like Multicast Source, Multicast Group ID and Sequence Number, the header of the multicast data packet includes three specialized fields: the 'More Packets' (*MP*) field, the 'Current Dispatch Time' (*CDT*) field and the 'Time Left for Next Dispatch' (*TNLD*) field. The *CDT* field stores the time as the number of milliseconds lapsed since Jan 1, 1970, 12 AM. These additional overhead (relative to that of the other ad hoc multicast routing protocols) associated with the header of each data packet amounts to only 12 more bytes per data packet.

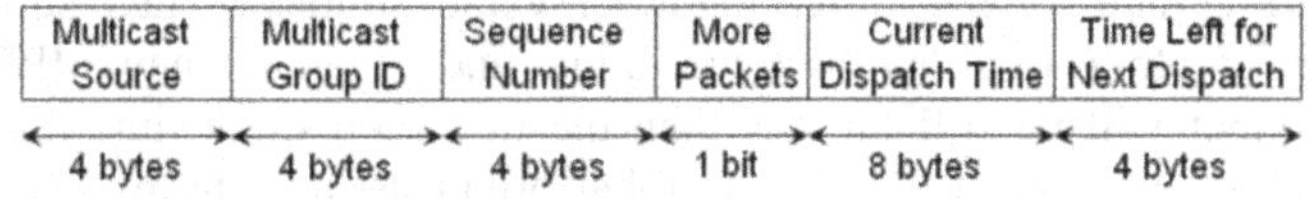

Fig. 4. Structure of the Header of the Multicast Data Packet

The source sets the *CDT* field in all the data packets sent. If the source has any more data to send, it sets the *MP* flag to 1 and sets the appropriate value for the *TLND* field, which indicates the number of milliseconds since the *CDT*. If the source does not have any more data to send, it will set the *MP* flag to 0 and leaves the *TLND* field blank. As we assume the clocks across all nodes are synchronized, a receiver will be able to calculate the end-to-end delay for the data packet based on the time the data packet reaches the node and the *CDT* field in the header of the data packet. An average end-to-end delay per data packet is maintained at the receiver for the current path to the source. If the source node has set the MP flag, the receiver computes the 'Next Expected Packet Arrival Time' (*NEPAT*), as the *CDT* field + *TLND* field + 2*Average end-to-end delay per data packet. A timer is started for the *NEPAT* value.

2.4 Multicast Tree Maintenance

If an intermediate node notices that its link with a downstream node has failed (i.e., the two nodes have moved away and are no longer neighbors), the intermediate node generates and sends a Multicast Path Error Message (MPEM) to the source of the multicast group entry. The MPEM has information about the receiver nodes affected (obtained from the multicast routing table) because of the link failure with the downstream node. Figure 5 shows the structure of an MPEM. The intermediate node removes the tuple(s) corresponding to the downstream node(s) and the affected receiver node(s). After these deletions, if no more <Downstream node, Receiver node> tuple exists for a <Source node, Multicast group ID> entry, the intermediate node removes the entire row for this entry from the routing table.

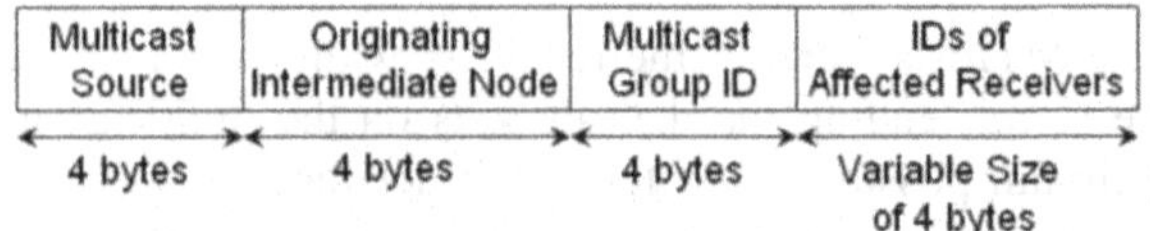

Fig. 5. Structure of a MPEM Message

The source, upon receiving the MPEM, will wait to receive a Multicast Predicted Path Message (MPPM) from each of the affected receivers, within a MPPM-timer maintained for each receiver. The source estimates a Tree-Repair Time (*TRT*) for each receiver as the time that lapsed between the reception of the MPEM from an intermediate node and the MPPM from the affected receiver. An average value for the TRT per receiver is maintained at the source as it undergoes several path failures and repairs before the next global broadcast based tree discovery. The MPPM-timer (initially set to the time it took for the source to receive the MTEM from the receiver) for a receiver will be then set to 1.5* Average *TRT* value, so that we give sufficient time for the destination to learn about the route failure and generate a new MPPM. Nevertheless, this timer will be still far less than the tree acquisition time that would be incurred if the source were to launch a global broadcast tree discovery. Hence, our approach will only increase the network throughput and does not decrease it.

2.5 Prediction of Node Location Using the LUVs

If a multicast receiver does not receive the data packet within the *NEPAT* time, it will attempt to locally construct the global topology using the location and mobility information of the nodes learnt from the latest broadcast tree discovery. Each node is assumed to be moving in the same direction with the same speed as mentioned in its latest LUV. Based on this assumption and information from the latest LUVs, the location of each node at the *NEPAT* time is predicted.

We now explain how to predict the location of a node (say node *u*) at a time instant *CTIME* based on the LUV gathered from node *u* at time *STIME*. Let (X_u^{STIME}, Y_u^{STIME}) be the X and Y co-ordinates of *u* at time *STIME*. Let $Angle_u^{STIME}$ and $Velocity_u^{STIME}$ represent the angle of movement with respect to the X-axis and the velocity at which node *u* is moving. The distance traveled by node *u* from time *STIME* to *CTIME* would be: $Distance_u^{STIME\text{-}CTIME} = (CTIME - STIME + 1) * Velocity_u^{STIME}$. We assume each node is initially configured with information regarding the network boundaries, given by [0, 0], [X_{max}, 0], [X_{max}, Y_{max}] and [0, Y_{max}]. Let (X_u^{CTIME}, Y_u^{CTIME}) be the predicted location of node *u* at time *CTIME*.

$$X_u^{CTIME} = X_u^{STIME} + Offset\text{-}X_u^{CTIME}\ ; \quad Y_u^{CTIME} = Y_u^{STIME} + Offset\text{-}Y_u^{CTIME}$$
$$Offset\text{-}X_u^{CTIME} = Distance_u^{STIME\text{-}CTIME} * \cos(Angle_u^{STIME})$$
$$Offset\text{-}Y_u^{CTIME} = Distance_u^{STIME\text{-}CTIME} * \sin(Angle_u^{STIME})$$

If $(X_u^{CTIME} < 0)$, then $X_u^{CTIME} = 0$; If $(X_u^{CTIME} > X_{max})$, then $X_u^{CTIME} = X_{max}$
If $(Y_u^{CTIME} < 0)$, then $Y_u^{CTIME} = 0$; If $(Y_u^{CTIME} > Y_{max})$, then $Y_u^{CTIME} = Y_{max}$

2.6 Multicast Path Prediction

NR-MLPBR: The receiver node locally runs the Dijkstra's minimum hop path algorithm [3] on the predicted global topology. If at least one path exists from the source to the receiver in the generated topology, the algorithm returns the minimum hop path among them. The receiver node then sends a Multicast Predicted Path Message, MPPM (structure shown in Figure 6), on the discovered path with the route information included in the message.

R-MLPBR: The receiver node uses the LUV obtained from each of the intermediate nodes during the latest global tree broadcast discovery to learn about the identification of its peer receiver nodes that are part of the multicast group. If there existed a direct path to the source on the predicted topology, the receiver chooses that path as the predicted path towards the source. Otherwise, the receiver determines a set of node-disjoint paths on the predicted global topology. The node-disjoint paths to the source are ranked depending on the number of non-receiver nodes that act as intermediate nodes on the path. The path that has the least number of non-receiver nodes as intermediate nodes is preferred. The reason is a path that has the least number of non-receiver nodes is more likely to be a minimum hop path and if a receiver node lies on that path, the number of newly added links to the tree would also be reduced. R-MLPBR thus aims to discover paths with the minimum hop count and at the same time attempts to conserve bandwidth by reducing the number of links that get newly added to the tree as a result of using the predicted path. The MPPM is hence sent on the predicted path that has minimum number of non-receiver nodes. If two or more paths has the same minimum number of non-receiver nodes, R-MLPBR breaks the tie by choosing the path with the minimum hop count to the source.

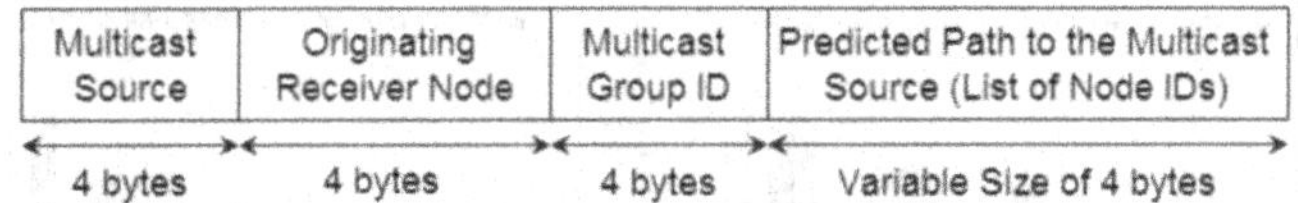

Fig. 6. Structure of the Multicast Predicted Path Message

2.7 Propagation of the Multicast Predicted Path Message towards the Source

An intermediate node on receiving the MPPM adds the tuple <One-hop sender of the MPPM, Originating Receiver node of the MPPM> to the list of <Downstream node, Receiver node> tuples for the multicast tree entry corresponding to the source node and the multicast group to which the MPPM belongs to. The MPPM is then forwarded to the next downstream node on the path towards the source. If the source node receives the MPPM from the appropriate receiver node before the MPPM-timer expires, it indicates that the predicted path does exist in reality. A costly global broadcast tree discovery has been thus avoided. If an intermediate node could not successfully forward the MPPM to the next node on the path towards the source, it informs the receiver node of the absence of the route through a MPPM-Error packet. The receiver node on receiving the MPPM-Error packet discards all the LUVs and does not generate any new MPPM. After the MPPM-timer expires, the multicast source initiates a new global broadcast-based tree discovery procedure.

3 Simulations

We use a 1000m x 1000m square network. The transmission range per node is 250m. The number of nodes used in the network is 25 and 75 nodes representing networks of low and high density respectively. We compare the performance of NR-MLPBR and R-MLPBR with that of the Multicast Extension [4] of the Ad hoc On-demand Distance Vector [5] (MAODV) routing protocol that minimizes the hop count per source-receiver path and the Bandwidth-Efficient Multicast Routing Protocol (BEMRP) [6] that minimizes the number of links in the multicast tree. We implemented all of these four multicast routing protocols in a discrete-event simulator developed in Java. The simulation parameters are summarized in Table 1.

Table 1. Simulation Conditions

Physical Layer	Propagation Model: Two-ray ground reflection model [1]
MAC Layer	IEEE 802.11 [7], Bandwidth: 2 Mbps, Queue Size: 100
Routing Protocols	BEMRP [6], MAODV [4], NR-MLPBR and R-MLPBR
Mobility Model	Random Way Point Model [8]: Min. Node Speed = 0 m/s,
	Pause Time: 0 s, Max. Node Speed = 10 m/s and 50 m/s
Traffic Model	Constant Bit Rate (CBR), UDP
	# Receivers: 2 (small), 4 and 8 (medium), 12 and 24 (high)
	Data Packet Size:512 bytes, Packet Sending Rate: 4/second

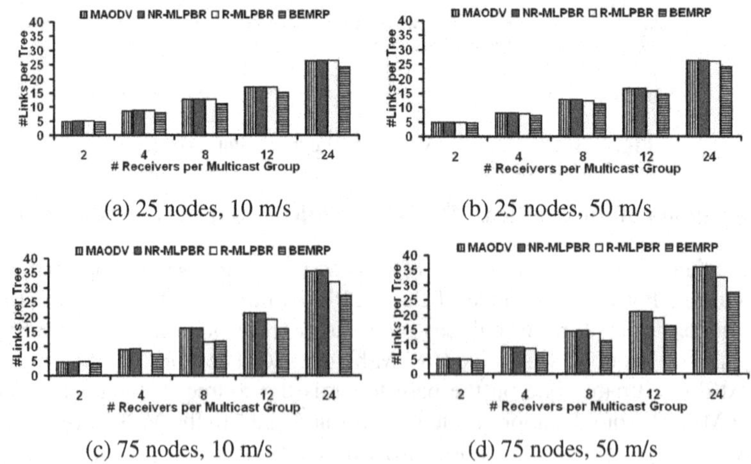

(a) 25 nodes, 10 m/s (b) 25 nodes, 50 m/s

(c) 75 nodes, 10 m/s (d) 75 nodes, 50 m/s

Fig. 7. Average Number of Links per Multicast Tree

The performance metrics studied through the simulations are the following computed over the duration of the entire multicast session. Each of the performance results in Figures 7 through 9 are an average of the results obtained from simulations conducted with 5 sets of multicast groups and 5 sets of mobility profiles.

- **Number of Links per Tree:** This is the time averaged number of links in the multicast trees discovered and computed over the entire multicast session.
- **Hop Count per Source-Receiver Path:** This is the time averaged hop count of the paths from the source to each receiver of the multicast group.
- **Time between Successive Broadcast Tree Discoveries:** This is the average of the time between two successive broadcast tree discoveries.

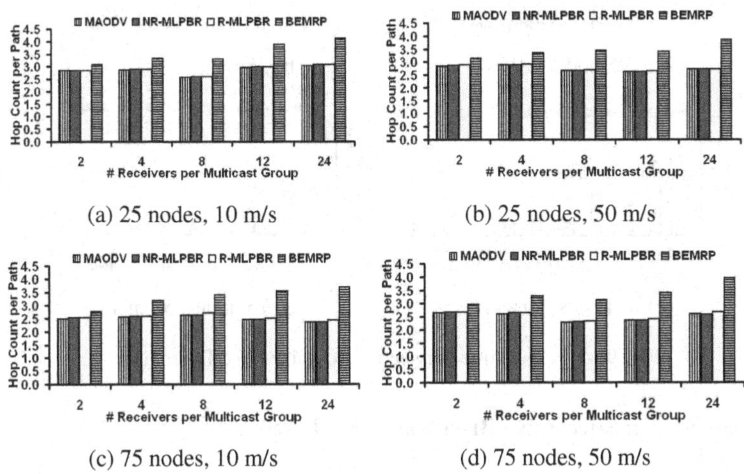

Fig. 8. Average Hop Count per Source-Receiver Path

3.1 Number of Links per Multicast Tree

R-MLPBR manages to significantly reduce the number of links vis-à-vis the MAODV and NR-MLPBR protocols without yielding to a higher hop count per source-receiver path. R-MLPBR is the first multicast routing protocol that yields trees with the reduced number of links and at the same time, with a reduced hop count (close to the minimum) per source-receiver path. However, R-MLPBR cannot discover trees that have minimum number of links as well as the minimum hop count per source-receiver path. The BEMRP protocol discovers trees that have a reduced number of links for all the operating scenarios. However, this leads to larger hop count per source-receiver paths for BEMRP as observed in figure 8.

3.2 Average Hop Count per Source-Receiver Path

All the three multicast routing protocols – MAODV, NR-MLPBR and R-MLPBR, incur almost the same average hop count per source-receiver path and it is considerably lower than that incurred for BEMRP. The hop count per source-receiver path is an important metric and it is often indicative of the end-to-end delay per multicast packet from the source to a specific receiver. BEMRP incurs a significantly larger hop count per source-receiver path and this can be attributed to the nature of this multicast routing protocol to look for trees with a reduced number of links. When multiple receiver nodes have to be connected to the source through a reduced set of links, the hop count per source-receiver path is bound to increase. The hop count per source-receiver path increases significantly as we increase the multicast group size.

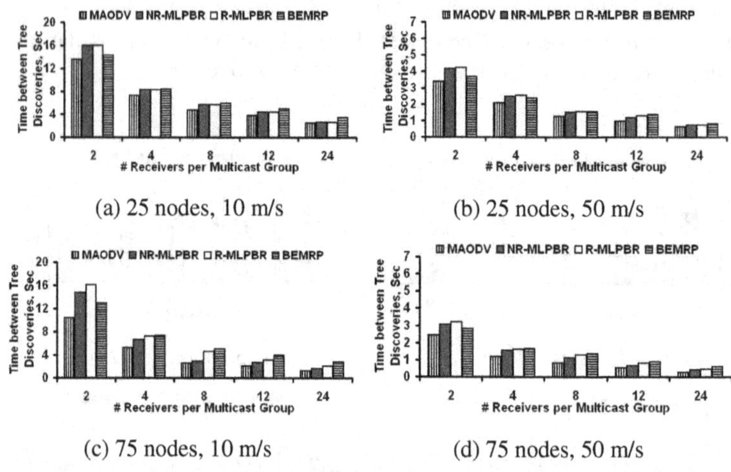

(a) 25 nodes, 10 m/s (b) 25 nodes, 50 m/s

(c) 75 nodes, 10 m/s (d) 75 nodes, 50 m/s

Fig. 9. Average Time between Successive Tree Discoveries

3.3 Time between Successive Broadcast Tree Discoveries

The time between successive broadcast tree discoveries is a measure of the stability of the multicast trees and the effectiveness of the location prediction and path prediction approach of the two multicast extensions. For a given condition of node density and node mobility, both NR-MLPBR and R-MLPBR incur relatively larger time between successive broadcast tree discoveries for smaller and medium sized multicast groups. MAODV tends to be more unstable as the multicast group size is increased, owing to the minimum hop nature of the paths discovered and absence of any path prediction approach. For larger multicast groups, the multicast trees discovered using BEMRP are relatively more stable by virtue of the protocol's tendency to strictly minimize only the number of links in the tree.

4 Conclusions and Future Work

The number of links per tree discovered using R-MLPBR is only about 15-20% more than that discovered using BEMRP, but the hop count per source-receiver path is significantly smaller (by about 40%-60%) than those observed in trees discovered using BEMRP and is the same as that discovered using MAODV. NR-MLPBR and R-MLPBR incur larger time between successive tree discoveries for smaller and medium sized multicast groups, where as BEMRP discovers stable trees for larger multicast groups. We conjecture that with the deployment of broadcast tree discovery strategies (such as DMEF [9]) that can discover inherently stable trees, the performance of NR-MLPBR and R-MLPBR with respect to the time between successive tree discoveries can be further improved vis-à-vis BEMRP and MAODV.

Acknowledgments. Research was sponsored by the Army Research Laboratory and was accomplished under Cooperative Agreement Number W911NF-08-2-0061. The views and conclusions in this document are those of the authors and should not be interpreted as representing the official policies, either expressed or implied, of the Army Research Laboratory or the U.S. Government. The U.S. Government is authorized to reproduce and distribute reprints for Government purposes notwithstanding any copyright notation herein.

References

1. Broch, J., Maltz, D.A., Johnson, D.B., Hu, Y.C., Jetcheva, J.: A Performance of Comparison of Multi-hop Wireless Ad hoc Network Routing Protocols. In: 4th International Conference on Mobile Computing and Networking, Dallas, pp. 85–97. ACM, New York (1998)
2. Meghanathan, N.: Location Prediction Based Routing Protocol for Mobile Ad Hoc Networks. In: Global Communications Conference, New Orleans. IEEE, Los Alamitos (2008)
3. Cormen, T.H., Leiserson, C.E., Rivest, R.L., Stein, C.: Introduction to Algorithms, 2nd edn. MIT Press/ McGraw Hill, New York (2001)
4. Royer, E., Perkins, C.E.: Multicast Operation of the Ad-hoc On-demand Distance Vector Routing Protocol. In: 5th Conference on Mobile Computing and Networking, Seattle, USA, pp. 207–218. ACM, New York (1999)
5. Perkins, C.E., Royer, E.M.: The Ad hoc On-demand Distance Vector Protocol. In: Perkins, C.E. (ed.) Ad hoc Networking, pp. 173–219. Addison-Wesley, New York (2000)
6. Ozaki, T., Kim, J.-B., Suda, T.: Bandwidth-Efficient Multicast Routing for Multihop, Ad hoc Wireless Networks. In: 20th International Conference of Computer and Communications Societies, Anchorage, USA, vol. 2, pp. 1182–1192. IEEE, Los Alamitos (2001)
7. Bianchi, G.: Performance Analysis of the IEEE 802.11 Distributed Coordination Function. IEEE Journal of Selected Areas in Communication 18(3), 535–547 (2000)
8. Bettstetter, C., Hartenstein, H., Perez-Costa, X.: Stochastic Properties of the Random-Waypoint Mobility Model. Wireless Networks 10(5), 555–567 (2004)
9. Meghanathan, N.: A Density and Mobility Aware Energy-Efficient Broadcast Strategy to Determine Stable Routes in Mobile Ad hoc Networks. submitted for journal publication (2009)

AGSMR: Adaptive Geo-Source Multicast Routing for Wireless Sensor Networks*

Sejun Song[1], Daehee Kim[1], and Baek-Young Choi[2]

[1] Dept. Electrical and Computer Engineering, Wichita State University Wichita, KS
{sejun.song,dxkim3}@wichita.edu

[2] Dept. Computer Science and Electrical Engineering, University of Missouri Kansas City, MO
choiby@umkc.edu

Abstract. We propose Adaptive Geo-Source Multicast Routing (AGSMR) for WSNs. It addresses the scalability issue of previous location based stateless multicast protocols in WSNs. AGSMR is a novel stateless multicast protocol that optimizes the location-based and source-based multicast approaches in various ways. First, it saves the cost of a tree building by using receiver's geographic location information during the receiver's the membership establishment stage without flooding. Second, it decreases computation time, in turn, energy usage by determining the multicast routing path at a multicast source node (or rendezvous point (RP)) rather than calculating and selecting neighbors at each forwarding node. Third, it reduces packet overhead by encoding with a small node ID instead of potentially large location information, and by adaptively using branch geographic information for common source routing path segments.

Keywords: Wireless Sensor Network, Geographic Multicast, Source Multicast.

1 Introduction

The marriage of wireless communication and sensing technology into a self-powered, low-cost, and tiny processing node provides an enabling method to build large self-organizing wireless sensor networks (WSNs). The sensor nodes can be deployed randomly close to or inside of the terrain of interest to create a cooperative and self-organizing wireless ad hoc network. The sensed data and control messages are exchanged between sensor nodes and the control (sink) nodes relayed by the neighbor nodes via a multi-hop routing protocol. Applications of WSN are countless including environmental monitoring, industrial monitoring and control, and military surveillance to name a few.

To build practical services over WSNs, especially considering that sensor nodes' limitations in power, computation, and local storage, it is both critical and

* This work was supported in part by the US National Science Foundation under Grant No. 0729197. Any opinions, findings, and conclusions or recommendations expressed in this material are those of the authors and do not necessarily reflect the views of the US National Science Foundation.

B. Liu et al. (Eds.): WASA 2009, LNCS 5682, pp. 200–209, 2009.

challenging to support network communications efficiently. Multicast routing is one of the most promising and essential routing services, as it provides an efficient means of distributing data to multiple recipients to minimize the network resource consumption using in-network duplication. In fact, many WSN applications such as mission assignment, configuration update, and phenomenon report are one-to-many group communication scenarios between sensor nodes and a sink node.

Various tree-based multicast algorithms including MAODV [12], ADMR [8], ODMRP [9], AMRoute [15], AMRIS [14], and PAST-DM [6] have been developed for the traditional wireless ad hoc networks and have evolved in support of WSNs. However, those traditional multicast routing techniques are designed as control-centric approaches focused on solving the mobility issues under the assumption of enough processing and local storage capacity on each node. They maintain a forwarding table on each node through a multicast routing tree for a group. The distributed group forwarding states should be updated via periodic control flooding messages. Due to the capacity limitations on sensor nodes, they may not be the most efficient choice for WSNs.

Several location-based multicast protocols such as DSM [1], PBM [10], and LGT [2] have been proposed to perform a centralized membership management on a multicast root instead of distributed states. The multicast root builds a multicast tree using the locally maintained network topology information, and encodes the tree information into the packet header. The forwarding nodes relay the packet according to the tree path information carried by the packet header. Although the stateless multicast protocols are considered to be better than stateful distributed tree based protocols, those stateless multicast protocols are not suitable for the large-scale networks due to the packet encoding constraint and flooding based location exchange.

Recently, various enhanced approaches such as GMR [7], HGMR [3], and HRPM [4], SPBM [13] have been proposed to resolve those WSN multicast issues. However, carrying all the group locations and the forwarding neighbor information in each data packet and calculating the next forwarding neighbors on each node, still cause scalability and performance problems.

In this paper, we present Adaptive Geo-Source Multicast Routing (AGSMR) protocol for WSNs. AGSMR is a novel stateless multicast protocol based on path information that optimizes the previous location-based multicast approaches in various ways. The unique contributions of the proposed protocol are as follows. 1) It builds a common path multicast tree during the group membership establishment period. This on-demand approach reduces the location flooding overhead of the network topology maintenance on each node. 2) It decreases the computational overhead of each forwarding node such as the forwarding decision and packet de/encoding, with simple serialized path information. 3) It reduces the packet encoding overhead by adaptively using geographic unicast and source multicast. Geographic unicast is more efficient for long non-branching path segments, and source multicast is desirable with branching path segments. 4) It further decreases the packet header size by using the multicast packet with a small node ID instead of potentially large position information.

The rest of the paper is organized as follows. Section 2 describes the AGSMR protocol. Section 3 evaluates AGSMR, and compare with GMR and SMR in various scenarios. Section 4 offers the conclusions and future work.

2 Adaptive Geo-Source Multicast Routing

In this section, first we give a brief background on two types of stateless multicast routing algorithms which we compare the performance of the proposed AGSMR with. We then provide an overview of AGSMR, and describe the proposed AGSMR for the following three main issues: 1) construction of a multicast tree, 2) state information encoding, and 3) forwarding methodology.

2.1 Background

The proposed AGSMR is a hybrid of geographic multicast routing (GMR) and source based multicast routing (SMR) approaches. Thus we provide a brief background on the algorithms.

GMR assumes a centralized membership management at the multicast root like other stateless protocols. However, it does not build an entire multicast tree on the root. The root node only selects a subset of its neighbors as forwarding nodes to the destinations according to the cost and progress ratio and it encodes selected neighbor IDs and a list of the destination sensor locations into the data message header. The message is broadcasted to all the neighbor nodes. Upon receiving the message, the selected forwarding nodes calculate a subset of its neighbors again, which eventually propagates multicast packets to the destinations. Each forwarding node performs approximately $O(min(neighbors, destinations)^3)$ calculations to select forwarding neighbors.

SMR constructs a multicast tree on the root node based upon either the entire network topology or the partial path information for the destinations. For example, DSM assumes each node has an entire network topology by location flooding. The source node locally computes a Steiner tree for the multicast group. It encodes the tree path information (node IDs) by using Prüfer sequence [5] to the packet header. The packet is broadcasted to all the neighbor nodes. Upon receiving the packet, each child node, which is inside of the tree path, creates a subtree, encodes its Prüfer sequence to the header, and relays the packet to its children until the subtree path reaches the end of the tree path. The subtree encoding complexity is $O(path\_node^3)$ on each child node.

2.2 Overview of AGSMR

AGSMR addresses the scalability issues of geographic routing and source based routing. It constructs a multicast tree on the root node based upon path information for the destinations. Instead of maintaining entire network topology on each node via location flooding, the path information is sent to the source node through the group management scheme. Each join request message carries its path information in addition to the location information. For example, when a member node joins by using geographic unicast, the source receives the reverse geographic shortest path information to the destination. According to the path information of each destination, the source builds a multicast tree with common path segments among the destinations. It encodes the multicast tree into the packet header by using LCRS (Left Child Right Sibling) binary tree [11], that serializes the subtree path information. To optimize the encoding size, it identifies long non-branching routing path segments and uses the branch locations for the source routing information instead of many node IDs along the path. Each forwarding node uses geographic unicast to the next branching node, if the next node is provided by location information. If the next node is given by the node IDs, a forwarding node relays the subtree path segment information to the neighbor nodes. In this case, there is no additional calculation overhead except the simple packet truncation for the next subtree.

2.3 Construction of Multicast Tree

In constructing a multicast tree, AGSMR does not assume every node has others' location information. That is, unlike dynamic source multicast routing, flooding of the location information among the nodes is not required. In our scheme, path information is created on-demand during the join stage in the request message. Then the source builds a multicast tree based on the received path information in $O(path)$. Intermediate nodes keep states only during the join stage temporarily, and do not need any state for forwarding. The small temporary states on intermediate nodes enable the source to make compressed path information to destinations.

The scheme works as follows. First a destination node, *dst* sends a join message, *join_msg*, toward the source, *src*. The message is sent only to next hops that are closer to *src*. Intermediate nodes keep simple information of [*dst, hop_cnt*] in a table called *MState*. *dst* is a destination node ID whose path to *src* goes through the intermediate node, and the hop count, *hop_cnt* from itself to the destination down the path, i.e., [*dst, hop_cnt*]. When a *join_msg* message arrives at an intermediate node, if *dst* is already recorded on the *MState* of the intermediate node and the number of hops down the path to the member is smaller than the new message, then the join message is dropped. Otherwise the state of [*dst, hop_cnt*] is updated or added in *MState*. A *join_msg* includes path segments so far, and the number of destinations that use the intermediate nodes on their paths to the *src* (e.g. $[< n1 - n2 >: 3dsts, < n2 - n3 >: 4dsts]$). Once the *join_msg*s are received, the *src* computes a multicast tree starting with a path segment that is used by the highest number of destinations, until it includes all the destinations. The algorithms used in the intermediate nodes and source are depicted in Algorithms 1 and 2, respectively.

```
MState: multicast state table, contains dst and hop_cnt pairs ;
if join_msg ∈ MState then
    if hop_cnt < MState(dst) then
        MState(dst) := hop_cnt;
        Add the path segment information to join_msg;
        Send the join_msg to prog_next_hops toward src;
    end
end
else
    Add [dst, hop_cnt] to MState ;
    Add the path segment information to join_msg ;
    Send the join_msg to prog_next_hops toward src ;
end
```

Algorithm 1. Group Management at Intermediate Nodes

```
D: the set of destinations;
while Set of dsts, D ≠ ∅ do
    Send mcast data onto a path that includes the most number of dsts;
    Remove dsts from D;
end
```

Algorithm 2. Multicast Path Selection at Source node

2.4 State Information Encoding and Forwarding Methodology

The source node creates a serialized path into the packet header by using the common paths of a multicast tree. First, the encoding algorithm translates the original *n-ary* multicast tree to a LCRS (Left Child Right Sibling) binary tree. Starting from the original root node, each node's leftmost child in the original tree is made its left child in the binary tree, and its nearest sibling to the right in the original tree is made its right child in the binary tree. Second, a serialized path information is created by walking along the LCRS binary tree in the order of 'sibling first, then child node.' Figure 1 illustrates an example to show how to translate the original spanning tree into the LCRS binary tree. By walking through the LCRS, the serialized path $\{d,i,j,e,f,g,h,a,c,b\}$ is created.

The state information is encoded as a 'serialized path,' that is consecutive data of the same size (given as 2 bytes) information block. The block can be a node ID, a location coordinate, and a delimiter. A 2-byte delimiter can be distinguished from other information blocks by setting 1 in the most significant bit. Each delimiter has two 7-bit offsets. The node ID block can be identified by setting 00 in the left 2 bits. With a 2 byte information block, the maximum number of node IDs can be about 16K (use only 14 bits). Branch delimiters are inserted next to the original tree branches' serialized path to indicate the original tree's sibling relationship (the subtree information for each sibling node). The root node broadcasts the multicast packet after encoding the final serialized path into the packet header. When the multicast packet is received at a forwarding node, the node selects the serialized path for its own subtree according to the branch delimiter information. The delimiter format is shown in Figure 2.

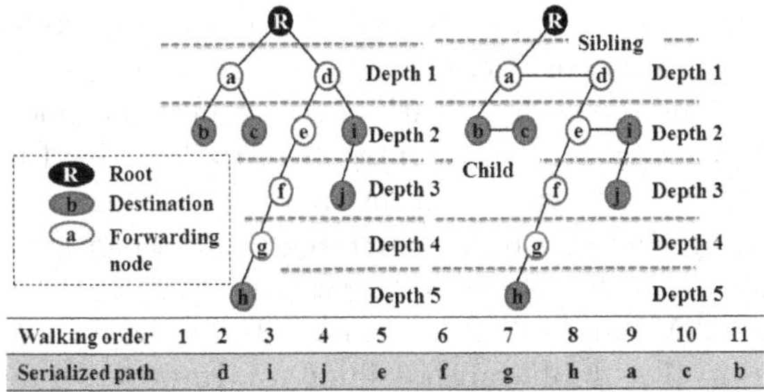

Fig. 1. Multicast Tree, LCRS Binary Tree, and a Serialized Path

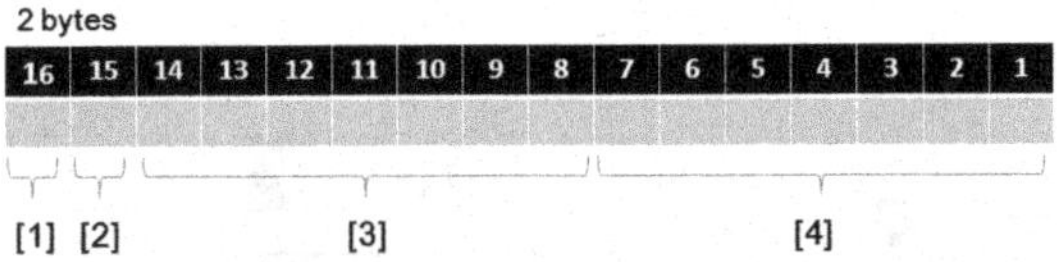

2 bytes

16	15	14	13	12	11	10	9	8	7	6	5	4	3	2	1
[1]	[2]	[3]						[4]							

Bit Condition	Type	Size
[1] = 1	Delimiter	[3], [3]+[4] is offset of sibling nodes under branch node in serialized path
[1] = 0 AND [2] = 1	X or Y coordinate	14 bits ([3]+[4])
[1] = 0 AND [2] = 0	Node ID	14 bits ([3]+[4])

Fig. 2. 2 bytes Delimiter Format

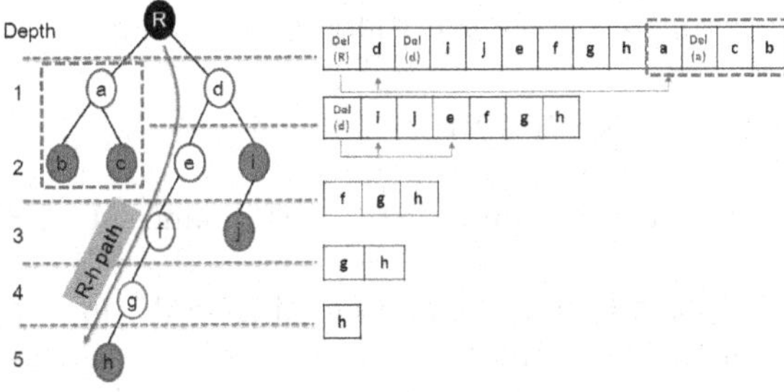

Fig. 3. R-h path Forwarding

Figure 3 illustrates how to utilize the serialized path information along the R to h forwarding track. For example, node d can make a new serialized path for its subtree by checking the offset from the first delimiter (R).

A longer non-branching path segment can be identified during the serialized path creation. The serialized path can be minimized using the location information (i.e., x and y coordinates) instead of putting the entire path node IDs. If a forwarding node finds the location information (delimiter value is 01) in the serialized path, it uses geographic unicast. Although it requires computations to find the next neighbor, geographic unicast algorithm complexity is very low unlike the original geographic multicast. In the example shown in Figure 4, there is a long (n nodes) non-branching path segment between node e and h. The serialized path segment size is represented by only 2 bytes, thus the information is reduced by $2(n-2)$ bytes resulting in a huge saving of packet size along the path. Comparing with the pure source multicast scenarios of the spanning tree with n number of nodes, the encoding ratio $(n-2)$ of the Prüfer sequence algorithm used in DSM can be better than our RSLC based serialized path encoding algorithm (n - 1 + # of branch delimiters). However, comparing with the geo-source multicast with several long paths, our algorithm is comparable to the Prüfer sequence algorithm. Furthermore, our algorithm is designed to have less computation overhead on the forwarding node. The computation complexity of our algorithm is $O(1)$ while Prüfer sequence algorithm has $O(n^2)$.

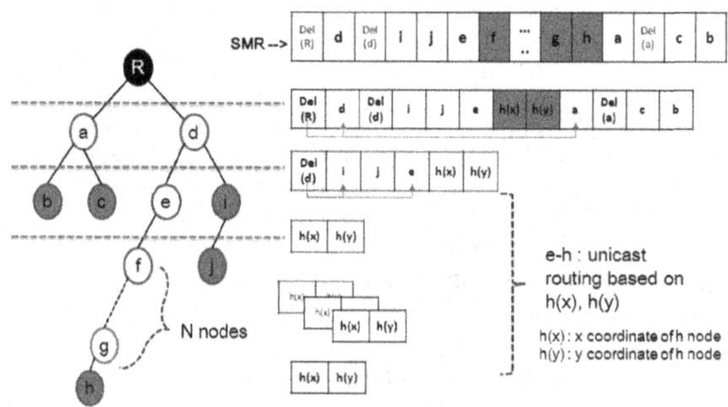

Fig. 4. Geo-Source Multicast Forwarding

3 Performance Evaluation

In this section, we evaluate and compare the performance of AGSMR with GMR and SMR.

To verify the efficiency, we have implemented AGSMR in ns2 (v2.33) simulator and compared with GMR and SMR. In the network setting, we use a grid topology and the maximum number of neighbor nodes is fixed as 12 nodes (fixed signal length). We assume no packet loss due to the packet collision. We use metrics of total packet size and computation time for the various system settings. The simulations were performed with 50 iterations for each system setting. The locations of a source and destinations are chosen randomly. We assume that the location coordinate of a node is 2 times bigger than the node identification.

We first evaluate the packet processing overhead on each multicast forwarding node. To see the overall system efficiency and scalability we use total packet size that is the accumulated packet usage of the entire multicast tree nodes. Figure 5 (a) shows the total packet sizes with varied number of destinations. The percentages of destinations are from 1% to 30% of the fixed network size (1024 sensor nodes). The results depict that AGSMR has smaller total packet sizes

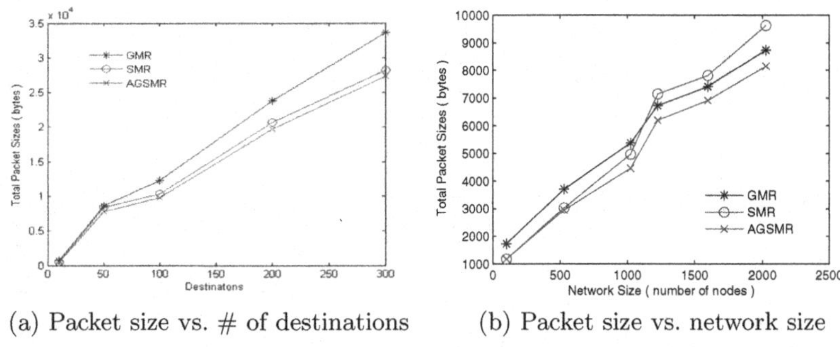

(a) Packet size vs. # of destinations (b) Packet size vs. network size

Fig. 5. Packet size overhead

than other protocols, as it minimizes the packet size for the non-branching path nodes. Meanwhile, the total packet size of GMR is always bigger than others, as GMR encodes its multicast packet with the destination locations. SMR's total packet size is larger than AGSMR's, because SMR encodes the packet with entire multicast path node ID.

Figure 5 (b) depicts the total packet sizes with varied network sizes. The network size ranges from 100 to 2000 while the destination number is fixed as 30 nodes. The results illustrate that the total packet size of GMR is bigger than that of SMR in the smaller network size, but SMR's packet size becomes bigger in case of the larger network size. It is because that SMR is more sensitive to the network size than other protocols, as SMR encodes the packet with the path information. Meanwhile, AGSMR has smaller total packet size and is less sensitive to the network size than other protocols, as it has more chance of having longer non-branching paths.

Both Figure 5 (a) and (b) show that the total packet size of AGSMR is less than other protocols in the condition of the larger network with more destinations. It indicates that AGSMR is more scalable than other protocols, as it spends less sensor node resources (i.e. energy) to transmit a multicast packet.

Next, we measured the computation time on each forwarding node that is used to process the incoming packet, in order to calculate the next forwarding neighbors, and prepare the corresponding packet to forward. To see the overall system performance we use the average computation time which divides total accumulated time by the number of nodes in the multicast tree.

Figure 6 (a) shows the average computation time with varied number of destinations. The percentages of destinations are from 1% to 30% of the fixed network size (1024 sensor nodes). The results show that GMR spends much higher computation time than other protocols and the time difference becomes bigger according to the increment of the number of destinations. It is because GMR calculates the next forwarding neighbors on each forwarding node and the algorithm complexity is increased according to the number of destinations. Meanwhile, in both SMR and AGSMR, the average computation time is minimal regardless of the number of destinations, as there is no need for the next forwarding node

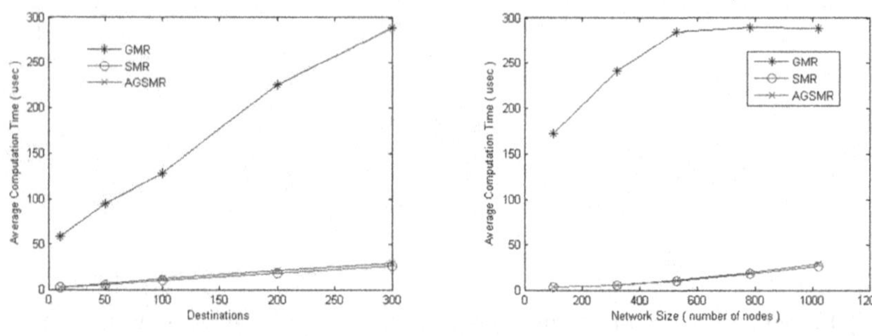

(a) Computation time vs. # of destinations (b) Computation time vs. network size

Fig. 6. Comparison of computation time

calculation. For the larger number of destinations, the computation time of AS-GMR is slightly higher than that of SMR due to the geographic unicast calculation.

Figure 6 (b) shows the average computation time with varied network sizes. The network size is varied from 100 to 1024, while the number of destinations is 30% of the network size. The results depict that GMR spends much higher computation time than other protocols, but the time difference is bounded and not proportional to the increment of the network size. Both SMR and AGSMR spend minimal computation time and have little dependency on the network size.

Figures 6 (a) and (b) indicate that AGSMR's computation time is much less than GMR's, its geographic unicast routing computation overhead is minimal, and its average computation time is as good as SMR.

4 Conclusions and Future Work

We have presented a novel stateless path information based multicast protocol called AGSMR (Adaptive Geo-Source Multicast Routing) for WSNs. AGSMR optimizes the previous location-based multicast approaches providing unique features including on-demand path information based tree construction, light-weight forwarding, adaptive usage of geographic unicast and source multicast, and enhanced state encoding capability. Our analysis and simulation results show that AGSMR outperforms GMR in computation time and packet overheads while maintaining the advantages of stateless protocols. Our future work includes two main directions. First, we are working on a structural extension of the proposed algorithm such as supporting hierarchical approaches. Second, we plan to investigate the reliability issues of the proposed multicast protocol.

References

1. Basagni, S., Chlamtac, I., Syrotiuk, V.: Location aware, dependable multicast for mobile ad hoc networks. Computer Networks 36, 659–670 (2001)
2. Chen, K., Nahrstedt, K.: Effective location-guided tree construction algorithms for small group multicast in manet. In: IEEE INFOCOM (June 2002)

3. Hu, Y.C., Stojmenovic, I., Koutsonikolas, D., Das, S.: Hierarchical geographic multicast routing for wireless sensor networks. In: SENSORCOMM (2007)
4. Das, S.M., Pucha, H., Hu, Y.C.: Distributed hashing for scalablemulticast in wireless ad hoc networks. IEEE TPDS 19(3), 347–361 (2008)
5. Gottlieb, J., Julstrom, B.A., Raidl, G.R., Rothlauf, F.: Prüfer numbers: A poor representation of spanning trees for evolutionary search. In: The Genetic and Evolutionary Computation Conference (GECCO), pp. 343–350 (2001)
6. Gui, C., Mohapatra, P.: Differential destination multicast-a manet multicast routing protocol for small groups. In: IEEE WCNC (March 2003)
7. Liu, X., Sanchez, J., Ruiz, P., Stojmenovic, I.: Gmr: Geographic multicast routing for wireless sensor networks. In: IEEE SECON (2006)
8. Jetcheva, J.G., Johnson, D.B.: Adaptive demand-driven multicast routing in multi-hop wireless ad hoc networks. In: ACM MobiHoc (October 2001)
9. Lee, S.-J., Gerla, M., Chiang, C.-C.: On-demand multicast routing protocol. In: IEEE WCNC (September 1999)
10. Mauve, M., Fuessler, H., Widmer, J., Lang, T.: Positionbased multicast routing for mobile ad-hoc networks. University of Mannheim, CS TR-03-004 (2003)
11. NIST Dictionary of Algorithms and Data Structures. Left child right sibling tree, `http://www.itl.nist.gov/div897/sqg/dads/HTML/leftChildrightSiblingBinaryTree.html`
12. Royer, E.M., Perkins, C.E.: Multicast operation of the ad-hoc on-demand distance vector routing protocol. In: MobiCom (August 1999)
13. Transie, M., Fuler, H., Widmer, J., Mauve, M., Effelsberg, W.: Scalable position-based multicast for mobile ad-hoc networks. In: International Workshop on Broadband Wireless Multimedia: Algorithms, Architectures and Applications (BroadWim) (October 2004)
14. Wu, C., Tay, Y.: Amris: A multicast protocol for ad hoc wireless networks. In: MILCOM (November 1999)
15. Xie, J., Talpade, R.R., Mcauley, A., Liu, M.: Amroute: ad hoc multicast routing protocol. Mobile Networks and Applications 7(6), 429–439 (2002)

On the Capacity of Hybrid Wireless Networks with Opportunistic Routing

Tan Le and Yong Liu

Department of Electrical and Computer Engineering,
Polytechnic Institute of New York University,
Six MetroTech Center, Brooklyn, NY 11201
tle04@students.poly.edu, yongliu@poly.edu

Abstract. This paper studies the capacity of hybrid wireless networks with opportunistic routing (OR). We first extend the opportunistic routing algorithm to exploit high speed data transmissions in infrastructure network through base stations. We then develop linear programming models to calculate the end-to-end throughput bounds from multiple source nodes to single, as well as, multiple destination nodes. The developed models are applied to study several hybrid wireless network examples. Through case studies, we investigate several factors that have significant impacts on the hybrid wireless network capacity under opportunistic routing, such as node transmission range, density and distribution pattern of base stations (BTs), number of wireless channels on wireless nodes and base stations, etc. Our numerical results demonstrate that opportunistic routing could achieve much higher throughput on both ad-hoc and hybrid networks than traditional unicast routing (UR). Moreover, opportunistic routing can efficiently utilize base stations and achieve significantly higher throughput gains in hybrid wireless networks than in pure ad-hoc networks especially with multiple-channel base stations.

1 Introduction

New portable devices, such as iPhone, PDAs are increasingly equipped with strong communication and computation capabilities. They can host a wide range of applications, such as web browsing, audio/video streaming, online gaming, etc. Most devices have multiple radio interfaces and support different wireless protocols, such as Bluetooth, Wi-Fi, and 3G. It has become critical for such devices to efficiently utilize resources available in a hybrid wireless networking environment to achieve high data throughput and support bandwidth-intensive applications.

Recently, Opportunistic Routing (OR) was proposed to improve the throughput for ad-hoc networks. In this paper, we explore the gain of integrating OR with hybrid wireless networks that consist of ad-hoc wireless nodes and base stations connected to a wireline infrastructure. We first extend the opportunistic routing algorithm to exploit high speed data transmissions in infrastructure network through base stations. We then develop linear programming models to calculate the end-to-end throughput bounds from multiple source nodes to single, as well as, multiple destination nodes. The developed models are applied to study several hybrid wireless network examples. Through case studies, we investigate several factors that have significant impacts on the hybrid

B. Liu et al. (Eds.): WASA 2009, LNCS 5682, pp. 210–223, 2009.

wireless network capacity under OR, such as density and distribution pattern of Base Stations, number of wireless channels on wireless nodes and BTs, etc.

The contribution of this paper is four-fold:

1. We propose a simple method to extend OR to hybrid wireless networks. We develop new transmission cost metrics and forwarding priority rules to take into account candidate routes through BTs and infrastructure network.
2. We develop linear programming models to calculate end-to-end throughput bounds from multiple source nodes to single, as well as, multiple destination nodes.
3. We demonstrate through case studies that OR can efficiently utilize BTs and achieve significantly higher throughput gains in hybrid wireless networks than in pure ad-hoc networks. And the throughput gain of OR is also higher than that of UR in hybrid networks.
4. We systematically evaluate several factors determining the throughput gains of OR in hybrid wireless networks.

The rest of the paper is organized as follows. We briefly review the related works in Section 2. In Section 3, we present the extension of OR to hybrid wireless networks and the LP models to characterize the throughput bounds from multiple sources to single destination, and from multiple sources to multiple destinations. Case studies on several example hybrid wireless networks are presented in Section 4. The paper is concluded in Section 5.

2 Background and Related Work

The throughput bound and capacity of ad-hoc and hybrid wireless networks have been studied extensively in the past. Well-known papers [13] and [14] developed analytical methods to calculate the capacity of mobile and ad-hoc networks. The works in [2][3][4][5][6][7] investigated the capacity of ad-hoc networks with infrastructure support in different cases and scenarios under UR. Recently, the topic Opportunistic Routing on ad-hoc networks attracted lots of interest [8][9][10][11][12]. In [11], the authors studied the opportunistic routing protocol ExOR, which dynamically chooses paths on a per-transmission basis in a wireless network to efficiently improve the throughput. To illustrate the idea of OR, in Figure 1, A wants to send packets to D. B_1, B_2 and B_3 are closer to D and are chosen as the candidate forwarders. After one broadcast from A, B_1, B_2, and B_3 all receive the packet. Assuming B_1 has the highest forwarding priority, so it will take over and broadcast the packet to its candidate forwarders C_1, C_2 and C_3. Assume highest priority node C_1 misses the packet, so C_2 will take over and forward the packet to its destination D. In [8], by integrating opportunistic routing with network coding, a new protocol MORE leads to significant throughput improvement in both unicast and multicast cases. In [9], the authors introduced the robust distribution opportunistic routing scheme base on ETX metric that can find the optimal path from source to destination. Authors of [12] conducted a systematic performance evaluation, taking into account node densities, channel qualities and traffic rates to identify the cases when opportunistic routing makes sense. The recent work from K.Zeng et al. [1] proposed the method to calculate the maximum throughput between two end nodes

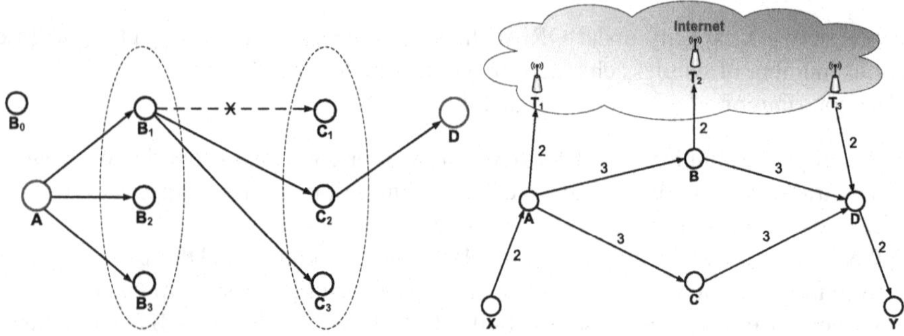

Fig. 1. Opportunistic Routing on ad-hoc network

Fig. 2. Simple example of hybrid wireless network

with Opportunistic Routing in ad-hoc networks. The main focus of this paper is to study the throughput improvement of OR in hybrid wireless networks.

3 Capacity of Hybrid Wireless Networks with OR

3.1 Network Model

We consider a hybrid wireless network consisting of wireless nodes and Wi-Fi Base Stations (BTs). Wireless nodes are equipped with radio interfaces and can communicate with each other through multi-hop ad-hoc transmissions. BTs are connected to the Internet using high bandwidth wireline connections. If a wireless node is within the coverage of a BT, it can communicate with the BT using single-hop infrastructure mode. Optionally, a wireless node might have a connection to a 3G base station that covers all wireless nodes under consideration. The optional 3G connection can be used as a control channel for nodes to exchange control information, such as the geographical locations of nodes. Packets can be transmitted using two transmission modes: ad-hoc mode and infrastructure mode. We assume all nodes in the network are cooperative and forward each other's packets to their destinations with Opportunistic Routing. Here are some assumptions on hybrid wireless networks under study:

- There are N_1 static wireless nodes randomly located in a square area. There are N_2 Wi-Fi Base Stations in the same area.
- Wireless nodes are homogeneous. They have the same set of transmission rates, and equivalent effective transmission ranges.
- Assume the coverage areas of BTs do not overlap with each other. Each wireless node could connect to at most one BT.
- Source node transmits data with OR through relay nodes to destination. If the relay node is a wireless node, it uses OR to forward the packet to the next-hop node (relay or the final destination). If a relay node is a BT, it forwards the packet to the next-hop node through direct single-hop transmission.
- Through a separate control channel (e.g., 3G), every node knows the geographical locations of its neighbors and the destination node.

- We study two different models for data transmissions in hybrid wireless networks:
  1. *Single-channel model:* In this model, all BT nodes and wireless nodes are equipped with a single radio interface. They use the same frequency spectrum to communicate with each other. In other words, infrastructure and ad-hoc transmissions share the same wireless channel. Wireless nodes use OR and BTs use UR to forward packets toward their destinations. Since every BT node only has a single wireless channel, it could communicate with no more than one wireless node at any given time.
  2. *Multiple-channel model:* In this model, infrastructure and ad-hoc transmissions operate at non-overlapping frequency ranges. Wireless nodes in the coverage of a BT can simultaneously communicate with the BT using infrastructure mode and other wireless nodes using ad-hoc mode. Moreover, every BT node has multiple wireless channels, so it can communicate with multiple wireless nodes simultaneously. Wireless nodes use OR and BTs use UR to forward packets. If the Candidate Relay Set (CRS) of a wireless node consists of a BT and some wireless nodes, the wireless node simultaneously employs infrastructure and ad-hoc transmissions to push the same packet to the BT and wireless nodes respectively.

3.2 Concurrent Transmitter Sets

The biggest challenge of studying the capacity of wireless networks is to model the conflicts between wireless links. The concept of Concurrent Transmitter Sets (CTS) was proposed in [1] to calculate the end-to-end throughput in ad-hoc networks with OR. We extend the CTS concept to study the capacity of hybrid wireless networks.

With OR, a transmitter has multiple forwarding candidates in its Candidate Relay Set (CRS). Let all links from a transmitter to nodes in its CRS as links associated with that transmitter. In a hybrid wireless network, Conservative CTS (CCTS) is a set of transmitters (including the BTs) that when all of them are transmitting simultaneously, all links associated with them are still usable (no interfere with any other link [1]). However, such a requirement is too restrictive. Data from a transmitter can be forwarded to the next hop as long as one forwarding candidate in its CRS receives the data. To account for this, Greedy CTS (GCTS) is a set of transmitters (including the BTs) that when all of them are transmitting data simultaneously, at least one link associated with each transmitter is usable. This leads to the maximum end-to-end throughput. A maximal CCTS (GCTS) is a CCTS (GCTS) that is not a true subset of any another CCTS (GCTS).

For the single-channel model, infrastructure transmissions could interfere with ad-hoc transmissions. A BT cannot send and receive data with more than one wireless node at a particular time. For the multiple-channel model, BTs can send and receive data with multiple nodes simultaneously in infrastructure mode. Infrastructure transmissions have no conflict with ad-hoc transmissions. Due to the assumed non-overlapped BT coverage areas, infrastructure transmissions of different BTs are also conflict-free. Data transmissions between BTs are in the wireline domain and will not interfere with any wireless transmissions. Consequently, directed links between BTs, and directed links between a BT and its associated end nodes can be activated at anytime without introducing interference to any other link in the network. With the assumption of the number of wireless channels on each BT is big enough that it could sending and receiving data with all associated nodes simultaneously, all BT nodes can be included in all CTSs. An example of CTS is illustrated in Figure 2. A link ij in the graph indicates node $j \in$ CRS of node i and they are in the transmission range of each other. Assume source node A needs to send data to destination node D with the relays B, C, base stations T_1, T_2 and T_3. We will find the CTSs for the two different models.

1. Single-channel model: Pairs of nodes (A, B), (B, C), (C, A) could not be included in the same CCTS. The reason is that two sets of links associated with each pair of nodes are not interference free. Also the pairs of of nodes (B, T_3) and (C, T_3) could not be included in the same CCTS because their links to node D are not interference free. So the maximal Conservative CTSs in this case are: $\{A, T_1, T_2, T_3\}$, $\{B, T_1, T_2\}$, $\{C, T_1, T_2\}$. The maximal Greedy CTSs in this case are exactly the same as the above maximal CCTSs. When all nodes in each of these GCTSs transmitting simultaneously, usable links associated with each node are: $\mathbf{A} : AT_1$; $\mathbf{B} : BT_2$; $\mathbf{C} : CD$; $\mathbf{T_1} : T_1T_3$; $\mathbf{T_2} : T_2T_3$, $\mathbf{T_3} : T_3D$.
2. Multi-channels model: For Conservative CTSs, pairs of nodes (A, B), (B, C), (C, A) could not be included in the same CCTS. So the maximal CCTSs in this case are: $\{A, T_1, T_2, T_3\}$, $\{B, T_1, T_2, T_3\}$, $\{C, T_1, T_2, T_3\}$. On the other hand, for GCTSs, there are only pairs of nodes (A, C) and (B, C) could not be included in the same GCTS. It is because the only link CD associated with node C will be not usable whenever nodes A or B activated to transmit data. So the maximal Greedy CTSs in this case are: $\{A, B, T_1, T_2, T_3\}$, $\{C, T_1, T_2, T_3\}$. When all nodes in each of these GCTSs transmitting simultaneously, usable links associated with each node are: $\mathbf{A} : AT_1$; $\mathbf{B} : BT_2$; $\mathbf{C} : CD$; $\mathbf{T_1} : T_1T_3$; $\mathbf{T_2} : T_2T_3$, $\mathbf{T_3} : T_3D$.

3.3 Opportunistic Routing Model

In OR, a transmitter selects neighbors "closer", i.e., with lower transmission cost, to the destination as candidate forwarders in CRS. Forwarders in CRS are ranked based on their "closeness" to the destination. Since there is no preset route to a destination with OR, it is impossible to determine the accurate transmission cost from a node to a destination. In a pure ad-hoc network, one can use the geographic distance between a node i and destination node j to measure the packet transmission cost from i to j through ad-hoc network. For hybrid wireless networks, we propose a new metric that takes into account the low transmission cost through the infrastructure network. We assume costs of the infrastructure transmissions between BTs are negligible. Then the cheapest transmission from i to j through infrastructure network is for i to transmit a packet destined to j first to its closest BT, T_i. Then T_i transmits the packet to a BT T_j that is the closest to node j. Finally, T_j sends the packet to j. If i is directly covered by T_i, we use geographic distance d_{iT_i} between i and T_i to estimate the transmission cost $\hat{d}_{iT_i}$ from i to T_i. If i is not in the coverage of T_i, we choose a node k_i in T_i's coverage that is the closest to i as a relay node. All packets from i to T_i will be first sent to k_i using the ad-hoc mode, then be relayed to T_i using the infrastructure mode. Consequently, the transmission cost is estimated as $\hat{d}_{iT_i} = d_{ik_i} + d_{k_iT_i}$. Similarly, the transmission cost from T_j to j can be estimated as $\hat{d}_{T_jj}$. The total transmission cost through the infrastructure network is then estimated as $\hat{d}_{ij} = \hat{d}_{iT_i} + \hat{d}_{T_j j}$. The effective transmission cost $\bar{d}_{ij}$ from i to j in the hybrid wireless network is the minimum of the cost of pure ad-hoc transmission and that of transmission through infrastructure:

$$\bar{d}_{ij} = \min(\hat{d}_{ij}, d_{ij}) \tag{1}$$

For the example in Figure 2, the source node is X and the destination node is Y. Assuming the geographic distances are $d_{XY} = 9$, $d_{XB} = 5$, $d_{XD} = 7$, $d_{AY} = 5$, $d_{BY} = 7$. The transmission cost using infrastructure network can be estimated as:

$$\hat{d}_{XY} = (d_{XA} + d_{AT_1}) + (d_{T_3 D} + d_{DY}) = (2+2) + (2+2) = 8 \tag{2}$$

So $\bar{d}_{XY} = min(\hat{d}_{XY}, d_{XY}) = 8$.

In OR, a forwarding candidate is utilized to transmit a packet if and only if it receives the packet and all other candidates with higher priority in the CRS don't receive the packet. To study the capacity of OR, we need to calculate the *effective forwarding rate* of a link between a transmitter i to each of its forwarding candidate k. Let i sends data to its forwarding candidate set with rate R. $J(i)$ be the candidate forwarding set for i, and $J(i) = \{i_1, i_2, ..., i_r\}$. The priority order to forward packets from i is $i_1 < i_2 < ... < i_q < ... < i_r$, $1 \leqslant q \leqslant r$. Let p_{ik} be the Packet Reception Ratio (PRR) between i and k. p_{ik} theoretically depends on distance between i and k, end node density around the position of nodes i and k, and the MAC scheduling scheme. Then the effective forwarding rate $\tilde{R}_{ii_q}$ on link $\langle ii_q \rangle$ is:

$$\tilde{R}_{ii_q} = Rp_{ii_q} \prod_{k=0}^{q-1} (1 - p_{ii_k}) \tag{3}$$

3.4 Throughput Bound to Single Destination

Given basic models studied in previous sections, we now proceed to study the capacity of hybrid wireless networks with OR. We start with the case that multiple sources send data to the same destination. As summarized in Table 1, there is a set S including N_s source nodes $\{S_1, \cdots, S_{N_s}\}$ sending traffic to the same destination node D. From the original network, we create a connected graph $G = (V, E)$. V is the set of nodes, including end nodes and BT nodes. E is the set of all available links, including ad-hoc links and infrastructure links. Let f_{ij} be the amount of traffic sent on link l_{ij}. We are interested in finding out the bound of end-to-end throughput from source nodes in S to D.

Assuming there are M maximal CTS's $(T_1, T_2, ..., T_M)$. At any time, when a CTS is scheduled to transmit, nodes in the scheduled CTS could transmit packets simultaneously. Let λ_α be the time fraction that CTS T_α is scheduled. We need to calculate the effective forwarding rate $\tilde{R}^\alpha_{ij}$ for each link $\langle i, j \rangle$ under each CTS T_α. If a CCTS T_α is scheduled and $i \in T_\alpha$, all links associated with i are usable, therefore $\tilde{R}^\alpha_{ij} = \tilde{R}_{ij}$, $\forall j \in J(i)$, which is calculated in (3); if $i \notin T_\alpha$, $\tilde{R}^\alpha_{ij} = 0$. If a GCTS T_α is scheduled and node $i \in T_\alpha$, some links associated with i maybe not usable. Let ψ^α_{ij} be a binary

Table 1. Notation on Linear Programming Formulations

$S_j, 1 \leqslant j \leqslant N_s$	Source nodes
D	Destination node
$G(V,E)$	The original graph. V is set of nodes. E is the set of all available links.
l_{ij}	Link between nodes i and j
f_{ij}	Amount of flow assigned to link l_{ij}
λ_α	Time fraction scheduled for CTS T_α
M	Number of maximal CTS's of the network: $(T_1, T_2, ..., T_M)$
$\tilde{R}^\alpha_{ij}$	Effective forwarding rate of link l_{ij} during the active phase of CTS T_α

variable for the usability of link $\langle i, j \rangle$ under a GCTS T_α, then we have $\tilde{R}^\alpha_{ij} = \psi^\alpha_{ij} \tilde{R}_{ij}$, $\forall j \in J(i)$.

Let H_{S_j} be the sending rate from source S_j toward the destination D. We have the following LP optimization formulation to characterize the throughput bound with single destination.

$$\max \sum_{j=1}^{N_s} H_{S_j} \tag{4}$$

subject to,

$$f_{ij} \geqslant 0, and \quad f_{ij} = 0, if \quad j \notin J(i), \forall \langle i, j \rangle \in E, \tag{5}$$

$$\sum_{\langle i,j \rangle \in E} f_{ij} = \sum_{\langle j,i \rangle \in E} f_{ji}, \forall i \in V - \mathcal{S} - \{D\} \tag{6}$$

$$\sum_{\langle S_j,k \rangle \in E} f_{S_j k} - \sum_{\langle i,S_j \rangle \in E} f_{iS_j} = H_{S_j}, \forall S_j \in \mathcal{S} \tag{7}$$

$$\sum_{\langle D,i \rangle \in E} f_{Di} = 0 \tag{8}$$

$$f_{ij} \leqslant \sum_{\alpha=1}^{M} \lambda_\alpha \tilde{R}^\alpha_{ij}, \quad \sum_{\alpha=1}^{M} \lambda_\alpha \leqslant 1; \lambda_\alpha \geqslant 0, 1 \leqslant \alpha \leqslant M \tag{9}$$

Equation (4) is to find the maximum amount of traffic sent out from all the source nodes $\{H_{S_j}\}$ to the destination. Constraint (5) specifies that the traffic on all links are none negative and there are no traffic from one node to its neighbor nodes that are not in its forwarding candidate set. Constraint (6) specifies flow conservation on all relay nodes. Constraint (7) specifies the flow conservations on all source nodes $S_{j, 1 \leqslant j \leqslant N_s}$. Constraint (8) states that no outgoing traffic from destination node D. Constraint (9) preserves that only one CTS could be activated to transmit at any given time and the traffic assigned on each link is no more than the aggregate effective forwarding rate of that link during all active phases of CTSs. Depending on what types of CTSs we used as the input of the above formulation, we will get different bounds. Conservative CTS (CCTS) leads to conservative upper bound, Greedy CTS (GCTS) leads to optimistic upper bound of the end-to-end throughput.

3.5 Throughput Bound to Multiple Destinations

Based on the formulation for the single destination, we develop a model to calculate the throughput bound from multiple sources to multiple destinations in hybrid wireless networks. Suppose there are a set $\mathcal{S}$ including N_s source nodes $\{S_i, 1 \leqslant i \leqslant N_s\}$, and a set $\mathcal{D}$ including N_d destination nodes $\{D_j, 1 \leqslant j \leqslant N_d\}$. In OR, at each node i, there are different candidate forward sets for different destinations. Let $J^d(i)$ be the candidate forwarding set for destination node d at node i, $J^d(i) = \{i_1^d, i_2^d, \cdots\}$ with the priority order $\{i_1^d < i_2^d < \cdots\}$. Similar to (3), for the q-th forward candidate i_q^d in $J^d(i)$, we can calculate the effective forwarding rate for destination d on link $\langle i, i_q^d\rangle$ as

$$\tilde{R}_{ii_q^d}^{(d)} = Rp_{ii_q^d}\prod_{k=0}^{q-1}(1-p_{ii_k^d}), \quad 1 \leqslant q \leqslant |J^d(i)|. \tag{10}$$

Since CTS is also defined based on forwarding sets for all nodes, we need to include destination information into the definition of CTS. More specifically, a Conservative CTS (CCTS) T_α is a set of transmitter-destination pairs $T_\alpha = \{(i, d(i)), i \in V, d(i) \in V\}$, such that all links $\{\langle i, j\rangle, \forall j \in J^{d(i)}(i), \forall (i, d(i)) \in T_\alpha\}$ are usable when all transmitters in CCTS are active. Similarly, a Greedy CTS (GCTS) T_α is a set of transmitter-destination pairs $T_\alpha = \{(i, d(i)), i \in V, d(i) \in V\}$ such that for each transmitter i in GCTS, there exists at least one link $\langle i, j\rangle$, $j \in J^d(i)$, that is usable when other transmitters in GCTS are active.

Similar to the single destination case, we need to calculate the effective forwarding rate $\tilde{R}_{ij}^{\alpha(d)}$ on each link $\langle i, j\rangle$ for destination d under each CTS T_α. If a CCTS T_α is scheduled and $(i, d) \in T_\alpha$, all links from i to nodes in $J^d(i)$ are usable, therefore $\tilde{R}_{ij}^{\alpha(d)} = \tilde{R}_{ij}^{(d)}, \forall j \in J^d(i)$, which is calculated in (10); if $(i, d) \notin T_\alpha$, $\tilde{R}_{ij}^{\alpha(d)} = 0$. If a GCTS T_α is scheduled and $(i, d) \in T_\alpha$, some links associated with i maybe not usable. Let ψ_{ij}^α be a binary variable for the usability of link $\langle i, j\rangle$ under a GCTS T_α, then we have $\tilde{R}_{ij}^{\alpha(d)} = \psi_{ij}^\alpha \tilde{R}_{ij}^{(d)}, \forall j \in J^d(i)$.

Let $H(S_i, D_j)$ be the sending rate from source i to the destination j, and $f_{ij}^{(d)}$ be the traffic on link $\langle i, j\rangle$ destined to d. We have the following LP optimization formulation to characterize the aggregate throughput bound.

$$\max \sum_{i=1}^{N_s}\sum_{j=1}^{N_d} H(S_i, D_j) \tag{11}$$

subject to,

$$f_{ij}^{(d)} \geqslant 0, \quad f_{ij}^{(d)} = 0, if \quad j \notin J^d(i), \forall \langle i, j\rangle \in E, \forall d \in \mathcal{D} \tag{12}$$

$$\sum_{\langle i,j\rangle\in E} f_{ij}^{(d)} = \sum_{\langle j,i\rangle\in E} f_{ji}^{(d)}, \forall i \in V - \mathcal{S} - \{d\}, \forall d \in \mathcal{D} \tag{13}$$

$$\sum_{\langle S_j,k\rangle\in E} f_{S_jk}^{(d)} - \sum_{\langle i,S_j\rangle\in E} f_{iS_j}^{(d)} = H(S_j,d), \forall S_j \in \mathcal{S}, \forall d \in \mathcal{D} \tag{14}$$

$$\sum_{\langle d,i\rangle\in E} f_{di}^{(d)} = 0, \forall d \in \mathcal{D} \tag{15}$$

$$f_{ij}^{(d)} \leqslant \sum_{\alpha=1}^{M} \lambda_\alpha \tilde{R}_{ij}^{\alpha(d)}, \forall d \in \mathcal{D}, \sum_{\alpha=1}^{M} \lambda_\alpha \leqslant 1; \lambda_\alpha \geqslant 0, 1 \leqslant \alpha \leqslant M \tag{16}$$

Similar to the single destination case, constraints (12), (13), (14) and (15) specifies legitimate per-destination traffic flow on all links, relay nodes, source nodes, and destinations. Constraint (16) preserves that one CTS can be activated to transmit at any time, for each destination, the traffic assigned on each link is no more than total amount of traffic that could be delivered on that link during all active phases of CTSs.

4 Performance Evaluation

In this section, we apply models developed in the previous section to study the throughput bound and capacity of hybrid wireless networks with OR in three different cases: Single Source to Single Destination, Multiple Sources to Single Destination and Multiple Sources to Multiple Destinations.

4.1 Methodology

We setup the case studies with different network sizes and different characteristics of the network in order to get the most accurate conclusions about the hybrid wireless network capacity. Based on the transmission range of transmitters, we developed a C++ program to calculate CTSs. Given node locations, the program calculates CTSs for both single-channel and multiple-channel models. The proposed LP method could be used for any type of packet loss model. For demonstration, we use a simple packet loss model on link $\langle i,j\rangle$: $p_{ij} = 1 - d_{ij}/L$, where d_{ij} is the distance between i and j, L is the maximum transmission range. The node transmission rate is fixed at 10 packets/timeslot. We then calculate the effective forwarding rate on each link $\tilde{R}_{ij}^{\alpha}$ for each CTS. Then we use AMPL - CPLEX to solve the LP Problem to find the maximum throughput in each case. For each case study, we conduct multiple simulation runs and report the average of all runs.

To understand the gain of OR in hybrid wireless networks, we also compare the performance of OR with that of hybrid unicast routing in the same network setting. To calculate the throughput bound of UR, we first build up the link conflict graph out of the original graph. In the conflict graph, each vertex corresponds to a link in the original graph. There is a link between two vertexes in the conflict graph if two corresponding links in the original graph interfere with each other. By finding all maximal independent sets of vertexes in the conflict graph, we can find the maximal sets of links in the original graph that can be activated at the same time. Assuming there are M maximal independent sets $(T_1, T_2, ..., T_M)$. At any time, one set can be scheduled to transmit and all links in the scheduled set can transmit simultaneously. Let λ_α be the time fraction that T_α is scheduled. The forwarding rate on link $\langle ii_q \rangle$ is:

$$\tilde{R}_{ii_q} = Rp_{ii_q} \tag{17}$$

Then, we can reuse the LP formulation from (4) to (9) and from (11) to (16) to calculate the capacity of hybrid wireless networks under either OR or UR routing method.

4.2 Single Source to Single Destination

At first, we run the case studies with a small network setting. The network area is 500m x 500m. There are 8 wireless ad-hoc nodes. Nodes are located at the special positions as in Figure 3(a). Node 1 is the source, node 8 is the destination. The initial radio range of nodes is 110m. Source node and relay nodes send out packets with rate 10 packets/timeslot. We start the experiment with pure ad-hoc transmissions. Then BTs are added with different parameters and positions. From this setup, we calculate the maximum end to end throughput at 6 different cases of BT locations. Case 1: no BT; Case 2: one BT in position T_1; Case 3: two BTs in positions T_2 and T_3; Case 4: two BTs in positions T_2 and T_3 with the radio range of every node from now on increased to 120m; Case 5: two BTs in position T_4 and T_5. Case 6: two BTs in position T_6 and T_3. We make the comparison between the OR and UR on the same network setting. The LP results of the bound of end to end throughput are showed on the Figure 3(b). First, we analyze throughput bound with OR. In ad-hoc mode, the bound of throughput from node 1 to node 8 is 0.3 packets/TS. All traffic routed through the path 1→2→3→ . . . →8. The bottom necks on the maximum throughput path are the links: 2→3, 3→4, 4→5, 5→6, 6→7. In case 2, when one BT is added to the network, throughput bound start gaining to 0.36 packets/TS since some additional traffic could be routed through infrastructure network over links 4→T_1→6. Case 3, when two BTs are located in the positions of T_2 and T_3, throughput bound increased to 1.0 packets/TS with more traffic could be

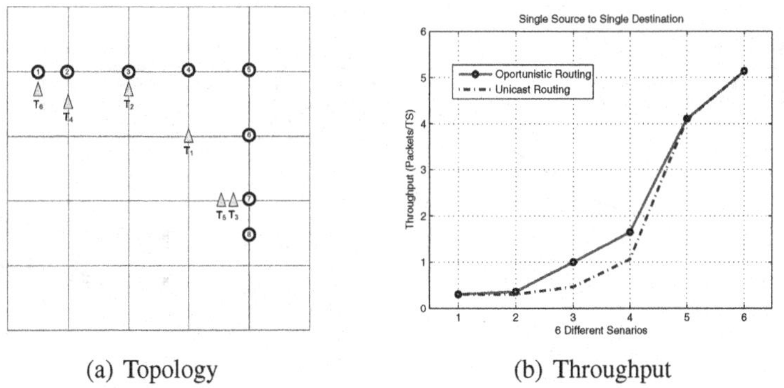

(a) Topology (b) Throughput

Fig. 3. End-to-End throughput improvement from single source to single destination routed through infrastructure network to get over "bottleneck" area. In case 4, when the radio range of each node is slightly increased, the throughput bound is increased to 1.65 packets/TS since the packet loss ratios on links are reduced. Consequently the effective forwarding rates on wireless links are increased. When the positions of two BTs are changed to positions T_4 and T_5 in case 5, the throughput is increased to 4.1 packets/TS. This is because all traffic is routed through high bandwidth infrastructure network through link $T_4 \rightarrow T_5$. In case 6, two BTs are located in position T_6 and T_3, closer to the source and destination nodes. That helps to improve the bound of throughput from node 1 to node 8 to 5.14 packets/TS. All traffic is routed through the infrastructure network from the source to the destination in a single path.

When wireless nodes use UR to forward data, throughput gets through a single path from the source node to the destination node. The throughput bound on each case is: Case 1: 0.3 packets/TS; Case 2: 0.3 packets/TS; Case 3: 0.47 packets/TS; Case 4: 1.06 packets/TS; Case 5: 4.09 packets/TS; Case 6: 5.14 packets/TS. Throughput bound of the network with OR will be higher than with UR when the optimal solution using more than one path to forward data toward the destination node. There for in cases 2, 3, 4 and 5, throughput gain with OR are higher than that with UR. But both routing methods get the same throughput bound for the cases 1 and 6. From the above results, we can see that infrastructure network could significantly increase the end-to-end throughput of ad-hoc network with OR. The numbers and locations of BTs are important and could significantly impact the end-to-end throughput. OR will outperform UR for the cases of using multi paths to get to the destination.

4.3 Multiple Sources to Single Destination

For the case of multiple sources and single destination, we studied two different settings. The first setting is to calculate the throughput bound with random demands, random nodes and BTs positions. The second setting is to study the impact of BT distribution patterns on the throughput bound of the network. For each setting, we make comparisons between two different node models and between OR and UR.

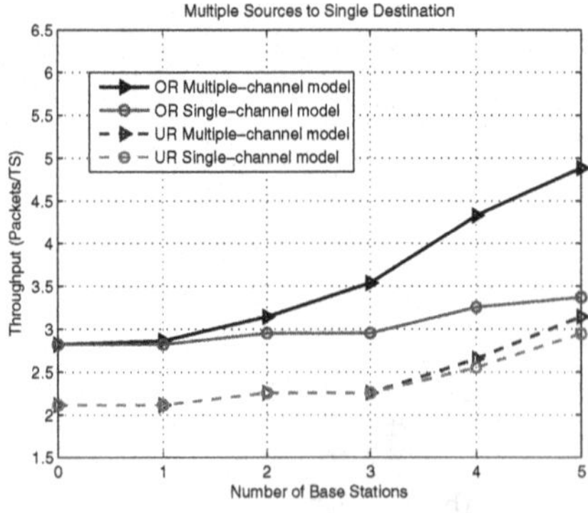

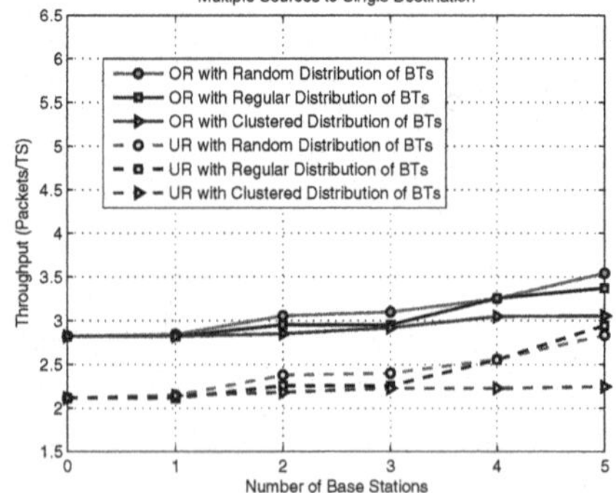

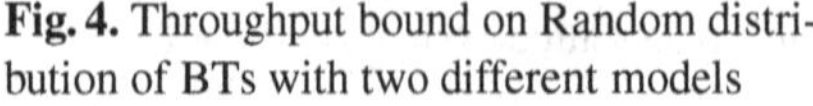

Fig. 4. Throughput bound on Random distribution of BTs with two different models

Fig. 5. Throughput bound on different distribution patterns of single-channel BTs

There are 35 nodes randomly located in an area of 1000m x 1000m. We randomly select 10 nodes as source nodes, and one node as destination node. The radio range of nodes is 150m. Source nodes and relay nodes send data with rate 10 packets/TS. We start with pure ad-hoc network, then add BTs randomly to the network. For the multiple-channel model, we assume that BTs have 4 wireless channels to communicate with wireless nodes.

Figure 4 presents the throughput bound of hybrid wireless networks as the number of BTs increases. The figure shows the average values of 10 samples. From the figure, we see the growth trend of the throughput bound in random hybrid network as the number of base stations increases. When the number of base stations gets to 5, the throughput bound of hybrid wireless network outperforms the pure ad-hoc case by more than 170% for multiple-channel model and by 125% for single-channel model (4.88 and 3.54 packets/TS compared to 2.86 packets/TS in ad-hoc case). Due to the increased capacity of BTs, the throughput bound increases higher on multiple-channel model than single-channel model. Analyzing the results in details, we found that when the number of base stations is increased, the traffic routed through the pure ad-hoc network decreases and the traffic through the infrastructure network increases. As a result, the end-to-end throughput is improved. Also for either models, OR always get significantly higher throughput than UR. The reason is that with multiple demands from multiple sources, at each hop, there are more chances for wireless nodes to forward packets through multi-nodes CRS under OR than a single relay node under UR. This makes the throughput bounds of OR much higher than UR.

For the second case study, we measure the throughput bound with the same network configuration as the first case but with three different BT's distribution patterns: random distribution, regular distribution and clustered distribution. For the regular distribution with n BTs, we evenly partition the whole area into n regions around the center of the area. One BT is placed at the center of each region. For the clustered distribution of BTs, we used a simple greedy scheme to add BTs one by one to the network at positions that could cover the highest number of uncovered wireless nodes. Again, we study the two models. Figure 5 shows the comparison of the throughput bounds under three BT distribution patterns with the single-channel model. With the same number of base stations deployed on the network, the throughput bound in regular distribution case is approximately as high as the throughput bound in the random distribution case, but higher than the throughput bound in the case of clustered distribution. This is because that, with the clustered BT distribution, many wireless nodes fall into the coverage of a same BT. Since each BT shares a single channel between ad-hoc transmission, the transmission through BT actually becomes the bottleneck and the bandwidth in the infrastructure network cannot be efficiently utilized. Meanwhile, for the multiple-channel model in Figure 6, the throughput bound in the case of clustered BT distribution is 15% $\sim$ 20% higher than the random and regular BT distributions. In the extreme case when number of base stations is 5, the throughput bound for 3 cases are: 4.81, 5.14 and 5.81 packets/TS respectively. The reason is: with clustered distribution, more wireless nodes can be covered with the same number of BTs, and with multiple channels, the transmissions through BTs are no longer bottleneck. This shows that the more nodes covered by BTs, the higher the throughput bound improvement. Also, in the studied

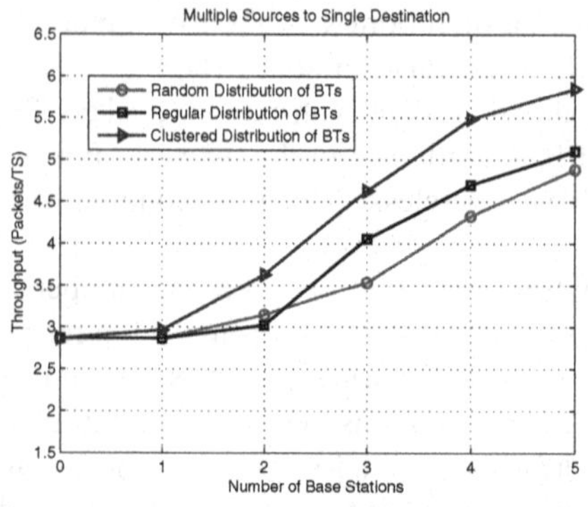

Fig. 6. Throughput bound on different distribution patterns of multi-channel BTs

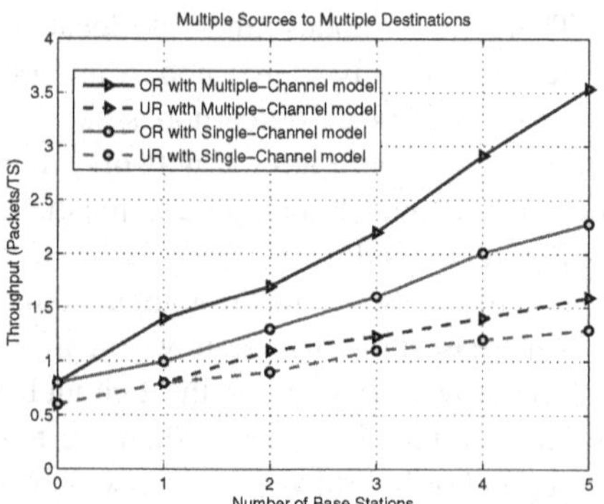

Fig. 7. Bound of throughput from Multiple Sources to Multiple Destinations

case, due to random source nodes distribution, the regular BT distribution only slightly outperforms the random BT distribution.

4.4 Multiple Sources to Multiple Destinations

For the case of Multiple Sources to Multiple Destinations, we set up a network area of 1000m x 1000m. There are 10 nodes randomly placed in the area. We then configure 3 random pairs of source and destination nodes. The radio range of nodes is 150m. Node transmission rate is 10 packets/TS. We start with pure ad-hoc network. We then gradually add BTs one by one to random locations of the network until 5 BTs are added. The throughput improvement result is shown in Figure 7. From this figure, we can see that the throughput bound increases as the number of base stations increases. Throughput bound for multiple-channel model is significantly higher than the single-channel model for both OR and UR. OR always got higher throughput bound than UR. For OR, the throughput bound with 5 BTs in case of multiple-channel model is 3.5 packets/TS, which is more than four times of the throughput bound of the pure ad-hoc case (0.79 packets/TS) and equals to 160 % throughput bound in case of single-channel model.

5 Conclusion

In this paper, we studied the throughput gain of OR routing schemes in hybrid wireless networks. We first extended OR to exploit the high throughput routes over infrastructure network. We then developed linear programming models to characterize the capacity of hybrid wireless networks with OR. Our models calculate the end-to-end throughput bounds from multiple source nodes to single, as well as, multiple destination nodes. Through case studies on example hybrid wireless networks, we demonstrated the throughput gain of OR in hybrid wireless networking environment. The impacts of several factors on OR performance, such as the radio range of nodes, the density and distribution pattern of BTs were evaluated in the case studies. We also demonstrated that OR got higher throughput gain than UR in both ad-hoc and hybrid wireless networks, single-channel and multiple-channel models. The current solving assumes simplified packet loss model. As a work for future direction, we will study the capacity of hybrid wireless networks with more realistic packet loss models. We used maximal CTS to calculate the throughput bounds. However it is time consuming to identify maximal CTS for large networks. We will study more efficient ways to model the conflicts between hybrid wireless links and characterize network capacity. We also plan to verify our capacity results using packet level simulations.

References

1. Zeng, K., Lou, W., Zhai, H.: On End-to-end Throughput of Opportunistic Routing in Multirate and Multihop Wireless Networks. In: IEEE Infocom 2008, Phoenix, AZ, April 15-17 (2008)
2. Liu, B., Liu, Z., Towsley, D.: On the capacity of hybrid wireless networks. In: Proc. IEEE Infocom (2003)
3. Kozat, U., Tassiulas, L.: Throughput capacity of random ad hoc networks with infrastructure support. In: Proc. of MobiCom (2003)
4. Agarwal, A., Kumar, P.: Capacity bounds for ad hoc and hybrid wireless networks. ACM SIGCOMM Computer Communications Review 34, 71–81 (2004)
5. Zemlianov, A., de Veciana, G.: Capacity of ad hoc wireless networks with infrastructure support. IEEE JSAC 23(3), 657–667 (2005)
6. Dai, Q., Rong, L., Hu, H.: Capacity, "Delay and Mobility in hybrid wireless networks". In: IEEE International Conference on Networking, Sensing and Control, 2008. ICNSC 2008 (2008)
7. Liu, B., Thiran, P., Towsley, D.: Capacity of a Wireless Ad Hoc Network with Infrastructure. In: Proc. ACM Mobihoc (2007)
8. Chachulski, S., Jennings, M., Katti, S., Katabi, D.: Trading structure for randomness in wireless opportunistic routing. In: Proc. ACM Sigcomm (2007)
9. Dubois-Ferriére, H., Grossglauser, M., Vetterli, M.: Least-Cost Opportunistic Routing. In: 2007 Allerton Conference on Communication, Control, and Computing, Monticello IL (September 2007)
10. De Couto, D.S.J., Aguayo, D., Bicket, J., Morris, R.: A high-throughput path metric for multi-hop wireless routing. In: Proceedings of the 9th annual international conference on Mobile computing and networking, San Diego, CA, USA, September 14-19 (2003)
11. Biswas, S., Morris, R.: Opportunistic routing in multi-hop wireless networks. In: Proceedings of the Second Workshop on Hot Topics in Networks (HotNets-II), Cambridge, MA (November 2003)
12. Shah, R.C., Wietholter, S., Wolisz, A., Rabaey, J.M.: When Does Opportunistic Routing Make Sense? In: IEEE PerSens (March 2005)
13. Gupta, P., Kumar, P.R.: The capacity of wireless networks. IEEE Transactions on Information Theory 46(2) (March 2000)
14. Grossglauser, M., Tse, D.N.C.: Mobility Increases the Capacity of Ad-hoc Wireless Networks. In: IEEE Infocom, pp. 1360–1369 (2001)

NQAR: Network Quality Aware Routing in Wireless Sensor Networks

Jaewon Choi[1,*], Baek-Young Choi[2], Sejun Song[3], and Kwang-Hui Lee[1]

[1] Dept. of Computer Engineering, Changwon National University,
9 Sarim-dong, Changwon, Gyeongnam 641-773, South Korea
[2] Dept. of Computer Science and Electrical Engineering,
Univ. of Missouri, Kansas City,
5100 Rockhill Road, Kansas City, MO 64110, United States
[3] Dept. of Electrical and Computer Engineering, Wichita State University,
1845 Fairmount, Wichita, KS 67260, United States

Abstract. We propose a network quality aware routing (NQAR) mechanism to provide an enabling method of the delay-sensitive data delivery over error-prone wireless sensor networks. Unlike the existing routing methods that select routes with the shortest arrival latency or the minimum hop count, the proposed scheme adaptively selects the route based on the network qualities including link errors and collisions with minimum additional complexity. It is designed to avoid the paths with potential noise and collision that may cause many non-deterministic backoffs and retransmissions. We propose a generic framework to select a minimum cost route that takes the packet loss rate and collision history into account. NQAR uses a data centric approach to estimate a single-hop delay based on processing time, propagation delay, packet loss rate, number of back-offs, and the retransmission timeout between two neighboring nodes. This enables a source node to choose the shortest expected end-to-end delay path to send a delay-sensitive data. The experiment results show that NQAR reduces the end-to-end transfer delay up to approximately 50% in comparison with the latency-based directed diffusion and the hop count-based directed diffusion under the error-prone network environments. Moreover, NQAR performs better than other routing methods in terms of jitter, reachability, and network lifetime.

Keywords: WSNs, Routing, Delay, Quality.

1 Introduction

Wireless Sensor Networks (WSNs) consist of a large number of battery-powered, low-cost, and tiny sensor nodes, which have the capability of sensing, data processing, and wireless communication. The sensor nodes can be deployed randomly close to or inside the terrain of interest to create a cooperative and self-organizing wireless ad hoc network with minimal provisioning. Unlike the traditional high cost and fixed

* This work was supported in part by the Korea Research Foundation Grant (KRF-2007-357-D00208) from the Korean Government (MOEHRD).

B. Liu et al. (Eds.): WASA 2009, LNCS 5682, pp. 224–233, 2009.

array of sensor systems, the WSN technology enables countless new applications including environmental hazard monitoring, military surveillance and reconnaissance, and health monitoring applications to name a few.

In WSNs, the sensed data and control messages are exchanged between sensor nodes and the control (sink) nodes relayed by the neighbor sensor nodes via a multi-hop routing protocol. To build practical services over WSNs, especially considering sensors' limitations in power, computation, and local storage, it is both critical and challenging to support efficient network layer multi-hop routing protocols. To cope with the characteristics of sensor nodes, various new routing protocols have been proposed in WSNs [1][2][3]. These protocols are mainly designed 1) to reduce redundant data (data aggregation) and unnecessary controls by using on-demand data centric approaches [4][5][6][7], 2) to limit the network scale by using structured approaches such as clustering and hierarchical architectures [8][9], and 3) to decrease distributed state overheads by using location based approaches [10][11]. To achieve an efficient resource usage, those routing protocols commonly select routes based upon the static quality factors such as maximum power availability, minimum energy usage, maximum position progress, minimum hop count, or the shortest arrival latency. However, those static quality based parameters have limitations in case of the error-prone and densely deployed WSNs, because they do not take retransmissions due to packet losses and backoffs due to collisions into consideration.

In this paper, we propose a network quality aware routing (NQAR) mechanism to provide an enabling method of the delay-sensitive data delivery over error-prone and densely deployed WSNs. The proposed scheme adaptively utilizes the dynamic network quality factors including link error rates and collision histories. It is designed to avoid the paths with potential noise and collision, which may cause many non-deterministic retransmissions and backoffs. NQAR uses a data centric on demand method to estimate the minimum cost end-to-end routing path. The summary of NQAR operation is as follows. First, each sensor node maintains its network quality information including the packet loss rate, the number of retransmissions, and the number of backoffs for a certain period. Second, during the interest dissemination period, each node relays interest with its network quality information to its neighbors. Third, each nodes estimates a single-hop delay based on processing time, propagation delay, packet loss rate, number of backoffs, and retransmission timeouts between two neighboring nodes, which in turn enables the calculations of expected end-to-end delays during the interest dissemination period. Finally, a source node can send delay-sensitive data to a sink node along the shortest expected end-to-end delay path. It is clearly noted that the proposed scheme simultaneously considers the dynamic qualities of wireless network links in addition to the overall static parameters including per-hop processing time and power in the routing decision process. To the best of our knowledge, NQAR is the first work to simultaneously consider the qualities of wireless links as well as processing time in the routing decision process. We perform extensive simulations under the various qualities of links and show that the NQAR reduces the end-to-end transfer delay up to 50% in comparison with the latency-based directed diffusion [5] and the hop count-based directed diffusion [7] under the error-prone (link error and collision) network environments. Moreover, NQAR performs better than other routing methods in terms of jitter. Since NQAR inherently avoids error-prone links, the reachability (reliability) is improved in case of no packet retransmission. We also find that NQAR prolongs the network lifetime as it prevents unnecessary energy consumption, resulting from the relative reductions of packet losses and retransmissions.

The remainder of this paper is organized as follows. Section 2 summarizes the related work to this research. Section 3 explains the details of the NQAR algorithm and Section 4 presents the experiment results. Finally, we conclude our work in Section 5.

2 Related Work

Routing protocols in WSNs have been designed as power efficient, data-centric, and cooperative approaches to address its unique characteristics (i.e. resource limitations). Sensor Protocols for Information via Negotiation (SPIN) [4] is one of the earliest data centric approaches, which allow any sensor nodes around the information data to initiate interest advertisements. Before sending the real data, it starts negotiation with the collected data description (meta-data). It achieves energy efficiency by reducing redundant data transmission (data fusion). However, if the sensor nodes around the information data are not interested in that data, the sensor node initiated advertisement mechanism cannot ensure the delivery of the information data. Directed diffusion (DD) [5][6] is one of the most popular data centric approaches, which starts the interest (a network task description) dissemination from the sink nodes. During the interest propagation, each sensor node keeps a time stamped interest to establish the gradients from the data source back to the sink. When the source has data to send, it transmits the data along the lowest latency path. It is energy efficient in that the message propagation and aggregation are done between neighbors. It is also better than SPIN from the data coverage point of view. However, it has additional overhead on sensor nodes to handle the control information and does not work well with time-sensitive or continuous data delivery applications due to its interest dissemination model. It also does not consider the global energy-balancing to increase network lifetime. Energy-efficient Differentiated Directed Diffusion (EDDD) [7] is an extension of the directed diffusion protocol to establish a path between a source and a sink with the minimum hop count and the minimum available energy to enhance the shortcomings of the original directed diffusion. However, both directed diffusion and EDDD do not reflect the error-prone (noise and collision) network link characteristics of WSNs [1]. It causes non-deterministic additional delays due to retransmission and/or re-processing in the MAC layer.

Low Energy Adaptive Clustering Hierarchy (LEACH) [8] is introduced to achieve an energy efficiency to arrange a structured traffic path by forming clusters. Only a few representative nodes (cluster heads) are involved in the cluster control (assigning transmission time for each sensor node: TDMA) and data transmission (including data aggregation). To support equal energy dissipation, the cluster head roles are evenly alternated among the sensor nodes. Power-Efficient Gathering in Sensor Information Systems (PEGASIS) [9] is a network lifetime enhancement work over LEACH protocol. It reduces communication overhead by arranging local coordination among the neighboring sensor nodes and by chaining the communication path to the sinks instead of the cluster formation. Nodes need only communicate with their neighbors and they take turns in communicating with the sink.

Greedy Perimeter Stateless Routing (GPSR) [10] is an earlier version of the location-based geographic routing protocol. It decreases the number of distributed states and the maintenance overheads by calculating the next forwarding node based only upon the destination location information on each forwarding node. It chooses a routing path according to the best position progression towards the destination. However, it will need an additional location service to map positions and node IDs. Geographic and Energy Aware Routing (GEAR) [11] adds an energy parameter to the geographical progress parameter in calculation of the best destination path. It refines the next estimated progression cost with the learned cost, which is the feedback information of the previously propagated packet cost to the destination. It also reduces interest dissemination to a certain region to conserve more energy.

None of the above methods, however, takes non-deterministic delays due to retransmissions and backoffs into consideration. NQAR is unique in that it uses dynamic network quality parameters to estimate the event-to-sink delay path.

3 Network Quality Aware Routing (NQAR) Algorithm

An important observation is that packets may be lost due to channel problems such as interference and collision. Then the link layer retransmission is performed after a packet loss is detected, and the time necessary to detect a packet loss is at least twice as much as one-way propagation delay. Furthermore, there can be repeated packet loss and retransmission attempts. Therefore, the problem of selecting a path with the shortest end-to-end propagation delay or minimum hop count is that the performance is significantly affected by packet loss rates of links. In such a case, the existing methods will undergo the additional delays that are not presupposed, and may fail to transmit time-critical data successfully.

We first describe our approach of a path selection that is based on directed diffusion[1], but takes packet loss rate into account in link costs. We then discuss how the cost can be used to meet various parameters such as delay and energy consumption.

Using the packet loss rate from a node i to its neighboring node j ($r_{loss(i,j)}$), the expected cost to successfully transmit a packet from i to j ($Cost_{(i,j)}$) is estimated by Equation (1). $c_{init(i,j)}$ and $c_{retrn(i,j)}$ are the initial packet transmission costs, and the additional cost to retransmit the packet in case of packet loss from i to j, respectively. Note that $c_{retrn(i,j)}$ is multiplied by the expected number of retransmissions given the link error rate. Nodes maintain the local packet loss rates and propagation delays from themselves to their neighboring nodes. This packet loss rate is the recent average of packet losses on a link and is maintained by each node in the MAC layer [12].

$$Cost_{(i,j)} = c_{init(i,j)} + \frac{r_{loss(i,j)}}{1 - r_{loss(i,j)}} \times c_{retrn(i,j)} \quad (1)$$

Then a node receiving the *interest* packet, i can estimate the end-to-end cost from itself to the sink node 0, ($Cost_{(i,0)}$) by the sum of hop costs along the path as shown in Equation (2).

[1] Note that we do not assume link symmetry. If links are symmetric, one-phase directed diffusion can be used. Otherwise, two-phase diffusion should be used.

$$Cost_{(i,0)} = \sum_{k=1}^{i} Cost_{(k,k-1)} \tag{2}$$

The nodes with data matching the query in the *interest* packet flooded by the sink node become the sources. A source node selects a path (gradient) whose $Cost_{(i,0)}$ value is the smallest among the $Cost_{(i,0)}$s of all the directed gradients it is maintaining.

Equation (1) can be applied for various considerations. For example, if the expected number of (re)transmissions is considered, we can set $c_{init(i,j)}$ and $c_{retrn(i,j)}$ to be 1 as in Equation (3).

$$Cost_{(i,j)} = \frac{1}{1 - r_{loss(i,j)}} \tag{3}$$

This enables us to select a path with the smallest number of (re)transmissions. The small number of (re)transmissions is important as excessive retransmissions cause energy depletion early. Moreover the different number of packet retransmissions over an error-prone link/path adversely affects jitter, in addition to delay.

We can also compute the expected energy consumption of a packet over the link between node i and j, by assigning an energy usage $c_{eng(i,j)}$ to $c_{init(i,j)}$ and $c_{retrn(i,j)}$ from the Equation (1), as below.

$$Cost_{(i,j)} = \frac{c_{eng(i,j)}}{1 - r_{loss(i,j)}} \tag{4}$$

Now we focus on the expected end-to-end delay. Let us consider the time necessary for node i to successfully transmit a packet to its neighboring node j. First, the delay should include a packet processing time (t_{prcs}) and propagation time (t_{prop}). Once a packet loss occurs, the packet should be retransmitted after a retransmission timeout (t_{rto}) that is typically set as multiples of the propagation delay and is greater than the round trip time. In this case, the packet should be processed again at node i. Thus, as for 1 hop delay, the initial cost ($c_{init(i,j)}$) in Equation (1) would be the sum of the processing time ($t_{prcs(i,j)}$) and propagation delay ($t_{prop(i,j)}$), and the additional cost ($c_{retrn(i,j)}$) will become the sum of the processing time ($t_{prcs(i,j)}$) and retransmission timeout ($t_{rto(i,j)}$), which leads to Equation (5).

$$Cost_{(i,j)} = (t_{prcs(i,j)} + t_{prop(i,j)}) + \frac{r_{loss(i,j)}}{1 - r_{loss(i,j)}} \times (t_{prcs(i,j)} + t_{rto(i,j)}) \tag{5}$$

There are several factors involved in a packet processing time (t_{prcs}). When a packet needs to be sent, a clear channel assessment (CCA) is first needed. Then possible queueing and actual transmission times are required. Thus, the processing time (t_{prcs}) is the sum of the channel assessment time (t_{chnasm}), transmission time (t_{trn}) and queueing time (t_{queue}) as in Equation (6).

$$t_{prcs(i,j)} = t_{chnasm(i,j)} + t_{trn(i,j)} + t_{queue(i,j)} \tag{6}$$

Channel assessment time (t_{chnasm}) varies depending on the channel condition. When a node has a packet to send, its micro-controller observes whether the channel is clear or not. If the channel is clear, the micro-controller signals the radio component such as CC2520 [13] to send out the packet. Otherwise, it will back off for some time (t_{chnbck}) and then test the channel again. The problem is that whether the channel is clear or not is nondeterministic. Thus, we predict the channel condition by the history of backoffs. A micro-controller can count up the number of channel backoffs and calculate the rate of channel busy to channel clear that is referred to as the channel backoff rate ($r_{chnbck(i,j)}$) in this paper. That is, a channel backoff rate represents the possibility of channel failure in the node. Thus the channel assessment time is estimated by Equation (7). Transmission time (t_{trn}) is deterministic in nature given a packet size and link bandwidth.

$$t_{chnasm(i,j)} = \frac{r_{chnbck(i,j)}}{1 - r_{chnbck(i,j)}} \times t_{chnbck(i,j)} \tag{7}$$

By Equations (5)-(7), we can calculate an expected transfer delay of a link. $Cost_{(i,j)}$ in Equation (5) then means the sum of the expected delays in successfully transferring data over 1 hop considering channel assessment time, transmission time, propagation delay, packet loss rate, and retransmission timeout. This in turn enables us to compute the expected end-to-end delay of a path via Equation (2).

Note that NQAR requires that each sensor should estimate and maintain its network quality information such as link loss rate and channel loss rate. Exponentially weighted moving average algorithm can be used for the estimations, and the memory and computation overhead involved is small. In summary, our route selection approach effectively takes into account of dynamic as well as static qualities of link and channel for the performance of delay, jitter, and energy consumption that are analyzed in Section 4.

4 Performance Evaluations

In this section, we compare the performance results of NQAR with the original latency-based directed diffusion [5] and the hop count-based directed diffusion EDDD [7]. The performance metrics used include the end-to-end delays, jitters, reachability (reliability), and network lifetime.

For the simulations, we implemented the interest dissemination mechanisms of the directed diffusion. Three different gradient generation algorithms are implemented in each sensor node. The simulations were conducted with 10 x 10 grid network topology. Network conditions including packet loss rates and channel backoff rates are randomly allocated within the range of error rate parameter configuration. For example, if the range of error rate is 20%, random rate values from 0% up to 20% are assigned to the packet loss rate and the channel backoff rate respectively. Propagation delays are proportional to the distance between two sensor nodes. We also assume that the retransmission timeout is four times as long as the one-way propagation delay. Each sensor node maintains the history of packet loss rates and propagation delays, and a channel backoff count. As shown in Table 1, we use various simulation parameters the same as the sensor motes implementation by using CC2520 [13] chipset specification. We set the channel backoff time the same as the TinyOS setting that is 6.6 *ms*. Transmission time is 4.0 *ms*, resulting from dividing packet size (1,024 bits) by bandwidth (250 Kbps).

Table 1. Configuration of experiment parameters

Item	Value
Number of nodes	100
Initial energy of each node	1 J
Transmitting power	77.4 mW
Receiving power	55.5 mW
Packet size	1,024 bits
Inter-arrival time	100 ms
Bandwidth	250 Kbps

4.1 Results

Figure 1 shows the end-to-end transfer delays of the three routing protocols under different range of error rates. The presented values are the average delays of 1,000 packet transmissions. In Figure 1, we observe that the improvement of delay values of NQAR becomes significant according to the increments of the range of error rates. For example, average delay of NQAR improves by approximately 43% in comparison with the latency-based protocol and by about 51% compared with the hop count-based protocol under 90% of the range of error rates[2]. Usually, if error rates are high, retransmissions and channel backoffs happen more frequently. The results clearly indicate that NQAR works very well, especially in error-prone networks.

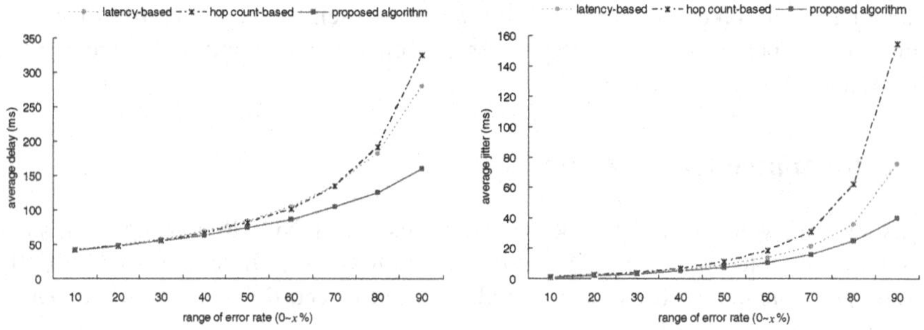

Fig. 1. End-to-end delay

Fig. 2. Average jitter

Figure 2 presents the average jitter values of the three routing protocols under different range of error rates. The values are measured by the standard deviation of the end-to-end delays. NQAR has smaller average jitters and increases the average jitters slower than other protocols along the increments of the range of error rates. For example, average jitter of NQAR is smaller than that of the latency-based protocol about 47% and that of the hop count-based protocol by approximately 74% under 90% of the range of error rates. The hop count-based protocol shows the worst average jitter values, because it has less consideration on various timing conditions related to the dynamic link quality. The results indicate that NQAR will work better for the various applications time-critical data transmissions and jitter-sensitive streaming data transmissions.

---

[2] Random rate values from 0% up to 90% are assigned to the packet loss rate and the channel backoff rate respectively.

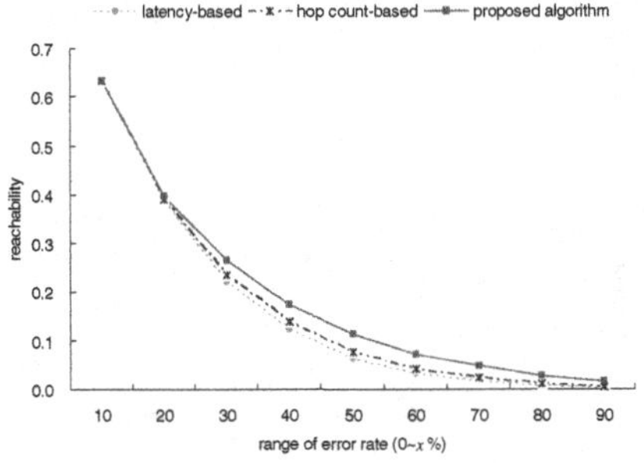

Fig. 3. Event-to-sink reachability

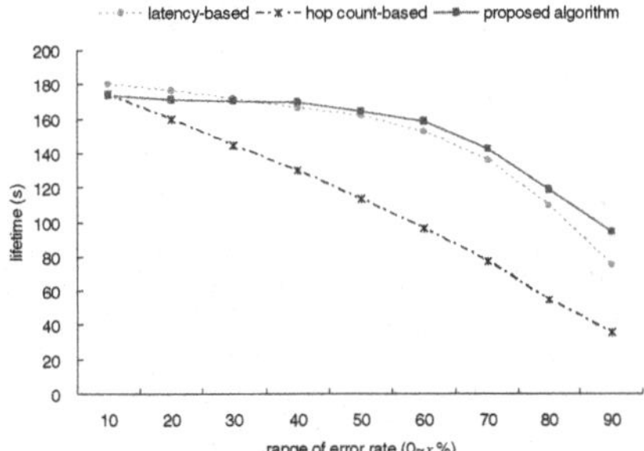

Fig. 4. Network lifetime

Figure 3 presents the event-to-sink reachability of the three routing protocols under different range of error rates. The event-to-sink reachability is the ratio of the number of packets arrived at the sink node to the number of packets sent by a source node after assuming no sensor node performs packet loss detection or retransmission. It is very important to choose a reliable routing path considering the overheads of the loss recovery mechanisms (packet loss detection and retransmission) that include memory overhead for caching, delay increase by retransmission, and additional energy consumption due to memory access and retransmission. As illustrated in Figure 3, NQAR has higher event-to-sink reachability than the other protocols. It is because NQAR protocol selects a path with a lower probability of packet losses, as in Equation (1).

Figure 4 exhibits the network lifetimes of the three routing protocols under different range of error rates. We define network lifetime as the operation time until the first sensor node runs out of the energy. From a routing protocol point of view, the network lifetime can be prolonged by reducing the number of unnecessary packet (re)transmissions and by spreading traffic equally over the network. It shows that the network lifetimes of NQAR are longer and the decrements are smoother than the other protocols along the increments of the range of error rates. It is because NQAR efficiently reduces unnecessary retransmissions by selecting a less error-prone routing path. We further analyze the impacts of routing protocols on the network lifetime with the number of retransmissions and standard deviations of the number of transmissions.

Figure 5 shows the number of retransmissions of the three routing protocols under different range of error rates. NQAR has much fewer number and slower increments of retransmissions than the other protocols along the increments of the range of error rates, since it takes the link quality into consideration. Compared to the latency-based protocol, the hop count-based protocol has fewer retransmissions, which is because the shorter distance path has the less chance of packet losses.

Figure 6 shows the standard deviation of the packet transmissions by each node. The smaller standard deviation means packets were sent evenly by each node. Although it shows similar traffic distribution trends, NQAR has smaller standard deviations than the hop count-based protocol and larger standard deviations than the latency-based protocol. It is because the hop count-based protocol may have a little more chance of selecting a certain node in the diagonal direction path to the sink node.

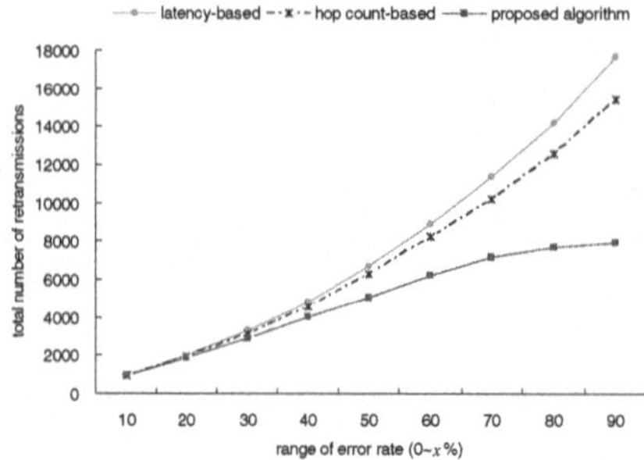

Fig. 5. Total number of retransmissions

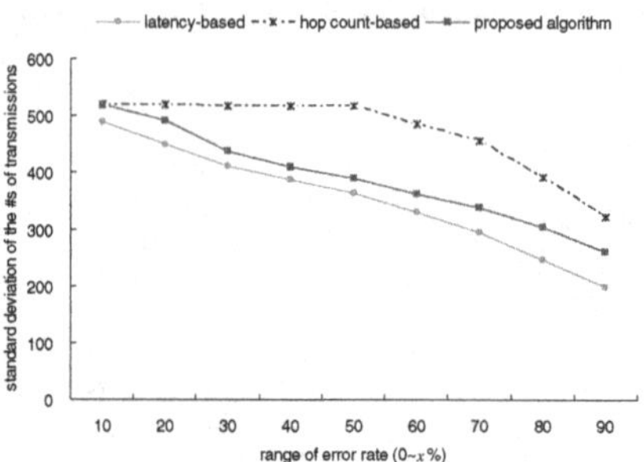

Fig. 6. Standard deviation of the packet transmissions

According to both Figure 5 and Figure 6, for the given similar traffic distribution trends, it is clear that NQAR prolongs the network lifetime in the error-prone networks by reducing the chance of retransmissions.

5 Conclusion

We have proposed a network quality aware routing (NQAR) protocol for error-prone and densely deployed WSNs. In addition to the existing routing methods that select routes with the least energy cost, the shortest arrival latency, or the minimum hop count, NQAR adaptively utilizes the network qualities including link error rates and collision histories in the route selection. It is designed to avoid the paths with potential noise and collision that may cause many non-deterministic delays due to backoffs and retransmissions. NQAR uses a data centric approach to estimate a single-hop delay based on processing time, propagation delay, packet loss rate, the number of backoffs, and retransmission timeouts between two neighboring nodes. This in turn enables the source to select the shortest expected end-to-end delay path to send data. NQAR is unique in that it holistically considers the qualities of wireless links as well as processing time in the routing decision process. Through extensive simulations, we have validated that NQAR improves the end-to-end transfer delay performance and decreases jitter significantly under the error-prone (link error and collision) network environments. We have shown that NQAR increases end-to-end reachability (reliability) in case of no data retransmission, because of its inherent nature of avoiding error-prone links. We have also found that NQAR prolongs the network lifetime, as it prevents unnecessary energy consumption resulting from the relative reductions of packet losses and retransmissions.

References

[1] Akyildiz, I.F., Su, W., Sankarasubramaniam, Y., Cayirci, E.: A Survey on Sensor Networks. IEEE Communications Magazine 40(8), 2–114 (2002)

[2] Al-Karaki, J.N., Kamal, A.E.: Routing Techniques in Wireless Sensor Networks: A Survey. IEEE Wireless Communications 11(6), 6–28 (2004)

[3] Akkaya, K., Younis, M.: A Survey on Routing Protocols for Wireless Sensor Networks. Ad Hoc Networks 3(3), 325–349 (2005)

[4] Heinzelman, W., Kulik, J., Balakrishnan, H.: Adaptive Protocols for Information Dissemination in Wireless Sensor Networks. In: Proc. 5th ACM/IEEE Mobicom Conference (MobiCom 1999), Seattle, WA, August 1999, pp. 174–185 (1999)

[5] Intanagonwiwat, C., Govindan, R., Estrin, D.: Directed Diffusion: A Scalable and Robust Communication Paradigm for Sensor Networks. In: Proc. of the 6th Annual International Conference on Mobile Computing and Networking (MobiCom 2000), Boston, Massachusetts, USA, August 6-11, pp. 56–67 (2000)

[6] Intanagonwiwat, C., Govindan, R., Estrin, D., Heidemann, J., Silva, F.: Directed Diffusion for Wireless Sensor Networking. IEEE/ACM Transactions on Networking (TON) 11(1), 2–16 (2003)

[7] Chen, M., Kwon, T., Choi, Y.: Energy-Efficient Differentiated Directed Diffusion (EDDD) in Wireless Sensor Networks. Computer Communications 29(2), 231–245 (2006)

[8] Heinzelman, W., Chandrakasan, A., Balakrishnan, H.: Energy-Efficient Communication Protocol for Wireless Microsensor Networks. In: Proceedings of the 33rd Hawaii International Conference on System Sciences (HICSS 2000) (January 2000)

[9] Lindsey, S., Raghavendra, C.: PEGASIS: Power-Efficient Gathering in Sensor Information Systems. In: IEEE Aerospace Conference Proceedings, vol. 3(9-16), pp. 1125–1130 (2002)

[10] Karp, B., Kung, H.T.: GPSR: Greedy perimeter stateless routing for wireless sensor networks. In: The Proceedings of the 6th Annual ACM/IEEE International Conference on Mobile Computing and Networking (MobiCom 2000), Boston, MA (August 2000)

[11] Yu, Y., Estrin, D., Govindan, R.: Geographical and Energy-Aware Routing: A Recursive Data Dissemination Protocol for Wireless Sensor Networks, UCLA Computer Science Department Technical Report, UCLA-CSD TR-01-0023 (May 2001)

[12] Felemban, E., Lee, C.-G., Ekici, E., Boder, R., Vural, S.: Probabilistic QoS Guarantee in Reliability and Timeliness Domain in Wireless Sensor Networks. In: Proc. of IEEE INFOCOM 2005, Miami, Florida, USA, March 13-17 (2005)

[13] Texas Instruments: CC2520 Datasheet, `http://focus.ti.com/docs/prod/folders/print/cc2520.html`

A Network Coding Approach to Reliable Broadcast in Wireless Mesh Networks*

Zhenyu Yang, Ming Li, and Wenjing Lou

Department of Electrical and Computer Engineering,
Worcester Polytechnic Institute, 100 Institute Road, Worcester, MA 01609
{zyyang,mingli,wjlou}@wpi.edu

Abstract. Reliable broadcast is an important primitive in wireless mesh networks (WMNs) for applications such as software upgrade, video downloading, etc. However, due to the lossy nature of wireless link, it is not trivial to achieve the reliability and efficiency at the same time. In this paper, we put forward R-Code, a reliable and efficient broadcast protocol based on intra-flow network coding. The key idea is to construct a minimum spanning tree as a backbone whose link weight is based on ETX metric. The broadcast overhead and delay are simultaneously reduced by enabling each node to be covered by the parent node in the tree which promise its reliable reception of the whole file. Opportunistic overhearing is utilized to further reduce the number of transmissions. Extensive simulation results show that R-Code always achieves 100% packet delivery ratio (PDR), while introducing less broadcast overhead and much shorter delay than AdapCode.

1 Introduction

Wireless mesh networks (WMNs) is an approach to provide high-bandwidth network access for a specific area, which becomes prosperous during the last decade. Broadcast is an important function in WMNs. For example, it is necessary for software code updates which may be done at the initial deployment and testing phase of the network, or being used in multimedia services like video/audio downloading. The salient feature of such kind of applications is that they require the PDR (Packet Delivery Ratio) to be strictly 100%, which means all the nodes have to download every byte of the broadcasting file. Also, since other normal unicast traffics may exist in the network at any time, broadcast applications are desired to have good coexistence with these traffics, which means consuming minimal amount of network bandwidth and complete the broadcast process quickly.

The fundamental challenge in the design of reliable and efficient broadcast protocol in WMNs is the unreliability of wireless links, which is mainly due to the path loss, interference and channel fading [12]. Previous schemes usually achieve reliability by applying the same mechanisms as used in wired broadcast protocols, such as ARQ mechanism [13], FEC mechanism [11], etc. However, these schemes tend to introduce large amount of redundant transmissions and incur problems like "ACK explosion", etc.

* This work was supported in part by the US National Science Foundation under grants CNS-0626601, CNS-0746977, CNS-0716306, and CNS-0831628.

B. Liu et al. (Eds.): WASA 2009, LNCS 5682, pp. 234–243, 2009.

Network coding (NC) has emerged as a promising technique to increase the network bandwidth-efficiency and reliability recent years. Briefly speaking, NC is a new communication paradigm for packet-based networks which breaks with the conventional store-and-forward way. It gives the intermediate nodes the flexibility of encoding different packets received previously together for subsequent transmission with the purpose of benefiting multiple receivers with single transmission. Those packets mixed together could be from different data flows, in which case it is called inter-flow nework coding [8]; otherwise if they are from the same data flow, it is called intra-flow network coding [2]. Moreover, NC makes the schedule of retransmission easier since now each encoded packet is the same and no specific packet is indispensable for the receivers.

Prior works that exploit the advantage of NC for reliable broadcasting in wireless networks are still at preliminary stage. As far as we know, AdapCode [7] is the only protocol designed purposely for reliable broadcasting. It combines probabilistic forwarding and NC together and promises perfect reliability by a "NACK+timer" mechanism.

In this paper, we propose R-Code, a NC-based reliable broadcast protocol in WMNs with unreliable links. In R-Code, we build a minimum spanning tree (MST) to behave as a "virtual backbone", whose link weight is based on ETX metric [4]. *The key idea of R-Code is that every node is covered by the best neighbor, the parent node in the MST, for its reliable reception and successful decoding.* R-Code continues to exploit the broadcast nature of wireless transmission to further reduce the transmissions. Simulation results show that, R-Code can guarantee 100% PDR with less broadcast overhead than AdapCode and achieve much lower broadcast delay at the same time.

The rest of the paper is organized as follows. Related work in given in Section 2. We describe the network model and network coding primitives in Section 3. The design of the protocol is shown in Section 4. In Section 5, we present the simulation results. In the end, we give conclusion in Section 6.

2 Related Work

Exploiting the idea of NC for reliable broadcast is still at a preliminary stage. MORE [2] is the first NC-based protocol for reliable routing. To the best of our knowledge, it is also the only one that is implemented and applied in real world scenario. MORE combines the idea of opportunistic routing (OR) [1] and network coding, which eliminates OR's requirement for complicated and costly coordination between receivers while enjoying the throughput benefit of NC. MORE is designed for supporting unicast flows and it can also be extended to support broadcast applications, although it does not perform very well in that case, because almost all the nodes become forwarders which incur heavy contention and congestion. Koutsonikolas *et.al.* proposed Pacifier [10], a high throughput, reliable multicast protocol based on MORE. Pacifier addresses the weakness of MORE by maintaining a multicast tree structure. It also alleviates the "crying baby" problem by a round-robin algorithm and further increases the throughput. Namely, when one of the destinations has very poor connection and if we try to satisfy its reliability requirement, then the rest of the destinations will experience performance degradation. We note that although both MORE and Pacifier can support broadcast applications, they are not purposely designed for that. In both protocols, the source node is the only active "pump" that transmits packet proactively and all the other intermediate nodes just play the role of forwarder, which passively relay what they received. Thus, for some missing packet, the destinations can only get it from the source rather than some node nearby that has already got the whole file, which will incur many redundant transmissions and is inefficient.

In comparison, since each node has to get the whole file ultimately, the schemes specially designed for broadcast make all the nodes within the network to be "temporary source" after receiving the whole file. AdapCode [7] is such a protocol, which aims at reliable broadcast in wireless sensor networks (WSNs) and studies the global code updates. It also tries to achieve load balance and rapid propagation. Since we will compare R-Code with AdapCode in this paper, a brief overview of it is presented below. AdapCode is motivated by probabilistic forwarding approach, which means for each received packet, the receiver just forwards it with some probability less than 1 in order to reduce the traffic introduced compared with naive flooding. AdapCode combines this idea with network coding which further reduces the traffic by letting a node send one coded packet after receiving every N coded packets from other nodes. The particular choice of such N is called *coding scheme*. Also, it applies a "NACK+Timer" mechanism to promise 100% reliability. During the code update process, each node keeps a count-down timer. If the node missed some packets, it will broadcast a NACK packet when the timer fires, within which contains the IDs of those missed packets. All the other nodes overheard this NACK and have already received those requested packets will take part in a response process and one of them will be randomly selected as the real responder. This process goes on until all the nodes get all the packets. However, since the NACK mechanism inherently tends to elongate the reception time, AdapCode still needs relatively long propagation delay. Also, the link quality is not explicitly considered in the design of AdapCode, which may result in additional transmissions in realistic networks.

3 Preliminaries

3.1 Network Model

In this paper, We only consider the wireless mesh network that consists of all the routers, one of which plays the role of gateway that connects to the Internet. The gateway is always the only source that wants to broadcast files through the network. Since we only consider the one-to-all scenario, intra-flow network coding [2] is adopted to reduce the number of transmissions and simplify the protocol design. The WMN is modelled as a weighted undirected graph $G(V, E)$, where V is the set of nodes and E is the set of links. The weight of link (i, j) is: $w_{i,j} = (1/p_{i,j} + 1/p_{j,i})/2$, where $p_{i,j}$ is the probability of successful packet reception from i to j, vice versa (the reason for taking the average of probabilities of both directional is that the construction of MST is based on undirected links). Since in reality mesh routers are often statically deployed, we assume the network topology and also the link quality keep stable during one broadcast session [14], which is usually finished within several minutes at most. Moreover, we assume the routers have enough memory that can store several generations simultaneously, each of which usually are tens of kilo-bytes. The definition of generation is presented in the following section.

3.2 Network Coding

For the purpose of reducing the complexity of encoding/decoding and storage requirement, the broadcasted file is divided into segments sequentially, called generation [3]. Each generation contains same number of k packets, denoted as $s_i, i = 1, 2, ..., k$. All the encoding/decoding operation is done within one generation, where a coded packet x is the linear combination of all these k original packets: $x = \sum_{j=1}^{k} \alpha_j s_j$. $< \alpha_1, \alpha_1, ..., \alpha_k >$ is the encoding vector, which identifies how to generate this coded packet from the original packets in this generation. Each element of the coding vector is independently randomly [6] selected from a Galois field $GF(2^q)$. Every coded packet includes this coding vector in the packet header for future decoding. Upon receiving a coded packet x of generation i, the receiver puts x into the buffer matrix for generation i and then tries to decode it along with all the other coded packets of this generation received previously by doing Gaussian elimination on the buffer matrix, whose complexity is $O(k^3)$.

3.3 Minimum Spanning Tree

Since applying MST for broadcast is well studied in both wired and wireless networks, many efficient and distributed algorithms of building and maintaining MST for a given network are proposed [5, 9],. In our protocol, since we assume the WMN is static, the MST can be computed and updated distributively along with the routing table at relatively long intervals and be shared by multiple broadcast sessions, thus the extra communication and computation overheads introduced can be amortized and are negligible [2].

4 R-CODE

In this section, we present the design of R-Code. At first, we use a simple example to explain the intuition behind R-Code; In the following, we present the details of the design.

4.1 Intuition of R-Code

The intuition underlying our approach is that for each node i , since all its neighbors capable of behaving as a "temporary source", it can always choose to be reliably covered by the best neighbor with minimum cost, where the word best means this neighbor can transmit one packet to i reliably with minimum expected number of transmissions. We believe a good global performance can be achieved through all those simple, optimal local decisions.

This can be illustrated with a simple example that is shown by Fig.1. This toy network consists of 4 nodes, with S being the only source and wants to broadcast a packet

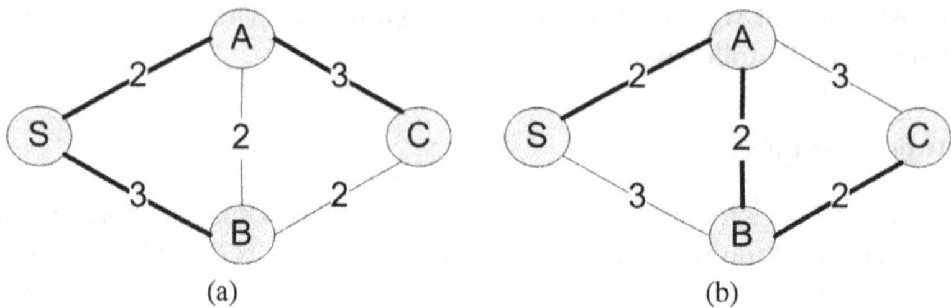

Fig. 1. A simple example to show the intuition of R-Code. The ETX value is assigned for each link.

reliably. If we build the broadcast tree like Pacifier does, which is to combine all the best unicast path from source to every other nodes, then we get the tree that is shown in Fig.1(a) with bold lines. The total expected number of transmissions introduced is 6, where both of S and B generates 3 transmissions; However, we observe that some nodes are not covered by the best choice. For example, C can get the packet from B with 2 transmissions, which is more efficient than getting it directly from the source S. If we make all nodes to be covered by their best neighbors, then we naturally build a MST as broadcast tree, which is shown in Fig.1(b). Now the total expected number of transmissions needed is $2 + 2/3 + 14/9 = 4.23$, which is generated by S, B, C respectively. Actually, this is also the minimum number of transmissions needed. However, we do not claim that this optimal result can always be achieved through R-Code. We note that our effort in this paper is put on designing practical and efficient protocol rather than pursing theoretically optimal performance.

4.2 Design of R-Code

Generally, R-code can be divided into two stages.

Initialization Stage. During this stage, each node i broadcasts "Hello" packets with period T to estimate the quality of links to other nodes nearby. Based on collected information, i builds up a neighbor table $Table_i$, $Table_i = \{j|w_{i,j} \leq W_{threshold}, j \in V \text{and } j \neq i\}$, where $W_{threshold}$ is some predefined threshold value. Further, based on this table, i builds a MST [9] and stores this tree structure by a node set which contains all the neighbors within the MST.

Above is the general initialization stage. For a specific broadcast session, the single source s makes the MST just built a directed tree originated from itself, which is the root. Each node i records the upstream node as its Guardian $Guardian_i$, and all the downstream nodes as $Children_i$. The $Guardian_s$ is s itself and the children sets of all the leaf nodes is empty.

Broadcast Stage. R-Code works on top of the IP layer and the packet header format is shown in Fig.2, which contains a type field that identifies data packet from ACK packet, the source's IP address, broadcast session id, generation index, generation size which

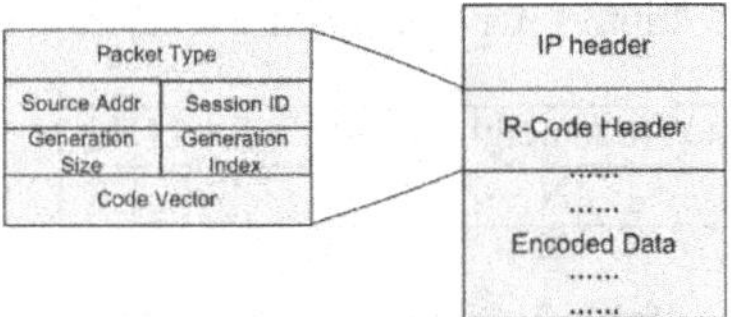

Fig. 2. R-Code packet header format

indicates the total number of generations and code vector that describes the packet content with respect to the original packets. The broadcast session starts by letting the source continuously send coded packets of the first generation with interval T_{pkt}. When a node i overhears a packet, it stores this packet in the corresponding buffer matrix and runs Gaussian elimination on the matrix to check if it received enough information to retrieve all the original packets of this generation. If so, it records this reception time and notifies the guardian by sending a positive ACK in unicast, whose reliability can be promised by MAC layer. Then, if i is currently not in the process of broadcasting for other generation, it begins to play the role of guardian for its children by keeping sending coded packets of this generation with interval T_{pkt}. Otherwise, if i is still not able to retrieve all the original packets of this generation, it keeps silent and waits for more packets;

In R-Code, guardian node needs to receive the ACKs from all its children before moving to the next generation. After receiving all those ACKs, the guardian node will deliver the packets of this generation to upper layer and flush the corresponding buffer matrix. Additionally, it should add the index of this generation into the successfully acknowledged ones and pause for a period of $T_{generation}$ time before broadcasting the next generation, allowing the children nodes to rebroadcast what they just received [15]. There are two challenges need to be solved to make R-Code run smoothly.

1. How to select the generation to be sent next? For source node, it moves sequentially, from generation n to generation $n+1$, until complete the last generation and then quit this broadcast session. We note that source's quit does not mean the termination of the broadcast session, which maybe still goes on in other nodes. For other transmitters, the selection of next generation follows FIFO policy: it chooses the earliest received generation from those successfully received but not successfully acknowledged ones, the index of which is always the smallest too. If there are no such generations currently, then this node checks the previous records of successfully acknowledged generations to see if all the generations have been acknowledged. If so, it quits this broadcast session; or else this node keeps silent and wait for future reception.

2. Dealing with ACKs. As presented above, the perfect reliability is guaranteed by the guardian-child relationship. Although multiple ACKs will be send back to the guardian, we argue that this will not incur "ACK explosion" problem for reasons listed below. (1) We make a requirement about the generation size used in R-Code, which should be relatively large, i.e, 32 or 64. Because those ACKs is in generation-level rather than packet-level, if one generation contains large number of packets, for some specific guardian node, the link qualities between it to its children are different and

Table 1. Optimal coding schemes

average neighbor	0-5	5-8	8-11	11-
N	1	2	4	8

Table 2. Simulation parameters

Simulation Parameter	Value
$W_{threshold}$	5
Random backoff time	10..30ms
pathloss model	two-ray
fading mode	rician
rician k factor	4
Hello packet interval(T)	1s
$T_{generation}$	100ms

those child nodes tend to receive the whole generation successfully at different times with very high probability. (2) Since the child nodes are usually a small subset of all the neighbors of the guardian node, thus even some of them really reply ACKs almost at the same time and cause a conflict at the guardian node side, the collision avoidance mechanism of 802.11 can easily handle this. Further, we require that each child backoffs a random short time before sending ACK.

5 Performance Evaluation

We evaluate the performance of R-Code and compare it with AdapCode through extensive simulations. In our implementation of AdapCode, for fairness, we always allow the nodes to generate coded packets by doing linear combination of all the k original packets rather than a portion of them, where the latter is AdapCode's intended consideration for WSNs. As claimed in [7], this relaxation could give adapCode better performance on bandwidth efficiency.

5.1 Simulation Settings

We use Glomosim simulator in our simulations. The network consists of a 7×7 grid of static nodes, where the grid size equals $200m$ and average number of neighbors per node is 9.51. For AdapCode, We follow the optimal coding schemes presented in [7], which is shown in Table 1.

The source is fixed to be node 0 in the left-bottom corner for all the simulations. The broadcasted file is 1MB and is divided into 4096 pieces, each of which is 256 byte long. The MAC layer runs $802.11b$ with some modification that fixes the data rate to be $11Mbps$. Other related simulation parameters are listed in Table 2. We run both protocols in this network 10 times with T_{pkt} varied from $11ms$ to $29ms$ and use the following metrics for comparison:

Average propagation delay: The total time required for a node to receive the whole file, average over all nodes.

Average number of transmissions: The total number of transmissions of all the nodes divided by the node number. It gives an estimate of the average traffic introduced by this broadcast session.

Average number of linearly dependent packets: The total number of linearly dependent packets received by all the nodes divided by the node number. We note that this number includes those packets overheard by some node who has already got the whole generation that this packet belongs to.

Note that we do not compare PDR performance, since both R-Code and AdapCode can guarantee 100% reliability.

5.2 Traffic

We first compare the average traffic introduced by both protocols. Besides data packets, we also count the NACKS of AdapCode and those unicast packets for maintaining the guard relation and ACKs of R-Code. From Fig.3(a) we can see that R-Code introduces fewer transmissions than AdapCode in all settings and the performance gain is greater when the per packet broadcast interval T_{pkt} is larger, where the maximal gain can be 15% when T_{pkt} is $29ms$. We also observe that as T_{pkt} increases, the average number of transmissions incurred by R-Code decreases while the average traffic introduced by AdapCode keeps almost the same and even increases a little. The key reason for this is R-Code's local optimal decision. For each node, it always choosing the best neighbor to be the guardian. In comparison, when a node i in AdapCode is requiring some more packets, it just randomly chooses a node from those who overheard i's NACK and also able to reply. This randomly selected node, we argue, maybe not the best one and thus needs more number of transmissions to satisfy the requirement of node i. The second cause for the more number of transmissions of AdapCode is presented below. Since the timer of each node in AdapCode is restored to initial value once this node receives a new packet due to the "lazy NACK" mechanism, on the opposite, this means if the node does not receive any packet for some period, its timer will fire firstly and it will broadcast the NACK. Unfortunately, this is just what happened to those nodes with bad connection to the sender. Further, because this bad connected node has received much fewer packets, it will require more retransmissions in its NACK and most of those retransmissions tend to be useless for those good connected receivers who only miss small number of innovative packets. This is shown clearly in Fig.3(b), where we can see that nodes in AdapCode encounter more linearly dependent reception in all cases.

5.3 Propagation Delay

Compared with the performance of introduced traffic, R-Code brings a larger gain over AdapCode when it comes to the metric of propagation delay. It is obviously to see that under all settings, the average propagation delay of R-Code performances much better than AdapCode, which is shown in Fig.4(a). The gain is higher when packet broadcast interval is small, i.e., when T_{pkt} is $11ms$, the reduction ratio can be almost 50%. This is consistent with our analysis in previous section, which indicates that NACK mechanism inherently tends to elongate the propagation delay. And we also observe that both protocols' broadcast delay grow almost linearly to the packet broadcast interval. This is

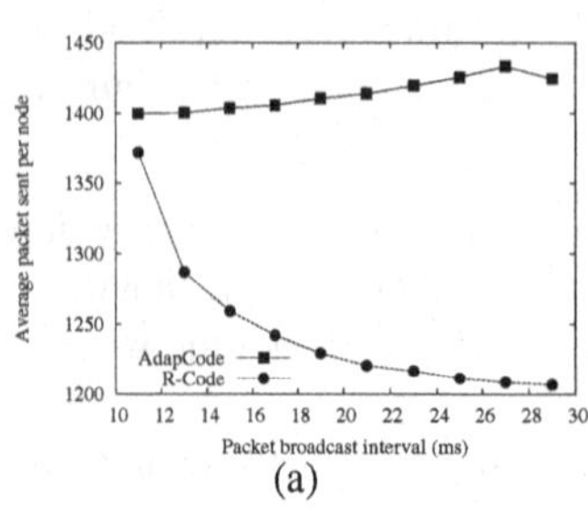

(a)

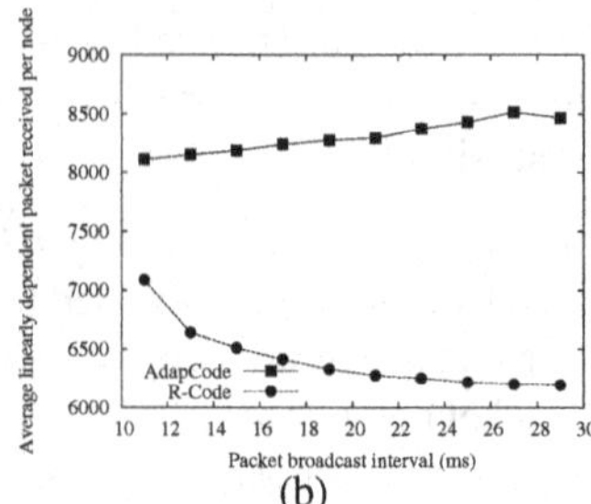

(b)

Fig. 3. Traffic

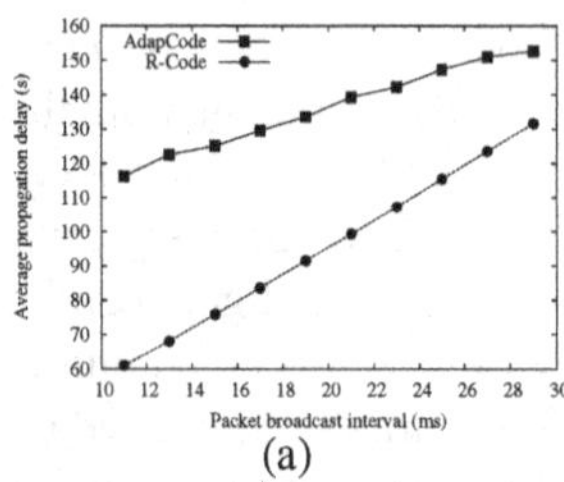

(a)

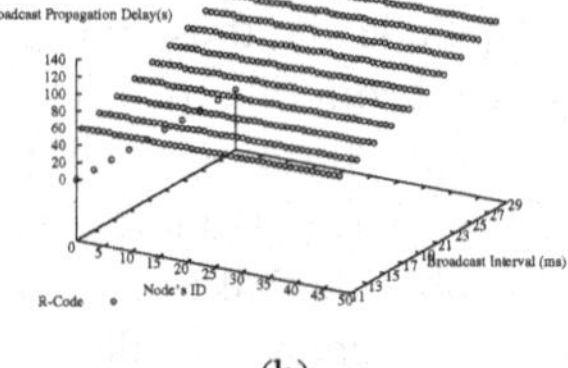

(b)

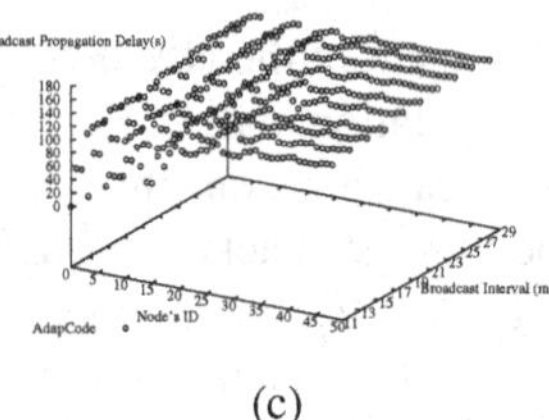

(c)

Fig. 4. Propagation Delay

because all the transmitters inject packets into network with a period of T_{pkt}. Besides shorter average propagation delay, R-Code can also achieves more consistent individual node propagation delay, which means all the nodes running R-Code can get the whole file at approximately the same time. This is shown in Fig.4(b); In comparison, nodes running AdapCode receive the whole file with delays that have much larger variation, which is shown in Fig.4(c). This makes R-Code more appropriate for applications like software updates where some subsequent operations will be done just after the reception of the whole file.

From the simulation results presented above, we can see that R-Code is a simple and high performance reliable broadcast protocol for WMNs, which achieves less transmission overhead and shorter broadcast delay without the need of complicated timer mechanism. However, we also observe that there is a tradeoff between those two metrics, both for R-Code and AdapCode. Thus for specific application, it should chooses proper parameter values according to its own requirement.

6 Conclusion

In this paper, we focus on designing a practical broadcasting protocol for wireless mesh networks, which provides 100% reliability for all receivers. We present R-Code, A simple, efficient and high-performance broadcast protocol with the help of network coding to reduce the number of total transmissions required and average propagation delay. The core idea is to promise each node to be covered by the best neighbor. Based on the intuition that local optimal solution can achieves better global performance, we apply MST as the broadcast tree. Extensive simulations showed that R-Code can reduce the number of required transmissions and propagation delay as high as 15% and 50%, respectively, compared with the state-of-the-art AdapCode.

References

1. Biswas, S., Morris, R.: Opportunistic routing in multi-hop wireless networks. SIGCOMM Computer Communications Review (2004)
2. Chachulski, S., Jennings, M., Katti, S., Katabi, D.: Trading structure for randomness in wireless opportunistic routing. In: SIGCOMM 2007 (2007)
3. Chou, P., Wu, Y., Jain, K.: Practical network coding. In: Proceedings of the 41st Allerton Conference on Communication, Control, and Computing (September 2003)
4. De Couto, D., Aguayo, D., Bicket, J., Morris, R.: A high-throughput path metric for multi-hop wireless routing
5. Garay, J.A., Kutten, S., Peleg, D.: A sub-linear time distributed algorithm for minimum-weight spanning trees. SIAM J. Comput. (1998)
6. Ho, T., Mdard, M., Koetter, R., Karger, D.R., Effros, M., Shi, J., Leong, B.: A random linear network coding approach to multicast. IEEE Trans. Inform. Theory (2006)
7. Hou, I.-H., Tsai, Y.-E., Abdelzaher, T., Gupta, I.: Adapcode: Adaptive network coding for code updates in wireless sensor networks. In: INFOCOM 2008 (April 2008)
8. Katti, S., Rahul, H., Hu, W., Katabi, D., Medard, M., Crowcroft, J.: Xors in the air: practical wireless network coding. SIGCOMM Computer Communications Review (2006)
9. Khan, Maleq, Pandurangan, Gopal: A fast distributed approximation algorithm for minimum spanning trees. Distributed Computing (April 2008)
10. Koutsonikolas, D., Hu, Y.-C., Wang, C.-C.: High-throughput, reliable multicast without crying babies in wireless mesh networks. In: INFOCOM 2009 (April 2009)
11. Koutsonikolas, D., Hu, Y.C.: The case for fec-based reliable multicast in wireless mesh networks. In: DSN 2007: Proceedings of the 37th Annual IEEE/IFIP International Conference on Dependable Systems and Networks, pp. 491–501 (2007)
12. Marco Zú, N.Z., Krishnamachari, B.: An analysis of unreliability and asymmetry in low-power wireless links. ACM Trans. Sen. Netw. 3(2), 7 (2007)
13. Pagani, E., Rossi, G.P.: Reliable broadcast in mobile multihop packet networks. In: MobiCom 1997, pp. 34–42 (1997)
14. Reis, C., Mahajan, R., Rodrig, M., Wetherall, D., Zahorjan, J.: Measurement-based models of delivery and interference in static wireless networks. SIGCOMM Comput. Commun. Rev. 36(4), 51–62 (2006)
15. Scheuermann, B., Lochert, C., Mauve, M.: Implicit hop-by-hop congestion control in wireless multihop networks. Ad Hoc Networks (2008)

Workload-Driven Compressed Skycube Queries in Wireless Applications

Zheng Fang[1], Jie Wang[1], and Donghui Zhang[2]

[1] Department of Computer Science, University of Massachusetts, Lowell, MA 01854
[2] College of Computer and Information Science, Northeastern University, Boston, MA 02115

Abstract. Compressed skycubes provide an efficient mechanism for skyline queries that are useful for wireless applications, where the size of a compressed skycube is often much smaller than that of the original skycube. However, even with compression, the entire compressed skycube may still be too large to be placed in the main memory of a wireless device. To overcome this obstacle we introduce the concept of workload-driven subspace compressed skycubes to meet the needs of an expected query profile. While it is NP-hard to find the best set of subspace compressed skycubes within the given memory constraint to serve the largest possible number of queries, we devise a polynomial-time approximation algorithms with a proven approximation guarantee. Our simulation results show that the approximation algorithm produces feasible solutions in reasonable amount of time with approximation ratios close to 1.

Keywords: Compressed skycube, approximation algorithm.

1 Introduction

Skyline queries [HJL$^+$06, LCY08] have made wireless and mobile applications more efficient, including applications in multi-criteria decision making, data mining [JHE04], and user-preference queries [HKP01]. For example, one can improve GPS service response by returning the requested POI (point of interest) based on skyline queries on distance, price, and other specific requirements of the POI, rather than returning all nearby POIs. To process such queries, a full skycube needs to be stored in the main memory to serve queries on all possible combinations of attributes. It may require a large size of main memory to store a full skycube of high-dimensional data, which may not be available in wireless devices. Compressed skycubes were introduced to address this problem [XZ06]. Although expected to be much smaller than a full skycube, a compressed skycube may still be too large, for most mobile devices have architectural limitations on main memories. We introduce a concept of workload-driven subspace compressed skycubes to tackle this problem. In particular, we study how to select a set of most frequently-queried subspace skylines into the main memory on a given user query profile to serve as many queries as possible. This is an NP-hard problem. We devise a polynomial-time approximation algorithm with a

B. Liu et al. (Eds.): WASA 2009, LNCS 5682, pp. 244–253, 2009.

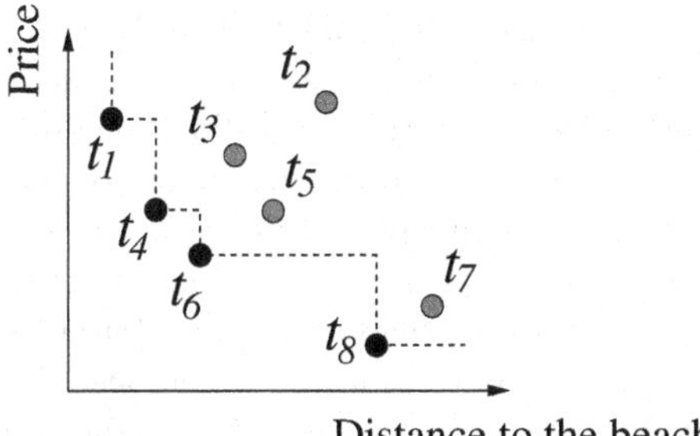

Fig. 1. An example of skyline query on hotel locations and price near a beach

proven guarantee for finding an efficient approximation of this problem. We carry out numerical experiments and show that the approximation algorithm produces feasible solution in reasonable amount of time with approximation ratios close to 1.

The rest of this paper is organized as follows. In Section 2 we review the existing work on skyline queries, skycubes, and compressed skycubes. In Section 3 we introduce the concept of workload-driven subspace skycube queries and define the *Multiple Compressed Skyline Cube* (MCSC) Problem. We show that MCSC is NP-hard. We present a polynomial-time approximation algorithm with a proven guarantee. Finally in Section 4 we provide numerical experiment results to show the performance of our approximation algorithm.

2 Related Work

The concept of skyline queries was originated in the 1960s, where the skyline was called the *Pareto set*, and the skyline objects were called the *admissible points* [BS66] or *maximal vectors* [BKS+78]. The corresponding problem in theoretical studies is also known as the *maximal vector problem* [KLP75, PS85]. Given a set of d-dimensional objects, the *skyline query* returns the "best" objects under given criteria that are not *dominated* by any other object. An object t_1 is said to *dominate* object t_2 if t_1's value in each dimension is less than or equal to t_2's value in the same dimension, and has a strictly smaller value in at least one dimension. The preference function of *"dominate"* can also be defined in other ways as long as it is monotone on all dimensions. A concrete example of the skyline query is to find hotels in the city that are the cheapest and closest to the beach. In figure 1, the 2-dimensional dots represent hotels with corresponding attribute of the data (e.g. the price and distance from the shore). The skyline consists of objects t_1, t_4, t_6, and t_8.

Skyline queries in the context of databases were first studied by Börzsönyi *et al.* [BKS01]. A number of algorithms have been devised to compute skyline queries since then. While conventional skyline computations are often restricted to a fixed set of dimensions (see, for example, [BG04,BGZ04,CET05,CGG+03] and [GSG05, KRR02,LYW+05,PTF+,TEO01]), recent research on skyline queries has shifted to *subspace skyline* computations [PJE+05, YLL+05, TXP06], which does not assume a priori knowledge of query dimensions. Given a set of objects with d dimensions, different users may be interested in different dimensions of the data. Therefore, skyline queries can be issued on any subset of the d dimensions. A d-dimensional space contains $2^d - 1$ subspaces, and a *subspace skyline query* asks for the skyline in one of the $2^d - 1$ subspaces. For convenience, we refer to the space of d dimensions as a *full space*. In the previous example of hotel locations, we assume that each hotel has three attributes: *distance* (to the beach), *price*, and *rating*. A user interested in price and rating of the hotels can issue a skyline query on the subspace $\langle$*price*, *rating*$\rangle$.

To provide answers to skyline queries on a subspace, a database system would need to compute skyline queries on the fly or store all possible subspace skylines in its main memory. The compute-on-the-fly approach often results in slow response time (e.g. [TXP06]). Thus, it may be necessary to pre-compute all possible subspace skylines and store them in the main memory to provide quick response to future queries. The concept of skycubs was introduced (see *et al.* [YLL+05]) for this purpose. A skycube consists of all possible subspace skylines.

The size of a full skycube of high dimensional data may be very large, for it may contain a large number of duplicates and it may need to maintain the complete subspace skylines in every cuboid or subspace. The concept of *compressed skycube* (CSC) was introduced recently to address this problem [XZ06]. Compressed skycubes provide a new method to improve the storage of skycubes and support efficient updates. A CSC represents concisely a complete skycube and preserves the essential information of subspace skylines. Each skyline object is stored in the cuboids that correspond to the minimum subspaces of the object to achieve compression, and the CSC contains only non-empty cuboids. Compared to the original skycube [YLL+05], the CSC has much fewer duplicates among cuboids, and does not need to contain all cuboids. The size of a CSC is therefore expected to be much smaller than that of the original skycube.

3 Workload-Driven Compressed Skycube

The CSC structure still suffers from the curse of dimensionality. In particular, when dimensionality is high, the CSC structure may become space inefficient, for the number of subspaces are exponential to the number of dimensions. Thus, the size of a CSC may exceed the size of the main memory of a devise. One way to solve this problem is to build multiple smaller CSC structures, referred to as "subspace CSCs", each of which corresponds to a *subset* of attributes. For example, with a 12-dimensional dataset, the total size of three subspace CSCs, corresponding to three non-overlapping 4-dimensional subspaces, is usually much smaller than the original CSC for the 12-dimensional space. Clearly, multiple subspace CSCs may not cover all subspace skyline queries. Since the benefit of using a CSC is to quickly answer any subspace query without scanning the original dataset, we would like to determine which subspace CSCs should be selected and placed in the main memory to serve the largest possible number of queries. A query profile is a collection of subspace skylines associated with an expected number of queries on each subspace skyline. In this section, we introduce a work-load driven CSC scheme based on a given query profile.

Example 1. This example motivates the concept of subspace CSC. Consider an NBA dataset with 17 dimensions indicating *points*, *rebounds*, *assists*, *foul*, *play_minutes*, *free_throws*, and a few other attributes. Over the past month, the query profile contains the following subspace skyline query distribution.

- 100 skyline queries over (points, rebounds)
- 80 skyline queries over (point, assists)
- 50 queries over (assists, foul, play_minutes)
- 5 queries over (free_throws, points)

Based on the query profile, maintaining a 17-dimensional CSC is not necessary, because the query distribution is highly biased and only a small portion of subspaces are used. In this example, two subspace CSCs, corresponding to (points, rebounds, assists, free_throws) and (assists, foul, play_minutes), can cover all the subspace skyline queries in the profile.

Given a query profile such as the one given in Example 1, suppose we can only build at most m CSCs, where each CSC has at most k attributes. The problem is to find the subspace CSCs to cover the maximum number of user queries.

For example, consider the user profile in Example 1. Suppose we can only build at most two subspace CSCs, where each CSC has at most three attributes. The two subspace CSCs that cover the maximum number of user queries have attributes (points, rebounds, assists) and (assists, foul, play_minutes), respectively. This scheme covers 230 out of 235 queries.

We will formulate this problem in Section 3.1 and show that the problem is NP-hard. In Section 3.2, we present a polynomial-time approximation algorithm for finding approximation solutions.

3.1 Problem Formulation

Let $\mathcal{A}$ be the set of attributes in a data set for skyline objects and B the memory size on a server available for storing CSC tables.

1. Let $q(D)$ denote the number of expected queries made on D. (This number may be obtained based on applications.)
2. Let $s(D)$ denote the size of the CSC table of D.
3. Let Q denote a given query profile on a given set of subspaces $S = \{D_1, \ldots, D_k\}$. That is,
$$Q = \{\langle D_1, q(D_1)\rangle, \ldots, \langle D_k, q(D_k)\rangle\}.$$

Let D_i and D_j be two subspaces. Denote by $D_i \cup D_j$ the new subspace consisting of all attributes in D_i and D_j. The following property is straightforward.

1. If $D_i \cap D_j = \emptyset$, then $s(D_i) + s(D_j) \leq s(D_i \cup D_j)$.
2. If $D_i \subseteq D_j$, then $s(D_i) \leq s(D_j)$.

Define a profit function p on S as follows: For each $D \in S$, let

$$p(D) = \sum_{D_i \subseteq D} q(D_i).$$

Note that $p(D)$ represents the number of queries that the CSC table of D can cover. For example, let $Q = \{\langle AB, 10\rangle, \langle AC, 2\rangle, \langle ABC, 5\rangle, \langle ABD, 5\rangle\}$. Then

$$\begin{aligned} p(AB) &= q(AB) = 10, \\ p(AC) &= q(AC) = 2, \\ p(ABC) &= q(ABC) + q(AB) + q(AC) = 17, \\ p(ABD) &= q(ABD) + q(AB) = 15. \end{aligned}$$

For each $W \subseteq S$, let

$$s(W) = \sum_{D \in W} s(D).$$

Let $u(W)$ denote the class of sets in S that are subsets of some set in W. (Note that each common subset is listed exactly once.) That is,

$$u(W) = \{D \mid D \in S \text{ and } (\exists D' \in W)[D \subseteq D']\}.$$

Let

$$p(W) = \begin{cases} 0, & \text{if } W = \emptyset, \\ \sum_{D \in u(W)} q(D), & \text{if } W \neq \emptyset, \end{cases} \tag{1}$$

Our goal is to select a subset $S^* \subseteq S$, where no set in S^* is a proper subset of another set in S^*, such that $p(S^*)$ is maximized. This is equivalent to putting as many as possible CSC tables in the memory to serve the largest possible number of queries. This gives rise to the following optimization problem.

MULTIPLE COMPRESSED SKYLINE CUBE PROBLEM (MCSC)

Input: A class of sets $S = \{D_1, \ldots, D_n\}$ and a positive integer B, where each D_i has a positive integer value $s(D_i)$ such that $s(D_i) \leq B$ for all i from 1 to n and a positive integer value $q(D_i)$.
Output: Find a subset $S^* \subseteq S$ that satisfies the following requirements:

1. **No proper subset:** No set in S^* is a proper subset of another set in S^*.
2. **Size constraint:** $s(S^*) \leq B$.
3. **Maximization:** $p(S^*)$ is maximum among all possible selections of S^* that satisfies the no-proper-subset and size-constraint requirements.

We note that when the elements in S are disjoint pairwise, that is, when $D_i \cap D_j = \emptyset$ for $i \neq j$, then MCSC includes the NP-hard Knapsack problem as a special case, and so MCSC is NP-hard. However, the standard polynomial-time approximation scheme (PTAS) for the Knapsack problem does not apply to MCSC because of the "no proper subset" constrain. We present a polynomial-time approximation algorithm for MCSC in the next section.

3.2 Polynomial-Time Approximation

Let J be a subset of S. We say that J is feasible if no element in J is a proper subset of another element in J. A set D is feasible to J if $J \cup \{D\}$ is feasible.

Let k be a fixed positive integer. We construct an algorithm to find a solution to MCSC. Our algorithm consists of two phases. The first phase finds all possible feasible subsets of up to k elements using brute force. There are $O(kn^k)$ many such subsets. For each such subset J, let

$$\begin{aligned} B_J &= B - s(J), \\ n(J) &= n - |J|, \\ S - J &= \{D_{j_1}, \ldots, D_{j_{n(J)}}\}, \text{ where } \frac{p_{j_1}}{s_{j_1}} \geq \cdots \geq \frac{p_{j_{n(J)}}}{s_{j_{n(J)}}} \end{aligned}$$

The second phase packs the remaining space using a greedy strategy based on profit density. In particular, find the first integer i such that D_{j_i} is feasible to J. Set $B_J \leftarrow B_J - s(D_{j_i})$. If $B_J \geq 0$, set $J \leftarrow J \cup \{D_{j_i}\}$. Repeat this process until $B_J < 0$ or there is no set left that is feasible to J.

Let A be the most profitable subset among all subsets J. That is, $p(A) = \max_J\{p(J)\}$ and $p(A) \leq B$. The total time for computing A is $O(kn^{k+1})$. Let S^* be an optimal solution. If S^* contains no more than k elements, then the algorithm will generate S^* and return S^* or another set with the same profit as $p(S^*)$.

If S^* contains more than k elements, let $H = \{D_{h_1}, \ldots, D_{h_k}\}$ be the set of the k most profitable elements in S^*. Because S^* is an optimal solution, H is feasible. Thus, H must be among the feasible k-element subsets generated by the algorithm. The greedy phase of the algorithm extends H by selecting elements in $S - H$ according to the profit density ratios. The elements selected may or may not be in $S^* - H$. Let $F \subseteq S^* - H$ and $G \subseteq S - S^*$ be the sets of elements selected. That is, the algorithm computes a feasible solution $H \cup F \cup G$. Let D_a be the element in $S^* - H \cup F$ with the highest profile density ratio in $S^* - H \cup F$ and let $D_b \in G$ be the last element placed in G.

For convenience, we refer to our approximation algorithm as a *2-phase approximation* algorithm.

Lemma 1. $p_a/s_a \geq p_b/s_b$.

Proof. Note that $S^* - H \cup F$ is a set of elements feasible to $H \cup F$. Thus, according to the greedy strategy, the first element selected in G must have a density ratio at least as large as p_a/s_a. Hence, $p_a/s_a \geq p_b/s_b$.

Let $B_a = B - s(H \cup F)$ and $B_b = s(G)$. Clearly, $B_b \leq B_a$.

Theorem 1

$$p(A) \geq \left(\frac{p_b s_a B_b}{p_a s_b B_a}\right) p(S^*).$$

Proof. It suffices to only consider the case when S^* contains more than k elements. We have

$$\begin{aligned} p(S^*) &= p(H \cup F) + \sum_{D \in S^* - H \cup F} p(D) \\ &\leq p(H \cup F) + s(S^* - H \cup F)\left(\frac{p_a}{s_a}\right) \\ &\leq p(H \cup F) + \Big(B - s(H \cup F)\Big)\left(\frac{p_a}{s_a}\right) \\ &= p(H \cup F) + B_a\left(\frac{p_a}{s_a}\right). \end{aligned}$$

Note that

$$p(G) \geq s(G)\left(\frac{p_b}{s_b}\right) = B_b\left(\frac{p_b}{s_b}\right).$$

Thus,

$$\begin{aligned} p(S^*) &\leq p(H \cup F) + \left(\frac{p_a}{s_a}\right)\left(\frac{s_b}{p_b}\right)\left(\frac{B_a}{B_b}\right) p(G) \\ &\leq \left(\frac{p_a}{s_a}\right)\left(\frac{s_b}{p_b}\right)\left(\frac{B_a}{B_b}\right) p(H \cup F \cup G). \end{aligned}$$

Finally, we have

$$p(A) \geq p(H \cup F \cup G) \geq \left(\frac{p_b s_a B_b}{p_a s_b B_a}\right) p(S^*).$$

To perform numerical analysis on performance of our approximation algorithm, it is desirable to compare its query coverage and running time with that of the optimal solutions to MCSC. In addition, we will also compare with a simple greedy algorithm. Finding the optimal solutions to MCSC may only be doable on instances of moderate sizes (i.e., with low dimensions) because of its NP-hardness.

We note that the standard dynamic programming to obtain optimal solutions for the knapsack problem does not work for MCSC because of the "no proper subset" constrain. We will instead perform an exhaustive search as follows: Enumerate all possible combinations of subspaces, calculate the profit of each combination, and choose the optimal solution from them.

The simple greedy algorithm first sorts all the subspaces according to the profit density, i.e., according to $profit/size$, then greedily chooses feasible subspace with the largest profit density to form a feasible solution.

4 Experimental Evaluation

In this section, we will compare the number of queries served by the optimal solution, the 2-phase approximation algorithm, and the simple greedy algorithm on different dimensionality. We will also compare their time complexity. In this experiment, we set the physical memory to 50% of the space required for storing the whole CSC. The number of queries made on each subspaces ranges randomly from 0 to 200. The size of each subspace is also generated randomly, with the constrain that if $D_i \cap D_j = \emptyset$, then $s(D_i) + s(D_j) \leq s(D_i \cup D_j)$.

Figure 2 depicts the numerical results with dimensionality ranging from 4 to 8, where the running-time figure is under logarithm. The performance of the 2-phase approximation algorithm depends on the value of k, where k should be set to a relatively small value to obtain approximation solutions in reasonable time. In our experiments we chose $k = 2$ and $k = 3$. At dimensionality of 4 and 5, setting $k = 3$ yields solutions that are close to being optimal. At dimensionality of 6, the approximation ratio can reach as high as 93.6% when $k = 2$ and 99.6% when $k = 3$. When dimensionality grows higher, it is almost impossible to get an optimal solution because of the exponentially increase of time complexity. We ran our brute-force algorithm for days trying to obtain the optimal solution for dimensionality of 7 and 8. Unfortunately, the program ran out of memory (4GB) without producing optimal solutions. The dash rectangles in Figure 2(a) represent the best results before the program used up the main memory. We also observe that the simple greedy algorithm, although fast, perform poorly. For example, at dimensionality of 8, it only only serve about 7% of the queries servable by the 2-phase approximation algorithm. The reason is that subspace CSCs that can only serve small number of queries may have large $profit/size$.

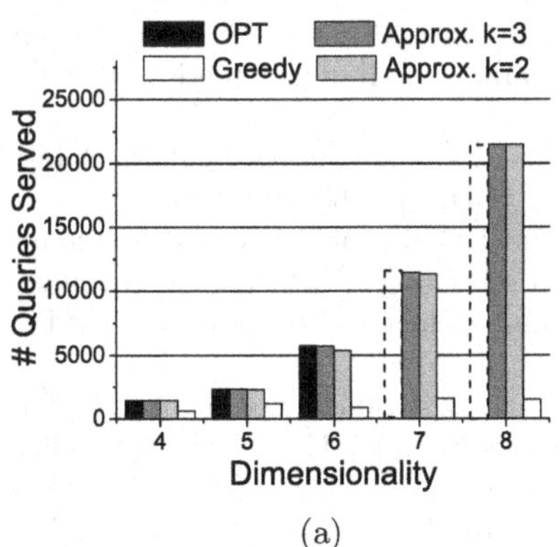

(a)

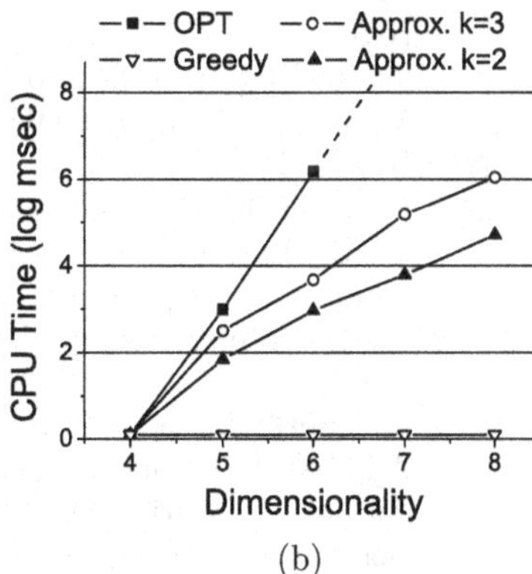

(b)

Fig. 2. Performance comparisons on different dimensionality. The dashed rectangles in (a) represent the best solutions we obtained before the program used up 4GB main memory of the underlying computer. The dashed line in (b) indicates the logarithm of the expected running time for achieving optimal solutions.

These poor choice of subspace CSCs are actually selected by the simple greedy algorithm, keeping most of the good candidates from being selected because of the "no proper subset" constrain.

5 Conclusions

In this paper, we dealt with the issue when the full CSC structure is too big to be stored in the main memory. We presented a new concept of subspace CSC. A subspace CSC is a projection of the full CSC on a smaller set of dimensions. How to select, based on user query profiles, multiple subspace CSCs that can be stored in the main memory to serve the largest possible number of queries is NP-hard. We devised a polynomial-time approximation algorithm with a small approximation ratio. Our experiments showed that the number of queries served by the approximation algorithm is close to that by the optimal solution.

Acknowledgements

Z. Fang and J. Wang were supported in part by the NSF under grant CNS-0709001 and CCF-0830314. D. Zhang was supported in part by the NSF under CAREER Award IIS-0347600. Points of view in this document are those of the authors and do not necessarily represent the official position of the NSF.

References

[JHE04] Jin, W., Han, J., Ester, M.: Mining Thick Skylines over Large Databases. In: Boulicaut, J.-F., Esposito, F., Giannotti, F., Pedreschi, D. (eds.) PKDD 2004. LNCS, vol. 3202, pp. 255–266. Springer, Heidelberg (2004)

[HKP01] Hristidis, V., Koudas, N., Papakonstantinou, Y.: PREFER: A System for the Efficient Execution of Multi-parametric Ranked Queries. In: SIGMOD, pp. 259–270 (2001)

[HJL+06] Huang, Z., Jensen, C., Lu, H., Ooi, B.: Skyline Queries Against Mobile Lightweight Devices in MANETs. In: ICDE, pp. 66–76 (2006)

[LCY08] Liang, W., Chen, B., Yu, J.: Energy-efficient skyline query processing and maintenance in sensor networks. In: Proceeding of the 17th ACM conference on Information and knowledge management (CIKM), pp. 1471–1472 (2008)

[BS66] Barndorff-Nielsen, O., Sobel, M.: On the Distribution of the Number of Admissable Points in a Vector Random Sample. Theory of Probability and its Application 11(2), 249–269 (1966)

[BKS+78] Bentley, J.L., Kung, H.T., Schkolnick, M., Thompson, C.D.: On the Average Number of Maxima in a Set of Vectors and Applications. Journal of ACM 25(4), 536–543 (1978)

[KLP75] Kung, H.T., Luccio, F., Preparata, F.P.: On Finding the Maxima of a Set of Vectors. Journal of ACM 22(4), 469–476 (1975)

[PS85] Preparata, F., Shamos, M.: Computational Geometry: An Introduction. Springer, Heidelberg (1985)

[BKS01] Börzsönyi, S., Kossmann, D., Stocker, K.: The Skyline Operator. In: ICDE, pp. 421–430 (2001)

[BG04] Balke, W.-T., Güntzer, U.: Multi-objective Query Processing for Database Systems. In: VLDB, pp. 936–947 (2004)

[BGZ04] Balke, W.-T., Güntzer, U., Zheng, J.X.: Efficient Distributed Skylining for Web Information Systems. In: Bertino, E., Christodoulakis, S., Plexousakis, D., Christophides, V., Koubarakis, M., Böhm, K., Ferrari, E. (eds.) EDBT 2004. LNCS, vol. 2992, pp. 256–273. Springer, Heidelberg (2004)

[CET05] Chan, C.Y., Eng, P.-K., Tan, K.-L.: Stratified Computation of Skylines with Partially-Ordered Domains. In: SIGMOD, pp. 203–214 (2005)

[CGG+03] Chomicki, J., Godfrey, P., Gryz, J., Liang, D.: Skyline with Presorting. In: ICDE, pp. 717–816 (2003)

[GSG05] Godfrey, P., Shipley, R., Gryz, J.: Maximal Vector Computation in Large Data Sets. In: VLDB, pp. 229–240 (2005)

[KRR02] Kossmann, D., Ramsak, F., Rost, S.: Shooting Stars in the Sky: An Online Algorithm for Skyline Queries. In: VLDB, pp. 275–286 (2002)

[LYW+05] Lin, X., Yuan, Y., Wang, W., Lu, H.: Stabbing the Sky: Efficient Skyline Computation over Sliding Windows. In: ICDE, pp. 502–513 (2005)

[PTF+] Papadias, D., Tao, Y., Fu, G., Seeger, B.: An Optimal and Progressive Algorithm for Skyline Queries. In: SIGMOD, pp. 467–478 (2003)

[TEO01] Tan, K.-L., Eng, P.K., Ooi, B.C.: Efficient Progressive Skyline Computation. In: VLDB, pp. 301–310 (2001)

[PJE+05] Pei, J., Jin, W., Ester, M., Tao, Y.: Catching the Best Views of Skyline: A Semantic Approach Based on Decisive Subspaces. In: VLDB, pp. 253–264 (2005)

[YLL+05] Yuan, Y., Lin, X., Liu, Q., Wang, W., Yu, J.X., Zhang, Q.: Efficient Computation of the Skyline Cube. In: VLDB, pp. 241–252 (2005)

[TXP06] Tao, Y., Xiao, X., Pei, J.: SUBSKY: Efficient Computation of Skylines in Subspaces. In: ICDE (2006)

[XZ06] Xia, T., Zhang, D.: Refreshing the sky: the compressed skycube with efficient support for frequent updates. In: SIGMOD, pp. 491–502 (2006)

Routing-Aware Query Optimization for Conserving Energy in Wireless Sensor Networks

Jie Yang and Jie Wang

Department of Computer Science
University of Massachusetts, Lowell, MA 01854
{jyang,wang}@cs.uml.edu

Abstract. Processing multiple real-time queries on a multi-hop wireless sensor network while conserving energy is a challenging issue. A naive approach would simply disseminate each query individually, even if the queries contain overlapping information. This imposes excessive energy consumption on sensor nodes in the data paths. We propose a routing-aware query optimization method to conserve energy on these nodes. In particular, we devise an algorithm to reduce query redundancy based on location information, attributes, and time constraints contained in the queries and the routing information of the underlying network. Our simulation results show that our approach can significantly reduce energy consumptions and improve the overall performance of the network.

1 Introduction

We consider a query system in a multi-hop wireless sensor network that consists of a base station and a number of sensor nodes (stationary or mobile), where sensor nodes can handle data queries independently or cooperatively. A wireless sensor network of this kind may be viewed as a distributed database system [10,14,5,7,9]. However, unlike in a conventional distributed database system where each node is equipped with sufficient power supply and abundant computing resources, a sensor node in a wireless sensor network typically has stringent power supply and insufficient computing resources. These limitations affect the design of energy-efficient query systems.

In the standard query model of wireless sensor networks, users submit queries to the base station. The base station processes the queries and disseminates them to the destination regions of the network using the underlying routing mechanism. When multiple queries are submitted, the base station may simply disseminate each query separately, even if they contain overlapping information. This would cause the sensor nodes on the data paths to consume excessive energy. Finding a way to reduce query redundancy is expected to significantly reduce energy consumption on these nodes and improve the overall performance of the network. This motivated the study of query optimization. Query optimization seeks to recompose queries received by the base station to a new set of queries that satisfies the needs of the users and reduces energy consumptions on sensor nodes on the data paths.

We observe that the location information of regions and the routing information of the underlying network may be used to select and combine queries to share a significant portion of the two data paths, which can help conserve energy. Based on this observation

B. Liu et al. (Eds.): WASA 2009, LNCS 5682, pp. 254–263, 2009.

we devise a query model for carrying out query optimization, and an energy-efficient routing-aware optimization algorithm based on the location information, attributes, and time constraints (e.g., deadlines) contained in the queries and the routing information of the underlying network. Our simulation results show that our approach can significantly reduce energy consumptions and improve the overall performance of the network.

The rest of the paper is organized as follows. In Section 2, we provide an overview of early work on query processing in sensor networks. In Section 3, we describe the system model and present the standard query model. We then describe our query model. In Section 4, we present a routing-aware query optimization algorithm. In Section 5, we present performance evaluations and analysis results. In Section 6 we conclude the paper.

2 Related Work

Data aggregation has been studied extensively in distributed database systems (see, e.g., AODV [1], Cougar [14], Directed Diffusion [8], ACQUIRE [12], and TAG [10]). Query processing and dissemination have also been studied intensively. In particular, Coman *at al.* [2] proposed a general framework to process spatial-temporal queries in a sensor network in a distributed manner. It routes the query to the destination specified in the query. It then collects the data based on the queries and processes them. Sensor nodes may also process data as they collect them. They then proposed a spatial-temporal query processing algorithm using local storage, and presented an energy consumption model for their algorithm [3]. Samuel *et al.* devised an acquisitional query processor (ACQP) to collect in wireless sensor networks [11]. They provided a query processor-like interface and used acquisitional techniques to reduce energy consumption. They also devised a semantic routing tree (SRT) to optimize query dissemination. The SRT tree provides an efficient mechanism for disseminating queries and collecting results for queries over constant attributes. Deshpande *et al.* presented a probabilistic model based on time-varying multivariate Gaussians [4] under the assumption that the queries sent by users include error tolerance and target confidence bounds that specify how much uncertainty the user is willing to tolerate. They were focused on multiple snap-shot queries over the current state of the network, rather than on continuous queries.

Early studies on query optimization in wireless sensor networks include [15,16]. Yu *et al.* proposed a multi-layered overlay-based framework consisting of a query manager and a number of access points (sensor nodes) [16]. The query manager provides a query optimization plan and the access points execute the plan. They presented an algorithm to reduce duplicate/overlapping queries based on location information contained in the original queries. However, the algorithm pays no attention to the underlying routing topology of the network and it does not consider attributes or the deadline information contained in the original queries. Yang *et al.* proposed a query optimization method [15] based solely on query regions and attributes, but does not take into consideration the routing topology of the underlying network.

3 Query Model

We consider a multi-hop wireless sensor network with only one base station. Our results can be easily extended to networks with multiple base stations. We assume that the network is divided into multiple regions (a.k.a clusters), which may be done dynamically. Each cluster elects a leader called a cluster head to act as a liaison between sensor nodes in the cluster and neighbor clusters or the base station. Users are aware of the division of the regions and the base station has the information of the cluster heads. For convenience, we use a cluster head to represent the region it is in.

The base station contains a query manager to handle queries. Users send queries to the base station, and the query manager processes queries and disseminates them with complete routing information of the network. Several mechanisms have been proposed to disseminate queries and route the data back to the base station. In this paper we will focus on query optimization.

Note that cluster heads may change dynamically and routes from the base station to cluster heads are also formed dynamically. We assume that such changes will only occur periodically. We also assume that there is a management component that updates cluster heads and routing information. Thus, without loss of generality, we assume that cluster heads and routes from the base station to cluster heads are fixed for the current set of queries.

We model queries in two categories: *simple queries* and *compound queries*. A simple query is a quintuple

$$q = (s, A, t, f, d),$$

where s is the location information of a cluster head, A is a set of attributes the user wants to know in region s, e.g., temperature, light, voltage, pressure, humidity, or wind speed; t (optional) denotes the temporal information, indicating the duration of the query in a given time unit; f (optional) denotes the frequency information, indicating how often the data should be reported; and d (optional) denotes the deadline information, indicating how soon the data should be reported. We set $d = \infty$ to indicate that the underlying query has no deadline. The temporal information t may be a single time instance or a time interval.

A compound query is a combination of several simple queries, written as a quintuple:

$$Q = (S, \mathcal{A}, T, F, D),$$

where S is a sequence of location values of m cluster heads: $\langle s_1, \ldots, s_m \rangle$, $\mathcal{A}$ a sequence of m attribute sets: $\langle A_1, \ldots, A_m \rangle$, T a sequence of m temporal values: $\langle t_1, \ldots, t_m \rangle$, F a sequence of m frequency values: $\langle f_1, \ldots, f_m \rangle$ a sequence of frequencies, and D a sequence of m deadlines: $\langle d_1, \ldots, d_m \rangle$, such that $(s_i, A_i, t_i, f_i, d_i)$ is a simple query. Depending on applications we may impose an upper bound for m.

For example, suppose the user submits the following query to the base station: "*Find the temperature and humidity in region s_1 from 8am to 4pm every ten minutes and report the data back before 5pm, and find the temperature in s_2 from 10am to 5pm every 30 minutes and report the data back before 6pm.*" In this example, $S = \langle s_1, s_2 \rangle$, $\mathcal{A} = \langle \{\text{temperature, humidity}\}, \{temperature\} \rangle$, $T = \langle$[8am, 4pm], [10am, 5pm]$\rangle$, $F = \langle 600, 1800 \rangle$ (in seconds), and $D = \langle$5pm, 6pm$\rangle$.

Queries without location information can be processed using the standard techniques such as the flooding and the direct diffusion technique [8].

For ease of presentation, we will present our algorithm on a simplified query model excluding f and t. It is straightforward to generalize our algorithm to the full query model.

When queries arrive, the query manager checks whether the requested data asked by the queries is available in the local cache to avoid redundant query dissemination and data collection. If not, the query manager starts the query optimization process. We use a *receiving buffer* (RB) to store unprocessed queries, and a *processing buffer* (PB) to execute query optimization. The deadline information d contained in a query is used to check whether there is sufficient time for optimization. If yes, the query manager stores the query in RB. If not, the query manager disseminates the query to the network without optimization to beat the deadline. We use the FIFO mechanism to manage buffers. Other storage mechanisms may be used based on applications. Fig. 1 depicts our query model

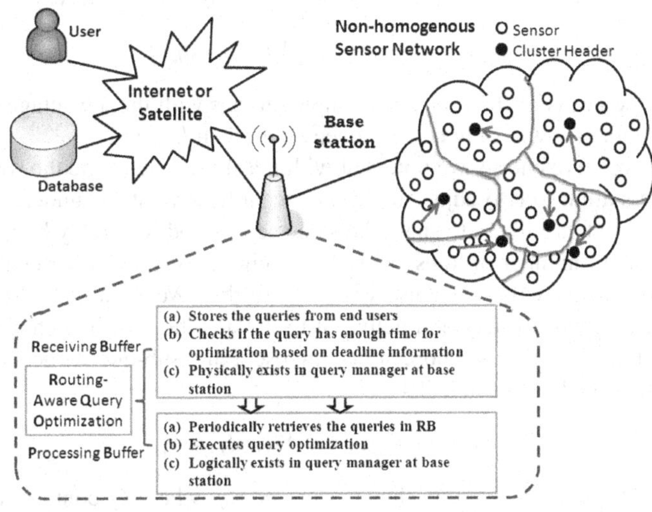

Fig. 1. Two-tier Buffer Query model

Queries stored in the RB buffer are processed once every epoch (e_p) [13]. Each epoch consists of a query optimization (QO) phase and a query process (QP) phase. In the QO phase, the query manager periodically retrieves the queries stored in RB and stores them in PB for optimization, making RB available for new queries. In the QP phase, the query manager disseminates optimized queries to the network and routes collected data corresponding to the query back from sensor nodes using the underlying routing mechanism. The duration of a QP phase is a tunable application-specific parameter.

4 Routing-Aware Query Optimization (RAQO)

The energy consumption for disseminating a query Q comes from two parts. One part is the energy cost for delivering Q from the base station to the destination region, denoted by $G(Q)$. The other part is the energy cost for transmitting the corresponding data from the destination sensor nodes back to the base station, denoted by $H(Q)$.

Let $Q_1, Q_2, \ldots, Q_n$ be n queries currently stored in the processing buffer to be optimized. The RAQO algorithm processes these queries and produces a new set of queries $Q'_1, Q'_2, \ldots, Q'_r$ that meet the needs of the original queries. The energy consumption of serving these queries is equal to

$$E_q = \sum_{i=1}^{r} (G(Q'_i) + H(Q'_i)) .$$

We want to find a way to produce $Q'_1, Q'_2, \ldots, Q'_r$ that minimizes E_q. To do so, we will want to combine queries for the same destinations into one query. Thus, we will first decompose queries into simple queries and then combine them. In particular, let $(s, A_1, d_1), \ldots, (s, A_k, d_k)$ $(k > 1)$ be simple queries with the same destination region s. Them we will replace these queries with the following simple query:

$$(s, A_1 \cup \cdots \cup A_k, \min\{d_1, \ldots, d_k\}),$$

which meets the needs of the k original simple queries with the advantage that sensor nodes on the data path will only be used once rather than k times.

To further conserve energy we note that within a short time frame the routing paths from the base station to two adjacent regions, regardless what the underlying routing mechanism is used, are likely to share the same sensor nodes as relay hops except the last hop or a small number of hops. Thus, combining two simple queries for adjacent regions into one query will help conserve energy further. We assume that sensor nodes can inspect a compound query and deliver it to the next hop, h, if each simple query contained in it has h as the next hop, or decompose it into sub-queries according to the routing information. For example, let

$$Q = (\langle s_1, s_2\rangle, \langle A_1, A_2\rangle, \langle d_1, d_2\rangle)$$

be a compound query received by the current node g, where Q contains two simple queries $q_1 = (s_1, A_1, d_1)$ and $q_2 = (s_2, A_2, d_2)$. If the next hops for both queries are the same node h, then g will deliver Q to h. If the next hop for q_1 is h_1 and for q_2 is h_2 with $h_1 \neq h_2$, then g will decompose Q and deliver q_1 to h_1 and q_2 to h_2.

For simplicity we will only consider how to merge two simple queries (Merging more than two simple queries can be done similarly). For this purpose we need to determine when two simple queries should be merged. Assume that there are N regions in the network, labeled as $1, 2, \ldots, N$. Denote by N_i the set of sensor nodes used as hops on the routing path from the base station to cluster head s_i (not including s_i). N_i may be different for different routing protocols. The definition of N_j is similar. Let

$$w_{ij} = \frac{|N_i \cap N_j|}{|N_i \cup N_j|}.$$

Let BS denote the base station. The weight w_{ij} indicates the relative common portion of sensor nodes shared by the two routing paths $BS \rightsquigarrow s_i$ and $BS \rightsquigarrow s_j$. Clearly, $0 \leq w_{ij} \leq 1$.

We list the cluster heads in a compound query in the increasing order on the labels (indexes) of the regions they are in. That is, cluster head s_i is in region i. We define the following merge operation $\circ$ for merging two simple queries. Let $q_i = (s_i, A_i, d_i)$ and $q_j = (s_j, A_j, d_j)$ be two simple queries with $i < j$. Then

$$q_i \circ q_j = q_j \circ q_i = (\langle s_i, s_j \rangle, \langle A_i, A_j \rangle, \langle d_i, d_j \rangle).$$

Let $L = \{Q_1, \ldots, Q_n\}$. Let $0 < \lambda \leq 1$ be a threshold value to indicate when two simple queries should be merged with the benefit of saving energy. The RAQO algorithm takes (L, λ) as input and outputs a set of new queries R as follows:

RAQO(L, λ):

1. Let $\{s_{n_1}, \ldots, s_{n_\ell}\}$ be the cluster heads contained in the queries in L. Set $R \leftarrow \emptyset$.
2. Set $I \leftarrow \emptyset$. Let $J = \{n_1, \ldots, n_\ell\}$. If $|J| \geq 2$, then for each $n_i \in J$, find the smallest index $n_{m(i)} \in J$ with $i \neq m(i)$ such that

$$w_{n_i, n_{m(i)}} = \max\{w_{n_i, n_j} \mid j \neq i \text{ and } 1 \leq j \leq \ell\}.$$

   That is, node s_{n_i} shares with $s_{n_{m(i)}}$ the most portion of their routes compared to other nodes s_{n_j}. If $w_{n_i, n_{m(i)}} > \lambda$ then place $(n_i, n_{m(i)})$ into I and remove n_i and $n_{m(i)}$ from J. Repeat Step 2. Otherwise, goto Step 3.
   We maintain I as a sorted list in a non-increasing order according to $w_{n_i, n_{m(i)}}$.
3. Decompose each $Q_i \in L$ into simple queries and place them in R.
4. Let $(s_{l_1}, A_{l_1}, d_{l_1}), \ldots, (s_{l_p}, A_{l_p}, d_{l_p})$ be all simple queries in R such that $s_{l_1} = \cdots = s_{l_p}$. Remove these queries from R and place the following new query to R:

$$(s_{l_1}, A_{l_1} \cup \cdots \cup A_{l_p}, \min\{d_{l_1}, \cdots, d_{l_p}\}).$$

5. Let $(n_i, n_{m(i)})$ be the first element in I. Remove $q_{n_i} = (s_{n_i}, A_{n_i}, d_{n_i})$ and $q_{n_{m(i)}} = (s_{n_{m(i)}}, A_{n_{m(i)}}, d_{n_{m(i)}})$ from R and place $q_{n_i} \circ q_{n_{m(i)}}$ into R. Remove $(n_i, n_{m(i)})$ from I. Repeat Step 5 until $I = \emptyset$. **End of the algorithm**

A number of small improvements can be made in the implementation of RAQO. For example, in Step 3, there is no need to generate a duplicate simple query if it is already generated. For another example, in Step 3 one may run through each pair in I, starting from the first element, and "merge" those compound queries of two simple queries whose region indexes match with the pair to keep this new query from decomposition. The definition of this "merge" operation, denoted by $\Box$, is defined as follows:

Let $Q_i = (S_i, \mathcal{A}_i, D_i)$ and $Q_j = (S_j, \mathcal{A}_j, D_j)$, where $S_i = S_j, |S_i| = |S_j| = k$, $\mathcal{A}_i = \langle A_{i_1}, \ldots, A_{i_k} \rangle$, $\mathcal{A}_j = \langle A_{j_1}, \ldots, A_{j_k} \rangle$, $D_i = \langle d_{i_1}, \ldots, d_{i_k} \rangle$, and $D_j = \langle d_{j_1}, \ldots, d_{j_k} \rangle$. Then

$$\begin{aligned} Q_i \Box Q_j &= (S_i, \mathcal{A}_i \Box \mathcal{A}_j, D_i \Box D_j) \\ \mathcal{A}_i \Box \mathcal{A}_j &= \langle A_{i_1} \cup A_{j_1}, \ldots, A_{i_k} \cup A_{j_k} \rangle, \\ D_i \Box D_j &= \langle \min\{d_{i_1}, d_{j_1}\}, \ldots, \min\{d_{i_k}, d_{j_k}\} \rangle. \end{aligned}$$

In addition to the $\Box$ operation, we will also need to define another "merge" operation to merge Q_i with Q_j when S_i is a proper subsequence of S_j. The definition of this operation is straightforward.

5 Performance Analysis

We analyze the RAQO algorithm through simulations. Our experiments use the experimental data given in [6]: formula (1) to calculate the energy consumption on transmitting a message of size x to a destination of distance y and formula (2) to calculate the energy consumption on receiving a message:

$$E_{Tx}(x, y) = E_{elec} \cdot x + E_{amp} \cdot x \cdot y^2, \tag{1}$$

$$E_{Rx}(x, y) = E_{elec} \cdot x, \tag{2}$$

where $E_{elec} = 50nJ/bit$, and $E_{amp} = 100pJ/(bit \times m^2)$, $1nJ = 1000pJ$, and $1MnJ = 1000nJ$. It is known that processing 100 million instructions consumes about the same energy as transmitting 10 bits of data, and so the energy consumption on processing is negligible.

Evaluation System. We call $|I|/N$ the *adjacent region degree* (ARD). The range of ARD is between 0 and 0.5, where 0 indicates that it is not worth one's effort to combine any simple queries, and 0.5 indicates that any simple query for a region can always be merged with another simple query for an adjacent region. In our experiments, we choose $\lambda = 0$. For a specific routing mechanism, we may choose a different positive value for λ. We compare RAQO with the following three existing query optimization methods:

1. *Location based query optimization* (LQO) [16]. LQO uses location information to reduce the number of duplicate/overlapping queries.
2. *Location and attribute based query optimization* (LAQO) [15]. LAQO uses both the location information and attributes to optimize queries. LAQO does not use storage buffers to store queries.
3. *Routing-blind query optimization* (RBQO). To illustrate the advantage of our query model with a receiving buffer and a processing buffer, we modify RAQO(L, λ) by not executing last merging step.

Comparison of Energy Consumption on the Number of Queries. Fig. 2(a) shows the comparison of energy consumption on the number of queries. We have the following observations:

1. RAQO and RBQO outperform both LQO and LAQO. For example, when the number of queries is large from 100 to 200, the energy consumption of LQO and LAQO can be $2 \sim 6$ times higher than that of RAQO and RBQO. This matches our expectation, for RAQO and RBQO can both optimize more queries using a receiving buffer and a processing buffer.
2. While compared to LQO and LAQO the performance of RBQO is similar to that of RAQO, we note that RAQO still costs less energy than RBQO. This is also expected, for knowing the network topology helps to optimize queries further.
3. LAQO performs better than LQO. This is expected, because LAQO also optimizes attributes while LQO does not.

4. While energy consumption is sensitive to the number of queries as expected, RAQO alleviates this problem. This is because when the number of queries increases, there will be more room for optimization because queries for the same region and for adjacent regions will also increase, which is effectively used by RAQO.
5. RAQO offers competitive performance even when the number of queries is medium or low. That is, RAQO can significantly reduce energy consumption regardless the number of queries.

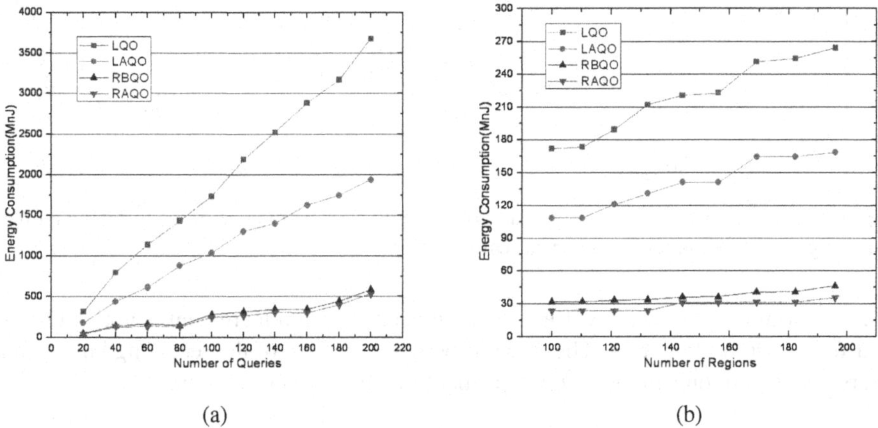

Fig. 2. (a) Energy consumption comparison on the number of queries. (b) Energy consumption on the number of regions contained in the queries.

Energy Consumption on the Number of Regions Contained in the Queries. Fig. 2(b) depicts the comparison of energy consumption on the number of regions contained in the queries. We see that as the the number of regions involved in queries is enlarged, the overall energy consumption also increases. This is because more sensor nodes are involved, or more query/data transmissions are performed. Nevertheless, RAQO outperforms all three other algorithms for the same reasons described in the energy comparison on the number of queries.

Energy Consumption and the Query Delivery Ratio on the Size of the Receiving Buffer. Fig. 3(a) shows the energy consumption and query delivery ratio on the size of the receiving buffer. The query delivery ratio is defined to be the ratio of total number of queries disseminated after optimization over the total number of queries received by the query manager. We can see that when the buffer size is increased, the query delivery ratio is also increased. This is because a larger buffer can hold more queries for optimization. If the buffer size is small and the number of query messages is large, the query manager will have to discard some of the queries when the buffer is full.

We can also see that when the size of the receiving is small, the query delivery ratio is small. Thus, only a small number of queries will be processed, and so the energy consumption is small. On the other hand, when the buffer size is increased, more queries can be processed and disseminated, and so the query delivery ratio is also increased,

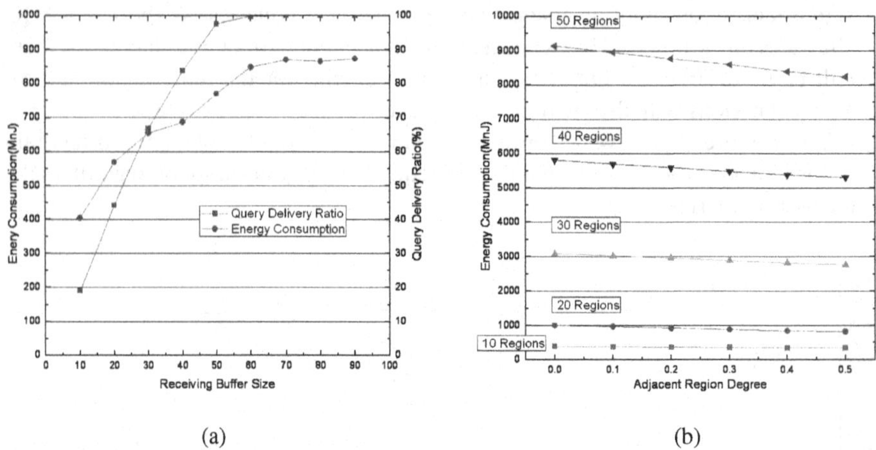

(a) (b)

Fig. 3. (a) Energy consumption and the ratio of query delivery on the size of the receiving buffer. (b) Energy consumption on the adjacent region degrees.

which consumes more energy. But the energy consumption increment is not as fast as that for smaller buffer sizes. The tradeoff between the size of the receiving buffer and energy consumption would be an interesting topic for further research.

Energy Consumption on the Adjacent Region Degree (ARD). Fig. 3(b) shows the energy consumption on ARDs. We can see that the energy consumption decreases when the ARD increases, for a larger ARD implies that there is more to share on routing paths to adjacent regions, and so more energy will be saved.

6 Conclusion

We presented in this paper a routing-aware query optimization algorithm on a two-tier buffer query model to conserve energy. Our simulation results show that our approach is superior to previously known approaches.

Acknowledgement

The authors were supported in part by the NSF under grants CNS-0709001 and CNF-0830314. Any opinions, findings, and conclusions or recommendations expressed in this paper are those of the authors, and do not necessarily reflect the views of the NSF.

References

1. Chakeres, I.D., Belding-Royer, E.M.: Aodv routing protocol implementation design. In: ICDCSW 2004: Proceedings of the 24th International Conference on Distributed Computing Systems Workshops - W7: EC (ICDCSW 2004), Washington, DC, USA, 2004, pp. 698–703. IEEE Computer Society, Los Alamitos (2004)

2. Coman, A., Nascimento, M.A., Sander, J.: A framework for spatio-temporal query processing over wireless sensor networks. In: DMSN 2004: Proceeedings of the 1st international workshop on Data management for sensor networks, pp. 104–110. ACM Press, New York (2004)
3. Coman, A., Sander, J., Nascimento, M.A.: An analysis of spatio-temporal query processing in sensor networks. In: ICDEW 2005: Proceedings of the 21st International Conference on Data Engineering Workshops, Washington, DC, USA, 2005, p. 1190. IEEE Computer Society Press, Los Alamitos (2005)
4. Deshpande, A., Guestrin, C., Madden, S.R., Hellerstein, J.M., Hong, W.: Model-driven data acquisition in sensor networks. In: VLDB 2004: Proceedings of the Thirtieth international conference on Very large data bases, pp. 588–599. VLDB Endowment (2004)
5. Gehrke, J., Seshadri, P.: Querying the physical world. IEEE Personal Communications 7, 10–15 (2000)
6. Heinzelman, W., Chandrakasan, A., Balakrishnan, H.: Energy-efficient communication protocol for wireless microsensor networks, vol. 2, p. 10 (January 2000)
7. Hellerstein, J.M., Hong, W., Madden, S., Stanek, K.: Beyond average: Towards sophisticated sensing with queries. In: Zhao, F., Guibas, L.J. (eds.) IPSN 2003. LNCS, vol. 2634, pp. 63–79. Springer, Heidelberg (2003)
8. Intanagonwiwat, C., Govindan, R., Estrin, D., Heidemann, J., Silva, F.: Directed diffusion for wireless sensor networking. IEEE/ACM Trans. Netw. 11(1), 2–16 (2003)
9. Jaikaeo, C., Srisathapornphat, C., Shen, C.-C.: Querying and tasking in sensor networks. In: SPIE, vol. 4037, pp. 184–194 (2000)
10. Madden, S., Franklin, M.J., Hellerstein, J.M., Hong, W.: Tag: a tiny aggregation service for ad-hoc sensor networks. SIGOPS Oper. Syst. Rev. 36(SI), 131–146 (2002)
11. Madden, S.R., Franklin, M.J., Hellerstein, J.M., Hong, W.: Tinydb: an acquisitional query processing system for sensor networks. ACM Trans. Database Syst. 30(1), 122–173 (2005)
12. Sadagopan, N., Krishnamachari, B., Helmy, A.: Active query forwarding in sensor networks. Journal of Ad Hoc Networks 3, 91–113 (2005)
13. Trigoni, N., Yao, Y., Demers, A., Gehrke, J.: Multi-query optimization for sensor networks. In: Prasanna, V.K., Iyengar, S.S., Spirakis, P.G., Welsh, M. (eds.) DCOSS 2005. LNCS, vol. 3560, pp. 307–321. Springer, Heidelberg (2005)
14. Woo, A., Madden, S., Govindan, R.: Networking support for query processing in sensor networks. Commun. ACM 47(6), 47–52 (2004)
15. Yang, J., Yan, B., Lee, S., Cho, J.: Saqa: Spatial and attribute based query aggregation in wireless sensor networks. In: Sha, E., Han, S.-K., Xu, C.-Z., Kim, M.-H., Yang, L.T., Xiao, B. (eds.) EUC 2006. LNCS, vol. 4096, pp. 15–24. Springer, Heidelberg (2006)
16. Yu, W., Le, T.N., Lee, J., Xuan, D.: Effective query aggregation for data services in sensor networks. Comput. Commun. 29(18), 3733–3744 (2006)

In-Network Historical Data Storage and Query Processing Based on Distributed Indexing Techniques in Wireless Sensor Networks

Chunyu Ai[1], Ruiying Du[1,2], Minghong Zhang[1,3], and Yingshu Li[1]

[1] Georgia State University, 34 Peachtree St., Atlanta, GA, USA
[2] Wuhan Computer School of Wuhan University, Wuhan, China
[3] Department of Mathematics, Graduate University, Chinese Academy of Sciences, Beijing, China

Abstract. Most of existing data processing approaches of wireless sensor networks are real-time. However, historical data of wireless sensor networks are also significant for various applications. No previous study has specifically addressed distributed historical data query processing. In this paper, we propose an Index based Historical Data Query Processing scheme which stores historical data locally and processes queries energy-efficiently by using a distributed index tree. The simulation study shows that our scheme achieves good performance on both query responding delay and network traffic.

Keywords: Historical Data, Distributed Index, Historical Data Query, Wireless Sensor Networks.

1 Introduction

Nowadays large-scale sensor networks are widely deployed around the world for various applications. Sensor networks are used to report live weather conditions, monitor traffic on highways, detect disasters, monitor habitat of animals, etc. Tremendous volumes of useful data are generated by these deployments. Most existing applications just process real-time data generated by sensor networks (e.g., [1,2]). However, historical data of sensor networks are also significant to us, especially statistical meaning of historical data. For instance, maximum, minimum, and average temperatures of the past two months in a specific area are concerned in the weather monitoring application. By capturing rush hours and the bottleneck of traffic according to historical data, a large quantity of useful information can be provided to improve traffic conditions. Through analysis of historical data, some knowledge, principles, and characteristics can be discovered.

One simple method to process historical data is that the base station collects all data and processes in a centralized manner. Nevertheless, sensor nodes will deplete energy rapidly for continually reporting and forwarding data. Another method is storing data locally, that is, data are stored at a sensor node where they are generated. Intuitively, a sensor node cannot store a large quantity of

B. Liu et al. (Eds.): WASA 2009, LNCS 5682, pp. 264–273, 2009.

historical data since its memory capacity is low. Popular motes such as Mica2 and Micaz [3] are equipped with a 512K bytes measurement flash memory, it can store more than 100,000 measurements. Another popular mote, TelosB [3], has a 1024K bytes flash memory. 512K or 1024K bytes are really small memory capacity. However, it is enough to store most of sensing data, sampling data, or statistical data during a sensor node's entire lifetime since the lifetime of a sensor node is short due to the limitation of batteries. For a Mica mote powered by 2 AA batteries, the lifetime is 5-6 days if continuously running, and it can be extended to over 20 years if staying sleep state without any activity [4]. For most applications, a sensor can live for several weeks or months [5]. Assume a Mica mote with a 512K bytes flash memory can live 3 months. $(100,000/90) = 1111$ measurements can be saved locally every day. Suppose we have 4 sensing attributes need to be saved, frequency of sampling can be 1 per 5 minutes which is normal in wireless sensor network applications. If proper compressing techniques are applied according to data's characteristics, much more data can be stored locally. Consequently, storing data locally at a sensor is feasible. The historical data can be downloaded when the battery is replaced or recharged if possible.

The motivation of storing historical data is to support historical data queries. However, locally storing data might cause a query to be flooded in the entire network to probe data when it is processed. We propose a scheme in this paper named Historical Data Query Processing based on Distributed Indexing (HDQP) which stores historical data in network and processes queries energy-efficiently by using index techniques. Historical data is stored at each sensor. For saving memory capacity, compressing and sampling techniques can be used according to data characteristics and users' requirements. To process queries quickly and energy-efficiently, in-network distributed tree-based indexes are constructed. Using indexes to process queries can reduce the number of involved sensors as many as possible, thus conserving energy consumption. To avoid load skew, index data are partitioned on different nodes according to their time stamp. That is, there exist multiple index trees in the network. Which index trees are used depends on query conditions.

The rest of this paper is organized as follows. Section 2 discusses related work. Section 3 describes how to store historical data at a sensor node. Constructing and maintaining the distributed index trees are addressed in Section 4. Section 5 explains how to process historical data queries. Simulation results and analysis are presented in Section 6. Finally, we conclude in Section 7.

2 Related Work

Many approaches have been proposed to describe how to store data for sensor networks. One category of such storage solutions is that the base station collects and stores all data. However, such approaches might be more applicable to answer *continuous queries* . Obviously, the mortal drawback of collecting all data is shortening the network lifetime.

For improving network lifetime, in-network storage techniques have been addressed to solve ad-hoc queries. These frameworks are primarily based on the

Data-Centric Storage (DCS) concept [6]. In DCS, relevant data are stored by *name* (e.g., tiger sightings). All data with the same general name will be stored at the same sensor node. Queries for data with a particular name can be sent directly to the node storing those named data. In-network DCS schemes differ from each other based on the events-to-sensors mapping method used.

The works in [7], [8], and [9] use a distributed hashing index technique to solve range queries in a multi-dimensional space. The work in [2] proposed a distributed spatio-temporal index structure to track moving objects.

Specially, most of these approaches just store partial data, which satisfy conditions or present events and moving objects, generated by sensors . To our best knowledge, no in-network distributed historical data storage, indexing, and query processing schemes have been presented in the literature.

3 Historical Data Storage

Since a sensor node's memory capacity is limited, we have to fully utilize it to store as many data as possible. The administrator of the sensor network can specify the attributes which need to be stored locally according to users' requirements. Suppose there are n attributes $(A_1, A_2, \cdots, A_n)$ need to be saved, and the sensor node senses the values $V_1, V_2, \cdots, V_n$ of $A_1, A_2, \cdots, A_n$ respectively at sensing intervals. For each sensing interval, a record with the format $(T, V_1, V_2, \cdots, V_n)$ (where T is a time-stamp) is written to the flash memory. However, if the sensing interval is very short such as 5 seconds, the flash memory will be full filled quickly. Then the rest of coming sensing data cannot be stored. To avoid this happen, whenever the flash memory is occupied more than 80%, a *weight-reducing* process is trigged. One record of every two consecutive records is erased. This weight-reducing process can make at least half of memory space available again. Applying the weight-reducing process repeatedly causes partial historical data lost. However, as we mentioned in Section 1, even though the flash memory capacity is small, it still can store 5 to 10 values per hour for each attribute. Consequently, the historical data stored in the flash memory can reflect the changing trend of each sensing attribute.

Each sensor node needs to calculate the maximum, minimum, and average for each attribute periodically. The administrator specifies an *update interval* which is much greater than the sensing interval. For instance, if the sensing interval is 5 minutes, the update interval can be 2 hours. At the end of each update interval, a sensor node sends the *index update message* including the maximum, minimum, and average values of that interval to its parent node of the index tree (we will discuss it in the next section).

4 Construct and Maintain Distributed Index Tree

Constructing effective distributed index structures can help process queries efficiently. In this section, we introduce how to construct and maintain distributed index trees.

4.1 Construct a Hierarchical Index Tree

We assume that any point in the monitored area is covered by at least one sensor node. Moreover, the sensor network is static, and absolute or relative locations (2-D cartesian coordinates) of sensor nodes are known via using GPS or location algorithms. This is necessary since users use the location as query conditions or results sometimes. At the base station, the entire network is divided into four subregions in vertical and horizontal directions, and each subregion has almost the same number of sensor nodes. Then, for each generated subregion, it is continuously divided into four subregions with almost the same number of sensor nodes. This partition process keeps going until there is no enough sensor nodes to promise that every generated subregion has at least one sensor node. A partition example is shown in Figure 1. The entire network is divided into a lot of rectangles called cells in this paper. Each cell has at leat one sensor node. In each iteration of the partition, a generated subregion is assigned an ID from 0 to 3 according to its relative position to others respectively. Finally, the cell id (CID) is the combination of IDs generated by all partition steps (as shown in Figure 1). After partition, the location and CID of each cell are recorded and sent to the sensor nodes within that cell. We use 2-D coordinates of the cell's top-left and bottom-right vertices, $\{(x_{tl}, y_{tl}), (x_{br}, y_{br})\}$, to describe the cell's geographical position.

For processing queries efficiently, a hierarchical index tree is constructed. An index tree example is shown in Figure 1 and 2. Firstly, each cell randomly chooses a sensor node as the leader of this cell. Other nodes in that cell set the leader as their parent. Since only the leader has a chance to be the index node, to maintain energy balance, sensor nodes in the same cell serve as the leader in turn. In the example, node $N13$, $N14$, and $N15$ are in the same cell, and node $N13$ is chosen to be the leader of $N14$ and $N15$. If a cell only has one sensor node, the only node is chosen to be the leader naturally. Then, the index tree is established in a reverse manner of network partition. In other words, the index tree is constructed from bottom to top. For each group of four cells which are

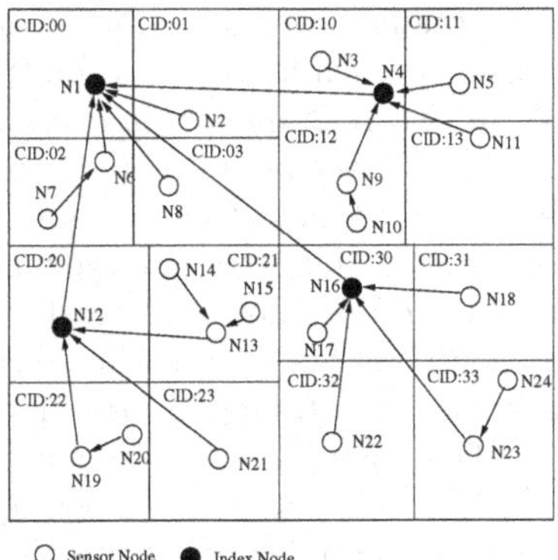

Fig. 1. Network Partition

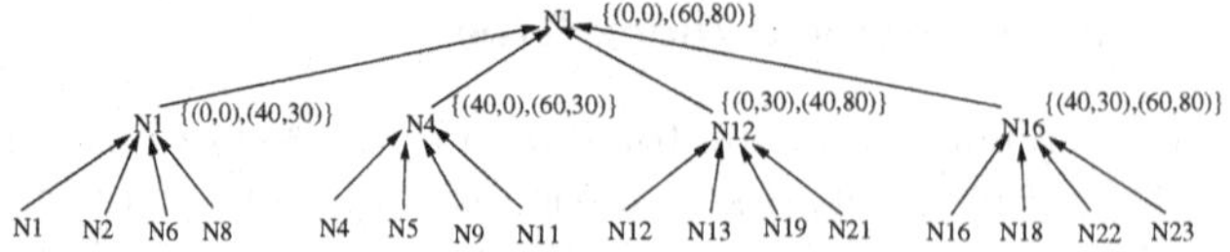

Fig. 2. Index Tree

generated from the same subregion, the leader of the top-left cell is chosen to be the parent of these four cells' leaders including itself. Then, for each group of four generated parent nodes which belong to the same subregion in the partition process, the top-left one is chosen to be the parent. The process continues until the root is generated. In the example shown in Figure 1, Node $N1$ is chosen to be the parent of Node $N1$, $N2$, $N6$, and $N8$. Node $N4$, $N12$, and $N16$ are chosen to be the parents of other three groups respectively. Next step, Node $N1$ is chosen to be the parent of $N1$, $N4$, $N12$, and $N16$, and the root $N1$ is generated. The structure of the index tree is shown in Figure 2. Obviously, the index tree is a quad-tree, and all inter nodes have four children.

If we use the same index tree during the entire network lifetime of networks, the accumulative index data will occupy most memory space quickly, especially the top layer nodes. Furthermore, index nodes will use up energy much earlier than others because the query processing frequently accesses these nodes. To balance index data distribution and energy consumption among sensor nodes, a set of index trees is generated by switching nodes' positions in the index tree periodically.

The administrator needs to specify a *tree switching period* P_S. The ideal value of P_S is the estimated network lifetime divided by the number of sensor nodes. Thus, every node has a chance to sever as an index node. Four children of the root serve as the root node in turn. For the root node (first layer), the switching period is P_S. Each node in the second layer also makes its four children serve as the parent in turn. However, the switching period of nodes in the second layer is $4 * P_S$. The switching period for nodes in the layer L is $4^{L-1} * P_S$. The lower the layer, the longer the switching period. In fact, in our index tree structure, a higher layer index node contains more data than a lower layer index node since an internal node appears at each layer of the subtree rooted at itself. For example, the root node $N1$ in Figure 2 appears in every layer of the index tree. Our schedule replaces the higher layer nodes more frequently than lower layer nodes, thus evenly distributing index data to all sensor nodes.

Through switching nodes in the index tree, a large number of index trees are available. However, a sensor node does not need to store all these index trees. Since we follow the rules to switch nodes, a sensor node can calculate its current parent according to the current time-stamp T. For a node in the (L)th layer of an index tree, its parent's CID at time T can be calculated by replacing its own CID's $(L-1)$th bit with $(\lfloor T/(4^{L-1} * P_S) \rfloor \%4)$. Geographic routing is used to generate routes among nodes of the index tree since the CID of a sensor node also indicates its relative position.

4.2 Index Maintaining

The leader of each cell is responsible for calculating the maximum, minimum, and average values of each attribute for the cell it belongs to periodically. If there are more than one sensor node in a cell, the maximum, minimum, and average values are calculated among all sensing values of the current interval from these sensor nodes. At the end of each update interval, the leader sends the update message, (T, max, min, avg) (where T is the beginning time stamp of the current time interval), to its parent in the index tree. The update message also includes the time stamp and node ID of the max and min values. The internal node in the index tree maintains the received index data with the structure as shown in Table 1. When an update message is received, it is inserted into the index structure. The internal node also merges four update messages for the current time interval T by calculating max, min, and avg, and sends this update message to its parent.

Table 1. Index Sturcture

Child0:	Child1:	Child2:	Child3:
Location: $\{(x_{tl}, y_{tl}), (x_{br}, y_{br})\}$	Location: $\{(x_{tl}, y_{tl}), (x_{br}, y_{br})\}$	...	...
Attribute1: T_i, max, min, avg T_{i+1}, max, min, avg	Attribute1: T_i, max, min, avg T_{i+1}, max, min, avg		
⋮	⋮		
Attribute2: T_i, max, min, avg	Attribute2: T_i, max, min, avg		
⋮	⋮		
⋮	⋮		

5 Historical Data Query Processing

Historical data queries can inquire max, min, and avg values for a past period of time in a specified geographic area. Also, the sensing values of specific sensor nodes or locations in the past can be retrieved. A historical query can be issued at the base station or a sensor node in the network which is named as *query node*.

Query Example1

SELECT S.temperature, S.humidity, S.location FROM sensor S

WHERE S.location WITHIN {(10, 10), (30, 30)} AND S.time BETWEEN now()-1 days AND now()

Query Example2

SELECT MAX(S.temperature), S.location FROM sensor S

WHERE S.location WITHIN{(0, 0), (50, 30)} AND S.time BETWEEN 02/01/2009 and /02/04/2009

If the query node receives a query like Query Example1, the query is forwarded to the query location {(10, 10), (30, 30)}. When a sensor node within {(10, 10), (30, 30)} receives this query, it forwards this query to the closest ancestor node (node $N1$ at the second layer in Figure 1) of the index tree, whose location contains the query location. Then, $N1$ accesses its indexes and sends the query to all its children which have intersection with the query location. Thus, the query is sent to sensor nodes which possibly satisfy the query conditions through the index tree. When a sensor node receives a query, it verifies itself. If the conditions are satisfied, it sends corresponding results back to the query node. In this query example, the index tree can bound the number of involved sensor nodes efficiently. Only cells which have intersection with location {(10, 10), (30, 30)} are probed.

For Query Example2, the query node forwards the query to the lowest layer index node (the root $N1$ in Figure 1), which contains the query location. Then, $N1$ probes MAX(S.temperature) within {(0, 0), (40, 30)} from $N1$ and MAX(S.temperautre) within {(40, 0), (50, 30)} from $N4$ between 02/01/2009 and /02/04/2009 separately. For location {(0, 0), (40, 30)}, we can calculate the index nodes, which store the MAX value between 02/01/2009 and /02/04/2009, and merge results from these index nodes to get MAX(S.temperautre) within {(40, 0), (50, 30)}. However, since {(40, 0), (50, 30)} does not perfectly match $N4$'s location {(40, 0), (60, 30)}, $N4$ has to further probe some of its children, then merges results returned by its children to get MAX(S.temperautre). Finally, the root $N1$ merges results returned by $N1$ and $N4$ to get the MAX(S.temperature) within {(0, 0), (50, 30)} and sends the results back to the query node. Usually, users send queries like Query Example2 to inquire statistical information from wireless sensor networks.

The distributed index tree can guide queries to be processed efficiently and restrict the number of involved sensor nodes. For some queries, the results are already stored in the index structure, so accessing one or several index nodes instead of a large number of sensor nodes can acquire the results.

6 Simulation

In this section, we evaluate the performance of our proposed HDQP. The sensing interval of a sensor is 5 minutes, and the update interval P_S of the index tree is 2 hours. Since network traffic greatly affects energy efficiency, we use it as the metric for performance evaluation.

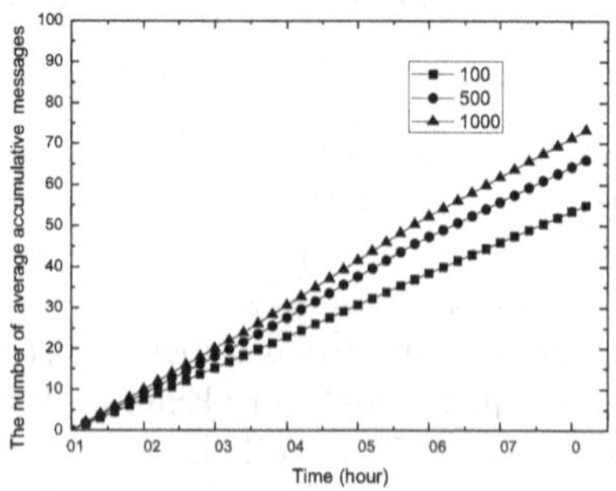

Fig. 3. Cost of maintaining the index tree with various network size

The main cost of maintaining the index tree is sending and forwarding update messages along the index tree periodically. Figure 3 shows the number of average accumulative messages of sensor nodes with 100, 500, and 1000 sensor nodes in the network respectively. The more sensor nodes the network has, the more cost of maintaining the index tree. The reason is that a bigger network must generate a bigger index tree structure, thus increasing the maintaining load. Since for a sensor node, one time index updating just causes about 2 messages averagely, and the index tree is not updated frequently, so the cost of maintaining the index tree is acceptable for wireless sensor networks with limited energy. Furthermore, as can be seen in Figure 3, the maintaining cost does not rapidly increase with the increasing of the network size. Therefore, the distributed index structure is also suitable for large-scale wireless sensor networks.

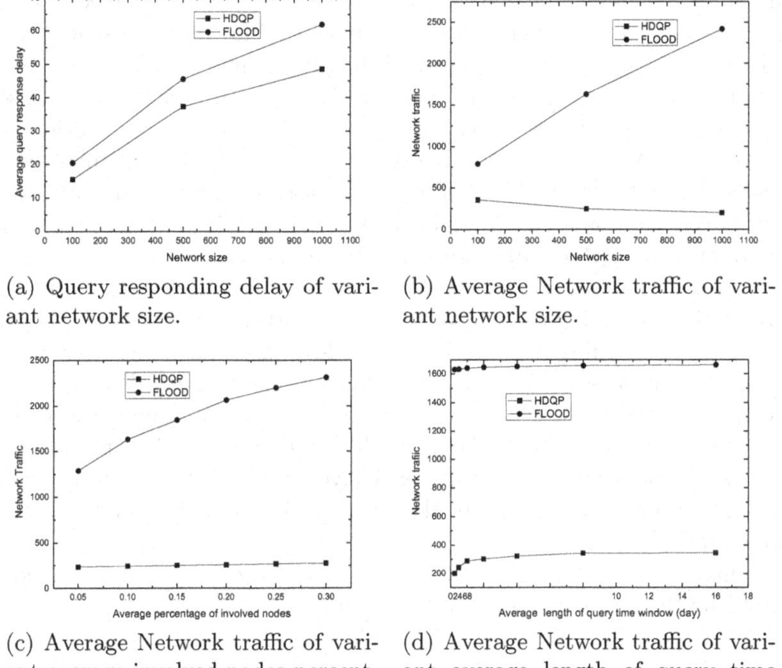

(a) Query responding delay of variant network size.

(b) Average Network traffic of variant network size.

(c) Average Network traffic of variant average involved nodes percentage of queries.

(d) Average Network traffic of variant average length of query time window.

Fig. 4. Query Processing Performance, 1000 queries during 72 hours

The performance of our HDQP is evaluated on two aspects, delay of query processing and cost of network traffic. The delay of query processing is query responding time since the query is issued until the user receives results. In our simulation, computation delay of sensor nodes is ignored, so this delay is measured by the number of hops of the longest path for sending a query and returning results. Network traffic is defined as the average number of messages sent and forwarded by all sensor nodes. Figure 4 shows the average query responding delay and network traffic (including cost of maintaining the index tree) of processing 1000 queries during 72 hours. We compare our HDQP with Flood method where the query node floods the query to entire network and all sensor nodes satisfied query conditions send corresponding data back to the query node. As seen in Figure 4(a), with the increasing of network size, query responding delay increases too since the length of pathes for sending queries and returning results increases with the network size. HDQP achieves shorter delay than Flood because it does not need to probe all qualified sensor nodes, and partial or all results can be acquired from the index tree. Figure 4(b) shows that HDQP is much better than Flood on network traffic especially for large-scale networks. This is because the index tree can help HDQP to answer queries by accessing index nodes and a small number of qualified sensor nodes if necessary. However, Flood method lets all qualified sensor nodes involve in the query processing. Network traffic of HDQP decreases with the network size increasing since for processing the same number of queries, a large-scale network has much more nodes to share work load. Figure 4(c) shows the average network traffic with variant involved sensor nodes percentage of queries. This parameter is decided by the location condition in a query. As shown in the figure, with the increasing of involved node percentage, the network traffic of Flood increases obviously since all involved nodes need to report results. However, HDQP is not affected by this parameter obviously, since HDQP acquire most of data from the index trees. The average network traffic with variant length of query time window is shown in Figure 4(d). With the increasing of time window length, the network traffic of HDQP increases too. Since index data are partitioned by time stamp, more index nodes are accessed for processing queries with a longer time window. When the length of time window reaches a certain value, the network traffic does not evidently increase any more. The reason is that when the time window is long than 4 times of partition period of the accessed layer, the number of accessed index nodes does not increase any more. However, an index node may include index data of several time slices.

In summary, our HDQP scheme can process historical data query quickly and energy-efficiently, and it is also suitable for large-scale networks.

7 Conclusion

In this paper, we have proposed a scheme, HDQP, to process historical data queries of wireless sensor networks. Our approach is the first work to study distributed historical data query processing by using an effective distributed index tree. The indexes can help process queries energy-efficiently and reduce the query responding delay. Index tree switching mechanism also can balance the load among sensor nodes to avoid data distribution and energy consumption skew.

Acknowledgment

This work is supported by the NSF under grant No. CCF-0545667 and CCF 0844829.

References

1. Aly, M., Gopalan, A., Zhao, J., Youssef, A.: Stdcs: A spatio-temporal data-centric storage scheme for real-time sensornet applications. In: 5th Annual IEEE Communications Society Conference on Sensor, Mesh and Ad Hoc Communications and Networks, 2008. SECON 2008, June 2008, pp. 377–385 (2008)
2. Meka, A., Singh, A.: Dist: a distributed spatio-temporal index structure for sensor networks. In: CIKM 2005: Proceedings of the 14th ACM international conference on Information and knowledge management, pp. 139–146. ACM, New York (2005)
3. Crossbow - wireless sensor networks - products - wireless modules, `http://www.xbow.com/Products/productdetails.aspx?sid=156` (accessed February 3, 2009)
4. Malan, D., Fulford-jones, T., Welsh, M., Moulton, S.: Codeblue: An ad hoc sensor network infrastructure for emergency medical care. In: International Workshop on Wearable and Implantable Body Sensor Networks (2004)
5. Madden, S.R., Franklin, M.J., Hellerstein, J.M., Hong, W.: Tinydb: an acquisitional query processing system for sensor networks. ACM Trans. Database Syst. 30(1), 122–173 (2005)
6. Shenker, S., Ratnasamy, S., Karp, B., Govindan, R., Estrin, D.: Data-centric storage in sensornets. SIGCOMM Comput. Commun. Rev. 33(1), 137–142 (2003)
7. Greenstein, B., Estrin, D., Govindan, R., Ratnasamy, S., Shenker, S.: Difs: a distributed index for features in sensor networks. In: 2003 IEEE International Workshop on Sensor Network Protocols and Applications, 2003. Proceedings of the First IEEE, May 2003, pp. 163–173 (2003)
8. Li, X., Kim, Y.J., Govindan, R., Hong, W.: Multi-dimensional range queries in sensor networks. In: SenSys 2003: Proceedings of the 1st international conference on Embedded networked sensor systems, pp. 63–75. ACM, New York (2003)
9. Aly, M., Pruhs, K., Chrysanthis, P.K.: Kddcs: a load-balanced in-network data-centric storage scheme for sensor networks. In: CIKM 2006: Proceedings of the 15th ACM international conference on Information and knowledge management, pp. 317–326. ACM, New York (2006)

Throughput Potential of Overlay Cognitive Wireless Mesh Networks

Jonathan Backens* and Min Song**

Department of Electrical and Computer Engineering
Old Dominion University
Norfolk, VA 23529, USA
{jback006,msong}@odu.edu
http://www.odu.edu/networking

Abstract. In this paper we consider a cognitive radio overlay model applied to single channel, single radio wireless mesh network and investigate the performance and fairness. Specifically we challenge the nominal mesh capacity of $O(\frac{1}{n})$ and provide proof that under certain constraints total mesh capacity can approach $O(\frac{1}{2})$ with an average per node throughput of $O(\frac{1}{n_a})$ where n_a is the number of data generating active nodes. We provide an analysis of overlay communication using dirty paper coding on the sequential transmissions in wireless mesh networks.

Keywords: Overlay Cognitive Radio, Wireless Mesh Networks, Throughput.

1 Introduction

The challenge of ubiquitous connectivity has given rise to the use of wireless mesh networks around the world as a cheap, effective and flexible real world solution. Specifically the challenges of providing higher capacity, better fairness and improved spectrum utilization are actively being researched. Most current cognitive mesh literature focuses on WMNs filling unused spectral holes, a technique known as dynamic spectrum access or *interweave* cognitive networking. This interweave model is often referred to as a switching model as primary and secondary users have mutually exclusive access the shared spectrum. In contrast, the cognitive *underlay* model allows for simultaneous primary and secondary user transmission through methods such as UWB[10]. By allowing the secondary transmission to use UWB, the overall incurred interference in the specific frequency range used by the primary user is small enough to be ignored. The final model typically considered is the cognitive *overlay* model. This model uses non-causal side knowledge of the primary message by the secondary transmitter and *dirty paper coding* or *Costa coding* to allow simultaneous transmission

* The research of Jonathan Backens is supported by US Department of Education GAANN Program.

** The research of Min Song is supported by NSF CAREER Award CNS-0644247.

B. Liu et al. (Eds.): WASA 2009, LNCS 5682, pp. 274–283, 2009.

within the same spectrum and with the same radio technology. Costa proved in [1] that given a large enough codeword set the AWGN optimal capacity can be achieved; namely $C = \frac{1}{2}\ln(1+\frac{P}{N})$. Although this realization requires complex coding schemes, the potential for capacity increase in a normally interfering channel between two node pairs is quite enticing.

Uniquely traffic in WMNs is by nature destined to or from a single gateway node. Thus all traffic generally follows routes with forwarding conducted by intermediary nodes. Messages being forwarded are known *a priori* to previous nodes in a transmission sequence and the non-causal knowledge requirement of the message to be forwarded is already satisfied. In addition, since the collision domain is the bottleneck to capacity in any nominal mesh network [4] it can be concluded that by reducing its influence, capacity can be increased.

The main contribution of this paper is an improved method for using cognitive overlay in WMN to achieve total network capacity of $O(\frac{1}{2})$ with an average node capacity of $O(\frac{1}{2n_a})$. Specifically, we consider randomly deployed mesh networks of variable size and traffic. The characterization of the performance over a large number of random networks using the overlay technique is unique to our work. The rest of the paper is organized as follows. In Section 2, a basic review of capacity of mesh networks and underlay cognitive radio models are presented as shown in related work. Section 3 provides a theoretical proof for our new approximations for capacity. In Section 4, the results of extensive simulations are presented to confirm our theoretical bounds and to show the fairness of our TDMA algorithm. Section 5 summarizes our results and main contributions.

2 Related Work

The discussion of capacity in wireless networks was defined in the seminal work [2] in which for an ad-hoc network an upper theoretical bound was determined to be $\theta(\frac{1}{\sqrt{n}})$. This constraint was given with an optimally chosen geometric configuration with all nodes at a one hop distance. However if this constraint is relaxed to randomly distributed nodes than the capacity falls significantly to $\theta(\frac{1}{\sqrt{n\log n}})$. The consideration for the multi-hop nature of WMNs specifically was presented in [4]. This work used the assumption that two nodes within the same collision domain must use different time slots to transmit. The subsequent throughput was determined by the collision domain to be worst case $O(\frac{1}{n})$.

There has been several attempts at using CR theoretical models applied to WMN for increasing throughput. The comparison between the overlay and interweave models is presented in [10]. The numerical results showed that clearly that cognitive overlay models performed significantly better than the two switch interweave model.

The specific model for such an overlay network is well defined in [3] for the two receiver two transmitter case. Specifically, the case where the secondary user has *non-causal* knowledge of the primary user message is considered. This model is shown in Fig. 1(a). As [3] concludes, the use of DPC or *Costa coding* in this model can achieve a capacity upper bounded by the interference free AWGN

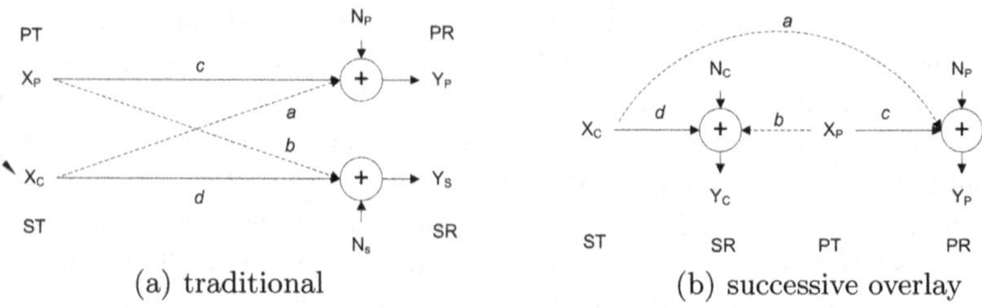

(a) traditional (b) successive overlay

Fig. 1. Cognitive Overlay Models

channel for both transmissions. This is an adaptive coding scheme which bases the secondary transmitters codeword on the primary transmissions codeword and thus falls into the category of CR. The specific rates achievable by this two receiver two transmitter model are defined in [3] as,

$$0 \leq R_p \leq \frac{1}{2} \log(1 + \frac{(\sqrt{P_P} + a\sqrt{\alpha P_c}^2)}{1 + a^2(1-\alpha)P_c}) \tag{1}$$

$$0 \leq R_c \leq \frac{1}{2} \log(1 + (1-\alpha)P_c) \tag{2}$$

Furthermore, [5] approaches throughput in WMN as a relaying problem with joint cooperation between the transmitters. Thus the concept of exploiting the redundant messages of the BC in WMN first considers an overlay model. However these techniques considered just the broadcast case and not general traffic across the network. In [6] a comparison of ad hoc cooperative broadcast techniques is presented. Specifically the performance of DPC was compared with both time-division successive broadcast and time-division relaying. It concludes with evidence that DPC can outperform other methods of relaying if messages are known non-causally. Further studies into the performance benefits of cooperation in the two TX two RX model were conducted in [7]. Here cooperation among the transmitters was shown to out perform cooperation among receivers. This performance benefit was dependent on the high SNR of the transmitter cooperation channel, since messages must be passed between the transmitters before DPC can take place. Thus the higher the quality of cooperation the greater the overall capacity gain of the channel.

Interestingly in the MIMO case as the collision domain is reduced and transmitter cooperation is exploited the utilization of the total channel capacity available increases. As shown in [9], when the capacity is maximized in a TDMA based MIMO network a natural by-product is increased fairness. This leads to assumptions that similar increases would occur in the sequential WMN case with DPC. This concept was further exploited in [8], where pairwise DPC in a WMN was considered. The throughput overall for the mesh topology was increased and the paper showed promise that overlay techniques could improve mesh capacity overall beyond nominal limits found in [4]. These results stem from theoretical work done in [3] and found that with small values of a the capacity of a single primary and single secondary user would be $R_p = R_c = \gamma B$ with $0.937 \leq \gamma \leq 0.999$ for $0.1 \leq a \leq 0.9$. However the extension of cognitive overlay beyond two node pairs was not considered. In addition the results were limited to only end to end network traffic and not arbitrary or saturated traffic conditions.The model we present in Section 3 takes this basic manipulation of the data forwarding characteristics inherent in WMN and extends it to models of arbitrary node size. Thus the true sequential nature of larger node networks can better be exploited.

3 Theoretical Analysis

As shown in [6] in order to achieve the desired $2B$ bandwidth allowed from two cognitive pairs the secondary user and the primary user are subject to fading constraints. Now although these constraints are important, the main interference range of each transmission in a WMN does lead to collision domains when the number of nodes considered exceeds the two TX two RX model. The challenge of successive dirty paper encoding results when continuous traffic is desired over the entire mesh chain. Whereas in [8] the collision domain was still a dominating factor when considering overall throughput in a chain topology (in addition to the more complex random topology), the following proof shows that continuous DPC can be used.

As given in [6] the following basic model can be used to model the relationship between the primary users and secondary users in a typical underlay cognitive model.

$$Y_1 = X_1 + aX_2 + Z_1 \tag{3}$$

$$Y_2 = bX_1 + X_2 + Z_2 \tag{4}$$

Now since X_n is formed using DPC we get

$$Y_1 = (1 + a\sqrt{\frac{\alpha P_2}{P_1}})X_1 + a\hat{X}_2 + Z_1$$

$$Y_2 = (b + \sqrt{\frac{\alpha P_2}{P_1}})X_1 + \hat{X}_2 + Z_2$$

In [3] the process at the receiver for decoding these messages is simple. Since X_1 and $\hat{X}_2$ are i.i.d. Gaussian and already power constrained by P_c, Receiver 1 treats the value of $a\hat{X}_2$ as independent Gaussian noise and thus can be ignored up to a certain rate(namely the AWGN channel capacity for small $a \leq 1$). In addition since Receiver 2 knows non-causally X_1 it can simply subtract $(b + \sqrt{\frac{\alpha P_2}{P_1}})X_1$ and recover $\hat{X}_2$. The extension from the pairwise case to the nth case is shown in the next section with proof that similar message recovery is possible.

3.1 Proof of nth Case

Now we extend the two transmitter two receiver pair for a chain of n nodes and find it useful to consider the scenario of Fig. 2. Thus we can extend Y_n to an arbitrarily large n such and determine if the coding scheme remains bounded by this two node example or increases in complexity and thus reduces overall capacity. This is a key proof since if nodes are constantly generating traffic then without some bounds on complexity eventually the throughput would be reduced to nothing. Simply put it is not possible to DPC code an infinite number of messages together without some level of message degradation unless an infinitely large codeword set is available. Since this is not possible, the proof of a limited interference range allows for limited codeword set sizes and thus achievable capacity gains with DPC.

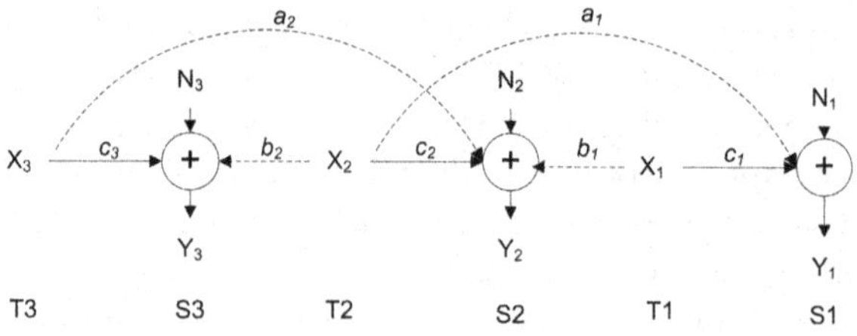

Fig. 2. Cognitive Overlay Model Extended

We consider first that each transmitter has *non-causal* knowledge of all previously transmitted messages and is in fact adjusting its codeword according to DPC rules. We then get a succession of transmissions generated of the form.

$$X_n = \hat{X}_n + \sum_{i=1}^{n-1} \sqrt{\frac{(\prod_{j=i}^{n-1} \alpha_j) P_n}{P_i}} \hat{X}_i \tag{5}$$

From (5) it is easy to see that previously transmitted messages are considered when forming each new message, however the scale of message is reduced by a factor relative to $\sqrt{\alpha_i}$ each time, thus eventually reducing the effect of the previous messages is negligible. The smaller α the quicker we can simplify the transmission method. This can also be seen in the received message as the interference of previously transmitted messages also falls off with relative to α. Thus we must constrain $\alpha \leq 1$ with coding complexity proportional to α.

Recall that the α value can be considered as the percentage of P_c used to transmit P_p's message and is related to only to the interference channel gain between the cognitive transmitter and the primary receiver (value a) and the values of P_p and P_c according to the following equation. We generalize for our n^{th} case.

$$\alpha_i = (\frac{\sqrt{P_i}(\sqrt{1 + a_i^2 P_{i+1}(1 + P_i)} - 1)}{a_i \sqrt{P_{i+1}(1 + P_i)}} \text{, } i = 1...n-1$$

Thus if we can constrain then we can guarantee that the successive DPC will not include an infinite many number of previous message values. Or simply, nodes need only consider a subset of all previously transmitted messages when DPC a new message. This conclusion is a substantial contribution and allows for network chains of any given length of nodes to be able to transmit at capacity. Thus we extend (3) and (4) and substitute with (5) to get

$$Y_k = a_{k+1}X_{k+1} + X_k + b_{k-1}X_{k-1} + a_{k-2}X_{k-2} + Z_k \tag{6}$$

$$= a_{k+1}(\hat{X}_{k+1} + \sum_{i=1}^{k} \sqrt{\frac{(\prod_{j=i}^{k} \alpha_j)P_{k+1}}{P_i}}\hat{X}_i) + (\hat{X}_k + \sum_{i=1}^{k-1} \sqrt{\frac{(\prod_{j=i}^{k-1} \alpha_j)P_k}{P_i}}\hat{X}_i)$$

$$+b_{k-1}(\hat{X}_{k-1}+\sum_{i=1}^{k-2} \sqrt{\frac{(\prod_{j=i}^{k-2} \alpha_j)P_{k-1}}{P_i}}\hat{X}_i)+a_{k-2}(\hat{X}_{k-2}+\sum_{i=1}^{k-3} \sqrt{\frac{(\prod_{j=i}^{k-3} \alpha_j)P_{k-2}}{P_i}}\hat{X}_i)+Z_i$$

However if the α values are again small then as shown in (5) we can rewrite this expression to only a few terms, viz. the following expression.

$$Y_k = (a_{k-2}+b_{k-1}\sqrt{\frac{\alpha_{k-2}P_{k-1}}{P_{k-2}}}+\sqrt{\frac{\alpha_{k-2}\alpha_{k-1}P_k}{P_{k-2}}}+a_{k+1}\sqrt{\frac{\alpha_{k-2}\alpha_{k-1}\alpha_k P_{k+1}}{P_{k-2}}})\hat{X}_{k-2}$$

$$+(b_{k-1} + \sqrt{\frac{\alpha_{k-1}P_k}{P_{k-1}}} + a_{k+1}\sqrt{\frac{\alpha_k\alpha_{k-1}P_{k+1}}{P_{k-1}}})\hat{X}_{k-1}$$

$$+(a_{k-2} + a\sqrt{\frac{\alpha_{k+1}P_{k+1}}{P_{k-1}}})\hat{X}_k + a_{k+1}\hat{X}_{k+1}, k = 2...n-1$$

which can be written in a simplified form as

$$Y_k = b^*\hat{X}_{k-2} + b^{**}\hat{X}_{k-1} + \hat{X}_k + a_{k+1}\hat{X}_{k+1} \tag{7}$$

Now we consider that the receiver Y_k already known non-causally the $b^*\hat{X}_{k-2} + b^{**}\hat{X}_{k-1}$ terms which it can simply subtract from the message. In addition due to the already stated characteristics of DPC code words, the $a_{k+1}\hat{X}_{k+1}$ values can be treated as simply independent Gaussian noise and thus ignored. Therefore the $\hat{X}_k$ message is recovered with only standard noise interference. This conclusion proves that a chain of nodes can achieve nearly the total throughput capacity of the AWGN channel individually using DPC regardless of length.

3.2 Fairness and TDMA

It is trivial to conclude that with increased density WMN have increased collision domains. Therefore a unique scheduling algorithm is needed to ensure collisions are reduced. A basic TDMA schedule algorithm is presented to resolve this.

- A TDMA window is created with unique time slots for each node
- Each node assigned a time slot
- All unused time slots are detected by downstream nodes and are marked available
- Active nodes are allocated additional unused time slots in a round robin fashion based on distance from the gateway.

As seen in this algorithm, if each time slot is of uniform length and the unused time slots are distributed evenly a basic level of fairness can be achieved. As shown in the simulations in the following section, our presented overlay model achieves nearly optimal fairness with this simple algorithm. The stated algorithm is clearly dependent on the individual characteristics of the mesh(ie node degrees and hop counts). Thus as shown in Figs. 3 and 4 the fairness of the nominal mesh clearly degrades as the network grows. This can also be seen in the original overlay model presented in [8]. However, since this collision domain is eliminated by our new overlay model, fairness becomes a natural result.

4 Simulation Results

In the following section simulations have been run to ensure that the improved capacity claims are realized. Specifically we will consider the case of the effects of node constraints on throughput in both the linear and nonlinear case. The simulation were run in Matlab using randomly generated mesh networks with single antenna nodes. The distance based routing with free space path loss model was used. In addition, since DPC requires a priori CSI, each node was aware of the locations of of other nodes via the routing tree. This ensured the TDMA method for communication and also enabled calculations for collision domains in the simple and non-overlay models. It should be noted that since nodes were designed as half-duplex the maximum channel capacity for a given mesh is 50%.

The simulations for performance were conducted for normalized channel capacity and thus only percentages of utilization are shown since individual channel capacity is dependent on coding scheme, channel bandwidth, and fading characteristics.

As shown in Fig. 3, the performance of the mesh network in a single linear model (viz. a single chain topology with node degree 1) gives the worst case performance in terms of collision domains as the number of nodes in the mesh is increased.The second part Fig. 3(a) shows the relative fairness of each of the models simulated. It is clear that under the worst possible constraints that the nominal mesh has a difference in fairness of as much as 2:1, this disparity is relative to the distance a given node is from the gateway. Therefore, this ratio can be seen as a starvation rate for distant nodes in a network. As projected, the general overlay model shows a significantly better performance than that nominal case with a channel utilization of roughly 35% over nominal's 26%. The proposed extended overlay presented in this paper approaches the maximum throughput potential and thus roughly doubles the throughput of the nominal case and increases the basic overlay by over 40%.

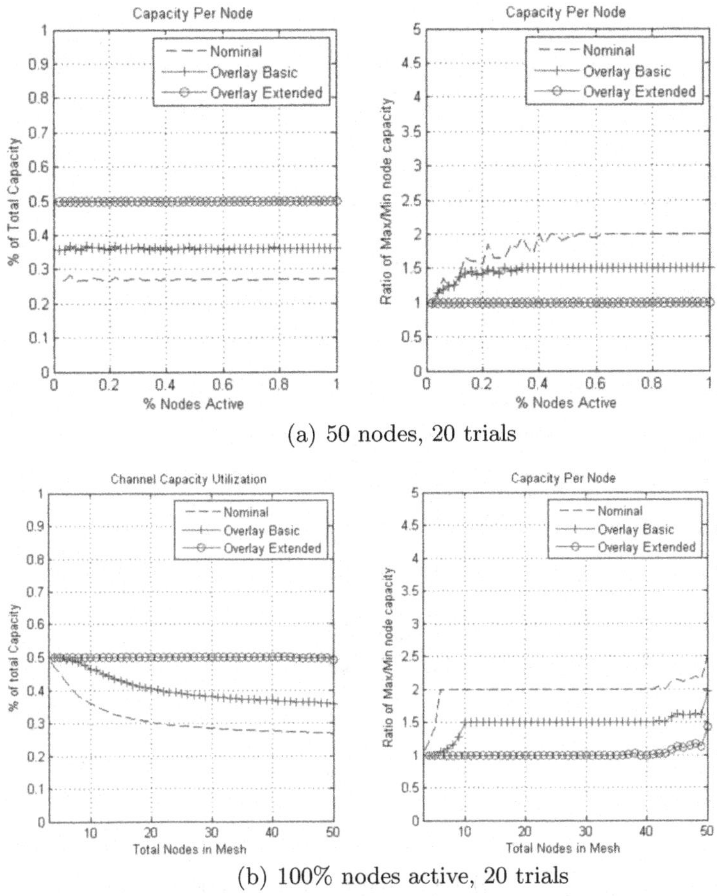

(a) 50 nodes, 20 trials

(b) 100% nodes active, 20 trials

Fig. 3. Chain Topology

It is clear from Fig 3. that smaller network sizes have similar performance regardless of model. However with networks greater than 20 nodes the performance is noticeably less for the nominal and basic models. In networks of greater than 10 nodes the fairness of the nominal stabilizes to 2:1 and the basic stabilizes to 1.5:1 with the extended maintaining overall fairness of 1:1. Thus node starvation takes place quickly in larger networks with higher numbers of active nodes with the basic overlay and nominal cases. it is clear that each model converges as both the total nodes and active nodes grows.

The extension of these worst case models to the 2D model allows for a more realistic modeling environment. These simulations were run with nodes placed randomly in a 2 dimensional environment allowing for nodes of higher degree. As shown in Fig. 4 the capacity remains constant independent of the number of active nodes in the mesh. However clearly fairness is dependent on the number of nodes. It is clear that this random case supports better overall performance than the basic overlay and the nominal cases, with values of 40% and 28% respectively.

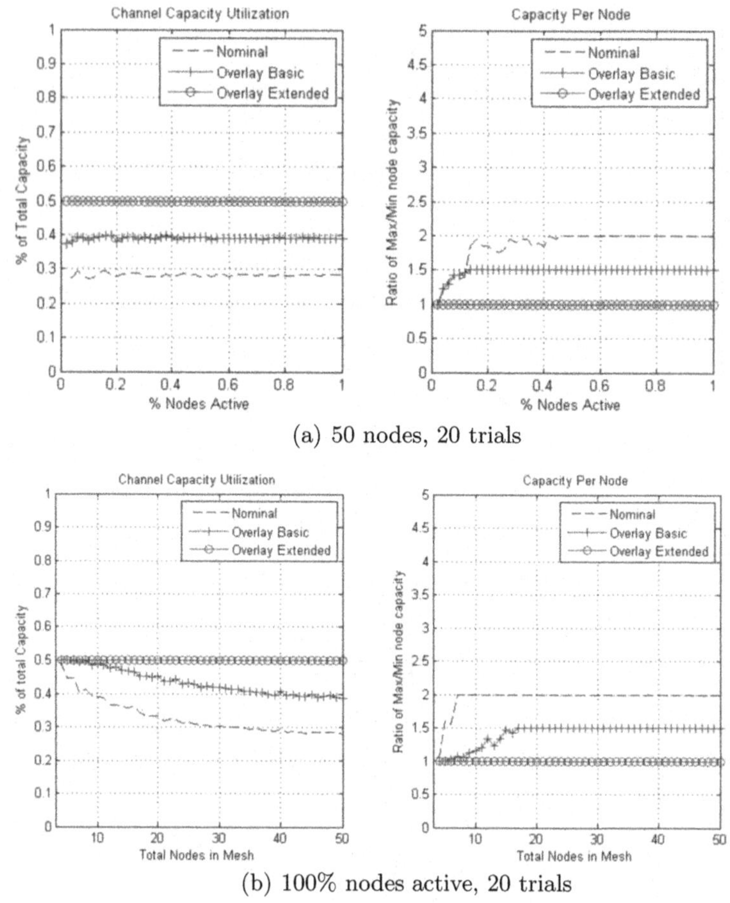

(a) 50 nodes, 20 trials

(b) 100% nodes active, 20 trials

Fig. 4. Arbitrary 2D Topology

Our extended overlay again provides consistent performance approaching the total capacity threshold.

The results of Fig. 4 provide the best overall viewpoint of the performance and fairness increase of our extended overlay network. The falloff of the performance of the basic overlay and nominal cases is much more gradual than the extreme case presented in Fig. 3. The capacities of these models do approach the worst case and it can be general considered equivalent to worst case after the total number of nodes exceeds 45. Similarly the fairness approaches worst case after only 5 nodes for the nominal case and 18 for the basic overlay case.

5 Conclusions

In this paper we have investigated the influence of cognitive overlay models on arbitrary wireless mesh networks. We have mitigated the problem of the collision domain in forwarding links in the mesh network by organizing the routing chains in the mesh network as simultaneous transmissions with *non-causal* side information and proving the potential for achievable capacity as approaching the AWGN channel capacity. Our simulated results clearly show that cognitive overlay WMN can achieve near optimal capacity of $\frac{B}{2}$ regardless of number of active nodes or total nodes. In addition this model also achieves a nearly perfect fairness between node capacity across the entire mesh network regardless of total number of nodes or number of active nodes. These results were substantial increases over both then nominal case and other overlay models proposed by earlier research.

References

1. Costa, M.: Writing on dirty paper (Corresp.). IEEE Transactions on Information Theory 29(3), 439–441 (1983)
2. Gupta, P., Kumar, P.R.: The capacity of wireless networks. IEEE Transactions on information theory 46(2), 388–404 (2000)
3. Jovicic, A., Viswanath, P.: Cognitive Radio: An Information-Theoretic Perspective. In: 2006 IEEE International Symposium on Information Theory, pp. 2413–2417 (2006)
4. Jun, J., Sichitiu, M.L.: The nominal capacity of wireless mesh networks. IEEE Wireless Communications 10(5), 8–14 (2003)
5. Kurniawan, E., Madhukumar, A.S., Chin, F., Liang, Y.-C.: Successive dirty paper coding: New relaying scheme for cooperative networks. In: IEEE 18th International Symposium on Personal, Indoor and Mobile Radio Communications, PIMRC 2007, September 2007, pp. 1–5 (2007)
6. Ng, C.T.K., Goldsmith, A.J.: Transmitter cooperation in ad-hoc wireless networks: Does dirty-paper coding beat relaying? In: IEEE Information Theory Workshop, 2004, pp. 277–282 (2004)
7. Ng, C.T.K., Jindal, N., Goldsmith, A.J., Mitra, U.: Capacity gain from two-transmitter and two-receiver cooperation. IEEE Transactions on Information Theory 53(10), 3822–3827 (2007)
8. Pereira, R.C., Souza, R.D., Pellenz, M.E.: Using cognitive radio for improving the capacity of wireless mesh networks. In: IEEE 68th Vehicular Technology Conference, 2008. VTC 2008. September 2008, pp. 1—5 (Fall 2008)
9. Sharif, M., Hassibi, B.: On the capacity of MIMO broadcast channels with partial side information. IEEE Transactions on Information Theory 51(2), 506–522 (2005)
10. Srinivasa, S., Jafar, S.A.: The throughput potential of cognitive radio: A theoretical perspective. IEEE Communications Magazine 45(5), 73 (2007)

Data Collection with Multiple Sinks in Wireless Sensor Networks

Sixia Chen, Matthew Coolbeth, Hieu Dinh, Yoo-Ah Kim, and Bing Wang*

Computer Science & Engineering Department, University of Connecticut

Abstract. In this paper, we consider Multiple-Sink Data Collection Problem in wireless sensor networks, where a large amount of data from sensor nodes need to be transmitted to one of multiple sinks. We design an approximation algorithm to minimize the latency of data collection schedule and show that it gives a constant-factor performance guarantee. We also present a heuristic algorithm based on breadth first search for this problem. Using simulation, we evaluate the performance of these two algorithms, and show that the approximation algorithm outperforms the heuristic up to 60%.

1 Introduction

A wireless sensor network, which consists of an ad hoc group of small sensor nodes communicating with one another, have a variety of applications such as traffic monitoring, emergency medical care, battlefield surveillance, and underwater surveillance. In such applications, it is often necessary to collect the data accumulated by each sensor node for processing. We call the operation of transmitting accumulated data from sensor nodes to the sinks *data collection*. In this paper, we consider the problem to find a schedule to quickly collect a large amount of data from sensor nodes to sinks. Data need to be collected without merging. If the data can be merged, the operation is called data aggregation.

One of the challenges in data collection in wireless networks is radio interferences that may prevent nearby sensor nodes from transmitting packets simultaneously. Scheduling data transmissions without carefully considering such inferences can result in significant delay in data collection.

When there is only one gateway (or sink) to collect data and the amount of data at all sensor nodes is similar, a greedy algorithm may work well. For example, there is a 3-approximation algorithm for general graphs and optimal algorithms for simpler graphs in this case [5]. When there are multiple gateways and the distribution of the data is not uniform, the problem becomes more challenging as the amount of data to be sent to each gateway need to be balanced to avoid congestion.

In this paper, we consider the problem of minimizing the latency of data collection in settings where (i) data cannot be merged, (ii) there are multiple

* Y. Kim and B. Wang were partially supported by UConn Faculty Large Grant and NSF CAREER award 0746841, respectively.

B. Liu et al. (Eds.): WASA 2009, LNCS 5682, pp. 284–294, 2009.

sinks, and (iii) the amount of data accumulated at sensor nodes as well as the capacity of links may not be uniform. We present an approximation algorithm to find a schedule with a constant-factor guarantee. We evaluate the performance of this algorithm as well as a greedy heuristic algorithm using simulation in various settings. Our simulation results show that the approximation algorithm outperforms the naive heuristic up to 60%.

The rest of the paper is organized as follows: We present related work and problem formulation in Sections 2 and 3, respectively. In Section 4, we introduce an LP-based approximation algorithm and show that it gives a constant-factor performance guarantee. We then present a greedy breadth-first-search (BFS) based heuristic algorithm in Section 5, and the experimental results in Section 6. Conclusion is presented in Section 7.

2 Related Work

Data broadcast and collection are among the most fundamental operations in many communication networks. Algorithms for broadcasting in wireless networks, in which the objective is to transmit data from one source to all the other nodes, have been extensively studied in the literature [1,3,7,13,12,8]. Data collection and aggregation problem in wireless networks, on the other hand, are relatively new but have recently received much attention [14,15,11,18,5].

Florens and McEliece [5] studied data distribution and collection problems with a single source/sink. They present data distribution/collection schedule for several types of graphs, and show that it provides 3-approximation for general graphs and optimal solution for simpler graphs such as trees. Their algorithm (and the analysis) cannot be easily extended to the case of multiple sinks. In addition, they assume that all the links have uniform capacity, i.e., one packet can be transmitted over a link at each time unit.

Another problem closely related data collection is the data aggregation problem (also called convergecast), in which gathered data can be merged by taking the maximum or minimum for example. Huang et al. [14] designed a nearly constant approximation algorithm for minimum latency data aggregation problem.

Cheng et al. [4] considered large-scale data collection problem in wired networks, in which a large amount of data need to be collected from multiple hosts to a single destination. They present coordinated data collection algorithm using a time-expanded graph to minimizes the latency. Unlike our problem, radio interference is not an issue in their problem as they consider data collection in wired networks.

3 Problem Formulation

3.1 Network Model

A wireless sensor network can be modeled as a graph $G = (V, E)$ in which each node in V represents a sensor node and each link, $e \in E$, represents a wireless communication link between two nodes. The capacity of a link, e, specifies the amount of data that can be transmitted over e during a unit time. For any two network nodes, $u, v \in V$, (u, v) and $C(u, v)$ respectively denote the link from u to v and its capacity. Finally, every link $(u, v) \in E$ has an *interference set*, denoted as $I(u, v)$, which represents the set of links in E that may not be used concurrently with (u, v) due to interference. Interference has been modeled in a variety of ways in the literature, including *protocol model* [9], *transmitter model (Tx-model)* [19], *transmitter-receiver model (Tx-Rx model)* [2,16], and so on. Our algorithm is applicable to any of those models by appropriately defining interference sets $I(u, v)$ according to the model.

3.2 Data Collection Problem

We consider the Multiple-Sink Data Collection Problem (MSDC), in which there are multiple sinks and a large amount of data from sensor nodes need to be transmitted to one of the sinks. Formally, we are given a wireless directed network graph, $G = (V, E)$. Each link (v_i, v_j) in the graph from node $v_i \in V$ to $v_j \in V$ is associated with a capacity, $C(v_i, v_j)$, and an interference set, $I(v_i, v_j) = \{(v_{i'}, v_{j'}) \in E \mid \text{link } (v_{i'}, v_{j'}) \text{ interferes with link } (v_i, v_j)\}$. A link cannot be used when another link in its interference set is activated. We have a set of sinks $D \subset V$. For node $v_i \in V \setminus D$, let s_i denote the amount of accumulated data at this node, and the data need to be sent to one of the nodes in D. Note that the data can be sent to *any* of the sinks. We want to find a data-collection schedule to transmit all the data to the sinks. The schedule must specify in each time slot which links are used for data transfer. In order for the schedule to be valid, it must not allow two interfering links to be used for data transfer at the same time. Our objective is to find a data-collection schedule of the minimum latency.

4 A Constant Approximation Algorithm

In this section, we present an approximation algorithm with a constant-factor guarantee. The algorithm consists of three components. The first component constructs a *time-expanded graph* [10,6], which represents the progression of the state of the network throughout a given time period T, during which data collection occurs. The second component uses a *linear programming* (LP) formulation to generate *feasible flows* to send data over edges in the time-expanded graph. The first and second components need to be repeatedly run until we can find a feasible flow with latency close enough to the optimal solution. The details of the iterations are given in the end of Section 4.2 and Algorithm 1. Once a feasible flow solution is obtained, the third component finds an *exact data collection schedule* for each time slot. We refer to this algorithm as *LP-based algorithm*. In Section 4.4 we show that it gives constant factor guarantees, with the constant depending on the interference model (e.g., it gives 5-approximation under unit disk model). We next describe the three components in the algorithm in detail.

4.1 Generating a Time-Expanded Graph

One core component of our algorithm is expanding the network graph, G, to a time-expanded graph, $G_T = (V_T, E_T)$, which represents the network over a period of T time units, and in which we can compute a network flow that corresponds to a valid data collection schedule. Figure 1 depicts an example network graph and its corresponding time-expanded flow graph.

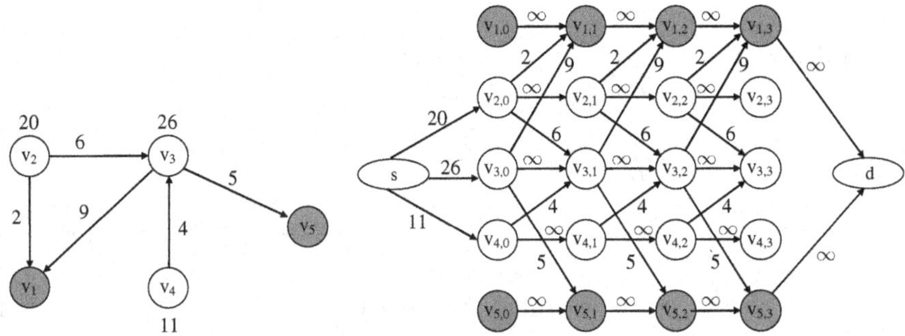

Fig. 1. A network graph, G, and its corresponding time-expanded graph, G_T, where $T = 3$, and the shaded nodes represent the sinks

Given a graph G and time T, the expanded time graph, $G_T = (V_T, E_T)$, can be constructed as follows. For each network node $v_i \in V$, and for every $t \in \{0...T\}$, we add a vertex $v_{i,t}$ to V_T. These vertices represent v_i at $T+1$ points of time, where $v_{i,t+1}$ is one time unit later than $v_{i,t}$. To represent the storage of data over time at a node in V, we assign an unlimited flow capacity, $C_T(v_{i,t}, v_{i,t+1}) = \infty$, to any $v_i \in V$ and $t \in \{0...T-1\}$. Furthermore, we assign a flow capacity $C_T(v_{i,t}, v_{j,t+1}) = C(v_i, v_j)$ to each edge $(v_{i,t}, v_{j,t+1}) \in E_T$, which represents the maximum amount of flow allowed on this edge in a time unit. In addition, we associate a flow interference set, $I_T(v_{i,t}, v_{j,t+1})$, to $(v_{i,t}, v_{j,t+1}) \in E_T$, which can be inferred from the interference set of the corresponding link in E. Specifically, for all $v_i, v_j, v_{i'}, v_{j'} \in V$ with $(v_{i'}, v_{j'}) \in I(v_i, v_j)$, and for all $t \in \{1...T-1\}$, $(v_{i',t}, v_{j',t+1}) \in I_T(v_{i,t}, v_{j,t+1})$. Last, we add a super source s and a super sink d into the time expanded graph. We also create a link from s to $v_{i,0}$ with capacity s_i for any node $v_i \in V \setminus D$. Meanwhile, for any node $v_j \in D$ in the original graph, we have a link from $v_{j,T}$ to d with unlimited capacity.

4.2 Computing a Data Flow

The constructed time-expanded graph G_T, along with the associated supplies, edge capacities, and interference constraints, form an interference-bound network flow problem. In this problem, if the maximum flow from s to d is $\sum_{v_i \in V \setminus D} s_i$, then in the original graph we can collect all the data to the sink in time T. We solve the network flow problem using a linear programming (LP) formulation as follows. Denote $f_{u,v}$ as the flow along the edge from vertex u to v for any $u, v \in V_T$ and $(u, v) \in E_T$. In particular, $f_{s,u}$ represents the flow along the link from the super source s to node $u \in V_T$, and $f_{v,d}$ represents the flow along the link from node $v \in V_T$ to the super sink d. Let $Out(u)$ denote the set of the endpoints of the outgoing links of u, $u \in V_T$, and let $In(v)$ denote the set of the endpoints of the incoming links of v, $v \in V_T$. Then the LP formulation is:

$$\textbf{Maximize:} \quad \sum_{u \in Out(s)} f_{s,u}$$

$$\textbf{Subject to:} \quad \sum_{u \in Out(s)} f_{s,u} - \sum_{v \in In(d)} f_{v,d} = 0 \tag{1}$$

$$\sum_{v \in In(u)} f_{v,u} - \sum_{v \in Out(u)} f_{u,v} = 0, \ \forall \ u \neq s, d \tag{2}$$

$$\frac{f_{u,v}}{C_T(u,v)} + \sum_{(u',v') \in I(u,v)} \frac{f_{u',v'}}{C_T(u',v')} \leq 1, \ \forall \ u, v \in V_T \tag{3}$$

$$f_{u,v} \leq C_T(u,v), \ \forall \ u, v \in V_T \tag{4}$$

$$f_{u,v} \geq 0, \ \forall \ u, v \in V_T \tag{5}$$

The above LP formulation represents a network flow problem with additional constraints to ensure interference-free property. More specifically, Constraints (1) and (2) are for flow conservation, and Constraint (4) is for link capacity. Constraint (3) provides a sufficient condition for interference-free schedule. In other words, the constraints ensure that, throughout any time slot, only one network link in each interference set can be active.

For a given time T, if the resulting maximum flow from s to d after solving the LP problem is $\sum_{v_i \in V \setminus D} s_i$, then we can infer a complete schedule for all data in the network to be collected in time at most T. By performing a standard doubling/binary search, we can find the minimum latency T_{min} necessary to have a valid network flow solution in logarithmic time. Once T_{min} is found, the solution of network flow in the time-expanded graph $G_{T_{min}}$ can be obtained, and will be used in the third step (see Section 4.3) to generate an exact data collection schedule. Algorithm 1 presents a high-level description of the above procedure.

Algorithm 1. Compute feasible data flow

1. Guess T_{min} in logarithmic time, using doubling and binary search:
   (a) Generate a time-expanded graph G_T of length T from the given network G.
   (b) Check whether there exists a valid flow in G_T using the LP formulation.
2. Compute the solution of network flow in time-expanded graph $G_{T_{min}}$.

4.3 Data Collection Schedule

We now present a scheduling algorithm for each time interval. We assume that the amount of data to be collected is sufficiently large, and so we can split the

Algorithm 2. Construct data collection schedule for interval $[t, t+1]$
for $i = 1$ to $|V_{I_t}|$ **do**

1. In interval $[t, t+1]$, find the earliest slot, $[t', t' + x_i^t]$, for $v_{i,t}^I$ while not causing any interference (i.e., this slot has no overlap with the slots already allocated to nodes in $N(v_{i,t}^I)$).
2. If no consecutive slot of duration x_i^t is found, split x_i^t into shorter durations and schedule each duration separately.

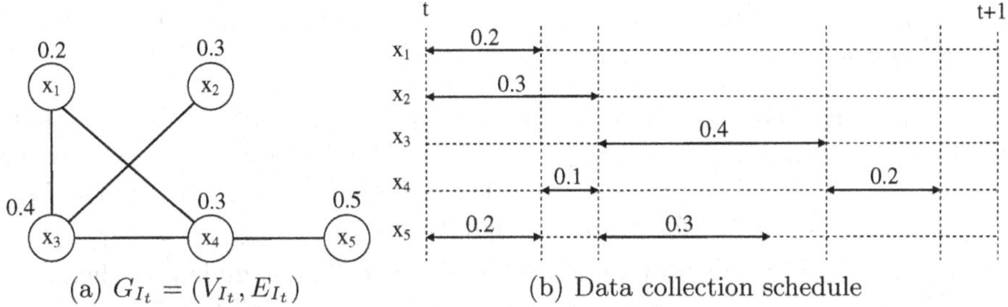

Fig. 2. An example illustrates Algorithm 2

data into pieces as small as necessary. Without loss of generality, we assume the time interval to be one second.

Consider time interval $[t, t+1]$. Let $G_t = (V_t, E_t)$ denote a subgraph of $G_T = (V_T, E_T)$, where $V_t = \{v_{i,t}, v_{i,t+1} \mid v_i \in V\}$ and $E_t = \{(v_{i,t}, v_{j,t+1}) \mid (v_i, v_j) \in E\}$. We derive an link interference graph $G_{I_t} = (V_{I_t}, E_{I_t})$ from $G_t = (V_t, E_t)$, where node $v_{i,t}^I \in V_{I_t}$ corresponds to an edge in E_t, and an edge in E_{I_t} connects two vertices, $v_{i,t}^I$ and $v_{j,t}^I$, if and only if $v_{i,t}^I$ and $v_{j,t}^I$ interfere with each other in G_t. Let f_i^t denote the amount of flow that is transmitted through $v_{i,t}^I$. Let $N(v_{i,t}^I)$ be the set of nodes in V_{I_t} that are connected to $v_{i,t}^I$. That is, $N(v_{i,t}^I)$ contains all the edges that interfere with $v_{i,t}^I$ in E_t. Let $x_i^t = f_i^t / C_T(v_{i,t}^I)$, where $C_T(v_{i,t}^I)$ represents the capacity along the edge $v_{i,t}^I \in E_t$. Then x_i^t represents the amount of time that $v_{i,t}^I$ needs to occupy in interval $[t, t+1]$.

Algorithm 2 describes how to construct a data collection schedule for interval $[t, t+1]$. Basically, for each node $v_{i,t}^I \in V_{I_t}$, it schedules a duration of x_i^t as early as possible while not causing any interference. An example illustrating the algorithm is shown in Figure 2. In the figure, (a) shows an example of link interference graph G_{I_t} where the number beside each node shows the amount of flow to be sent over the link. A valid data collection schedule for the link interference graph can be constructed as shown in (b). That is, the flows for x_1 and x_2 can be scheduled starting from time t. Transmission for x_3 can be scheduled only after $t + 0.3$ due to the interference with x_2 which is already scheduled. For x_4, 0.1 is scheduled after x_1 is finished and before x_3 starts sending, and the remaining is scheduled after $t + 0.7$. x_5 can be scheduled in a similar way.

In Section 4.4, we prove that this algorithm produces a schedule of length at most 1 for time interval $[t, t+1]$. Therefore, we can concatenate the T unit schedules to produce a complete schedule of length at most T. In practice, the length of the schedule for each interval may be substantially less than one, leading to a complete schedule substantially less than T. In our experiments, we found that a computed complete schedule is often below T (it is often less than $0.7T$).

4.4 Analysis

Theorem 1. *The data collection schedule ultimately produced by our algorithm is valid and satisfies the interference constraints.*

Proof. We only sketch the proof due to space limit. First, it is easy to see that, in Algorithm 2, any two nodes, $v^I_{i,t}, v^I_{j,t} \in V_{I_t}$, that interfere with each other will not be scheduled during the same time slot in $[t, t+1]$. Secondly, since Constraint (3) in the LP formulation is equivalent to $x^t_i + \sum_{v^I_{k,t} \in N(v^I_{i,t})} x^t_k \leq 1$, in each unit time interval, an amount of x^t_i for v^t_i will be completely scheduled. Last, Constraints (1) in the LP formulation guarantee that all the data from the sources will be delivered to the sinks at the end of the schedule. Therefore, the above claim holds. □

We next establish that, under several network models, our algorithm approximates an optimal schedule within a constant factor. In particular, under a unit disk model, it approximates the optimal schedule within a factor of five. To prove the approximation guarantee, we use the following lemma from [17].

Lemma 2. *[17] For every edge $(u, v) \in E$, there are at most c edges in $I(u, v)$ that can transfer data at the same time, where c is a constant depending on the model used to determine the network's interference constraints. Under a unit disk model, $c = 5$.*

Theorem 3. *The LP-based algorithm gives c-approximation for Multi-sink Data Collection problem.*

Proof. Let LP_k refer to a linear programming formulation, which differs from that in Section 4.2 in that the interference constraint (3) is replaced by

$$\frac{f_{u,v}}{C_T(u,v)} + \sum_{(u',v') \in I(u,v)} \frac{f_{u',v'}}{C_T(u',v')} \leq k, \ \forall\ u, v \in V_T. \tag{6}$$

That is, LP_k allows using k edges simultaneously in each interference set (our original LP formulation is LP_1).

By Lemma 2, an optimal data collection schedule may use no more than c edges in a given interference group simultaneously. It has been shown that Constraints (6) provide a necessary condition to obtain a valid flow without interferences when k is set to c (c depends on the interference model) [17]. Therefore, the optimal solution is lower bounded by the solution to LP_c. We can also see that, at any point in time, the schedule produced by LP_c allows c edges in each interference group to be active. If the amount of time available is multiplied by c, then each of these potentially interfering transmissions can be placed in its own time period. The resulting schedule satisfies the constraints imposed in LP_1. Let OPT refer to an optimal algorithm, and let $\mathcal{T}(X)$ denote the latency of the schedule produced by an algorithm, X. Therefore, $\mathcal{T}(LP_1) \leq c \cdot \lceil \mathcal{T}(LP_c) \rceil \leq c \cdot \lceil \mathcal{T}(OPT) \rceil$. □

5 A Greedy BFS-Based Algorithm

In this section, we design a heuristic algorithm for the special case where all the links have the same capacity. This heuristic algorithm is greedy in nature and uses breadth first search. Therefore, we call it *Greedy BFS-based Algorithm.*

The main idea of the algorithm is to divide nodes into layers according to their distance to the set of sinks, and let nodes far away from the sinks transmit data to nodes close to the sinks, which in turn forward the data to the sinks. More specifically, let $Dist(u, v)$ denote the distance between u and v in graph G, which is the length (in hop counts) of the shortest path connecting u and v in G. Let $Dist(v, U)$ denote the distance from u to a set of nodes U, which is defined to be $\min_{u \in U} Dist(u, v)$. We divide nodes into layers according to their distance to the sink set, D. More specifically, let L_i denote the set of nodes whose distance to D is i. Let l_{max} denote the index of the layer that is farthest away from D. We can obtain L_i using breadth first search, $i = 1, \ldots, l_{max}$. Let $Data(u, t)$ denote the amount of data at node u at time t. Consider a heuristic function, $F(t) = \sum_{u \in V} Dist(u, D) Data(u, t)$. At the end of the schedule (i.e., after all data have been transmitted to the sinks), this function equals zero. Our heuristic takes a greedy approach to reduce $F(t)$ as fast as possible by maximizing the number of

Algorithm 3. Greedy BFS-based Algorithm

Classify nodes into layers using breadth first search
$t \leftarrow 0$
while $F(t) > 0$ **do**
  $X \leftarrow \emptyset$ /* *the set of transmitting links at time t* */
  for $i = l_{max}$ to 1 **do**
    sort $Data(u, t)$ in decreasing order, $u \in L_i$
    for each $u \in L_i$ such that $Data(u, t) > 0$ **do**
      if u has neighbor $v \in L_{i-1}$ such that the link (u, v) does not interfere with any link in X **then**
        $X \leftarrow X \cup \{(u, v)\}$
      end if
    end for
  end for
  Transmit data on every link in X
  Update $Data(u, t)$ for all $u \in V$
  $t \leftarrow t + 1$
end while

nodes that transmit data at every time t, while ensuring that (i) the transmissions do not create any interference, and (ii) nodes in L_{i+1} transmit to nodes in L_i (so that $F(t)$ decreases over time). We repeat the above procedure until $F(t)$ goes to zero. The pseudo-code of the algorithm is given in Algorithm 3.

6 Experimental Results

Network Setting: We generate a unit disk graph by placing n nodes uniformly at random over a square region of size $\sqrt{2n} \times \sqrt{2n}$, where n is the number of nodes. The area of the network, as a result, increases in proportion to the number of nodes, maintaining an approximately constant network density. We vary the number of nodes n in the random network from 30 to 70 with increments of five. There is an edge between two nodes if their geometric distance is no more than one. The capacities of all the links are the same. For convenience, we set all capacities to be 1. A random subset of the nodes is chosen as sinks. The number of sinks is set to be $1, 2, 4$ and 8. We consider two distributions for the initial amount of data at non-sink nodes: uniform distribution, where the initial data at each non-sink node is set to be 1, and skewed distribution, where the initial data s_i at node i is $1/i$.

Interference Model: Our algorithm is applicable to any interference model. In our experiments, we use two-hop interference model, in which two edges can interfere with each other if they are within two-hop distance [16].

Performance Comparison. For each setting, we generate ten independent inputs and compare the average latencies of the two algorithms over the ten inputs. Figure 3(a) and (b) depict the ratio between average latencies of Greedy BFS-based Algorithm and LP-based Algorithm for uniform and skewed distribution, respectively (the results using 8 sinks are similar and omitted for clarity).

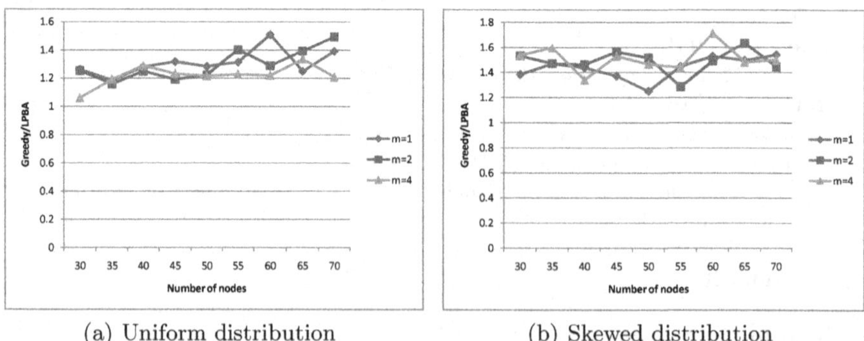

(a) Uniform distribution (b) Skewed distribution

Fig. 3. Ratio between average latencies of Greedy BFS-based Algorithm and LP-based Algorithm. m is the number of sinks.

The confidence intervals are tight and hence omitted. We observe that the latency of LP-based Algorithm is around 20% to 70% shorter than that of Greedy BFS-based Algorithm. For uniform distribution, the gain of LP-based Algorithm increases from 1.1 to 1.5 as the number of nodes increases. For skewed distribution, LP-based algorithm outperforms Greedy Algorithm by 40%-60%, even for small networks. Last, we observe similar results for different number of sinks.

7 Conclusion

We proposed a constant approximation algorithm and a heuristic for Multiple-Sink Data Collection Problem in wireless sensor networks. The constant approximation algorithm first constructs a time-expanded graph, then generates feasible flows in the expanded graph, and finally finds an exact data collection schedule. The heuristic algorithm is based on greedy breadth first search. Our experimental results show that the approximation algorithm can significantly outperform the simple heuristic (up to 60%).

References

1. Alon, N., Bar-Noy, A., Linial, N., Peleg, D.: A lower bound for radio broadcast. Journal of Computer and System Sciences 43(2), 290–298 (1991)
2. Balakrishnan, H., Barrett, C., Anil Kumar, V.S., Marathe, M., Thite, S.: The distance 2-matching problem and its relationship to the mac layer capacity of adhoc wireless networks. IEEE J. Selected Areas in Connunications 22(6) (August 2004)
3. Bar-Yehuda, R., Goldreich, O., Itai, A.: On the time-complexity of broadcast in multi-hop radio networks: An exponential gap between determinism and randomization. Journal of Computer and System Sciences 45(1), 104–126 (1992)
4. Cheng, W.C., Chou, C.-F., Golubchik, L., Khuller, S., (Justin) Wan, Y.-C.: Large-scale data collection: a coordinated approach. In: IEEE Infocom (2003)
5. Florens, C., McEliece, R.: Packets distribution algorithms for sensor networks. In: IEEE Infocom (2003)
6. Ford, L.R., Fulkerson, D.R.: Flows in networks. Princeton University Press, New Jersey (1962)
7. Gandhi, R., Parthasarathy, S., Mishra, A.: Minimizing broadcast latency and redundancy in ad hoc networks. In: ACM MobiHoc 2003, pp. 222–232 (2003)
8. Gandhi, R., Kim, Y.-A., Lee, S., Ryu, J., Wan, P.-J.: Approximation algorithm for data broadcast and collection in wireless networks. In: IEEE Infocom (Mini conference) (2009)
9. Gupta, P., Kumar, P.R.: The capacity of wireless networks. IEEE Transactions on Information Theory 46(2), 388–404 (2000)
10. Hopper, B., Tardors, E.: Polynomial time algorithms for some evacuation problems. In: SODA: ACM-SIAM Symposium on Discrete Algorithms, pp. 512–521 (1994)
11. Huang, Q., Zhang, Y.: Radial coordination for convergecast in wireless sensor networks. In: LCN 2004: Proceedings of the 29th Annual IEEE International Conference on Local Computer Networks, Washington, DC, USA, 2004, pp. 542–549. IEEE Computer Society Press, Los Alamitos (2004)

12. Huang, S.C.-H., Wan, P.-J., Deng, J., Han, Y.S.: Broadcast scheduling in interference environment. IEEE Trans. on Mobile Computing 7(11), 1338–1348 (2008)
13. Huang, S.C.-H., Wan, P.-J., Jia, X., Du, H., Shang, W.: Minimum-latency broadcast scheduling in wireless ad hoc networks. In: Proceedings of 26th IEEE Infocom, pp. 733–739 (2007)
14. Huang, S.C.-H., Wan, P.-J., Vu, C.T., Li, Y., Yao, F.: Nearly constant approximation for data aggregation scheduling in wireless sensor networks. In: Proceedings of 26th IEEE Infocom, pp. 366–372 (2007)
15. Kesselman, A., Kowalski, D.R.: Fast distributed algorithm for convergecast in ad hoc geometric radio networks. J. Parallel Distrib. Comput. 66(4), 578–585 (2006)
16. Anil Kumar, V.S., Marathe, M., Parthasarathy, S., Srinivasan, A.: End-to-end packet scheduling in ad hoc networks. In: ACM-SIAM symposium on Discrete Algorithms, SODA, pp. 1014–1023 (2004)
17. Anil Kumar, V.S., Marathe, M.V., Parthasarathy, S., Srinivasan, A.: Algorithmic aspects of capacity in wireless networks. In: SIGMETRICS, Banff, Alberta, Canada (June 2005)
18. Upadhyayula, S., Annamalai, V., Gupta, S.K.S.: A low-latency and energy-efficient algorithm for convergecast in wireless sensor networks. In: IEEE Global Telecommunications Conference, pp. 3525–3530 (2003)
19. Yi, S., Pei, Y., Kalyanaraman, S.: On the capacity improvement of ad hoc wireless networks using deirectional antennas. In: Proceedings of 4th ACM international symposium on Mobile ad hoc networking and computing, pp. 108–116 (2003)

Communication in Naturally Mobile Sensor Networks

Donghua Deng[1] and Qun Li[2]

[1] Juniper Networks, Sunnyvale, CA 94089
ddeng@juniper.net
[2] Department of Computer Science, College of William and Mary
liqun@cs.wm.edu

Abstract. Naturally mobile sensors networks are ad-hoc sensor networks in which nodes move under the control of the environment, for example for nodes attached to animals or for nodes drifting with currents on the surface of the water. In this paper we study communication in one type of naturally mobile network, where motion can be modeled as a random walk approximation to Brownian motion. This model captures the movement of societies of animals such as grazing herds. We analyze information propagation in such networks using a reaction-diffusion approach.

1 Introduction

Recent advances have shown great possibilities for low cost wireless sensors, with developments such as the MICA Mote [8,7], all the way along the path to the ultimate goal of smart dust recently implemented on a single chip called Spec [8]. Such small sensors could bound to birds or animals to monitor and collect data about its habitat, environment, and behavior. Pollen-sized sensors can drift in the air to monitor the environment or conduct surveillance tasks. In this paper our goal is to begin understanding this new kind of naturally mobile sensor network. To this end, there are many very interesting questions: How do the sensors communicate with each other? How does data collected in a naturally mobile sensor network get transmitted to a base station? How does the natural mobility affect the communication performance? We wish to answer these questions and show how to design a mobile sensor network for various applications.

In this paper, we focus on information diffusion in a naturally mobile network for two problems. In the first problem, we assume that sensors drift in a closed space, collect data, and send back the data to an access point. Sensors exchange data when they are in each other's proximity. This is called the data transmission problem. In the second problem we ask how fast a piece of information can be spread to the whole network. The answer to this question will provide a bound for programming the sensors in the network with a new task, or for propagating new parameters in the network. This is called the network coverage problem. We present analyses for each of these problems. Although our work has been

B. Liu et al. (Eds.): WASA 2009, LNCS 5682, pp. 295–304, 2009.

motivated by the naturally mobile network model, they also apply to engineered mobile networks where the control of the network results in Brownian-like motion for the nodes.

2 Related Work

Related work on mobile sensors includes [15],[9],[16],[11],[2],[13],[6],[17],[5],[10]. Compared with the previous work, we consider a different aspect of mobility in this paper. Mobility maintains sporadic and localized connections to some sensors in a sparse network, which gives a long delay network if we regard mobility as an information delivery means. Instead of increasing the capacity, we aim at a sparse network that uses less energy by eliminating long range communications.

3 The Model: Random Sensor Networks

In this section we describe the mathematical model we use to characterize a class of naturally mobile systems. We focus on the class of systems whose movement can be described as a random walk approximation to Brownian motion. Other interesting classes of natural mobility will be the focus of future papers. We consider systems that move along two-dimensional surfaces; our results can also be extended to three-dimensional spaces, but we leave it to the future work.

Random walk can be used to model and simulate Brownian motion by using Donsker's theorem [4]. It states the following. If $X_1, X_2, \cdots$ denote a sequence of independent, identically distributed random number and $S_m := X_1 + \cdots + X_m$, then for all m large, the curve generated by linearly interpolating over points $S_1/\sqrt{m}, S_2/\sqrt{m}, \cdots, S_m/\sqrt{m}$ is close to a Brownian motion run until time one. The intuition behind this theorem is that Brownian motion is a continuous random walk, that is, when the time step of the random walk approaches infinitesimal, random walk becomes Brownian motion.

A naturally mobile sensors is modeled with random walks on a $n \times n$ grid in a square of size l as follows. For the convenience of analysis, we also use torus to approximate grid in the following. Each time the clock ticks, the mobile sensor moves to the next position (any of the four neighboring positions) on the grid randomly. We assume all the events happen on the points of the grid. Only when the sensor placed at the same position as the event can sense the event. We also assume that $b \times b$ base stations are installed on the points of the grid evenly. Similarly, only the mobile sensor placed at the same position as a base station can transmit its data to the base station. We assume the base stations have wired network to connect to the monitor center and the latency to notify the center is zero. In this model we wish to know how long it takes to report an event to one of the base stations after the event happens.

The time for an event to be reported to one of the base stations, T is composed of two parts. This first part T_1 is the *detect time*, defined as the time from the occurrence of the event till the time the event is detected. The second part T_2 is the report time, defined as the time from the detection of the event till the event is notified to the base station.

4 Data Transmission for Communication with No Propagation

Suppose a mobile sensor randomly walks on a nxn grid in a square with each side length l. Each time the clock ticks, the mobile sensor moves to the next position (any of the four neighboring positions) on the grid randomly. We assume all the events happen on the points of the grid. When a sensor is at the same position as the event, it can sense the corresponding event. We also assume bxb base stations are installed on the points of the grid evenly. Similarly, when the mobile sensor is at the same position as a base station, it can transmit the data collected to the base station. We assume the base stations are connected by wired network to the monitor center and the latency to notify the center is zero. The question we ask is: how long does it take to report an event to one of the base stations after the event happens?

The time for an event to be reported to one of the base stations, T is composed of two parts: (1) the time for the sensor to sense the event, T_1; and (2) the time for the sensor to approach a base station and report the event after that, T_2. We now estimate T_1 and T_2.

The detection time T_1 can be characterized as:
(http://www.math.tamu.edu/~rellis/comb/torus/torus.html)
$P\{T_1 > t\} \approx exp(\frac{-t}{cn^2 \log n^2})$ where $c \approx 0.34$ as $n^2 \to \infty$ (valid for $n \geq 5$).

We now want to estimate how much time it takes until a sensor encounters a base station after reaching an event point on the grid.

In our model, the $b \times b$ base stations are installed on the $n \times n$ torus field uniformly. Now let's fold the whole grid to a small $\frac{n}{b} \times \frac{n}{b}$ torus field such that only one base station is contained in this smaller field. The random walk on the original torus can be mapped onto a random walk on this smaller torus. Every time a sensor passes by the location of a base station on the original torus, it reaches the only base station in the small torus.

Therefore, we have

$$P\{T_2 > t\} \approx exp(\frac{-t}{c(\frac{n}{b})^2 \cdot \log(\frac{n}{b})^2})$$

Let $f_1(t)$ and $f_2(t)$ be the pdf (probability density function) of T_1 and T_2. We have

$$f_1(t) = \frac{1}{c_1} exp(-\frac{t}{c_1}), \quad f_2(t) = \frac{1}{c_2} exp(-\frac{t}{c_2})$$

(where $c_1 = cn^2 \log n^2$ and $c_2 = c(n/b)^2 \log(n/b)^2$).

Then the pdf of T is

$$f(t) = \int_0^t f_1(x) f_2(t-x) dx = \frac{e^{-\frac{t}{c_1}} - e^{-\frac{t}{c_2}}}{c_1 - c_2}$$

and

$$P\{T > t\} = \int_t^\infty f(x) dx = \frac{c_1 e^{-\frac{t}{c_1}} - c_2 e^{-\frac{t}{c_2}}}{c_1 - c_2}$$

Now let's look at the expectation and the variance of T, the time for an event to be detected and reported to an access point. Since

$$\int xe^{-\frac{x}{c}}dx = -cxe^{-\frac{x}{c}} - c^2e^{-\frac{x}{c}}$$

we have

$$E(T) = \int_0^\infty tf(t)dt = c_1 + c_2$$

Also because

$$\int x^2e^{-\frac{x}{c}}dx = -cx^2e^{-\frac{x}{c}} - 2c^2xe^{-\frac{x}{c}} - 2c^3e^{-\frac{x}{c}}$$

we have

$$\int_0^\infty t^2f(t)dt = 2(c_1^2 + c_1c_2 + c_2^2)$$

Then

$$var(T) = E(T^2) - E^2(T) = c_1^2 + c_2^2$$

We can have the following theorem:

Theorem 1. *In the random walk model the time for data transmission $T = T_1 + T_2$ has expectation $c_1 + c_2$ and variance $c_1^2 + c_2^2$.*

Suppose we have s sensors. Let the time it takes for any sensor report an event to any of the base stations be T_s. We have

$$P\{T_s > t\} = (P\{T > t\})^s = (\frac{c_1e^{-\frac{t}{c_1}} - c_2e^{-\frac{t}{c_2}}}{c_1 - c_2})^s$$

To approximate T_s, let's consider time t after an event happens. Since there are n^2 grid points and a sensor can be at any grid point, the stationary distribution of the sensor on that specific spot of event is $1/n^2$. During time t, roughly st/n^2 sensors will visit the event spot. The probability for one of st/n^2 sensors to visit a base station during time interval t is $st/n^2 \cdot b^2t/n^2 = sb^2t^2/n^4$. Thus, T_s should be on the order of $\frac{n^2}{b\sqrt{s}}$.

5 Information Diffusion for Communication with Propagation

In this section we address the information diffusion problem: how fast can a message or some data be spread over an entire mobile network, where mobility can be modeled as Brownian motion approximated as a random walk. Two sensors exchange information when they arrive within transmission range. To reason about how fast a piece of information can diffuse through the network, we note that the relative movement of two sensors is also a random walk. Thus, we may approximate the meeting probability between two sensors and derive a formula for the information spread.

Suppose many particles do random walk on a 2-d grid defined as in Section 3. Recall that this space is a square or a torus. When the clock ticks, each sensor moves in any of the four directions on the grid and the direction is chosen randomly. Two particles can only communicate when they meet at a grid point. Suppose one particle has a piece of information that needs to be sent to all the other particles. The particle will transmit the information to all the other particles it meets. This process will be repeated by all the new particles that are now holding the piece of information. We wish to quantify the amount of time it takes to propagate the information to all the particles (or some fraction of particles).

We can use random walk on 2-D grid (or, without loss of generality on a 3-D torus) or Brownian motion to characterize the motion of the particles. An approximation of the data diffusion problem can be described by Fisher's equation [12]:

$$\frac{\partial u}{\partial t} = ku(1-u) + \frac{\partial^2 u}{\partial x^2} + \frac{\partial^2 u}{\partial y^2}$$

which is a reaction diffusion equation that is used to model other natural processes such as gene mutation, population growth, and flame propagation. In this equation u is the density of the informed particles (or the probability that there is a node at that position that is infected. Initally there is only one position has probability 1 and all other positons have probability 0), (x, y) is the location in consideration, u_t is the partial derivative to time t, and $u_{xx}+u_{yy}$ is the Laplacian (the partial derivative at location (x, y)). The equation states that the change of the density of informed particles at a given time depends on the infection rate $ku(1-u)$ and the diffusion from places nearby (diffusion process in macroscopic level is the same as Brownian motion in microscpic level). The first term measures the infection rate as being proportional to the product of the density of the infected and uninfected particles, which is an approximation in a continuum case. We can understand this by considering a small area in which all infected and uninfected particles are distributed evenly. The second term shows how fast the infected particles are diffusing, and the Laplacian is a measure of how high the density is at one location (x, y) with respect to the density nearby. If nearby places have a higher density, then the Laplacian will be positive and infected particles will diffuse toward this position. Otherwise, the infected particles will diffuse away from this position.

To use Fisher's equation, we have to know the reaction rate and the diffusion rate. The reaction rate k is related to the number of particles an individual particle meets in a unit time.

5.1 Meeting Rate

We first consider the meeting rate of a particle for the Brownian Motion model. Suppose a particle has k meets with other particles on average in a time unit on

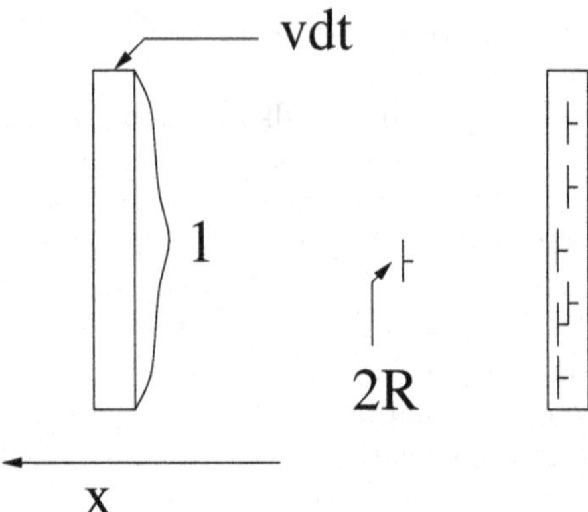

Fig. 1. Computation of the meeting rate of a particle

a 1×1 field. We define two sensors meet when they are within distance r of each other. Then the average time between two meets is $\tau = \frac{1}{k}$. We know that the average sojourn time for a particle in the transmission range of another particle is $t_s = r^2 \log(\frac{1}{r})$ [1,3]. In a time unit, the total sojourn time of other particles is kt_s, which should be $\lambda \pi r^2$ on average where λ is the particle density. Thus, we have $kt_s = \lambda \pi r^2$. We get $k = \lambda \pi r^2 / t_s = \lambda \pi / \log(\frac{1}{r})$.

The following gives the meeting rate for the case in which a particle moves in a straight line most of the time. This is not relevant to our analysis here, but we feel it may be useful for people who are interested in applying the results to other mobility models.

Suppose a particle has k meets with other particles on average in a time unit. Then the average time between two meets is $\tau = \frac{1}{k}$. The chance that the particle has a meeting in time dt is $\frac{dt}{\tau} = kdt$. The average time between two meetings and thus the meeting rate depend on the density of the particles and the transmission range. Consider a moving particle that moves parallel to x-axis (see Fig. 1) and focus on the unit segment that is perpendicular to the x-axis. During a time interval of dt, the particle travels a distance of vdt. There are λvdt particles in the area. The probability that the particle will meet one of the particles in the area is $\sigma_c \lambda vdt$ where σ_c is the length of the *meeting cross section*, defined as the interval within which the particle must be located if it is to communicate with a particular particle. We have $\sigma_c = 2R$ where R is the transmission range. Combining the above equation for meeting probability, we establish $2R\lambda vdt = kdt$ and $k = 2vR\lambda$.

5.2 Diffusion Time Bound

After knowing the sensor meeting rate and diffusion rate of the sensor motion, we can specify Fisher equation to describe the information propagation (for 1-d case):

$$\frac{\partial u}{\partial t} = ku(1-u) + D\frac{\partial^2 u}{\partial x^2}$$

where k is the meeting rate among sensors and D is the diffusion coefficient of the Brownian motion (the original Fisher's equation assumes unit diffusion coefficient)[1]. For 2-d case, we can simply add another term $D\frac{\partial^2 u}{\partial y^2}$. Then we can estimate how much time it takes for the information to cover a spot, that is, with sufficiently large density sensors at that location are infected with the information.

Theorem 2. *The time for a point x (x can be thought of as the distance to the origin of the information) being covered by the information is on the order of $O(\ln(\frac{D}{k^2 x_o^2}) + \frac{x}{2\sqrt{kD}})$ where x_0 is the radius of the initial information coverage.*

Proof. Let $t^* = kt$ and $x^* = x\sqrt{\frac{k}{D}}$, we get

$$\frac{\partial u}{\partial t^*} = u(1-u) + \frac{\partial^2 u}{\partial x^{*2}}$$

The equation for 2-d case can be obtained by adding one term $D\frac{\partial^2 u}{\partial y^2}$.

Consider

$$\frac{\partial u}{\partial t} = u(1-u) + \frac{\partial^2 u}{\partial x^2}$$

$$u(x,0) = u_0 \cdot \delta(0)$$

The second equation is the initial condition describing the initial distribution of infected sensors (ideally only origin point has sensors being infected in the beginning). The analytical solution to the equation for d dimension in general [14] is

$$u(x,t) = [1 + u_0^{-1}(4\pi t)^{d/2} \cdot exp(\frac{x^2 - 4t^2}{4t})]^{-1}$$

Suppose $d = 2$, which is the case for two dimension. Consider a point at position x. To cover x, we would like its $u(x,t)$ to be considerably large, say α. We analyze the required time t.

---

[1] A smaller particle, a less-viscous fluid, and a higher temperature each would increase the amount of motion one could expect to observe. Over a period of time, the particle would tend to drift from its starting point, and, on the basis of kinetic theory, it is possible to compute the probability (P) of a particle moving a certain distance (x) in any given direction (the total distance it moves will be greater than x) during a certain time interval (t) in a medium whose coefficient of diffusion (D) is known, D being equal to one-half the average of the square of the displacement in the x-direction. This formula for probability "density" allows P to be plotted against x. The graph is the familiar bell-shaped Gaussian "normal" curve that typically arises when the random variable is the sum of many independent, statistically identical random variables, in this case, the many little pushes that add up to the total motion. The equation for this relationship is $\frac{e^{-x^2/4Dt}}{2\sqrt{\pi Dt}}$.

$$[1 + u_0^{-1}(4\pi t)^{d/2} \cdot exp(\frac{x^2 - 4t^2}{4t})]^{-1} > \alpha$$

$$4\pi t \cdot exp(\frac{x^2 - 4t^2}{4t}) < u_0(\frac{1}{\alpha} - 1)$$

$$4\pi t \cdot exp(\frac{x^2}{4t} - t) = \frac{4\pi t}{e^t} \cdot e^{\frac{x^2}{4t}} < u_0(\frac{1}{\alpha} - 1)$$

Consider the predominant part $\frac{e^{x^2/4t}}{e^t}$. When $t = \frac{x}{2}$, we get $\frac{x^2}{4t} = t$. Thus, when x is large, $t = \frac{x}{2}$. When x is small, $\frac{x^2}{4t} < t$, then $\frac{1}{e^t}$ is the dominant part. We should have $\frac{1}{e^t} = u_0$.

In summary, $t = \frac{x}{2}$ when x is large; $t = -\ln u_0$ when x is small or u_0 is small. Thus, $t = O(-\ln u_0 + \frac{x}{2})$.

If the initial covered area has radius x_0, we have $u_0 = \pi(\sqrt{\frac{k}{D}}x_0)^2 = \frac{\pi k x_o^2}{D}$. $t = \frac{t^*}{k} = \frac{1}{k} \cdot O(-\ln u_0 + \frac{x^*}{2}) = \frac{1}{k} \cdot O(\ln \frac{D}{kx_0^2} + \frac{x}{2}\sqrt{\frac{k}{D}}) = O(\ln(\frac{D}{k^2 x_o^2}) + \frac{x}{2\sqrt{kD}})$

The analytical solution of the Fisher equation on $u(x,t)$ is given in the proof of the theorem. The diffusion efficiency depends on the motion of the particles. It can be computed by knowing the speed, expectation and deviation of the motion intervals. The diffusion efficiency also capture the notion of "almost connecting a network" which is a very useful routing parameter and may lead to better routing performance in mobile sensor networks using diffusion-style routing.

5.3 Simulation Experiments

Our diffusion analysis relies on Brownian motion equations which are hard to simulate. However, we can use Donsker's theorem to define a random walk simulation for Brownian motion.

We built a simulator that models this random walk approximation as follows. Each particle at position (x, y) goes to its eight neighbors on the grid with the same probability. Each grid cell has side $1/\sqrt{2m}$. After m steps, the expectation and the variance of the displacement are 0 and 1 respectively. We choose a large m so that the random walk is able to simulate the Brownian motion.

In Figure 2, we plot three curves obtained from three simulation runs. In each simulation, we fix the number of nodes at 1000, the transmission range at 1.0, and the network space at 100x100. Each particle moves with variance 1 in a time unit. Particles bounce back when they hit the network boundary. We assume that two particles within each other's transmission range can and will communicate. To initialize the data diffusion process we select a particle and load it with a certain piece of data. After the data is loaded into this particle, it starts to diffusing the information opportunistically, as soon as it encounters a new particle. All particles with the data diffuse it. In Figure 2, the three curves are the diffusion time when diffusion starts at different particles, placed at different locations in the field. The x-axis is the time elapsed and y-axis is the percentage of particles that are "infected" with the information. The dotted

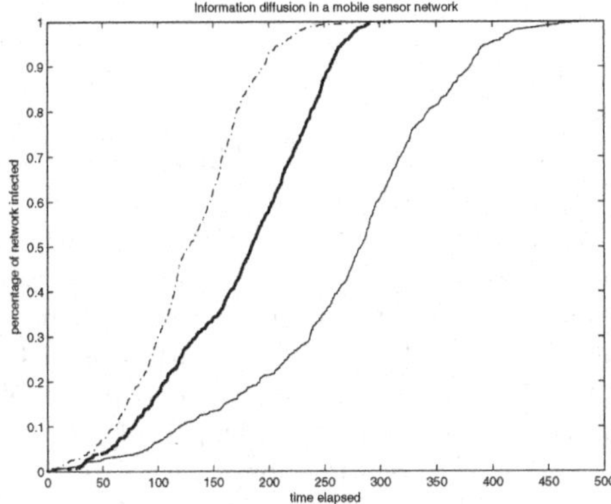

Fig. 2. Simulation results about the information diffusion with time

curve presents the results when the data diffusion starts in the middle of the field. We observe that information diffusion is location dependent. The fastest spread occurs when the diffusion starts in the middle of the field which makes sense intuitively.

6 Conclusion

In this paper we have discussed information propagation in mobile sensor networks where nodes move according to Brownian processes. We model Brownian motion as random walks on a grid. This motion model captures the movement of a class of naturally mobile systems (such as grazing animals) and can also be applied to engineered mobility (such as teams of robots controlled to move this way.) We have computed a time bound for information diffusion throughout the network when nodes can exchange data when in each other's proximity. This analysis provides some insight into the design and utility of this kind of network. The relationship between sensor density and the time for information propagation and/or data transmission allows us to decide on the number of sensors to be deployed in an application-specific way. These results also impact network design protocols and designing controllers for teams of robots. Many open questions remain for this type of network. In the future we wish to consider new motion models for naturally mobile systems and we wish to add determinism and a notion of goals to the framework.

Acknowledgment

The authors would like to thank all the reviewers for their helpful comments. This project was supported in part by US National Science Foundation grants CNS-0721443, CNS-0831904, and CAREER Award CNS-0747108.

References

1. Aldous, D.J.: Probability approximations via the Poisson clumping heuristic. Springer, New York (1989)
2. Bansal, N., Liu, Z.: Capacity, delay and mobility in wireless ad-hoc networks. In: INFOCOM, San Francisco, CA (April 2003)
3. Dembo, A., Peres, Y., Rosen, J., Zeitouni, O.: Cover Times for Brownian Motion and Random Walks in Two Dimensions. Ann. Math., 160 (2004)
4. Donsker, M.: Justification and extension of doob's heuristic approach to the kolmogorov-smirnov theorem. The Annals of Math. Stat. 23, 277–181 (1952)
5. Grossglauser, M., Tse, D.: Mobility increases the capacity of adhoc wireless networks. IEEE/ACM Transactions on Networking 10(4), 477–486 (2002)
6. Grossglauser, M., Vetterli, M.: Locating nodes with ease: Mobility diffusion of last encounters in ad hoc networks. In: INFOCOM, San Francisco, CA (April 2003)
7. Hill, J., Bounadonna, P., Culler, D.: Active message communication for tiny network sensors. In: INFOCOM (2001)
8. Hill, J., Szewczyk, R., Woo, A., Hollar, S., Culler, D., Pister, K.: System architecture directions for network sensors. In: ASPLOS (2000)
9. Juang, P., Oki, H., Wang, Y., Martonosi, M., Peh, L.-S., Rubenstein, D.: Energy-efficient computing for wildlife tracking: Design tradeoffs and early experiences with zebranet. In: ASPLOS, San Jose, CA, pp. 96–107 (2002)
10. Kesidis, G., Konstantopoulos, T., Phoha, S.: Surveillance coverage of sensor networks under a random mobility strategy. In: Proc. IEEE Sensors, Toronto (October 2003)
11. Liu, B., Liu, Z., Towsley, D.: On the capacity of hybrid wireless networks. In: INFOCOM, San Francisco, CA (April 2003)
12. Murray, J.D.: Mathematical Biology. Springer, Heidelberg
13. Perevalov, E., Blum, R.: Delay limited capacity of ad hoc networks: Asymptotically optimal transmission and relaying strategy. In: INFOCOM, San Francisco, CA (April 2003)
14. Puri, S., Elder, K.R., Desai, R.C.: Approximate asymptotic solutions to the d-dimensional fisher equation. Physics Letters A 142(6,7), 357–360 (1989)
15. Shah, R.C., Roy, S., Jain, S., Brunette, W.: Data mules: Modeling a three-tier architecture for sparse sensor networks. In: First IEEE International Workshop on Sensor Network Protocols and Applications (SPNA), Anchorage, AK (May 2003)
16. Small, T., Haas, Z.J.: The shared wireless infostation model: a new ad hoc networking paradigm (or where there is a whale, there is a way). In: ACM Mobihoc, Annapolis, pp. 233–244 (2003)
17. Yuen, W., Yates, R., Mau, S.: Exploiting data diversity and multiuser diversity in noncooperative mobile infostation networks. In: INFOCOM, San Francisco, CA (April 2003)

Void Avoidance in Three-Dimensional Mobile Underwater Sensor Networks

Peng Xie, Zhong Zhou, Zheng Peng, Jun-Hong Cui, and Zhijie Shi

Computer Science & Engineering Department,
University of Connecticut, Storrs, CT 06269
{xp,zhongzhou,zhengpeng,jcui,zshi}@engr.uconn.edu

Abstract. Mobile underwater sensor networks are usually featured with three-dimensional topology, high node mobility and long propagation delays. For such networks, geographic routing has been shown to be very suitable. However, routing voids pose great challenges on the greedy policy used in most geographic routing protocols. The problem is more severe for underwater sensor networks because of node mobility and three-dimensional topology. In this paper, we propose a void avoidance protocol, called Vector-Based Void Avoidance (VBVA), to address the routing void problem in mobile underwater sensor networks. VBVA adopts two mechanisms, vector-shift and back-pressure, to handle voids. Vector-shift mechanism is used to route data packets along the boundary of a void. Back-pressure mechanism routes data packets backward to bypass a concave void. VBVA handles the routing void problem on demand and thus does not need to know network topology and void information in advance. Therefore, it is very robust to cope with mobile voids in mobile networks. To the best of our knowledge, VBVA is the first void avoidance protocol to address the three-dimensional and mobile void problems in underwater sensor networks. Our simulation results show that VBVA works effectively and efficiently in mobile underwater sensor networks.

1 Introduction

Underwater sensor networks have received growing interests recently [3,11]. In application scenarios such as estuary monitoring and submarine detection, mobile underwater sensor networks are urgently demanded [3,8]. In such three-dimensional mobile networks, efficient routing faces great challenges.

It is shown that geographic routing protocols [10,14] such as VBF are suitable for mobile underwater networks. Geographic routing protocols rely on the geographical information of the nodes to determine the next data-forwarding node. Various packet forwarding polices, especially greedy-based ones, have been explored in these protocols. However, most of the greedy policies, which try to select one or more neighbors that are the nearest to the destination, may not be effective or efficient in certain network scenarios. For example, in sparse networks, a node probably cannot forward its data packets based on its greedy policy if none of its neighbors is closer to the destination. This phenomena is referred to as a routing void in [4]. How to cope with routing voids in geographic

B. Liu et al. (Eds.): WASA 2009, LNCS 5682, pp. 305–314, 2009.

routing protocols is quite challenging. The characteristics of underwater sensor networks make this problem even more difficult. First of all, a void in underwater sensor networks is three-dimensional. Second, the mobility of underwater nodes makes the void mobile.

In this paper, we propose a new protocol, called vector-based void avoidance (VBVA) routing protocol, to address this issue in mobile underwater sensor networks. VBVA is a vector-based approach. Initially, the forwarding path of a data packet is represented by a vector from the source to the destination. If there is no presence of voids in the forwarding path, VBVA is essentially the same as vector-based forwarding (VBF) [14]. When there is a void in the forwarding path, VBVA adopts two methods, vector-shift and back-pressure, to handle the void. In the vector-shift mechanism, VBVA attempts to route the packet along the boundary of the void by shifting the forwarding vector of the data packet. If the void is convex, vector-shift mechanism can successfully route the packet around the void and deliver it to the destination. However, if the void is concave, the vector-shift method may fail. In this case, VBVA resorts to back-pressure method to route the data packet back to some nodes suitable to do vector-shift. We prove that if the network is connected, VBVA can always find an available path. Since VBVA avoids voids on demand, it can handle the mobile network and mobile voids efficiently and effectively. To the best of our knowledge, VBVA is the first protocol to address the three-dimensional and mobile void problem in underwater sensor networks.

The rest of the paper is organized as follows. In Section 2, we review existing work on the routing protocol for underwater sensor networks and the void avoidance algorithms. Then, we present VBVA in detail in Section 3. We evaluate the performance of VBVA in different network settings in Section 4. In Section 5, we conclude our work and point out the future work.

2 Related Work

In this section, we will first review routing protocols for underwater sensor networks. After that, we will review existing void avoidance algorithms and show their differences from our work.

2.1 Routing Protocols in Underwater Sensor Networks

A lot of research has been done in the last few years on the routing protocols for underwater networks. The challenges and the state of arts for the routing protocols in underwater networks have been discussed in details in [6,3]. A pioneering work is done in [13] on the routing protocol for underwater networks. In this work, a central master node is used to probe the network topology and do the route establishment. In [1], the authors propose a novel method to improve the efficiency of the flood-based routing protocol in underwater sensor networks. Focus beam routing appears in [7], which dynamically establish a route as the data packet traverses the network towards its final destinations. An adaptive routing protocol for underwater Delay Tolerant Networks (DTN) has been proposed in [5], which divides the network into multiple layers and every node adaptively find its routes to the upper layer according to its past memory. Vector-Based-Forwarding (VBF)protocol appears in [14], which takes advantages of the location information to form one or multiple routing pipes from the source to the destination. Multiple routes might be used simultaneously in VBF to improve the reliability.

Different from all of the above work, our VBVA protocol is a geographic routing protocol with void avoidance capacity. To the best of knowledge, VBVA is the first geographical routing protocol which can deals with voids efficiently in underwater sensor networks.

2.2 Void Avoidance Algorithms

There are numerous work proposed to handle the void problem in radio sensor networks. In [16], a graph traversal algorithm *right-hand rule* is proposed to bypass the void in the network. A node bypasses a void by forwarding the data to the node first traversed by the arriving edge of the packet counterclockwise. However, this algorithm requires that the underlying graph is planar. A flooding algorithm appears in [12]. Here, when a node cannot forward a packet further, it floods the packet one-hop, and then its neighbors will forward the packet in a greedy way. Distance upgrading algorithm (DUA) is proposed in [2]. In this algorithm, each node records its virtual distance to the destination. A packet is forwarded from the nodes with larger virtual distances to the nodes with lower virtual distances.

However, all of the existing void avoidance routing protocols address stationary and two-dimensional wireless networks. They are not suitable for three-dimensional mobile underwater sensor networks, which are the target of the VBVA protocol.

3 Vector-Based Void Avoidance Protocol

In this section, we describe our vector-based void avoidance protocol(VBVA). VBVA extends the vector-based forwarding protocol(VBF) [14]. When there is no void, VBVA works in the same way as VBF. If a void is detected, VBVA resorts to its vector-shift mechanism which tries to shift its forwarding vector to bypass the void. If the vector-shift mechanism does not work, VBVA will use its back-pressure mechanism to retreat the data packet back to some nodes that can use vector-shift mechanism to bypass the void. We will first give a brief introduction to VBF. Then, we will discuss how to detect a void in VBVA and present its vector-shift and back-pressure mechanism.

3.1 Vector-Based Forwarding (VBF)

VBF is a geographic routing protocol [14]. Each node in the network knows its position, which can be obtained by localization algorithms [17]. If no localization service is available, the sensor nodes can still estimate its relative position to the forwarding node by measuring its distance to the forwarder and the angle of arrival (AOA) if it is equipped with some hardware device. This assumption is justified by the fact that acoustic directional antennae are much smaller than RF directional antennae due to the extremely small wavelength of sound. Moreover, underwater sensor nodes are usually larger than land-based sensors and thus have room for such devices.

In VBF, the forwarding path follows a vector from the source to the sink, which is called forwarding vector. The position information of the source, sink, and forwarder is carried in the header of the data packet. When a node receives a packet, it calculates its distance to the forwarding vector. If the distance is less than a pre-defined threshold, called radius, this node is qualified to forward the packet. In VBF, the forwarding path is virtually a pipe from the source to the sink, called forwarding pipe.

VBVA extends VBF with the capability to handle voids. It has the same assumptions as VBF, i.e., a node can overhear the transmission of its neighbors. Because of broadcasting nature of underwater acoustic channels, this can be easily satisfied. Similar to VBF, the forwarding path of a packet is also represented as a vector and carried in the packet in VBVA. If there is no presence of void in the forwarding path, VBVA behaves the same as VBF. However, VBVA significantly differs from VBF in that VBVA can detect the presence of the void in the forwarding path and bypass the void. With its void avoidance mechanism, VBVA can potentially find multiple forwarding vectors for a data packet, thus significantly improving the robustness of the network.

3.2 Void Detection

In VBVA, a node detects the presence of a void by overhearing the transmission of the packet by its neighboring nodes. In VBVA, the information about the forwarding vector of a packet is carried in the packet. When a node overhears the transmission of a data packet, the node records the position information of the forwarding nodes. We denote the start point and the end point of the forwarding vector by S and T respectively. For any node N, we define the *advance* of node N on the forwarding vector of the packet is the projection of the vector $\overrightarrow{SN}$ on the forwarding vector $\overrightarrow{ST}$. We call a node a *void node* if all the advances of its neighbors on the forwarding vector carried in a packet are smaller than its own advance. An example is shown in Fig. 1, the forwarding vector of a packet is $\overrightarrow{ST}$, the advances of nodes B, C and F on the forwarding vector are denoted as A_B, A_C and A_F, respectively. As shown in Fig 1, all the neighbors of node F have smaller advances than F on the forwarding vector $\overrightarrow{ST}$. Thus node F is a void node. In VBVA, if a node finds out that it has the largest advance on the current forwarding vector among all the neighboring nodes within the forwarding pipe, the node concludes that it is a void node and has detected a void on the current forwarding vector.

Unlike VBF where the forwarding vector of a packet is defined to be the vector from the source to the sink and is kept unchanged during the packet delivery. In VBVA, once a forwarding node detects a void, the node tries to bypass the void

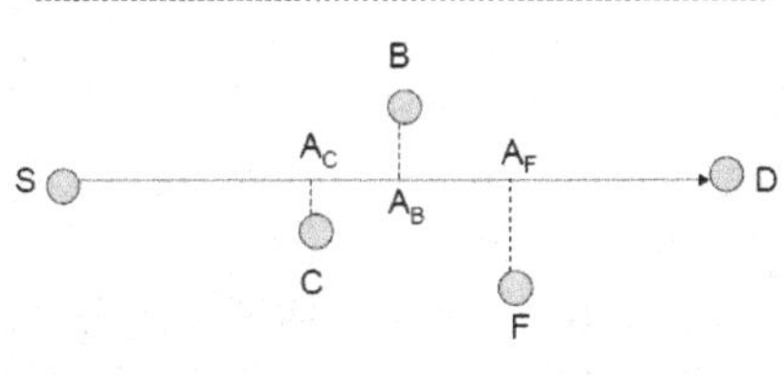

Fig. 1. An example of void node

by changing the forwarding vector of the packet to find alternative routes. Two mechanisms, *vector-shift* and *back-pressure*, are used in VBVA for bypassing the void. We describe the two mechanisms in detail next.

3.3 Vector-Shift Mechanism

In VBVA, when a node determines that it is a void node for a packet, it will try to bypass the void by shifting the forwarding vector of the packet. To do the vector shifting, the node broadcasts a vector-shift packet to all its neighbors. Upon receiving this control packet, all the nodes outside the current forwarding pipe will try to forward the corresponding data packet following a new forwarding vector from themselves to the sink. This process is called *vector-shift* and we say the void node *shifts* the forwarding vector.

As shown in Fig. 2(a), the dashed area is the void area. Node S is the sender and node T is the sink node. At the beginning, node S forwards the packet along the forwarding vector $\overrightarrow{ST}$, and then it keeps listening the channel for some time. Since the neighboring node D and A of node S are not within the forwarding pipe, they will not forward this packet. Thus node S cannot overhear any transmission of the same packet and concludes that it sits at the edge of a network void. It then broadcasts a vector-shift control packet, asking its neighbors to change the current forwarding vector to $\overrightarrow{DT}$ and $\overrightarrow{AT}$ as shown in Fig. 2(a). Nodes D and A repeat the same process. The arrowed lines in Fig. 2(a) are the forwarding vectors used by the forwarding nodes. From this figure, we can see that if the void area is convex, it can be bypassed by the vector-shift mechanism.

After shifting the forwarding vector of a packet, a node keeps listening the channel to check if there is a neighboring node forwarding the packet with the new forwarding vector. If the node does not hear the packet being forwarded even if it has shifted the current forwarding vector, the node is defined as an *end node*. For an end node, the vector-shift mechanism cannot find an alternative routing path and we have to use our back-pressure mechanism.

3.4 Back-Pressure Mechanism

When a node finds out that it is an end node, it broadcasts a control packet, called **BP**(Back Pressure) packet. Upon receiving a **BP** packet, every neighboring node tries to shift the forwarding vector of the corresponding packet if it has

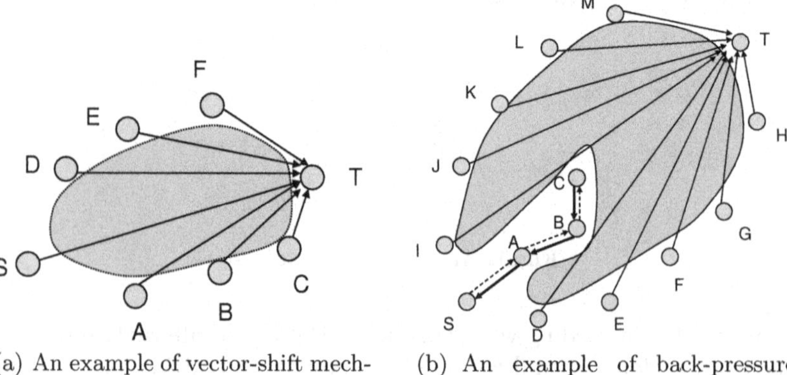

(a) An example of vector-shift mechanism

(b) An example of back-pressure mechanism.

Fig. 2. Two mechanisms of VBVA

never shifted the forwarding vector of this packet before. Otherwise, the node broadcasts the **BP** packet again. We call the process of repetitively broadcasting the **BP** packet the *back-pressure* process . The **BP** packet will be routed back in the direction moving away from the sink until it reaches a node which can do vector shifting to forward the packet toward the sink.

Fig. 2(b) shows an example for the back-pressure process. Here, the shadowed area is a concave void. The node S is the sender and node T is the sink. When node S forwards the packet with forwarding vector $\overrightarrow{ST}$ to node C, since node C cannot forward the packet along the vector $\overrightarrow{ST}$ any more, it will first use vector-shift mechanism to find alternative routes for the data packet. Since node C is an end node, it cannot overhear the transmission of the packet. Node C then broadcasts a **BP**(Back Pressure) packet. Upon receiving the **BP** packet, node B first tries to shift the forwarding vector but fails to find routes for the data packet. Then node B broadcasts **BP** packet to node A and so on. Finally, a **BP** packet is routed from node A to the source S. Node S then shifts the forwarding vector to $\overrightarrow{HT}$ and $\overrightarrow{DT}$. The data packet is then forwarded to the sink by the vector-shift method from nodes H and D as shown in Fig. 2(b). It is clear from Fig. 2(b) that our back-pressure mechanism can handle the end-node problem and the concave void.

We have proved that with our vector-shifting and back-pressure mechanisms, VBVA can guarantee to find a path from the source to the sink if the underlying MAC is collision free and the topology of the networks is connected and stable during a data transmission. Interested readers can refer to our technical report for the proof as well as the protocol details [15].

4 Performance Evaluation

In this section, we evaluate the performance of VBVA by simulations. We implement a simulator for underwater networks based on ns-2. The underlaying MAC used here is a broadcast MAC protocol. In this MAC, if a node has data to send, it first senses the channel. If the channel is free, then the node broadcasts the packet. Otherwise, it backs off. The maximum number of backoffs is 4 for one data packet.

4.1 Simulation Settings

In all our simulations, we set the parameters similar to UWM1000 [9]. The bit rate is 10 kbps, and the transmission range is 100 meters. The energy consumption on sending mode, receiving mode and idle mode are 2 W, 0.75 W and 8 mW respectively. The size of the data packet and large control packet for VBF and VBVA in the simulation is set to 50 bytes. The size of the small control packet for VBVA is set to 5 bytes. The pipe radius in both VBVA and VBF is 100 meters. The maximum delay window, T_{delay} of VBVA is set to 1 second.

In all the simulation experiments described in this section, sensor nodes are randomly distributed in a space of 1000 m $\times$1000 m $\times$500 m. There are one data source and one sink. The source sends one data packet per 10 seconds. For each setting, the results are averaged over 100 runs with a randomly generated topology. The total simulation time for each run is 1000 seconds.

Performance Metrics. We examine three metrics: success rate, energy cost and energy tax. The *success rate* is the ratio of the number of packets successfully received by the sink to the number of packets generated by the source. The *energy cost* is the total energy consumption of the whole network. The *energy tax* is the average energy cost for each successfully received packet.

4.2 Performance in Mobile Random Networks

In this simulation setting, the source is fixed at $(500, 1000, 250)$, while the sink is at located at $(500, 0, 250)$. Besides the source and sink, all other nodes are mobile as follows: they can move in horizontal two-dimensional space, i.e., in the X-Y plane (which is the most common mobility pattern in underwater applications). Each node randomly selects a destination and speed in the range of $0 - 3$ m/s, and moves toward that destination. Once the node arrives at the destination, it randomly selects a new destination and speed, and moves in a new direction.

From Figure 3(a), we can see that the success rate of VBVA is very close to that of flooding and much higher than that of VBF when the number of nodes is low. When the number of nodes in the networks increases, the probability of the presence of void is decreased, the difference among these three protocols is becoming smaller. When the network is very sparse, flooding algorithm and VBVA outperform VBF. Moreover, VBVA shows almost the same capability to overcome the voids in the networks as flooding. And the success rate of flooding roughly is the upper bound for all the routing protocols proposed for mobile networks.

As shown in Figure 3(b), VBF is the most energy efficient among these three protocols since VBF never attempts to consume more energy to overcome the

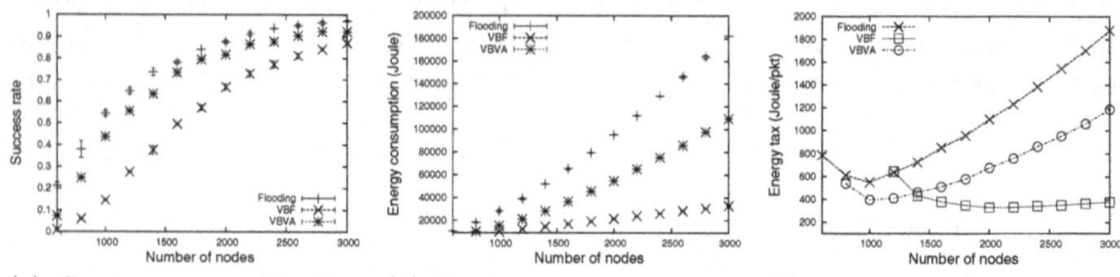

(a) Success rate: flooding, VBF and VBVA. (b) Energy cost: Flooding, VBF and VBVA. (c) Energy tax: Flooding, VBF and VBVA.

Fig. 3. Comparison between Flooding, VBF and VBVA

voids in the networks. VBVA is energy efficient than flooding under all the network deployments. Notice that the difference between the energy cost of VBVA and flooding algorithm increases as the network becomes denser. This is attributed to the fact that VBVA overcomes voids with an energy efficient way. On the other hand, VBVA consumes more energy than VBF.

The energy taxes of the Flooding, VBF and VBVA are shown in Figure 3(c). From this figure, we can see that when the network is sparse, both flooding and VBVA consume less energy to successfully deliver one packet than VBF does. However, when the number of nodes exceeds 1200, flooding algorithm consumes more energy per packet than VBF and VBVA. VBVA consumes more energy per packet than VBF when the number of nodes in the network exceeds 1400. VBVA has lower energy tax than flooding algorithm under all the network topologies. Notice that after some point (1400), although VBVA has higher energy tax than that of VBF, it is still preferable over VBF for some application scenario where success rate is important. Since VBVA is based on VBF, it is easy to integrate VBVA as an option for VBF such that the application can determine if it is worth turning on void-avoidance.

From this simulation setting, we can see that VBVA approximates flooding algorithm on the success rate, but at much less energy cost. VBVA can avoid voids in mobile networks effectively and efficiently.

4.3 Handling Concave and Convex Voids

In this simulation setting, the sink is fixed at location $(500, 0, 250)$ and the the source is fixed at location $(500, 1000, 250)$. We generate two different voids: concave and convex voids for the network. In order to generate concave and convex voids, we divide the whole space into smaller cubes $(50 \times 50 \times 50)$. A node is randomly deployed in each cube. We generate an ellipsoid centered at $(500, 500, 250)$ with radius $(300, 300, 150)$. The larger ellipsoid is the convex void in which there no nodes deployed. In order to generate a concave void, we generate another smaller ellipsoid centered at $(500, 300, 250)$ with radius $(200, 200, 150)$. These two ellipsoids overlap each other. The cubes in the overlapped part within the larger ellipsoid are deployed with sensor nodes, other cubes inside other parts of the large ellipsoid are empty. By doing this, we created an approximate concave void and the simulation results are shown in Table 1.

Table 1. Concave void vs convex void

Void	Success rate	Energy tax (Joule/pkt)
Concave void	0.992600	606.450097
Convex void	0.99700	603.503211

Table 1 demonstrates that VBVA can effectively bypass both the concave and the convex voids. From the table, we can see also that it costs more energy to bypass the concave void than convex void since there involves back-pressure mechanism in VBVA when it addresses the concave void. We have proved that our VBVA can definitely find a route for a packet if the network is connected. Here, we can see that our VBVA can always achieve at least 99% success rate. only less than 1% packets get lost because no path exists from the source to the destination in the simulated random network.

We have also conducted simulations when a void is mobile. The results show that VBVA can handle mobile void efficiently and effectively. When the mobility speed of a void is less than 3 meters/s, the success rate and energy efficient is not affected as long as there exists a path from the source to the sink. Due to space limit, we omit the results. Interested readers can refer to our technical report for details [15].

5 Conclusions

The routing void problem in underwater sensor networks is characterized as three dimensional space, highly mobile nodes and mobile voids, which pose the most challenging problem for geographic routing protocols.

In this paper, we propose a void avoidance protocol, called vector-based void avoidance (VBVA) to address the routing void problem in mobile underwater sensor networks. VBVA is the first protocol to address the three-dimensional and mobile voids. VBVA adopts two mechanisms, vector-shift and back-pressure to bypass voids in the forwarding path. VBVA detects a void only when needed and handles the void on demand. It does not require the topology information of the network and is very robust against mobile nodes and mobile voids.

We evaluate the performance of the VBVA under various network scenarios. The simulation results show that VBVA can handle both concave and convex voids as well as mobile voids effectively and efficiently.

References

1. Goel, I.K.A., Kannan, A.G., Bartos, R.: Improveing Efficiency of a Flooding-based Routing Protocol for Underwater Networks. In: Proceedings of the 3rd ACM international workshop on Underwater networks, September 2008, pp. 91–94 (2008)
2. Chen, S., Fan, G., Cui, J.: Avoid Void in Geographic Routing for Data Aggregation in Sensor Networks. International Journal of Ad Hoc and Ubiquitous Computing,Special Issue on Wireless Sensor Networks 2(1) (2006)

3. Cui, J., Kong, J., Gerla, M., Zhou, S.: Challenges:Building scalable mobile underwater wireless sensor networks for aquatic application. IEEE network, Special Issue on Wireless Sensor Networking 20(3), 12–18 (2006)
4. Fang, Q., Gao, J., Guibas, L.: Locating and Bypassing Routing Holes in Sensor Networks. In: Proc. of IEEE INFOCOM 2004, Hong Kong, China (March 2004)
5. Guo, Z., Colmbo, G., Wang, B., Cui, J.-H., Maggiorini, D., Rossi, G.P.: Adaptive Routing in Underwater Delay/Disruption Tolerant Sensor Networks. In: Proceedings of the WONS, January 2008, pp. 31–39 (2008)
6. Heideman, J., Ye, W., Wills, J., Syed, A., Li, Y.: Research Challenges and Applications for Underwater Sensor Networking. In: IEEE Wireless Communication and networking Conference, Las Vegas, Nevada, USA (April 2006)
7. Jornet, J.M., Stojanovic, M., Zorzi, M.: Focused Beam Routing Protocol for Underwater Acoustic Networks. In: Proceedings of the 3rd ACM international workshop on Underwater networks, September 2008, pp. 75–81 (2008)
8. Kong, J., Cui, J.-H., Wu, D., Gerla, M.: Building Underwater Ad-hoc Networks for Large Scale Real-time Aquatic Applications. In: IEEE Military Communication Conference (MILCOM 2005) (2005)
9. LinkQuest, `http://www.link-quest.com/`
10. Nicolaou, N.C., See, A.G., Xie, P., Cui, J.-H., Maggiorini, D.: Improving the Robustness of Location-Based Routing for Underwater Sensor Networks. In: Oceans 2007, Aberdeen, Scotland (June 2007)
11. Proakis, J.G., Rice, J.A., Sozer, E.M., Stojanovic, M.: Shallow Water Acoustic Networks. John Wiley and sons, Chichester (2001)
12. Stojmenovic, I., Lin, X.: Loop-Free Hybrid Single-Path/Flooding Routing Algorithm with Guaranteed Delivery for Wireless Networks. IEEE Transactions on Parallel and Distributed Systems 12 (October 2001)
13. Xie, G.G., Gibson, J.H.: A Network Layer Protocol for UANs TO Address Propagation Delay Indcued Performance Limitations. In: Proceedings of the MTS/IEEE Oceans, November 2001, pp. 1–8 (2001)
14. Xie, P., Cui, J.-H., Lao, L.: VBF: Vector-Based Forwarding Protocol for Underwater Sensor Networks. In: Proceedings of IFIP Networking 2006, Coimbra, Portugal (May 2006)
15. Xie, P., Zhou, Z., Peng, Z., Cui, J.-H., Shi, Z.: Void Avoidance in Three Dimensional Mobile Underwater Sensor Netwroks. In: UCONN CSE Technical Report:UbiNet-TR09-01 (June 2009), `http://www.cse.uconn.edu/~jcui/publications.html`
16. Xu, Y., Lee, W.-C., Xu, J., Mitchell, G.: PSGR: Priority-based Stateless Geo-Routing in Wireless Sensor Networks. In: MASS 2005, Washington, D.C., USA (November 2005)
17. Zhou, Z., Cui, J.-H., Zhou, S.: Localization for Large-Scale Underwater Sensor Networks. In: Akyildiz, I.F., Sivakumar, R., Ekici, E., de Oliveira, J.C., McNair, J. (eds.) NETWORKING 2007. LNCS, vol. 4479, pp. 108–119. Springer, Heidelberg (2007)

Distributed Range-Free Localization Algorithm Based on Self-Organizing Maps

Pham Doan Tinh and Makoto Kawai

Graduate School of Science and Engineering, Ritsumeikan University, Kusatsu, Japan
gr036088@ed.ritsumei.ac.jp

Abstract. In Mobile Ad-Hoc Networks (MANETs), determining the physical location of nodes (localization) is very important for many network services and protocols. This paper proposes a new Distributed Range-free Localization Algorithm Based on Self-Organizing Maps (SOM) to deal with this issue. Our proposed algorithm utilizes only connectivity information to determine the location of nodes. By utilizing the intersection areas between radio coverage of neighboring nodes, the algorithm has maximized the correlation between neighboring nodes in distributed implementation of SOM and reduced the SOM learning time. An implementation of the algorithm on Network Simulator 2 (NS-2) was done with the mobility consideration to verify the performance of the proposed algorithm. From our intensive simulations, the results show that the proposed scheme achieves very good accuracy in most cases.

1 Introduction

Recently, mobile ad-hoc network localization has received attention from many researchers [1]. Many algorithms and solutions have been presented so far. These algorithms are ranging from simple to complicated schemes, but they can be categorized as range-based and range-free algorithms. Range-free algorithms utilize only connectivity information and the number of hops between nodes. The others utilize the distance measured between nodes by either using the Time-Of-Arrival (TOA) [2], Time-Differential-Of-Arrival (TDOA) [3], Angle-Of-Arrival (AOA) [4] or Received-Signal-Strength-Indicator (RSSI)[5] technologies. However, they usually need extra hardware to achieve such measurement. When calculating the absolute location, most schemes need at least three anchors (nodes that are equipped with Global Positioning System or know their location in advance).

DV-HOP is a typical range-free algorithm. It was proposed by D.Niculescu and B.Nath [6] as an Ad-hoc Positioning System (APS). DV-HOP uses distance-vector forwarding technique to get the minimum hop count from a node to heard anchors. By using corrections calculated by anchors (average hop-distance between anchors), nodes estimate their location by using lateration (triangulation) method. Besides DV-HOP, some other algorithms seem to be more complicated, but have better accuracy. The Multi-Dimensional Scaling Map (MDS-MAP) proposed by Yi Shang et al. [7] is an example. MDS-MAP is originated from a data analytical technique by displaying distance-like data in geometrical visualization.

B. Liu et al. (Eds.): WASA 2009, LNCS 5682, pp. 315–324, 2009.

It computes the shortest paths between all pairs of nodes to build a distance matrix and then applies the classical Multi-Dimensional Scaling (MDS) to this matrix to retain the first two largest eigenvalue and eigenvector to a 2-D relative map. After that, with three given anchors, it transforms the relative map into an absolute map based on anchors' absolute location. There are some variances of MDS-MAP such as centralized method - MDS-MAP(C), and distributed one-MDS-MAP(P). But, in the distributed method, to get the absolute location, nodes need global information about the sub-network's map that contains at least three anchors. Tran et al. [8] proposed a new localization scheme based on Support Vector Machine (SVM). The authors have contributed another machine learning method to the localization problem, and proved the upper bound error of this method.

Regarding the localization based on Self-Organizing Maps, some researchers have employed SOM directly or with some modification. The method presented by G.Giorgetti [9] employed the classical SOM to the localization. This method uses centralized implementation and requires thousands of learning steps in convergence of network topology. The authors also realize that this method is good for small and medium size networks of up to 100 nodes. S.Asakura et al. proposed a distributed localization scheme[10] based on SOM. Jie Hu et al. [11] also proposed another version of distributed localization based on SOM. In this work, the authors employed a deduced SOM version[12]. But, this method still needs too many iterations (at least 4000) to make the topology to be converged with a relatively low accuracy. In another work[13], the authors use SOM to track a mobile robot with the utilization of surrounding environments from readings of sensor data. In the work presented by E.Ertin et al.[14], another version of SOM was used to implement the localization in wireless sensor networks. This paper extends one of our previous work[15] to improve and adapt it with mobility scenarios. The main contribution of this paper is the utilization of intersection between radio coverage of neighboring nodes in our modified SOM, and the adaptation of the algorithm to the mobility scenarios.

2 Motivation for SOM Based Distributed Localization

The Self-Organizing Maps (SOM) was invented by T.Kohonen [16]. SOM provides a technique for representation of multi-dimensional data into much lower dimensional spaces (usually one or two dimensions). It uses a process known as vector quantization. The nature of SOM is a neural network working in unsupervised learning manner. Suppose that we have a mobile ad-hoc network of connected nodes, in which only a small number of nodes know their location in advance (anchor nodes). Now we have to determine the location of the remaining nodes that do not know their location, especially in distributed manner. In our proposed scheme, one can think that a mobile ad-hoc network itself is an SOM network, in which each neuron is a node in that network, and these neurons are connected to their 1-hop neighboring nodes (nodes have direct radio links). The topological position and the weight of each neuron are associated with its estimated location. The learning process includes two phases. The first phase takes place locally at each node, where the input pattern is its estimated location (this input is dynamically changed over time except that the anchors use their known location) and neighborhood nodes are its 1-hop neighboring nodes. It is obvious that each node becomes the Best-Matching Unit (BMU) at its local region. So when updating weights at the BMU, only its 1-hop neighbors' weights are updated. The BMU node also receives updates from other nodes when it becomes 1-hop neighbor of other nodes. Anchors do not update their known positions during the learning process, so if the network has some nodes know their location in advance (anchors), then each node will utilize the information from these anchors by adjusting its location towards the estimated absolute location based on the information from these heard anchors. At the end of the learning process, the weight at each node (SOM neuron) is its estimated location.

3 Proposed Distributed Localization Algorithm Based on SOM

In this section, we will introduce about our proposed Distributed Range-free Localization Algorithm (LS-SOM). The first two sections describe about initialization and learning stages of the main algorithm. The mobility consideration is presented in the third section.

3.1 Initialization Stage

At a predefined interval, each anchor in the network broadcasts a packet to its neighboring nodes. This packet contains the anchor's location and a hop count initialized to one. When a node receives a packet contains anchor information, node then decides to discard or forward the packet to its neighboring nodes or not with the following rules.

1. If the packet is already in the cache, the node then compares the hop count of the packet with that of the cached packet. If the hop count of the arrival packet is less than that of the cached packet, then the cached packet is replaced with a new arrival packet, and forwarded to its neighboring nodes with hop count modified to add one hop. If the hop count of the arrival packet is greater than or equal to that of cached packet, then it is dropped.
2. If the packet is not in the cache, then it is added to the cache and forwarded to its neighboring nodes with hop count modified to add one hop.

Having information from some anchors, the nodes now initialize their location ready for SOM learning process. In our proposed method, the initial location of a node is calculated based on either randomized value (if node does not receive enough three anchors) or a value calculated using a trilateral method. In this initialization stage, nodes also exchange information (using short "HELLO" message broadcast) so that each node has information about its neighboring nodes (1-hop neighbors). Nodes also exchange information about 1-hop neighbors with its neighboring nodes, so that all nodes in the network have information about both 1-hop and 2-hop neighboring nodes.

3.2 Learning Stage

Before going into our algorithm details, let us formulate the mathematical notations which will be used in this paper. We represent a wireless ad-hoc network as an undirected connected graph. The vertices are nodes' locations, and edges are the connectivity information (direct connection between neighboring nodes). The target wireless ad-hoc network is formed by G anchors with known locations $\Omega_i(i = 1,2,...,G)$ and N nodes with unknown locations. The unknown nodes have actual locations denoted as $\omega_i(i = 1,2,...,N)$ and estimated locations denoted as $\varpi_i(i = 1,2,...,N)$.

1. Estimated location exchange
   At this step, each node forwards its estimated location to all of its neighbors, so that it also knows the estimated location of its neighbors as $\varpi_{i,j}(j = 1,2,...,N_i)$ with N_i is the number of nodes within its communication range.
2. Local update of relative location
   We will now shape the topology at each region formed by the node with location ϖ_i together with all of its neighboring nodes. The node ϖ_i plays as the input vector and becomes the winning neuron for that region. Consequently, the neighboring nodes of ϖ_i will receive the updating vector from node ϖ_i. Suppose that the node with the estimated location ϖ_i has N_i neighbors. The locations of these neighbors are denoted as $\varpi_{i,j}(j = 1,...,N_i)$. Based on classical SOM, neighboring nodes of the node with location ϖ_i will update their weight with the following formula.

   $$\varpi_{i,j}(m+1) = \varpi_{i,j}(m) + \Delta(m) \tag{1}$$

   where $\Delta(m)$ is calculated using (2).

   $$\Delta(m) = \alpha(m)(\varpi_i - \varpi_{i,j}(m)) \tag{2}$$

   in which $\alpha(m)$ is the learning rate exponential decay function at iteration $m-th$ defined in (3).

   $$\alpha(m) = \exp(-\frac{m+1}{T}) \tag{3}$$

   where m denotes the $m-th$ time step of the total T learning steps. But, updating by using (1) means that the neighboring nodes will move toward the location determined by ϖ_i. This will lead to the problem as showed in Fig.1. From Fig.1, the nodes with location ϖ_j and ϖ_k are the neighbors of the node with location ϖ_i, but ϖ_j is not the neighbor of ϖ_k. In the worst case, the estimated location of the node with location ϖ_j falls into the radio range of the node with location ϖ_k, then the node with location ϖ_j may not escape from that wrong location throughout the learning process (dead location). In this paper, we propose an algorithm to solve this problem as follows. Suppose that at the node with location ϖ_i, we have to update location for the neighbor node with location $\varpi_{i,j}(j = 1,...,N_i)$. First, we find out other $L_{i,j}$ neighbor node $\varpi_{i,j,k}(k = 1,...,L_{i,j})$ of the node with location

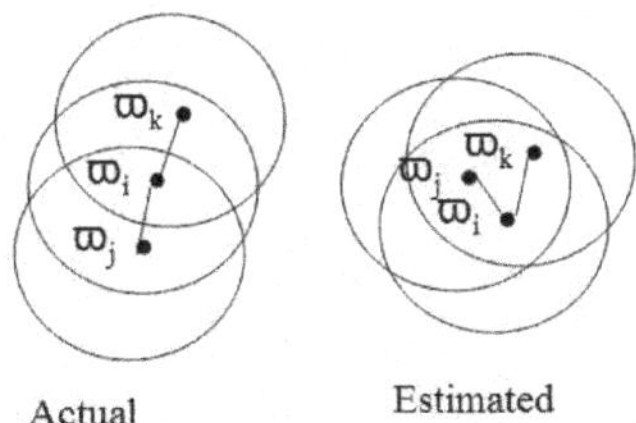

Fig. 1. The case where node ϖ_j has wrong estimated location

ϖ_i that are not the neighbor of the node with location $\varpi_{i,j}$ (this is done easily because each node knows its neighbors' neighbors). Now we calculate the vector that has the direction towards the intersection area (the dashed area) in Fig.2. As illustrated in Fig.3, this vector is calculated using (4).

$$\xi_{i,j} = \frac{1}{L_{i,j}} \sum_{k=1}^{L_{i,j}} \frac{r - \mid \varpi_{i,j} - \varpi_{i,j,k} \mid}{\mid \varpi_{i,j} - \varpi_{i,j,k} \mid} (\varpi_{i,j} - \varpi_{i,j,k}) \tag{4}$$

where r denotes the maximum communicable range between $\varpi_{i,j}$ and $\varpi_{i,j,k}$ $(k = 1, ..., L_{i,j})$. We use vector $\xi_{i,j}$ as a guidance to update the location of the node with location $\varpi_{i,j}$ by changing (1) to (5).

$$\varpi_{i,j}(m+1) = \varpi_{i,j}(m) + \Delta(m) + \mid \Delta(m) \mid (\frac{\xi_{i,j}}{\mid \xi_{i,j} \mid})\beta \tag{5}$$

The update by (5) makes each node move toward the intersection area as showed in Fig.2. This update also maximizes the correlation between the neighboring nodes that is the key problem for the speed and accuracy of topological convergence using SOM. In (5), β is a learning bias parameter calculated using (6).

$$\beta = \begin{cases} 0 \; m <= \tau \\ 1 \; m > \tau \end{cases} \tag{6}$$

with τ is a learning threshold. This threshold determines the step to apply this modification. Basically, we can apply this modification after several steps of SOM learning. At the end of this step, the node with location ϖ_i transmits its neighbor location updates based on (5) to all of its neighbors. As a result, it also receives the similar updates from its N_i neighboring nodes as $\varpi_{j,i} (j = 1, ..., N_i)$. Node with location ϖ_i now calculates its newly estimated location by averaging its current location and the updates from the neighboring nodes using (7).

$$\varpi_i = \frac{1}{N_i + 1} (\sum_{j=1}^{N_i} \varpi_{j,i} + \varpi_i) \tag{7}$$

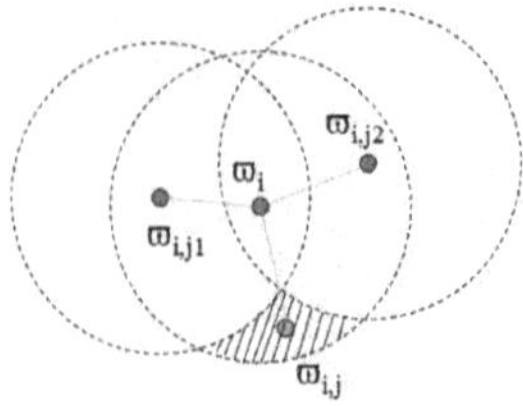

Fig. 2. Possible location of neighboring node $\varpi_{i,j}$

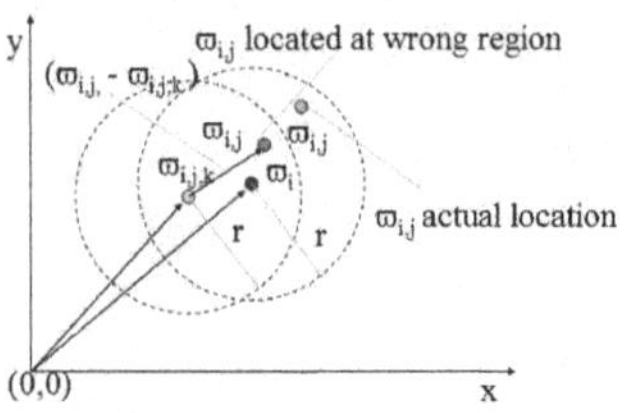

Fig. 3. The case where neighboring node $\varpi_{i,j}$ is located at wrong location

3.3 Mobility Consideration

In MANETs, nodes may move in arbitrarily manner, so the movement of nodes will affect the performance of the algorithm. To adapt LS-SOM with MANETs, we proposed a repeated learning algorithm as follows.

1. First Time Initialization
   Anchors participate in localization will flood the network just one time, so that nodes can calculates the initial location for fast topology convergence.
2. Repeated Learning
   At specified interval, nodes perform neighboring detection by exchanging a short "HELLO" messages. Having neighboring information, nodes now proceed with the learning process.

4 Simulation Evaluations

To evaluate the performance of our proposed method, we use the average error ratio in comparison with the radio range of the nodes presented in (8).

$$Error(r) = \frac{1}{N}\sum_{i=1}^{N}\frac{\mid \varpi_i - \omega_i \mid}{r} \tag{8}$$

4.1 Simulation Parameters

To ease the comparison, we call the method in the existing work[10] as SOM, and our proposed method as LS-SOM. We conducted the simulation for static and mobile scenarios by using MATLAB (we integrated SOM, DV-HOP, and LS-SOM into the program received from[7]) and NS-2, respectively. For static scenarios, each experiment is done on thousands of randomly generated networks on an area of 10 by 10. For mobile scenarios, we simulated on networks with 25 randomly distributed nodes on an area of 300 by 300 square meters. The propagation model is TwoRayGround and transmission range of each node is

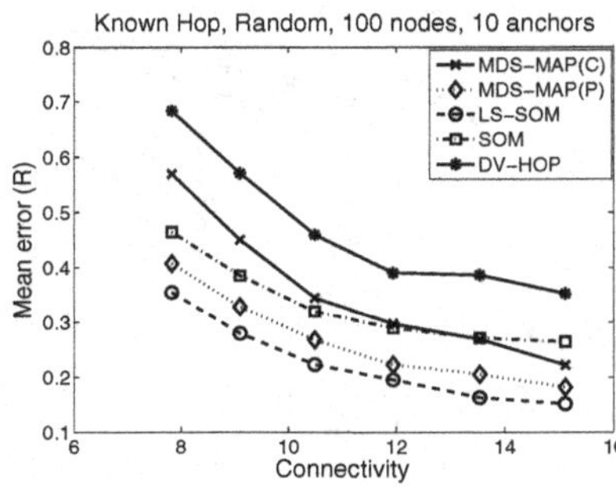

Fig. 4. Performace by connectivity

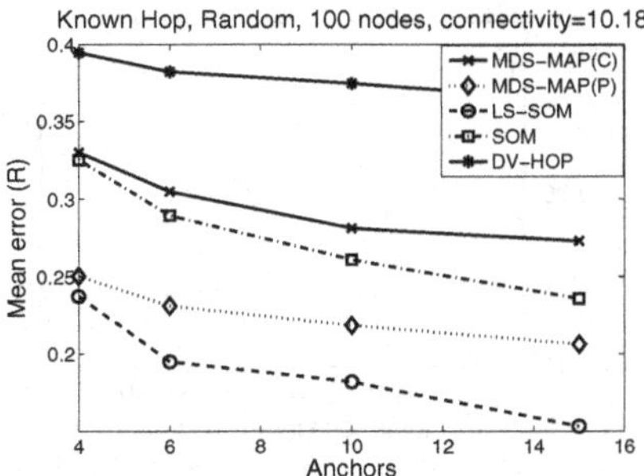

Fig. 5. Performace by anchors

100 meters. The common parameters used in simulation are as follows. Number of SOM learning steps T is 15, and Learning bias threshold τ is 1.

4.2 Static Networks

With static networks, we study how the accuracy is influenced by the connectivity level (the average number of neighbor nodes that a node has direct communication with), and the number of anchor nodes deployed. Fig.4 shows the average error with different connectivity levels. The result indicates that LS-SOM achieves very good accuracy over the SOM, DV-HOP, MDS-MAP(C), and even MDS-MAP(P) from sparse to dense networks. Especially with very sparse networks, LS-SOM still performs better than the others. The performance with the variance of anchors is showed in Fig.5. We find that LS-SOM increases accuracy when the number of anchors increases. When the number of anchors increases, LS-SOM improves accuracy much better than the others. We have tested and realized that on the grid deployment with 50% position error, LS-SOM gets better accuracy than the random deployment. Fig.6 shows the average error through each SOM learning step. LS-SOM needs only 15 to 30 learning steps to achieve a stable result. Comparing to thousands of learning steps in the traditional SOM, LS-SOM decreases network overhead and computational cost. Fig.8(a) shows one of the actual topology that is generated during the simulation. Fig.8(b), Fig.8(c), and Fig.8(d) show the topologies estimated with DV-HOP, SOM and LS-SOM, respectively. In these figures, the rectangles and the circles denote the anchor nodes and the unknown nodes, respectively. From the figures, one can realize that LS-SOM outperforms the topology regeneration. It is resistant to the perimeter effect that other schemes encounter. Fig.7 shows the distribution of nodes localized for 1000 randomly generated networks with 100 nodes, number of anchors ranging from 4 to 15, and connectivity is selected randomly from 7 to 15. From Fig.7, 80% of nodes localized with the error around 30% for LS-SOM.

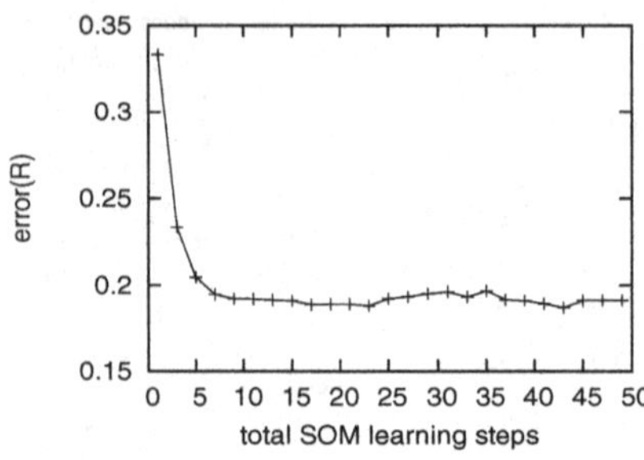

Fig. 6. Performace by SOM learning steps

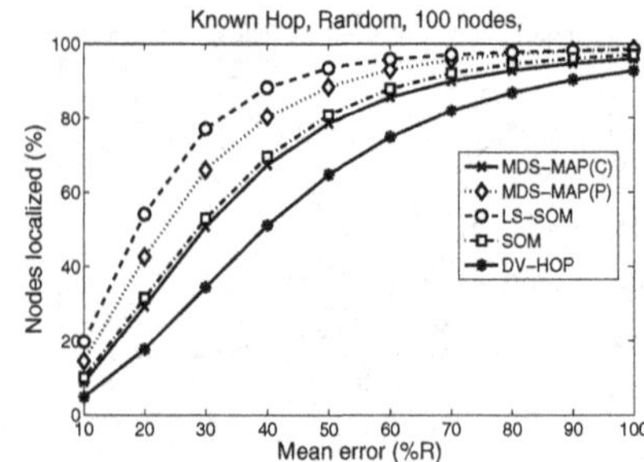

Fig. 7. Distribution of nodes localized (G=4 to 15)

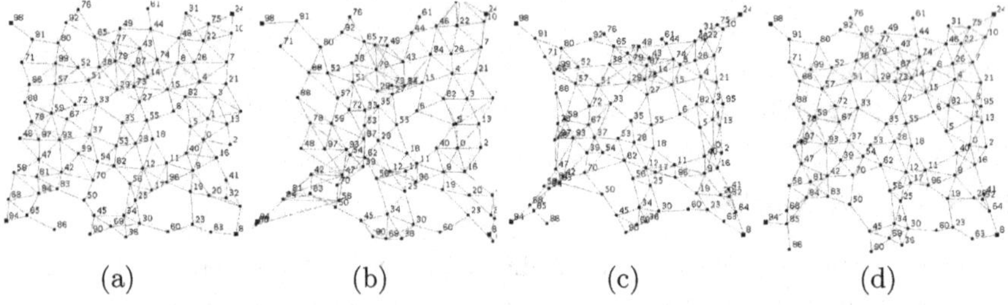

Fig. 8. Topology regeneration (N=100, G=4, connectivity=4.88) a) Actual topology, b)DV-HOP (error=0.50), c)SOM (error=0.35), d)LS-SOM (error=0.23)

4.3 Mobile Networks

We have implemented LS-SOM in NS-2 environment, in which LS-SOM is designed as an agent installed on each node and runs completely in parallel manner. In our simulation scenarios, anchors nodes are also moving. The Fig.9 shows the performance of LS-SOM by simulation time. From Fig.9, we can see that LS-SOM will give a stable estimation accuracy after the time period for initialization and initial learning. The delay period depends on the network configuration. In our simulation on NS-2, the difficulty is that the transmission delay and packet collision at MAC layer. We just simply solve the packet collision by using randomized packet exchange scheduling. Fig.10 shows the throughput for generated packets by simulation time. We see a burst of traffic at the beginning because of the anchor flooding in the initialization stage. From this observation, we can easily find that the cost for network flooding is very expensive. Fig.11 shows the throughput of dropping packets due to collision. We realize that during the learning process that about 30% of exchanging messages was dropped. Fig.12 shows the distribution of dropping packets at each node. Number of dropped packets of nodes near the center of topology is greater than that of nodes near the perimeters. It is to infer that the number of packet dropped will increase with the connectivity level, and we should consider this problem when designing a practical localization system.

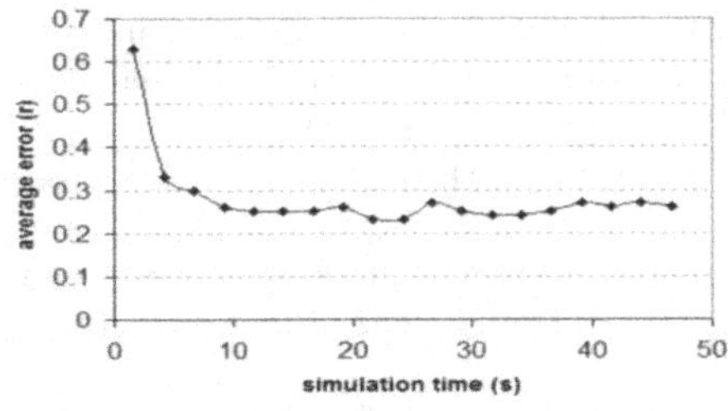

Fig. 9. Performace by simulation time (N=25, G=4, nodes speed=10m/s)

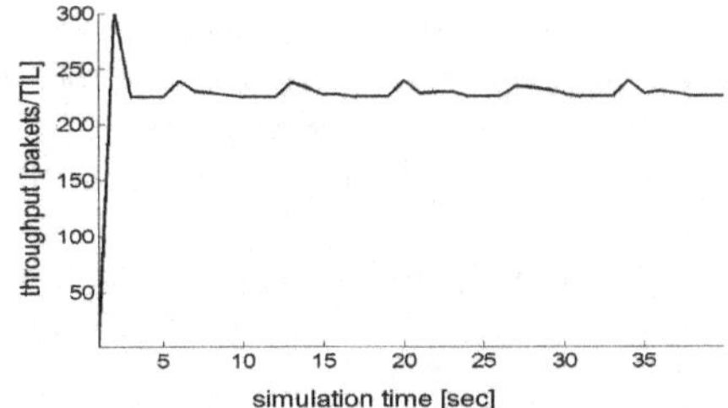

Fig. 10. Generating packets (N=25, G=4, nodes speed=10m/s)

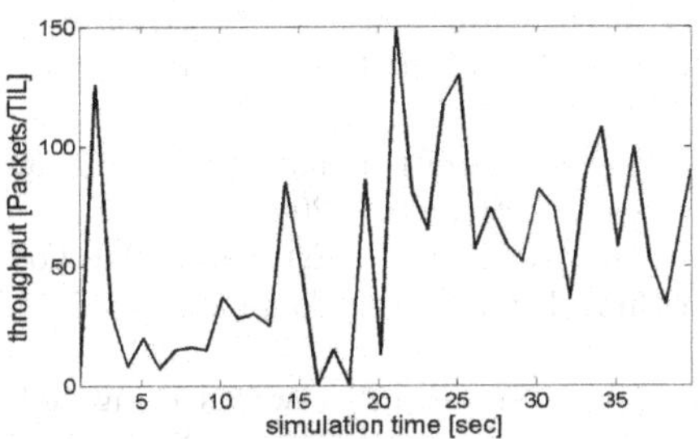

Fig. 11. Dropping packets (N=25, G=4, nodes speed=10m/s)

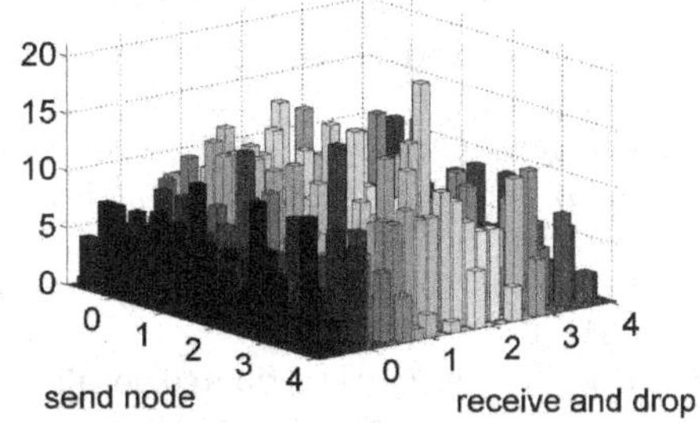

Fig. 12. Distribution of dropping packets

5 Conclusions

We have presented our proposed Distributed Range-free Localization Algorithm Based on Self-Organizing Maps (LS-SOM) in this paper. By introducing the utilization of intersection areas between radio coverage of neighboring nodes, the algorithm maximizes the correlation between neighboring nodes in distributed SOM implementation. With this correlation maximization, our method increases the quality of the topology estimation and reduces the time of the topological convergence. With our proposed solution for mobility management, LS-SOM is capable of working with networks having high mobility. From intensive simulations, the results show that LS-SOM has achieved good accuracy over the original SOM and other algorithms. LS-SOM has reduced the SOM learning steps to just around 15 to 30 steps. Besides that, LS-SOM is capable of working not only with static networks, but also with mobile networks. Future work will investigate in a more precise distance measurement method to make LS-SOM to be more flexible.

References

1. Poovendran, R., Wang, C.L., Roy, S.: Secure Localization and Time Synchronization for Wireless Sensor and Ad Hoc Networks. Springer, Heidelberg (2007)
2. Wellenhoff, B.H., Lichtenegger, H., Collins, J.: Global Positioning System: Theory and Practice, 4th edn. Springer, Heidelberg (1997)

3. Savvides, A., Han, C.C., Strivastava, M.B.: Dynamic fine-grained localization in ad-hoc networks of sensors. In: Proc. The 7th annual international conference on Mobile computing and networking (MobiCom), pp. 166–179 (2001)
4. Niculescu, D., Nath, B.: Ad hoc positioning system (APS) using AoA. In: Proc. INFOCOM, pp. 1734–1743 (2003)
5. Patwari, N., Hero III, A., Perkins, M., Correal, N., O'Dea, R.: Relative Localization Estimation in Wireless Sensor Networks. IEEE Trans. Signal Processing 51(8), 2137–2148 (2003)
6. Nicolescu, D., Nath, B.: Ad-Hoc Positioning Systems (APS). In: Proc. IEEE GLOBECOM (2001)
7. Shang, Y., Ruml, W., Zhang, Y., Fromherz, M.: Localization from Connectivity in Sensor Networks. IEEE Trans. Parallel and Distributed Systems 15(11), 961–974 (2004)
8. Tran, D.A., Nguyen, T.: Localization In Wireless Sensor Networks Based on Support Vector Machines. IEEE Trans. Parallel and Distributed Systems 19(7), 981–994 (2008)
9. Giorgetti, G., Gupta, S.K.S., Manes, G.: Wireless localization using self-organizing maps. In: Proc. IPSN 2007, Cambridge, Massachusetts, USA (2007)
10. Asakura, S., Umehara, D., Kawai, M.: Distributed Location Estimation Method for Mobile Terminals Based on SOM Algorithm. IEICE Trans. Commun. J85-B(7), 1042–1050 (2002)
11. Hu, J., Lee, G.: Distributed localization of wireless sensor networks using self-organizing maps. In: Proc. Multisensor Fusion and Integration for Intelligent Systems, pp. 284–289 (2008)
12. Sum, J., Leung, C.S., Chan, L.W., Xu, L.: Yet another algorithm which can generate topograph map. IEEE Trans. Neural Networks 8, 1204–1207 (1997)
13. Janet, J., Gutierrez, R., Chase, T., White, M., Sutton, J.: Autonomous mobile robot global self-localization using Kohonen and region-feature neural networks. Journal of Robotic Systems 14, 263–282 (1997)
14. Ertin, E., Priddy, K.: Self-localization of wireless sensor networks using self-organizing maps. In: Proc. SPIE 2005, vol. 5803, pp. 138–145 (2005)
15. Tinh, P.D., Noguchi, T., Kawai, M.: Localization scheme for large scale wireless sensor networks. In: Proc. ISSNIP 2008, pp. 25–30 (2008)
16. Kohonen, T.: Self-Organizing Maps, 3rd edn. Springer, Heidelberg (2001)
17. Cordeiro, C.D.M., Agrawal, D.P.: Ad-hoc & Sensor Networks Theory and Applications. World Scientific, Singapore (2006)
18. Niculescu, D., Nath, B.: Error Characteristics of Ad Hoc Positioning Systems (APS). In: Proc. MobiHoc 2004 (2004)

Location Discovery in SpeckNets Using Relative Direction Information

Ryan McNally and D.K. Arvind

School of Informatics, University of Edinburgh,
10 Crichton St. Edinburgh, EH8 9AB, UK
http://www.inf.ed.ac.uk

Abstract. A speck is intended to be a miniature (5X5X5mm) semiconductor device that combines sensing, processing, wireless communication and energy storage capabilities. A specknet is an ad-hoc wireless network of specks. The location of specks in the network is useful in processing information, for reasons ranging from routing data to giving the data sensed a spatial context. This paper presents an algorithm for discovering the location of specks and updating that information in the face of movement. The proposed algorithm exploits the location constraints implied by the sensed directions to a speck's one-hop neighbours in order to compute a likely location. Direction information may be gleaned in a robust manner through the use of free-space optical communications systems. The algorithm is fully distributed, requires no special infrastructural support, has modest requirements in terms of computation and communication and does not rely on range measurement or anchor nodes. The performance of the location discovery algorithm is evaluated in the SpeckSim simulator under a range of adverse conditions.

Keywords: Networks, localization.

1 Introduction

A speck [23] is designed to combine sensing, processing, wireless networking capabilities and a captive power source, all integrated in a minimal volume.

The specknet is a programmable computational network of hundreds of specks - in effect a fine-grained distributed computation platform built on a substrate of an ad-hoc wireless network of resource-constrained nodes. The model of distributed computation takes into account some specific features of specknets, such as the unreliability of wireless communication, and a higher than normal failure rate of specks due to the harsh operating conditions, meagre power supply, and very large volume manufacturing where individual specks cannot be fully tested.

A feature that will be important in many applications of specknets in pervasive and ubiquitous computing is the ability to map the data being sensed, and the information subsequently extracted, to its location within the specknet. In addition location data is very useful when routing messages across the network [1], especially in large networks where conventional routing tables become infeasible on resource-constrained devices.

B. Liu et al. (Eds.): WASA 2009, LNCS 5682, pp. 325–337, 2009.

Developing location algorithms for specknets poses unique problems. The specks will have extremely limited power (~1mW power budget), computation, bandwidth and storage (~2KB), and communication is expensive in comparison to computation (~x10). Any location algorithm should require minimal processing and storage, be robust against unreliable specks and communications, and be fully distributed across the specknet. The algorithm proposed in this paper satisfies each of these constraints at the cost of the requirement that the specks be equipped with appropriate sensory capability.

In the rest of this paper, Section 2 outlines existing algorithms for location discovery and their weaknesses in the face of the requirements of specknets; Section 3 describes the proposed algorithm; Section 4 describes the metric chosen to evaluate the performance of the algorithm and presents the results, with conclusions and possible improvements outlined in Section 5.

2 Related Work

Algorithms for location discovery in sensor networks can be classified according to various factors:

2.1 Infrastructure

Some localisation algorithms require infrastructural support over and above the network nodes themselves. This infrastructure is typically of two forms:

The first is to use a small number of devices separate to the network that enables nodes to locate themselves, as in the Lighthouse [2], Thunder [3] and similar approaches [4][5], and those approaches using mobile robots [6][7]. These algorithms share a common drawback, namely that the operation of the algorithm is entirely dependent on the operation of these scarce resources. If the devices break down, no localisation is possible. In addition, these devices must advertise themselves to the entire network and so are by necessity conspicuous. This requirement may be problematic for some applications where stealthy deployment is valued.

The other approach to infrastructure is to have a subset of nodes in the deployed network that is more capable than normal nodes. These so-called *anchor nodes* have knowledge of their location through some other means, such as GPS or simply explicit programming. Other nodes can then compute their location with respect to these anchor nodes. Such approaches have requirements ranging from only a few anchor nodes [8][9] to requiring that a anchor nodes be present throughout the deployed network [10][11].

The drawback to using anchor nodes lies in their deployment. Algorithms that use few anchor nodes typically operate by having other nodes measure the distance to the anchors and trilaterating their own location. Thus if the anchors are deployed to be almost collinear or coincident, the trilateration against these positions using noisy distance measurements is error-prone and even ambiguous. Algorithms that use many anchor nodes require that they are distributed evenly throughout the deployment area.

In both cases, such careful placing of the anchor nodes is difficult to guarantee in a true ad-hoc deployment.

2.2 Centralisation

Centralised algorithms [12][13][14] operate by gathering information, such as network connectivity or sensor readings, for the entire network onto the central computer, where it can undergo substantial analysis before the computed locations for nodes are disseminated back into the network. These approaches reduce the amount of computation required of the nodes but represent a single point of failure and limit the scalability of the network.

The increased amount of data that must be routed across the network is extremely undesirable due to the relatively high power expenditure of communication when compared to computation. In order to collect the network information at the central computer, the amount of data transfer necessarily increases rapidly closer to the central computer, leading to a problematic disparity in power consumption (and hence node lifetimes) across the network.

Centralised algorithms also suffer in networks with node mobility. The latency burden of information making two full traversals of the network in addition to the processing time can easily render the computed locations irrelevant by the time they are received by the nodes.

2.3 Available Data

Algorithms can also be categorised according to what information is available to the nodes. The baseline is usually connectivity (the set of neighbours that a node can contact directly), but nodes may also have distance information about their neighbours, gained through received signal strength information (RSSI) [15][16] or ultrasonic time-of-flight [17].

Using RSSI as a very rough *indicator* of distance is easy to implement and can help refine location estimates and resolve ambiguities. However, it has been shown [18][19] that RSSI is a poor *measure* of distance in the general case, and can vary dramatically with apparently subtle environmental factors that are extremely difficult for nodes to account for.

Using ultrasonics and measuring the time-difference of arrival of a sonic and radio signal can give much greater accuracy when computing inter-node distances. However, ultrasonic systems suffer from relatively high power consumption and physical bulk. Ultrasonic transceivers also suffer from issues of interference, low data rates and interference, reducing their utility in high-density networks [20].

Akella et al.[21] propose an algorithm that uses direction information in addition to range measurement. Direction information can be gathered in a robust fashion by using a free-space optical (FSO) communication system. This system comprises a number of optical transceivers, essentially a light-emitting diode (LED) paired with a light sensor, such that a node can transmit a signal in a particular known direction, and receive signals coming from that direction. The transceivers are arrayed on the node to provide communication capability in any direction.

This system gives the nodes the ability to determine the relative direction to a neighbouring node based on which light sensor received the neighbour's signal. If the neighbour details which transceiver is being used to transmit the received signal, a node is able to compute that neighbour's orientation relative to itself.

The algorithm combines the computed orientation with the range measurement in order to compute the neighbour's relative location. If the node knows its own location, this relative location estimate for the neighbour can be converted to an absolute estimate by simple vector addition, and communicated to the neighbouring node. This neighbouring node is then able to compute absolute location estimates for its neighbours, and so on. In this way, the number of nodes that know their own location can grow from a single elected origin node to encompass the entire network.

The primary problem with this approach is that each relative location estimate has an error factor determined by the fidelity of the FSO communication system. A system with many individual transceivers is able to estimate the direction and orientation of neighbouring nodes with greater accuracy than that with fewer transceivers. As each node's location estimate is based on the location estimate of a single node that is one hop closer to the origin node, the location errors compound as the hop count from the origin node increases. This accumulation of location error severely limits the utility of the algorithm in large networks.

3 Algorithm Description

The algorithm proposed in this paper, dubbed the Sectoring algorithm, requires a similar level of node capability as the FSO algorithm due to Akella et al.[21], namely, the ability to sense the direction of neighbouring nodes. Note that the inter-node ranging ability assumed by the FSO algorithm is not required for the Sectoring algorithm.

The direction sensing capability can be implemented in a robust fashion with the use of optical communications. A node equipped with an array of LED transmitters and a corresponding array of light sensors can make directed transmissions and detect the direction of incoming transmissions. The fidelity of a sensed direction is based purely on the number of transceivers that a node is equipped with: i.e. a node with 8 transceivers can transmit and sense in 8 different directions. Such optical communications systems have been used previously to aid in robot swarm organisation [22].

The fundamental premise of the algorithm is to exploit the direction constraints implied upon a node by its neighbours' communications. A node that knows its location restricts the locations of those neighbours that receive its transmission to lie within the area of effect of that transmission. In contrast to radio communication, the extent of an optical transmission is easy to control with the physical design of the node. Baffles around the LED and light sensor can limit their effect to a known segment of the area around the node. In addition, the area of effect can be easily approximated as a circle segment. The individual constraint on a node's location implied by a single neighbour may not be enough to compute a sufficiently accurate location estimate, but the combination of many constraints implied by many neighbours is likely to increase the accuracy of the location estimate.

The algorithm operates as a feedback loop: each node gathers information about its immediate neighbours' locations and orientations, uses this information to compute a location estimate, and then shares this estimate with its neighbours, thus contributing to their own location estimates. The algorithm does not require any infrastructure external to the network or anchor nodes that have perfect knowledge of their location, and so the resulting coordinate system is consistent internally to the network but will differ by an affine transform to the positions of the nodes as measured by some external observer.

Each node in the network must agree on a common point to use as the origin of the coordinate system. This is achieved by calculating the coordinate system relative to the node with the lowest ID number. The algorithm operates by having every node make periodic transmissions from each of its optical transceivers. Each transmission details:

- The ID of the transmitting node
- The origin ID that the transmitting node is located with respect to
- The computed location of the transmitting node
- The predicted direction of the transmission. This is obtained by adding the orientation of the transceiver onto the computed orientation of the node.

Each node will store the details of recently received transmissions, in addition to the angle of the optical receiver that the transmission was detected on. Each node also keeps track of the lowest origin ID yet encountered. When a transmission is received, the origin ID contained therein is examined to determine the data's validity:

- If the received origin ID is greater than that held, then the transmission is ignored
- If the received origin ID is lower than that held, then all stored data is discarded and the stored origin ID is updated to the new lower value
- If the received origin ID is the same as that held, then the stored data is updated with the received details as normal

This procedure allows the network to converge on using a single reference point for the coordinate system. It is important to note that the node with the lowest ID has no special responsibilities as the origin, and participates in the algorithm as any other node does. All that is required is that the network agree on a common reference point around which to build a coordinate system, and it is of no consequence to the algorithm if the origin node subsequently expires.

At the outset of the algorithm, every node considers itself to be the origin of the coordinate system, i.e.: its location estimate is (0,0), its computed orientation is 0 degrees, and the origin ID field is set to its own ID. In order to predict the area of effect of a transmission, each node must be able to estimate its own location and orientation relative to the rest of the network.

3.1 Orientation Estimation

Nodes can calculate their orientation relative to each neighbour by examining the direction of incoming transmissions and the orientation of the transceivers that they were detected on. As illustrated in Figure 1, node A calculates the direction of its transmission t by adding the orientation of the transceiver to its own orientation estimate a. Node B detects the transmission on the transceiver that has relative orientation r, and can the calculate its own orientation b as $180\text{-}r\text{+}t$ degrees. Each neighbour can imply a different orientation for a node, and so the average of each implied orientation is used to predict transmission directions. This averaging allows the nodes to estimate their orientation with greater accuracy than the fidelity of their FSO system would suggest.

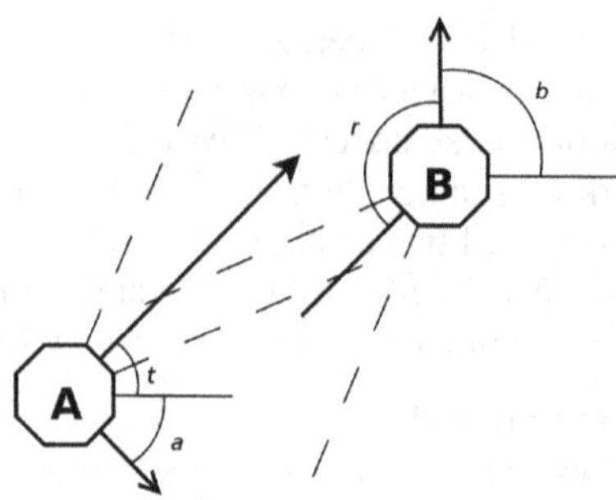

Fig. 1. Calculating relative orientation

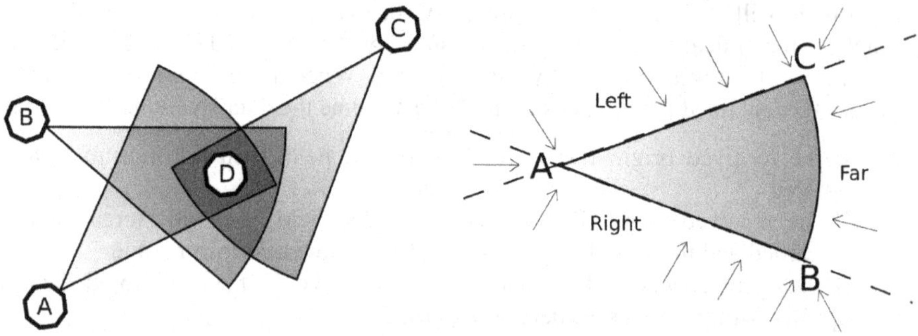

Fig. 2. Location estimate constraints and constraint compliance procedure

3.2 Location Estimation

In order to compute a location estimate, each node examines the stored transmission records and constructs a set of circle segments using the received transmission direction information and location estimate taken with knowledge of the divergence angle of the FSO transceivers. The node then calculates a point that lies in the intersection of the circle segments as the location estimate, as illustrated on the left of Figure 2, where node *D* computes a location that lies within the transmissions of nodes *A*, *B* and *C*.

The location estimate is made using an iterative approach. Each circle segment constraint *C* implied by the transmission from a neighbour is compared with the current location estimate *E*. If a node has no existing estimate *E*, it simply takes the centroid of *C* as an initial guess that is then refined. If *E* lies outwith *C*, then the minimum alteration vector *V* is calculated such that *E*+*V* lies within *C*. Alteration vectors are calculated for every neighbours' circle segment constraint, and the average of these vectors is applied to the location estimate.

The procedure to calculate *V* is simple, given the vertices *A*, *B* and *C* of the circle segment. If the current location estimate *E* lies to the right of the line passing through *A* and *B*, then *V* is calculated as the shortest vector between *E* and the line segment *AB*. *V* is calculated similarly if *E* lies to the left of *AC*. If *E* lies to the left of *AB* and to the right of *AC*, the distance between *E* and *A* is calculated and compared with the assumed transmission range. If E lies outwith the transmission range, then V is calculated as the minimum vector to satisfy the constraint, i.e.: that moves E directly towards A. The right-hand side of Figure 2 illustrates these tests.

In addition to the rigid constraint that a node's location estimate must lie within the circle segments implied by its neighbours' transmissions, a further elastic constraint is applied to reflect the fact that a node is more likely to lie further from a neighbour, where the circle segment is wider. This is achieved by applying a repulsive force to each node's location estimate in the direction of each neighbour's transmission. The repulsive force is scaled such that it is stronger when two nodes' estimated locations are closer together, and conversely much weaker when the nodes are more distant.

3.3 Summary

The Sectoring algorithm uses a modest level of storage capacity (2 node IDs and 3 numbers with low precision requirements – it was found that using more than 8 bits per number gave negligible performance improvements) per neighbour, and a modest amount of computation (ranging from 18 arithmetic and 2 trigonometric to 24 arithmetic and 4 trigonometric operations) per neighbour in order to compute or refine a location estimate. The sensory requirements for operation are straightforward to implement and robust in the face of environmental effects such as electromagnetic interference and background noise. There is a requirement, however, for deployed nodes to have line-of-sight contact with immediate neighbours.

While the Sectoring algorithm uses a similar level of hardware capability to the algorithm due to Akella et al., it distinguishes itself by exploiting information from multiple sources. In the case of Akella's algorithm each node is only located with respect to one of its neighbours. This reliance on a single source of information leads to the accumulating error that severely limits the scalability of the approach.

When using the Sectoring algorithm, nodes locate themselves with respect to their entire neighbourhood. This fusion of multiple sources of location information, and the feedback process of continually sharing location information with neighbours in order to refine location estimates, eliminates error accumulation and allows the localisation of even very large networks.

4 Algorithm Assessment

4.1 Simulation Parameters

Simulations were performed using the SpeckSim simulator to determine the performance of the algorithm. The baseline scenario is 100 nodes distributed randomly over a unit square. Each node is equipped with 8 optical transceivers arrayed to give complete and non-overlapping coverage around the node. Each transceiver has a transmission range of 0.2 units. Each node attempts to transmit once every second. The primary metric shown is the location error: this is simply the distance between a node's computed and physical locations, disregrading a network-wide skew transformation. All simulations were repeated 100 times with different network layouts and communication timing, and the results averaged. Error bars where present indicate the standard deviation of that metric over the repetitions of the simulations.

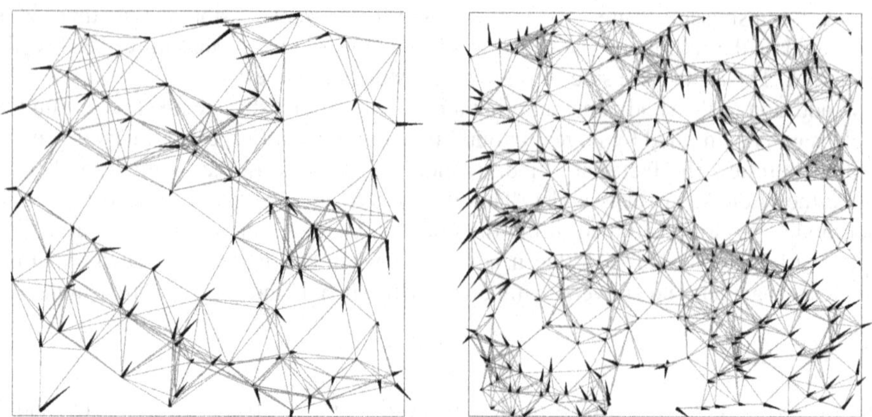

Fig. 3. Location estimate error

4.2 Results

Perhaps the easiest way to illustrate the performance of the algorithm is with a diagram of the output. Figure 3 shows the error between each node's actual and computed position, disregarding any network wide skew, after the network has reached a settled state. The light lines denote network links.

The network on the left is comprised of 100 nodes with a communications range of 0.2 units, while the network on the right is double the magnitude, with 400 nodes each with a communication range of 0.1 units. These images demonstrate that location error does not increase with the number of hops to the origin node as in Akella's approach. A feature of note is that neighbouring errors tend to have similar magnitudes and directions, indicating that nodes have located themselves with respect to their immediate neighbours with a high degree of accuracy, but that errors creep in between clusters of tightly-connected nodes.

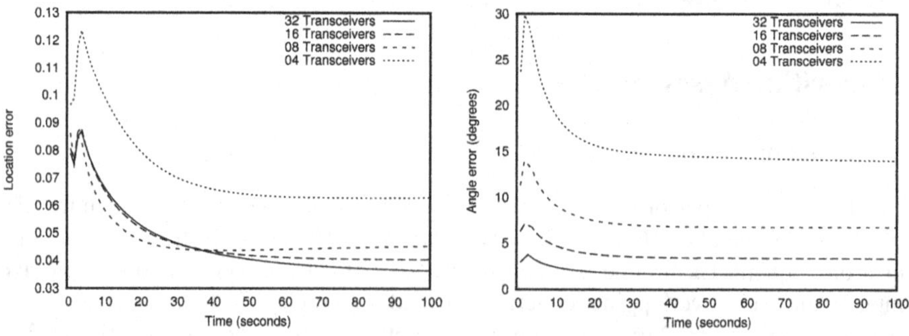

Fig. 4. Location error and angle error over time

One of the most important factors for the accuracy of the location estimates is the fidelity of the FSO system. The first graph in Figure 4 charts the magnitude of location error over time, and shows the effect of varying the number of transceivers that each node is equipped with. As can be seen, nodes are able to locate themselves to within 35% of their communication range while having the ability to sense that their neighbours are in one of only four possible directions. Although not shown on the graph for reasons of clarity, the standard deviation of the location error metric for networks of nodes with 8 or more transceivers remains steady at around 0.012 units.

The second graph shows the benefits of combining several sources of angle information. For instance, nodes with only 4 transceivers are only able to sense their orientation to within 45 degrees based on a single source, but can achieve an average accuracy of 15 degrees by combining readings from many neighbours. The second graph also demonstrates the dependence of location error on angle error, with both graphs showing a rise in error as the network converges on using the same seed node, and then a gradual decrease as the system of constraints approaches a globally-satisfied state. As expected, increasing the number of transceivers leads to lower location and angle errors.

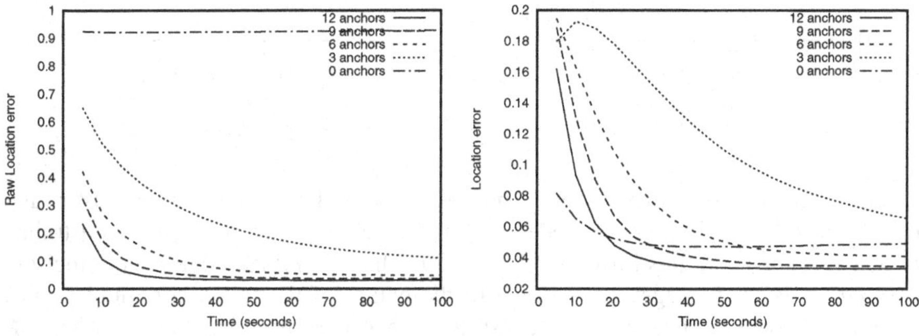

Fig. 5. Effects of location anchor nodes

Unlike many localisation algorithms, the Sectoring algorithm does not require anchor nodes in order to compute a consistent location map for the entire network. The algorithm will, however, seamlessly integrate the information from any anchor nodes that may be present such that the location map for the entire network converges on the physical truth of the network deployment. The algorithm operates exactly as before, with the caveat that the anchor nodes turn their receiving hardware off - their location estimate is not based on that of their neighbours. The graph on the left of Figure 5 shows the raw error in the location estimates - simply the average distance between a node's computed and actual locations. The network with no anchor nodes present is steady at a high level of raw error, reflecting the error due to the network-wide skew between computed location map and physical truth, but networks with anchor nodes converge on having a raw error level similar to the corrected error levels shown in Figure 4. The graph on the right of Figure 5 shows the corrected error metric over the same networks, and demonstrates how the presence of the anchor nodes leads to an initially high corrected error metric that falls with time as nodes converge on knowing their true physical locations and the corrective transform approaches the identity matrix.

It is unlikely that a network will be deployed in an ideal environment, or that large-scale device manufacture is flawless, and so it is important to explore algorithm behaviour under adverse conditions. The left-hand graph in Figure 6 shows the effects of introducing randomly-placed 0.1 unit long walls into the deployment area that block transmissions. The right-hand graph charts location error under various levels of imperfect manufacture. For example, when the "transceiver defect rate" is 0.2, there is a 20% chance that a given transceiver on a node is non-operative, and can neither transmit nor receive data.

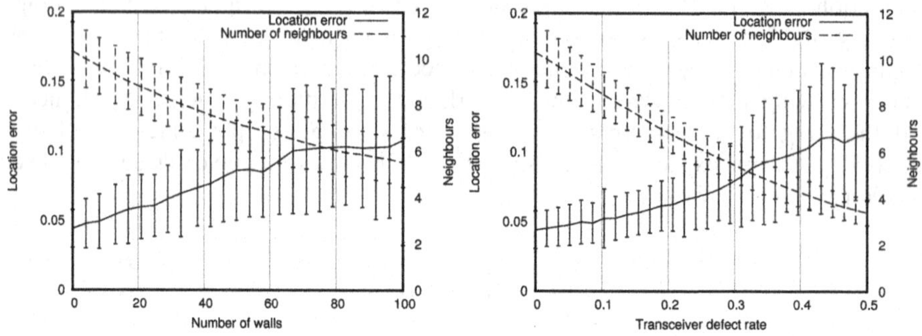

Fig. 6. Effects of opaque walls and transceiver defects

These graphs both demonstrate the relationship between location error and neighbourhood size: in general, nodes with more neighbours have tighter constraints on their locations and thus lower levels of error. That this relationship is not precisely mirrored between these graphs is down to the nature of the failed communications. Given three nodes A, B and C, the constraints on A's location are tightest when AB and AC are orthogonal. If A is situated next to a wall, there is 50% less chance of this orthogonal arrangement occurring than if A were situated in open space. In contrast, nodes that have faulty transceivers are still able, on average, to communicate in all directions, and so the optimal orthogonal arrangement can still occur.

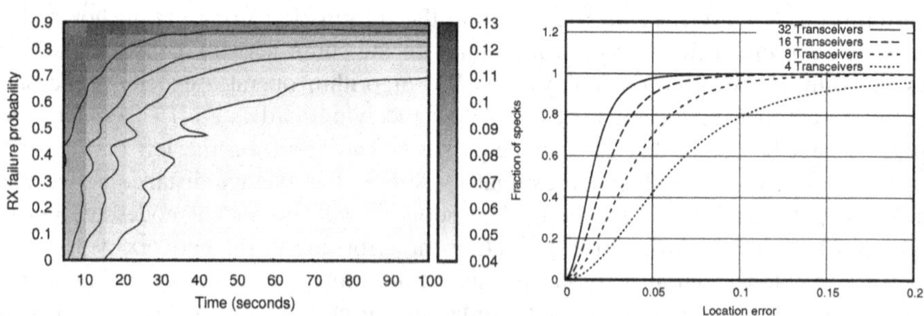

Fig. 7. Effects of noisy channel | Location error distribution

The graph on the left-hand side of Figure 7 explores the effects of a failure-prone communications channel. For instance, when "RX failure probability is 0.5, there is a 50% chance that the reception of a particular broadcast will fail, and the receiving speck will not get the transmitted data. The shading of the graph gives an indication of location error at that particular level of channel failure and simulation time, with darker shades indicating larger errors. The contour line plots are placed at location error levels of 0.05, 0.06, 0.07 and 0.09 units in order to clarify the shading. As can be seen, increasing levels of channel unreliability only serve to delay a network's attainment of a low error rate, rather than preclude it. As expected, as the chance of a reception failure approaches 100%, the delay in the network attaining a settled state grows dramatically.

The graph on the right-hand side of Figure 7 shows the cumulative distribution function of location error in 1000 random network layouts of 100 nodes each. From this we can assert that for a randomly deployed network of nodes equipped with 8 transceivers each, there is a 70% chance that a given node will compute its location to within 0.05 units, or 25% of its own communication range. Indeed, even nodes with only 4 transceivers are able to locate themselves to within 50% of their own communication range with a probability of 80%.

5 Conclusion

We have described a novel algorithm that calculates location information to a high degree of accuracy, is simple to implement, and that requires minimal bandwidth, computation and storage. In addition to performing location discovery, the algorithm's requirements are slight enough that it can be run continually in order to maintain each node's computed location in the face of movement.

The algorithm is entirely distributed, and thus reliable in the face of node failures, and runs on a homogeneous network. In addition, anchor nodes that know their own location can be introduced into the network, which will seamlessly integrate the higher-grade location information and so reduce errors.

Algorithm performance has been shown to scale gracefully in the face of adverse conditions such as grievous node manufacturing defect rates and communication channel faults, both persistent and intermittent.

In network deployments where node complexity and cost is limited, acceptable performance can be obtained with even a minimal number of optical transceivers. This characteristic highlights the value and utility of direction information in network localisation.

Although not addressed in this paper, the performance of the algorithm could be improved, especially in sparse networks, by taking range information into account. Unlike radio communications, the energy of an optical transmission reduces in a predictable manner with increasing distance. In addition, the emission pattern of LEDs is very simple to characterise. This allows nodes to make accurate estimations of inter-node distances based on the received power of a transmission. The range information would further limit the range of possible locations for a node, and thus reduce location error.

References

[1] Karp, B., Kung, H.T.: GPSR: greedy perimeter stateless routing for wireless networks. In: Mobile Computing and Networking, pp. 243–254 (2000)

[2] Römer, K.: The lighthouse location system for smart dust. In: Proceedings of MobiSys 2003 (ACM/USENIX Conference on Mobile Systems, Applications, and Services), San Francisco, CA, USA, May 2003, pp. 15–30 (2003)

[3] Zhang, J., Yan, T., Stankovi, J., Son, S.: Thunder: Towards Practical, Zero Cost Acoustic Localization for Outdoor Wireless Sensor Networks. ACM SIGMOBILE Mobile Computing and Communications Review 11(1), 15–28 (2007)

[4] Wang, L., Zeadally, S.: Landscape: a high performance distributed positioning scheme for outdoor sensor networks. In: Wireless And Mobile Computing, Networking And Communications, 2005 (WiMob 2005), IEEE International Conference on 3 (2005)

[5] Stoleru, R., Vicaire, P., He, T., Stankovic, J.A.: Stardust: a flexible architecture for passive localization in wireless sensor networks. In: SenSys 2006: Proceedings of the 4th international conference on Embedded networked sensor systems, pp. 57–70. ACM, New York (2006)

[6] Sichitiu, M., Ramadurai, V.: Localization of wireless sensor networks with a mobile beacon. In: 2004 IEEE International Conference on Mobile Ad-hoc and Sensor Systems, pp. 174–183 (2004)

[7] Pathirana, P., Bulusu, N., Savkin, A., Jha, S.: Node localization using mobile robots in delay-tolerant sensor networks. IEEE Transactions on Mobile Computing 4(3), 285–296 (2005)

[8] Niculescu, D., Nath, B.: Ad hoc positioning system (APS). Globecom-New York 5, 2926–2931 (2001)

[9] Nagpal, R., Shrobe, H., Bachrach, J.: Organizing a global coordinate system from local information on an ad hoc sensor network. In: Zhao, F., Guibas, L.J. (eds.) IPSN 2003. LNCS, vol. 2634, pp. 333–348. Springer, Heidelberg (2003)

[10] Bulusu, N., Heidemann, J., Estrin, D.: Gps-less low cost outdoor localization for very small devices. IEEE Personal Communications Magazine 7(5), 28–34 (2000)

[11] He, T., Huang, C., Blum, B., Stankovic, J., Abdelzaher, T.: Range-free localization schemes in large scale sensor networks (2003)

[12] Doherty, L., Pister, K.S.J., Convex, L.E.G.: position estimation in wireless sensor networks. In: Proc. of the IEEE Infocom, pp. 1655–1663 (2001)

[13] Shang, Y., Ruml, W., Zhang, Y., Fromherz, M.: Localization from Mere Connectivity. In: Proceedings of the 4th ACM international symposium on Mobile ad hoc networking & computing, pp. 201–212. ACM, New York (2003)

[14] Moses, R., Krishnamurthy, D., Patterson, R.: A Self-Localization Method for Wireless Sensor Networks. EURASIP Journal on Applied Signal Processing 2003(4), 348–358 (2003)

[15] Moore, D., Leonard, J., Rus, D., Teller, S.: Robust Distributed Network Localization with Noisy Range Measurements. In: Proceedings of the 2nd international conference on Embedded networked sensor systems, pp. 50–61. ACM, New York (2004)

[16] Ma, J., Gao, M., Zhu, Y., Ni, L.: Anchor-free Localization with Refinement in Sensor Networks (submitted for publication) (July 2004)

[17] Priyantha, N.B., Chakraborty, A., Balakrishnan, H.: The Cricket Location-support System. In: MobiCom 2000: Proceedings of the 6th annual international conference on Mobile computing and networking, pp. 32–43. ACM Press, New York (2000)

[18] Elnahrawy, E., Li, X., Martin, R.: The limits of localization using signal strength: a comparative study. In: 2004 First Annual IEEE Communications Society Conference on Sensor and Ad Hoc Communications and Networks. IEEE SECON 2004, pp. 406–414 (2004)

[19] Whitehouse, K., Karlof, C., Culler, D.: A practical evaluation of radio signal strength for ranging-based localization. ACM SIGMOBILE Mobile Computing and Communications Review 11(1), 41–52 (2007)

[20] Hazas, M., Hopper, A.: Broadband ultrasonic location systems for improved indoor positioning. IEEE Transactions on Mobile Computing 5(5), 536–547 (2006)
[21] Akella, J., Yuksel, M., Kalyanaraman, S.: A Relative Ad hoc Localization Scheme using Optical Wireless. In: 2nd International Conference on Communication Systems Software and Middleware. COMSWARE 2007, pp. 1–8 (2007)
[22] Kelly, I., Martinoli, A.: A scalable, on-board localisation and communication system for indoor multi-robot experiments. Journal of Sensor Review 24(2), 167–180 (2004)
[23] Arvind, D.: Speckled computing. In: Technical Proceedings of the 2005 NSTI Nanotechnology Conference (May 2005)

Providing Source-Location Privacy in Wireless Sensor Networks

Yun Li and Jian Ren

Department of Electrical and Computer Engineering,
Michigan State University,
East Landing, MI 48864-1226, USA
{liyun1,renjian}@egr.msu.edu

Abstract. Wireless sensor networks (WSN) have been widely used in many areas for unattended event monitoring. Mainly due to lack of a protected physical boundary, wireless communications are vulnerable to unauthorized detection, interception and and even node capture. Privacy is becoming one of the major issues that jeopardize the successful deployment and survivability of wireless sensor networks. While confidentiality of the message can be ensured through content encryption, it is much more difficult to adequately address the source-location privacy. For WSN, source-location privacy service is further complicated by the fact that the sensor nodes consist of low-cost and low-power radio devices, computationally intensive cryptographic algorithms (such as public-key cryptosystems) and large scale broadcasting-based protocols are not suitable for WSN. In this paper, we propose a two-step routing strategy for the messages to be routed from the actual source node to the SINK node through either a single, or multiple, randomly selected intermediate node(s) away from the source node so that it is to make it infeasible for the adversaries to trace back to the source node through hop-by-hop routing analysis. In the first protocol, the messages will be routed to a single intermediate node. This scheme can provide very good local source-location privacy. We also propose routing through multiple randomly selected intermediate nodes based on angle and quadrant to further improve the performance and security. While providing source-location privacy for WSN, our simulation results demonstrate that the proposed schemes are very efficient in energy consumption, and transmission latency. The proposed schemes can also assurance high message delivery ratio. Therefore, they can be used for many practical applications.

1 Introduction

Wireless sensor networks have been envisioned as a technology that has a great potential to be widely used in both military and civilian applications. Sensor networks rely on wireless communications, which is by nature a broadcast medium that is more vulnerable to security attacks than its wired counterpart due to lack of a physical boundary. In the wireless sensor domain, anybody with an appropriate wireless receiver can monitor and intercept the sensor network communications. The adversaries may use expensive radio transceivers and powerful

B. Liu et al. (Eds.): WASA 2009, LNCS 5682, pp. 338–347, 2009.

workstations to interact with the network from a distance since they are not restricted to using sensor network hardware. It is possible for the adversaries to identify the message source or even identify the source location, even if strong data encryption is utilized.

Location privacy is an important security issue. Lack of location privacy can expose significant information about the traffic carried on the network and the physical world entities. While confidentiality of the message can be ensured through content encryption, it is much more difficult to adequately address the source-location privacy. Privacy service in WSN is further complicated since the sensor nodes consist of only low-cost and low-power radio devices and are designed to operate unattended for long periods of time. Battery recharging or replacement may be infeasible or impossible. Therefore, computationally intensive cryptographic algorithms, such as public-key cryptosystems, and large scale broadcasting-based protocols, are not suitable for WSN. This makes privacy preserving communications in WSN an extremely challenging research task. To optimize the sensor nodes for the limited capabilities and the application specific nature of the networks, traditionally, security requirements were largely ignored. This leaves the WSN vulnerable to security attacks. In the worst case, the adversaries may be able to undetectably take control of some sensor nodes, compromise the cryptographic keys and reprogram the sensor nodes.

In this paper, we propose to provide source-location privacy through a two-phase routing process. In the first routing phase, the message source randomly selects an intermediate node, or multiple intermediate nodes, in the sensor domain and then transmits the message to the randomly selected intermediate node(s) before it is transmitted to the SINK node. For single intermediate node case, the intermediate node is expected to be far away from the source node in the sensor domain. This scheme can provide very good local source-location privacy. To further improve the performance and security, we propose angle-based and quadrant-based multiple intermediate nodes selection schemes in this paper. These two schemes can offer network-level (global) source-location privacy for WSN. Our simulation results also demonstrate that the proposed schemes are very efficient and can be used for many practical applications.

2 Related Works

In the past two decades, originated largely from Chaum's mixnet [1] and DC-net [2], a number of source-location private communication protocols have been proposed [3,4,5,6,7,8,9,10,11,12,13,14,15]. The mixnet family protocols use a set of "mix" servers that mix the received packets to make the communication source ambiguous. The DCnet family protocols [2,6,5] utilize secure multiparty computation techniques. However, both approaches require public-key cryptosystems and are not quite suitable for WSN.

Multiple schemes were proposed to provide destination location privacy. In [9, 10] base station location privacy based on multi-path routing and fake messages injection was proposed. In this scheme, every node in the network has to transmit messages at a constant rate. Another base station location privacy scheme was introduced in [16], which involves location privacy routing and fake message injection. In this paper, we will address the source location privacy in wireless sensor networks.

In [11,12], source location privacy is provided through broadcasting that mixes valid messages with dummy messages. The main idea is that each node needs to transmit messages consistently. Whenever there is no valid message, the node has to transmit dummy messages. The transmission of dummy messages not only consumes significant amount of sensor energy, but also increases the network collisions and decreases the packet delivery ratio. Therefore, these schemes are not quite suitable for large scale sensor networks.

Routing based protocols can also provide source-location privacy through dynamic routing so that it is infeasible for the adversaries to trace back to the source-location through traffic monitoring and analysis. The main idea is to, first, route the message to a node away from the actual message source randomly, then forward the message to the SINK node using single path routing. However, both theoretical and practical results demonstrate that if the message is routed randomly for h hops, then the message will be largely within $h/5$ hops away from the actual source, see Fig. 1. To solve this problem, several approaches have been proposed. In phantom routing protocol [13,14] the message from the actual source will be routed to a phantom source along a designed directed walk through either sector-based approach or hop-based approach. Take the section-based directed walk as an example, the source node first randomly determines a direction that the message will be sent to. The direction information is stored in the header of the message. Then every forwarder on the random walk path will forward this message to a random neighbor in the same direction determined by the source node. In this way, the phantom source can be away from the actual source. Unfortunately, once the message is captured on the random walk path, the adversaries will be able to get the direction information stored in the header of the message. Therefore, the exposure of direction information decreases the complexity for adversaries to trace back to the actual message source in the magnitude of 2^h. Random walk from both the source node and the SINK node was also proposed in [15]. In this scheme, Bloom Filter was proposed to store the information of all the visited nodes in the network for each message to prevent the messages from hopping back. However, this design allows the adversaries to recover significant routing information from the received messages. In fact, this design is "not realistic" for large scale sensor networks.

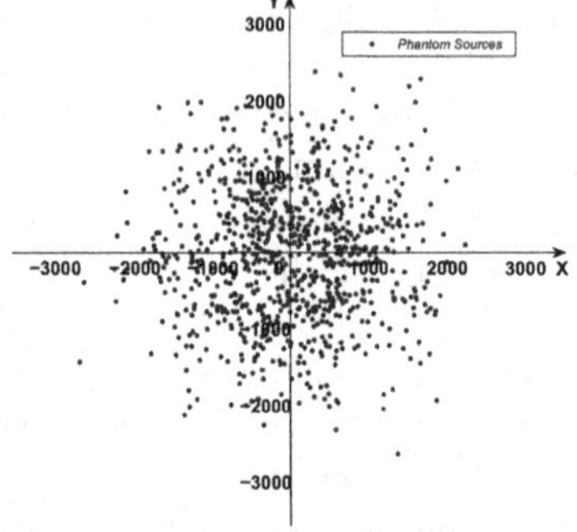

Fig. 1. Random routing: packets=1000, hops=50, routing range=250 meters, average distance=4.2 hops from source, longest distance=12.2 hops from source

3 Models and Design Goals

3.1 The System Model

We make the following assumptions about our system:

- The network is evenly divided into small grids. The sensor nodes in each grid are all fully connected. In each grid, there is one header node responsible for communicating with other header nodes nearby. The whole network is fully connected through multi-hop communications.
- The information of the SINK node is public. It is the destination location that all data messages will be transmitted to through a multi-hop routing path.
- The content of each message will be encrypted using the secret key shared between the node/grid and the SINK node. However, the encryption operation is beyond the scope of this paper.
- The sensor nodes are assumed to have the knowledge of the relative locations and their adjacent neighboring nodes. The information about the relative location of the sensor domain may also be achieved through network broadcasting [17, 18].

3.2 The Adversarial Model

We assume that there are some adversaries in the target area, who try to locate the source location through traffic analysis and tracing back. The adversaries have the following characteristics in this paper:

- The adversaries will have unbounded energy resource, adequate computation capability and sufficient memory for data storage. The adversaries may also compromise some sensor nodes in the network.
- The adversaries will not interfere with the proper functioning of the network, such as modifying packets, altering the routing path, or destroying sensor devices, since such activities can be easily identified. However, the adversaries may carry out passive attacks, such as eavesdropping of the communications.
- The adversaries are able to monitor the traffic in an area and get all of the transmitted messages. On detecting an event, they could determine the immediate sender by analyzing the strength and direction of the signal they received. However, we assume that the adversaries are unable to monitor the entire wireless sensor network.

4 Proposed Source-Location Privacy Scheme

In this section, we propose a source-location privacy scheme through randomly selected intermediate node(s).

4.1 Routing through Single-Intermediate Node

In this scheme, the message will be routed through a randomly selected intermediate node (RRIN) based on the relative location of the sensor node. The intermediate node is expected to be far away from the source node so that it is difficult for the adversaries to get the actual source location information.

Since we assume that each sensor node only has knowledge of its adjacent nodes. The source node may not have accurate information of the sensor nodes multiple hops away. In particular, the randomly selected intermediate node may not even exist. However, the relative location can guarantee that the message packet will be forwarded to the area of the intermediate node. The last node in the routing path adjacent to the intermediate node should be able to tell whether such a randomly selected intermediate node exists or not. In the case that such a node does not exist, this node will become the intermediate node. The intermediate node then routes the received message to the destination node.

Suppose the source node is located at the relative location (x_0, y_0), to transmit a data message, it first determines the minimum distance, d_{min}, that the intermediate node has to be away from the source node. We denote the distance between the source node and the randomly selected intermediate node as d_{rand}. Then we have $d_{rand} \geq d_{min}$.

Whenever the source node wants to generate a d_{rand}, it will first generate a random number x. The value of this random variable is normally distributed with mean 0 and variance σ^2, i.e., $X \sim N(0, \sigma)$. Then the source node can calculate d_{rand} as follows: $d_{rand} = d_{min} \times (|x| + 1)$.

Therefore, the probability [19] that d_{rand} is located in the interval $[d_{min}, \rho d_{min})$ is: $2\varphi_{0,\sigma^2}(\rho - 1) - 1 = 2\frac{1}{\sigma\sqrt{2\pi}}e^{-\frac{(\rho-1)^2}{2\sigma^2}} - 1 = 2\varphi\left(\frac{\rho-1}{\sigma}\right) - 1$, where $\rho > 1$, φ_{0,σ^2} is the Gaussian probability density function [20].

If we choose σ to be 1.0, then the probability that d_{rand} falls within the interval $[d_{min}, 2d_{min})$ will be $2\Phi(\frac{1}{1}) - 1 = 0.6827$. The probability that d_{rand} is in the interval $[d_{min}, 3d_{min})$ will be $2\Phi(\frac{2}{1}) - 1 = 0.9545$.

After d_{rand} is determined, the source node randomly generates an intermediate node located at (x_d, y_d) satisfies: $d_{rand} = \sqrt{(x_d - x_0)^2 + (y_d - y_0)^2} \geq d_{min}$.

Upon receiving data message, the intermediate node forwards the message to the SINK node. Unlike the directed walk proposed in phantom routing, in RRIN the selection of the intermediate node is totally random. Therefore, it does not have the security drawbacks of phantom routing discussed before.

However, the possibility for a node to be selected as an intermediate node is proportional to the distance between this sensor and the source node. Therefore, for large scale sensor networks, the intermediate nodes tend not to be too far away from the source node. In other words, the intermediate nodes are highly likely to concentrate in a circle area centered at the source node. So for large scale sensor networks, this scheme could only provide local location privacy.

In order to provide global location privacy over the sensor network, the selection of intermediate nodes have to be totally random, i.e., every sensor nodes in the networks has the same probability of being selected as the intermediate node for any source nodes.

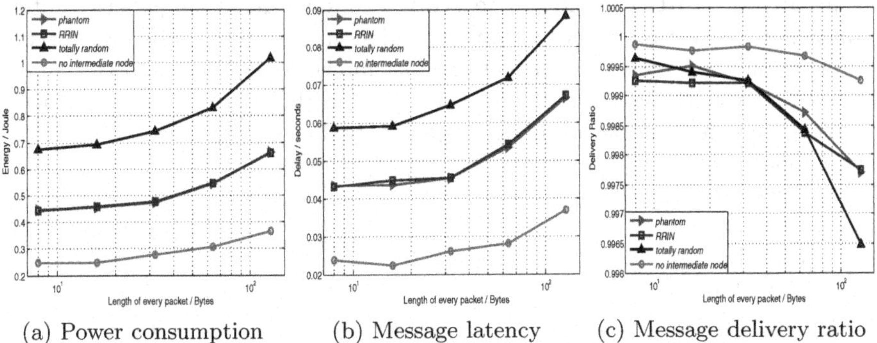

(a) Power consumption (b) Message latency (c) Message delivery ratio

Fig. 2. Performance of routing by single-intermediate node

We compared the performance of our proposed schemes and the phantom routing through simulation using NS2 on Linux. In our simulation, 400 nodes are distributed randomly in a 3360×3360 meters area. The SINK node is located in the center of the area. For phantom routing, the average distance between the phantom source and the actual source is 506.12 meters after four routing hops, while for RRIN, the average distance between the intermediate node and the source is 529.14 meters.

We also compared power assumption, message latency and message delivery ratio of multiple routing schemes in Fig. 2. Direct message transmission without source privacy gives the best performance. Random selection of intermediate nodes has the worst performance. However, it provides the highest level of security. The performance of RRIN and phantom routing are comparable, while RRIN can provide better location privacy protection.

Random intermediate node selection without restriction may also have some limitations. First, the length of the routing path tends to be too long. As a result, this routing path consumes much more energy than our proposed scheme. Second, because the path is too long, the message drop rate may increase, which will reduce the message delivery ratio. Third, if a single path is too long, once a packet is captured by the adversaries in path, the adversaries may get the direction of the source-location according to the transmission direction of the captured packet.

4.2 Routing through Multi-intermediate Nodes

From the discussion in last section we can see that routing through single-intermediate node is more suitable for small scale sensor networks. In this section, we propose routing through multiple randomly selected intermediate nodes for large sensor networks.

The intermediate nodes are preselected before a message is sent out from the source node. The information of the intermediate nodes is stored in the header of the messages. However, no information of the former intermediate node(s) will be maintained in the header. In this section, we propose *angle-based* and *quadrant-based* intermediate nodes schemes.

Angle-Based Multi-intermediate Nodes Selection. In angle-based intermediate nodes selection, prior to data transmission, the source node needs to determine a maximum angle β between the last intermediate node and the source node. As shown in Fig. 3.(a), $S, I_1, \cdots, I_n, D$ are the source node, intermediate nodes and the destination node, respectively. Let the distance between the source node and the SINK node be d, the average distance between two adjacent intermediate nodes be r, then the angle generated for each hop transmission is at most: $\alpha = arcsin(\frac{r}{d})$. Therefore, the number of intermediate nodes needed for an angle β is at least: $n = \beta/\alpha$.

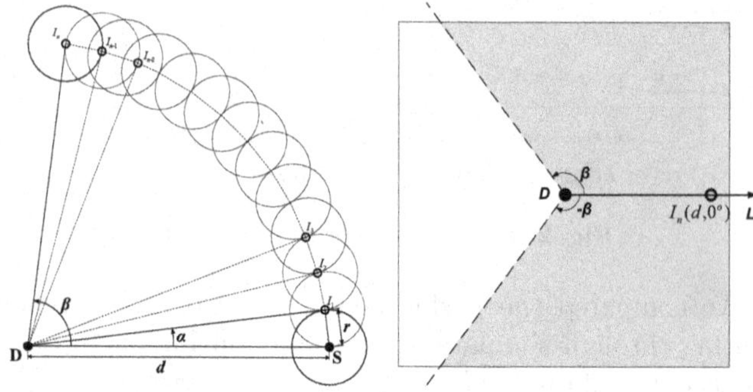

(a) Angle-based approach (b) Possible source location

Fig. 3. Angle-based intermediate nodes selection

After β is determined, the source node needs to choose an actual angle θ between the last intermediate node and itself according to the destination node D, where θ is a random variable evenly distributed in the range $(-\beta, \beta)$. Therefore, the last intermediate node I_n could be determined based on θ. Then the source node could select the other intermediate nodes $I_1, I_2, \cdots, I_{n-1}$ between S and I_n to generate all the intermediate nodes.

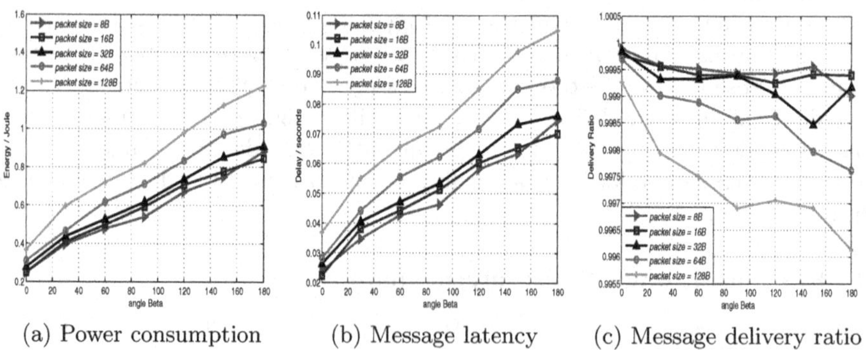

(a) Power consumption (b) Message latency (c) Message delivery ratio

Fig. 4. Performance of angle-based multi-intermediate nodes

Security Analysis. We will analyze that even if the adversaries are able to successfully identify the location of the last intermediate node I_n, the determination of the source location S is still very difficult according to our assumption, as shown in Fig. 3.(b), where D, I_n are the SINK node and the last intermediate node, respectively. In the case that the location of I_n is known, a polar coordinate system is built on the network with D located at the origin and I_n at $(d, 0°)$, where d is the distance from D to I_n. The possible location of S is in the shaded area shown in Fig. 3.(b), i.e, the radian measure range of $(-\beta, \beta)$, where β is a configurable parameter range from 0° to 180°. The larger β is, the higher level of location privacy we could achieve. Moreover, β can also be dynamic, in which case the adversaries are unable to determine the actual β, the possible location of the source node S can be anywhere in the whole domain.

Simulation Results. We carried out simulations to evaluate the performance of the angle-based multi-intermediate nodes scheme using NS2 on Linux system. In the simulation, the target area is a square field of size 3360 × 3360 meters. The SINK node is located at the center of the network area. The SINK node is also the destination for all packet transmissions. In this simulation, the curve with $\beta = 0$ means the messages are transmitted to the SINK node directly without relying on any intermediate nodes. Simulation results are provided in Fig. 4 to demonstrate the tradeoff relationship between performance and the angle β.

Quadrant-Based Multi-Intermediate Nodes Selection. In quadrant-based approach, for each source node, the whole network is divided into four quadrants according to its location and the SINK node's location.

First, the source node has to determine the formation of the quadrants. As shown in Fig. 5.(a), S, I, D are the source node, the last intermediate node and the destination nodes, respectively. The distance between S and D is d. A reference frame is built on this network for source node S. The SINK node D is located at the origin with coordinate $(0, 0)$, S's (x_S, y_S) location in *quadrant* 1 is: $x_S = d \times cos(\alpha)$, $y_S = d \times sin(\alpha)$, where α is a evenly distributed random variable located in the range of $(0°, 90°)$. From the reference frame, the source node S could select a random node located in *quadrant* 2 or *quadrant* 4, which is the shaded area in Fig. 5.(a), as the last intermediate node I. In this way, the possible angle between S and I according to D falls in the range $(0°, 180°)$. Even if the adversaries can determine the location of I, they still cannot get the information about the location of the source node. For

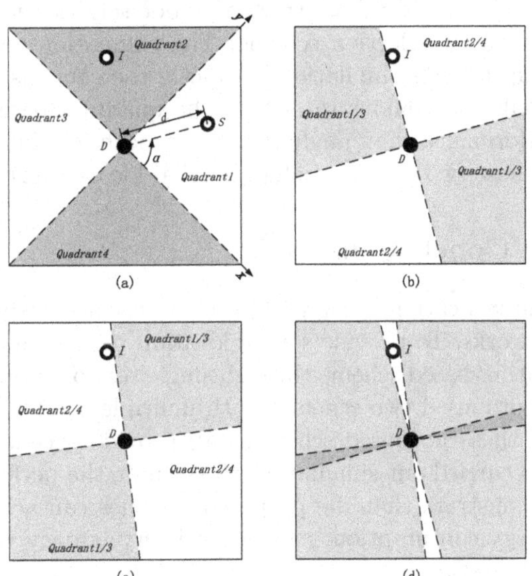

Fig. 5. Quadrant-based intermediate nodes selection

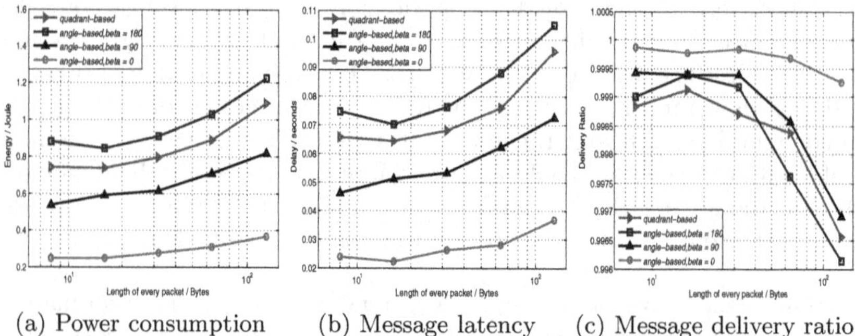

(a) Power consumption (b) Message latency (c) Message delivery ratio

Fig. 6. Performance of quadrant-based multi-intermediate nodes

example, in Fig. 5.(b)-(d), for the same I, the formation of the quadrants could be the one shown in Fig. 5.(b), or the one shown in Fig. 5.(c). In another word, the source node S can be located in the shaded area in Fig. 5.(b), or the shaded area in Fig. 5.(c). Therefore, the possible location area of the source node is the shaded area in Fig. 5.(d), which is almost the whole network area. In this way, global source location privacy is achieved.

Simulation Results. We also conducted simulations to compare the performance of quadrant-based intermediate node selection scheme and angle-based intermediate node selection scheme. The simulation results are shown in Fig. 6. The setup for this simulation is exactly the same as the angle-based approach. Our simulation demonstrates that the quadrant-based approach can provide better performance than angle-based approach for the case that $\beta = 180°$, while both of these two schemes achieve global location privacy.

5 Conclusions

Source location privacy is critical to the successful deployment of wireless sensor networks. To provide source location privacy, in this paper, we first proposed a routing-based scheme through single randomly selected intermediate node. Then we proposed two schemes with multiple randomly selected intermediate nodes. All these proposed schemes can provide excellent source location privacy. We also carried out simulations to evaluate the performance. The simulation results demonstrate that the proposed schemes can achieve very good performance in energy consumption, message delivery latency while assuring high message delivery ratio.

References

1. Chaum, D.: Untraceable electronic mail, return addresses, and digital pseudonyms. Communications of the ACM 24 (February 1981)
2. Chaum, D.: The dinning cryptographer problem: Unconditional sender and recipient untraceability. Journal of Cryptology 1(1), 65–75 (1988)

3. Ahn, L., Bortz, A., Hopper, N.: *k*-anonymous message transmission. In: Proceedings of the 10th ACM conference on Computer and Communications Security, Washington D.C., USA, pp. 122–130 (2003)
4. Beimel, A., Dolev, S.: Buses for anonymous message delivery. J. Cryptology 16, 25–39 (2003)
5. Golle, P., Juels, A.: Dining cryptographers revisited. In: Cachin, C., Camenisch, J.L. (eds.) EUROCRYPT 2004. LNCS, vol. 3027, pp. 456–473. Springer, Heidelberg (2004)
6. Goel, S., Robson, M., Polte, M., Sirer, E.G.: Herbivore: A Scalable and Efficient Protocol for Anonymous Communication. Tech. Rep. 2003-1890, Cornell University, Ithaca, NY (February 2003)
7. Reed, M., Syverson, P., Goldschlag, D.: Anonymous connections and onion routing. IEEE J. on Selected Areas in Coomunications, Special Issue on Copyrigh and Privacy Protection 16(4), 482–494 (1998)
8. Reiter, M.K., Rubin, A.D.: Crowds: anonymity for web transaction. ACM Transactions on Information and System Security 1(1), 66–92 (1998)
9. Deng, J., Han, R., Mishra, S.: Intrusion tolerance and anti-traffic analysis strategies for wireless sensor networks. In: Proceedings of the DSN, Washington, DC, USA, p. 637. IEEE Computer Society Press, Los Alamitos (2004)
10. Deng, J., Han, R., Mishra, S.: Countermeasures against traffic analysis attacks in wireless sensor networks. SecureComm., 113–126 (September 2005)
11. Yang, Y., Shao, M., Zhu, S., Urgaonkar, B., Cao, G.: Towards event source unobservability with minimum network traffic in sensor networks. In: Proceedings of the WiSec, pp. 77–88 (2008)
12. Shao, M., Yang, Y., Zhu, S., Cao, G.: Towards statistically strong source anonymity for sensor networks. IEEE INFOCOM, 51–55 (April 2008)
13. Kamat, P., Zhang, Y., Trappe, W., Ozturk, C.: Enhancing source-location privacy in sensor network routing. IEEE ICDCS, 599–608 (June 2005)
14. Ozturk, C., Zhang, Y., Trappe, W.: Source-location privacy in energy-constrained sensor network routing. In: SASN, pp. 88–93. ACM Press, New York (2004)
15. Xi, Y., Schwiebert, L., Shi, W.: Preserving source location privacy in monitoring-based wireless sensor networks. In: IEEE IPDPS (2006)
16. Jian, Y., Chen, S., Zhang, Z., Zhang, L.: A novel scheme for protecting receiver's location privacy in wireless sensor networks. IEEE Transactions on Wireless Communications 7, 3769–3779 (2008)
17. Zhang, Y., Liu, W., Fang, Y., Wu, D.: Secure localization and authentication in ultra-wideband sensor networks. IEEE Journal on Selected Areas in Communications 24, 829–835 (2006)
18. Cheng, X., Thaeler, A., Xue, G., Chen, D.: Tps: a time-based positioning scheme for outdoor wireless sensor networks. IEEE INFOCOM 4, 2685–2696 (2004)
19. Wikipedia, Normal distribution, `http://en.wikipedia.org/wiki/Normal_distribution`
20. Stigler, S.M.: Statistics on the Table, ch. 22. Harvard University Press

Fully Decentralized, Collaborative Multilateration Primitives for Uniquely Localizing WSNs*

Arda Cakiroglu[1] and Cesim Erten[2]

[1] Computer Science and Engineering,
Işık University, Sile 34980 Turkey
[2] Computer Engineering,
Kadir Has University, Istanbul 34083 Turkey

Abstract. We provide primitives for uniquely localizing WSN nodes. The goal is to maximize the number of uniquely localized nodes assuming a fully decentralized model of computation. Each node constructs a cluster of its own and applies unique localization primitives on it. These primitives are based on constructing a special order for multilaterating the nodes within the cluster. The proposed primitives are fully collaborative and thus the number of iterations required to compute the localization is fewer than that of the conventional iterative multilateration approaches. This further limits the messaging requirements. With relatively small clusters and iteration counts we can localize almost all the uniquely localizable nodes.

1 Introduction

Many applications and systems from areas such as environment and habitat monitoring, weather forecast, and health applications require use of many sensor nodes organized as a network collectively gathering useful data; see [1] for a survey. In such applications it is usually necessary to know the actual locations of the sensors. Sensor network localization is the problem of assigning geographic coordinates to each sensor node in a given network. Although Global Positioning System (*GPS*) can determine the geographic coordinates of an object, a GPS device has to have at least four line of sight communication lines between different satellites in order to locate itself. Thus, in cluttered space or indoor environments GPS may be ineffective. Additional disadvantages including the power consumption, cost, and size limitations allow only a small portion of nodes in a large scale sensor network have GPS capabilities. It is important to design methods that achieve localization with limited use of such systems. A common paradigm introduced to overcome this difficulty is the *iterative multilateration* where only a small portion of the nodes are assumed to be *anchor* nodes with a priori location information. Every node uses its ranging sensors to measure distances to the neighbors and shares the measurement and location information if available. Multilateration techniques are then employed in an iterative manner

* Partially supported by TUBITAK grant 106E071.

B. Liu et al. (Eds.): WASA 2009, LNCS 5682, pp. 348–357, 2009.

to collectively estimate node locations from such information [13]. Assuming no measurement errors, "unique" localization of a sensor node is achieved via trilateration from three anchor positions if distance to those anchors are known. Although this is a sufficient condition for uniqueness it is rarely necessary in wireless sensor networks settings. A finite number of possible locations for a set of neighbor nodes for which range information is available may also provide unique location for a sensor node. In this paper we propose primitives for unique localization of nodes in a sensor network. Assuming measurements with no noise, the goal is to maximize the number of uniquely localized nodes employing iterative multilateration. The proposed primitives are fully decentralized, fully collaborative. The suggested collaboration model gives rise to a high rate of unique localization. Moreover this is achieved with reasonably low energy requirements for message exchanges as the average number of iterations per node is low.

2 Related Work

We can classify the previous work based on where the computation takes place and the type of localization solution produced. Centralized methods assume the availability of global information about the network at a central computer where the computation takes place [7, 8, 11]. whereas in decentralized methods each node usually processes some local information gathered via a limited number of message exchanges [4, 17]. A second distinction between different methods is the localization output produced. In *unique localization* a single position is assigned to each node in the network [2]. Even though the topology of the underlying graph may not give rise to a unique localization, it may still be possible to assign a finite set of positions for each node, called *finite localization* [8]. There has been recent interest and theoretical results on uniquely localizing networks. However the suggested methods usually rely on centralized models [8]. To overcome this difficulty cluster-based approaches or collaborative multilateration have been suggested. Moore *et al.* propose the idea of localizing clusters where each cluster is constructed using two-hop ranging information [17]. Only trilateration is employed as the localization primitive which results in fewer nodes being uniquely localized as compared to the primitives we propose. Savvides *et al.* propose n-hop collaborative multilateration. The nodes organize into *collaborative subtrees*, then using simple geometric relationships each node constructs a position estimate and finally the estimate is refined using a least-squares method. The collaboration is on sharing distance and position information within n-hops but each node is still responsible for locating itself. With our model of full collaboration not only does a node receive information to compute its position but it may also receive information regarding its own location from neighboring nodes as well.

3 Unique Localization Primitives

Our unique network localization method relies on two low level primitives: Reliable internode distance measurement and internode communication mechanisms. Several techniques such as TDoA, RSSI, ToA may be used to obtain distance between two sensor nodes [10, 15]. The gathered distance information is assumed to be error-free. We also assume that the communication between sensor nodes is through broadcasting and that the broadcasted data is received by all neighboring nodes within the sensing range of the broadcaster.

The main unit of localization is a *cluster*. Each node u in the sensor network $\mathbb{N}$ goes through an initial setup phase constructing C_u^r, the $r-radius$ cluster centered at u. Let N_u denote the immediate neighborhood of node u. We assume that u has already gathered $d(u, v_i)$, distance to $v_i \in N_u$. With this information every u creates its own cluster C_u^1 where u is at the center, there is an edge (u, v_i) with weight $d(u, v_i)$ for every $v_i \in N_u$. At the second round of information exchange every node shares its cluster with all the nodes in its neighborhood. As a result each node u can construct C_u^2, and so on. After the final iteration of broadcasting/gathering of packets the cluster C_u^r is constructed with the collected data. With this construction C_u^1 is a *star* graph centered around u and C_u^2 is a *wheel* graph centered at u, together with the edges connecting to the wheel. We note that with this model a pair of clusters may share many nodes. Although this may seem like a waste, we show that these overlaps give rise to efficient collaboration in terms of unique localization. The collaboration is modelled via the iterative localization. At each iteration, each node constructs a new set of uniquely localized nodes in its cluster C_u^r using our proposed primitives, broadcasts this set to the neighbors, gathers analogous information and iterates the same process.

3.1 Bilaterations and Unique Localization

The network localization problem can be converted into that of *graph realization problem.* Let $\mathbb{G}(V, E)$ be the graph corresponding to a physical sensor network $\mathbb{N}$. Each vertex $v_i \in V = \{v_1, ..., v_m, v_{m+1}, ..., v_n\}$ corresponds to a specific physical sensor node i in $\mathbb{N}$. Vertices $v_1, ..., v_m$ are the nodes with known positions, called *anchors.* There exists an edge $(v_i, v_j) \in E$ if nodes i and j are within sensing range or both $i, j \leq m$. Each edge (v_i, v_j) where $v_i, v_j \in V$ and $i \neq j$ is associated with a real number which represents the Euclidean distance between the two nodes i, j. Formally, the graph realization problem is assigning coordinates to the vertices so that the Euclidean distance between any two adjacent vertices is equal to the real number associated with that edge [3, 9]. The graph realization problem has intrinsic connections with the graph rigidity theory. If we think of a graph in terms of bars and joints, a *rigid* graph means 'not deformable'or 'not flexible' [9]. Formally, the rigidity of a graph can be characterized by Laman's condition: A graph with n vertices and $2n-3$ edges is rigid if no subgraph with n' vertices contains more than $2n'-3$ edges [14]. Obviously if the graph is not rigid infinite number of realizations are possible through continuous deformations. However, even when the graph is rigid there may be ambiguities that give rise to more than one possible realization. In order to formalize these ambiguities the term *globally rigid* is introduced [6]. A graph is globally rigid if and only if it is *3-connected* and *redundantly rigid.* Global rigidity is a necessary and sufficient condition for unique realizations. We note that the discussions of rigidity and global rigidity apply to "generic" frameworks, i.e. those with algebraically independent vertex

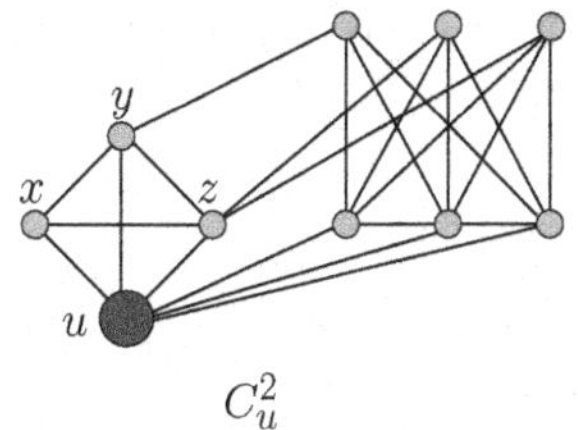

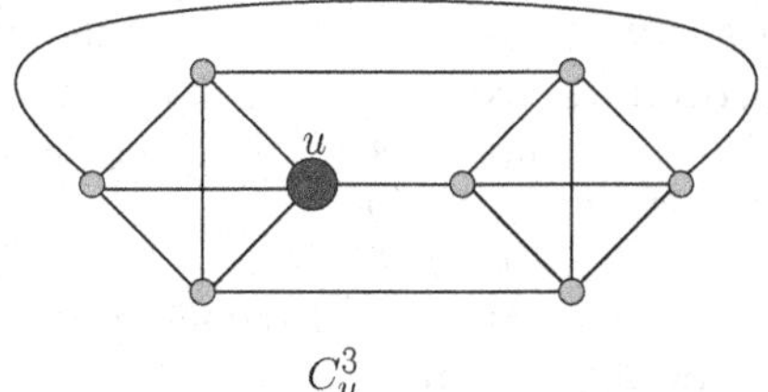

Fig. 1. *Left:* Order should be picked carefully for C_u^2. *Right:* No order exists for C_u^3.

coordinates over the rationals [2, 6]. As almost all point sets are generic and the generic global rigidity can be described solely in terms of combinatorial properties of the graph itself, in what follows the term globally rigid assumes the genericity of the frameworks.

It is NP-Hard to find a realization of $\mathbb{G}(V, E)$ even if $\mathbb{G}$ is globally rigid [5, 12]. However there exists an exceptional graph class called *trilateration graphs* that is uniquely localizable in polynomial time. A graph is a trilateration graph if it has a trilateration ordering $\pi = \{u_1, u_2, ..., u_n\}$ where u_1, u_2, u_3 forms a K_3 and each u_i has at least three neighbors that come before u_i in π. Although easily localizable, trilateration is a strong requirement for unique localization. C_u^2, for instance, contains a wheel graph centered at u. A wheel graph is uniquely localizable although it is not a trilateration graph. If the graph is not 3-connected, there exists a pair of vertices whose removal disconnects the graph. The graph can be flipped through the line passing through the disconnecting pair. Although flipping introduces nonunique realizations, the fact that finite possibilities arise as a result is the main motivation behind *bilateration graphs*. A graph is a bilateration graph if it has a bilateration ordering $\pi = \{u_1, u_2, ..., u_n\}$ where u_1, u_2, u_3 forms a K_3 and each u_i has at least two neighbors that come before u_i in π. For the localization application, fixing the initial K_3 allows one to neglect the global rotations and translations. Our main focus is on localizing bilateration graphs that arise within the defined cluster C_u^r. For $r = 1$ the constructed model is no different than the usual trilateration primitive. We provide useful remarks regarding bilateration graphs and the clusters, more specifically for small values of r, since for the sensor network settings those are of special interest.

Remark 1. (For $r = 2$) If C_u^r is globally rigid, then it is a bilateration graph. We defer the proof to the full paper. We note that even if C_u^r is globally rigid, not every ordering is a bilateration ordering. For instance C_u^2 in Figure 1 is globally rigid. Starting an ordering with any one of the four triangles formed between u, x, y, z bilateration does not contain C_u^2 completely. However starting an ordering with any other triangle in the cluster provides a complete bilateration of C_u^2.

Remark 2. (For $r = 3$) There exist globally rigid clusters which are not bilateration graphs. C_u^3 in Figure 1 is globally rigid and therefore uniquely localizable, but it is not a bilateration graph.

Algorithm 1. Iterated at u each time new anchors in A_u are received from N_u

procedure UNIQUELOCALIZATION(A_u)
  Let L indicate the set of finitely localized nodes.
  for all $a \in A_u$ **do**
    UPDATE(L, a)
  $\pi \leftarrow$ FINDBILATERATIONORDER
  for all $v \in \pi$ **do**
    MULTILATERATE(v, $N_\pi(v)$),
    where $N_\pi(v)$ are neighbors of v that are to the left of it in π
  Broadcast new anchors in C_u^r to N_u

3.2 Unique Localization within Iterative Collaboration

The goal is to finitely localize as many nodes as possible and share the resulting unique node positions with the neighbors. The main localization method is iterative. Each node u executes the localization method on its own cluster. If u creates the unique positions of some new nodes within C_u^r, then it shares this information with the neighbors, some of which may have overlapping clusters with C_u^r. Those neighbors may benefit this exchange if the shared nodes are part of a globally rigid component within their clusters. This procedure continues iteratively until no node creates any new unique positions and gathers any new information from the neighbors. The main localization procedure is shown in Algorithm 1 which is repeated at every iteration.

At the beginning of each iteration node u gathers a recently discovered set of anchors, A_u, by listening to the broadcasts made by nodes in N_u. We note that we use *anchor* as a more general term in the sense that every node that is uniquely localized throughout the localization process is called an anchor. If a newly discovered anchor node a is not finitely localized, a and its position are appended to L, the set of finitely localized nodes and their positions. Otherwise all positions other than the real one are *removed.* Next a bilateration order π of the nodes in C_u^r is found. As stated in Remark 1, not every ordering covers C_u^r completely. To find a bilateration order π in general, we select a *seed* set as the first level in the ordering. We continue a breadth-first traversal to construct new levels of nodes while making sure every node in a level has at least two neighbors in the preceding levels. As iterations of the localization procedure increase, the set of finitely localized nodes grows, therefore it constitutes a good candidate for the seed set. However for the initial iterations we try every possible triple as a candidate for the seeds and take the maximum size set. Following the order in π multilaterations are done to compute position possibilities for each node. The traversal is done in a breadth-first manner rather than a depth-first manner so as to decrease the number of position possibilities as early as possible during this process. The rest of the localization procedure where each node in π is multilaterated in order is the same as the centralized localization method of [8]. Going through π, finite positions are created for each v using two *consistent* positions p_b, p_c of immediate ancestors b, c. This is via *bilateration*, computing the intersection points of two circles centered at p_b, p_c with appropriate radii.

Each generated position has a localization history in the form of an *ancestors* list which stores the consistent positions of b, c and the ancestors of those positions. Checking the consistency of a pair of points then involves comparing their ancestries. If a node exists in the ancestries of both, but with different positions, then they are not consistent. Finally positions of the rest of the immediate ancestors of v in π are checked for consistency with the new positions of v. Throughout bilateration and update bilateration every position that has been found inconsistent is *removed* immediately and thus further localizations do not take into account any unnecessary data. We note that all *removals* in the unique localization are recursive in the sense that the removal of a point p_b causes the removal of positions containing p_b in their ancestries as well.

3.3 Analysis

Let k denote the average degree of a node in $\mathbb{N}$. The size of a packet broadcasted by a node in the jth iteration of the initial setup is $O(k^j)$. The total size of all packets broadcasted throughout the network in this phase is $O(n \times k^r)$, where n is the number of nodes in the network. During the unique localization within iterations each recently discovered anchor is broadcasted at most once. The number of nodes in a cluster C_u^r is bounded by $O(k^r)$. Therefore the total size of all packets broadcasted throughout the network is the same as the first phase, $O(n \times k^r)$ which is the total size overall. Assuming k, r are constants the total packet size is linear in terms of the size of the network. In terms of running time, a single execution of the localization takes $O(2^{k^r})$ time in the worst case. Although exponential on the size of a cluster, assuming the cluster sizes are constant, each iteration requires constant time. Same argument holds for the memory requirements of a sensor node. For practical considerations, the value of r is of crucial importance in determining the efficiency in terms of the messaging overhead, time and space requirements. For most of the experiments the maximum number of position possibilities for the whole cluster rarely exceeds 2^{10} for all practical values of r.

Assuming the iterative model of collaboration, the value of r is also important for determining the unique localizability as the next lemma shows.

Lemma 1. *(For $\forall r \geq 2$) Within the defined model of collaboration between clusters, there exists a class of graphs that have $O(1)$ uniquely localizable nodes for $r-1$, whereas $\Theta(n)$ uniquely localizable nodes for r.*

Proof (Sketch). The *flower* graphs of Figure 2-a is such a class. The middle part called the *sepal* is a circulant graph of vertices $x_1, \ldots x_c$. Within the sepal each x_i has edges to $x_{i-2}, x_{i-1}, x_{i+1}, x_{i+2}$. Thus the sepal is the circulant graph of c vertices, $Ci_c(1, 2)$, which is globally rigid. Corresponding to each x_i there is a *petal* P_{x_i} which is a wheel centered at x_i. P_{x_i} itself is globally rigid and shares exactly two vertices with the two neighboring petals $P_{x_{i-1}}$ and $P_{x_{i+1}}$. Vertices x_i, x_{i-1} are shared with the petal of x_{i-1} and x_i, x_{i+1} are shared with that of x_{i+1}. We set $c = 4r - 2$. The cluster $C_{x_i}^r$ includes the sepal in its entirety and is globally rigid. If three anchors belong to the same petal, the center of the petal

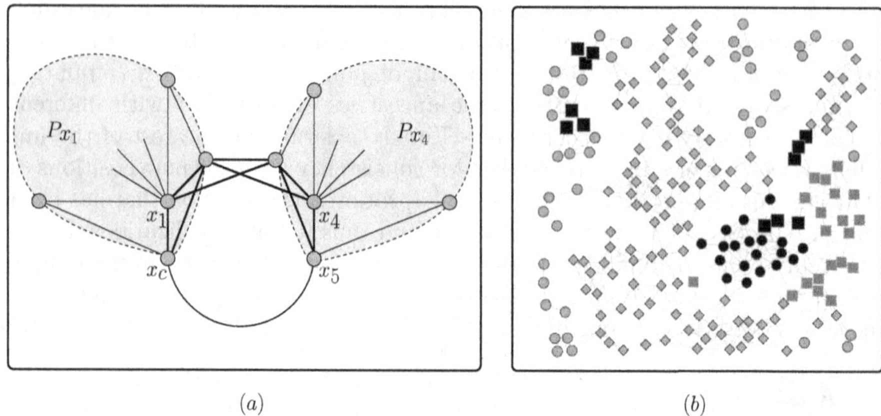

Fig. 2. (a) The flower graph not localizable for $r-1$, uniquely localizable for r. (b) Random network with $n = 200$ and $k = 6$. Black squares are localized for $r = 0$ (anchors), black circles for $r = 1$, gray squares for $r = 2$, diamonds for $r = 3$, and gray circles are unlocalizable.

can collapse its petal, and therefore the sepal completely, which further enables the unique localization of every petal in the graph and the whole network is uniquely localized. However $C_{x_i}^{r-1}$ is not globally rigid. Unless each petal contains at least three anchors, i.e. it is independently localizable, unique localization is not possible. □

We can assign equal sizes to the petals such that each petal consists of almost (n/c) nodes. An immediate consequence then is that, assuming a random assignment of anchors, the probability of localizing $n/(4r-2)$ nodes under the C_u^{r-1} cluster model is the same as that of localizing the complete network under the C_u^r cluster model. This is true since in C_u^{r-1} a petal is uniquely localizable either in its entirety or none at all. Moreover a uniquely localizable petal in C_u^{r-1} gives rise to uniquely localizable network in C_u^r. It implies that, deploying the same number of anchors, with $r = 3$ we can localize the complete network, whereas only ten percent of the network is localizable for $r = 2$. We note that in practical deployment scenarios the likelihood of flower-like configurations is higher for small values of r. Therefore the contrast between the uniquely localizable node ratios for $r = 2, 3$ is quite remarkable and is verified with the experiments of the following section.

4 Experiments and Discussion of Results

The implementation is coded in C++ using LEDA library [16]. The implementations are available at `http://hacivat.khas.edu.tr/~cesim/uniloc.rar`. Experiments are performed on a computer with the configuration of AMD X2 3800+ of CPU and 3GB of RAM. Because we propose a distributed algorithm, a discrete event simulation system has been designed. We start by generating a random network with parameters n and k. Firstly n random points in the plane are generated using the random number generation of LEDA [16]. All nodes are assumed to have equal sensing range which is increased iteratively until average degree equals k. All experiments are reproducible in any platform. Network size is fixed at $n = 200$ and four randomly chosen K_3s are declared as anchors. The experiments are run for r, k values where r varies from 1 to 8 and k varies from 4 to 16. Every unique configuration is repeated 10 times. The recorded results are divided into two when appropriate. First phase results are those arising from the cluster construction and the second phase results correspond to those of the actual unique localization.

We select performance measures in order to analyze and construe localization, messaging performances, and running time and space requirements. LNR (Localized Node Ratio) is the number of uniquely localized nodes divided by n. BC (average Broadcast Count per node) is total number of broadcasted messages divided by n. The size of each broadcasted packet differs especially in the second phase. Thus BC alone does not fully represent bandwidth usage per node. BA (average Broadcast Amount per node) is the total size of all broadcasted packets divided by n. AT (Average Time per node) is the average time spent for computations required by the localization algorithm on a physical sensor node. MP (Maximum possibilities per node) is defined as $\underset{u \in \mathbb{N}}{\text{Max}} \, (\underset{v \in C_u^r}{\text{Max}} \, |v.Positions|)$. In our implementation we bound $|v.Positions|$ to be at most 1024. Finally, TP (average Total Possibilities per cluster) is $(\sum_{u \in \mathbb{N}} \sum_{v \in C_u^r} |v.Positions|)/n$, which is a measure of the average space requirements of a sensor node. Figure 2-b is a visual illustration of our unique localization method. All the uniquely localizable nodes (almost 80% of the whole network) are uniquely localized with $r = 3$, whereas 6% of the network is uniquely localizable for $r = 0$ (anchors), 13% for $r = 1$, and 23% for $r = 2$. We note that in the simplest case, for $r = 1$, our method is analogous to iterative trilateration [17].

Figure 3 (top-left) shows the growth of LNR with respect to r and k. As r increases LNR grows as expected. There exist partial graphs, such as the one in Figure 2-a, that are localizable only for a specific r. However since the occurrence probability of such graphs is inversely proportional to r, for $r > 5$ when $6 \leq k \leq 10$, LNR does not grow drastically. The change in BC values with respect to r, k is plotted in Figure 3 (top-right). Since the number of broadcasts in the Initial Setup phase is constant, the irregularity of the plot is caused by the broadcasts in the Iterative Localization phase. Number of broadcasts in this phase depends on how many new anchors are localized at each iteration. The BC values are maximum for $6 \leq k \leq 10$. For sparse networks when $k < 6$, the messaging overhead is low since not that many nodes are localized to be broadcasted in the first place. In contrast when $k > 10$ each localization iteration uniquely localizes many nodes at once therefore requires few broadcasts. However as can be verified in Figure 3 (bottom-left), the BA values indicating the broadcast size per node grows proportionally in terms of k and r. Figure 3 (bottom-right) shows the MP values. The peak values are reached at $7 \leq k \leq 10$ for almost all r values,

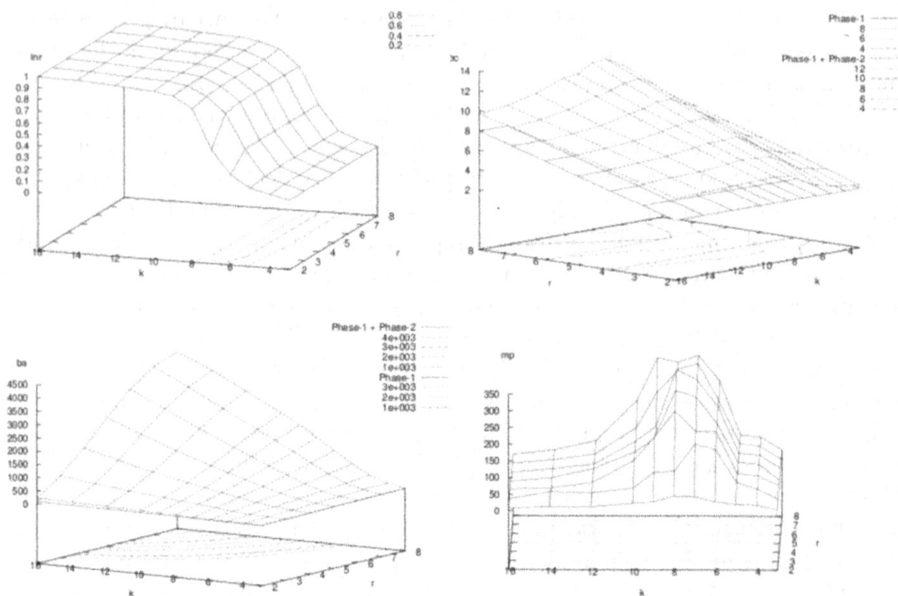

Fig. 3. *Top-left:* The ratio of localized nodes. *Top-right:* Average number of broadcasts per node *Bottom-left:* Average amount of data broadcasted in units *Bottom-right:* Average memory requirements (maximum possibilities per node).

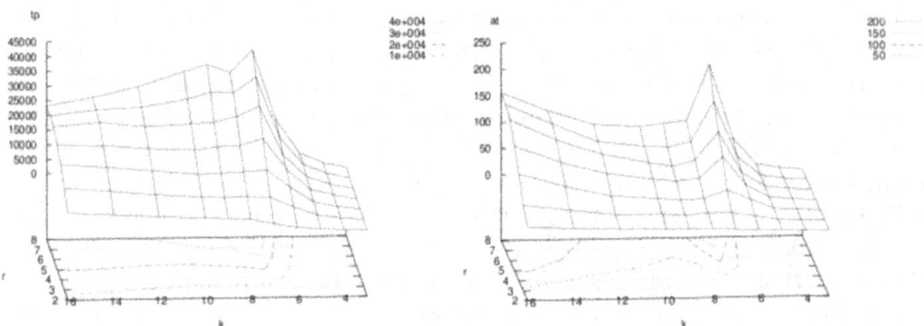

Fig. 4. *Left:* Total possibilities stored in each cluster at any time during unique localization. *Right:* Running time in seconds during localization.

since low connectivity does not enable too many bilaterations, therefore possible locations, whereas high connectivity leads to unique localization too quickly. Similar reasoning could apply to TP except that cluster size plays an important role as well in this case; see Figure 4-left. The average cluster size is k^r, therefore for large values of k ($k \geq 9$), TP is constant or grows slightly even though MP decreases. High connectivity leads to ease of unique localization but also gives rise to large clusters, which seem to cancel out each others' affects in terms of space requirements of a sensor node. It is interesting to analyze the time spent for localization computations at each node since it depends on both MP and TP. As can be seen in Figure 4-right the growth seems to be similar to that of MP for $k \leq 9$. However the large cluster sizes reflected in TP seem to overcome the advantages created by low MP for larger connectivities and running time increases.

References

[1] Akyildiz, I., Su, W., Sankarasubramaniam, Y., Cayirci, E.: A survey on sensor networks. IEEE Communications Magazine 40(8), 102–114 (2002)

[2] Aspnes, J., Eren, T., Goldenberg, D., Morse, A., Whiteley, W., Yang, Y., Anderson, B., Belhumeur, P.: A theory of network localization. IEEE Trans. on Mobile Computing 5(12), 1663–1678 (2006)

[3] Aspnes, J., Goldenberg, D., Yang, Y.: On the computational complexity of sensor network localization. In: Proc. of 1st Int. Workshop on Algorithmic Aspects of Wireless Sensor Networks, pp. 32–44 (2004)

[4] Basu, A., Gao, J., Mitchell, J., Sabhnani, G.: Distributed localization using noisy distance and angle information. In: Proc. of the 7th ACM Int. Symp. on Mobile ad hoc networking and computing, pp. 262–273 (2006)

[5] Berg, A., Jordán, T.: A proof of connelly's conjecture on 3-connected circuits of the rigidity matroid. J. Comb. Theory Ser. B 88(1), 77–97 (2003)

[6] Connelly, R.: Generic global rigidity. Discrete Comput. Geom. 33(4), 549–563 (2005)

[7] Efrat, A., Erten, C., Forrester, D., Kobourov, S.: A force-directed approach to sensor localization. In: Proc. 8th ACM/SIAM Alg. Eng. and Exp., pp. 108–118 (2006)

[8] Goldenberg, D., Cao, P.B.P.M., Fang, J.: Localization in sparse networks using sweeps. In: Proc. of ACM MobiCom, pp. 110–121 (2006)

[9] Hendrickson, B.: Conditions for unique graph realizations. SIAM Journal on Computing 21, 65–84 (1992)

[10] Hightower, J., Borriello, G.: Location systems for ubiquitous computing. Computer 34(8), 57–66 (2001)

[11] Hu, L., Evans, D.: Localization for mobile sensor networks. In: Proc. of the 10th Int. Conf. on Mobile computing and networking, pp. 45–57 (2004)

[12] Jackson, B., Jordán, T.: Connected rigidity matroids and unique realizations of graphs. J. Comb. Theory Ser. B 94(1), 1–29 (2005)

[13] Krishnamachari, B.: Networking wireless sensors. Cambridge University Press, Cambridge (2006)

[14] Laman, G.: On graphs and rigidity of plane skeletal structures. Journal of Engineering Mathematics 4, 331–340 (1970)

[15] Mao, G., Fidan, B., Anderson, B.: Wireless sensor network localization techniques. Comput. Netw. 51(10), 2529–2553 (2007)

[16] Mehlhorn, K., Naher, S.: Leda: A platform for combinatorial and geometric computing. Communications of the ACM 38 (1999)

[17] Moore, D., Leonard, J., Rus, D., Teller, S.: Robust distributed network localization with noisy range measurements. In: Proc. of the 2nd Int. Conf. on Embedded Networked Sensor Systems, pp. 50–61 (2004)

Relative Span Weighted Localization of Uncooperative Nodes in Wireless Networks

Christine Laurendeau and Michel Barbeau

School of Computer Science, Carleton University,
1125 Colonel By Drive, Ottawa, ON Canada K1S 5B6
Tel.: 613-520-2600; Fax: 613-520-4334
{claurend,barbeau}@scs.carleton.ca

Abstract. Increasingly ubiquitous wireless technologies require novel localization techniques to pinpoint the position of an uncooperative node, whether the target be a malicious device engaging in a security exploit or a low-battery handset in the middle of a critical emergency. Such scenarios necessitate that a radio signal source be localized by other network nodes efficiently, using minimal information. We propose two new algorithms for estimating the position of an uncooperative transmitter, based on the received signal strength (RSS) of a single target message at a set of receivers whose coordinates are known. As an extension to the concept of centroid localization, our mechanisms weigh each receiver's coordinates based on the message's relative RSS at that receiver, with respect to the span of RSS values over all receivers. The weights may decrease from the highest RSS receiver either linearly or exponentially. Our simulation results demonstrate that for all but the most sparsely populated wireless networks, our exponentially weighted mechanism localizes a target node within the regulations stipulated for emergency services location accuracy.

1 Introduction

Given the pervasiveness of cellphones and other wireless devices, compounded with the associated expectation of permanent connectivity, it is perhaps not surprising that the abrupt dashing of such presumptions makes headline news. A recent spate of cases in Canada have highlighted the tragic consequences of failing to locate the source of an emergency 911 cellphone call. These events have spurred the Canadian Radio-television Telecommunications Commission (CRTC) to regulate the same wireless Enhanced 911 (E911) provisions [1] as the Federal Communications Commission (FCC) in the U.S. [2] Under Phase II of the FCC and CRTC plans, network-based localization, where other nodes (whether base stations or other handsets within range) estimate the position of a device, must accurately reveal a target location within 100 meters 67% of the time and within 300 meters in 95% of cases.

Self-localization achieved with handset-based localization techniques can produce granular results. For example with the Global Positioning System (GPS), a precision of ten meters may be achieved [3]. But self-localization is not feasible in all scenarios. An uncooperative node is one that cannot be relied upon to determine its coordinates, for example a defective sensor, a malicious device engaging in a security exploit or a low-battery handset in a critical situation.

B. Liu et al. (Eds.): WASA 2009, LNCS 5682, pp. 358–367, 2009.

In a sufficiently densely populated wireless network, the source location of a given message may be approximated from the coordinates of receiving devices, assuming an omnidirectional propagation pattern. We propose two localization algorithms that estimate a transmitting node's position as the weighted average of receiver coordinates, assuming a single message is received from the target node. We describe a *relative span weighted localization* (RWL) mechanism, where the concept of weighted moving average is adapted to provide a linear mapping between the weight assigned to a receiver's coordinates and the relative placement of its received signal strength (RSS) value within the overall RSS span. We further propose an exponential variation of RWL, dubbed *relative span exponential weighted localization* (REWL). This approach is conceptually related to an exponential moving average and relies on an exponential weight correspondence between a receiver's coordinates and its relative situation within the RSS span. We evaluate the RWL and REWL algorithms using simulated RSS reports featuring a variety of node densities, number of receivers, and amount of signal shadowing representative of environment-based RSS fluctuations. We also test our localization mechanisms with RSS values harvested from an outdoor field experiment.

Section 2 provides an overview of existing work in centroid-based localization techniques. Section 3 outlines the centroid localization schemes on which our new algorithms are based. Section 4 describes our linearly and exponentially weighted location estimation mechanisms. Section 5 evaluates the performance of both algorithms using simulated and experimental RSS values. Section 6 concludes the paper.

2 Related Work

Centroid localization (CL) has been suggested as an efficient location estimation method that never fails to produce a solution, unlike existing geometric and algebraic localization approaches [4, 5, 6]. The original incarnation of CL is described by Bulusu *et al.* [7], and localizes the transmitting source of a message to the (x, y) coordinates obtained from averaging the coordinates all receiving devices within range. Weighted centroid localization (WCL), as proposed by Blumenthal *et al.* [8], assigns a weight to each of the receiver coordinates, as inversely proportional to either the known transmitter-receiver (T-R) distance or the link quality indicator available in ZigBee/IEEE 802.15.4 sensor networks [9]. Behnke and Timmermann [10] extend the WCL mechanism for use with normalized values of the link quality indicator. Schuhmann *et al.* [11] conduct an indoor experiment to determine a set of fixed parameters for an exponential inverse relation between T-R distances and the corresponding weights used with WCL. Orooji and Abolhassani [12] suggest a T-R distance-weighted averaged coordinates scheme, where each receiver's coordinates are inversely weighted according to its distance from the transmitter. But this approach assumes that the receivers are closely co-located and that the T-R distance to at least one of the receivers is known *a priori*.

3 Centroid Localization

We outline the centroid localization approaches on which our novel algorithms are based, and introduce the notation used throughout the description of our mechanisms.

Notation. The estimated coordinates of the transmitter we are striving to locate are denoted as $\widehat{p} = (\widehat{x}, \widehat{y})$. Each receiver R_i is situated at a point of known coordinates $p_i = (x_i, y_i)$. For the sake of simplicity in our algorithm descriptions, we depict operations on receiver points p_i. In fact, two separate calculations occur. The approximated $\widehat{x}$ coordinate is computed from all the receiver x_i coordinates, and $\widehat{y}$ is calculated from the y_i coordinates.

Given a set of known points p_i in a Euclidian space, for example a number of receivers within radio range of a target transmitter to be localized, Bulusu *et al.* [7] approximate the location $\widehat{p}$ of a node from the *centroid* of the known points p_i as follows:

$$\widehat{p} = (1/n) \times \sum_{i=1}^{n} p_i \tag{1}$$

where n represents the number of points.

In the simple CL approach, all points are assumed to be equally near the target node. Blumenthal *et al.* [8] argue that some points are more likely than others to be close to target node. Their WCL scheme aims to improve localization accuracy by assigning greater weight to those points which are estimated to be closer to the target and less weight to the farther points. The *weighted centroid* is thus computed as:

$$\widehat{p} = \sum_{i=1}^{n} (w_i \times p_i) \ / \ \sum_{i=1}^{n} w_i \tag{2}$$

with $w_i = (d_i)^{-g}$ where d_i is the known distance between the target node and point p_i, and the exponent g influences the degree to which remote points participate in estimating the target location $\widehat{p}$. Values of g are determined manually, with Blumenthal *et al.* and Schuhmann *et al.* [11] promoting different optimal values, depending on the experimental setting.

4 Relative Span Weighted Localization

Assuming an uncooperative node, we cannot presume to know *a priori* the set of T-R distances d_i or the optimal value of g in a given outdoor environment. Further, we cannot estimate values of d_i from the log-normal shadowing model, as the transmitter effective isotropic radiated power (EIRP) may not be known. We therefore introduce the concept of relative span weighted localization in order to estimate the location of a transmitter with minimal information available at a set of receivers. Our approach adapts the concept of moving average from a weighting method over time and applies it to WCL in the space domain. But rather than ascribing weights according to known or approximated T-R distances, we weigh each receiver coordinates according to the relative placement of its RSS value within the span of all RSS reports for a given transmitted message. We assign greater weight to the receiver coordinates whose RSS value is closer to the maximum of the RSS span and thus closer to the transmitter. Conversely, lesser weight is ascribed to receivers with lower RSS values, as they are deemed farther from the transmitter. The receiver coordinates may be weighted linearly or exponentially.

Definition 1 (Minimal/Maximal RSS). *Let $\mathbb{R}$ be the set of all receivers within range of a given message $\mathcal{M}_T$ originating from an uncooperative transmitter T. Let Υ denote the set of RSS values measured at each receiver $R_i \in \mathbb{R}$ for message $\mathcal{M}_T$, such that: $\Upsilon = \{\upsilon_i : \upsilon_i$ is the RSS value for message $\mathcal{M}_T$ at R_i for all $R_i \in \mathbb{R}\}$*

Then we define the minimal and maximal RSS values, $\mathcal{V}_{min}$ and $\mathcal{V}_{max}$, for message $\mathcal{M}_T$, as the smallest and largest RSS values in Υ, such that: $\mathcal{V}_{min} = \min\{\upsilon_i \in \Upsilon\}$ and $\mathcal{V}_{max} = \max\{\upsilon_i \in \Upsilon\}$.

Definition 2 (RSS Span). *Let the minimal and maximal RSS values for a message $\mathcal{M}_T$ be as stated in Definition 1. We define the RSS span $\mathcal{V}^{\Delta}$ for this message at a set of receivers $\mathbb{R}$ as the maximal range in RSS values over all receivers, such that: $\mathcal{V}^{\Delta} = \mathcal{V}_{max} - \mathcal{V}_{min}$.*

We describe two relative span weighted localization algorithms, both computing a weighted centroid as defined in Equation (2), but with novel approaches for computing the weights assigned to each receiver coordinates.

4.1 Linearly Weighted Localization

The RWL algorithm computes a centroid of receiver coordinates, each weighted linearly according to the relative position of the receiver's RSS value within the RSS span.

Algorithm 1 (RWL Algorithm). *The* relative span weighted localization *(RWL) algorithm estimates a transmitter's coordinates $\widehat{p}$ as the weighted centroid of all receiver coordinates p_i, as defined for WCL in Equation* (2)*, but with a linearly increasing weight assigned to each receiver according to its presumed proximity to the transmitter. Given the RSS values in Υ, as found in Definition 1, and the RSS span $\mathcal{V}^{\Delta}$ determined according to Definition 2, the weight w_i of each receiver R_i is computed from the relative placement of its RSS value υ_i in the RSS span, as $w_i = (\upsilon_i - \mathcal{V}_{min})/\mathcal{V}^{\Delta}$, for each $R_i \in \mathbb{R}$.*

The relative span weighted centroid *thus becomes:*

$$\widehat{p} = \frac{\sum_{i=1}^{n} \left[(\upsilon_i - \mathcal{V}_{min}) \times p_i\right]}{\sum_{i=1}^{n} (\upsilon_i - \mathcal{V}_{min})} \qquad \textit{where } n = |\mathbb{R}| \tag{3}$$

4.2 Exponentially Weighted Localization

Exponentially weighted moving averages (EMAs) have been used for a variety of forecasting applications, for example in Muir [13], to predict future values based on past observations, with more weight exponentially ascribed to more recent data. A *weighting factor* λ is used as a parameter to control the proportion of weight assigned to recent observations with respect to past ones.

We adapt the EMA concept, as described by Roberts [14], from rating observations over time for the purpose of weighting receiver coordinates over the space domain.

While EMA favors more recent observations in time with a weighting factor of λ, we bolster receivers that are likely to be closer to a transmitter and thus feature higher RSS values. In addition, rather than increasing the weighting factor exponent by one for each observation in time, we correlate the exponent with the relative position of each receiver's RSS value within the RSS span.

Algorithm 2 (REWL Algorithm). *The* relative span exponentially weighted localization *(REWL) algorithm estimates a transmitter's coordinates $\widehat{p}$ as the weighted centroid of all receiver coordinates p_i, as defined for WCL in Equation* (2)*, but with exponential weight assigned to each receiver according to a weighting factor λ. Given the RSS values in Υ as found in Definition 1, the weight w_i of each receiver R_i is computed from the relative placement of its RSS value v_i in the RSS span, as $w_i = (1-\lambda)^{(\mathcal{V}_{max}-v_i)}$, for each $R_i \in \mathbb{R}$.*

The relative span exponentially weighted centroid *thus becomes:*

$$\widehat{p} = \frac{\sum_{i=1}^{n} \left[(1-\lambda)^{(\mathcal{V}_{max}-v_i)} \times p_i\right]}{\sum_{i=1}^{n}(1-\lambda)^{(\mathcal{V}_{max}-v_i)}} \qquad \textit{where } n = |\mathbb{R}| \tag{4}$$

5 Performance Evaluation

We evaluate the performance of the RWL and REWL algorithms using simulated RSS values and experimental ones harvested from an outdoor field experiment.

5.1 Simulation Results

We ran the RWL and REWL mechanisms on simulations featuring a variety of node densities and number of receivers. For each of 10 000 executions, we generate a random transmitter position within a 1000×1000 m^2 simulation grid. We define our node densities as the number of nodes per 100×100 m^2. For every node density $d \in \{0.25, 0.50, 0.75, 1.00, 2.00, 3.00, 4.00, 5.00, 6.00, 7.00, 8.00, 9.00, 10.00\}$, we position d nodes per 100×100 m^2 in uniformly distributed positions on our simulation grid. For each node, we compute a RSS value based on the log-normal shadowing model [15], with a random amount of signal shadowing generated along a log-normal probability distribution. We assume two different radio propagation environments with path loss constants obtained from outdoor experiments. For the 2.4 GHz WiFi/802.11g frequency, we use propagation values measured by Liechty *et al.* [16,17], where a signal shadowing standard deviation is measured at nearly $\sigma = 6$ dBm. For the 5.8 GHz frequency, licensed for vehicular networks [18], we make use of the constants determined by Durgin *et al.* [19], with a signal shadowing standard deviation close to $\sigma = 8$ dBm. Similar experiments by Schwengler and Gilbert corroborate the amount of signal shadowing commonly experienced at this frequency [20]. Our setup allows us to gauge the performance of relative span weighted localization based on propagation environments featuring different amounts of signal fluctuations. Once our simulated nodes are positioned, we determine which ones can be used as receivers. We set all receiver sensitivity to -90 dBm, and the nodes that feature a RSS value above the sensitivity are deemed within range of the transmitter and thus become receivers. The non-receiver nodes are subsequently ignored as out of range.

For each execution, we use the known coordinates of all receivers to compute a possible position for the transmitter, according to four algorithms: the maximum RSS receiver method, where a transmitter is assumed to be at exactly the receiver position with the highest RSS value; the CL approach, as set out by Bulusu *et al.* in Equation (1); the RWL algorithm using Equation (3); and the REWL algorithm as set forth in Equation (4), given three different values for the weighting factor $\lambda \in \{0.10, 0.15, 0.20\}$. We assess the performance of each mechanism according to its location accuracy, computed as the Euclidian distance between the estimated position $\widehat{p}$ and the actual transmitter location, averaged over all executions. Our results are deemed accurate within ± 3 meters in a 95% confidence interval.

Figure 1 plots the average location error for each tested algorithm, given all defined node densities, for frequency 2.4 GHz. The corresponding results at the 5.8 GHz frequency may be found in [21]. We find that while higher densities consistently yield greater location accuracy, a larger amount of signal shadowing results in higher location errors. For example, for all densities, the REWL algorithm, with the 2.4 GHz frequency and $\sigma = 6$ dBm, yields a location error consistently less than 75 meters, while the same mechanism at the 5.8 GHz frequency and $\sigma = 8$ dBm reaches an error of 105 meters. In general, we find an error increase of roughly 50% for every 2 dBm of additional signal shadowing standard deviation. For both frequencies and all node densities, the REWL algorithm with weighting factor of 15% ($\lambda = 0.15$) achieves optimal results.

We assessed the performance of each algorithm, and in particular the REWL ($\lambda = 0.15$) mechanism, when compared to the E911 regulations for location accuracy. While

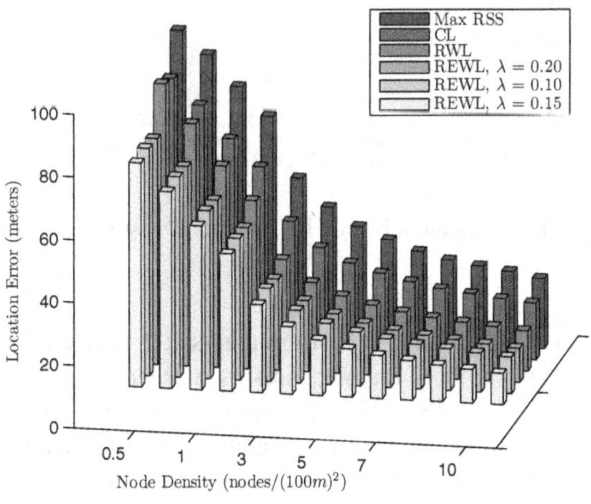

Fig. 1. Algorithm Location Error by Node Density for 2.4 GHz

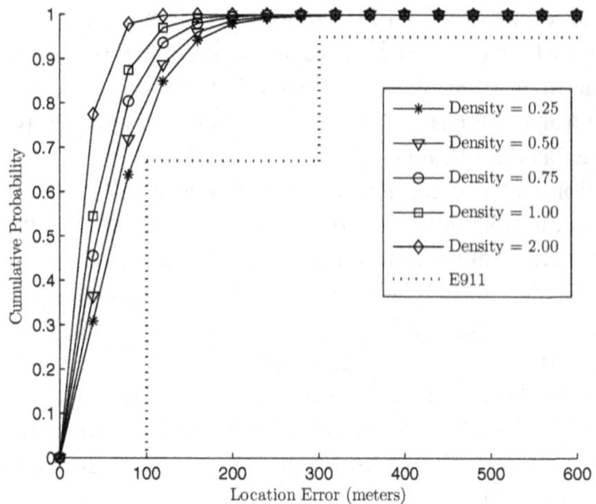

Fig. 2. REWL Location Error CDF by Node Density for 2.4 GHz

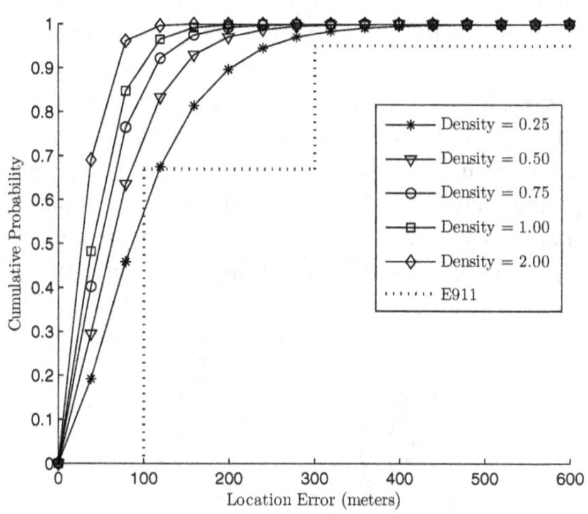

Fig. 3. REWL Location Error CDF by Node Density for 5.8 GHz

every method evaluated meets the E911 requirements at 2.4 GHz with moderate signal shadowing ($\sigma = 6$ dBm), none of the mechanisms succeed with 5.8 GHz and a larger amount of shadowing ($\sigma = 8$ dBm) [21]. However, even in the latter case, the REWL approach is nearly adequate. Given the smaller amount of signal shadowing found at 2.4 GHz, the REWL ($\lambda = 0.15$) algorithm meets the E911 location accuracy requirements for every node density, as seen in Figure 2. For larger amounts of shadowing at 5.8 GHz, only the smallest node density of 0.25 per 100×100 m^2 fails to meet the E911 standard, as shown in Figure 3. Even in a heavily shadowed environment, higher node densities can accurately localize a transmitter within 100 meters 67% of the time and within 300 meters in 95% of cases.

Orooji *et al.* [12] simulate a cluster of seven cells, each featuring a base station with a one kilometer radius, in order to compute the location of a mobile station. A very small amount of signal shadowing $\sigma \in \{1, 2\}$ dBm is taken into account. Even though their proposed T-R distance-weighted method assumes a known distance to one of the base stations, the mean location error is 48 meters, with 95% of executions resulting in a location error less than 103 meters. Our RWL and REWL ($\lambda = 0.15$) algorithms for 2.4 GHz with eight receivers yield an average 37 and 34 meter location error respectively. RWL locates a transmitter within 100 meters 98% of the time, while REWL does so in 99% of cases. Thus over a similarly sized simulation grid, our RWL and REWL mechanisms consistently yield more accurate results.

5.2 Experimental Results

We conducted an outdoor field experiment with four desktop receivers statically arranged in the corners of a rectangular area 80×110 m^2 in size. Each receiver collected the RSS values of packets transmitted by a laptop from each of ten separate locations. Only the messages simultaneously received by the four desktops were retained. The localization algorithms were executed on each message, and the location error for each algorithm averaged over all transmitter locations can be found in Table 1. We find that the RWL and REWL mechanisms perform far better than the maximum RSS receiver and CL approaches, with a gain in location accuracy of up to 40%. On average, the RWL, REWL with $\lambda = 0.15$, and REWL with $\lambda = 0.20$ mechanisms perform equally well, with no algorithm emerging as clearly superior to the others. This may be due to our small experimental data set (approximately 400 messages), when compared to simulation results obtained over 10 000 executions. While our simulations also found consistently similar results between the RWL and REWL mechanisms, the larger amount of simulated data allows us to draw more fine-tuned conclusions.

Table 1. Average Location Error for All Experimental Transmitter Locations

Algorithm	Max RSS	CL	RWL	REWL		
				$\lambda = 0.10$	$\lambda = 0.15$	$\lambda = 0.20$
Average Location Error (meters)	40	46	28	33	29	28

6 Conclusion

We propose a wireless network-based localization mechanism for estimating the position of an uncooperative transmitting device, whether it be a malfunctioning sensor, an attacker engaging in a security exploit or a low-battery cellphone in a critical emergency. We extend the concept of weighted centroid localization and describe two additional receiver coordinate weighting mechanisms, one linear and the other exponential, that assume no knowledge of the T-R distances nor of the transmitter EIRP. We adapt the concept of moving averages based on observations over time to the space domain. We ascribe linear and exponential weights to each receiver coordinates, based on the relative positioning of the receiver's RSS value within the RSS span of all receivers.

We tested our relative span weighted localization algorithms with simulated and experimental RSS values, using two frequencies featuring different amounts of signal shadowing. We found that our algorithms yield lower location errors than the existing centroid localization method. As expected, the location accuracy increases as more nodes participate in the localization effort. For example with REWL ($\lambda = 0.15$) at 2.4 GHz, one node per 100×100 m^2 localizes a transmitter within 44 meters, while ten nodes per 100×100 m^2 do so in less than ten meters. Yet the location accuracy decreases as the amount of signal shadowing between different receivers increases, with an average decrease of approximately 50% for every 2 dBm of additional signal shadowing standard deviation. We conclude that the exponential variation of our relative span weighted localization algorithm achieves a location accuracy that meets the FCC regulations for Enhanced 911, for all densities with moderate amounts of signal shadowing and for all but the smallest node densities with extensive shadowing.

Acknowledgment

The authors gratefully acknowledge the financial support received for this research from the Natural Sciences and Engineering Research Council of Canada (NSERC), and the Automobile of the 21st Century (AUTO21) and Mathematics of Information Technology and Complex Systems (MITACS) Networks of Centers of Excellence (NCEs).

References

1. Canadian Radio-television Telecommunications Commission: Implementation of Wireless Phase II E9-1-1 Service. Telecom Regulatory Policy CRTC 2009-40 (2009)
2. Federal Communications Commission: 911 Service. FCC Code of Federal Regulations, Title 47, Part 20, Section 20.18 (2007)
3. Nielson, J., Keefer, J., McCullough, B.: SAASM: Rockwell Collins' Next Generation GPS Receiver Design. In: Proceedings of the IEEE Position Location and Navigation Symposium, March 2000, pp. 98–105 (2000)
4. Liu, C., Wu, K., He, T.: Sensor Localization with Ring Overlapping Based on Comparison of Received Signal Strength Indicator. In: Proceedings of the IEEE International Conference on Mobile Ad-hoc and Sensor Systems, October 2004, pp. 516–518 (2004)
5. Liu, B.C., Lin, K.H., Wu, J.C.: Analysis of Hyperbolic and Circular Positioning Algorithms Using Stationary Signal-Strength-Difference Measurements in Wireless Communications. IEEE Transactions on Vehicular Technology 55(2), 499–509 (2006)
6. Liu, B.C., Lin, K.H.: Distance Difference Error Correction by Least Square for Stationary Signal-Strength-Difference-based Hyperbolic Location in Cellular Communications. IEEE Transactions on Vehicular Technology 57(1), 227–238 (2008)
7. Bulusu, N., Heidemann, J., Estrin, D.: GPS-less Low-Cost Outdoor Localization for Very Small Devices. IEEE Personal Communications 7(5), 28–34 (2000)
8. Blumenthal, J., Grossmann, R., Golatowski, F., Timmermann, D.: Weighted Centroid Localization in Zigbee-based Sensor Networks. In: Proceedings of the IEEE International Symposium on Intelligent Signal Processing (WISP), October 2007, pp. 1–6 (2007)

9. LAN/MAN Standards Committee of the IEEE Computer Society: IEEE Standard for Information Technology - Telecommunications and Information Exchange Between Systems - Local and Metropolitan Area Networks - Specific Requirements - Part 15.4: Wireless Medium Access Control (MAC) and Physical Layer (PHY) Specifications for Low-Rate Wireless Personal Area Networks (WPANS) - Amendment 1: Add Alternate PHYs. IEEE Std 802.15.4a-2007 (2007)
10. Behnke, R., Timmermann, D.: AWCL: Adaptive Weighted Centroid Localization as an Efficient Improvement of Coarse Grained Localization. In: Proceedings of the 5th Workshop on Positioning, Navigation and Communication (WPNC), March 2008, pp. 243–250 (2008)
11. Schuhmann, S., Herrmann, K., Rothermel, K., Blumenthal, J., Timmermann, D.: Improved Weighted Centroid Localization in Smart Ubiquitous Environments. In: Sandnes, F.E., Zhang, Y., Rong, C., Yang, L.T., Ma, J. (eds.) UIC 2008. LNCS, vol. 5061, pp. 20–34. Springer, Heidelberg (2008)
12. Orooji, M., Abolhassani, B.: New Method for Estimation of Mobile Location Based on Signal Attenuation and Hata Model Signal Prediction. In: Proceedings of the IEEE 27th Annual Conference of the Engineering in Medicine and Biology Society, September 2005, pp. 6025–6028 (2005)
13. Muir, A.: Automatic Sales Forecasting. The Computer Journal 1(3), 113–116 (1958)
14. Roberts, S.W.: Control Chart Tests Based on Geometric Moving Averages. Technometrics 1(3), 239–250 (1959)
15. Rappaport, T.S.: Wireless Communications: Principles and Practice, 2nd edn. Prentice-Hall, New Jersey (2002)
16. Liechty, L.C.: Path Loss Measurements and Model Analysis of a 2.4 GHz Wireless Network in an Outdoor Environment. Master's thesis, Georgia Institute of Technology (2007)
17. Liechty, L.C., Reifsnider, E., Durgin, G.: Developing the Best 2.4 GHz Propagation Model from Active Network Measurements. In: Proceedings of the 66th IEEE Vehicular Technology Conference, September 2007, pp. 894–896 (2007)
18. ASTM International: Standard Specification for Telecommunications and Information Exchange Between Roadside and Vehicle Systems – 5 GHz Band Dedicated Short Range Communications (DSRC) Medium Access Control (MAC) and Physical Layer (PHY) Specifications. ASTM E2213-03 (2003)
19. Durgin, G., Rappaport, T.S., Hao, X.: Measurements and Models for Radio Path Loss and Penetration Loss In and Around Homes and Trees at 5.85 GHz. IEEE Transactions on Communications 46(11), 1484–1496 (1998)
20. Schwengler, T., Gilbert, M.: Propagation Models at 5.8 GHz - Path Loss & Building Penetration. In: Proceedings of the IEEE Radio and Wireless Conference (RANCOM), September 2000, pp. 119–124 (2000)
21. Laurendeau, C., Barbeau, M.: Wireless Network-based Relative Span Weighted Localization of Uncooperative Nodes. Technical Report TR-09-04, School of Computer Science, Carleton University (2009)

A Consistency-Based Secure Localization Scheme against Wormhole Attacks in WSNs*

Honglong Chen[1], Wei Lou[1], and Zhi Wang[2]

[1] Department of Computing,
The Hong Kong Polytechnic University, Kowloon, Hong Kong
{cshlchen,csweilou}@comp.polyu.edu.hk
[2] State Key Laboratory of Industry Control Technology,
Zhejiang University, Hangzhou, P.R. China
wangzhizju@gmail.com

Abstract. Wormhole attacks can negatively affect the localization in wireless sensor networks. A typical wormhole attack can be launched by two colluding external attackers, one of which sniffs packets at one point in the network, tunnels them through a wired or wireless link to another point, and the other of which relays them within its vicinity. In this paper, we investigate the impact of the wormhole attack on the localization process and propose a novel consistency-based secure localization scheme against wormhole attacks, which includes wormhole attack detection, valid locators identification and self-localization. We also conduct the simulations to demonstrate the effectiveness of our proposed scheme.

Keywords: Consistency, secure localization, wormhole attack, wireless sensor networks.

1 Introduction

Wireless sensor networks (WSNs) consist of a large amount of sensor nodes which cooperate among themselves by wireless communications to solve problems in fields such as emergency response systems, military field operations, and environment monitoring systems. Nodal localization is one of the key techniques in WSNs. Most of current localization algorithms estimate the positions of location-unknown nodes based on the position information of a set of nodes (*locators*) and the inter-node measurements such as distance measurements or hop counts. Localization in WSNs has drawn growing attention from the researchers and many range-based and range-free approaches [1, 2, 3] have been proposed. However, most of the localization systems are vulnerable under the hostile environment where malicious attacks, such as the *replay attack* or *compromise attack* [4], can disturb the localization procedure. Security, therefore, becomes a significant concern of the localization process in hostile environments.

The *wormhole attack* is a typical kind of secure attacks in WSNs. It is launched by two colluding *external attackers* [4] which cannot compromise legitimate nodes or their cryptographic keys. One of the wormhole attackers overhears packets at one point

* This work is supported in part by grants PolyU 5236/06E, PolyU 5232/07E, PolyU 5243/08E, ZJU-SKL ICT0903, and NSFC No. 60873223 and No. 90818010.

B. Liu et al. (Eds.): WASA 2009, LNCS 5682, pp. 368–377, 2009.

in the network, tunnels them through the wormhole link to another point in the network, and the other wormhole attacker broadcasts the packets among its neighborhood nodes. This may cause a severe impact on the routing and localization procedures in WSNs. Khabbazian et al. [5] point out how the wormhole attack impacts on building the shortest path in routing protocols. For the localization procedure under wormhole attacks, some range-free approaches have been proposed [6, 7]; however, range-based approaches have not been well addressed.

In this paper, we propose a consistency-based secure localization scheme to defend against the wormhole attack on the range-based localization. It makes the following contributions: 1) A novel wormhole attack detection scheme is proposed to detect the existence of a wormhole attack and further distinguish the types of the wormhole attack; 2) A valid locator identification approach is designed to identify the valid neighboring locators of the sensor. Two independent algorithms are proposed to handle different wormhole attacks; 3) The simulations are conducted to demonstrate that our proposed scheme outperforms other existing schemes.

2 Related Work

The secure localization in hostile environment has been investigated for several years and many secure localization systems have been proposed.

To resist the compromise attack, Liu et al. [8] propose the range-based and range-free secure localization schemes respectively. SPINE [4] utilizes the verifiable multilateration and verification of positions into the secure localization in hostile network. ROPE [9] is a robust positioning system with a location verification mechanism that verifies the location claims of the sensors before data collection. TSCD [10] proposes a novel secure localization approach to defend against the distance-consistent spoofing attack using the consistency check on the distance measurements.

To detect the existence of wormhole attacks, researchers propose some wormhole attack detection approaches. In [11], *packet leashes* based on the notions of geographical and temporal leashes is proposed to detect the wormhole attack. Wang et al. [12] detect the wormhole attack by means of visualizing the anomalies introduced by incorrect distance measurements between two nodes caused by the wormhole attack. [13] further extends the method in [12] for large scale network by selecting some feature points to reduce the overlapping issue and preserving the major topology features. In [14], a detection scheme is elaborated by checking whether the maximum number of independent neighbors of two non-neighbor nodes is larger than the threshold.

To achieve secure localization in a WSN suffered from wormhole attacks, SeRLoc [6] detects the wormhole attack based on the *sector uniqueness* property and *communication range violation* property, then filters out the attacked locators. HiRLoc [7] further utilizes antenna rotations and multiple transmit power levels to improve the localization resolution. The schemes in [8] can also be applied into the localization against wormhole attacks. However, SeRLoc and HiRLoc needs extra hardware such as directional antennae and cannot obtain satisfied localization performance in that some attacked locators may still be undetected. [8] requires a large amount of computation and possibly becomes incompetent when malicious locators are more than the legitimate ones. In [15], Chen et al. propose to make each locator build a conflicting-set and then the sensor can use all conflicting sets of its neighboring locators to filter out incorrect distance measurements of its neighboring locators. The limitation of the scheme is that it only works properly when the system has no packet loss. As the attackers may drop the packets purposely, the packet loss is inevitable when the system is under a wormhole attack. Compared to the scheme in [15], the consistency-based secure localization scheme proposed in this paper can obtain high localization performance when the system has certain packet losses. Furthermore, it works well even when the malicious locators are more than the legitimate ones, which causes the malfunction of the scheme in [8].

3 Problem Formulation

In this section, we build the network model and the attack model, describe the related definitions and analyze the effect of the wormhole attack on the range-based localization, after which we classify the locators into three categories.

3.1 Network Model

Three different types of nodes are deployed in the network, including locators, sensors and attackers. The locators, with their own locations known in advance (by manual deployment or GPS devices), are randomly deployed in an Euclidean two-dimensional plane. The location-unknown sensors conduct self-localization based on their distances to neighboring locators. The attackers collude in pair to launch a wormhole attack to disrupt the localization of the sensors. All the nodes are assumed to have the same transmission range R. However, the communication range between two wormhole attackers can be larger than R, as they can communicate with each other using certain communication technique.

The sensors measure the distances to their neighboring locators using the Received Signal Strength Indicator (RSSI) method. For simplicity, we assume that the measurement error of the distance follows a normal distribution $N(\mu, \sigma)$ with the mean value $\mu = 0$ and the standard deviation σ. The sensors estimate their locations using the Maximum Likelihood Estimation (MLE) method [2].

3.2 Attack Model

The network is assumed to be deployed in hostile environment where wormhole attacks exist to disrupt the localization of sensors. During the wormhole attack, one attacker sniffs packets at one point in the network, tunnels them through the wormhole link to another point. Being as *external attackers* that cannot compromise legitimate nodes or their cryptographic keys, the wormhole attackers cannot acquire the content, e.g., the type, of the sniffed packets. However, the attackers can drop off the sniffed packets purposely to further deteriorate the sensor's localization process. The length of the wormhole link is assumed to be larger than R to avoid the endless packet transmission loops caused by the both attackers.

The wormhole attack endured by a node can be classified into *duplex wormhole attack* and *simplex wormhole attack* according to the geometrical relation between the node and the attackers. A node is under a duplex wormhole attack when it lies in the

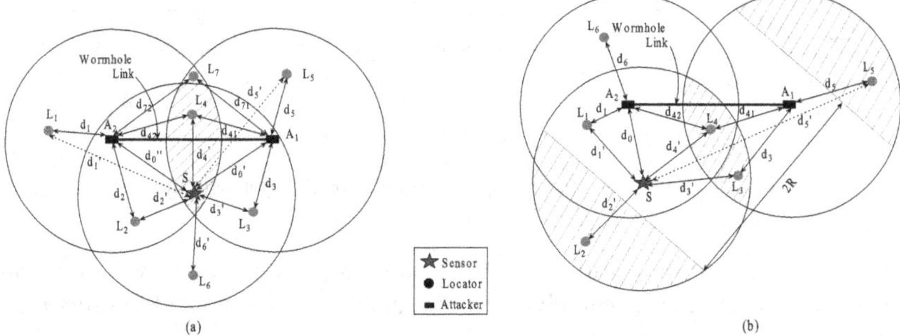

Fig. 1. (a) Duplex wormhole attack; (b) Simplex wormhole attack

common transmission area of the two attackers. On the other hand, a node is under a simplex wormhole attack when it lies in the transmission area of only one of the two attackers but not in the common transmission area. Fig. 1 shows the impact of the wormhole attack on the distance measurement of the sensor. When measuring the distance, the sensor broadcasts a request signal and waits for the responding beacon signals from the locators within its neighboring vicinity, based on which the sensor can use the RSSI method to estimate the distances to neighboring locators. For the duplex wormhole attack as shown in Fig. 1(a), when L_1 sends a beacon message to the sensor S, S will only get the distance measurement as d'_0 instead of the actual distance d'_1 because the RSSI received by S just reflects the propagational attenuation from A_1 to S. For L_2's beacon message, as the packet will travel through two different paths to reach S, $L_2 \to S$ and $L_2 \to A_2 \to A_1 \to S$ respectively, S will obtain two distance measurements d'_2 and d'_0. For L_4's beacon message, it travels through three paths to reach S, $L_4 \to S$, $L_4 \to A_2 \to A_1 \to S$ and $L_4 \to A_1 \to A_2 \to S$ respectively, thus S will get three distance measurements as d'_4, d'_0 and d''_0. For the simplex wormhole attack as shown in Fig. 1(b), when S receives the beacon message from L_5, it will measure the distance to L_5 as d_0. For L_3, two different distance measurements d'_3 and d_0 will be obtained. Thus, the locators which can communicate with the sensor via the wormhole link will introduce incorrect distance measurements.

All the locators which can exchange messages with the sensor, either via the wormhole link or not, are called *neighboring locators* (N-locators) of the sensor. Among these neighboring locators, the ones which can exchange messages with the sensor via the wormhole link are called *dubious locators* (D-locators), as their distance measurements may be incorrect and mislead the localization; the locators which lie in the transmission range of the sensor are called *valid locators* (V-locators), as the sensor can obtain correct distance measurements with respect to them and assist the localization.

In this paper, we denote the set of N-locators, D-locators and V-locators as $\mathcal{L}_N$, $\mathcal{L}_D$ and $\mathcal{L}_V$. For the scenario in Fig. 1(a), $\mathcal{L}_N = \{L_1, L_2, L_3, L_4, L_5, L_6, L_7\}$, $\mathcal{L}_D = \{L_1, L_2, L_3, L_4, L_5, L_7\}$ and $\mathcal{L}_V = \{L_2, L_3, L_4, L_6\}$. It is obvious that $\mathcal{L}_N = \mathcal{L}_V \cup \mathcal{L}_D$.

4 Secure Localization Scheme against Wormhole Attack

As the D-locators will negatively affect the localization of the sensor, it is critical for the sensor to identify the V-locators before the self-localization. In this section, we

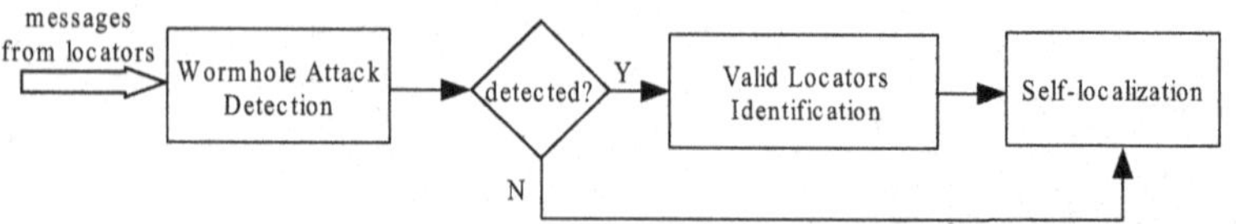

Fig. 2. Flow chart of the proposed secure localization scheme

propose a novel secure localization scheme against wormhole attack, which includes three phases shown in Fig. 2, namely wormhole attack detection, valid locators identification and self-localization:

- *Wormhole Attack Detection:* The sensor detects the wormhole attack using the proposed detection schemes and identifies the type of the wormhole attack.
- *Valid Locators Identification:* Corresponding to the duplex wormhole attack and the simplex wormhole attack, the sensor identifies the V-locators using different identification approaches.
- *Self-localization:* After identifying enough V-locators, the sensor conducts the self-localization using the MLE method with the correct distance measurements.

4.1 Wormhole Attack Detection

We assume that each locator periodically broadcasts a beacon message within its neighboring vicinity. The beacon message will contain the ID and location information of the source locator. When the network is threatened by a wormhole attack, some affected locators will detect the abnormality through beacon message exchanges. The following scenarios are considered abnormal for locators: (1) a locator receives the beacon message sent by itself; (2) a locator receives more than one copy of the same beacon message from another locator via different paths; (3) a locator receives a beacon message from another locator which is outside the transmission range of receiving locator. When the locator detects the message abnormality, it will consider itself under a wormhole attack. Moreover, if the locator detects the message abnormality under the first scenario, i.e., the locator receives the beacon message sent by itself, it will further derive that it is under a duplex wormhole attack. The beacon message has two additional bits to indicate these two statuses for each locator:

- detection bit: this bit will be set to 1 if the locator detects the message abnormality through beacon message exchanges; otherwise, this bit will be 0;
- type bit: this bit will be 1 if the locator detects itself under a duplex wormhole attack; otherwise, this bit will be 0.

When the sensor performs self-localization, it broadcasts a *Loc_req* message to its N-locators. As soon as the locator receives the *Loc_req* message from the sensor, it replies with an acknowledgement message *Loc_ack* similar to the beacon message, which includes the ID and location information of the locator. The *Loc_ack* message also includes above two status bits. When the sensor receives the *Loc_ack* message, it can measure the distance from the sending locator to itself using the RSSI. The sensor also calculates the response time of each N-locator based on the *Loc_ack* message using the approach in [10] to countervail the random delay on the MAC layer of the locator.

Detection scheme D1: If the sensor S detects that it receives the *Loc_req* message sent from itself, it can determine that it is currently under a duplex wormhole attack. For example, when the sensor is under the duplex wormhole attack as shown in Fig. 1(a), the *Loc_req* message transmitted by the sensor can travel from A_1 via the wormhole link to A_2 and then arrive at S after being relayed by A_2. Thus, S can determine that it is currently under a duplex wormhole attack.

Detection scheme D2: If the sensor S detects that the detection bit of the received *Loc_ack* message from any N-locator is set to 1, S can determine that it is under a simplex wormhole attack. Note that when using the detection scheme D2, the sensor may generate a false alarm if the sensor is outside the transmission areas of the attackers but any of its N-locators is inside the transmission areas of the attackers. However, this will only trigger the V-locators identification but not affect the self-localization result.

Algorithm 1. Wormhole Attack Detection Scheme

Sensor broadcasts a *Loc_req* message.
Each N-locator sends a *Loc_ack* message to the sensor, including the message abnormality detection result.
Sensor waits for the *Loc_ack* messages to measure the distance to each N-locator and to calculate the response time of each N-locator.
if sensor detects the attack using scheme D1 **then**
    A duplex wormhole attack is detected.
else if sensor detects the attack using scheme D2 **then**
    A simplex wormhole attack is detected.
else
    No wormhole attack is detected.

The pseudocode of wormhole attack detection is shown in Algorithm 1. The sensor broadcasts a *Loc_req* message for self-localization. When receiving the *Loc_req* message, each N-locator replies a *Loc_ack* message including whether it has detected the abnormality. The sensor measures the distances to its N-locators based on the *Loc_ack* messages using RSSI method and calculates the response time of each N-locator. If the sensor reccives the *Loc_req* message sent by itself, it determines that it is under duplex wormhole attack. Otherwise, if the sensor is informed by any N-locator that the abnormality is detected, it declares that it is under simplex wormhole attack. If no wormhole attack is detected, the sensor conducts the MLE localization.

4.2 Valid Locators Identification Approach

Duplex Wormhole Attack: When detecting that it is currently under a duplex wormhole attack, the sensor tries to identify all its V-locators for secure localization. Take L_2 in Fig. 1(a) for example, when receiving the *Loc_req* message from the sensor, L_2 responds a *Loc_ack* message. As the sensor lies in the transmission range of L_2, the *Loc_ack* message can be received by the sensor directly. In addition, the *Loc_ack* message can also travel from A_2 via the wormhole link to A_1 then arrive at the sensor. Therefore, the sensor can receive the *Loc_ack* message from L_2 for more than once. However, there will be three different scenarios: (1) the locator lies in the transmission range of the sensor and its message is received by the sensor for three times (such as

L_4 in Fig. 1(a)); (2) the locator lies out of the transmission range of the sensor and its message is received by the sensor for twice (such as L_7 in Fig. 1(a)); (3) the locator lies in the transmission range of the sensor and its message is received by the sensor for twice (such as L_2 in Fig. 1(a)). We can see that L_2 and L_4 are V-locators, but not V_7. The sensor will use the following valid locator identification scheme to find the V-locators.

Identification scheme I1: When the sensor is under a duplex wormhole attack, if the sensor receives the *Loc_ack* message from a N-locator for three times and the type bit in the *Loc_ack* message is set to 1, this N-locator will be considered as a V-locator (such as L_4 in Fig. 1(a)). As the sensor only countervails the MAC layer delay of the locators but not the attackers when calculating the response time, the message traveling via the wormhole link is considered to take a longer response time. Thus, the distance measurement based on the *Loc_ack* message from this V-locator which takes the shortest response time will be considered correct. If the sensor receives the *Loc_ack* message of a N-locator for just twice and the type bit in the *Loc_ack* message is set to 1, this N-locator will be treated as a D-locator (such as L_7 in Fig. 1(a)). For the last scenario, if the sensor receives the *Loc_ack* message of a N-locator for twice and the type bit in the *Loc_ack* message is set to 0, this N-locator will be considered as a V-locator, and the distance measurement based on the *Loc_ack* message with a shorter response time will be considered as correct (such as L_2 in Fig. 1(a)).

Distance consistency property of V-locators: Assuming a set of locators $\mathbb{L} = \{(x_1, y_1), (x_2, y_2), ..., (x_m, y_m)\}$ and corresponding measured distances $\mathbb{D} = \{d_1, d_2, ..., d_m\}$, where (x_i, y_i) is the location of L_i and d_i is the measured distance from the sensor to L_i, $i = 1, 2, ..., m$. Based on $\mathbb{L}$ and $\mathbb{D}$, the estimated location of the sensor is $(\tilde{x}_0, \tilde{y}_0)$. The mean square error of the location estimation is $\delta^2 = \sum_{i=1}^{m} \frac{[d_i - \sqrt{(\tilde{x}_0 - x_i)^2 + (\tilde{y}_0 - y_i)^2}]^2}{m}$. The distance consistency property of V-locators states that the mean square error of the location estimation based on the correct distance measurements is lower than a small threshold while the mean square error of the location estimation based on the distance measurements which contains some incorrect ones is not lower than that threshold.

Identification scheme I2: If the sensor determines no less than two V-locators using the identification scheme I1, it can identify other V-locators by checking whether the distance estimation is consistent. A predefined threshold τ^2 of the mean square error is determined, that is, a distance estimation with a mean square error smaller than τ^2 is considered to be consistent. As shown in Fig. 1(a), the sensor can identify L_2, L_3 and L_4 as V-locators and obtain the correct distance measurements to them. For other undetermined locators, the sensor can identify them one by one. For example, to check whether L_1 is a V-locator, the sensor can estimate its own location based on the distance measurements to L_1, L_2, L_3 and L_4. As the distance measurement to L_1 is incorrect, the mean square error of the estimated location may exceed τ^2, which means that L_1 is not a V-locator. When the sensor checks the distance consistency of L_2, L_3, L_4 and L_6, it can get that the mean square error is lower than τ^2, thus L_6 is treated as a V-locator, and the distance measurement to L_6 is correct. After checking each of the undetermined N-locators, the sensor can identify all V-locators with the correct distance measurements.

Simplex Wormhole Attack: If the sensor detects that it is under a simplex wormhole attack, it will adopt the following valid locators identification schemes.

Identification scheme I3: When the sensor is under a simplex wormhole attack as shown in Fig. 1(b), if it receives the *Loc_ack* message from a N-locator twice, this N-locator will be considered as a V-locator. For example, when L_3 in Fig. 1(b) replies a *Loc_ack* message to the sensor, this message will travel through two different paths to the sensor, one directly from L_3 to the sensor and the other from L_3 to A_1 via the wormhole link to the sensor. Therefore, the sensor can conclude L_3 is a V-locator. To further obtain the correct distance measurement to L_3, the sensor compares the response times of the *Loc_ack* message from L_3 through different paths and the one with a shorter response time is considered correct. Similarly, L_4 can also be identified as a V-locator and its correct distance measurement can be obtained.

Spatial property: The sensor cannot receive messages from two N-locators simultaneously if the distance between these two N-locators is larger than $2R$.

Identification scheme I4: When the sensor is under a simplex wormhole attack as shown in Fig. 1(b), if the spatial property is violated by two N-locators, it is obviously that one of them is a V-locator and the other is a D-locator. For instance, the distance between L_2 and L_5 in Fig. 1(b) is larger than $2R$, after receiving *Loc_ack* messages from them, the sensor can detect that the spatial property is broken. As the *Loc_ack* message from L_5 travels via the wormhole link to the sensor, it will take a longer response time than that from L_2. The sensor will regard the locator with a shorter response time (L_2 in this case) as a V-locator, and the other (L_5) as a D-locator. The distance measurement to L_2 is also considered correct.

Identification scheme I5: When the sensor is under a simplex wormhole attack, similar to the identification scheme I2, if the sensor detects at least two V-locators using the identification schemes I3 and I4, it can identify other V-locators based on the distance consistency property of V-locators. Take the scenario in Fig. 1(b) for example, the sensor can identify L_2, L_3 and L_4 as V-locators and obtain the correct distance measurements to them. The sensor can further identify other V-locators by checking the distance consistency. A mean square error smaller than τ^2 can be obtained when the sensor estimates its location based on L_1, L_2, L_3 and L_4 because they are all V-locators. So the sensor can conclude L_1 is a V-locator and the distance measurement to L_1 is correct.

The procedure of valid locators identification approach is listed in Algorithm 2: If the sensor detects that it is under a duplex wormhole attack, it will conduct the identification scheme I1 to identify V-locators. As the distance consistency check needs as least 3 locators, if the sensor identifies no less than 2 V-locators, it can use the identification scheme I2 to identify other V-locators. On the other hand, if the sensor detects that it is under a simplex wormhole attack, it adopts the identification schemes I3 and I4 to identify the V-locators. After that, if at least 2 V-locators are identified, the sensor conducts the scheme I5 to detect other V-locators.

5 Simulation Evaluation

In this section, we present the simulation results to demonstrate the effectiveness of the proposed consistency-based secure localization scheme. The network parameters are set as follows: the transmission range R of all types of nodes is set as $15m$; the standard deviation of the distance measurement $\sigma = 0.5$; the threshold for the distance

Algorithm 2. Valid Locators Identification Approach

```
if S detects a duplex wormhole attack then
    Conduct scheme I1 to identify V-locators.
    if the identified V-locators ≥ 2 then
        Conduct scheme I2 to identify other V-locators.
else if S detects a simplex wormhole attack then
    Conduct schemes I3 and I4 to identify V-locators.
    if the identified V-locators ≥ 2 then
        Conduct scheme I5 to identify other V-locators.
```

consistency $\tau^2 = 1$; the network packet loss rate is 5%. We show the performance results of the proposed scheme when the density of locators, denoted as ρ_l, and the ratio of the length of the wormhole link (i.e., the distance between two attackers) to the transmission range, denoted as L/R, are various.

Fig. 3(a) demonstrates the performance comparison of wormhole attack detection probability between our scheme and SeRLoc scheme when $\rho_l = 0.006/m^2$ (with the average degree around 4) and L/R is from 1 to 5. It can be observed that our scheme obtain a performance with the probability higher than 97%. Although the two schemes gain the similar performance when $L/R > 3.5$, our scheme outperforms SeRLoc scheme, especially when $L/R < 2$.

Fig. 3(b) shows the performance of our proposed scheme, SeRLoc scheme, the consistency scheme [8] and the scheme without any detection process when $\rho_l = 0.006/m^2$ and L/R is from 1 to 5. The SeRLoc scheme identifies some D-locators first, then conducts self-localization based on the rest locators. However, SeRLoc scheme does not distinguish the duplex wormhole attack and simplex wormhole attack, and it may be invalid when under the duplex wormhole attack. The consistency scheme identifies the D-locators based on the consistency check of the estimation result, the locator which is the most inconsistent one will be considered as a D-locator. The localization result is considered as successful when $d_{err1} \leq d_{err2} + f_{tol} * R$, where d_{err1} (and d_{err2}) denotes the localization error with (and without) using the secure localization scheme, f_{tol} is the factor of the error tolerance of the localization (f_{tol} is set as 0.1 in our simulations). The performance of the scheme without any detection process shows the severe impact of the wormhole attack on the localization process, which makes the localization totally fail when L/R is larger than 2. Fig. 3(b) shows that our proposed scheme obtains much better performance than the other schemes.

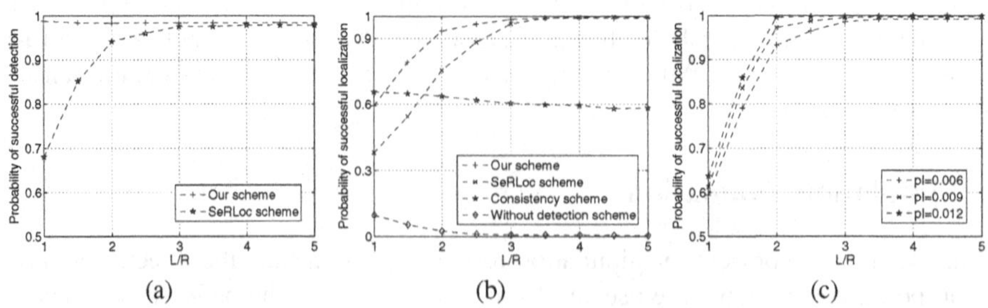

Fig. 3. Performance evaluation: (a) Probability of wormhole attack detection; (b) Probability of successful localization; (c) Probability of successful localization under different locator densities

Fig. 3(c) shows the performance of successful localization of the proposed scheme under different locator densities. We can see that the increase of locator density only has some slight improvement on the probability of the successful localization.

6 Conclusion and Future Work

In this paper, we analyze the impact of the wormhole attack on the range-based localization. We propose a novel consistency-based secure localization mechanism against wormhole attacks. The simulation results are presented to demonstrate the effectiveness of our proposed scheme on the wormhole attack detection and secure localization. Although the proposed approach is described based on the RSSI method, it can be easily applied to the localization based on the time-of-arrival or time-difference-of-arrival methods. In the future, our work will focus on the secure localization when the sensor is under multiple wormholes' attack simultaneously and we also intend to consider the secure localization when different nodes have different transmission radii.

References

1. Savvides, A., Han, C., Srivastava, M.: Dynamic Fine-Grained Localization in Ad-hoc Networks of Sensors. In: Proc. of ACM MOBICOM (2001)
2. Zhao, M., Servetto, S.D.: An Analysis of the Maximum Likelihood Estimator for Localization Problems. In: Proc. of IEEE ICBN (2005)
3. Bahl, P., Padmanabhan, V.N.: RADAR:An In-building RF-based User Location and Tracking System. In: Proc. of IEEE INFOCOM (2000)
4. Capkun, S., Hubaux, J.P.: Secure Positioning of Wireless Devices with Application to Sensor Networks. In: Proc. of IEEE INFOCOM (2005)
5. Khabbazian, M., Mercier, H., Bhargava, V.K.: Wormhole Attack in Wireless Ad Hoc Networks: Analysis and Countermeasure. In: Proc. of IEEE GLOBECOM (2006)
6. Lazos, L., Poovendran, R.: SeRLoc: Robust Localization for Wireless Sensor Networks. ACM Trans. on Sensor Networks, 73–100 (2005)
7. Lazos, L., Poovendran, R.: HiRLoc: High-Resolution Robust Localization for Wireless Sensor Networks. IEEE Journal on Selected Areas in Communications 24, 233–246 (2006)
8. Liu, D., Ning, P., Du, W.: Attack-Resistant Location Estimation in Sensor Networks. In: Proc. of IEEE IPSN (2005)
9. Lazos, L., Poovendran, R., Capkun, S.: ROPE: Robust Position Estimation in Wireless Sensor Networks. In: Proc. of IEEE IPSN (2005)
10. Chen, H., Lou, W., Ma, J., Wang, Z.: TSCD: A Novel Secure Localization Approach for Wireless Sensor Networks. In: Proc. of the 2nd Int'l Conf. on Sensor Technologies and Applications (2008)
11. Hu, Y.C., Perrig, A., Johnson, D.B.: Packet Leashes: A Defense Against Wormhole Attacks in Wireless Networks. In: Proc. of IEEE INFOCOM (2003)
12. Wang, W., Bhargava, B.: Visualization of Wormholes in Sensor Networks. In: Proc. of ACM WiSe (2004)
13. Wang, W., Lu, A.: Interactive wormhole detection and evaluation. Information Visualization 6, 3–17 (2007)
14. Maheshwari, R., Gao, J., Das, S.R.: Detecting Wormhole Attacks in Wireless Networks Using Connectivity Information. In: Proc. of IEEE INFOCOM (2007)
15. Chen, H., Lou, W., Wang, Z.: Conflicting-Set-Based Wormhole Attack Resistant Localization in Wireless Sensor Networks. In: Proc. of the 6th International Conference on Ubiquitous Intelligence and Computing (2009)

Can You See Me? The Use of a Binary Visibility Metric in Distance Bounding

Michelle Graham and David Gray

School of Computing, Dublin City University, Dublin, Republic of Ireland
mgraham@computing.dcu.ie, dgray@computing.dcu.ie

Abstract. Wireless networks are becoming more and more commonplace, with ubiquitous computing flourishing in this ever expanding environment. As this occurs, the demand for a reliable method of locating devices has also increased dramatically. Locating devices with no a prioi knowledge is a very large problem, requiring much special equipment. Instead, we focus on the issue of location verification, a smaller aspect of the location issue. Distance bounding is a well respected technique used in this area, however it relies on precise calculations to locate a device. We propose a method of locating a device which does not rely on these calculations. Instead, we employ a binary "yes/no" visibility metric, where neighbouring devices indicate whether they can "see" or communicate directly with the claiming device. We confirm the existence of a direct link through excluding the possibility of a proxied connection being employed. The intersection of the ranges of these devices can then be used to extract a location area, without relying on calculating exact distances through precise timings.

1 Introduction

The issue of location verification is relatively new to the area of research. Previously, focus was upon locating a device with no a priori knowledge. However, location verification simplifies this problem through limiting the field in which the device may possibly be located. This reduces the location verification issue to discovering whether or not a device is present within a specific area.

Location verification has a number of uses within the area of security. For example, a device may need to be granted access to some facilities within a secure network. This access should only be granted when the device is physically present within the area of the network. The system must therefore first ascertain whether the device is physically located in the area of the network, or merely using some form of proxy to gain access. We propose a method of location verification employing distance bounding which guards against proxy attacks such as this.

The technique of distance bounding was first proposed by Brands and Chaum in [1] as a method of determining the upper bound on the physical distance between two parties. This is achieved using a challenge-response scenario, where the delay between sending a bit and receiving the corresponding response bit

B. Liu et al. (Eds.): WASA 2009, LNCS 5682, pp. 378–387, 2009.

is timed and a distance extrapolated. This method of location extraction has been employed in varying approaches [2,3,4], however as the calculations are of such a precise nature, the resulting location is often inaccurate. We propose a method of verifying the location of a device in a wireless network without requiring these precise measurements. Instead, a device claiming its location (a *claimant*) distance bounds with multiple neighbouring devices (*verifiers*) in the claimed area. Each of the verifiers produce a binary yes/no verdict concerning the visibility of the claimant to them. A claimant can communicate with a verifier through either a direct or proxied connection. A direct connection is deemed to be where the claimant and the verifier are within one hop of each other in an ad hoc network. We propose that receiving a positive visibility verdict indicates that a claimant has completed the distance bounding process satisfactorily and does not appear to be utilising a proxy connection. As the only other method of communication between a claimant and its verifier is through a direct connection, it follows that a positive visibility verdict indicates that the claimant is present in the area of that verifier. This binary metric and its related issues are explained further in sect. 3.

The remainder of our paper is structured as follows: In Sect. 2, we discuss the technique of distance bounding in greater detail and examine other work in the area. In Sect. 3, we describe the use of a binary metric and how it can result in the calculation of a location. In Sect. 4, we detail the results of simulated "honest" distance bounding exchanges and those involving a proxy. In Sect. 5, we outline our plans for future work in the area of this binary metric and finally in Sect. 5, we present our conclusions regarding this work.

2 Literature Review

Distance bounding was first proposed in 1993 by Brands and Chaum [1]. The process involves a device A sending a challenge bit to device B and timing the delay between transmission and receiving the corresponding responce bit back. This delay is used to calculate an upper bound on the distance between devices A and B. In practice, a series of these exchanges is done to lessen the effects of network delays on the overall result.

Without any protection or additional security, distance bounding is vulnerable to a number of attacks, most notably the mafia and proxy attacks. The *mafia fraud* [5] is a form of *man-in-the-middle* attack where an intruder acts as both a malicious claiming device and a malicious verifying device in between an honest claiming device and an honest verifiying device. The intruder interacts with an honest claiming device as a verifier and with an honest verifying device as a claiming device, passing off the honest claimant's responses as his own. In essence this allows him to identify himself as the honest claimant to the honest verifier. The *proxy attack* is an extension of the mafia fraud, where both the claiming device and the intruder collaborate to deceive the verifying device. As in the mafia fraud, the intruder passes off messages to the verifying device from the claiming device as his own. However, unlike in the mafia fraud, the claiming device is fully aware that this is happening, and has enlisted the intruder to act as its proxy. This attack allows the claiming device to convince the verifying device that it is physically closer than it actually is.

The concept of distance bounding is used across a range of communication technologies in order to verify a claimed location. Sastry, Shankar and Wagnar presented a method for distance bounding called the Echo protocol [2] utilising the difference in propagation time between ultrasound and radiofrequency (RF) transmissions. However, this approach leaves the protocol open to a proxy attack as a colluding device inserted between the proving device and the verifying device allows the prover to transmit its reply to the colluder over RF. The colluding device can then replay the reply back to the verifier over ultrasound. As RF has a faster propagation than ultrasound, the attack would not be detected.

Hancke and Kuhn [4] have proposed a protocol for distance bounding based on ultra-wideband pulse communication, using RFID devices. Again, precise timings are employed to calculate whether the device in question is within a specific distance from the verifying device. In this approach, a single nonce is sent from the verifying device to the proving device and used in a pseudorandom function in combination with the secret key shared by both parties. The resulting bits are then inserted into two shift registers and used over a series of exchanges. The inclusion of a secret key ties the resulting bits to the prover. However, the bit calculation stage is not timed and therefore the resulting bits can still be passed on to a proxy. In addition to this, RFID devices are extremely limited in range, from a matter of centimeters up to a metre, and a location verification scheme based upon this technology would not be practical outside of a select set of circumstances.

Waters and Felten [3] presented a protocol for distance bounding for use within wireless networks known as the proximity-proving protocol. The use of wireless networks makes this a more useful approach for general location verification than that put forth by Hancke & Kuhn. In this approach, a proving device contacts a trusted Location Manager (LM) to prove that it is in the area of that LM. Unlike in Brands & Chaum's approach, the LM & proving device distance bound using nonces, rather than single bit challenge and responses. However, the precise timings are again used to calculate an exact upper bound on the possible distance between the prover and the LM.

3 The Binary Metric

3.1 Introduction

In this section, we outline the premise of a binary metric for use with distance bounding in a wireless network and examine its usefulness. As described in Sect. 1, the proposed binary metric is a yes/no "visibility" metric. A device can only participate in a distance bounding exchange via either a direct connection to a verifying device or through at least one proxying device. Digital signatures are employed on the return leg of the distance bounding to tie the results of the exchange to that claimant. Therefore if a claimant is visible to a verifier, i.e. it can communicate with the verifier, it is either participating honestly or is attempting to mount a proxy attack. The binary metric is designed to detect whether or not a claimant is a single wireless network hop from its verifier. As the distance over which a message can travel in a single hop on a wireless network is limited, this definition provides an upper bound on the possible distance between the claimant and its verifier.

The binary metric is designed for use within a location verification protocol which protects the proof gathering exchange from mafia frauds and proxy attacks through the use of encryption. A device provides a location claim to a central system server, supplying it with its current location. This location does not have to be provided by a specific device, but can be sourced from any suitable device, such as either a user inputting a location or coordinates supplied by a GPS [6] device. Neighbouring devices (*verifiers*) within the wireless network produce a yes or no verdict indicating whether the claiming device (*claimant*) is able to communicate with them within a reasonable time limit. These verdicts are employed as a tool to verify the location claim, in place of the round trip times used by other approaches. Instead of calculating an upper bound on the distance between the claimant and verifier, a yes verdict indicates that the claimant is somewhere within direct communication range of the verifier.

3.2 Honest vs. Proxy Exchanges

The proposed use of a binary metric in distance bounding removes the reliance on timing to calculate an upper bound on the possible distance between the claimant and a verifier. However, when dealing with this binary metric we employ a time limit on the acceptable delay time between the verifier sending its challenge and receiving the claimant's response. This is included as a security measure, to distinguish between a proxy attack and an honest exchange. When a verifier engages in distance bounding with an honest claimant, the response time is 2x+s+d, where s is the fixed time required to digitally sign the response, d is the computational delay and x is the message's transmission time for a single network hop. However, when a verifier engages in distance bounding with a malicious claimant who launches a proxy attack on the process, the response time must be greater than 2x+s+d. This is due to the fact that during the course of a proxy attack, the message being transmitted does not undergo a single network hop in each direction, but many.

In an honest exchange, a challenge is sent from the verifier to the claimant and the claimant's response is sent directly back. However, during a proxy attack, the verifier's challenge is sent to the proxy device, who then forwards it on through at least one hop on the network to reach the true claimant. The true claimant's response must then also travel the extra steps to reach the proxy before being relayed back to the verifier. It is these additional message hops that increase the response time of a proxy attack. We propose to use this flaw in the proxy attack's design to detect its occurance. A claimant cannot communicate with its verifiers without either a direct or proxied connection. Therefore, the ability of the binary metric to detect the presence of a proxy attack also allows it to function as a verification method, proving that the claimant is in the claimed area.

In order for this attack detection to function, the time difference between a proxy attack's distance bounding run and an honest distance bounding exchange must be significant enough for there to be little to no overlap in times. If there is no overlap between the possible times taken for an honest claimant to complete its distance bounding and a malicious claimant to perform a proxy attack, then the occurance of a proxy attack is easily detectable. One danger when dealing with the detection of a proxy attack using timings such as these is that the computational delay will drown out the difference in transmission times between an honest exchange and a proxy attack. In order to confirm that this issue does not pose a threat to the functionality of the approach, we have conducted multiple network simulations, which are discussed in Sect. 4. However, digitally signing the reply message does not impact the detection of a proxy attack as this process is standardised. As the keys employed within this process are kept within a tamper-resistant unit, the time require for signing is standardised by this unit. Due to its constant value, this time can be subtracted out of the round trip time prior to attempting the detection of a proxy.

3.3 What Does a "Yes" Verdict Mean?

There are two possible verdicts which a verifier may provide regarding a claimant: the claimant is visible to it during distance bounding or the claimant is not visible. While these two verdicts appear to be straightforward, their meanings are not so. If a claimant is found by a verifier to be visible during distance bounding and a proxy attack is not deemed to have occured, then that claimant is deemed to be within the area of that verifier. It is impossible for a verifier to mistakenly find that a claimant is in the area when it is not, due to the fact that the exchange is tied to that particular claimant through the use of digital signatures.

If a verifier judges that a claimant is visible to it during distance bounding, it must first have received multiple valid responses to its challenges from that claimant within an acceptable time frame. Without the aid of a proxy device located closer to the verifier than itself, the claimant is not capable of proving itself to be in the area of the verifier. Proxy attacks are ruled out through the use of time limits, and so any positive visibility results on the part of a verifier cannot be a mistake. Therefore, if a verifier gives a positive verdict, either the verifier is acting maliciously and supplying a false positive, or the claimant is behaving honestly and communicating directly with the verifier.

3.4 What Does a "No" Verdict Mean?

When a verifier uses the binary visibility metric, it can result in either a positive visibility verdict (where it can "see" the claimant) or a negative visibility metric (where the claimant is not visible at all or does not respond within the time limit, indicating the employment of a proxied connection). Unlike in the case of a positive visibility verdict, there are multiple possible reasons for a verifier stating that the claimant is not visible during the distance bounding process.

The three main reasons for a negative visibility verdict are: the claimant is not present in the area, the claimant is in the area but not within range of the verifier or that there are network issues preventing the claimant from completing distance bounding within the time limit.

The simplest reason for a negative verdict is that the claimant is not present in the area. In this case, the claimant could either have mistakenly made a false location claim, it could have moved on from that location before the distance bounding occurred (a distinct danger if the system is based in the area of Vehicular Ad-Hoc Networks [7], where participants are usually in motion during exchanges) or finally, it could have attempted to deceive the system through claiming to be in a specific location and hoping that the system's detection measures would be flawed.

The remaining reasons outlined for a negative verdict on the part of the verifier are caused by a failure in the technology upon which this system is built. Although the claimant is in the area in both cases, a falsely negative verdict is received. Either the range of the verifier is too limited to allow for the claimant to distance bound directly with it, removing its chance for a positive verdict, or the network over which distance bounding is to occur is too unreliable to allow it. Although distance bounding is undertaken multiple times to lessen the effects of network issues on the eventual outcome, it the network is consistantly poor, either too noisy or too lossy, then the claimant will not be able to distance bound successfully within its allowed time frame. It is for these reasons that we do not factor negative visibility verdicts into the calculation of location at the end of the distance bounding process. While there are some cases in which the negative verdict is genuinely deserved, there are also multiple scenarios in which a false negative is received, which could pollute the location calculations. As there can be no mistaken positive verdicts due to the inclusion of digital signatures, we employ only these in the final location calculation.

3.5 The Binary Metric vs. Precise Calculations – What's Changed?

The typical approach to location verification with regard to distance bounding is in order to verify that a device is within range of a specific resource or location ([4,8,9,10]) through calculating an upper bound on the possible distance between the device and required resource/location. This is done by precisely timing the delay between a verifier sending a challenge and receiving the appropriate response back from the claimant. This round trip time is then used to calculate a greatest possible distance, through using the speed at which the signal can travel in that time. In the case of the Echo protocol, both the speed of sound and the speed of light are factored into the calculation of distance. When dealing with distance bounding in wireless networks, such as with the proximity proving protocol, the processing time on the part of the verifier is subtracted from the round trip time. This figure is halved and multiplied by the speed of light (approximately $3 * 10^8$m/s) to calculate an upper bound on the possible distance between the claimant and the verifier.

This approach differs greatly to the approach proposed in this work. Receiving a positive visibility verdict from multiple verifiers regarding the same location claim allows for the area in which that claimant could be located in to be reduced down through a form of triangulation. In this process, the possible broadcast ranges for each of the verifiers contacted are noted, and the broadcast areas (usually circles or spheres) are overlaid. The area of intersection between all of these areas is the only region in which the claimant could possibly be located, thus proving the location claim of the claimant.

4 Results to Date

4.1 Introduction

In order for the binary visibility metric to be considered practical for reliable location verification, it must be able to detect whether or not a proxy attack is underway during the distance bounding exchange. If the metric does not detect this attack, results gained in this approach would not be trustworthy. The nature of a proxy attack on a distance bounding exchange at least doubles the transmission time of any given message. It is this increase in response time which the verifier checks for when calculating its visibility verdict, in order to confirm that a proxy attack is not being carried out. However, one of the main issues with this method of proxy attack detection is that the time lost to network latencies and computational delays would drown out the difference between the time required for an honest exchange to complete and that required by a proxy attack. In order to confirm that this issue does not threaten the integrity of the detection approach, we have carried out distance bounding simulations and analysed the resulting times. We discuss these simulations and their results in this section.

4.2 Theoretical Calculations and Simulation Outline

The direct exchange of a message between two honest agents in a network is simulated by the transmission of a single ethernet frame to the ethernet address of the receiving agent (modelling the claimant). The receiving agent then creates a new frame and transmits this frame back to the ethernet address of the initial agent (modelling the verifier). In the case of a proxy attack, this situation is extended to include three devices, the claimant, a verifier and a proxying device. The message being sent is transmitted from the verifier to the proxy device, who then forwards it on to the claimant. This was chosen as it is the simplest possible proxy scenario. Therefore, if this situation is detectable using the binary metric, all proxy scenarios are vulnerable to detection.

Prior to the execution of the round trip simulations, we first completed theoretical estimations. These estimations are based on the theoretical maximum possible speeds at which the network equipment to be used could perform within the network specified. The figures were calculated as an indicator of whether or not the theory being put forth regarding proxy attack detection was theoretically possible. In addition to this, the estimates were used as a baseline with which the simulation results could be compared. These comparisons allowed for the detection of flaws in the simulation software, preventing inaccurate results from being given creedence and employed within this work.

The network equipment employed for these simulations was comprised of 2 laptop computers, each running ubuntu with a 802.11 b/g [11] network card. The units were connected to an ad-hoc network with a connection speed of 11mb/s. Using this information, the estimate figures were calculated as follows: In the direct exchange of a message, the message contents are sent in an ethernet frame. This frame is 10944 bits (1368 bytes) in size, including all ethernet headers. It is sent over a 11 mb/s connection twice, with the time required to transmit a single bit over this connection being $\frac{1}{11534336}$ seconds. The transmission of a single ethernet frame of this size once takes $\frac{1}{11534336} * \frac{10944}{1} = \frac{10944}{11534336}$. This is equivililant to 948.819 microseconds. Therefore the total round trip transmission time is $948.819 * 2 = 1897.638$ microseconds.

From these calculations, we can infer that the theoretical round trip time for a proxy scenario such as the one described above, situated in the same ad hoc network is at best $948.819 * 4$, or 3795.276 microseconds. These calculations do not take into account the computation latencies incurred at each point in the journey, and their results are therefore the absolute minimum that the exchanges could be completely in.

4.3 Round Trip Timing Simulation Results

After completing the direct scenario simulations and analysing the resulting times, it was discovered that the time required for a message to complete a round trip between two devices fluctuated over several thousand microseconds. However, upon further analysis of these figures, a *window of acceptance* emerged, within which an average of 93.58% of the results were received over 28 simulation runs, each containing 10000 exchanges. This window of acceptance was discovered to extend to within 2000 microseconds of the fastest round trip time achieved within that simulation's run.

The average fastest time achieved for a round trip was found to be 3264 microseconds, with an average of 9356 frames per simulation received within 2000 microseconds of this time (5264 microseconds). Therefore if this figure were enacted as an upper limit on the time in which a frame could acceptably be received in during direct distance bounding, 93.56% of the frames transmitted during these experiments would be accepted by a verifier. The inclusion of multiple iterations of distance bounding in the interaction removes the issue that a single frame's slow round trip would remove the ability of the claimant to prove itself visible. The odds of network problems repeating over a series of exchanges are very low, and multiple accepted frames cancel the negative effects of one or two failures.

As yet, no simulation data dealing with the proxy scenario is available. However, using the minimum time in which a direct exchange was achieved as a baseline (3256 microseconds) and employing the theoretical minimum required time to complete an exchange between two devices, we can infer that a proxied exchange set within this network enviroment would require at least 3256 + 1897.638, or 5153.638 microseconds at a minimum to complete. While this does fall within the window of acceptance defined above, computational delay on two devices is not taken into account, an unavoidable delay. In addition to this, network delays on two message transmissions are also omitted, which also increases the time required to complete the exchange. The odds of these increases amounting to less than 110.362 microseconds are extremely low. However, if it were possible that the absolute minimum time for a proxied exchange to be completed was within the window of acceptance, it is still highly unlikely that a proxy attempt would not be detected. This is due to the inclusion of multiple iterations of distance bounding. In order for the proxy attempt to succeed, the absolute minimum time required would need to be achieved not just once, but many times over.

Whilst carrying out these simulations, it was discovered that employing devices with vastly varied specifications and capabilities led to inaccurate and inconclusive distance bounding results. This is due to the need for predictability in the resulting round trip times. If claimant A) can complete an exchange in 3564 microseconds, but claimant B) has slower equipment and can only complete the exchange in 12834 microseconds, it will appear to the verifier as though claimant B) is attempting to carry out a proxy attack even if claimant B) is behaving honestly. For this reason, equipment used to carry out distance bounding employing the binary metric must be standardised to achieve roughly the same speed of exchange. An alternative approach to standardisation could be employed whereby the verifier is informed of the speed to be expected from a claimant prior to completing distance bounding. However, this is vulnerable to attack, as the claimant could lie about its minimum possible exchange speed, thus allowing enough time to carry out a proxy attack without detection.

5 Conclusion and Future Work

In this paper, we introduced the issue of location verification and how distance bounding has traditionally functioned as a technique in this area. We then put forth the concept of distance bounding using only a binary visibility metric, in which a verifying device indicates only whether a claiming device can respond within a reasonable time limit. Although the binary metric does not result in a specific location, distance bounding which relies on precise timing calculations also does not result in a single point of location. The use of a binary metric requires fewer precise calculations, yet still produces a similar quality of location verification information. We have outlined simulations carried out over an 802.11 network which support our theory that employing a reasonable time limit on the response time from a claimant can detect proxy attacks, rather than leaving the technique vulnerable to them.

One aspect of the visibility metric which has not been discussed here is the selection of verifying devices for use by a claimant. The location of verifiers in relation to both the claimant and to each other plays a vital role in the size of the eventual location area in which a claimant could be present. Our intention is to optimise the selection process in order to extract the maximum amount of location information from the final result and minimise the resulting possible location area. The most naive approach to this issue would be to simply select the verifiers whose broadcast areas overlap the least. However, although this would provide the smallest possible final location area, it is also vulnerable to tampering through planted malicious verifiers colluding with a claimant. Therefore, we must also weigh protection from tampering against location information extraction.

References

1. Brands, S., Chaum, D.: Distance-bounding protocols (extended abstract). In: Theory and Application of Cryptographic Techniques, pp. 344–359 (1993)
2. Sastry, N., Shankar, U.: Wagner, D.: Secure verification of location claims. Technical report (2003)
3. Waters, B., Felten, E.: Secure, private proofs of location. Technical report, Princeton University (2003)
4. Hancke, G.P., Kuhn, M.G.: An rfid distance bounding protocol. In: SECURECOMM 2005: Proceedings of the First International Conference on Security and Privacy for Emerging Areas in Communications Networks, Washington D.C., pp. 67–73. IEEE Computer Society Press, Los Alamitos (2005)
5. Desmedt, Y.: Major security problems with the 'unforgeable' (feige)-fiat-shamir proofs of identity and how to overcome them. In: Proceedings of SECURICOM 1988, Sixth Worldwide Congress on Computer and Communications Security and Protection, pp. 147–159 (1988)
6. Gabber, E., Wool, A.: How to prove where you are: racking the location of customer equipment. In: CCS 1998: Proceedings of the 5th ACM conference on Computer and communications security, pp. 142–149. ACM, New York (1998)
7. Raya, M., Hubaux, J.P.: The security of vehicular ad hoc networks. In: SASN 2005: Proceedings of the 3rd ACM workshop on Security of ad hoc and sensor networks, pp. 11–21. ACM Press, New York (2005)
8. Čapkun, S., Buttyán, L., Hubaux, J.P.: Sector: secure tracking of node encounters in multi-hop wireless networks. In: SASN 2003: Proceedings of the 1st ACM workshop on Security of ad hoc and sensor networks, pp. 21–32. ACM, New York (2003)
9. Capkun, S., Hubaux, J.: Secure positioning in wireless networks. IEEE Journal on Selected Areas in Communications: Special Issue on Security in Wireless Ad Hoc Networks 24, 221–232 (2006)
10. Reid, J., Nieto, J.M.G., Tang, T., Senadji, B.: Detecting relay attacks with timing-based protocols. In: ASIACCS 2007: Proceedings of the 2nd ACM symposium on Information, computer and communications security, pp. 204–213. ACM, New York (2007)
11. Association, I.S.: Ieee standards for information technology – local and metropolitan area network – part 11: Wireless lan medium access control (mac) and physical layer (phy) specifications. Published online (1999)

A Secure Framework for Location Verification in Pervasive Computing

Dawei Liu, Moon-Chuen Lee, and Dan Wu

Department of Computer Science and Engineering,
Chinese University of Hong Kong, Hong Kong
{dwliu,mclee,dwu1}@cse.cuhk.edu.hk

Abstract. The way people use computing devices has been changed in some way by the relatively new pervasive computing paradigm. For example, a person can use a mobile device to obtain its location information at anytime and anywhere. There are several security issues concerning whether this information is reliable in a pervasive environment. For example, a malicious user may disable the localization system by broadcasting a forged location, and it may impersonate other users by eavesdropping their locations. In this paper, we address the verification of location information in a secure manner. We first present the design challenges for location verification, and then propose a two-layer framework VerPer for secure location verification in a pervasive computing environment. Real world GPS-based wireless sensor network experiments confirm the effectiveness of the proposed framework.

1 Introduction

The prevalence of mobile networks together with the pervasive use of wireless and embedded computing devices has changed the landscape of wireless localization in the following aspects: (1) **Interactivity**: In mobile ad hoc networks (MANET), mobile users can be localized by a cooperative approach [1]. Compared with traditional localization methods which rely on a centralized localization system, this approach has the advantage of being inexpensive, scalable, and easily deployable without using a specialized infrastructure. (2) **Pervasiveness**: According to [2], the number of mobile devices is expected to increase to 3.3 billion by 2011. This allows the provision of location-based services beyond the scope of traditional mobile computing. For example, being able to know whether a nearby store is having a certain product on sale could be useful or helpful to both a business person and a customer. Also location-based access control in wireless networks should be friendly and naturally combined with physical security. Apparently, the customer should not be required to establish shared secret keys in advance for getting any product sales promotions information.

However, there are potential risks associated with the localization and location-based services in pervasive computing environments. An attacker could mislead

B. Liu et al. (Eds.): WASA 2009, LNCS 5682, pp. 388–397, 2009.

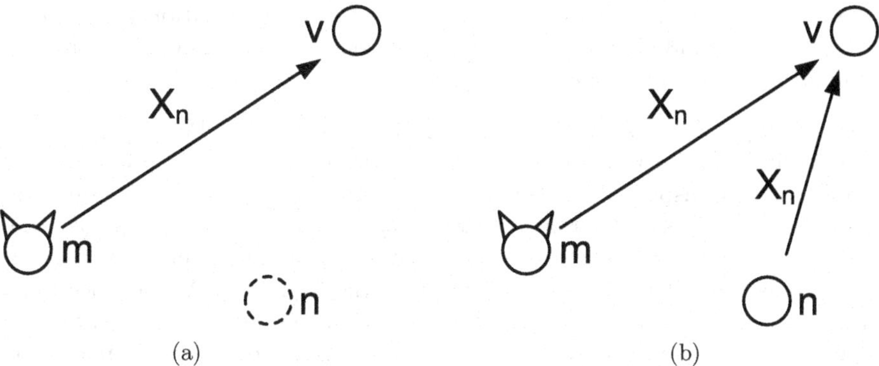

Fig. 1. A malicious user m forges a location claim X^c to a neighbor v. (a) m reports a fabricated location with $X^c = X_n$. (b) m impersonates another user n by eavesdropping and claiming the location $X^c = X_n$.

the localization system and disable the location-based service as illustrated in the examples below:

Example 1. In a cellular network, a mobile station (MS) could mislead the cellular positioning system (CPS) by reporting a forged distance or forged location coordinate [3] to the base stations (BS). This can be seen in Fig. 1(a) where m is the malicious MS and v is a BS.

Example 2. In wireless sensor networks (WSN), a group of beacons with GPS receivers attached are usually deployed to localize other sensors. A malicious beacon may impersonate other users by eavesdropping their locations, as shown in Fig. 1(b). According to [3], traditional WSN localization is highly vulnerable to this kind of attacks.

To solve these problems, it is important to verify the location of a mobile user before granting it to the access of network resources. The verification process could involve a group of verifiers for collecting the location claim X^c from the mobile user, and measuring the location-related information accordingly. If the user gave a forged location X^c, X^c would be inconsistent with the measurement. Based on the foregoing approach, various verification methods have been proposed recently. Generally, they have not considered fully the two important issues as outlined below:

- *User verification in pervasive computing environments.* Existing verification methods focus mainly on specific measurement models, such as the time-of-arrival (TOA) [4], the time-difference-of-arrival (TDOA) [3], the round trip time (RRT) [5], or the angle sector [6] which assume the presence of certain properties of all mobile devices. This assumption usually does not hold in pervasive computing environments where the mobile devices may differ significantly from each other. A general framework is needed in order to meet the requirements for location verification.
- *Protecting the user against eavesdropping.* User location claim information could be used by other malicious users for location spoofing, as discussed in

Example 2. Also any undesired disclosure of such information may violate the privacy of individuals [7]. For these reasons, secure communication is an important issue in location verification.

In this paper we propose a framework, referred to as VerPer, for secure location verification in pervasive computing environments. It is characterized by the following two aspects: A general location estimation method that integrates measurement models of different networks; and a secure protocol involving a Location Dependent Key (LDK) for communication. The remainder of the paper is organized as the following. Section 2 presents the framework VerPer. Section 3 analyzes the security of the proposed framework under various attacks. Section 4 demonstrates the effectiveness of the proposed framework by some real world GPS-based sensor network experiments. Section 5 concludes the paper.

2 VerPer: A Framework for Location Verification

In this section, we present VerPer, a framework for secure location verification. It is a middleware agent running at each verifier, which could be a BS, beacon or access point (AP) in different networks. This middleware consists of two layers: namely, LocaEs, a layer enables location estimation using different measurement models; and LocaVe, a layer for secure verification. The major functional blocks and their relations are shown in Fig. 2, where the shaded arrow represents data flow between the verifier and a mobile user, and the white arrow represents the data flow within two layers.

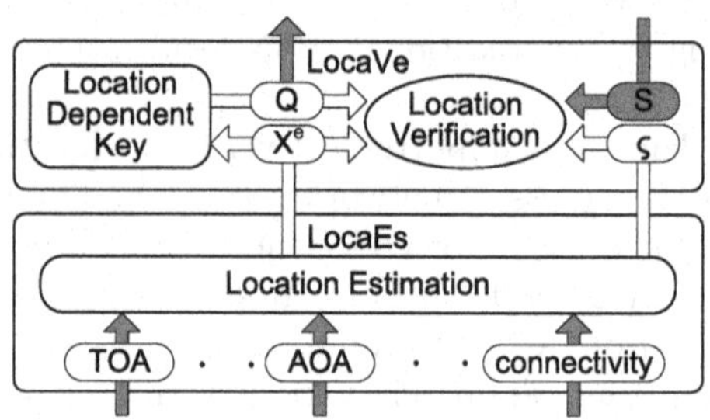

Fig. 2. VerPer Architecture

2.1 LocaEs Architecture

The layer LocaEs is aimed to support location estimation in various network scenarios. Since measurement models may differ significantly in CPS, GPS, WLAN and WSN localization systems, it is very difficult to implement existing verification schemes in a pervasive computing environment. We deal with this problem by separating location estimation from location verification. Specifically, LocaEs estimates a (or a group of) location which could subsequently be verified by the upper layer LocaVe. Depending on the measurement models used, the location of a mobile user could be related to the measurement information as follows:

- *Distance-based measurement model.* Take the TOA measurement as an example, the distance between a verifier v to a user u can be measured by $r_{vu} = (t_v - t_u) \times c$, where, t_u is the time at which a signal is sent out from u, t_v is the time at which the signal arrives at v, and c is the signal transmission speed. Then, the user's location X_u, can be related to the TOA measurements as following,
$$r_{vu}^2 = (x_v - x_u)^2 + (y_v - y_u)^2 \tag{1}$$
The above equation represents a circle in a 2D plane with its centre at X_v, location of v, and a radius r_{vu}. If more than 3 verifiers are available, X_u can be uniquely determined. A similar analysis can be carried out for TDOA [3] and RTT [5] measurement models.
- *Angle-based measurement model.* The use of antenna array in cellular networks allows the measurement of arriving angle of radio signals at BSs. Take the CDMA CPS [8] as an example. The location X_u can be related to the arriving angle in a 2D plane[1] via the following equation
$$\theta = atan(\frac{y_u - y_v}{x_u - y_v}) \tag{2}$$
where θ is the measured arriving angle of the radio signal sent from the user to the verifier (a BS). Similar analysis can be carried out in sensor networks [6], where the antenna sector is fixed for each beacon.
- *Connectivity-based measurement model.* Recent advance in WSN has suggested a connectivity-based measurement model. Without the distance or angle information, location X_u of a mobile node can be roughly estimated as the covering area of a neighboring beacon node. If there are several neighboring beacons, an approximate point in triangle (APIT) scheme has been proposed in [9] where better estimation accuracy can be expected.

A straightforward solution for location verification is to let $X_u = X^c$ and test the consistency of the measurement models presented above, e.g. the consistency of equations (1) and (2). Based on this principle, many verification schemes have been proposed for, and they all suffer from the drawback that they can only be applied to one specific model. To solve this problem, we introduce the operation of location estimation before proceeding to the verification. This additional operation has two advantages: (i) It separates physical measurement and estimation from location verification, and hence allows greater flexibility in the design and implementation of a verification system. As can be seen in Fig.2, LocaEs may operate in the same way in estimating X^e as existing localization systems, as a result, our scheme does not need to change any functional modules of those systems, compared with existing verification schemes which require a change of the infrastructure to enable consistency test. (ii) It provides valuable information which is essential for secure communication: common knowledge. Originally, it is inappropriate to assume any pre-shared secret key between u and v in a pervasive computing environment. However, if u gives an honest location claim and cooperates well in the location-related measurements, X^e should be identical to

1. $v \rightarrow u$: request for information
2. $v \leftarrow u$: echo
3. v: estimate X^e and ς (measurement noises)

Fig. 3. Location Estimation

the real location of u, so it should be identical to X^c. This common knowledge could be used for u and v to establish a secure link in the communication.

The operation of location estimation is summarized in Fig.3. Note that steps 1 and 2 may not be necessary necessary in the case of angle-based and connectivity-based measurement models in which v does not need cooperation of u in measuring θ. In addition to estimating X^e, LocaEs computes another set of information in step 3: the range of measurement noise ς. This information is important since X^e of a benign user u may not be identical to X^c due to the presence of noises in r_{vu} in equation (1) or in θ in equation (2). Moreover, X^e may not be uniquely determined in connectivity-based measurement models. Based on the information of X^e and ς, the location verification problem can be defined as: Determine whether the estimation X^e is consistent with the claim X^c.

2.2 LocaVe Architecture

On receiving the estimated location X^e, the verifier v will ask u to report its location claim X^c for verification. Different from the traditional concept of verification, we try to verify and protect X^c at the same time. Specifically, there are two issues that must be addressed (i) how to test the consistency between X^e and X^c, and (ii) how to protect X^c against eavesdropping. We are concerned about eavesdropping attacks because if u is an honest user and reports X^c without any protection, a malicious neighbor may eavesdrop X^c and then impersonate u by claiming to have the same location. It is obvious that eavesdropping attacks can be thwarted by encryption. Another solution could be letting u use the k-anonymity model in reporting X^c, a technique that has been widely used for privacy preserving [10] [7]. Generally, the second solution is not preferred for location verification, since it gives u, if malicious, a chance to "hide" itself among several other users.

We present above a secure location verification method based on a novel location-dependent key (LDK) distribution. This method is novel because (i) It does not require any pre-shared secret key between v and u for encryption; however, existing location-based key management schemes [11] [12] require a pre-shared secret key. (ii) It allows consistency test between X^e and X^c via decryption. In particular, u will encrypt X^c before transmitting it to v, and the message will be accepted only if it can be decrypted. The overview of this method is as depicted in Fig. 4.

At the beginning, v generates, based on a location-dependent index scheme, an $n \times n$ matrix Q of random keys. A location-dependent index scheme is used in the generation of Q. For a given key $q_{(l,m)}$ located in the l-th column and

1. v: generate an $n \times n$ matrix Q with random keys
2. $v \rightarrow u$: Q together with the indexes $X(x_1, \dots x_n)$ and $Y(y_1, \dots y_n)$
3. u: find a key $q_{(a,b)}$ by mapping X^c to the index (x_a, y_b) and encrypt X_i^c with $q_{(a,b)}$, i.e., $S = E_{q_{(a,b)}}(X^c)$
4. $u \rightarrow v$: S
5. v: find a key $q_{(a',b')}$ by mapping X^e to the index $(x_{a'}, y_{b'})$, select a sub-matrix Q' sized of $(\frac{2\varsigma}{c}+1) \times (\frac{2\varsigma}{c}+1)$, where $q_{(a',b')}$ is the center element
   for each key in Q'
     if S can be decrypted
       return true
     else return false

Fig. 4. Location Verification

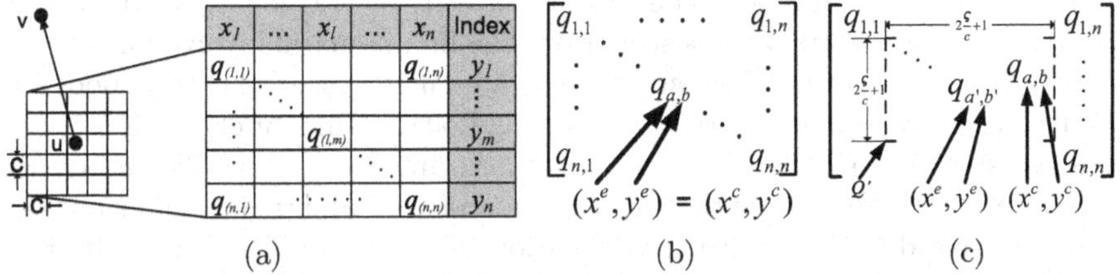

Fig. 5. Location-dependent key management. (a) Location-dependent index scheme. (b) Key selection in the ideal case. (c) Key selection in the presence of measurement noises.

the m-th row of Q, the index (l, m) is defined as the geographic coordinate (x_l, y_m), which is the center point of an area $c \times c$ in the network. Fig. 5(a) shows the location-dependent index scheme used by Q. Based on this scheme, any location coordinate can be uniquely mapped to a key such that the Euclidian Distance between the location coordinate and the index of the key (also a location coordinate) is the least. Then Q and its indices are sent to u in step 2.

In step 3, u first finds a key $q_{(a,b)}$ by mapping X^c to the index (x_a, y_b) using the same method discussed above. Then u encrypts X^c with the key $q_{(a,b)}$ such that $S = E_{q_{(a,b)}}(X^c)$. In the next step, u sends S to v. After receiving S, v decrypts it in step 5. Obviously, v does not know the key $q_{(a,b)}$ used by u for encryption. However, v has an estimated X^e which could be used in indexing the key for decryption. First, consider a simple scenario where there is no measurement noise in LocaEs such that $\varsigma = |X^e - X^c| = 0$. In this situation, $X^c(x^c, y^c)$ and $X^e(x^e, y^e)$ map to the same key $q_{(a,b)}$, as shown in Fig. 5(b). As a result, v can decrypt S successfully as long as u used the proper key to encrypt S.

In step 2 and 4, a neighboring malicious user may collect Q and S by eavesdropping; however, without the location of u, it cannot find $q_{(a,b)}$ to decrypt S. The only attack we need to consider is the "brute force attack" in which a malicious user tries all the keys in Q. A simple solution to this problem is to set a large number n for matrix Q. As long as the searching space for an attacker is big enough, S could hardly be decrypted for launching an attack quickly.

Now let us consider a practical scenario in which the measurement noises do exist in LocaEs. In this case, $X^c(x^c, y^c)$ could deviate from $X^e(x^e, y^e)$ and consequently the key $q_{(a',b')}$ found by using according to X^e may not be the same as $q_{(a,b)}$, the key used by v to encrypt S. One solution is to perform a local search around $q_{(a',b')}$ based on the noise threshold ς. Specifically, v selects a $(\frac{2\varsigma}{c}+1) \times (\frac{2\varsigma}{c}+1)$ submatrix Q' with $q_{(a',b')}$ as its center element, as shown in Fig.5(c). After testing all keys in Q', S can be finally decrypted, provided that v is honest. Apparently, the decryption computational cost would depend on the size of Q'.

3 Security Analysis

In this section we analyze VerPer's resistance to several location attacks. We consider particularly two attack scenarios. The first scenario involves one verifier v and one mobile user u. u is assumed to be a malicious user who may spoof v by forging the measurement information (during LocaEs) and/or claiming incorrect location (during LocaVe). The second scenario involves one verifier v and two users u_1 and u_2. We assume that u_2 is an honest user and u_1 is a malicious user who may eavesdrop the location verification between v and u_2. In both of the attack scenarios, we show that v is capable of identifying forged location claims.

3.1 One User

For location estimation, v measures the radio signal sent from u to estimate X^e. Some of this information could be forged depending on the measurement model used. Take the TOA measurement as an example, u could send a forged t_u to v. Thus, r_{uv} obtained by equation (1) would be biased and X^e would deviate from the real location. A smart u may then try to forge an X^c in order to make X^c and X^e consistenct. Note v does not release any location related information during the process of LocaEs. Due to the existence of unknown variables X_v in (1), u cannot predict the location of X^e. Therefore, u can hardly keep the consistency by forging t_u and X^c. A similar analysis can be carried out in angle-based and connectivity-based measurement models in which v does not require any cooperation from u in the measurement.

After obtaining the estimated location X^e, u will be required to send v a encrypted location claim S. As discussed in Section 2.2, each location uniquely maps to a key for encryption. If the encrypted message S from u is based on a forged claim X^c, S cannot be decrypted by v, since the key used by v would deviate from the one used for encryption. Similarly, S cannot be decrypted by v, if u reports the real location but lies to LocaEs. Finally, the malicious u would be excluded from the location verification.

3.2 Two Users

Based on the above analysis, we can identify forged location information from one malicious user. In the presence of another benign user, the problem of impersonation attacks, such as the sybil attack [13], arises when u_1 impersonates u_2 by simply eavesdropping the location verification between v and u_2, and claiming a forged location X_2^c. Since all information of u_1 comes from the honest user u_2, it would be difficult for v to find out whether u_1 is spoofing. Moreover, direct release of location information X_2^c may violate the privacy of individuals. To solve this problem, it is necessary to protect the location information of u_2 from being eavesdropped. Clearly it is inappropriate to assume any pre-shared secret key between a pair of verifier and mobile user in a pervasive environment, as a result, previous methods [6] [14] cannot deal with this kind of problem. The proposed location verification method can solve this problem as described below. In the verification phase, u_2 is asked to encrypt its location claim X_2^c by using a key from the key matrix sent by v. Since u_1 does not have an accurate estimation X_2^e, u_1 cannot find an appropriate key for decryption and hence fails to know X_2^c. In other words, u_1 cannot cheat v by impersonating u_2.

Remarks. In the above analysis, we focus only on two basic scenarios of location verification. In a network with multiple mobile users, a malicious user may be able to attack by coordinating with other malicious ones. A typical scenario is the wormhole attack which involves an attacker tunneling its the location and distance information to another attacker who can replay it during a location verification. Previous studies [6] [5] [14] have suggested many effective solutions to this problem as well as similar ones arising from the scenario of multiple malicious users. We will not elaborate too much here.

4 Experiments

In this section, we present our testing of the proposed VerPer in real world applications. A GPS-based WSN platform is used in the experiment. It is configured as follows: 4 computers are deployed in an outdoor sports field, and denoted by verifiers $\{v_0, v_2, v_3\}$ and the user u_1. Each computer has a GPS module attached, consisting of a SiRF III GPS receiver and an on-chip antenna. LocaEs operates in the distance-based measurement model, and u_1 is assumed honest. All verifiers can communication with u_1 using 802.11 netcards attached.

Fig. 6 shows the location of u_1 and v_0 during 20 *seconds*. For 2D demonstration, only longitude and latitude coordinates are displayed, and the distance between two nodes is $36.4m$. There are three groups of location records including: X_0 of v_0, X_1 ($X_1 = X_1^c$ given a honest user) and X_1^e of u_1. The former two groups are collected directly from GPS receivers, and the last group is estimated by using the distance-based measurement model. Let us consider first an ideal situation where the distances $\{r_{01}, r_{21}, r_{31}\}$ are free from any measurement noise. As can be seen in Fig. 6(a), there are slight drifts of all three sets of records, which, ideally, should be three points. Moreover, drifts for X_1^c and X_1^e are almost identical, since their trajectories overlap. Enlarged view of location

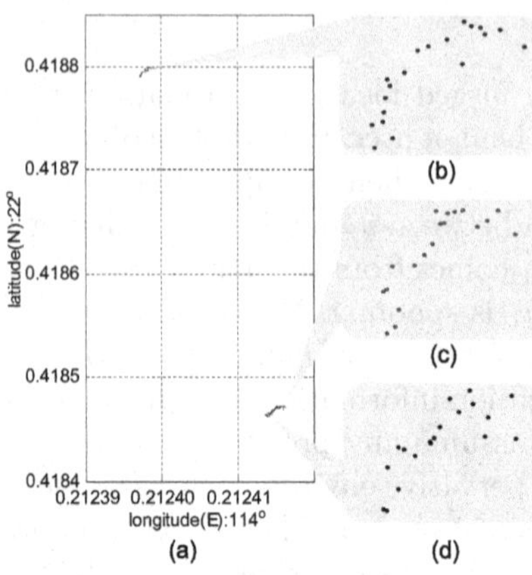

Fig. 6. Location records of v_0 and u_1 during 20 *seconds*. (a) Relative locations of u_1 and v_0. (b) X_0. (c) X_1 (or X_1^c). (d) X_1^e.

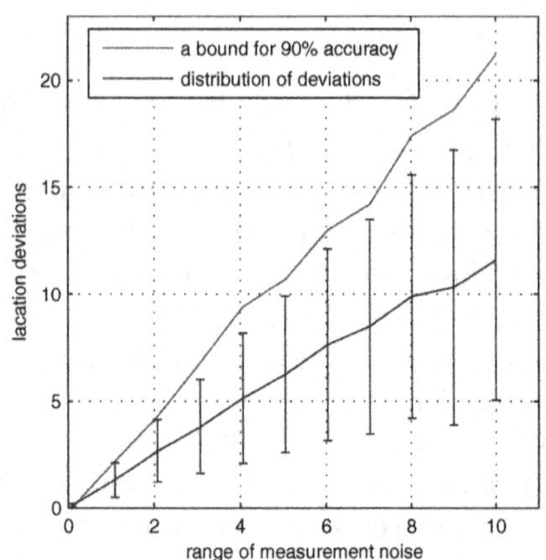

Fig. 7. The size of Q' in the presence of different distance measurement noises

records are shown in Fig. 6 (b)-(d), where each dote represents a location at a time. Clearly, all three trajectories tend to follow the same direction and are in a similar form. These observations agree well with previous discussion about LDK. In particular, the indices for keys for encryption and encryption may not be identical, as a result, a local search in Q' would be necessary. To minimize the risk of false verification caused by such noises, it is important to verify user's location information in real time.

Then we consider a practical scenario where measurement noise ς varies from centimeters [15] [16] to meters [9]. Fig. 7 shows the distribution of the differences between X_1^c and X_1^e in 1000 independent experiments where different noises are added to distances $\{r_{01}, r_{21}, r_{31}\}$. Clearly, in order to keep a 90% acceptance rate of the honest u_1, we need to enlarge the size of Q' as the increase of ς. Given a $80*80m^2$ localization area, when the noise is small, say $\varsigma < 10cm$, a typical range in UWB measurement [15], we will have $sizeof(Q) : sizeof(Q') = 3 \times 10^4$; when the noise increases to the range of $1m$, we will have $sizeof(Q) : sizeof(Q') = 330$. Since the ratio of $sizeof(Q)$ to $sizeof(Q')$ is directly related to the noise range, the security of the proposed LocaVe against brute force attack depends primarily on the measurement model used in LocaEs.

5 Conclusions

The existing location verification schemes are mostly inadequate in pervasive computing environments. One major reason is that most of them rely on specific measurement models and hence cannot work effectively in different networks. Another major reason is that they fail to protect the location claim of a mobile user against eavesdropping attack. In this paper, we have presented a two-layer framework for location verification, VerPer, to address the above issues. It is a general framework that can work in different localization systems and does not require any changes to the infrastructures of existing localization systems. Further, it is a secure framework, which uses a novel location-dependent key for secure communication. Two field tests in a GPS-based wireless sensor network demonstrate the effectiveness of VerPer. An interesting direction for future work is to combine the privacy preserving in location verification.

References

1. Patwari, N., Ash, J., Kyperountas, S., Hero III, A., Moses, R., Correal, N.: Locating the nodes: cooperative localization in wireless sensor networks. IEEE Signal Processing Magazine 22(4), 54–69 (2005)
2. Kokku, R., Sundaresan, K., Jiang, G.: Enabling location specific real-time mobile applications. In: Proceedings of ACM MobiArch, pp. 19–24 (2008)
3. Capkun, S., Rasmussen, K.C.M.S.M.: Secure Location Verification with Hidden and Mobile Base Stations. IEEE Transactions on Mobile Computing 7(4), 470–483 (2008)
4. Capkun, S., Hubaux, J.: Secure positioning of wireless devices with application to sensor networks. Proceedings of IEEE INFOCOM 2005 3, 1917–1928 (2005)
5. Liu, D., Ning, P., Du, W.: Detecting Malicious Beacon Nodes for Secure Location Discovery in Wireless Sensor Networks. In: Proceedings of IEEE ICDCS, pp. 609–619 (2005)
6. Lazos, L., Poovendran, R.: SeRLoc: secure range-independent localization for wireless sensor networks. In: Proceedings of ACM Workshop on Wireless Security, pp. 21–30 (2004)
7. Beresford, A., Stajano, F.: Location Privacy in Pervasive Computing. IEEE Pervasive Computing, 46–55 (2003)
8. Cong, L., Zhuang, W.: Hybrid TDOA/AOA mobile user location for wideband CDMA cellularsystems. IEEE Transactions on Wireless Communications 1(3), 439–447 (2002)
9. He, T., Huang, C., Blum, B., Stankovic, J., Abdelzaher, T.: Range-free localization schemes for large scale sensor networks. In: Proceedings of ACM MobiCom, pp. 81–95 (2003)
10. Gedik, B., Liu, L.: Location Privacy in Mobile Systems: A Personalized Anonymization Model. Proceedings of IEEE ICDCS 25, 620 (2005)
11. Liu, D., Ning, P.: Location-based pairwise key establishments for static sensor networks. In: Proceedings of ACM workshop on security of ad hoc and sensor networks, pp. 72–82 (2003)
12. Huang, D., Mehta, M., Medhi, D., Harn, L.: Location-aware key management scheme for wireless sensor networks. In: Proceedings of ACM workshop on security of ad hoc and sensor networks, pp. 29–42 (2004)
13. Newsome, J., Shi, E., Song, D., Perrig, A.: The sybil attack in sensor networks: analysis & defenses. In: Proceedings of ACM/IEEE IPSN, pp. 259–268 (2004)
14. Zhang, Y., Liu, W., Lou, W., Fang, Y.: Location-based compromise-tolerant security mechanisms for wireless sensor networks. IEEE Journal on Selected Areas in Communications 24(2), 247–260 (2006)
15. Fontana, R.: Experimental results from an ultra wideband precision geolocation system. Ultra-Wideband, Short-Pulse Electromagnetics 5, 215–224 (2000)
16. Hazas, M., Kray, C., Gellersen, H., et al.: A relative positioning system for co-located mobile devices. In: Proceedings of ACM Mobisys, pp. 177–190 (2005)

Introduction to Mobile Trajectory Based Services: A New Direction in Mobile Location Based Services

Sarfraz Khokhar[1] and Arne A. Nilsson[2]

[1] Cisco Systems, Inc.,
Raleigh, NC, USA
khokhar@cisco.com

[2] Department of ECE, North Carolina State University,
Raleigh, NC, USA
nilsson@ncsu.edu

Abstract. The mandate of E911 gave birth to the idea of Location Based Services (LBS) capitalizing on the knowledge of the mobile location. The underlying estimated location is a feasible area. There is yet another class of mobile services that could be based on the mobility profiling of a mobile user. The mobility profile of a mobile user is a set of the routine trajectories of his or her travel paths. We called such services as Mobile Trajectory Based Services (MTBS). This paper introduces MTBS and functional architecture of an MTBS system. Suitability of different location estimation technologies for MTBS has been discussed and supported with simulation results.

Keywords: Location Estimation Technologies, Location Based Services, GIS, Map Matching, Mobility Profile, Mobile Trajectory Based Services.

1 Introduction

The study of location determination of wireless transmitters has a long history. Applications that previously had used such wireless positioning systems primarily were for military, public safety and marine science research. Within the last few years there has been a massive surge of interest in wireless positioning methods and applications that can use wireless positioning information. The reasons for this surge are Legislation in the United States that requires cellular phone operators to provide location information to 911 call centers and new wireless positioning technologies that have the capability to alleviate shortcomings of GPS (Global Positioning Systems), such as high power consumption and slow to acquire initial position. The FCC (Federal Communications Commission) mandate (docket 94-102) requires mobile network operators to provide positional information to emergency services accurate within 125 meters [1]. This regulatory requirement has provided a stimulus for the commercial development of wireless positioning technologies and service applications built on these technologies, i.e., Location Based Services (LBS) [2] [3]. Such applications are very attractive to the operators who are seeking for additional revenue to the existing voice and data services. The variety of LBS is quite diverse and covers various disciplines of everyday life. Examples are: news, gaming, M-commerce, emergency, point

B. Liu et al. (Eds.): WASA 2009, LNCS 5682, pp. 398–407, 2009.

of interest, directions, traffic information, tracking, navigation, advertisement, location sensitive billing, electronic toll collection, directory assistance, and security, to name a few. Currently known LBS capitalize on the present location of a mobile user. We introduce another class of mobile location services that are based on mobile user's mobility profile. Mobility profiles are essentially collection of routine mobile traces or trajectories. We called this class of services Mobile Trajectory Based Services (MTBS). Fig. 1 shows a conceptual comparison of LBS and MTBS.

MTBS examples: A mobile user is sitting in his or her office and invokes a mobile trajectory based service, "Find a flower shop on my way home with a sale on roses". Such a service could be invoked anytime before leaving the office. This is an example of user initiated service (pull service). For an example of operator's initiated MTBS (push service), consider a location based service where you are passing by a clothing store from which you bought a pair of pants few weeks ago, the store sends you a soft discount coupon on your mobile phone to attract you to buy a matching jacket. MTBS version of this service would be that the vendor would know in advance even when you are still on the trajectory towards the store and may send you the soft coupon in advance. Actually the vendor may provide you the push service even when you are at home or a few days in advance.

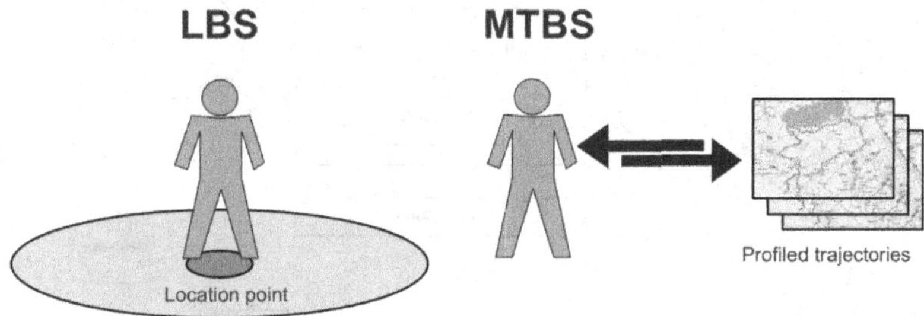

Fig. 1. Conceptual comparisons of MTBS with LBS. LBS are based on location of a mobile user whereas MTBS are based on profiled trajectories.

Another example of MTBS could be that you receive an alert from your service provider that there is an accident on your path to office and may suggest you an alternative route. There is a plethora of such applications where MTBS could be provided to a mobile user in an attractive and useful way. MTBS may be used for roadwork alert, weather alert, route advisory, emergency, advertisement, convenient social networking (dating), reminders, concierge, shopping, entertainment, directory assistance, and en-route planning.

This paper focuses on the functional architecture of an MTBS system and suitability of different location estimation technologies for MTBS. There are three key components of MTBS architecture: location estimation network, GIS database, and mobility profiler. We discuss these components in the following section. Location estimation and mobility profiling is accomplished by the mobile network operator using the mobile network, Mobile Station (MS), i.e., handset and GIS database. The mobility profile database produced by the mobility profiler could be shared with the content provider or provided to an application on per user basis.

2 Functional Architecture of MTBS

A high level end-to-end proposed architecture for MTBS is depicted in Fig. 2. It is partitioned into two sub systems: mobility profiling system and service provisioning system. Location estimation network, GIS database and mobility profiler including location polling agent, and mobility profile database comprise the mobility profiling system. The mobility profile database, application server and radio provisioning network make up a MTBS provisioning system. Location profiling agent triggers location estimation network using MLP (Mobile Location Protocol) to estimate location of the mobile user. The decision when to poll for location is based on the geographical layout of the road network and previous location. The basic idea is to capture the corners (turns) in the course of trajectory. The detail is provided in the following subsections. Mobility profiler estimates the trajectory of the mobile users and sends it to subscribers' mobility profiles database, from where application sever uses it as needed to accomplish MTBS.

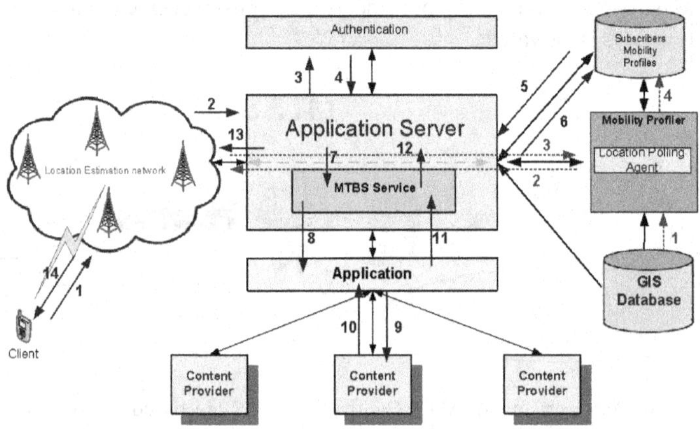

Fig. 2. A conceptual comparison of MTBS with LBS

The key components of MTBS functional architecture are described in the following subsections.

2.1 Location Estimation System

A cellular-based location takes advantage of the existing transceivers, communication bandwidth, two-way messaging, and well established infrastructure, but also inherits the disadvantages imposed by the design of the communication systems [4]. There are several technology alternatives for locating cellular telephones. If one considers modifications to the telephone, Assisted-GPS is the most commonly discussed option. The basic idea in Assisted-GPS is to establish a GPS reference network whose receivers have clear views of the sky and can operate continuously. This reference network is also connected with the mobile network. At the request of an MS or network-based application, the assistance data from the reference network is transmitted to the MS to increase performance of the GPS sensor [5]. For locating unmodified cellular telephones, signal attenuation, angle of arrival (AOA), time of arrival (TOA), time difference of arrival (TDOA), enhanced observed time difference (E-OTD), and time of advance (TA), are used. All time based mobile location estimation technologies are based on knowing where the existing reference points (cellular radio base stations) are and then relating them to the location of the mobile station. Signal strength method has not got as much attention as most of the other methods have. However some remarkable results have been reported [6]. AOA and TDOA are most discussed methods. AOA which operates with no modification on the mobile device was first developed for military and government organizations. It was later applied to cellular signals. It is based on the estimation of MS signal angle at the base stations (BS's). It requires an array of antenna elements. Future wireless systems may have more sophisticated and intelligent antenna systems [7]. Because of the fact that in TDMA (Time Division Multiple Access) system knows how much time signal takes to reach MS is also exploited for location estimation. This is called Time Advance. However a large error is associated with this method [8]. The error in all location estimation methods is inevitable. Please see Table 1. There are several sources of location error such as hearability of Remote BS's [9] [10], multipath conditions [11], non-line of sight conditions [12], and geometric dilution of precision [13]. Location error is the biggest challenge in mobile trajectory estimation. There is large body of literature on trajectory estimation using low error GPS but there is very little on trajectory estimation using erroneous mobile location.

Table 1. A comparison of location estimation technologies and the associated error

Technology	Handset impact	Error
TA	None	500m
TOA	None	100-300m
TDOA	None	100-200m
AOA	None	100-200m
E-OTD	Yes	20-200m
Assisted-GPS	Yes	25-100m

2.2 GIS Database

The very nature of MTBS makes geo-spatial technologies a necessary element. The geo-spatial technology used in MTBS is called GIS . GIS has been used in all disciplines of life that have any relation to geo-spatial data. GIS is a system for creating, storing, analyzing and managing spatial data and associated attributes [14]. In the strictest sense, it is a system capable of integrating, storing, editing, analyzing, sharing, and displaying geographically-referenced information. In GIS, features of the spatial data are organized into layers. A layer is a collection of all the features in the map that share some common characteristic [15]. The various physical aspects of the map: political boundaries, roads, railroads, waterways, and so forth, are assigned to layers according to their common spatial data values, Fig. 3.

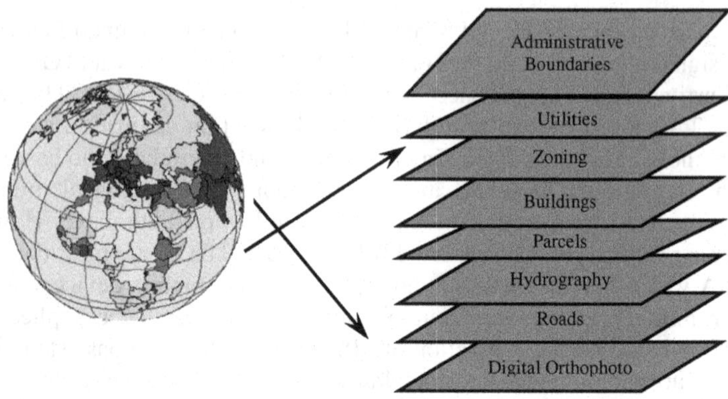

Fig. 3. GIS data is stored as different layers of features

For MTBS we are most interested in roads data. The roads are modeled as polylines or arcs [16][17]. Arcs are represented with starting and ending nodes, which imparts directionality to the arcs. The arcs pass through several vertices along its way. Each of the nodes and vertices are stored with coordinate values representing real-world locations in a real-world coordinate system such as longitude/latitude angles, State Plane feet, or Universal Transverse Mercator (UTM) meters. Along with the direction of a road other important associated information like speed and direction is also available. The constraints of direction and speed further help in decision making of map matching during mobility profiling. Fig. 4 depicts a pictorial view of actual GIS data we used in our mobility profiling simulation.

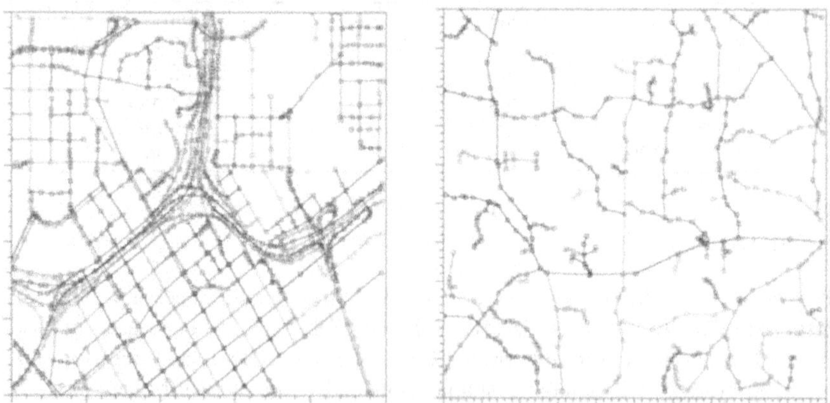

Fig. 4. Graphical view of road network GIS data of urban area of St. Paul Minnesota(left) and suburban area of North Carolina (right). We used this data in our mobility profiler.

2.3 Mobility Profiler

Mobility models used in location management and elsewhere wouldn't suffice for the mobility profiling of a mobile user. It has to be the actual mobility traces of mobile user's daily activities to do mobility profiling. Being creatures of habit and perhaps for maximum efficiency, we tend to use our routine routes in our daily commute. Therefore, it is a reasonable assumption that we are able to predict correctly the route on which a mobile user would travel based on his or her mobility pattern. However this may not be true for all the mobile users. We can categorize the mobile users in three categories: predictable, partially predictable, and unpredictable. Most of the mobile users with a routine job fall under the first two categories. For providing MTBS, the profiled trajectories do not have to be strictly predictable and accurate. As an analogy, location in LBS does not have to be perfectly accurate for most of the services. If a mobile stays predictable for most of the trajectories of the day, it is good enough basis for providing quite a large number of MTBS. The polled location points of the trajectory are time stamped. So the trajectory is a spatiotemporal distribution. All interpolated points on the curve have inclusive times association.

In our mobility model, a mobile user traces different trajectory for each day of the week. Most of the people (mobile users) follow the same path for multiple days of the week. If a user traverses the same trajectory for different days of the week, we still save each day's mobility separately. This makes the model more generic. Secondly we assume that the mobility of the mobile users is restricted to road networks. This is a reasonable constraint and provides a basis for correcting the erroneous estimated location using GIS database.

Mobility profiler collects the erroneous location points of a mobile user and applies trajectory estimation algorithm to correct the erroneous location points and interpolates them to produce the trajectory during the profiling week. Please refer to Fig. 2 for a complete flow sequence of mobility profiling.

Step 1. From the cell ID, the mobility profile knows which geographical area the mobile user is in. It pulls the relevant road network GIS data.

Step 2. The location polling agent in the mobility profiler collects the location points. The profiler corrects the erroneous location point and place on the appropriate road segment consulting the GIS data using a method called map matching [18] [19]. To minimize the usage of air resources, it attempts to collect the location of a mobile user in an adaptive manner. From the present location and the speed constraint, it can determine when a mobile user is approaching an intersection or turn. It polls the location only at those intersection and turns. We called this algorithm IPM (Intersection Polling Method) [20]. The mobility profiler applies map matching algorithms and constraints to construct a trajectory out of the erroneous location points.

Step 3. After estimating the trajectories for the whole week, the profiler saves these trajectories as mobility profile for that particular user in mobility profiles database.

A complete flow chart of mobility profiling algorithm is depicted in Fig. 5. Let $\mathbf{G}$ be the GIS road network database of the area, $\mathbf{D}$ be the days of the week, and $\mathbf{T}_{ri}$ be the trajectory for a day, $i \in \mathbf{D}$, the mobility profile of a mobile user,

$$\mathbf{T}_r \equiv \{\bigcup \mathbf{T}_{ri} \mid \forall i \in \mathbf{D}, \forall \mathbf{T}_{ri} \in \mathbf{G}, \bigcap \mathbf{T}_{ri} \neq \varnothing\}. \tag{1}$$

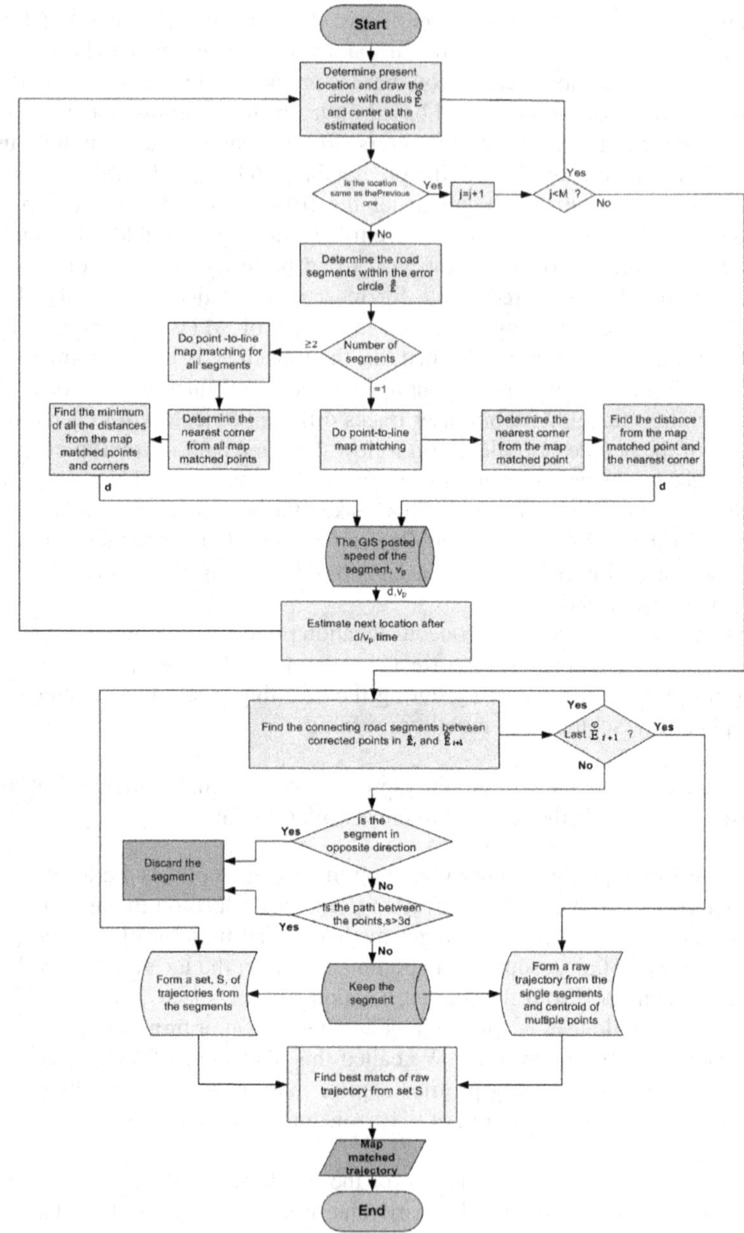

Fig. 5. Flow chart of mobility profiling algorithm used in MTBS system. The mobile user is polled for the current location around the intersections. The erroneous location points are map matched to road networks. Topological constraints further help to identify the trajectory.

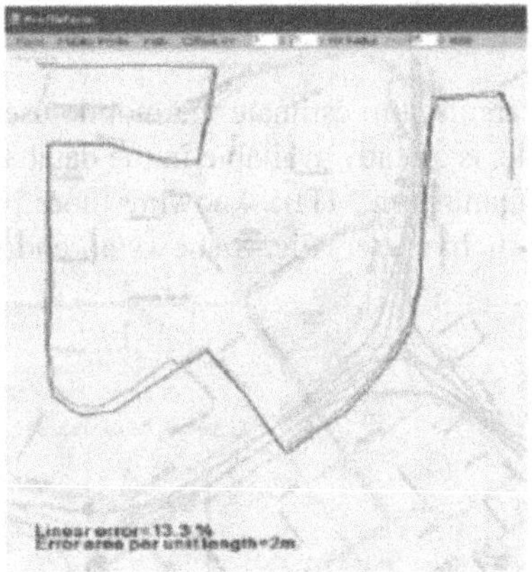

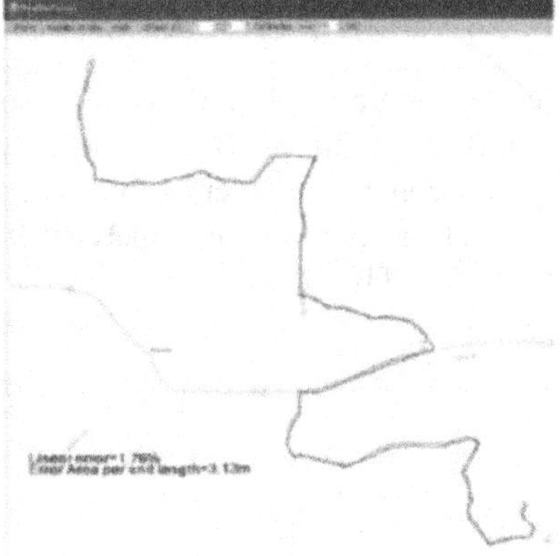

Fig. 6. Mobile trajectory estimation: In urban area with low location error of 25m the trajectory error is only along the parallel road (left). For suburban area even with a large location error (300m) trajectory estimation only missed a very small corner (right).

Implementing the mobility profiler algorithm of Fig. 5 we developed a Microsoft Window based application in C# (C Sharp). A mobile user traveling on green (dark line if black and white) path in (Fig. 6) was simulated both in urban and suburban areas. The mobility simulation was run at different location errors that correspond to different location estimation technologies. In suburban area all location errors up to 300m gave similar (good) result as shown in Fig. 6. The estimated trajectories are shown in blue (light if black and white). In urban area larger location errors missed few more intersections as shown in Fig. 7.

Fig. 7. In urban area with location error of 50m, the algorithm missed 2 intersections (left). On the same route a location error of 100m missed 4 intersections.

3 MTBS Provisioning Flow

While provisioning an MTBS, no air resources are used to estimate the mobile user's location. The basis of MTBS, the mobility profile, is already available in the database. However a content provider can provide more features in MTBS knowing more precise present location than just the Cell ID of a mobile user. Fig. 8 shows an end-to-end flow of MTBS provisioning.

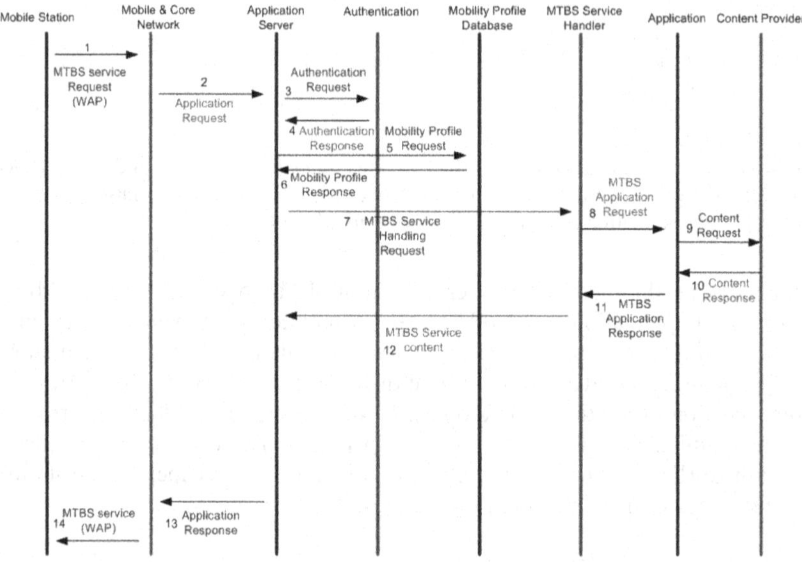

Fig. 8. An end-to-end flow diagram of MTBS provisioning. In this MTBS scenario the mobility profile is provided to the content provider (application server) on per usage basis.

4 Conclusion

A new direction in mobile location based services was introduced. In this paper we laid out functional architecture required to deliver MTBS. The most important component in MTBS architecture is mobility profiler. A complete, patented design of a mobility profiler was described in Section 2. MTBS could be built on several location estimation technologies. In urban areas Assisted-GPS and E-OTD are best suited. Because of their low error in location estimation they are suitable for any urban area. For suburban areas all major location estimation technology described in Section 2 such as Assisted-GPS, TOA, TDOA, AOA, and E-OTD are suitable for MTBS provisioning. MTBS provides many new and attractive applications which shall provide yet another revenue source for a mobile operator.

References

1. F.C.C., `http://www.fcc.gov/Bureaus/Wireless/Orders/1996/fcc96264.txt`
2. LBSzone, `http://www.lbszone.com/`
3. Kolodziej, K.W., Hjelm, J.: Local Positioning Systems-LBS Applications and Services. CRC Press, Boca Raton (2006)
4. Pi-Chun, C.: A cellular based mobile location tracking system. In: 49th Vehicular Technology Conference, pp. 1979–1983. IEEE Computer Society Press, Los Alamitos (1999)
5. Djuknic, G., Richton, G.: Geolocation and Assisted-GPS, Bell Laboratories, Lucent Technology (2001)
6. Hellebrandt, M., Mathar, R.: Location tracking of mobiles in cellular radio networks. IEEE Transactions on Vehicular Technology, 1558–1562 (1999)
7. Deblauwe, N., Van, B.L.: An Angle of Arrival Location Estimation Technique for Existing GSM Networks. In: IEEE International Conference on Signal Processing and Communications, pp. 1527–1530 (2007)
8. Yost, G.P., Panchapakesan, S.: Errors in automatic location identification using timing advance. In: 48th IEEE Vehicular Technology Conference, pp. 1955–1958 (1998)
9. Sattarzadeh, S.A., Abolhassani, B.: TOA Extraction in Multipath Fading Channels for Location Estimation. In: 17th International Symposium on Personal, Indoor and Mobile Radio Communications, pp. 1–4. IEEE Computer Society Press, Los Alamitos (2006)
10. Zhang-Xin, C., Wan, Q., Yang, W.L., Peng, Y.N.: Mobile Location Based on Scatterer Information. In: International Conference on Communications, Circuits and Systems Proceedings, pp. 1415–1418 (2006)
11. Paulraj, A., Papadias, C.: Space–time Processing for Wireless Communications. Signal Processing Magazine number 14, 49–83 (1997)
12. Wylie, M., Holtzmann, J.: The Non–Line of Sight Problem in Mobile Location Estimation. In: IEEE ICUPC, pp. 827–831 (1996)
13. Misra, P., Enge, P.: Global Positioning System: Signals, Measurements, and Performance, 2nd edn. (2006)
14. Schuurman, N.: GIS: A Short Introduction. Blackwell Publishing, Malden (2004)
15. Heywood, D.I.: An introduction to geographical information systems. Prentice-Hall, Englewood Cliffs (2002)
16. Christian, S., Jensen, et al.: Nearest Neighbor Queries in Road Networks. In: GIS 2003, New Orleans, pp. 7–8 (2003)
17. Dueker, K.J., Butler, J.A.: GIS-T Enterprise Data Model With Suggested Implementation Choices. Center for Urban Studies School of Urban and Public Affairs (1997)
18. Taghipour, S., Meybodi, M.R., Taghipour, A.: An Algorithm for Map Matching For Car Navigation System. In: 3rd International Conference on Information and Communication Technologies: From Theory to Applications, pp. 1–5 (2008)
19. Brakatsoulas, S., Pfoser, D., Salas, R., Wenk, C.: On map-matching vehicle tracking data. In: 31st Int. Conf. on Very Large Data Bases, pp. 853–864. ACM Press, New York (2005)
20. Khokhar, S., Nilsson, A.A.: Estimation of Mobile Trajectory in a Wireless Network. In: 3rd International Conference on Sensor Technologies and Applications, Athens (2009)

Spectrally Efficient Frequency Hopping System Design under Hostile Jamming*

Lei Zhang and Tongtong Li

Michigan State University, East Lansing MI 48824, USA
{zhangle3,tongli}@egr.msu.edu

Abstract. This paper considers spectrally efficient anti-jamming system design based on message-driven frequency hopping (MDFH). As a highly efficient frequency hopping scheme, MDFH is particularly robust under strong jamming. However, disguised jamming from sources of similar power strength can cause performance losses. To overcome this drawback, in this paper, we first propose an anti-jamming MDFH (AJ-MDFH) system. The main idea is to transmit an ID sequence along with the information stream. The ID sequence is generated through a cryptographic algorithm using the shared secret between the transmitter and the receiver. It is then exploited by the receiver for effective signal detection and extraction. It is shown that AJ-MDFH is not only robust under strong jamming, but can also effectively reduce the performance degradation caused by disguised jamming. Second, we extend AJ-MDFH to a multi-carrier scheme for higher spectral efficiency and more robust jamming resistance. Based on secure group generation, MC-AJ-MDFH can increase the system efficiency and jamming resistance significantly through jamming randomization and enriched frequency diversity. Moreover, by assigning different carriers to different users, MC-AJ-MDFH can readily be used as a collision-free multiple access system. Simulation examples are provided to illustrate the performance of the proposed approaches.

Keywords: Anti-jamming, physical layer security, message-driven frequency hopping.

1 Introduction

As a widely used spread spectrum technique, frequency hopping (FH) was originally designed for secure communication under hostile environments [1]. In conventional FH [2], each user hops independently based on its own PN sequence, a collision occurs whenever there are two users transmitting over a same frequency band. Mainly limited by the collision effect, the spectral efficiency of the conventional FH is very low [3,4].

Recently, a *three-dimensional* modulation scheme, known as message-driven frequency hopping (MDFH) is proposed in [5]. The basic idea of MDFH is that

* This research is partially supported by NSF under awards CNS-0746811 and CNS-0716039.

B. Liu et al. (Eds.): WASA 2009, LNCS 5682, pp. 408–417, 2009.

part of the message acts as the PN sequence for carrier frequency selection at the transmitter. More specifically, selection of carrier frequencies is directly controlled by the encrypted information stream rather than by a pre-selected pseudo-random sequence as in conventional FH. At the receiver, the carrier frequencies are captured using a filter bank which selects the strongest signals from all the frequency bands. The most significant property of MDFH is that: by embedding a large portion of the input bits into the hopping selection process, additional information transmission is achieved with no extra cost on either bandwidth or power [3]. *In fact, transmission through hopping frequency control essentially adds another dimension to the signal space, and the resulting coding gain can increase the system spectral efficiency by multiple times.*

It is observed that: under single band jamming, MDFH is particularly powerful under *strong jamming* scenarios, and outperforms the conventional FH by big margins. The underlying argument is that: for MDFH, even if the signal is jammed, strong jamming can enhance the power of the jammed signal and hence increases the probability of correct detection. When the system experiences *disguised jamming*, that is, when the jamming power is close to the signal power, it is difficult for the MDFH receiver to distinguish jamming from true signal, resulting in performance losses.

To improve the performance of MDFH under disguised jamming, in this paper, first we propose a single carrier anti-jamming MDFH (AJ-MDFH) scheme. The main idea is to insert some signal identification (ID) information during the transmission process. This ID information is generated through a cryptographic algorithm using the shared secret between the transmitter and the receiver. Therefore, it can be used by the receiver to locate the true carrier frequency or the desired channel. At the same time, it is computationally infeasible to be recovered by malicious users. Comparing with MDFH, AJ-MDFH can effectively reduce the performance degradation caused by disguised jamming and deliver significantly better results when the jamming power is close to that of the signal power. At the same time, it is robust under strong jamming just as MDFH. Second, we extend the single carrier AJ-MDFH to multi-carrier AJ-MDFH (MC-AJ-MDFH). Based on secure group generation, MC-AJ-MDFH can increase the system efficiency and jamming resistance significantly through *jamming randomization and enriched frequency diversity.* Moreover, by assigning different carrier groups to different users, MC-AJ-MDFH can also be used as a collision-free MDFH based multiple access system. Simulation examples are provided to demonstrate the effectiveness of the proposed approaches.

2 MDFH Brief Review

2.1 System Description

Let N_c be the total number of available channels, with $\{f_1, f_2, \cdots, f_{N_c}\}$ being the set of all available carrier frequencies. The number of bits used to specify an individual channel here is $B_c = \lfloor \log_2 N_c \rfloor$, where $\lfloor x \rfloor$ denotes the largest integer less than or equal to x. If N_c is a power of 2, then there exists a 1-1 map between the B_c-bit strings and the total available channels; otherwise, when N_c is not a power of 2, we will allow some B_c-bit strings to be mapped to more than one channel. Without loss of generality, here we assume that $N_c = 2^{B_c}$.

Let Ω be the selected constellation that contains M symbols, each symbol in the constellation represents $B_s = \log_2 M$ bits. Let T_s and T_h denote the symbol period and the hop duration, respectively, then the number of hops per symbol period is given by $N_h = \frac{T_s}{T_h}$. We assume that N_h is an integer.

The transmitter structure of MDFH is shown in Fig. 1a. We start by dividing the *encrypted* information stream into blocks of length $L \triangleq N_h B_c + B_s$. Each block is parsed into $N_h B_c$ *carrier bits* and B_s *ordinary bits*. The carrier bits are used to determine the hopping frequencies, and the ordinary bits are mapped to a symbol which is transmitted through the selected channels successively. Denote the nth block by X_n. Note that in MDFH, the whole block X_n is transmitted within one symbol period.

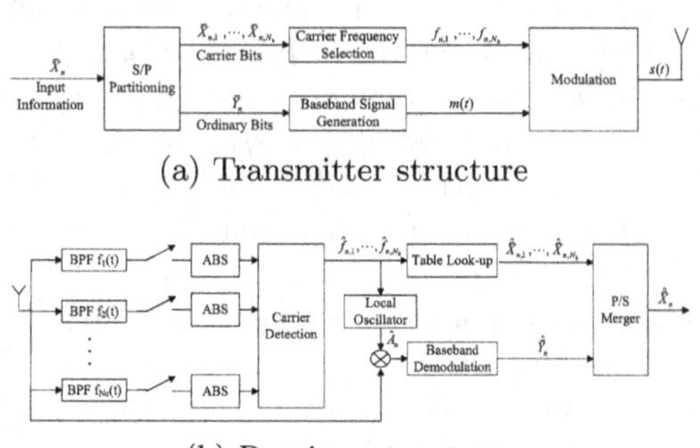

(a) Transmitter structure

(b) Receiver structure

Fig. 1. Transmitter and receiver structure of MDFH. ABS means taking the absolute value.

The receiver structure of MDFH is shown in Fig. 1b, in which the transmitting frequency is captured using a filter bank as in the FSK receiver rather than using the frequency synthesizer. Recall that $\{f_1, f_2, \cdots, f_{N_c}\}$ is the set of all available carrier frequencies. To detect the active frequency band, a bank of N_c bandpass filters (BPF), each centered at f_i $(i = 1, 2, \cdots, N_c)$, and with the same channel bandwidth as the transmitter, is deployed at the receiver front end. In the case that only one frequency band is occupied at any given moment, we measure the outputs of bandpass filters at each possible carrier frequency, and the actual carrier frequency at a certain hopping period is detected by selecting the one that captures the strongest signal. As a result, the carrier frequency (hence the information embedded in frequency selection) can be blindly detected at each hop.

To further enhance the spectral efficiency, MDFH can be extended to a multi-carrier system where the subcarriers hop over non-overlapping subsets of the total available frequency bands [6]. The design of multi-carrier MDFH is not unique. Through careful hopping process design, multi-carrier MDFH can randomize jamming interference and enhance the jamming resistance of the system. This topic is further discussed in Section 4.

2.2 Performance of MDFH under Jamming Interference

In this section, we consider the performance of single carrier MDFH under single band jamming, as multi-band jamming can be combatted with multi-carrier diversity. For robust jamming resistance, the jamming detection feature needs to be added to the MDFH receiver. Let E_i denote the received signal power over the ith channel. We propose to use the following threshold based detector.

1. Classify each channel according to the power detection threshold η. If $E_i < \eta$, then there is only noise over channel i, we say that the channel is *inactive*; otherwise, if $E_i \geq \eta$, we say that the channel is *active*.
2. Let $A = \{i_1, i_2, \cdots, i_m\}$ be the set of the index of all the active channels, then the estimated hopping frequency index, denoted by $\hat{k}$, is determined by $\hat{k} = \arg\min_{i \in A}\{E_i\}$. The carrier bits can be recovered based on $\hat{k}$.
3. The ordinary bits are extracted from $r_{\hat{k}}$ following the regular demodulation process.

Let p_e denote the error probability of the hopping frequency index $\hat{k}$ detection in MDFH. As can be seen, p_e is a function of the threshold η. The optimal threshold value η_{opt} can be obtained as $\eta_{opt} = \arg\min_\eta\{p_e\}$.

We compare the performance of MDFH under single band jamming with that of the conventional FH in AWGN channels, and the result (with no channel coding) is shown in Fig. 2. The jamming-to-signal ratio is defined as $JSR = \frac{N_J}{E_s}$, where N_J and E_s denote the jamming power and signal power, respectively. As can be seen, *MDFH delivers excellent performance under strong jamming scenarios*, and outperforms the conventional FH by big margins. The underlying argument is that: strong jamming can enhance the power of the jammed signal and hence increase the correct detection probability. Note that in this case, spectral efficiency of MDFH is $\frac{11}{3}$ times that of the conventional FH.

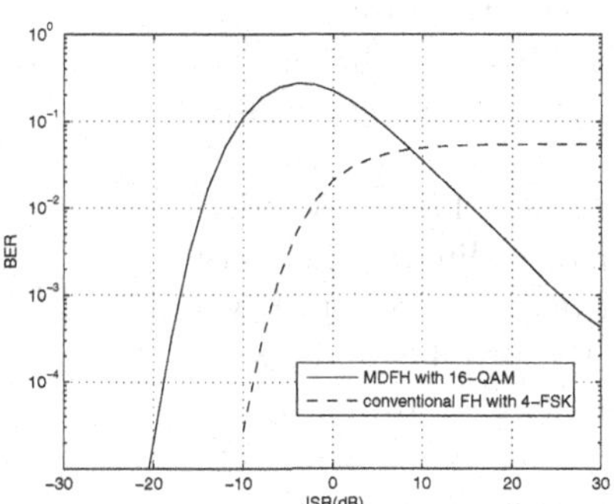

Fig. 2. Performance comparison under single band jamming, $E_b/N_0 = 10$dB, $N_h = 3$

However, we also notice that when the jamming power is close to the signal power, it is difficult for the MDFH receiver to distinguish jamming from true signal, resulting in unsatisfying performance. For conventional FH, once the jamming power reaches a certain level, the system performance is mainly limited by the probability that signal is jammed. For MDFH, the situation is more complex. We classify the jamming into two categories: strong jamming and disguised jamming. Strong jamming denotes the case where the jamming power is much higher than the signal power. Disguised jamming denotes the case where the jamming power is close to the signal power. MDFH is robust under strong jamming, but is sensitive to disguised jamming. To enhance the jamming resistance of MDFH under disguised jamming, in this paper, we introduce the anti-jamming MDFH system, named AJ-MDFH.

3 AJ-MDFH: System Description

In this section, we describe the transmitter and receiver design of the proposed AJ-MDFH scheme.

3.1 Transmitter Design

The main idea here is to insert some signal identification (ID) information during the transmission process. This ID information is shared between the transmitter and the receiver so that it can be used by the receiver to locate the true carrier frequency. Our design goal is to improve jamming resistance while maximizing the spectral efficiency of MDFH.

For AJ-MDFH, we propose to replace the ordinary bits in MDFH with the ID bits. The transmitter structure of AJ-MDFH is illustrated in Fig. 3a. As can be seen, each user is now assigned an ID sequence. Note that in MDFH, the same ordinary bits are transmitted at each hop. If we replace the ordinary bits with ID bits, the spectral efficiency is only reduced by a small factor $\frac{B_s}{N_h B_c + B_s}$. Take $N_h = 5, B_c = 8, B_s = 4$, for example, $\frac{B_s}{N_h B_c + B_s} = \frac{1}{11}$.

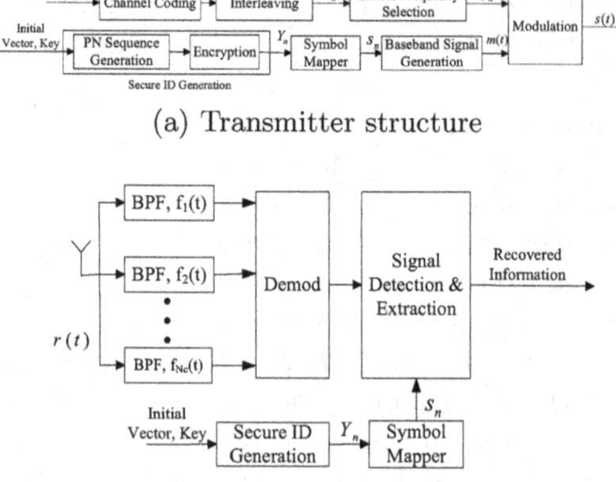

(a) Transmitter structure

(b) Receiver structure

Fig. 3. AJ-MDFH Transmitter and receiver

It should be noted that, in order to prevent impersonate attack, each user's ID sequence need to be kept secret from the malicious jammer. Therefore we generate the ID sequence through a reliable cryptographic algorithm, such as the Advanced Encryption Standard (AES) [7], so that it is computationally infeasible for the malicious user to recover the ID sequence. For the same reason, in AJ-MDFH, the ID bits will be varying at each hop. The ID sequence generation process is summarized as follows:

1. Generate a pseudo-random binary sequence using a 42-bit linear feedback shift register (LFSR) specified by the characteristic polynomial

$$x^{42} + x^{35} + x^{33} + x^{31} + x^{27} + x^{26} + x^{25} + x^{22} + x^{21} + x^{19}$$
$$+x^{18} + x^{17} + x^{16} + x^{10} + x^{7} + x^{6} + x^{5} + x^{3} + x^{2} + x + 1.$$

2. Take the output of LFSR as the plaintext, group it into blocks of length K_L bits ($K_L = 128, 192$ or 256), and feed it into the AES encrypter of key size K_L. The AES output is then used as our ID sequence.

As will be demonstrated in Section 5, AJ-MDFH is robust under strong jamming, and can effectively reduce the performance degradation caused by disguised jamming. It will also be observed that jamming resistance of AJ-MDFH can be further improved through channel coding, which corrects the residue errors using controlled redundancy.

3.2 Receiver Design

The receiver structure for AJ-MDFH is shown in Fig. 3b. The receiver regenerates the secure ID through the shared secret (including the initial vector, the LFSR information and the key). At each hop, the received signal is first fed into the bandpass filter bank. The output of the filter bank is first demodulated, and then used for carrier bits (i.e., the information bits) detection.

Demodulation. Let $s(t)$, $J(t)$ and $n(t)$ denote the ID signal, the jamming interference and the noise, respectively. For AWGN channels, the received signal can be represented as $r(t) = s(t)+J(t)+n(t)$. We assume that $s(t)$, $J(t)$ and $n(t)$ are independent of each other. If the spectrum of $J(t)$ overlaps with the frequency band of $s(t)$, then the signal is *jammed*; otherwise, the signal is *jamming-free*. If $J(t)$ spreads over multiple channels, we have multi-band jamming; otherwise, we have single band jamming. Note that the true information is embedded in the index of the active carrier over which the ID signal $s(t)$ is transmitted.

For $i = 1, 2, \cdots, N_c$, the output of the ith ideal bandpass filter $\mathrm{f}_i(t)$ is

$$r_i(t) = \mathrm{f}_i(t) * r(t) = \alpha_i(t)s(t) + J_i(t) + n_i(t). \tag{1}$$

Here $\alpha_i(t) \in \{0, 1\}$ is a binary indicator for the presence of signal in channel i at time instant t. At each hopping period, $\alpha_i(t)$ is a constant: $\alpha_i(t) = 1$ if and only if $s(t)$ is transmitted over the ith channel during the mth hopping period; otherwise, $\alpha_i(t) = 0$. $J_i(t) = \mathrm{f}_i(t) * J(t)$ and $n_i(t) = \mathrm{f}_i(t) * n(t)$. When there is no jamming presented in the ith channel, $J_i(t) = 0$.

For demodulation, $r_i(t)$ is first shifted back to the baseband, and then passed through a matched filter. At the mth hopping period, for $i = 1, \cdots, N_c$, the sampled matched filter output corresponds to channel i can be expressed as

$$r_{i,m} = \alpha_{i,m}s_m + \beta_{i,m}J_{i,m} + n_{i,m}, \tag{2}$$

where s_m, $J_{i,m}$ and $n_{i,m}$ correspond to the ID symbol, the jamming interference and the noise, respectively; $\alpha_{i,m}, \beta_{i,m} \in \{0, 1\}$ are binary indicators for the presence of ID signal and jamming, respectively. Note that the true information is carried in $\alpha_{i,m}$.

Signal Detection and Extraction. Signal detection and extraction is performed at each hopping period. *For notation simplicity, without loss of generality, we omit the subscript m in (2).* That is, for a particular hopping period, (2) is reduced to:

$$r_i = \alpha_i s + \beta_i J_i + n_i, \quad \text{for } i = 1, \cdots, N_c. \tag{3}$$

Define $\mathbf{r}=(r_1,\ldots,r_{N_c})$, $\boldsymbol{\alpha}=(\alpha_1,\ldots,\alpha_{N_c})$, $\boldsymbol{\beta}=(\beta_1,\ldots,\beta_{N_c})$, $\mathbf{J}=(J_1,\ldots,J_{N_c})$ and $\mathbf{n}=(n_1,\ldots,n_{N_c})$, then (3) can be rewritten in vector form as: $\mathbf{r}=s\boldsymbol{\alpha}+\boldsymbol{\beta}\cdot\mathbf{J}+\mathbf{n}$.

For single carrier AJ-MDFH, at each hopping period, one and only one item in $\boldsymbol{\alpha}$ is nonzero. That is, there are N_c possible information vectors: $\boldsymbol{\alpha}_1=(1,0,\ldots,0)$,..., $\boldsymbol{\alpha}_{N_c}=(0,0,\ldots,1)$. If $\boldsymbol{\alpha}_k$ is selected, and the binary expression of k is $b_1b_2\cdots b_{B_c}$, where $B_c=\lfloor\log_2 N_c\rfloor$, then estimated information sequence is $b_1b_2\cdots b_{B_c}$.

So at each hopping period, the information symbol $\boldsymbol{\alpha}$, or equivalently, the hopping frequency index k, needs to be estimated based on the received signal and the ID information which is shared between the transmitter and the receiver. Here we use the *maximum likelihood* (ML) detector. If the input information is equiprobable, that is, $p(\alpha_i)=\frac{1}{N_c}$ for $i=1,2,\ldots,N_c$, then MAP detector is reduced to the ML detector. For the ML detector, the estimated hopping frequency index $\hat{k}$ is given by

$$\hat{k}=\arg\max_{1\le i\le N_c} p\{\mathbf{r}|\boldsymbol{\alpha}_i\}. \tag{4}$$

Recall that the information signal (including $\boldsymbol{\alpha}$ and s), the jamming interference and the noise are independent to each other. Assume both the noise and the jamming interference are totally random, that is, $n_1,\ldots,n_{N_c}$, $J_1,\ldots,J_{N_c}$ are all statistically independent, then $r_1,\ldots,r_{N_c}$ are also independent. In this case, the joint ML detector in (4) can be decomposed as:

$$\hat{k}=\arg\max_{1\le i\le N_c}\prod_{j=1}^{N_c}p\{r_j|\boldsymbol{\alpha}_i\}=\arg\max_{1\le i\le N_c}\prod_{j=1,j\neq i}^{N_c}p\{r_j|\alpha_j=0\}\cdot p\{r_i|\alpha_i=1\} \tag{5}$$

Since $\prod_{j=1}^{N_c}p\{r_j|\alpha_j=0\}$ is independent of i, (5) can be further simplified as $\hat{k}=\arg\max_{1\le i\le N_c}\frac{p\{r_i|\alpha_i=1\}}{p\{r_i|\alpha_i=0\}}$, where $p\{r_i|\alpha_i=1\}=\sum_{\beta_i}p(r_i|\alpha_i=1,\beta_i)p(\beta_i)$ and $p\{r_i|\alpha_i=0\}=\sum_{\beta_i}p(r_i|\alpha_i=0,\beta_i)p(\beta_i)$, with $\beta_i\in\{0,1\}$. Define $\Lambda_i\triangleq\frac{p\{r_i|\alpha_i=1\}}{p\{r_i|\alpha_i=0\}}$ be the likelihood ratio for channel i, then (5) can be rewritten as: $\hat{k}=\arg\max_{1\le i\le N_c}\Lambda_i$.

If we further assume that $n_1,\ldots,n_{N_c}$ are i.i.d. Gaussian random variables of zero mean and variance $\sigma_n^2=\frac{N_0}{2}$, and $J_1,\ldots,J_{N_c}$ are i.i.d. Gaussian random variables of zero mean and variance $\sigma_J^2=\frac{N_J}{2}$, then it follows that:

$$\hat{k}=\arg\max_{1\le i\le N_c}\frac{\frac{p\{\beta_i=0\}}{\pi N_0}e^{-\frac{\|r_i-s\|^2}{N_0}}+\frac{p\{\beta_i=1\}}{\pi(N_0+N_J)}e^{-\frac{\|r_i-s\|^2}{N_0+N_J}}}{\frac{p\{\beta_i=0\}}{\pi N_0}e^{-\frac{\|r_i\|^2}{N_0}}+\frac{p\{\beta_i=1\}}{\pi(N_0+N_J)}e^{-\frac{\|r_i\|^2}{N_0+N_J}}}. \tag{6}$$

If $q=\sum_{i=1}^{N_c}\beta_i$ bands are jammed, then $p\{\beta_i=1\}=\frac{q}{N_c}$ and $p\{\beta_i=0\}=\frac{N_c-q}{N_c}$; and s is the ID symbol shared between the transmitter and the receiver.

In the case of successive *multi-band jamming*, as in partial-band jamming, $J_1,\ldots,J_{N_c}$ are no longer statistically independent, and hence the joint detector in (4) can no longer be decomposed as in (5). To resolve this problem, in the following section, we propose the multi-carrier AJ-MDFH scheme by exploiting rich frequency diversity. The multicarrier AJ-MDFH can ensure much better jamming resistance and spectral efficiency through successful jamming randomization.

4 Multi-carrier AJ-MDFH System

The multi-carrier AJ-MDFH (MC-AJ-MDFH) transmitter is illustrated in Fig .4. The basic idea is to split all the N_c channels into N_g non-overlapping groups, denoted by $G_l, l = 1, 2, \ldots, N_g$. The lth subcarrier hops over group G_l based on the AJ-MDFH scheme. To maximize hopping randomness of all the subcarriers, the channel groups need to be reorganized or regenerated after a pre-specified period, named group period. A secure group generation algorithm can be developed as in [5] to ensure that: (i) Each subcarrier hops over a new group of channels during each group period, so that it eventually hops over all the available channels in a pseudo-random manner; (ii) Only the legitimate receivers can recover the transmitted information correctly. Secure G_l generation is synchronized at the transmitter and the receiver. At the receiver, the received signal is fed to N_g single carrier AJ-MDFH receiver for signal extraction and recovery.

4.1 Increased Spectral Efficiency

With simultaneous transmission from multiple carriers, the spectral efficiency of the AJ-MDFH system can be increased significantly. Let $B_c = \log_2 N_c$ and $B_g = \log_2 N_g$, then each group has $N_{gc} = 2^{B_c - B_g}$ channels. The number of bits transmitted by the MC-AJ-MDFH within each hopping period is $B_{MC} = N_g(B_c - B_g)$. B_{MC} is maximized when $B_g = B_c - 1$ or $B_g = B_c - 2$, which results in $B_{MC} = 2^{B_c - 1}$. Note that the number of bits transmitted by the AJ-MDFH within each hopping period is B_c, it can be seen that $B_{MC} > B_c$ as long as $B_c > 2$. Let $N_c = 256$, for example, then the transmission efficiency of AJ-MDFH can be increased up to $\frac{B_{MC}}{B_c} = \frac{2^{B_c-1}}{B_c} = 16$ times.

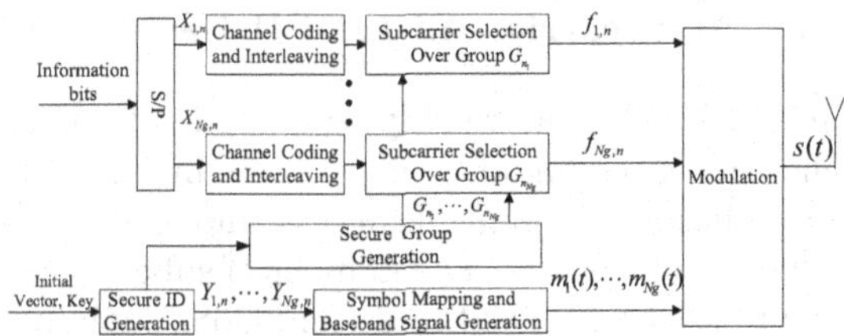

Fig. 4. MC-AJ-MDFH Transmitter

4.2 Enhanced Jamming Resistance

MC-AJ-MDFH can reinforce the jamming resistance of AJ-MDFH significantly through jamming randomization and increased frequency diversity. As we mentioned earlier, multi-band jamming is a serious challenge for single carrier AJ-MDFH. However, with secure group assignment, MC-AJ-MDFH can successfully randomize multi-band jamming, just in the way that burst errors are randomized by interleavers. If all together q bands are jammed, then on average, only $\frac{q}{N_g}$ bands are jammed within each group.

To further increase the jamming resistance of MC-AJ-MDFH under multi-band jamming, the frequency diversity of the system can be increased by transmitting the same or correlated information over more than one subcarriers. At the receiver, the received signal corresponding to each subcarrier can be combined for joint signal detection. Note that different subcarrier may transmit different ID symbols, the conventional diversity combination methods can not be applied directly. So instead of combining the received signal, we will combine the likelihood ratio Λ (defined in Section 3.2) of the channels corresponding to each subcarrier.

Assume that the same information is transmitted through the hopping frequency index of N_d subcarriers over N_d groups $\{G_{n_1}, G_{n_2}, \ldots, G_{n_{N_d}}\}$. As before, each group has N_{gc} channels. That is, the information is transmitted over the same hopping frequency index in each group. Note that for randomization purpose, the channel index in each group is random, and does not necessarily come in ascending or descending order.

Let Λ_i^l denote the likelihood ratio of channel i in group n_l, then the active hopping frequency index can be estimated by $\hat{k} = \arg\max_{1 \le i \le N_{gc}} \prod_{l=1}^{N_d} \Lambda_i^l$. The diversity order N_d can be dynamic in different jamming scenarios to achieve tradeoff between performance and efficiency.

4.3 Multi-carrier AJ-MDFH Based Multiple Access Scheme

MC-AJ-MDFH can readily be extended to a collision-free anti-jamming MDFH scheme to accommodate more users in the multiple access environment. To ensure collision-free multiple access among all users, different users will be assigned different subcarriers. The number of subcarriers assigned to each user can be different based on the data rate and QoS requirement of the user. The secure group generation algorithm ensures the randomness of the subcarrier frequencies occupied by each user.

5 Simulation Results

In this section, we illustrate the performance of the proposed AJ-MDFH and MC-AJ-MDFH through simulation examples. We assume that the signal is transmitted through AWGN channels under hostile jamming. The number of available channels is $N_c = 64$ ($B_c = 6$). For AJ-MDFH and MC-AJ-MDFH, we choose to use a two-level 16-QAM which has a circular star constellation, where each level has 8 symbols. For conventional FH, we use the 4-FSK modulation scheme.

We examine the performance of conventional FH, AJ-MDFH and MC-AJ-MDFH under partial band jamming, where four successive bands are jammed. The SNR is chosen to be $\frac{E_b}{N_0} = 15$dB. To maximize the spectral efficiency of

MC-AJ-MDFH, the group number is chosen to be $N_g = 32$. We observe that MC-AJ-MDFH can successfully randomize the successive multi-band jamming through secure group generation. At the same time, in this particular example, the spectral efficiency of MC-AJ-MDFH is 16/3 times that of AJ-MDFH. The system performance can be further enhanced by exploiting frequency diversity. As shown in Fig. 5, if we choose to transmit the same information through two subcarriers, then the jamming resistance is significantly improved.

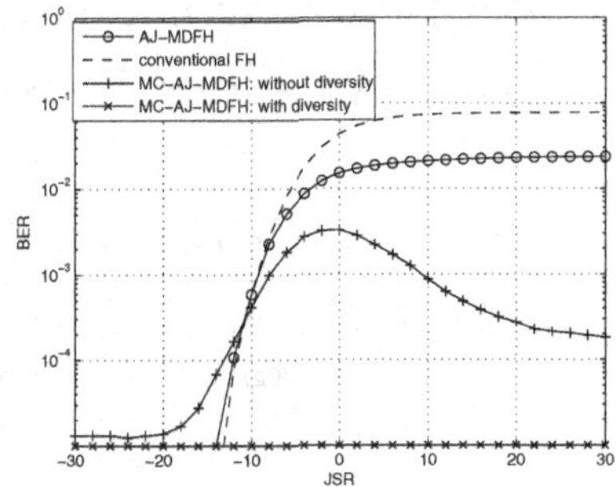

Fig. 5. Performance comparison under partial-band jamming

6 Conclusion

In this paper, we proposed a highly efficient anti-jamming scheme AJ-MDFH based on message-driven frequency hopping. It was shown that AJ-MDFH is robust under strong jamming and can effectively reduce the performance degradation caused by disguised jamming. Moreover, AJ-MDFH can be extended to multi-carrier AJ-MDFH for higher spectral efficiency and more robust jamming resistance. The proposed approaches can be applied to both civilian and military applications for reliable communication under hostile jamming, especially for satellite communications.

References

1. Simon, M., Polydoros, A.: Coherent detection of frequency-hopped quadrature modulations in the presence of jamming–part I: QPSK and QASK modulations. IEEE Trans. Commun. 29, 1644–1660 (1981)
2. Viterbi, A.: A processing-satellite transponder for multlple access by low rate mobile users. IEEE J. Sel. Areas Commun. (October 1978)
3. Ling, Q., Ren, J., Li, T.: Spectrally efficient spread spectrum system design: message-driven frequency hopping. In: Proc. IEEE Intl. Conf. Commun, May 2008, pp. 4775–4779 (2008)
4. Glisic, S., Nikolic, Z., Milosevic, N., Pouttu, A.: Advanced frequency hopping modulation for spread spectrum WLAN. IEEE J. Sel. Areas Commun. 18(1), 16–29 (2000)
5. Li, T., Ling, Q., Ren, J.: A spectrally efficient frequency hopping system. In: Proc. IEEE Global Telecommun. Conf., November 2007, pp. 2997–3001 (2007)
6. Ling, Q., Li, T.: Message-driven frequency hopping design and analysis. IEEE Trans. Wireless Commun. (accepted)
7. Daemen, J., Rijmen, V.: The Design of Rijndael: AES–the Advanced Encryption Standard. Springer, Heidelberg (2002)

A QoS Framework with Traffic Request in Wireless Mesh Network*

Bo Fu and Hejiao Huang

Harbin Institute of Technology Shenzhen Graduate School, China
fb8fb8@gmail.com, hejiao0@yahoo.com.cn

Abstract. In this paper, we consider major issues in ensuring greater Quality-of-Service (QoS) in Wireless Mesh Networks (WMNs), specifically with regard to reliability and delay. To this end, we use traffic request to record QoS requirements of data flows. In order to achieve required QoS for all data flows efficiently and with high portability, we develop Network State Update Algorithm. All assumptions, definitions, and algorithms are made exclusively with WMNs in mind, guaranteeing the portability of our framework to various environments in WMNs. The simulation results in proof that our framework is correct.

Keywords: Quality of service, traffic request, multi-path.

1 Introduction

Wireless Mesh Networks(WMNs) are being applied as a solution for providing last-mile Internet access for mobile clients, and thus many of these networks have been pushed to the market to provide complete commercial solution[1, 2, 3]. WMN is composed of mesh routers that are equipped with multi-radios and multi-channels. Among all the standards to evaluate the performance of the network, Quality of Service (QoS) describes the reliability and the delay of the data delivery through the links. The data in the network is delivered under requirements of reliability and delay in the network. There are some differences between WMN and other wireless networks, such as Ad-Hoc network. In WMN, the mesh routers are rarely mobile to avoid topology changes, limited node or power failures etc. Hence, we can not easily use the strategy in Ad-Hoc network to guarantee QoS in WMN. An altered method for QoS aiming at WMN is urgently needed.

Motivated by this research trend, much research work concerning QoS is appeared. In our previous work [1], we solve the QoS problem in the commodity network by maximize the throughput. And In this paper we focus on the QoS of different flows, but not different nodes in the WMN. In [4] the authors introduce the development of QoS architectures and present a generalized QoS framework in distributed systems. Some characters about QoS in WMN are introduced in

* This work was supported in part by National Natural Science Foundation of China with Grant No. 10701030.

B. Liu et al. (Eds.): WASA 2009, LNCS 5682, pp. 418–427, 2009.

[5], such as the propagation that affects the capacity of WMN. Providing a centralized management infrastructure in WMN, [6] presents a software package that allows gateways to get a balance between distance and load to guarantee QoS.

In [7], the authors propose an investigation on the tradeoffs among QoS, capacity, and coverage in a scalable multichannel ring-based WMN. The authors also develop a cross-layer analytical model that is based on physical/medium access control to evaluate the delay and jitter. [8] indicates that integrating packet-level and connection-level QoS control is significant to support applications with diverse QoS performance requirements in WMN. In [9], the authors analyze the QoS problem in WiMAX. Traffic load of each mesh router changes infrequently in WMN, since each router may aggregate traffic flows for a large number of clients in its coverage. Under this condition current traffic may be predicted by previous traffic. Similar to [10, 11], we use traffic request as quasi-static information to guarantee QoS requirement.

The contributions of this paper are as follows.

1. Traffic request is used to record requirement of QoS.
2. We use probability QoS constraint to simulate the real network environment.
3. All the definition and algorithms are based on multi-path.
4. Our Network State Update Algorithm is designed with portability.

The rest of this paper is organized as follows: We propose related terminologies and describe the problem in Section 2. Network state description is introduced in Section 3. Network State Update Algorithm is presented in Section 4. Then we present evaluation of our framework in Section 5 and conclude our work in Section 6.

2 Terminologies and Problem Description

Wireless mesh network is represented as an undirected communication graph $G = (V, E)$ in general. V is the set of nodes representing the routers. The neighborhood of $v \in V$, denoted by $\triangle(v)$, is the set of nodes residing in its transmission range, and $E \subseteq V \times V$ is the set of edges representing the links between two routers. $e = (a, b)$ is an edge whose two endpoints are a and b. Multi-orthogonal channels and multi-radios are used in WMN to avoid interference and increase throughput. For convenience, we design our algorithm and deploy simulation in the homogeneous network in which routers are equipped with the same radios, and for the same reason in this paper channels mean orthogonal channels for simplicity.

We introduce the definition of *coverage* which derives from [12] to confirm the range of transmission. Coverage of $e = (u, v)$, denoted as $Cov(e)$, represents the set of nodes that can be affected by e. $Cov(e) = \{x \in V | x \text{ stands inner } D(u, |uv|)\} \cup \{y \in V | y \text{ stands inner } D(v, |vu|)\}$, where $|uv|$ is physical length of edge (u, v) , and $D(u, |uv|)$ denotes the disk which centers at node u with radius $|uv|$. $e_1 = (a, b)$ interferes with $e_2 = (u, v)$ if and only if $a \in Cov(e_2)$ or $b \in Cov(e_2)$, and vice versa.

Similar as in [13], *traffic request* is defined as a 6-tuple $(i, in_i, eg_i, m_i, r_i, d_i)$, where i is the request ID, in_i is the ingress router (source router), eg_i is the egress router (destination router), m_i is bandwidth required, r_i denotes required reliability of this traffic request, and d_i denotes required maximum delay. Reliability and delay of traffic request is explained in Section 3. Traffic request records QoS constraint of the flows. The route the packet transmitted from ingress to egress is called *Path(ingress, egress)* that contains all the nodes and edges in the route. Edges must be assigned at least one channel when transmitting data in WMN. If C denotes the set of channel and T denotes the set of time slots, then we can use tuple $(e, c, t) \in E \times C \times T$ to denote that edge e is assigned channel c at the tth time slot.

In this paper our goal is to provide an algorithm with both time efficiency and high portability to satisfy requirement of QoS of flows. To achieve this goal, we present the standard to judge QoS and introduce probability QoS constraint in next section.

3 QoS Constraint Description

3.1 Reliability and Delay

Packet delivery ratio is proportion of the packets received by the destination nodes to the packets sent by the source nodes in a relative long time. We can also use this concept to judge the reliability of two neighbor nodes. For one hop between two neighbor nodes, for a path from source node to destination node, and for the entire network, reliability is a significant standard to the performance of the mesh network. Packet delivery ratio between two neighbor nodes u and v determine the reliability in this hop, which is denoted as $r_{u,v}$. Moreover, we can easily get that the reliability of a path is the product of all the reliability in the entire path. For a $Path(a, b)$, its *reliability* $r_{Path(a,b)} = \prod_{(u,v)\in Path(a,b)} r_{(u,v)}$.

Because our definition of *reliability of* $Path(a, b)$ is based on traffic request, the reliability of a path is reasonably related to data delivery. And the reliability of a path is also evidently affected by the hops in the path. In [13], the authors provide a network of 4% packet dropping probability in each hop, and we can assume the reliability of these hops are all 96%. Then the reliability of a 5 hops path, which is common in a mesh network, is 81%. Considering this seriously loss of reliability, we should not deploy QoS guarantee method based on any pure static network state, which will be introduced in Section 4. Some concepts and process below are derived from [14].

The definition of $Path(a, b)$ is based on single-path. If a traffic request which requires a data transmission from node a to b can be achieved by multi-path, the *reliability of the traffic request* is decided by each path that the data of this traffic request transmitted. The set of all the paths on which the data of a traffic request tr transmits is denoted as $PathSet_{tr}$. For traffic request tr, we have $r_{tr} = 1 - \prod_{Path(a,b)\in PathSet_{tr}} (1 - r_{Path(a,b)})$.

Delay of data transmission relates to time constraint of the QoS in WMN. We can easily get that the delay of a path is the sum of all the delay in the entire path. For a $Path(a,b)$, its *delay* $d_{Path(a,b)} = \sum_{(u,v)\in Path(a,b)} d_{(u,v)}$.

Similarly as the definition of reliability of the traffic request, we need to consider delay in multi-path routing of a traffic request. If traffic request requests 3 units data transmitting from the source node to destination node, these 3 units data can be routed into 3 different paths. In [1] we mention that IEEE 802.11 can satisfy 3 to 12 channels. Hence if there are also enough radios in the mesh network, these 3 units data can be transmitted simultaneously. The delay here is determined by the largest delay among all the paths. The situations are similar if we deploy different protocols mentioned in [2]. In application, if a traffic request requires low delay, it must send small amount of data frequently, because packets of small size that is sent to destination node do not make longer time waiting than packets of large size at the destination node. The main problem we need to consider here is the delay at each path, but not the delay resulted by the sequence of the data transmission or channel allocation. So we assume that for a traffic request with low delay requirement, its bandwidth m_i must be relative small in order to gain low delay. For traffic request tr, we have $d_{tr} = \mathrm{Max}_{Path(a,b)\in PathSet_{tr}} d_{Path(a,b)}$.

3.2 Probability QoS Constraint

It is nearly impossible that requirements of reliability and delay can always be satisfied in real network. Similar as [14, 15], we extend QoS constraint by probability. Given a probability, if QoS constraints are satisfied in this probability, we can deploy traffic request in the mesh network. Based on the equations of calculating r_{tr} and d_{tr}, for traffic request tr, we can get $\begin{cases} P(r_{tr} > R) > P_r \\ P(d_{tr} < D) > P_d \end{cases}$, where $P(condition)$ represents the probability that this condition is true, r_{tr} is reliability of the traffic request, R is a given reliability of the traffic request we need to satisfy in a network by the probability P_r, d_{tr} is delay of the traffic request, and D is a given delay of the traffic request we cannot exceed in a network by the probability P_d.

Section 3 shows an integrated method to describe the QoS constraints combined with traffic request in WMN by considering its characteristic distinct from wired network and other wireless networks.

3.3 Network State Description

As data described by traffic request is supposed to be transmitted through the nodes in mesh network, we need to develop a method to describe the network state related to the reliability and delay that the nodes in the network can guarantee. A network state table is maintained to record the satisfaction to the constraints of reliability and delay at each node. For a node A, a *node state table* shown in Table 1 is established to record the reliability and delay that this node can guarantee.

Table 1. Network State Table

	Node A	
neighbor nodes	reliability	delay
B	95%	1
D	98%	1
un-neighbor nodes	reliability	delay
L	95%	2
M	93%	3

The network state table may cause storage and updating overhead, but this kind of overhead is not too high to lower the performance of the network because of the brief data in the table. If we maintain node state table at each node in the network, data transmitted with traffic request can be routed by the nodes based on the state of this node to get sufficient reliability and to avoid long delay. The priority that either reliability or delay is more urgent also affects the routing direction to next hop router. The delivery of data will change the state of the network, so the update of node state table should be executed to adapt with altered network state. The strategy and frequency of this update will be introduced in Section 4. It is inevitable that an algorithm records reliability and delay in order to get QoS constraint in WMN, so our network state description can be easily deployed to the algorithm. This brings our algorithm proposed in Section 4 portability.

4 QoS Guarantee Method

Without considering the characteristic of a particular kind of wireless network, we still need to satisfy the constraint of reliability and delay of the network, but the distinction between mesh network and Ad-Hoc network makes some common methods aimed at the latter inapplicable. In this section, we propose our QoS guarantee algorithms adapting to static and dynamic network state.

4.1 Static QoS Guarantee Method

In [1], we proposed a throughput maximization method to guarantee QoS constraint. We maximize the throughput by resource contention graph and then provide data of high QoS constraint with high delivery priority. We mention this method here in order to make use of it in Section 4.2. And some previous work such as [4, 8, 9, etc.] can also guarantee QoS constraint.

Here we propose another method which is easier deployed than [15], and this method also adapts with wireless mesh network, because the network state is assumed to be static. Because there are already plenty of algorithms proposed, we just present the main frame of our algorithm in this section. Besides the field we introduced in Section 3, traffic request also records a time stamp which records the time when the data packet is sent from the source node. Based on reliability and delay of the traffic request, the router routes the traffic data by comparing its neighbor nodes in the node state table.

After one hop, an ACK packet will be sent back to the router to update the node state table, so we can get altered network state. Moreover, the ACK packet is also sent back backward to the source node through the routing path. This is the reason why we keep reliability and delay from to un-neighbor nodes in the node state table. According to the definition of probability QoS constraint in Section 3.2, we can analyze the QoS of this traffic request at the destination node, so the ACK packet is also used to revise QoS constraint of the traffic request at the source node. As traffic and route are relatively stable in static mesh network, this ACK backward process does not cost too much network resource.

4.2 Dynamic QoS Guarantee Method

The basic QoS guarantee method in dynamic state network can be gained by repetition of the static QoS guarantee methods mentioned in Section 4.1. Whenever network state changes or state update cycle time arrives, all the node state tables need to be updated, so we can get real-time network state to make sure the data routing to satisfy QoS constraint. But this strategy cost too much network resource and in WMN the network state does not always change frequently. We need to deduce a method to satisfy QoS and save network resource.

To achieve portability by making use of the algorithm we proposed in Section 4.1 and other algorithms in related works, we present a Network State Update Algorithm in this section. The algorithm in last paragraph is deployed by putting the QoS guarantee algorithm that already exists into a loop whose executing condition is the change of network state. But our NSUA algorithm is to revise the QoS guarantee algorithm that already exists by inserting network update conditions into the algorithm. To deploy NSUA algorithm, we need to calculate node state table of each node.

We need to examine network update conditions in the QoS guarantee algorithm that already exists. If a packet arriving at its destination node does not satisfy the probability QoS constraint, the destination node need to send ACK packet backward to the source node to revise QoS constraint of the future packets. Moreover, a node should be aware of the state of its neighbor nodes in order to confirm route strategy. This method effectively adapts with the change of the network state when one node becomes inefficacy. A node can detect the state of its neighbor nodes actively, or receive the ACK packet from its neighbor passively. The nodes in WMN do not change their state as frequently as in Ad-Hoc, so we tend to use passive detection to avoid too much overhead in the network.

As WMN can be deployed as last mile access of Internet, the particularity of the gateway node should be considered. The gateway nodes affect the performance of the connection between WMN and Internet[16]. If a gateway node is the forward node to Internet, we view it as destination node in WMN. Normally WMN with gateway nodes needs to maintain an interface to the application level, so in NSUA algorithm we provide the QoS information to the interface.

Table 2. Network State Update Algorithm

```
Network State Update Algorithm
1  Initial node state table of each node
2  Execute QoS guarantee algorithm that already exists
3    If probability QoS constraint is not satisfied at destination node X
4      node X sends ACK packet to source node
5      Update QoS constraint of this application at the source node
6    End If
7    If neighbor node of node Y is inefficient by passive detection
8      Update node state table of node Y
9    End If
10   If destination node Z is gateway node receiving packet
11     Update node state table of node Z by time stamp in the packet
12     Inform node state table of node Z to application level
13   End If
```

For a wireless mesh network of n nodes, the time that Network State Update Algorithm increases to the QoS guarantee algorithm that already exists is $O(n)$. In this Algorithm, Lines $3-13$ increase time cost of the QoS guarantee algorithm that already exists. Lines $3-6$ run in $O(n)$ time, because the length of longest path from X to the source node is less than n; Lines $7-9$ run in $O(n)$ time, because the updating node state table of node Y relates at most all the n nodes in WMN; Lines $10-13$ run in $O(1)$ time, because updating node state table of node Z and informing it to application level both cost constant time. Above all, NSUA Algorithm increases linear time to the existed QoS guarantee algorithm.

NSUA Algorithm is also with high portability, because the frame of the algorithm is to execute the network state update process in the executing of the QoS guarantee algorithm that already exists. Although NSUA Algorithm makes use of traffic request, probability QoS constraint and network state description, they are easily to be revised into those existed algorithms, because they are basic elements of a QoS guarantee algorithm. NSUA Algorithm is with both time efficiency and high portability.

5 Evaluation

We examine the performance of our framework in this section. According to Section 4, we deploy our NSUA Algorithm with the algorithm in [1]. The simulation environments are listed as follows.

1. The network is formed as a 4×5 grid topology.
2. There are at least four (ingress, egress) pairs in this network.
3. In different simulation environments, the number of channels varies from 3 to 12.
4. One link can only deliver 2 units flow in a time slot by one channel. The packet delivery ratio is set to be low on purpose to distinguish flows of different reliability requirements.

5.1 Packet Dropping Ratio under Different Reliability Requirements

There are many flows delivered by 4 channels in our simulation, and the reliability requirements of these flows are various. Table 3 shows the packet dropping ratio of three flows, whose reliability requirements are from high to low.

Table 3. Packet Dropping Ratio

Traffic Load	28	32	36	40
Flow 1	0	0	0	2/61
Flow 2	0	2/49	4/57	7/63
Flow 3	6/49	14/56	20/67	29/68

Table 3 shows that the packet dropping ratio of each flow increases while traffic load of each flow increases, but the packet dropping ratio of the flow of low reliability requirement is always higher than that of high reliability requirement. NSUA Algorithm can route flows effectively under the requirement of reliability. The packet dropping ratio of each flow decreases while the number of channels increases, because more channels can lead to less interference, and more packets of low reliability requirement can be delivered.

5.2 Delivery Time of Flows with Different Delay Constraints

We configure the simulation environment as: there are 4 to 8 channels in the network and traffic load varies from 28 to 36. Fig.1(a, b) record the result of our simulation when there are 6 and 8 channels, respectively. In each situation, the delay requirement of Flow 1 to 4 is from low to high.

The delivery time of the four flows in this simulation shows that the flow of higher delay requirement delivers in shorter time than that of lower delay requirement. And Fig.1(c) shows the delivery time of three flows with different

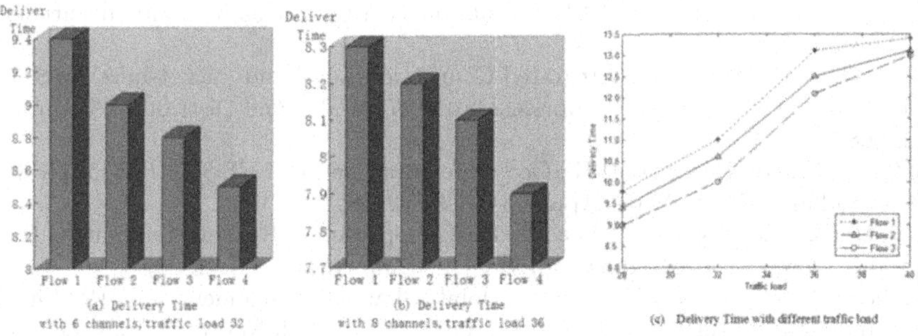

(a) Delivery Time with 6 channels, traffic load 32
(b) Delivery Time with 8 channels, traffic load 36
(c) Delivery Time with different traffic load

Fig. 1. Delivery Time of Flows with Traffic Load

traffic load when there are 5 channels in the simulation, in which the delay requirement of Flow 1 to 3 is from low to high. Fig.1(c) shows that delivery time of each flow increases while the traffic load increases, but the flow of higher delay requirement delivers in shorter time than that of lower delay requirement.

We mention at least 10 flows previously to show our result. According to NSUA Algorithm, if the destination node of a flow is a gateway node of WMN, this gateway node can update its node state table based on the QoS condition of this flow. In sum, the result of the simulation proves that our NSUA Algorithm can route the packet in the network under the QoS constraint effectively.

6 Conclusion

In this paper, we use traffic request to record QoS of the data flow, and we introduce the standard to judge the quality of service, probability QoS constraint and network state description in WMN. Then we develop Network State Update Algorithm to guarantee QoS in WMN with network state description. By making use of the existed QoS guarantee method, our time efficient NSUA Algorithm is with high portability.

References

1. Huang, H., Peng, Y.: Throughput Maximization with Traffic Profile in Wireless Mesh Network. In: Proceedings of the 14th Annual International Computing and Combinatorics Conference, pp. 531–540 (2008)
2. Akyildiz, I.F., Wang, X., Wang, W.: Wireless Mesh Networks: a Survey. Computer Networks 47, 445–487 (2005)
3. Mesh Dynamics Inc., `http://www.meshdynamics.com`
4. Aurrecoechea, C., Campbell, A.T., Hauw, L.: A Survey of QoS Architectures. In: Conference on Information Sciences and Systems (2004)
5. Gallego, D.M., Medeiros, A.M., Cardieri, P., Yacoub, M.D., Seo, C.E., Leonardo, E.J.: Capacity and QoS of Wireless Mesh Networks. In: 4th International Information and Telecommunication Technologies Symposium (2005)
6. Bortnikov, E., Kol, T., Vaisman, A.: QMesh: a QoS Mesh Network with Mobility Support. Mobile Computing and Communications Review 12 (2007)
7. Huang, J.H., Wang, L.C., Chang, C.J.: Capacity and QoS for a Scalable Ring-Based Wireless Mesh Network. IEEE Journal on Selected Areas in Communications 24 (November 2006)
8. Yu, O., Saric, E., Li, A.: Integrated Connection-Level and Packet-Level QoS Controls over Wireless Mesh Networks. Journal of Parallel and Distributed Computing (2008)
9. Zhang, Y., Hu, H., Chen, H.H.: QoS Differentiation for IEEE 802.16 WiMAX Mesh Networking. Mobile Netw. Appl. 13, 19–37 (2008)
10. Matta, I., Bestavros, A.: A Load Profiling Approach to Routing Guaranteed Bandwidth Flows. In: Proceedings of INFOCOM, pp. 1014–1021 (1998)
11. Alicherry, M., Bhatia, R., Li, L.: Joint Channel Assignment and Routing for Throughput Optimization in Multi-radio Wireless Mesh Networks. In: Proceedings of the 11th Annual International Conference on Mobile Computing and Networking, pp. 58–72 (2005)

12. Burkhart, M., Rickenbach, P., Wattenhofer, R., Zollinger, A.: Does Topology Control Reduce Interference. In: MobiCom 2004, pp. 24–26 (2004)
13. Suri, S., Waldvogel, M., Bauer, D., Warkhede, P.R.: Profile-Based Routing and Traffic Engineering. Computer Communications 26, 351–365 (2003)
14. Huang, X., Fang, Y.: Multiconstrained QoS Multipath Routing in Wireless Sensor Networks. Wireless Networks 14, 465–478 (2008)
15. Kim, S.H., Jang, Y.M.: Soft QoS-Based Vertical Handover Scheme for WLAN and WCDMA Networks Using Dynamic Programming Approach. Mobile Communications (2003)
16. Aoun, B., Boutaba, R., Iraqi, Y., Kenward, G.: Gateway Placement Optimization in Wireless Mesh Networks with QoS Constraints. IEEE Journal on Selected Areas in Communications 24, 2127–2136 (2006)
17. Tabatabaee, V., Kashyap, A., Bhattacharjee, B., La, R.J., Shayman, M.A.: Robust Routing with Unknown Traffic Matrices. In: 26th IEEE International Conference on Computer Communications, pp. 2436–2440 (2007)

An Approximation Algorithm for Conflict-Aware Many-to-One Data Aggregation Scheduling in Wireless Sensor Networks

Qinghua Zhu and Deying Li*

School of Information, Renmin University of China, Beijing 100872, China
{qinghuazhu,deyingli}@ruc.edu.cn

Abstract. A network of many sensors and a base station that are deployed over a region is considered. Each sensor has a transmission range, a interference range, and a carrier sensing range, which is r, αr, and βr, respectively. In this paper, we study the minimum latency conflict-aware many-to-one data aggregation scheduling problem: Given locations of sensors along with a base station, a subset of sensors, and parameters r, α, and β, find a schedule in which the data of each sensor in the subset can be transmitted to the base station with no conflicts, such that the latency is minimized. We designed an nearly a constant ratio approximation algorithm and a heuristic algorithm for the problem. Extensive simulations have been done to show the performances of the two algorithms.

Keywords: Conflict-aware, many-to-one data aggregation, latency, approximation algorithm, wireless sensor network.

1 Introduction

A wireless sensor network is a set of sensor nodes using radio transmissions, in which there is no infrastructure and sensors are to organize themselves arbitrarily. It has a wide variety of applications like emergency medical situations, battlefield surveillance, traffic monitoring. In these applications, quite often we need to gather data from those nodes to a fixed sink and process them. If the data gathered can be merged such as taking the maximum or minimum of them, we call this type of application as data aggregation. Real-time is very important in data aggregation applications, therefore, reducing the data aggregation latency is important issue in wireless sensor networks.

In this paper, we focus on conflict-aware data aggregation and try to reduce its latency by constructing a good schedule. Typically, the area of a wireless sensor network is larger than the transmission range of any individual node. Therefore, carrying out the data aggregation in general involves relaying the message by intermediate nodes. This necessitates computing a data aggregation

* Corresponding author.

B. Liu et al. (Eds.): WASA 2009, LNCS 5682, pp. 428–437, 2009.

schedule. The data aggregation schedule determines which nodes must transmit the message at what time slot. In addition, the broadcast nature of the wireless medium can cause two parallel transmissions to fail due to collision and interference. We call such parallel transmissions to be conflicting with each other. A data aggregation scheduling algorithm must avoid scheduling parallel transmissions which are very likely to fail based on the collision and interference. Huang et al [10] studied the minimum latency data aggregation schedule. But they only considered that transmission range was equal to the interference range. However, we consider more general cases, and study the minimum latency conflict-aware many-to-one data aggregation scheduling problem, in which we take parameters, the interference range and carrier sensing range, into account, so that we can avoid scheduling conflicting parallel transmissions in one time slot and latency is minimized. In this problem, there is only a subset of sensor nodes, and each node in the subset produces data which need to be aggregated to the base station. We propose an approximation algorithm for the problem.

The rest of the paper is organized as follows. Section 2 gives conflicts and conflict-aware communication model. In section 3, we review related works. In section 4, we describe the system model and the problem definition. Section 5 proposes an approximation algorithm for minimum latency conflict-aware many-to-one data aggregation scheduling problem. In section 6, we present the experimental results and finally we conclude the paper in section 7.

2 Conflicts and Conflict-Aware Communication

In this paper, we consider potential conflicts in parallel transmissions, which is similar with in [2]. Two parallel transmissions can be expected to succeed only if they avoid all following types of conflicts.

1. Collision at Receiver: If a node is within the transmission range of two or more transmitting nodes, it cannot correctly receive either of the messages.
2. Interference at Receiver: If a node is within the interference range of a transmitting node, it cannot correctly receive a message from any of its neighbors.
3. Contention at Sender: If a node is within the carrier sensing range of another transmitting node [6], the node cannot transmit a message to its neighbors.

We denote transmissions which avoid all the above types of conflicts to be conflict-aware transmissions.

3 Related Work

In wireless ad hoc networks, broadcast and data aggregation are the most fundamental and useful operations.

Broadcast algorithms for minimum latency have been studied extensively. Gandhi *et. al.* [7] studied the minimum latency broadcast problem in ad hoc networks. Authors proposed an approximation algorithm with ratio 648 in UDG.

Huang *et.al.* [4] presented a more efficient solution to this problem in UDG. They proposed approximation algorithm with ratio $16R - 15$, which is better than algorithm in [7]. They also extended pipelined algorithm [8] on arbitrary graphs to the UDG to get a lower bound of $R + O(logR)$. Chen *et. al.* [5] studied the minimum latency interference-aware broadcast scheduling considering the interference range, and proposed IAB algorithm with performance ratio $2\pi\alpha^2$, where interference range is α times of the transmission range. Mahjourian *et.al.* [2] studied the minimum latency conflict-aware broadcast scheduling considering transmission range, interference range, and carrier sensing range, and proposed CABS algorithm with performance ratio $O((max(\alpha, \beta))^2)$, where α, β is the ratio of the interference range and the carrier sensing range to the transmission range, respectively. [2] is the only work so far to study the carrier sensing range of the nodes.

Data aggregation for minimum latency is still relatively new but its importance cannot be overemphasized. Yu *et. al.* [9] studied the problem of scheduling transmissions for data gathering in wireless sensor networks. Algorithms were proposed to minimize the overall energy of the sensor nodes in the aggregation tree subject to the latency constraint. Chen *et. al.* [3] studied the Minimum Data Aggregation Time(MDAT) problem with uniform transmission range of all sensors. They designed a $(\Delta - 1)$-approximation algorithm for MDAT problem, where Δ is the maximum number of sensors within the transmission range of any sensor. Huang *et. al.* [10] also studied the MDTA problem and proposed algorithm with a nearly constant performance ratio 23.

To our best knowledge, none of the exist works for data aggregation considers the interference range or carrier sensing range of the wireless nodes. In this paper, we study the minimum latency conflict-aware many-to-one data aggregation scheduling problem which considers the transmission range, interference range, and carrier sensing range, in which latency is defined as the number of time slots until all the data of nodes in the subset get to the base station.

4 System Model and Problem Definition

We consider a network consisting of n sensors along with a base station. We consider an omni-antennae only, and a sensor node's transmission range, interference range and carrier sensing range are roughly disks centered at the node. For simplicity, we further assume that all nodes have the same transmission range r, same interference range αr, $\alpha \geq 1$, and same carrier sensing range βr, $\beta \geq 1$, respectively. Therefore, the communication network is represented by a UDG $G = (V, E)$. An edge exists between node u and node v if and only if $d(u, v) \leq r$, where $d(u, v)$ is the Euclidean distance between u and v. There exists an arc between node u and the base station b if and only if $d(u, b) \leq r$.

Given a UDG $G = (V, E)$ along with a base station $b \in V$, a subset $S \subseteq V - \{b\}$, and each node in S has data need to be aggregated to the base station, and parameters r, α, β, where $\alpha \geq 1$, and $\beta \geq 1$.

A data aggregation schedule can be thought of as a sequence of transmissions, each of which is consist of a sender and a receiver. Let $Sch = \{T_1, T_2, \cdots, T_l\}$ be a data aggregation schedule satisfying the many-to-one aggregation property, where $T_i = \{(u, v)|$ transmission (u, v) is scheduled in time slot $i\}$, $\forall 1 \leq i \leq l$. Let $S_i = \{u|(u, v) \in T_i\}$ and $R_i = \{v|(u, v) \in T_i\}$ for $\forall 1 \leq i \leq l$, then S_i and R_i are consist of all senders and receivers of transmissions scheduled in time slot i, respectively.

A conflict-aware many-to-one data aggregation schedule can be formulated as a sequence of transmissions $Sch = \{T_1, T_2, \cdots, T_l\}$ satisfying the following formal definition of the many-to-one aggregation property.

(1) $S_i \cap R_i = \emptyset, \forall 1 \leq i \leq l$
(2) $S_i \cap S_j = \emptyset, \forall i \neq j, 1 \leq i, j \leq l$.
(3) $S \subseteq \bigcup_{i=1}^{l} S_i$.
(4) $\bigcup_{i=1}^{k} S_i \bigcap \bigcup_{j=k}^{l} R_j = \emptyset, \forall 1 \leq k \leq l$.
(5) $G_{Sch} = (V_{Sch}, E_{Sch})$ is a tree rooted at the base station, where $V_{Sch} = \bigcup_{i=1}^{l}(S_i \cup R_i)$ and $E_{Sch} = \bigcup_{i=1}^{l} T_i$.
(6) T_i is conflict-aware, that is, non-conflicting.

The number l is called the data aggregation latency. The item (1) guarantees that a node can either send or receive data at one time slot. The item (2) satisfies that each node in the schedule transmits data once. The item (3) guarantees that the data of nodes in S can be transmitted. The item (4) satisfies that a node transmits data once and doesn't receive data after being scheduled to transmit. The item (5) guarantees that the data of nodes in S can get to the base station. The item (6) guarantees that the transmissions in each time slot are non-conflicting.

Now, *the minimum latency conflict-aware many-to-one data aggregation scheduling problem* can be formulated as follows: Given a UDG $G = (V, E)$ along with a base station $b \in V$, a subset $S \subseteq V - \{b\}$, and parameters r, α, β, find a conflict-aware many-to-one data aggregation schedule with minimum latency.

5 Our Data Aggregation Algorithms

5.1 Many-to-One Data Aggregation Tree Construction

In this subsection, we will construct a many-to-one data aggregation tree. Since we need to find a many-to-one schedule with minimum latency, there may be some nodes not needed to take part in schedule. Firstly, we take the breadth first search to find subgraph G_p and T_{BFS_p} for (S, b). Secondly, based on the subgraph, construct a maximal independent set and its partition. We divide all the nodes in G_p into layers according to T_{BFS_p} (where the 0-th layer is the base station) and find a maximal independent set U of G_p layer by layer and a partition $\{U_0, U_1, U_2, \cdots\}$ of U according to the layers of all nodes. The details are given in Algorithm 1.

Algorithm 1. Construct a maximal independent set and its partition.
Input: A connected network $G = (V, E)$, the base station b and $S \subseteq V$.
Output: A maximal independent set and its partition.
Procedure: MIS-Partition(G, S, b)

Using a breadth first search to get tree T_{BFSp} and G_p for (S, b)
Let R denote the depth of T_{BFSp}
Divide all nodes in T_{BFSp} into $L_1, L_2, \cdots, L_R$
$U = \emptyset$
For $i = 1$ to R **do**
  $U_i = \emptyset$
  For each node $v \in L_i$ **do**
    If v is independent of each node in U in G_p **do**
      $U = U \cup \{v\}$
      $U_i = U_i \cup \{v\}$
$U_0 = \emptyset$
Return U and $U_0, U_1, U_2, \cdots, U_R$

Finally, based on the maximal independent set U and its a partition $\{U_0, U_1, \cdots, U_R\}$, we construct the many-to-one data aggregation tree, on which we will make conflict-aware data aggregation schedule. For a node v, if there is a node u such that $(u, v) \in E$, we call that node v is a dominator of nodes v. The details are given in Algorithm 2.

Algorithm 2. Construct a many-to-one data aggregation tree.
Input: A network $G_p = (V_p, E_p)$ along with the base station b, a breadth first search tree T_{BFSp}, a maximal independent set U of G_p and the partition $U_0, U_1, U_2, \cdots, U_R$.
Output: A many-to-one data aggregation tree and some subsets of V_p.
Procedure: Many-to-OneDAT$(G_p, T_{BFSp}, U, U_0, U_1, U_2, \cdots, U_R)$

Using a breadth first search to get tree T_{BFSp} and G_p for (S, b), let R denote the depth of T_{BFSp}
$T = (V_T, E_T)$,where $V_T = V_p, E_T = \emptyset$
$C_1 = \{b\}$
For each node $v \in U_1$ **do**
  $E_T = E_T \cup \{(b, v)\}$
$D_1 = \emptyset$
For $i = 2$ to R **do**
  $C_i = \emptyset$
  $D_i = \emptyset$
  For each node $v \in U_i$ **do**
    Find its parent $p(v)$ in T_{BFSp}
    $C_i = C_i \cup \{p(v)\}$
    Find one of $p(v)$'s dominators $d_{p(v)}$ in $U_{i-1} \cup U_{i-2}$
    $D_i = D_i \cup \{d_{p(v)}\}$
    $E_T = E_T \cup \{(p(v), v)\} \cup \{(d_{p(v)}, p(v))\}$

$D = \emptyset$
For each node $v \in V_p$ not in $\bigcup_{i=1}^{R} C_i \bigcup U$ **do**
    Find one of v's dominators d_v in U
    $E_T = E_T \cup \{(d_v, v)\}$
    $D = D \cup \{d_v\}$
Return T and $C_1, D_1, C_2, D_2 \cdots, C_R, D_R$ and $V_p - \bigcup_{i=1}^{R} C_i \bigcup U, D$.

5.2 Many-to-One Data Aggregation Scheduling

The data aggregation tree obtained from Algorithm 2 doesn't prevent conflicts. We invoke Sub-Scheduler routine (Algorithm 3) to obtain conflict-aware sub-scheduling in tree obtained from Algorithm 2.

Before showing the details of algorithm 3, there is a lemma need to set out. Two transmissions "$t_1 \rightarrow r_1$" and "$t_2 \rightarrow r_2$" are said to be parallel if they are scheduled in the same time slot.

Lemma 1. *Two parallel transmissions "$t_1 \rightarrow r_1$" and "$t_2 \rightarrow r_2$" are non-conflicting if and only if the following three conditions are satisfied: (1) $d(t_1, r_2) > \alpha r$; (2) $d(t_2, r_1) > \alpha r$; (3) $d(t_1, t_2) > \beta r$.*

The details are given in Algorithm 3.

Algorithm 3. Construct sub-scheduling for conflict-aware data aggregation.
Input: A sender set S, a receiver set R, a data aggregation tree T, transmission range r, and parameters α, β.
Output: A conflict-aware schedule for S and R.
Procedure: Sub-Scheduler($S, R, T, r, \alpha, \beta$)

$X \leftarrow \emptyset$
$Sch \leftarrow \{\emptyset\}$
Let $p(u)$ be the parent of u in T
While $S \neq \emptyset$ **do**
    For each node $u \in S$ **do**
        If $\forall (v, p(v)) \in X, d(u, p(v)) > \alpha r, d(v, p(u)) > \alpha r$ and $d(u, v) > \beta r$ **do**
            $X \leftarrow X \cup \{(u, p(u))\}$
            $S \leftarrow S - \{u\}$
    $Sch \leftarrow Sch \cup \{X\}$
    $X \leftarrow \emptyset$
Return Sch

Based on the Sub-Scheduler routine, we can construct the conflict-aware data aggregation schedule. The details are given in Algorithm 4.

Algorithm 4. Construct conflict-aware many-to-one data aggregation scheduling.
Input: A network $G(V, E)$ along with a base station b, a subset $S \subseteq V - \{b\}$, transmission range r, and parameters α and β.
Output: A conflict-aware many-to-one data aggregation scheduling.

Let R be the depth of T_{BFS_p}
$[U, U_0, U_1, U_2, \cdots, U_R] \leftarrow$ MIS-Partition(G, S, b)
$[T, C_1, D_1, C_2, D_2 \cdots, C_R, D_R, NC, D] \leftarrow$
Many-to-OneDAT$(G_p, T_{BFS_p}, U, U_0, U_1, U_2, \cdots, U_R)$
$Sch \leftarrow Sch \cup$Sub-Scheduler$(NC, D, T, r, \alpha, \beta)$
If $R \geq 2$ **do**
  For $i = R$ to 2 **do**
    $Sch \leftarrow Sch \cup$Sub-Scheduler$(U_i, C_i, T, r, \alpha, \beta)$
    $Sch \leftarrow Sch \cup$Sub-Scheduler$(C_i, D_i, T, r, \alpha, \beta)$
$Sch \leftarrow Sch \cup$Sub-Scheduler$(U_1, C_1, T, r, \alpha, \beta)$
Return Sch

Theorem 1. *The time complexity of algorithm 4 is $O(|V|^2)$, where $|V|$ is number of nodes in the network.*

5.3 Performance Analysis

In this section, we study the approximation ratio of the Algorithm 4 which is for the minimum latency conflict-aware many-to-one data aggregation scheduling problem. We compare the performance of our algorithm against the trivial lower bound of R, where R is the depth of the T_{BFS_p}. Before analyzing the performance, we need to introduce a lemma in [2] which will be used to analyze the upper bound of latency obtained from our algorithm.

The following lemma shows the sufficient conditions for avoiding the three types of conflict.

Lemma 2 ([2]). *In order for two parallel transmissions "$t_1 \rightarrow r_1$" and "$t_2 \rightarrow r_2$" to be non-conflicting according to the network model, it is sufficient to have: $d(t_1, t_2) > max(\alpha + 1, \beta)r \vee d(r_1, r_2) > (max(\alpha, \beta) + 2)r$.*

Note that these conditions are in general stronger than what is needed for avoiding conflicting transmissions.

We construct two conflict graphs which are denoted by GC_t and GC_r according to Lemma 2. The graphs have the same vertices as the pruned graph G_p. In GC_t there is an edge between two nodes u, v if and only if $d(u, v) \leq max(\alpha + 1, \beta)r$. In GC_r there is an edge between two nodes u, v if and only if $d(u, v) \leq (max(\alpha, \beta) + 2)r$. Suppose two parallel transmissions "$t_1 \rightarrow r_1$" and "$t_2 \rightarrow r_2$" to be non-conflicting, it is sufficient to have $(t_1, t_2) \notin E(GC_t)$ or $(r_1, r_2) \notin E(GC_r)$.

Theorem 2 ([11]). *The area of the convex hull of any $n \geq 2$ non-overlapping unit-radius circular disks is at least $2\sqrt{3}(n-1) + (2-\sqrt{3})\lceil\sqrt{12n-3} - 3\rceil + \pi$.*

Definition 1. *$f(x)$ is the maximum integer n to make $2\sqrt{3}(n-1) + (2-\sqrt{3})\lceil\sqrt{12n-3} - 3\rceil + \pi \leq x$.*

Note that the value of $f(x)$ is a constant integer, which is easy to obtain for a given x.

Lemma 3. *Let $G_p = (V_p, E_p)$, $S \subseteq V_p$ and the nodes in S be independent in G_p, the the inductivities of $GC_t[S]$ and $GC_r[S]$ have an upper-bound of $f(2\pi h^2 + 2\pi h - 4h)$ and $f(2\pi k^2 + 2\pi k - 4k)$ respectively, where $h = max(\alpha + 1, \beta)$ and $k = max(\alpha, \beta) + 2$.*

Theorem 3. *Algorithm 4 has a latency upper bound $(a + 19b)R + \Delta b - a + 5$, where $a = 1 + f(2\pi h^2 + 2\pi h - 4h)$, $b = 1 + f(2\pi k^2 + 2\pi k - 4k)$, $h = max(\alpha + 1, \beta)$ and $k = max(\alpha, \beta) + 2$, Δ and R are the maximum degree of pruned network G_p and the depth of the pruned BFS tree T_{BFSp}, respectively. Here Δ contributes to an additive factor instead of a multiplicative one, thus algorithm 4 has a nearly constant $(a + 19b)$ ratio.*

The following table shows some instances of parameters α, β and obtained constant integer a, b.

α	β	a	b	α	β	a	b
1.10	1.40	9	22	1.20	1.50	10	24
1.30	1.60	11	25	1.40	1.70	12	26
1.50	1.80	13	28	1.60	1.90	14	29
1.70	1.30	15	26	1.80	1.50	16	28

5.4 Heuristic Algorithm

In this subsection we present Algorithm 5. In Algorithm 4, we schedule all the transmissions layer by layer after scheduling transmissions from NC to D. Algorithm 5 adopt a different order to schedule all the edges in the tree. The details are shown in Algorithm 5.

Algorithm 5. Construct conflict-aware many-to-one data aggregation scheduling.
Input: A network $G(V, E)$ along with a base station b, a subset $S \subseteq V - \{b\}$, and parameters α and β.
Output: A conflict-aware many-to-one data aggregation scheduling.

$Sch \leftarrow \{\emptyset\}$
Using a breadth first search to get tree T_{BFSp} and G_p for (S, b)
Let R be the depth of T_{BFSp}
$[U, U_0, U_1, U_2, \cdots, U_R] \leftarrow$ MIS-Partition(G_p, T_{BFSp})
Let T be the data aggregation tree returned by Many-to-OneDAT$(G_p, T_{BFSp}, U, U_0, U_1, U_2, \cdots, U_R)$
While there are edges in tree T **do**
  $S \leftarrow$ all the leaves of tree T
  $P \leftarrow$ all the parents of nodes in S in tree T
  $S' \leftarrow S$
  $Sch \leftarrow Sch \cup$Sub-Scheduler$(S, P, T, r, \alpha, \beta)$
  Delete all edges incident to nodes in S' from tree T
  Delete all the nodes in S'
Return Sch

6 Simulations

In the simulations, we focus on comparing the latencies obtained from algorithm 4 and algorithm 5. We study how the latencies are affected by varying four parameters: the total number of nodes in the network (N), and the number of sources ($|S|$) and the parameters α and β for interference range and carrier sensing range respectively.

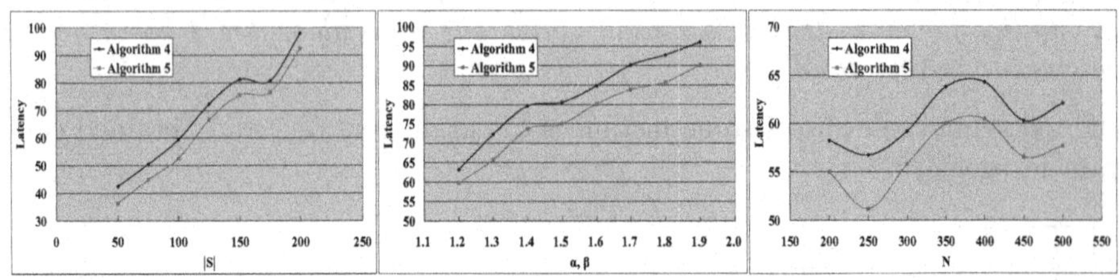

Fig. 1. (1.5, 1.8, 300) **Fig. 2.** (300, 150) **Fig. 3.** (1.5, 1.8, 100)

The simulations are conducted in a 100×100 2-D free-space by randomly allocating N nodes. The transmission range of each node is 30. We present average of 100 separate runs for each result shown in the following figures. In each run of the simulations, for given N and $|S|$, we randomly place N nodes and the base station in the free-space, and randomly select $|S|$ sources. Any topology which is not connected is discarded. Then we compute the many-to-one conflict-aware schedule latency using algorithm 4 and algorithm 5.

In Fig. 1, we fix $\alpha = 1.5$, $\beta = 1.8$ and $N = 300$, while varying $|S|$ from 50 to 200 in increments of 25. As shown in the figure, algorithm 5 consistently outperforms algorithm 4. It is also shown that the latencies obtained from both algorithm 4 and algorithm 5 are increasing as the number of sources increasing. It is easy to explain this phenomenon. Intuitively, the more is the number of the sources, the more is the number of nodes in the pruned networks and in the many-to-one data aggregation tree (the more is the number of edges need to schedule in many-to-one data aggregation tree). So, the the latencies obtained from algorithm 4 and algorithm 5 are increasing as the number of the sources increasing is comprehensible.

In Fig. 2, we fix $N = 300$ and $|S| = 150$, while varying parameters α and β from 1.1 to 1.9 in increments of 0.1. We make the interference range is equal to carrier sensing range in this simulation. Algorithm 5 also consistently outperforms Algorithm 4 in this simulation. It is also shown that the latencies obtained from both Algorithm 4 and Algorithm 5 are increasing as the parameters (α, β) increasing. It is easy to make this phenomenon clear. Intuitively, the more is the parameters of interference and carrier sensing range, the more is the area which will be intervened by each node, i.e., there less edges (transmissions) can be scheduled in the same time slot. So, the the latencies obtained from Algorithm 4 and Algorithm 5 are increasing as the parameters increasing is apprehensible.

In Fig. 3, we fix $\alpha = 1.5$, $\beta = 1.8$ and $|S| = 100$, while varying N from 200 to 500 in increments of 50. Algorithm 5 also consistently outperforms Algorithm 4 in this simulation.

Sum up the above simulations, it is concluded that algorithm 5 consistently outperforms algorithm 4, and algorithm 4 is an approximation algorithm.

7 Conclusion

In this paper, we study the minimum latency conflict-aware many-to-one data aggregation scheduling problem: Given locations of sensors along with a base station, a subset of all sensors, and parameters $r, \alpha,$, and β, find a schedule in which the data of each sensor in the subset can be transmitted to the base station with no conflicts, such that the latency is minimized. We designed nearly a constant $(a + 19b)$-ratio approximation algorithm and a heuristic algorithm for the problem. Simulations show our algorithms are efficient.

Acknowledgment

This work was supported in part by the NSF of China under Grant No. 10671208.

References

1. Cristescu, R., Beferull-Lozano, B., Vetterli, M.: On network correlated data gathering. In: IEEE INFOCOM, pp. 2571–2582. IEEE Press, Los Alamitos (2004)
2. Mahjourian, R., Chen, F., Tiwari, R., Thai, M., Zhai, H., Fang, Y.: An approximation algorithm for conflict-Aware broadcast scheduling in wireless ad hoc networks. In: MOBIHOC 2008, Hong Kong, pp. 331–340 (2008)
3. Chen, X., Hu, X., Zhu, J.: Minimum data aggregation time problem in wireless sensor networks. In: Jia, X., Wu, J., He, Y. (eds.) MSN 2005. LNCS, vol. 3794, pp. 133–142. Springer, Heidelberg (2005)
4. Huang, H., Wan, J., Jia, X., Du, H., Shang, W.: Minimum-latency broadcast scheduling in wireless ad hoc networks. In: INFOCOM 2007, Alaska, pp. 733–739 (2007)
5. Chen, Z., Qiao, C., Xu, J., Lee, T.: A constant approximation algorithm for interference aware broadcast in wireless networks. In: INFOCOM 2007, Alaska, pp. 740–748 (2007)
6. Deng, J., Liang, B., Varshney, P.: Tuning the carrier sensing range of ieee 802.11 mac. In: GLOBECOM 2004, pp. 2987–2991 (2004)
7. Gandhi, R., Parthasarathy, S., Mishra, A.: Minimizing broadcast latency and redundancy in ad hoc networks. In: MOBIHOC 2003, pp. 222–232 (2003)
8. Gasieniec, L., Peleg, D., Xin, Q.: Faster communication in known topology radio networks. In: PODC 2005, pp. 129–137 (2005)
9. Yu, Y., Krishnamachari, B., Prasanna, V.K.: Energy-latency tradeoffs for data gathering in wireless sensor etworks. In: IEEE INFOCOM 2004 (2004)
10. Huang, H., Wan, P., Vu, T., Li, Y., Yao, F.: Nearly constant approximation for data aggregation scheduling in wireless sensor networks. In: IEEE INFOCOM 2007 (2007)
11. Wegner, G.: Über endliche kreispackungen in der ebene. Studia Scientiarium Mathematicarium Hungarica 21, 1–28 (1986)

On Approximation Algorithms for Interference-Aware Broadcast Scheduling in 2D and 3D Wireless Sensor Networks

Ravi Tiwari, Thang N. Dinh, and My T. Thai*

CISE Department,
University of Florida,
Gainesville, Fl-32611
{rtiwari,tdinh,mythai}@cise.ufl.edu

Abstract. Broadcast scheduling is a mechanism for performing interference-aware broadcasting in multi-hop wireless sensor networks (WSNs). Existing studies assume all the WSN nodes lie on a 2D plane. This assumption is not always appropriate, as in practice the sensor nodes may acquire positions in the 3D space. In this paper, we study the broadcast scheduling problem in which we consider two different models of the transmission graph: Disk Graph (DG) in 2D and Ball Graph (BG) in 3D. We consider each node may have different transmission ranges and the interference range is α time of the transmission range (where $\alpha > 1$). We devise efficient coloring methods for coloring a hexagonal tiling in 2D and truncated octahedragonal tiling in 3D, which leads to $O(1)$-approximation ratio for broadcast scheduling problem in 2D and 3D, respectively.

Keywords: Approximation Algorithm, Broadcast Scheduling, Interference-aware.

1 Introduction

A Wireless Sensor Network (WSN) is a set of nodes deployed to sense some phenomena, collect information and send it to the base station for further processing on multi-hop paths. The sensor nodes in WSNs communicate via radio transmission. The broadcast nature of the radio transmission is called Wireless Broadcast Advantage (WBA) . This enables a transmitting sensor node to broadcast to all the receiving nodes within its transmission range in a single transmission. However, more than one sensors transmitting simultaneously may result in interference at receiving sensors. Therefore, their transmissions need to be scheduled to avoid interference, such scheduled transmissions are said to be interference-aware. In WSNs, the broadcast scheduling is one of the fundamental operations on which various distributed applications and protocols are based. In addition, broadcast scheduling is a far more effective mechanism in comparison to flooding [7] for mitigating the adverse effect of interference on the performance of broadcasting.

* Supported in part by NSF grant number CNS-0847869.

B. Liu et al. (Eds.): WASA 2009, LNCS 5682, pp. 438–448, 2009.

All existing research related to broadcast scheduling in WSNs consider that the sensor nodes are deployed in a 2D plane [1,2,5,3,4]. This may be appropriate in some cases, but in general the sensor nodes may acquires locations in a 3D space. For instance, the fire sensors are deployed on trees in the forests at different levels to percept the intensity of forest fire. The underwater sensors reside at different depth of sea in order to sense and collect vital information about aquatic life or to predict the disastrous Tsunami. The WSNs are also deployed on different buildings and bridges at different heights to measure the structural integrity. Furthermore, most of the existing work in 2D [1,2,3,4,5] consider all nodes in the network have the same transmission range. Only [1] considers different transmission ranges, however, they assume interference range and transmission range are the same, which is not quite practical.

In this paper, we study the interference-aware broadcast scheduling problem for WSNs in 2D and 3D. We model the WSNs using Disk Graphs (DGs) and Ball Graphs (BGs) in 2D and 3D respectively. We also consider a more realistic network model, in which nodes may have different transmission ranges and their interference range is α times larger than their transmission range (where $\alpha > 1$). This model has not been considered earlier for broadcast scheduling problem in the existing literature.

Since the broadcast scheduling in wireless network is NP-hard [1], we propose an $O(1)$-approximation algorithm for the interference-aware broadcast scheduling problem for WSNs in 2D and 3D. For this, we study two sub-problems: 1) Tiling and coloring 2D plane using identical regular hexagons. 2) Tiling and coloring 3D space using truncated octahedrons. The solutions of these two problems lead to the approximation ratio for interference-aware broadcast scheduling problem in 2D and 3D respectively.

In order to study the tiling and coloring of 2D plane using identical regular hexagons problem, we consider a hexagonal lattice H in the 2D plane. Further, we color all the hexagons in H in such a way that two hexagons h_1 and h_2 having the same color are at least a distance $d \in \Re$ apart. The distance d is considered between two closest points p_1 and p_2, such that p_1 is in h_1 and p_2 is in h_2. We optimally solve this problem for any arbitrary distance $d \in \Re$. Notice that a closely related problem to the above problem is studied in [8], where the distance d is considered between the centers of two hexagons. This problem has lot of motivation to channel assignment in cellular network [8,6,10,11,12], where the base station is located in the center of the hexagon cell. The solution of this problem cannot be trivially applied to optimally solve the tiling and coloring of 2D plane using hexagonal.

Furthermore, we consider a lattice structure TOC generated by tilling the 3D space using identical truncated octahedrons. All the truncated octahedrons in TOC are colored in such a way that two truncated octahedrons to_1 and to_2 having the same color are least distance $d \in \Re$ apart, the distance d is the distance between two closest points p_1 and p_2 in 3D space, where p_1 is in to_1 and p_2 is in to_2. We provide the lower bound for this problem along with an approximation algorithm in section 4.

Due to scarcity of space, detailed proofs of various lemmas and theorem are not given in this paper, but they will be accessible in the journal version.

The rest of the paper is organized as follows: In section 2, we describe the network model and formally define the interference-aware broadcast scheduling problem in WSNs, along with the interference model. We introduce the tilling and coloring of 2D plain using identical regular hexagon in section 3. Section 4 describes the tiling and coloring of 3D space using identical truncated octahedrons. The $O(1)$-approximation algorithm for broadcast scheduling in 2D and 3D WSNs, along with theoretical analysis are described in section 5. Finally, section 6 concludes the paper.

2 Network Model and Problem Definition

2.1 Network Model

In this paper, we consider each sensor node v_i has a transmission range $r_i^T \in [r_{min}^T, r_{max}^T]$ (where r_{min}^T and r_{max}^T are the minimum and maximum transmission range in the WSN, respectively and $\frac{r_{max}^T}{r_{min}^T} = \beta$) and an interference range $r_i^I = \alpha r_i^T$ $(\alpha > 1)$.

1. **The 2D Network Model:** In this model, each sensor node is represented by a point in 2D plane $\Re^2$. The transmission graph is represented by a disk graph $G = (V, E)$. Each node $v_i \in V$ is associated to two concentric disks D_i^T and D_i^I, centered at v_i, called the transmission disk and the interference disk, with radius r_i^T and r_i^I respectively. If a sensor node $v_j \in V$ lies within the disk D_i^T associated to node v_i, then there exists an edge (v_i, v_j) in E, which enables v_j to receive any message transmitted by v_i.
2. **The 3D Network Model:** In this model, each sensor represents a point in 3D space $\Re^3$. The transmission graph is modeled as a ball graph $G = (V, E)$. Each node $v_i \in V$ is associated to two concentric balls B_i^T and B_i^I, called the transmission ball and the interference ball centered at v_i with radius r_i^T and r_i^I, respectively. If a sensor node $v_j \in V$ lies within the the ball B_i^T of sensor node v_i, then there exists a directed edge (v_i, v_j) in E, which enables v_j to receive any message transmitted by v_i.

Based on our network model, we define our **interference model** as follows:

- If any receiving node v_j is within r_i^T of transmitter v_i, then the energy level of the transmitted signal from v_i is sufficient at v_j to receive and interpret the transmitted data.
- If v_j is outside r_i^T but within r_i^I, then the energy level of the transmitted signal from v_i at v_j is sufficient to interfere its reception from any other node.
- If v_j is outside r_i^I, then the energy level of the transmitted signal from v_i is beyond the perception of v_j.
- The simultaneous transmission of any two nodes v_i and v_j involves interference at some node v_k receiving from v_i, iff $d(v_i, v_k) \leq r_i^T$ and $d(v_j, v_k) \leq r_j^I$.

2.2 Problem Definition

Interference-Aware Broadcast Scheduling (IABS) problem: Given a WSN modeled as above and a designated sensor node s called the source holding a message m, which is to be broadcasted to all the sensor nodes in the WSN. The problem is to generate an interference-aware broadcast schedule with minimum latency for the transmission of message m from source s to all other nodes in the network. The interference-aware broadcast schedule must follow the following constraints:

- The source s is scheduled to transmit in the first timeslot t_1.
- A node u is scheduled to transmit in time slot t_j, iff it had already received the message in timeslot t_i, where $i < j$.
- Two nodes u and v are scheduled to transmit in parallel, iff their simultaneous transmission does not interfere each other's receivers.
- The number of schedules generated, i.e the maximum timeslots required for the broadcast to complete, called the broadcast latency should be minimized.

3 Tilling 2D Plane Using Regular Hexagons

In this section, we consider the Euclidean plane is divided into regular hexagons of sides $\frac{1}{2}$ to form a hexagonal tilling, as shown in Figure 1(a). We then study the Distance-d Hexagon Coloring problem defined as follows:

Distance-d Hexagon Coloring problem: *Given a hexagonal lattice H on a 2D plane and a distance $d \in \Re$, find the minimum number of colors needed to color the entire hexagonal lattice, such that two hexagons h_1 and h_2 having the same color must have the Euclidean distance $dist(h_1, h_2) \geq d$, here the distance $dist(h_1, h_2)$ is measured between two closest points p_1 and p_2, such that, p_1 lies within h_1 and p_2 lies within h_2.*

To study the Distance-d Hexagon Coloring problem, we enforce a new coordinate system in the plane, with axes inclined at 60°. This new coordinates system has two units vectors $\hat{i}(\frac{\sqrt{3}}{2}, 0)$ and $\hat{j}(\frac{\sqrt{3}}{4}, \frac{3}{4})$, as shown in Figure 1(a). The centers of each hexagon h coincide with the integral coordinates in this coordinate system. Now, each hexagon h can be identified by the coordinates (i, j) of its center as $h(i, j)$. The Euclidean distance between two hexagon centers $h(i_1, j_1)$ and $h(i_2, j_2)$ is given as $\frac{\sqrt{3}}{2}\sqrt{(i_1 - i_2)^2 + (i_1 - i_2)(j_1 - j_2) + (j_1 - j_2)^2}$, hence, the Euclidean distance between a hexagon center $h(i, j)$ from the origin $h(0, 0)$ is given as $\frac{\sqrt{3}}{2}\sqrt{i^2 + ij + j^2}$.

To provide solution for Distance-d Hexagon coloring problem, we first compute the coordinates of hexagon $h(i, j)$ closest to $h(0, 0)$ in the first quadrant, such that two closest points, p_1 in $h(0, 0)$ and p_2 in $h(i, j)$ are at least distance d apart.

We observe that the closest points p_1 and p_2 can appear in three ways as shown in Figure 1(b):

- p_1 is the upper right corner of $h(0, 0)$ and p_2 is the lower left corner of $h(i, j)$, in Figure 1(b) $(i = 3, j = 5)$.

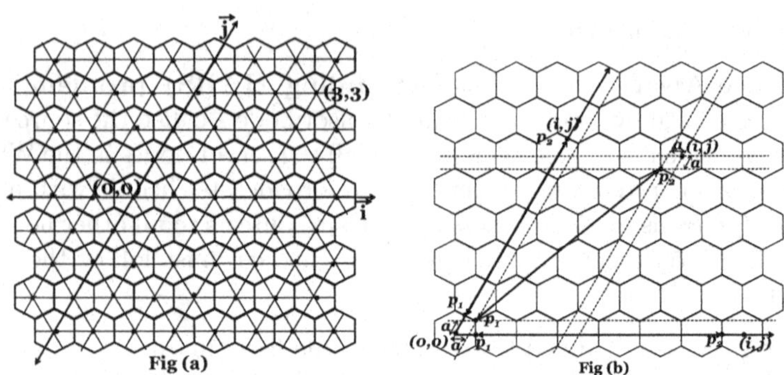

Fig. 1. Hexagonal Lattice

- p_1 is the mid point of upper right side of $h(0,0)$ and p_2 is the mid point of lower left side of $h(i,j)$, in Figure 1(b) $(i = 0, j = 7)$.
- p_1 is the mid point of right side of $h(0,0)$ and p_2 is the mid point of left side of $h(i,j)$, in Figure 1(b) $(i = 0, j = 7)$.

Without loss of generality, we considered $i \leq j$, therefore, we get rid of the third case. Now, for the given distance d, we compute (i,j) as follows:

- First we calculate two pairs (i_1, j_1) and (i_2, j_2) as follows:
  - Compute (i_1, j_1) in first quadrant using the inequality $d^2 \leq \frac{3}{4}((i_1-2a)^2 + (j_1 - 2a)^2 + (i_1 - 2a)(j_1 - 2a))$, such that $\sqrt{i_1^2 + j_1^2 + i_1 j_1}$ is minimum among all integral solution of this inequality. Here a is as shown in Figure 1(b) and is equal to $\frac{1}{3}$.
  - Compute $(i_2 = 0, j_2)$ in first quadrant using the Inequality $d^2 \leq \frac{3}{4}(j_2 - 1)^2$, such that j_2 is minimum among all integral solution of this inequality.
- Finally, if $(i_1^2 + i_1 j_1 + j_1^2) < (i_2^2 + i_2 j_2 + j_2^2)$, we select i, j as i_1, j_1 else we select i, j as i_2, j_2.

Subsequently, the distance between the centers of all the **co-color hexagons** (hexagons having the same color) in H will be $\frac{\sqrt{3}}{2}\sqrt{i^2 + j^2 + ij}$. We are now ready to describe the algorithm which optimally finds the co-color hexagons for a given hexagon $h(i', j')$ in H, for any arbitrary distance $d \in \Re$. The algorithm is illustrated as Algorithm 1. The Figure 2 shows an example for distance $d = \frac{\sqrt{31}}{2}$ and $i = 2,\ j = 3$.

Lemma 1. *The Algorithm 1 optimally identifies the co-color hexagons for a given distance $d \in \Re$.*

As shown in Figure 2, notice that the centers of the co-color hexagons for a given hexagon (considering it as origin $h(0,0)$ with out loss of generality) forms a rhombic Sub-Lattice S with basis vectors $\bar{A} = i\hat{i} + j\hat{j}$ and $\bar{B} = j\hat{i} - (i+j)\hat{j}$. Now, the number of colors needed to color H is equal to the number of rhombic

Algorithm 1. Co-color hexagon algorithm $(H, d, h(i', j'), c)$

Input: The hexagonal lattice H, distance d, hexagon $h(i', j')$ and a color number c assigned to $h(i', j')$.
Output: Set of co-color hexagons of $h(i', j')$
Compute i, j
$A \leftarrow \phi$;
$Queue \leftarrow h(i', j')$;
while (Queue is not empty) **do**
  $H(a, b) \leftarrow Queue.Remove()$
  $A \leftarrow H(a, b)$;
  $Color(H(a, b)) \leftarrow c$
  Insert each of the following hexagons in the Queue if they are not inserted in the queue:
    $H(a + i, b + j)$
    $H(a + (i + j), b - i)$
    $H(a + j, b - (i + j)j)$
    $H(a - i, b - j)$
    $H(a - (i + j), b + i)$
    $H(a - j, j + (i + j))$
end while
Return A;

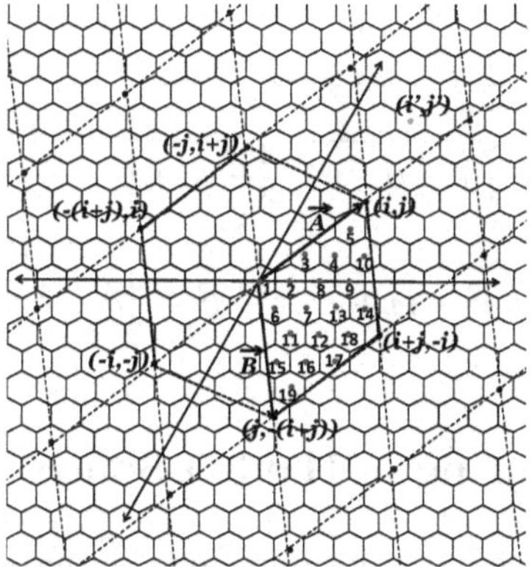

Fig. 2. An instance for Co-Color Hexagon Algorithm for $i = 2$ and $j = 3$

sub-lattice similar to S that can be identified in H. This number is equivalent to the index of classes of S in H, which is equal to $|det(\bar{A}.\bar{B})| = i^2 + j^2 + ij$ [9]. This is also the number of integral points of lattice H within the basic rhombic cell (excluding the lower side and the right side) of S formed by its generator (basis) vectors $\bar{A}$ and $\bar{B}$. These integral points are shown as red color points in Figure 2, lets refer this set of points as X. The set of hexagons centered at these integral points are assigned a unique color number among the points in X, ranging from 1 to $|X| = i^2 + j^2 + ij$. Further, these hexagons collectively forms a basic pattern which can be repeatedly used to color the entire hexagonal lattice, repeating the color numbers assigned to these hexagons. The coordinates of these integral points can be identified in $O(d^2)$ time, for any given d. Now in order to color the entire 2D hexagonal lattice, the Algorithm 1 can be repeatedly run on each of these integral points in X, assigning its color number to all the co-color hexagons. This will result in the coloring of the entire hexagonal lattice using $i^2 + j^2 + ij$ colors.

Theorem 1. *The coloring generated by the above method is an optimal solution to the Distance-d Hexagon Center Coloring problem.*

Theorem 2. *The number of colors for Distance-d Hexagon coloring problem for an arbitrary d is bounded by* $\frac{4}{3}d^2 + \frac{8}{3}d + \frac{4}{3}$

Proof. Consider the hexagon $h(0,0)$, one of its closest co-color neighbors in first quadrant is $h(i,j)$. Without loss of generality, we consider $j \geq i$, so now we have two cases: 1) $i = 0, j > 0$ and 2) $i > 0, j > 0$.

Case 1: We use j^2 colors to obtain the distance $d \leq (j-1)\frac{\sqrt{3}}{2}$. Therefore, the number of color is equal to $\frac{4}{3}d^2 + \frac{4}{\sqrt{3}}d + 1 < \frac{4}{3}d^2 + \frac{8}{3}d + \frac{4}{3}$

Case 2: As shown in the proof of Theorem 1, the number of colors used is $i^2 + ij + j^2$ and the guaranteed minimum distance between the closest points of two co-color hexagons is as follows:

$$d \leq \sqrt{\frac{3}{4}\left[(i-\frac{2}{3})^2 + (i-\frac{2}{3})(j-\frac{2}{3}) + (j-\frac{2}{3})^2\right]}$$
$$= \sqrt{\frac{3}{4}(i^2 + ij + j^2 + \frac{4}{3} - 2(i+j))}$$

It is easy to prove that $i^2 + ij + j^2 \leq \frac{4}{3}d^2 + \frac{8}{3}d + \frac{4}{3}$ for $i, j > 0$. The equality happens iff $i = j$. □

4 Tiling and Coloring of the 3D Space

In this paper, we study the uniform tilling and coloring of 3D space using identical truncated octahedrons. We consider each truncated octahedron has the maximum distance 1 unit within it. Such a truncated octahedron has the side length $\frac{1}{2\sqrt{3}}$ and the distance between its two parallel hexagonal faces is $\frac{1}{2}$, whereas the distance between its two parallel square faces is $\sqrt{\frac{2}{3}}$. Figure 3 shows the tilling of 3D space using truncated octahedrons. Based on this tilling, we study the Distance-d truncated octahedron coloring problem and propose its theoretical lower bound in Lemma 2 along with an approximation algorithm illustrated as Algorithm 2.

Distance-d truncated octahedron coloring problem: *Assume that the entire 3D space is tilled using truncated octahedrons of sides* $\frac{1}{2\sqrt{3}}$. *Find the minimum number of colors needed to color all the truncated octahedrons in the 3D space, such that any two truncated octahedrons* to_1 *and* to_2 *with the same color are at least distance* $d \in R^+$ *apart. Here the distance considered between* to_1 *and* to_2*, represented as* $dist(to_1, to_2)$ *is the Cartesian distance between two closest points* p_1 *and* p_2 *in 3D space, such that* p_1 *is within* to_1 *and* p_2 *is within* to_2.

In order to study the Distance-d truncated octahedron coloring problem, we introduce a new coordinate system in 3D space in which the X, Y, and Z axis are inclined as shown in Figure 3. The angle between X and Y axis is $\theta_1 = 2cos^{-1}(\sqrt{\frac{2}{3}})$, whereas, the angle between X and Z axis and Y and Z axis is $\theta_2 = sin^{-1}(\sqrt{\frac{2}{3}})$. Further, the distance along the X, Y and Z axis are the multiple of vectors $\vec{i}$ $(\frac{1}{2}, 0, 0)$, $\vec{j}$ $(\frac{1}{2}cos\theta_1, \frac{1}{2}sin\theta_1, 0)$, and $\vec{k}$ $(\sqrt{\frac{2}{3}}cos\theta_2, 0, \sqrt{\frac{2}{3}}sin\theta_2)$, respectively. The centers of each truncated octahedron in the 3D space coincides with the integral coordinates in the new coordinate system. Hence, every truncated octahedron can be identified by the coordinates (i, j, k) of its center as $to(i, j, k)$.

We define a graph $G_d = (TOC, E_d)$, such that TOC represents the set of vertices representing the truncated octahedrons in 3D space tiling. And the set E_d is a set of edges $E_d = \{(to_1, to_2)|dist(to_1, to_2) < d\}$. Consequently, the chromatic number $\chi(G_d)$ is the solution to the Distance-d truncated octahedron coloring problem i.e. the minimum number of colors needed to color all the truncated octahedrons in the 3D space tiling.

Lemma 2. *For any* $d \in R^+$, *the chromatic number* $\chi(G_d)$ *of the graph* $G_d = (TOC, E_d)$ *is at least* $\frac{\pi}{2}\sqrt{\frac{3}{2}}(d + \frac{1}{2})^3$.

The m^2n-coloring Algorithm

The m^2n-coloring algorithm is illustrated in Algorithm 2 and it guarantees that for any two truncated octahedrons to_1 and to_2 having $distance(to_1, to_2)$ less than $d = (m-1)\frac{1}{2} = (n-1)\sqrt{\frac{2}{3}}$, (here $d \in \Re^+$), have different colors. Figure 3 shows the basic coloring pattern generated by the m^2n-coloring algorithm for $d = 1$. In general the algorithm uses $\lceil(2d+1)\rceil^2 \left\lceil d\sqrt{\frac{3}{2}} + 1\right\rceil$ colors.

Theorem 3. *The approximation ratio of* m^2n*-coloring Algorithm is* $\frac{8\sqrt{2}}{\pi}$.

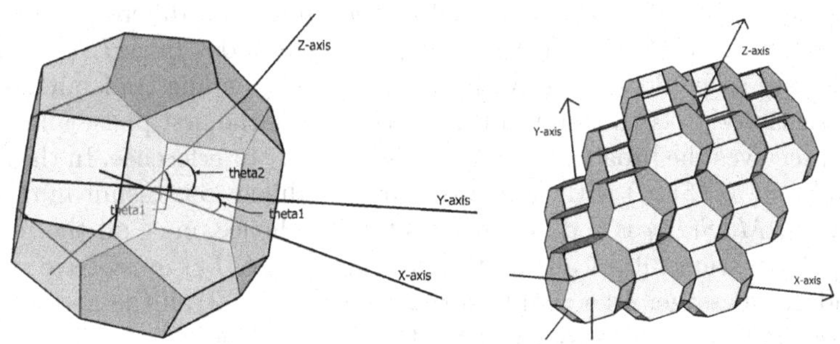

Fig. 3. Truncated octahedron tiling in 3D space

Algorithm 2. m^2n-coloring Algorithm

for all hexagon $TOC(i,j,k)$ **do**
  $Color_{TOC(i,j,k)} \leftarrow (k \bmod \lceil n \rceil)\lceil m \rceil^2 + (j \bmod \lceil m \rceil)\lceil m \rceil + (i \bmod \lceil m \rceil) + 1$
end for

5 Broadcast Scheduling Algorithm (BSA)

In this section, we first describe the Broadcast Scheduling Algorithm (BSA) and then provide the analysis of $O(1)$-approximation ratio for interference-aware broadcast scheduling problem in 2D and 3D WSNs, respectively.

5.1 Algorithm Description

The BSA takes as input transmission graph $G = (V, E)$ of the WSN and a source node $s \in V$ and runs BFS to partitions the G in to a set of layers $\{L_1, L_2, \ldots, L_R\}$ (here R is the radius of G with respect to s). Thenafter, BSA sequentionally transfers the broadcast message between the consecutive layers starting from layer $L_1 = \{s\}$. Consequently, all the nodes in the network receives the broadcast message.

During the first time slot the source node $s \in L_1$ transmits the broadcast message to the nodes in layer L_2. Thenafter, BSA runs $R - 2$ iterations of the Interlayer Scheduling Algorithm (ISA). In each iteration, ISA generates the interference-aware schedules for transmission between two consecutive layers.

The ISA takes as input two consecutive layers L_i and L_j and generates an interference-aware transmission schedule from L_i to L_j. For this, ISA first generates a maximal independent set $MIS(L_j)$ of the sub-graph $G(L_j)$ induced by the nodes in L_j in a way that $MIS(L_j)$ is the dominating set of L_j. After that ISA colors the nodes in $MIS(L_j)$ in such a way that no two nodes $u, v \in MIS(L_j)$ with Euclidean distance $d(u, v) < (\alpha + 1)r_{max}$ have the same color (see Lemma 3).

Subsequently, ISA schedules the transmission in two phases. In each phase it generates number of time slots equal to the number of different colors used to color nodes in $MIS(L_j)$. In the first phase the nodes in $MIS(L_j)$ having same color are scheduled to receive from their corresponding transmitters in L_i in the same timeslot. As a result of this, in the end of the first phase all nodes in $MIS(L_j)$ receives the broadcast message without any interference. In the second phase nodes in $MIS(L_j)$ with same color are scheduled to transmit in the same timeslot. As, $MIS(L_j)$ is a dominating set of L_j, hence, once all the nodes in $MIS(L_j)$ have transmitted all the nodes in $L_j \setminus MIS(L_j)$ must have received the broadcast message. As a result, in the end of phases 2, all the nodes in layer L_j receive the broadcast message without any interference.

Lemma 3. *For two transmissions $v_1^t \rightarrow v_1^r$ and $v_2^t \rightarrow v_2^r$ scheduled in the same time slot the sufficient condition for ensuring interference awareness is $d(v_1^t, v_2^t) > (\alpha + 1)r_{max}$ or $d(v_1^r, v_2^r) > (\alpha + 1)r_{max}$.*

5.2 $O(1)$-Approximation Ratio for IABS Problem in 2D WSN

In case of a 2D WSN, we consider the 2D Euclidean plane is divided into regular hexagons of sides $\frac{r_{min}}{2}$ to form a hexagonal tiling. This hexagonal tiling is colored using the coloring method described in section 3, keeping $d = (\alpha+1)r_{max}$. This ensures that when ISA is applied on a 2D WSN only one $MIS(L_j)$ node can be there in a hexagon. Further, a node in $MIS(L_j)$ is assigned the color of the hexagon it belongs to, this ensures no two nodes $u, v \in MIS(L_j)$ have the same color if $d(u,v) < (\alpha+1)r_{max}$.

BSA when applied to a 2D WSN provides an approximation ratio of $2\left\lceil \frac{4}{3}(\alpha+1)^2\beta^2 + \frac{8\beta(\alpha+1)}{3} + \frac{4}{3}\right\rceil$ for IABS problem. Lemmas 4 and Theorem 4 provides the theoretical analysis.

Lemma 4. *The $MIS(L_j)$ node in ISA are colored using at most $\left\lceil \frac{4}{3}(\alpha+1)^2\beta^2 + \frac{8\beta(\alpha+1)}{3} + \frac{4}{3}\right\rceil$ colors in case of a 2D WSN.*

Theorem 4. *The BSA algorithm provides an approximation ratio $2\left\lceil \frac{4}{3}(\alpha+1)^2\beta^2 + \frac{8\beta(\alpha+1)}{3} + \frac{4}{3}\right\rceil$ for a 2D WSN.*

5.3 $O(1)$-Approximation Ratio for IABS Problem in a 3D WSN

In case of a 3D WSN, we consider the 3D space is partitioned into identical truncated octahedrons of sides $\frac{r_{min}}{2\sqrt{3}}$ to form a truncated octaheragonal tiling. This truncated octaheragonal tiling is colored using the coloring method described in section 4, keeping $d = (\alpha+1)r_{max}$. This ensures that when ISA is applied on a 3D WSN only one $MIS(L_j)$ node can be there in a truncated octahedron. Further, a node in $MIS(L_j)$ is assigned the color of the truncated octahedron it belongs to, this ensures no two nodes $u, v \in MIS(L_j)$ have the same color if $d(u,v) < (\alpha+1)r_{max}$.

BSA when applied to a 3D WSN provides an approximation ratio of $2\lceil 2(\alpha+1)\beta+1\rceil^2 \left\lceil (\alpha+1)\beta\sqrt{\frac{3}{2}}+1\right\rceil$ for IABS problem. Lemmas 5 and Theorem 5 provides the theoretical analysis.

Lemma 5. *When ISA is applied to a 3D WSN, the $MIS(L_j)$ nodes are colored using at most $\lceil 2(\alpha+1)\beta+1\rceil^2 \left\lceil (\alpha+1)\beta\sqrt{\frac{3}{2}}+1\right\rceil$ colors.*

Theorem 5. *The BSA algorithm provides an approximation ratio $2\lceil 2(\alpha+1)\beta+1\rceil^2 \left\lceil (\alpha+1)\beta\sqrt{\frac{3}{2}}+1\right\rceil$ for a 3D WSN.*

6 Conclusion

In this paper, we studied the interference-aware broadcast scheduling problem in WSNs in 2D and 3D. We considered a more realistic scenario, where the nodes have different transmission range and their interference range is larger than their transmission range. We modeled the transmission graph of a WSN in 2D and 3D using a disk graph (DG) and a ball graph (BG), respectively. Since the interference-aware broadcast scheduling is NP-hard, we propose a $O(1)$-Approximation algorithm for WSNs in 2D and 3D WSN. To the best of our knowledge, we are the first to study the interference-aware broadcast scheduling problem in 3D WSNs.

References

1. Gandhi, R., Parthasarthy, S., Mishra, A.: Minimizing broadcast latency and redundancy in ad hoc networks. In: Mobihoc 2003, Proceedings of the 4th international symposium on Mobile Ad hoc Networking and Computing, pp. 222–232 (2003)
2. Chen, Z., Qiao, C., Xu, J., Lee, T.: A constant approximation algorithm for interference -aware broadcast in wireless networks. In: INFOCOM, pp. 740–748 (2007)
3. Huang, S.C.-H., Wan, P.-J., Jia, X., Du, H., Shang, W.: Minimum-latency broadcast scheduling in wireless ad hoc networks. In: INFOCOM, pp. 733–739 (2007)
4. Huang, S.C.-H., Wan, P.-J., Deng, J., Han, Y.S.: Broadcast Scheduling in interference Environment. IEEE Transaction on Mobile Computing 7(11) (2008)
5. Mahjourian, R., Chen, F., Tiwari, R., Thai, M.T., Zhai, H., Fang, Y.: An approximation algorithm for conflict-aware broadcast scheduling in wireless ad hoc networks. In: MobiHoc 2008, Proceedings of the 9th ACM international symposium on Mobile Ad hoc Networking and Computing, pp. 331–340 (2008)
6. Sen, A., Roxboroough, T., Sinha, B.P.: On an Optimal Algorithm for Channel Assignment in Cellur networks. In: ICC 1999, International Conference on Communication, vol. 2, pp. 1147–1151 (1999)
7. Ho, C., Obraczka, K., Tsudik, G., Vishvanath, K.: Flooding for reliable multicast in multi-hop ad hoc networks. In: The proceeding of the 3rd international workshop on discrete algorithms and methods for mobile communication, pp. 64–71 (1999)
8. Gamst, A.: Homogeneous distribution of frequencies in a regular hexagonal cell system. IEEE Transaction on Vehicular Technology 31(3), 132–144 (1982)
9. Cassels, J.W.S.: An introduction to the geometry of numbers. Springer, Berlin (1971)
10. Griggs, J.R., Jin, X.T.: Optimal Channel Assignment for Lattices with Conditions at Distance Two. In: Proceedings of the 19th IEEE International Parallel and Distributed Processing Symposium (IPDPS 2005), vol. 13, p. 238 (2005)
11. Leese, R.A.: A Unified Approach to the Assignment of Radio Channels on a Regular hexagonal Grid. IEEE Transactions on Vehicular Technology 46 (November 1997)
12. Arnaud, J.F.: Frequency Planning for Broadcast Services in Europe. Proceedings of the IEEE 68 (December 1980)

Dynamic Scheduling of Pigeons for Delay Constrained Applications*

Jiazhen Zhou, Jiang Li, and Legand Burge III

Department of Systems and Computer Science,
Howard University, Washington DC, 21000

Abstract. Information collection in the disaster area is an important application of pigeon networks - a special type of delay tolerant networks (DTN). The aim of this paper is to explore highly efficient dynamic scheduling strategies of pigeons for such applications. The upper bound of traffic that can be supported under the deadline constraints for the basic on-demand strategy is given through the analysis. Based on the analysis, a waiting based packing strategy is introduced. Although the latter strategy could not change the maximum traffic rate that a pigeon can support, it improves the efficiency of the pigeon largely. The analytical results are verified by the simulations.

1 Introduction

After disasters (e.g. earthquakes, fires, tornadoes) happen, it is urgent to rescue people and protect property. To ensure the rescuing work can be timely and correctly executed, accurate live information (e.g. in the the format of videos) is needed by the commanding headquarter. As the instant communications of large amount of message is usually unrealistic, especially after the disasters which probably destroy the communication infrastructure, a feasible solution is to send special vehicles (like helicopters) to the disaster areas to collect the information generated on live using a local wireless network. This special type of communication belongs to the range of delay tolerant communications.

Pigeon networks [1,2], which borrows the ancient idea of employing pigeons as the communication tool, can be viewed as a special type of delay tolerant networks that use special-purpose message carrier. Of course, the "pigeons" used here are not the real pigeons. Instead, they are vehicles that are equipped with much better moving ability and partial instant wireless communication ability. For instance, it can be an unmanned aviation vehicle or a robotic insect.

Different from a regular delay tolerant network, a pigeon network has the character of being private and secure [1,2], which is especially suitable for the purpose of disaster rescue and recovery. Thus, in the remained part of this paper, pigeon is used in place of the vehicle mentioned above and in the literatures of vehicle routing problems (VRP).

* The work was funded in part by NSF grant CNS-0832000 and the Mordecai Wyatt Johnson Program of Howard University.

B. Liu et al. (Eds.): WASA 2009, LNCS 5682, pp. 449–458, 2009.

Although the rescuing task has to be time tolerant due to the long time (compared with instant communications) needed by the travel of pigeons, the delay that can be tolerated is still limited. For example, the best time to rescuing people in an earthquake disaster should be within 48 hours, and the time is largely shortened (to hours) if someone is wounded or if the building that people are locked in are in dangerous situation. In conclusion, this becomes a *constrained delay tolerant problem*, and *the delay is the most important metric* to be considered for this type of problems.

Superficially, the delay that each message demand suffers is the only important factor, and the travel cost of pigeons is not that important, so it sounds like a pigeon can stay in an area as long as it can to make sure the demands in that area can be satisfied. However, another fact is that the pigeons available for the disaster rescue and recovery task are also limited. If the pigeons can be schedule more efficiently, more disaster areas can be covered. As a result, more lives and properties can be saved if the pigeons are scheduled more efficiently.

The problem presented in this paper is very close to the dynamic vehicle routing problem (VRP) [3,4,5]. The arrival of new demands are stochastic, and there is no ending of time horizon. Thus, a complete solution of routing and scheduling plan like in the static vehicle routing problem is impossible. This character makes policies rather than the solution the primary goal to pursue in the area of dynamic VRP. The representative work include those by Bersimas and Van Ryzin [6,7], and extended work by Swihart and Papastavrou [8].

While this paper borrows the important results from Bersimas and Van Ryzin [6,7], and Swihart and Papastavrou [8], it is also obviously different:

(1) The problem in this paper is more like a dynamic traveling salesman problem (TSP) rather than a dynamic VRP. The main reason is that essentially there is no capacity constraints. The amount of information that can be picked up by a pigeon is huge due to the advanced storage technique, thus it can be viewed as no limit.
(2) There is only one source and destination node, which is the headquarter. All pigeons must start from the headquarter, and deliver all information to the headquarter rather than random destinations like in [8]. This difference makes the delay considered here is totally different from what are in [6] and [8].
(3) There is deadline on the messages to be picked up. This deadline must not be violated when evaluate a scheduling policy. In contrast, in [6] and [8], the only goal is to minimize the average delay.

The rest of this paper is organized as follows: The basic model is described in Section 2, and the analysis on the two main strategies– the on-demand strategy and the waiting based packing strategy are presented in Section 3 and Section 4 respectively. In Section 5, the numerical results are shown, and Section 6 concludes this paper.

2 Model Description

Due to the consideration of safety for emergency staff and the availability of resources, the headquarter for information precessing and commanding rescue is usually away from the disaster area. As shown in Fig. 1, t_r is the travel time for a pigeon between the headquarter and the disaster area with the assumption that the velocity of a pigeon is constant. The pigeon has enough communication ability to know the demands of the information collectors in the disaster area in time. For the facility of analysis, the disaster area is assumed to be a square with the area being A, which is similar to most study on dynamic vehicle routing problem like in [6], [8]. The demands are generated in the disaster area with average rate being λ, and the time spent on picking up each message is $\overline{s}$. For each demand generated, it must be delivered to the headquarter within time T_D. T_D is also called the deadline of a message in the following part of this paper. A key question here is how should a pigeon be scheduled upon the message demands. If the goal is merely guaranteeing minimum delay for each message as in [6], [8], it is often beneficial to let the pigeon start picking up the messages whenever they are available. This approach can be viewed as an *on-demand* strategy.

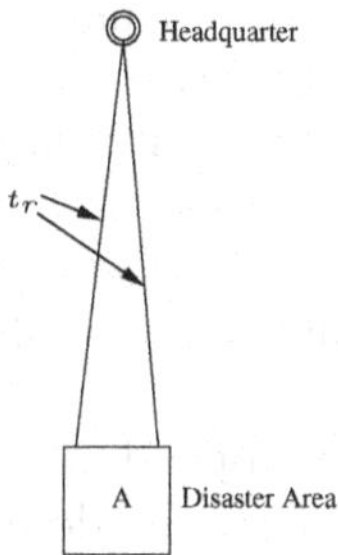

Fig. 1. System view of headquarter and disaster area

However, there is a big disadvantage of the on-demand strategy in the scenario considered in this paper. As the headquarter is far away from the disaster area, if the demand rate is not high, then the number of messages picked up on each trip is very limited. In other words, the throughput that can be achieved compared with the travel cost, which is defined as *efficiency* in Section 4.2, can be very low for the low load case. In fact, the pigeons are also a scarce resource, a high efficient scheduling scheme can allow a pigeon to be shared among different disaster areas.

Based on this fact, a waiting based scheduling is introduced here. The idea is that the pigeon can wait a certain amount of messages accumulated before starting picking up them. An important constraint for this strategy, however, is that the deadline of each message should not be violated.

In the following part of this paper, these two strategies are evaluated. The main performance metrics studied include the maximum throughput of the system, the maximum number of messages allowed to be picked up on each trip, and the comparison of efficiency of these two strategies under different load cases.

3 On-Demand Strategy

Denote the time point that the message demands are firstly generated as time 0, a pigeon is sent out to the disaster area right away. The dynamic flow of traveling and picking up is described as in Fig. 2.

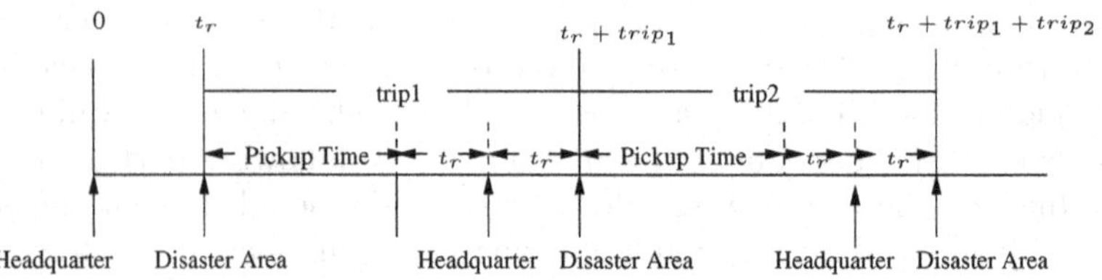

Fig. 2. The trips of a pigeon

With the assumption that a pigeon is able to communicate with the information collection equipments, it is reasonable for a pigeon to determine the messages to be picked up when it arrives at the disaster area. The pickup strategies in the disaster area is a dynamic traveling salesman problem (TSP). As shown by Bertsimas and Van Ryzan [6], possible strategies including *Shortest TSP*, *Nearest Neighbor*, and *Space Fill Curve*. Since the focus of this paper is analysis of the scheduling of the pigeon, only Shortest TSP policy is considered due to its tractability on analysis.

With the *Shortest TSP* strategy applied, a shortest TSP will be formed after the messages for the current trip have been determined. Then the pigeon will go through those sites according to the shortest tour to pick up their messages.

3.1 Basic Scenario – A Single Pickup Point

To facilitate the analysis and get better insight, a simpler scenario with a single pickup point is firstly considered. For example, there is a sensor network and a collector in the disaster area . The pigeon just need to pick up messages from the collector. For this simple case, there is no additional travel cost involved with picking up messages.

Denote the number of messages picked up at k^{th} trip as n_k, the total time spent on each trip (calculated as from the moment that start picking up messages to the moment that the pigeon returns to the disaster area for next pick up) is the summation of the time spent on picking up ($n_k\overline{s}$) and the travel time back and forth between the headquarter and the disaster area ($2t_r$):

$$TripTime_k = n_k\overline{s} + 2t_r. \tag{1}$$

The total number of messages picked up during k_{th} trip are generated during $(k-1)_{th}$ trip, which is the product of the average arrival rate and the $(k-1)_{th}$ trip time:

$$n_k = \lambda(n_{k-1}\overline{s} + 2t_r). \tag{2}$$

For a stable system, the number of messages picked up at each trip should converge to a value. Let $k \to \infty$ and denote the steady state solution for n_k as n^*, equation (2) becomes

$$n^* = \lambda \overline{s} n^* + 2\lambda t_r = \rho n^* + 2\lambda t_r. \tag{3}$$

Thus,

$$n^* = \frac{2\lambda t_r}{1 - \rho}. \tag{4}$$

Note that in the above equation, $\rho = \lambda \overline{s}$ is the system utilization, which is surely ≤ 1. As to be shown later, the allowed value of ρ could be much lower with the deadline constraint considered.

Theorem 1. The upper bound of system utilization without violating the deadlines of messages can be approximated as $\frac{T_D - 3t_r}{T_D + t_r}$.

Proof. For the scenarios considered here, if the deadline of the message at the head of each trip can be met, the deadlines of all other messages can also be met.

Denote the delay of the message at the head of k_{th} trip as D_k. As can be seen from Fig. 2, the starting point of pickup for $(k-1)_{th}$ trip is between the time points of the arrival of the tail message of $(k-1)_{th}$ trip and the head message of k_{th} trip. It is reasonable to estimate that the waiting of the head message of the k_{th} trip starts at $1/(2\lambda)$ after the starting of $(k-1)_{th}$ trip. Thus the waiting time before being picked up is $n_{k-1}\overline{s} + 2t_r - 1/(2\lambda)$, and the time spent on picking up the messages on the k_{th} trip is $n_k \overline{s}$. Also consider the time returning to the headquarter (t_r), D_k can be expressed as:

$$D_k = n_{k-1}\overline{s} + 2t_r - 1/(2\lambda) + n_k \overline{s} + t_r. \tag{5}$$

Similar to the derivation for the number of messages on each trip, the steady state solution for equation (5) can be obtained by letting $k \to \infty$. The resulting expression of delay for the head message, denoted as D^*, is confined by the deadline:

$$D^* = 2n^* \overline{s} + 3t_r - 1/(2\lambda) <= T_D. \tag{6}$$

As the goal is to get the maximum allowed arrival rate, which means that the arrival rate should be quite high, and the interarrival time is rather short. So it is reasonable to omit the $1/(2\lambda)$ part to make the expression neater. So the inequality (6) becomes

$$\frac{4t_r \lambda \overline{s}}{1 - \rho} + 3t_r <= T_D. \tag{7}$$

Note that $\rho = \lambda \overline{s}$, after solving above inequality, it can be obtained that

$$\rho^{Max} = \frac{T_D - 3t_r}{T_D + t_r}. \tag{8}$$

Remarks 1
(1) The maximum system utilization that can be supported is constrained by the deadline requirement and the travel costs between the headquarter and the disaster area. The longer is the tolerant delivery delay, the higher is the traffic rate that can be supported.
(2) To make sure the traffic supported by using this scheme is valid, it is necessary that $T_D - 3t_r > 0$. Thus, the time spent on single-trip travel between the headquarter and the disaster area should be $< T_D/3$.

3.2 Scenario with Multiple Pickup Locations

As a more general case, there are multiple collectors in a disaster area, and a Shortest TSP policy introduced in [6] is to be employed. To not lose generality, it is assumed that n messages to be picked up are located on n sites, one for each.

As a classical problem, the shortest travel cost for going though n locations in a square area in the Euclidean plane can be approximated as [9]:

$$TrvCst \approx \beta_{TSP}\sqrt{An}, \tag{9}$$

in which $\beta_{TSP} \approx 0.72$ [10]. Using normalized velocity of the pigeon (=1), the time spent on travel for picking up messages is $\beta_{TSP}\sqrt{An}$. Thus equation (2) becomes

$$n_k = \lambda(n_{k-1}\overline{s} + \beta_{TSP}\sqrt{An_{k-1}} + 2t_r). \tag{10}$$

The steady state solution of n_{k-1} and n_k - n^* can be obtained as

$$n^* = \frac{\lambda^2\beta_{TSP}^2 A + 4\lambda t_r(1-\rho) + \lambda\beta_{TSP}\sqrt{A(\lambda^2\beta_{TSP}^2 A + 8\lambda t_r(1-\rho))}}{2(1-\rho)^2}. \tag{11}$$

The delay of the head message is

$$D^* = 2n^*\overline{s} + 2\beta_{TSP}\sqrt{An^*} + 3t_r - 1/(2\lambda) \leq T_D. \tag{12}$$

Solving above inequality (with the $1/(2\lambda)$ part omitted), the highest system utilization that will ensure no violation of deadline is:

$$\rho^{Max} = \frac{(T_D - 3t_r)\overline{s} + \beta_{TSP}^2 A - \sqrt{(\beta_{TSP}^4 A^2 + 2\beta_{TSP}^2 A\overline{s}(T_D - 3t_r))}}{(T_D + t_r)\overline{s}} \tag{13}$$

4 Waiting Based Packing Strategy

The on-demand strategy studied above has at least two disadvantages: (1) The pigeon might never get any rest; (2) The number of messages picked up on each trip might be quite limited, which causes low efficiency of the pigeon. To avoid these shortcomings, a *waiting based packing strategy* is introduced and analyzed in this section.

As shown in Section 3.1, the number of messages picked up on each trip for the on-demand strategy is n^*. If the pigeon wait some additional time in the disaster area (or the headquarter), more demands can be formed during the pigeon's waiting (can be for taking a rest, or going to other areas for a trip). Thus, the amount of messages to be picked up is more than n^*. In the practical operation, a fixed amount of messages N (or say a *batch* with size N) can be packed for the pigeon to pick up.

4.1 Maximum Number of Messages That Can Be Picked Up

Since there is a deadline associated with each message, the number of messages picked up at each trip is limited. As the pigeon chooses to wait before starting pickup, the waiting time for the head message before the pickup process is $\frac{N}{\lambda}$. For the single pickup point scenario, the travel time for picking up and delivery is $N\overline{s} + t_r$. As a result, the total delay for the head message (denoted as D_w) is

$$D_w = \frac{N}{\lambda} + N\overline{s} + t_r \leq T_D. \tag{14}$$

It can be derived that

$$N < \frac{\lambda(T_D - t_r)}{1 + \rho} = N^*. \tag{15}$$

For the multiple pickup point case, the delay for the head message is

$$D_w = \frac{N}{\lambda} + N\overline{s} + \beta_{TSP}\sqrt{AN} + t_r. \tag{16}$$

With the deadline constraint applied, the maximum message that can be packed on a trip is

$$N^* = \frac{\lambda^2\beta_{TSP}^2 A + 4\lambda(1+\rho)(T_D - t_r) - \sqrt{\lambda^4\beta_{TSP}^4 A^2 + 4\lambda^3\beta_{TSP}^2 A(1+\rho)(T_D - t_r)}}{2(1+\rho)^2}. \tag{17}$$

4.2 Comparison of Efficiency

Efficiency measures the amount of message that can be picked up by a round trip of the pigeon. To facilitate the comparison, it is defined as *the ratio of time spent on serving customers compared with the total time spent on the trip.* Here the waiting time is not counted as the time on the trip as the pigeon can use this time period for resting or picking up messages from other areas.

According to the above definition, the efficiency of on-demand strategy, denoted as Eff_{od}, is

$$Eff_{od} = \frac{n^*\overline{s}}{n^*\overline{s} + 2t_r} = \rho. \tag{18}$$

For the waiting based packing strategy, the highest efficiency can be achieved when $N = N^*$:

$$Eff_{packing}^{Max} = \frac{N^*\overline{s}}{N^*\overline{s} + 2t_r} = \frac{\rho(T_D - t_r)}{\rho(T_D + t_r) + 2t_r}. \tag{19}$$

For the multiple pickup scenario, the efficiency can be computed similarly with travel cost for pickup considered based on equation (18) and (19).

5 Numerical Results

In this section, the above analysis is firstly verified with the simulation results, in which CSIM [11] simulation tool is employed. After the verification of correctness, the improvement of efficiency by the waiting based packing scheme is shown.

The main parameters used here are: the time spent on picking up a message is $\overline{s} = 0.01$ hour (36 seconds), the single trip time between the headquarter and the disaster area $t_r = 0.2$ hour (12 minutes), and the deadline for a message is 4 hours. The travel time of a side of the disaster area, which is normalized as $\sqrt{A}$, is 0.05 hour (3 minutes).

5.1 Comparison of Simulation and Analytical Results

In Fig. 3, the change of delay according to the arrival rate is shown for the on-demand scheduling. For both the single pickup point and multiple pickup points cases, the analytical results match the simulation results very well. From the X axis of two graphs it can be observed that the maximum supported traffic is $\lambda^{Max} = 80.95$ for the single pickup point case, and it is $\lambda^{Max} = 61.47$ for the multiple pickup points case due to additional travel costs needed for picking up the messages.

For the waiting based packing strategy, the effect of batch size on the delay of head message is shown in Fig. 4. Here $\lambda = 30$, and $n^* < N < N^*$, n^* and N^* can be computed using equations (4, 11), 15,17). For single pickup point case, the rounded values are $n^* = 18, N^* = 88$. For the multiple pickup location case, it is $n^* = 25, N^* = 80$.

As can be seen from Fig. 4, the delay goes up as the batch size becomes larger and larger. Also it can be seen that less number of messages can be packed when

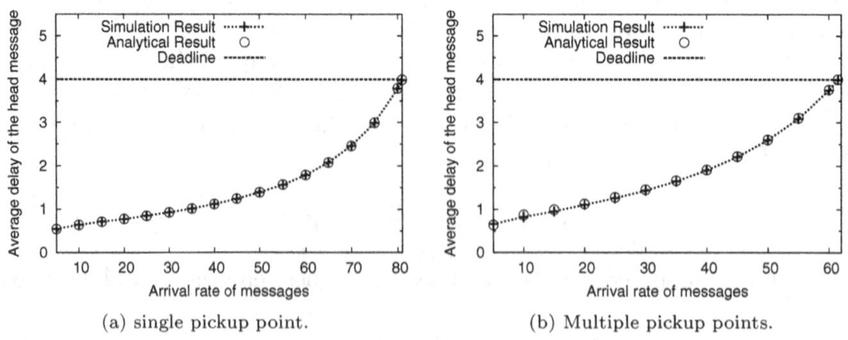

(a) single pickup point. (b) Multiple pickup points.

Fig. 3. Comparison of delay for on-demand strategy

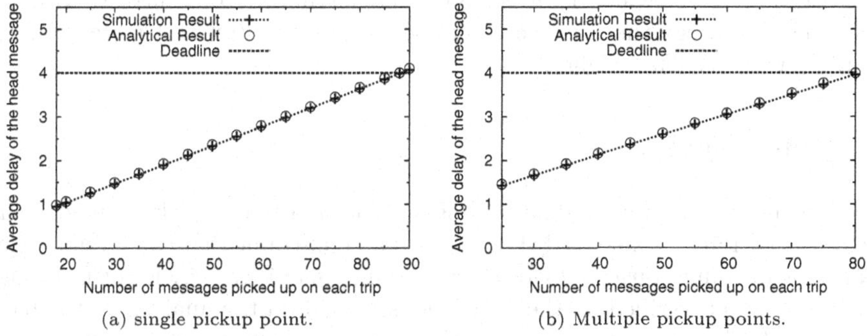

(a) single pickup point.

(b) Multiple pickup points.

Fig. 4. Comparison of delay with different packing size

there are travel costs associated with pickup. In addition, the simulation results show that the analytical results are very accurate.

5.2 Comparison of Efficiency

As shown in Fig. 5, the efficiency of the waiting based scheme is obviously higher (*as much as 500% higher*) than the on-demand strategy, especially when the load is not heavy. However, the difference of the two strategies disappear as $\rho \rightarrow \rho_{Max}$. In fact, this is because as the load increases, the demands accumulated on the former trip in the on-demand strategy is close to the maximum number of messages that the pigeon can pick up without violating the deadline, and the two schemes become the same when $\rho = \rho^{Max}$.

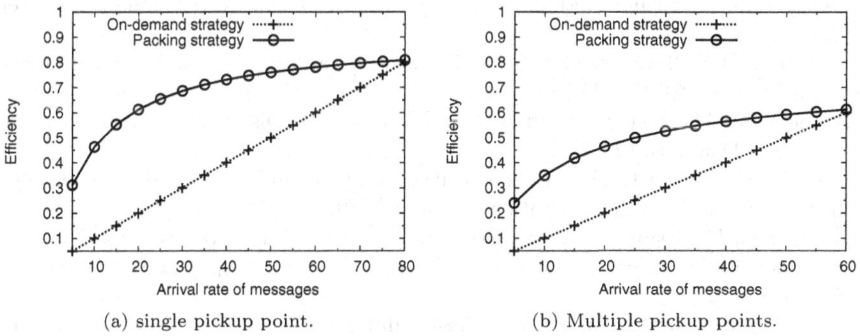

(a) single pickup point.

(b) Multiple pickup points.

Fig. 5. Comparison of efficiency for the two strategies

Another benefit of the waiting based packing strategy is that, the efficiency of the pigeon is not so sensitive to the arrival rate as the on-demand strategy. For example, for the single pick up point case (Fig. 5 (a)), the efficiency of the pigeon under the waiting based strategy when $\lambda = 20$ is 0.61, and it becomes

0.81 when $\lambda = 80$, which is about 30% percent higher. In contrast, with the on-demand strategy the efficiency increases from 0.2 to 0.8 as λ increases from 20 to 8, which is 300% higher.

6 Conclusion

The dynamic scheduling strategies of pigeons for information pickup and delivery in the disaster area is analyzed. The upper bound of traffic that can be supported under the deadline constraints for the basic on-demand strategy is given through the analysis and verified by the simulations. Based on the analysis of the basic on-demand scheduling strategy, a waiting based packing strategy is introduced. Although the latter strategy could not improve the maximum traffic rate that a pigeon can support, it improves the efficiency of the pigeon largely.

Possible future work include more detailed investigations of the dynamic routing strategies other than the shortest TSP policy, and the effect of the different distributions of the arrival rate, service rate, deadlines on the conclusion and bounds obtained in this paper.

References

1. Guo, H., Li, J., Qian, Y.: HoP: Pigeon-Assisted Forwarding in Partitioned Wireless Networks. In: Li, Y., Huynh, D.T., Das, S.K., Du, D.-Z. (eds.) WASA 2008. LNCS, vol. 5258, pp. 72–83. Springer, Heidelberg (2008)
2. Guo, H., Li, J., Qian, Y., Tian, Y.: A practical routing strategy in delay tolerant networks using multiple pigeons. In: Proceedings of Milcom 2008, San Diego, CA, November 17-19 (2008)
3. Psaraftis, H.N.: Dynamic vehicle routing problems. In: Golden, B.L., Assad, A.A. (eds.) Vehicle routing: Methods and studies, pp. 223–248. North Holland, Amsterdam (1988)
4. Psaraftis, H.N.: Dynamic vehicle routing: Status and prospects. Annals of Operations Research 61(1), 143–164 (1995)
5. Larsen, A.: The Dynamic Vehicle Routing Problem. Dissertation, Technical University of Denmark (2000)
6. Bertsimas, D., van Ryzin, G.: A stochastic and dynamic vehicle routing problem in the Euclidean plane. Operation Researches 39, 601–615 (1991)
7. Bertsimas, D., Ryzin, G.: Stochastic and Dynamic Vehicle Routing with General Demand and Interarrival Time Distribution. Advanced Applied Probability 25, 947–978 (1993)
8. Swihart, M., Papastavrou, J.: A stochastic and dynamic model for the single-vehicle pick-up and delivery problem. European Journal of Operational Research 114(3), 447–464 (1999)
9. Beardwood, J., Halton, J., Hammersley, J.: The shortest path through many points. Proc. Camb. Phil. Soc. 55, 299–327 (1959)
10. Johnson, D.: Presented at the Mathematical Programming Symposium, Tokyo (1988)
11. Mesquite Software, Inc.: CSIM19 User's Guide, Austin, Texas (2001)

Energy Efficient DNA-Based Scheduling Scheme for Wireless Sensor Networks

Shan Suthaharan[1], Abhinav Chawade[1], Rittwik Jana[2], and Jing Deng[1]

[1] Department of Computer Science, University of North Carolina at Greensboro, Greensboro, NC 27402, USA
{s_suthah,archawad,jing.deng}@uncg.edu
[2] AT&T Labs - Research, New Jersey, USA
rjana@research.att.com

Abstract. Wireless sensor networks are currently deployed in many areas, particularly for surveillance related applications. Sensors have very limited energy and processing capabilities, hence, it becomes necessary to introduce energy efficient algorithms to maximize the lifetime of a sensor node. We propose a new scheduling scheme based on Discrete Time Markov chain models used in genetics for DNA evolution prediction. The proposed scheduler uses a single control parameter to control state changes in order to obtain a compromise between network lifetime and throughput. We discuss the design of such a Discrete Time Markov chain based scheme and compare it to a standard approach in terms of node throughput and lifetime of entire network. Finally, we show the effectiveness of this scheme by simulating various network topologies in a realistic sensor network. Our observations show that just after 75% of simulation steps 90% more nodes are alive with the proposed scheduler. The residual battery power is 82% more and the packet reception rate is increased by 51% for the entire network when compared to the standard approach.

Keywords: Sleep-active scheduling, sensor node, wireless sensor network, DNA-based scheduling, WSN simulator.

1 Introduction

Wireless sensor networks (WSN) are promising particularly in environmental, agricultural, military and astronomy applications. A wireless sensor network can be formed by using several sensors, called *sensor nodes* and a processing center/sink node, called *command node* which receives data from the sensors and processes it [1]. A sensor is typically a tiny device which has limited resources such as a small memory footprint, tiny processor, slow access speeds and limited battery power. With these limitations in place, a sensor node must often act as both, an information source and an information router/sink, in a wireless sensor network [2]. Sensor node cannot remain active for a very long time continuously since transmission and sensing are typically energy consuming activities. One major problem in WSN occurs when nodes expire due to its limited battery power, the consequence being performance

B. Liu et al. (Eds.): WASA 2009, LNCS 5682, pp. 459–468, 2009.

degradation of the entire network in terms of information generation and information routing. Therefore, it becomes more and more important to develop sensor network protocols that extend the lifetime of the sensors. An obvious way of extending the lifetime of a sensor is to put the sensor node to sleep if it is idle. This way, a significant amount of battery power can be saved. However, this may lead to network performance degradation, because while a node is in sleep state data may arrive (to be routed) or a critical sensing event may be missed (to sense and generate information). As a result, data may not be delivered on time (transmission delay) or data may be lost completely (reduced throughput). Several sleep/active models and analysis have been recently proposed [3-8], but the question of trade-off between energy savings and improved network performance still remains partially answered. To address this problem, we propose a scheduler that changes the sensor behavior using a scheduling scheme that is built around the concept of three states Discrete Time Markov Chain (DTMC). In the standard approach (i.e. random schedules [3]) a sensor node has only 2 states which are, 1) *Sleep* (S) – low power state where minimal energy is consumed by sensor 2) *Active* (R) – node is fully functional. In the active state the sensor node can detect events as well as forward packets received. Energy consumption in sleep state is in the order of μwatts and in active state is in the order of milliwatts. Our scheme adds another state *No sensing*. In this state a node transmits packets stored in its buffer, however, it does not sense any data. This additional *No sensing* state facilitates compromise between node power consumption and its throughput. The paper is organized in the following manner. Section 2 presents some background information on energy saving schemes proposed in the WSN literature. Section 3 explains the derivation of the scheduling scheme based on DTMC models used in DNA mutation sequence prediction. Section 4 provides the simulation setup to test the proposed scheme followed by performance evaluation in Section 5. We provide a discussion and concluding remarks in Section 6.

2 Background

Energy savings is one of the important requirements in wireless sensor networks. The main concept used to save energy in WSN is to allow sensor nodes to follow some form of sleep/active duty cycles. Today, we can hardly find any WSN without a sleep/active scheduler. Various schemes have been proposed to date to reduce the sensors energy expenditure. MAC layer schemes like PAMAS allow for turning off nodes' RF chains to conserve power by not listening to all extraneous transmissions. Others propose different wake-up strategies at the MAC layer that wake up just in time to avoid severe network throughput degradation [6,9]. Smart algorithms on network routing proposed in [10] is also applicable to this work especially when nodes are continuously transitioning from the proposed Sleep, Wake-up and No Sensing states. Other analytic models exist for computing the scaling laws of large scale ad hoc sensor networks. Gupta and Kumar characterize the network throughput degradation as more nodes are introduced in a WSN [11]. According to [11] adopting conventional single-user packet decoding and forwarding in classical multihop architectures can only achieve a scaling up to $O(\sqrt{n})$, where n is the total number of nodes. An improvement on this was shown recently by Ozgur *et al.* [12]. They show the scaling of network capacity forms a linear relationship with respect to n for a dense network with fixed area and increasing node density. The results in the scaling information-theoretic laws do not directly apply to our model since they do not attempt to explicitly model sleep/active behavior rather a set of nodes that transmit data to a unique destination at random. The sleep/active schedulers proposed in the WSN literature can be grouped into Asynchronous (standard approach) and Synchronous (systematic approach) schemes. The standard approach adopts random scheduling of sleep/active cycles, while a systematic approach adopts organized scheduling. One such systematic approach is SMAC [6] which allows a node to select its listen/sleep schedule (called frame) and share the frame with its neighbors. This frame sharing capability provides synchronization between nodes. Later, to eliminate data forwarding interruption problem, DMAC [8] scheduling algorithm was proposed. DMAC imposes rigorous synchronization using data-gathering unidirectional tree. As an improvement to SMAC a new scheduling scheme called TMAC was introduced. TMAC [7] uses an adaptive sleep/active duty cycle to handle load variations in time and location. This can help to reduce energy wasted on what they call idle listening. All of the three methods are discussed in paper [3]. As stated in [3], SMAC is non flexible and non adaptive, TMAC scheme is complex and demands nodes synchronization and DMAC scheme demands rigorous synchronization. In [3] a model is developed to evaluate and measure sleep/active mechanisms using probability theory. This model verifies that the standard approach can reduce the complexity and the overhead of a WSN under increased node density than systematic approaches. Hence, we enhance the random scheduling scheme by integrating a simple and flexible, but an organized scheduler using the concepts of DTMC and DNA (Deoxyribonucleic Acid) evolution. We then compare the proposed scheme with the standard approach. Of particular relevance is the sleep/active model introduced by Chiasserini *et al.* [2,13]. They propose a complex DTMC model similar in spirit to our work. However, the fundamental difference in our work is that we propose a biologically inspired model (namely Jukes-Cantor [14]) that results in a very simple state transition matrix and subsequent analysis controlled by a single parameter. In contrast, the complete state space in [13] utilizes four parameters to be estimated using fixed point approximation (α, β, f, w). Furthermore, the DTMC is solved using a linear set of equations of dimension greater than 20 (4L, L=5 for acceptable convergence). Our work alleviates this complex fixed point approximation and uses just a single parameter to estimate the DTMC.

3 Proposed Scheduling Scheme

In this section we first discuss the DNA-based Jukes-Cantor model and K2MC models. The JCMC is designed to model DNA evolution. The main information contained in DNA is the genetic instructions that resemble the development and functioning of all living organisms [15-17]. Its four bases are called Adenine (A), Cytosine (C), Guanine (G) and Thymine (T) [15]. The JCMC model with 4 states has been explained simply in [18]. Here we define the JCMC of three states with the steady-state probabilities (1/3,1/3,1/3) and the following transition probability matrix:

$$\begin{array}{c} \\ S \\ N \\ R \end{array} \begin{array}{c} \begin{array}{ccc} S & N & R \end{array} \\ \begin{bmatrix} (1-\alpha_1) & \frac{\alpha_1}{2} & \frac{\alpha_1}{2} \\ \frac{\alpha_1}{2} & (1-\alpha_1) & \frac{\alpha_1}{2} \\ \frac{\alpha_1}{2} & \frac{\alpha_1}{2} & (1-\alpha_1) \end{bmatrix} \end{array}$$

The main conditions for JCMC model are (i) the steady state probabilities should be the same and (ii) row-wise and column-wise additions of the transition probabilities should be equal to 1. This model has a single parameter α_l which is time and DNA sequence dependent. The K2MC model is a two-parameter model and this model also explained in [18] using a DNA sequence with four states. K2MC's steady state probability is also defined for three states as (1/3, 1/3, 1/3) but the transition probability matrix is defined differently as follows:

$$\begin{array}{c} \\ S \\ N \\ R \end{array} \begin{array}{c} \begin{array}{ccc} S & N & R \end{array} \\ \begin{bmatrix} (1-\alpha_1-\beta_1) & \alpha_1 & \beta_1 \\ \alpha_1 & (1-\alpha_1-\beta_1) & \beta_1 \\ \beta_1 & \alpha_1 & (1-\alpha_1-\beta_1) \end{bmatrix} \end{array}$$

This model has two parameters α_1 and β_1 and it also satisfies the same conditions as of JCMC. We can see one common property in the transition matrix of DNA models is that the probabilities both column-wise and row-wise add to 1. Proposed scheme adopts Jukes-Cantor model as its foundation but uses 3 states instead of 4 states (bases) to define the rate matrix. We named the proposed scheme RDNA to represent Restricted DNA. Fig.1 and Fig. 2 show the state diagram and rate matrix used by RDNA scheme respectively.

$$\begin{array}{c} \\ S \\ N \\ R \end{array} \begin{array}{c} \begin{array}{ccc} S & N & R \end{array} \\ \begin{bmatrix} (1-\alpha) & 0 & \alpha \\ \frac{\alpha}{2} & (1-\alpha)+\frac{\alpha}{2} & 0 \\ \frac{\alpha}{2} & \frac{\alpha}{2} & (1-\alpha) \end{bmatrix} \end{array}$$

Fig. 1. Rate matrix for RDNA scheme - S: Sleep; R: Active and N: No Sensing

JCMC makes assumptions about initial distribution, that all 4 states (bases) are equiprobable and defines transition rates between every possible state combination. Our scheme is restricted in the sense that a node cannot go to state N just after state S since, when a node wakes up its data buffer can be empty such that additional packets can be queued for transmission. Also, once a node is in state N, it can either stay in state N or can go to state S. This restriction reduces chances of buffer overflow since a node's sensing and receiving units are deactivated in No Sensing and Sleep states. These state transition characteristics can be seen in state diagram presented in Fig. 2.

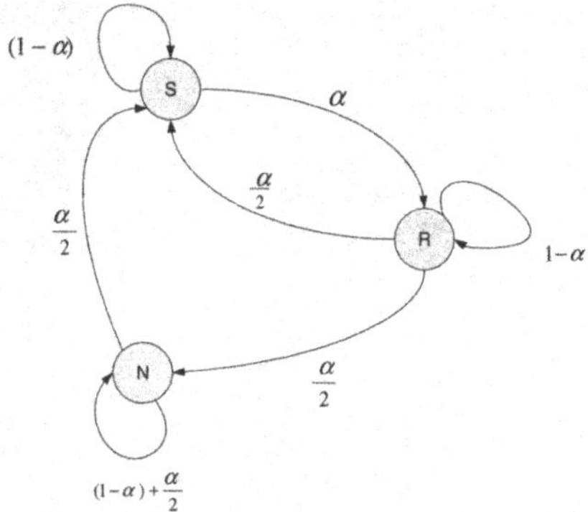

Fig. 2. State diagram for node transition, it shows the transition probabilities for the transitions

In our proposed scheduler the following steps are carried out: (i) the rate matrix is calculated by selecting an appropriate value for the control parameter α (selection of α will be explained later in section 5); (ii) number of each state is selected for the first *m* state transitions (called segment) using R as the initial state and the rate matrix; (iii) the states are randomly placed within the segment using uniform distribution; (iv) number of each state is selected for the subsequent segments (*m* states) using the last state of the preceding segment and the rate matrix while randomly placing them using uniform distribution. For example, if the last state of a segment is state R, then the next segment will have $\alpha m/2$ of state S, $\alpha m/2$ of state N and $(1\text{-}\alpha)\ m$ of state R using the rate matrix in Fig. 1. Similarly if the last state of a segment is state S, then the next segment will have $(1\text{-}\alpha)\ m$ of state S and αm of state R. The parameter α is used by the scheduler to control state transitions of a sensor node. Empirically, we have found out that the value of α should be within the range of (0.5, 0.7) with the peak at 0.6 to offer good compromise between network throughput, energy consumption and nodes alive.

4 Simulation Setup

RDNA scheme has been tested on random ad-hoc topologies using a modified version of the Wireless Sensor Network Simulator (WSNS) [19,20]. Fig. 3 depicts one of many sensor topologies. The topology is generated at the beginning of each simulation and the location of each sensor is randomly selected. Each sensor node is connected to its neighbors who fall within a certain radius. These connections are shown as solid black lines. The channel that currently transmits data is shown in a solid red line throughout the transmission duration. Routing can be directed or random and the internal routing algorithm is based on the energy level as described in [21]. Routing parameters can be tuned from GUI as seen in the Figure 3.

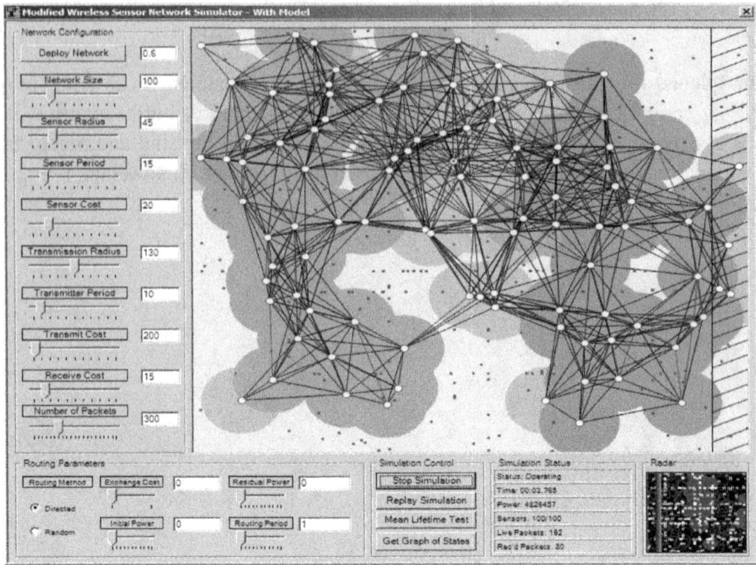

Fig. 3. Wireless Sensor Network Simulator's GUI showing network configuration

We have used the same default routing values for parameters such as transmission cost, reception cost and routing period in each simulation run. Command nodes are located in the rightmost region (shown with vertical and tilted solid black lines) and these nodes always remain active. The information to be sensed is contained in a data vector (which is shown as dots on the topology in Fig. 3). All data vectors move in a straight path over the network area at different speeds. One packet is generated by sensor node for each sensing event. One data vector may be sensed multiple times, till it lies in sensing radius of a node. Number of data vectors in network is always maintained at a constant level implying that network has steady load condition. These data vectors are generated periodically from all directions. In the case of our simulations, this number is kept to 300 for all simulation runs. The parameters t (state duration) and m (length of segment) are two of the important players in the development of our scheduler. Our study indicates a suitable mathematical relationship between t and m as $m = 100t$. After each 100 steps, an entry is created in the internal log by each node indicating its current state, battery power left and packets received and generated. This data is used at the end to generate simulation report. For the purpose of comparing our proposed scheme, we used a standard approach that adopts two states S and R. We have configured the WSNS to have this standard approach. It has same simulation parameters as in table 1, but the state scheduling is performed with a random number generator following uniform distribution. Simulation reports from this version of the WSNS are then compared with one which has the proposed scheme incorporated. We incorporated ZedGraph [22] for report generation and utilized .Net random numbers and distributions library [23]. We tested the scheme for 30 different simulation runs using parameter values given in Table 1.

Table 1. Wireless Sensor Network simulator parameters used in the simulation shown in Fig. 3

Number of nodes :	100
Value of α :	0.6
Routing method :	Directed
Initial energy for each node :	50000 units
Length of each segment (*m*) :	100*t*
Length of each simulation run :	37 x m
State duration (t) :	10 simulation steps
Sleep(S) state power consumption	0.045 units
Transmit and receive(R) state power consumption :	15 units
No Sensing(N) state power consumption :	12 units
Transmission Radius :	130 units
Sensing Radius :	45 units

5 Performance Evaluation

We tested the proposed scheme and the standard approach using several random topologies. Figs. 4 and 5 show results from the simulator *with* (proposed scheme) and *without* (standard approach) the proposed scheduler. Graphs have been drawn from average of 5 simulations (that are selected randomly) where value of α is same. Plots show result for different values of α. Fig. 4 shows the curves for average remaining battery power and Fig. 5 shows packet reception rate. It is evident from Fig.4 and Fig. 5 that the standard approach starts off with the good performance in terms of packet reception, but it quickly starts to lose the energy of the entire network as it progresses. Packet reception rate increases as value of α decreases. It is also evident from these figures that in general, packet reception rate is much higher with the proposed scheme, than that of the standard approach. The reason for this is integration of state N and its corresponding scheduling within the proposed scheme. The advantage is that the node checks and ensures that if one of its neighbors is awake it forwards the packet before proceeding to its next state. This ensures that there are less buffer overflows in each node. Hence, average reception rate is considerably higher even with certain degree of randomness. The state duration *t*=10 units also makes certain that node does not change state very frequently and hence saves energy. In contrast, the random sleeping policy in standard approach results in unpredictable battery power consumption. We are also interested to know the performance of the entire WSN when the proposed RDNA and the standard random scheduler (RS) are used. We measured the performance metric after completing 75% of the simulation epochs using:

$$R_{RDNA} = \frac{P_{RDNA} - P_{RS}}{P_{RDNA}} \times 100 \quad (1)$$

where P_{RDNA} and P_{RS} represent the performance metrics of RDNA and RS approaches. As our simulations have about 40 simulation steps we measured the performance metrics at 30th simulation step. Our results show that at 30th simulation steps 90%

more nodes are alive with the proposed scheduler. Its calculated as ((62-6)/62)*100 using the above equation, where 62 and 6 are number of nodes alive at 30th step when RDNA and RS are used (see Fig. 6). Similarly the residual battery power and packet reception rate increases are 82% and 51% respectively for the RDNA.

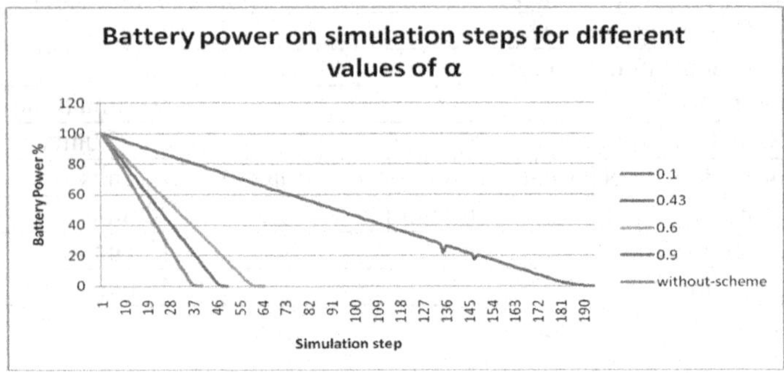

Fig. 4. Battery power consumption of the entire network is plotted here at each simulation step

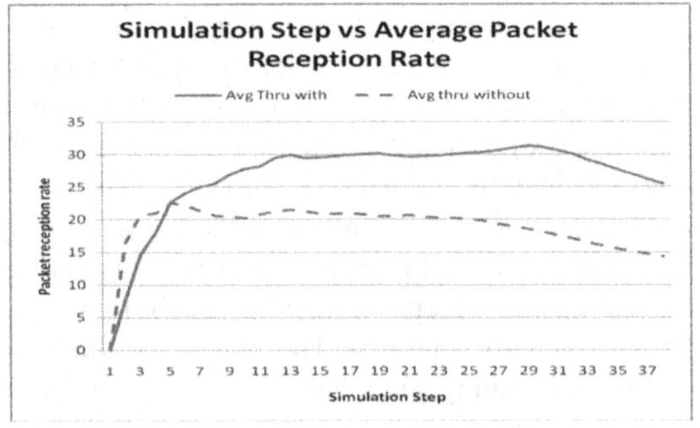

Fig. 5. Packet reception rate is monitored and calculated at each simulation step and plotted

In Fig. 6 we present number of nodes alive at each simulation step for proposed and standard approaches. As we can see until about 19 epochs all nodes are alive in both schemes. Beyond that the death rate of nodes is high in case of standard approach. In the proposed scheme the nodes start to die from step 27. We wanted to find a suitable range for α that offers good compromise between packet reception rate (RRates), remaining battery power (BPower) and number of nodes alive (NNodes). We have conducted simulations with different values of α however we present the performance metrics NNodes, RRates and BPower values observed at 30th step (which is about 75% of total simulation time or the step at which no nodes are alive) in Fig. 7. From lots of the three metrics at different α values we choose the values between 0.5 and 0.7 centered at 0.6 as suitable values for α. In our simulations we used α=0.6.

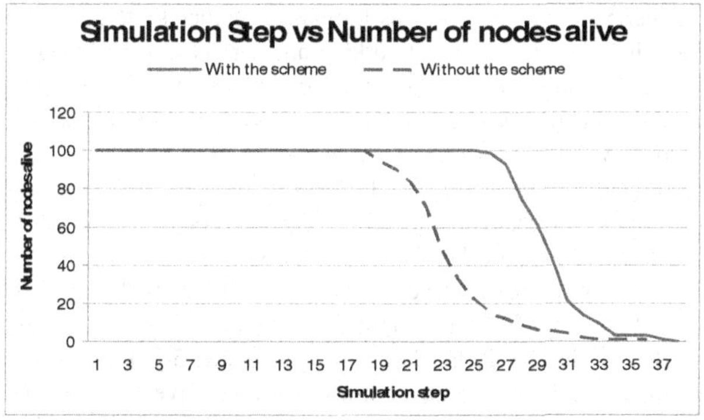

Fig. 6. Nodes alive at each simulation step plotted: Propose scheme verses standard appraoch

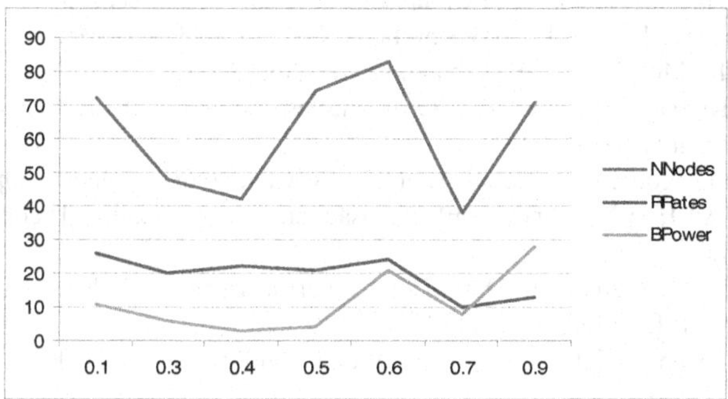

Fig. 7. Effect of different α values on the 3 performance metrics NNodes, Rrates and BPower

6 Conclusion

In this paper, we have proposed a new simplified scheme to schedule sleep and active states in a sensor node. The proposed scheme has a single control parameter α which offers a direct compromise between network lifetime and its throughput. The proposed scheme has also been verified by a WSN simulator under various realistic scenarios and compared to a traditional "standard" model. Simulation results show that the proposed scheme improves upon extending the average battery life, and the packet reception rate. Our future work will focus on evolving this model to incorporate wireless channel degradations based on fluctuating network load conditions and the residual node energy and deciding alpha as a function of various network parameters like traffic, node density, topology size etc.

References

[1] Akyildiz, I.F., Su, W., Sankarasubramaniam, Y., Cayirci, E.: A survey on sensor networks. IEEE Comm. Magazine, 102–114 (August 2002)

[2] Chiasserini, C.F., Garetto, M.: An analytical model for wireless sensor networks with sleeping nodes. IEEE Trans. on Mobile Comp. 5(12), 1706–1718

[3] Galiotos, P.: Sleep/Active schedules as a tunable characteristic of a wireless sensor network. In: Proc. Int. conference on networking and services, p. 51 (2006)
[4] Lin, C., He, Y.X., Xiong, N.: An energy-efficient dynamic power management in wireless sensor networks. In: Proc. 5th international symposium on parallel and distributed computing, pp. 148–154 (2006)
[5] Dousse, O., Mannersalo, P., Thiran, P.: Latency of wireless sensor networks with uncoordinated power saving mechanisms. In: MobiHoc 2004, pp. 109–120 (2004)
[6] Ye, W., Heidemann, J., Estrin, D.: An energy-efficient MAC protocol for wireless sensor networks. In: Proc. of the IEEE Infocom, New York, June 2002, pp. 1567–1576 (2002)
[7] Dam, T.V., Langendoen, K.: An adaptive energy-efficient MAC protocol for wireless sensor networks. In: SenSys 2003, California, November 5-7, pp. 171–180 (2003)
[8] Lu, G., Krishnamachari, B., Raghavendra, C.: An adaptive energy-efficient and low latency MAC for data gathering in wireless sensor networks. In: Proc. of the international workshop on algorithms, ad hoc and sensor networks, April 26-30, pp. 224–235 (2004)
[9] Singh, S., Raghavendra, C.S.: PAMAS: Power Aware Multi-Access Protocol with Signaling for Ad Hoc Networks. ACM Comp. Comm. Review, 5–26 (1998)
[10] Zheng, R., Hou, J., Sha, L.: Asynchronous Wakeup for Power Management in Ad Hoc Networks. In: MobiHoc 2003, Annapolis, MD (June 2003)
[11] Gupta, P., Kumar, P.R.: The Capacity of Wireless Networks. IEEE Trans. on Information Theory 46 (March 2000)
[12] Ozgur, A., Leveque, O., Tse, D.: Hierarchical Cooperation Achieves Optimal Capacity Scaling in Ad Hoc Networks. IEEE Transactions on Information Theory 53(10), 3549–3572 (2007)
[13] Chiasserini, C.F., Garetto, M.: Modeling the performance of wireless sensor networks. In: Proceedings of IEEE INFOCOM (2004)
[14] Jukes, T.H., Cantor, C.R.: Evolution of Protein Molecules, pp. 21–132. Academic Press, New York (1969)
[15] http://en.wikipedia.org/wiki/DNA
[16] http://en.wikipedia.org/wiki/Evolution_of_DNA
[17] Kimura, M.: A simple method for estimating evolutionary rates of base substitutions through comparative studies of nucleotide sequences. J. of Molecular Evolution 16, 111–120 (1980)
[18] Allman, E.S., Rhodes, J.A.: Mathematical models in biology: an introduction. Cambridge Univ. Press, Cambridge (2004)
[19] Wireless sensor network simulator Version 1.1, http://www.djstein.com/projects/WirelessSensorNetworkSimulator.html
[20] Chawade, A., Suthaharan, S.: DNA-based modeling of sleep-active behavior for wireless sensor networks. In: INFOCOM 2008 (Software Demo) (2008)
[21] Chang, J.H., Tassiulas, L.: Maximum lifetime routing in wireless sensor networks. IEEE/ACM Trans. on Networking 12(4), 609–619 (2004)
[22] ZedGraph .Net charting library, http://zedgraph.org/wiki/index.php?title=Main_Page
[23] Net random number generators and distributions, http://www.codeproject.com/KB/recipes/Random.aspx

Minimum-Latency Schedulings for Group Communications in Multi-channel Multihop Wireless Networks*

Peng-Jun Wan[1], Zhu Wang[1], Zhiyuan Wan[2], Scott C.-H. Huang[2], and Hai Liu[3]

[1] Illinois Institute of Technology, Chicago IL 60616, USA
[2] City Univesrsity of Hong Kong, Kowloon, Hong Kong
[3] Hong Kong Baptist University, Kowloon, Hong Kong

Abstract. This paper is motivated by exploring the impact of the number of channels on the achievable communication latency for a specific communication task. We focus on how to utilize the multiple channels to speed up four group communications including broadcast, aggregation, gathering, and gossiping in wireless networks under protocol interference model. Four scheduling algorithms are developed for these four group communications. We derive explicit tight bounds on the latencies of the four communication schedules produced by these algorithms. These latency bounds in general decrease with the number of channels and are also within constant factors of the respective minimum.

1 Introduction

With the rapid technology advances, many off-the-shelf wireless transceivers (i.e., radios) are capable of operating on multiple channels. For example, the IEEE 802.11 b/g standard and IEEE 802.11a standard provide 3 and 12 channels respectively, and MICA2 sensor motes support more than 50 channels. This paper aims to conduct comprehensive algorithmic studies of minimizing the communication latency by utilizing multiple channels under the following network model. All network nodes V lies in plane. Every node has a communication radius normalized to one, and an interference radius ρ for some parameter $\rho \geq 1$. The communication (respectively, interference) range of a node $v \in V$ is the disk centered at v of one (respectively, ρ). A node v can receive the message successfully from a transmitting node u if v is within the transmission range of u but is outside the interference range of any other node transmitting simultaneously at the same channel. Let λ be the number of available channels. Then, each network is associated with a pair of parameters (λ, ρ). We further assume that all communications proceeds in synchronous time-slots and each node can either transmit or receive at most one packet of a fixed size in each time-slot.

* This work was supported in part by NSF under grant CNS-0831831, and by the Research Grant Council of Hong Kong under the project CERG CityU 113807.

B. Liu et al. (Eds.): WASA 2009, LNCS 5682, pp. 469–478, 2009.

In this paper, we focus on the communication schedules for the following four group communication tasks in multihop wireless networks: broadcast, data aggregation, data gathering, and gossiping. The problem of computing a broadcast (respectively, aggregation, gathering, gossiping) schedule with minimum latency is referred to **Minimum-Latency Broadcast** (respectively, **Aggregation, Gathering, Gossiping**) **Schedule**. There are a number of recent works on the scheduling for broadcasting [7,8,11], aggregation [3,12,14], gathering [1,2,6] and gossiping [7,8,10] subject to the protocol interference constraint or the k-hop interference model. All of them assume $\lambda = 1$ (i.e. single-channel) and most of them assume $\rho = 1$ (i.e. the interference radius equal to the communication radius). Consequently, the impact of multiple channels on communication latency in the more general and practical case with $\rho > 1$ remains unexplored. In this paper, we develop four scheduling algorithms for the four group communications. We derive explicit tight bounds on the latencies of the four communication schedules produced by these algorithms. These latency bounds in general decrease with the number of channels and are also within constant factors of the respective minimum.

2 Preliminaries

Let $G = (V, E)$ be an undirected graph. The subgraph of G induced by a subset U of V is denoted by $G[U]$. The maximum (respectively, minimum) degree of G is denoted by $\Delta(G)$ (respectively, $\delta(G)$). The *inductivity* of G is defined by

$$\delta^*(G) = \max_{U \subseteq V} \delta(G[U]).$$

The *graph radius* of G with respect to a node v is the maximum depth of the breadth-first-search (BFS) tree rooted at v. A *graph center* of G is a node in G with respect to which the graph radius of G is the smallest.

A subset U of V is an *independent set* of G if no two nodes in U are adjacent. If U is a independent set of G but no proper superset of U is a independent set of G, then U is called a *maximal independent set* (MIS) of G. Any node ordering $v_1, v_2, \cdots, v_n$ of V induces an MIS U in the following first-fit manner: Initially, $U = \{v_1\}$. For $i = 2$ up to n, add v_i to U if v_i is not adjacent to any node in U. A subset U of V is a *dominating set* of G if each node not in U is adjacent to some node in U. Clearly, every MIS of G is also a dominating set of G. If U is a dominating set of G and the subgraph of G induced by U is connected, then U is called a *connected dominating set* (CDS) of G.

A (vertex) *coloring* of G is an assignment of colors to V satisfying that adjacent vertices are assigned with distinct colors. Equivalently, a vertex coloring corresponds to a partition of V into independent sets. First-fit coloring is a simple coloring algorithm. Consider a vertex ordering $\langle v_1, v_2, \cdots, v_n \rangle$ of V. For each $1 \leq i \leq n$, denote

$$N_{\prec}(v_i) = \{v_j : 1 \leq j < i, v_j \in N(v_i)\}.$$

The *first-fit coloring* in the ordering $\langle v_1, v_2, \cdots, v_n \rangle$ use colors represented by natural numbers and runs as follows: Assign the color 1 to v_1. For $i = 2$ up to n, assign to v_i with the smallest color not used by node in $N_{\prec}(v_i)$. Clearly, the output coloring uses at most $1 + \max_{1<i\leq n} |N_{\prec}(v_i)|$ colors. The parameter $\max_{1<i\leq n} |N_{\prec}(v_i)|$ is referred to as its *inductivity* of $\langle v_1, v_2, \cdots, v_n \rangle$.

Among all vertex orderings, a special vertex ordering, known as *smallest-last ordering* [13], achieves the smallest inductivity. It is produced iteratively as follows: Initialize H to G. For $i = n$ down to 1, let v_i be a vertex of the smallest degree in H and delete v_i from H. Then the ordering $\langle v_1, v_2, \cdots, v_n \rangle$ is a smallest-last ordering. Its inductivity is equal to the *inductivity* of G, which is defined by $\delta^* (G) = \max_{U \subseteq V} \delta (G[U])$.

Let $D = (V, A)$ be a digraph. The subgraph of D induced by a subset U of V is denoted by $D[U]$. The out-degree (respectively, in-degree) of a node u in D is denoted by $\deg_D^{out}(u)$ (respectively, $\deg_D^{in}(u)$). The maximum out-degree (respectively, in-degree) of D is denoted by $\Delta^{out}(D)$ (respectively, $\Delta^{in}(D)$).

An *orientation* of an undirected graph G is a digraph obtained from G by imposing an orientation on each edge of G. Suppose that the digraph $D = (V, A)$ is an orientation of $G = (V, E)$. We claim that $\delta^*(G) \leq 2\Delta^{out}(D)$. Indeed, for any $U \subseteq V$, $D[U]$ contains at least one node u satisfying $\deg_{D[U]}^{in}(u) \leq \deg_{D[U]}^{out}(u)$. Thus,

$$\begin{aligned}\delta(G[U]) &\leq \deg_{G[U]}(u) = \deg_{D[U]}^{in}(u) + \deg_{D[U]}^{out}(u) \\ &\leq 2\deg_{D[U]}^{out}(u) \leq 2\deg_D^{out}(u) \leq 2\Delta^{out}(D).\end{aligned}$$

So, $\delta^*(G) \leq 2\Delta^{out}(D)$.

3 Dominating Tree

Let G denote the unit-disk graph on V, which represents the communication topology. In this section, we describe a rooted spanning tree T of G constructed from the CDS presented in [14]. This tree will be used in the routings of all the four group communications. Depending on the type of the group communications, the root of T, denoted by s, is chosen as follows. For broadcast, s is the source the broadcast; for aggregation or gathering, s is the sink node; for gossiping, s is a graph center of G. In either case, we use L to denote the graph radius of G with respect to s.

We begin with the construction of a small, short and sparse CDS of G presented in [14]. We first select a maximal independent set (MIS) I of G in the first-fit manner in a breadth-first-search (BFS) ordering (with respect to s) of V. All nodes in I form a dominating set, and hence are referred to as dominators. Then, we select a set C of connectors to interconnect I as follows. Let G' be the graph on I in which there is edge between two dominators if and only if they have a common neighbor. The radius of G' with respect to s is denote by L'. Clearly, $L' \leq L - 1$. For each $0 \leq l \leq L'$, let I_l be the set of dominators of depth l in G'. Then, $I_0 = \{s\}$. For each $0 \leq l < L'$, let P_l be the set of nodes adjacent to at least one node in I_l and at least one node in I_{l+1}, and compute a minimal cover $C_l \subseteq P_l$ of I_{l+1}. Set $C = \bigcup_{l=0}^{L'-1} C_l$. Then, $I \cup C$ is a CDS of G. The following sparse properties of $I \cup C$ were proved in [14]:

- $|C_0| \leq 12$.
- For each $2 \leq l \leq L' - 1$, each dominator in I_l is adjacent to at most 11 connectors in C_l.
- For each $1 \leq l \leq L' - 1$, Each connector in C_l is adjacent to at most 4 dominators in I_{l+1}.

Now, we construct T by specifying the parent of each node other than s. First, each dominator in I_l with $2 \leq l \leq L'$ chooses the neighboring connector of the smallest ID in C_{l-1} as its parent. Second, each connector in C_l with $0 \leq l \leq L'-1$ chooses the neighboring dominator of the smallest ID in I_l as its parent. Third, each other node, referred to as dominatee, chooses the neighboring dominator of the smallest ID as its parent. Clearly, T is a spanning tree, and is called a *dominating tree*.

We introduce two geometric packing parameters. For any $r > 0$, let α_r (resp. β_r) denote the maximum number of points in a disk (resp., a half-disk) of radius r whose mutual distances are greater than one. Then, by Groemer's Inequality [9],

$$\alpha_r \leq \left\lfloor \frac{2\pi}{\sqrt{3}} r^2 + \pi r \right\rfloor + 1,$$

$$\beta_r \leq \left\lfloor \frac{\pi}{\sqrt{3}} r^2 + \left(\frac{\pi}{2} + 1 \right) r \right\rfloor + 1.$$

We use H_1 to denote the $(\rho + 1)$-disk graph on I. In other words, a pair of dominators in I are adjacent in H_1 if and only if their Euclidean distance is at most $\rho + 1$. Consider an arbitrary set of dominators U. It's easy to show that $\delta(H_1[U]) \leq \beta_{\rho+1} - 1$. Therefore, $\delta^*(H_1) \leq \beta_{\rho+1} - 1$. Consequently for any subset U of dominators, $\delta^*(H_1[U]) \leq \beta_{\rho+1} - 1$. Hence, the first-fit coloring of $H_1[U]$ in the smallest-last ordering uses at most $\beta_{\rho+1}$ colors, and such coloring is simply referred to as the *first-fit coloring* of U.

We also define a conflict graph H_2 on C as follows. A pair of connectors u and v are adjacent in H_2 if and only if either a dominator child of v is within the interference range of u, or a dominator child of u is within the interference range of v. We claim that $\delta^*(H_2) \leq 2(\alpha_\rho - 1)$. To prove this claim, we introduce an orientation D of H_2 as follows. Consider an arbitrary edge uv in H and assume that u has smaller ID than v. If a dominator child of v is within the interference range of u, we orient the edge uv to a link (u, v); otherwise, we orient the edge uv to a link (v, u). It's sufficient to show that $\Delta^{out}(D) \leq \alpha_\rho - 1$. Consider a connector u in D with maximum out-degree. Let X denote the set of dominators within the interference range of u. Then, $|X| \leq \alpha_\rho$. For each out-neighbor v of u in D, v has at least one child in X. On the other hand, all child dominators of u are also in X. Hence,

$$\Delta^{out}(D) \leq |X| - 1 \leq \alpha_\rho - 1.$$

So, our claim holds. Therefore, the first-fit coloring of H_2 in the smallest-last ordering uses at most $2(\alpha_\rho - 1) + 1 = 2\alpha_\rho - 1$ colors. This coloring is simply referred to as the *first-fit coloring* of C.

Using similar argument, we can show that for $1 \leq l \leq L' - 1$, $\delta^* (H_2 [C_l]) \leq 2(\alpha_\rho - 2)$. Therefore, the first-fit coloring of $H_2 [C_l]$ in the smallest-last ordering uses at most $2(\alpha_\rho - 2) + 1 = 2\alpha_\rho - 3$ colors. This coloring is simply referred to as the *first-fit coloring* of C_l.

4 Broadcast Scheduling

Let s be the source of the broadcast. We first construct the dominating tree T rooted as s as in Section 3. The routing of the broadcast is the spanning s-aborescence oriented from T. The broadcast schedule is then partitioned in $2L' + 1$ rounds sequentially dedicated to the transmissions by

$$I_0, C_0, I_1, C_1, \cdots, I_{L'-1}, C_{L'-1}, I_{L'}$$

respectively. The individual rounds are then scheduled as follows:

- In the round for I_0, only the source node s transmits, and hence this round has only one time-slot.
- In the round for C_0, we sort C_0 arbitrarily and let the i-th node in C_0 transmit in the $\lfloor i/\lambda \rfloor$-th time slot at channel $i \bmod \lambda$. Since $|C_0| \leq 12$, this round takes at most $\lceil 12/\lambda \rceil$ time-slots.
- In the round for I_l with $1 \leq l \leq L'$, we compute a a first-fit coloring of I_l, and let each dominator of the i-th color transmit in the $\lfloor i/\lambda \rfloor$-th time slot at channel $i \bmod \lambda$. This round takes at most $\lceil \beta_{\rho+1}/\lambda \rceil$ time-slots.
- In the round for C_l with $1 \leq l \leq L' - 1$, we compute a a first-fit coloring of C_l, and let each connector of the i-th color transmit in the $\lfloor i/\lambda \rfloor$-th time slot at channel $i \bmod \lambda$. This round takes at most $\lceil (2\alpha_\rho - 3)/\lambda \rceil$ time-slots.

Thus, the latency of the entire broadcast schedule is at most

$$\begin{aligned} & 1 + \left\lceil \frac{12}{\lambda} \right\rceil + L' \left\lceil \frac{\beta_{\rho+1}}{\lambda} \right\rceil + (L' - 1) \left\lceil \frac{2\alpha_\rho - 3}{\lambda} \right\rceil \\ & \leq \left\lceil \frac{\beta_{\rho+1}}{\lambda} \right\rceil (L - 1) + \left\lceil \frac{2\alpha_\rho - 3}{\lambda} \right\rceil (L - 2) + \left\lceil \frac{12}{\lambda} \right\rceil + 1. \end{aligned}$$

Since $\beta_{\rho+1} \geq 12$, it's easy to show that

$$\left\lceil \frac{\beta_{\rho+1}}{\lambda} \right\rceil (L - 1) + \left\lceil \frac{2\alpha_\rho - 3}{\lambda} \right\rceil (L - 2) + \left\lceil \frac{12}{\lambda} \right\rceil + 1 \leq \left(\left\lceil \frac{\beta_{\rho+1}}{\lambda} \right\rceil + \left\lceil \frac{2\alpha_\rho - 3}{\lambda} \right\rceil \right) L.$$

As L is a trivial lower bound on the minimum broadcast latency, the approximation ratio of the our broadcast schedule is at most $\left\lceil \frac{\beta_{\rho+1}}{\lambda} \right\rceil + \left\lceil \frac{2\alpha_\rho - 3}{\lambda} \right\rceil$.

5 Aggregation Scheduling

Let s be the sink of the aggregation. Let Δ denote the maximum degree of G, and L be the graph radius of G with respect to s. For the trivial case that $L = 1$, we simply let all nodes other than s transmit one by one. Such trivial schedule has latency $n - 1 = \Delta$. Subsequently, we assume that $L > 1$. We first construct the dominating tree T rooted as s as in Section 3. The routing of the aggregation schedule is the spanning inward s-aborescence oriented from T. Let W denote the set of dominatees. The aggregation schedule is then partitioned in $2L' + 1$ rounds sequentially dedicated to the transmissions by

$$W, I_{L'}, C_{L'-1}, I_{L'-1}, \cdots, C_1, I_1, C_0$$

respectively. We describe a procedure used by the scheduling in the round for W and the round for each C_l with $1 \leq l \leq L' - 1$.

Let B be a set of links whose receiving endpoints are all dominators. Suppose that ϕ is the maximum number of links in B with a common dominator endpoint. We first partition B into ϕ subsets B_j with $1 \leq j \leq \phi$ such that each dominator is incident to at most one link in each B_j. The schedule of B is then further partitioned into ϕ sub-rounds dedicated to $B_1, B_2, , \cdots, B_\phi$ respectively. In the sub-round for B_j, we compute a first-fit coloring of the dominators incident to the links in B_j, and then each link in B_j whose dominator endpoint receives the i-th color is scheduled in the $\lceil i/\lambda \rceil$-th time-slot at the channel $i \bmod \lambda$. Thus, each of the ϕ sub-rounds consists of at most $\lceil \beta_{\rho+1}/\lambda \rceil$ time-slots. Hence, the total number of slots is at most $\phi \lceil \beta_{\rho+1}/\lambda \rceil$.

Now, we are ready to describe the schedule in the individual rounds.

- In the round for W, we adopt the above procedure to produce a schedule in this round. Since each dominator is adjacent to at least one dominatee, the maximum number of nodes in W adjacent to a dominator is at most $\Delta - 1$. Hence, this round takes at most $(\Delta - 1) \lceil \beta_{\rho+1}/\lambda \rceil$ time-slots.
- In the round for C_l with $1 \leq l \leq L' - 1$, we also adopt the above procedure to produce a schedule in this round. Since each dominator in I_{l-1} is adjacent to at most 11 connectors in C_l, this round takes at most $11 \lceil \beta_{\rho+1}/\lambda \rceil$ time-slots.
- In the round for C_0, all nodes in C_0 transmit one by one, and thus this round takes at most 12 time-slots.
- In the round for I_l with $1 \leq l \leq L'$, we compute a a first-fit coloring of I_l, and let each dominator with the i-th color transmit in the i-th time slot. This round takes at most $\lceil \beta_{\rho+1}/\lambda \rceil$ time-slots.

Thus, the latency of the entire aggregation schedule is at most

$$\begin{aligned} &(\Delta - 1) \left\lceil \frac{\beta_{\rho+1}}{\lambda} \right\rceil + 11 \left\lceil \frac{\beta_{\rho+1}}{\lambda} \right\rceil (L' - 1) + 12 + L' \left\lceil \frac{\beta_{\rho+1}}{\lambda} \right\rceil \\ &= \left\lceil \frac{\beta_{\rho+1}}{\lambda} \right\rceil (\Delta + 12L' - 12) + 12 \leq \left\lceil \frac{\beta_{\rho+1}}{\lambda} \right\rceil (\Delta + 12L - 24) + 12. \end{aligned}$$

A trivial lower bound on the minimum aggregation latency is L. We claim that $\lceil \Delta / (\lambda \alpha_{1/(\rho-1)}) \rceil$ is also a lower bound for any $\rho > 1$. Indeed, let u be a node with maximum degree in G, and S be the unit-disk centered at u. Then, S contains $\Delta + 1$ nodes. If s is not in S, then all these $\Delta + 1$ nodes in S have to transmit; otherwise, exactly Δ nodes in S have to transmit. In either case, at least Δ nodes in S have to transmit. Since all nodes transmitting in the same time-slot at the same channel must be apart from each other by a distance greater than $\rho - 1$, at most $\lambda \alpha_{1/(\rho-1)}$ nodes in S can transmit in a time-slot. Hence, the Δ transmissions by the nodes in S takes at least $\lceil \Delta / (\lambda \alpha_{1/(\rho-1)}) \rceil$ time-slots. So, our claim holds. Therefore, the approximation bound of the aggregation schedule is at most $\lceil \beta_{\rho+1} / \lambda \rceil (\lambda \alpha_{1/(\rho-1)} + 12)$.

6 Gathering Scheduling

Let s be the sink of the gathering. If $L = 1$, then all other nodes transmit to s one by one, and this schedule is optimal. So, we assume subsequently that $L > 1$. We first construct the dominating tree of G rooted at s. The routing of the gathering schedule is the spanning inward s-aborescence oriented from T. Our gather schedule utilizes a labelling of the edges of T, which is described below.

Let $\langle v_1, v_2, \cdots, v_{n-1} \rangle$ be an ordering of $V \setminus \{s\}$ in the descending order of depth in T with ties broken arbitrarily. For $1 \le i \le n$, we assign the j-th edge in the tree path from s to v_j with a label $2(i-1)+j$ (see an example in Figure 1). Clearly, the number of labels received by an edge connecting v and its parent is equal to the number of descendents (including v itself) of v in T. If v is connector (respectively, dominator), all labels received by the edge between v and its parent are odd (respectively, even). In addition, all edges across two consecutive layers of the dominating tree receive distinct labels. We further claim that the largest label is $2n-3$. Consider a node v_i and let h be the length of the path from s to v_i. The maximum label assigned to the edges in the path from s to v_i is $2(i-1)+h$. It's sufficient to show that $2(i-1)+h \le 2n-3$. Since none of $v_1, v_2, \cdots, v_{i-1}$ belongs to the path from s to v_i, we have $h + i - 1 \le n - 1$ and hence $i \le n - h$. Therefore,

$$2(i-1)+h \le 2(n-h-1)+h = 2n-h-2 \le 2n-3.$$

So, the claim holds.

For each $1 \le k \le 2n-3$, let E_k denote the set of edges of T which has been assigned with a label k, and A_k denote the links in the inward s-arborescence oriented from the edges in E_k. Then, for odd (respectively, even) k, all the receiving (respectively, transmitting) endpoints of links in A_k are dominators. In addition, for each $1 \le k \le 2n-3$, every dominator is incident to at most one link in A_k.

Now, we are ready to describe the gathering schedule. The schedule are partitioned in $2n-3$ rounds sequentially dedicated to $A_{2n-3}, A_{2n-2}, \cdots, A_2, A_1$ respectively. For each $1 \le k \le 2n-3$, the round for A_k is scheduled as follows.

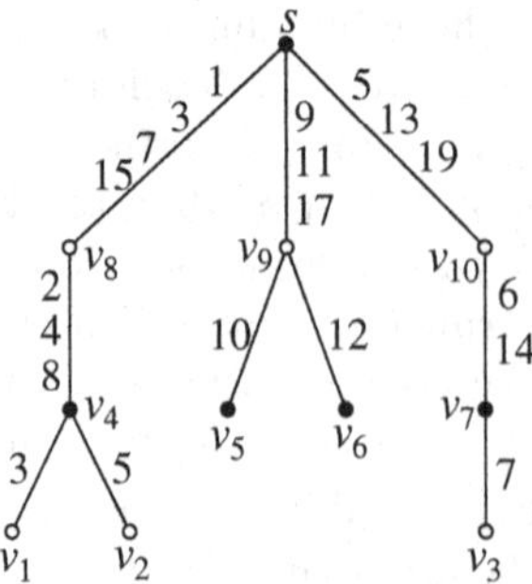

Fig. 1. A multi-labelling of the edges in the dominating tree

We first compute a first-fit distance-$(\rho+1)$ coloring of the dominator endpoints of the links A_k. Then each link whose dominator endpoint receives the i-th color is scheduled in the $\lceil i/\lambda \rceil$-th time-slot at the channel $i \bmod \lambda$.. Thus, each round takes at most $\lceil \beta_{\rho+1}/\lambda \rceil$ time-slots.

It's obvious that the latency of the gathering schedule is $\lceil \beta_{\rho+1}/\lambda \rceil (2n-3)$. Since $n-1$ is a trivial lower bound on the minimum gathering latency, the approximation ratio of the gathering schedule presented in this section is at most $2 \lceil \beta_{\rho+1}/\lambda \rceil$.

7 Gossiping Scheduling

Let s be the graph center of G. Our gossiping schedule consists of two phases. In the first phase s collects all the packets from all other nodes, and in the second phase s broadcasts all the n packets to all other nodes. We adopt the gathering schedule presented in the previous section for the first phase. In the second phase, the node s disseminates all received packets and its own packet to all other nodes. We present a schedule for the second phase next.

We construct the dominating tree T of G rooted at s. The routing of the second phase is the spanning s-aborescence oriented from T. We compute the first-fit coloring of dominators, and let k_1 be the number of colors used by this coloring. By proper renumbering of the colors, we assume that s has the first color. We then compute a first-fit coloring of all connectors, and let k_2 be the number of colors used by this coloring. We group the time-slots into frames of length $\lceil k_1/\lambda \rceil + \lceil k_2/\lambda \rceil$. In each frame, the first $\lceil k_1/\lambda \rceil$ slots form a dominator subframe, and the remaining $\lceil k_2/\lambda \rceil$ slots form a connector subframe. The source node s transmits one packet in each frame. Each connector (respectively, dominator) of color i receiving a packet in a dominator (respectively, connector) subframe transmits the received packet at the channel $i \bmod \lambda$ in the $\lceil i/\lambda \rceil$-th time-slot of the subsequent connector (respectively, dominator) subframe.

The correctness of the above schedule is obvious. The latency of the second phase can be bound as follows. After $n-1$ frames, s transmits the last packet. After another L' frames, the last packet reaches all nodes in $I_{L'}$. Finally, after another dominator sub-frame, the last packet reaches all nodes. So, the total number of time-slots takes by the second phase is at most

$$\left(\left\lceil\frac{k_1}{\lambda}\right\rceil+\left\lceil\frac{k_2}{\lambda}\right\rceil\right)(n-1+L')+\left\lceil\frac{k_1}{\lambda}\right\rceil \leq \left(\left\lceil\frac{k_1}{\lambda}\right\rceil+\left\lceil\frac{k_2}{\lambda}\right\rceil\right)(n+L-2)+\left\lceil\frac{k_1}{\lambda}\right\rceil$$
$$\leq \left(\left\lceil\frac{\beta_{\rho+1}}{\lambda}\right\rceil+\left\lceil\frac{2\alpha_\rho-1}{\lambda}\right\rceil\right)(n+L-2)+\left\lceil\frac{\beta_{\rho+1}}{\lambda}\right\rceil.$$

Since the first phase takes at most $\lceil\beta_{\rho+1}/\lambda\rceil(2n-3)$ time-slots, the total number of time-slots taken by the two phases is at most

$$\left(\left\lceil\frac{\beta_{\rho+1}}{\lambda}\right\rceil+\left\lceil\frac{2\alpha_\rho-1}{\lambda}\right\rceil\right)(n+L-2)+\left\lceil\frac{\beta_{\rho+1}}{\lambda}\right\rceil(2n-2)$$
$$=\left\lceil\frac{\beta_{\rho+1}}{\lambda}\right\rceil(3n+L-4)+\left\lceil\frac{2\alpha_\rho-1}{\lambda}\right\rceil(n+L-2)$$

Next, we show that the minimum gossiping latency is at least $n-1+L$. The broadcasting of each message requires at least L transmissions. So, the total number of transmissions in any gossiping schedule is at least nL. This implies that some node must take at least L transmissions. On the other hand, every node must take $n-1$ receptions. Therefore, some node takes at least $n-1+L$ transmissions and receptions. So, $n-1+L$ is a lower bound on the minimum gossiping latency. Therefore, the approximation ratio of our gossiping schedule is at most $3\lceil\beta_{\rho+1}/\lambda\rceil+\lceil(2\alpha_\rho-1)/\lambda\rceil$.

8 Summary

In this paper, we developed four communications schedules for broadcast, aggregation, gathering and gossiping respectively in multi-channel multihop wireless networks under the protocol interference model. Table 1 summarizes the upper bounds on the latencies of these communication schedules. The parameter L is the graph radius with respect to the source of the broadcast, sink of the aggregation, sink of the gathering, and the graph center respectively.

Table 1. Summary on the approximations bounds of the scheduling algorithms

Communication	Upper bound on latency
broadcast	$\left\lceil\frac{\beta_{\rho+1}}{\lambda}\right\rceil(L-1)+\left\lceil\frac{2\alpha_\rho-3}{\lambda}\right\rceil(L-2)+\left\lceil\frac{12}{\lambda}\right\rceil+1$
aggregation	$\left\lceil\frac{\beta_{\rho+1}}{\lambda}\right\rceil(\Delta+12L-24)+12$
gathering	$\left\lceil\frac{\beta_{\rho+1}}{\lambda}\right\rceil(2n-3)$
gossiping	$\left\lceil\frac{\beta_{\rho+1}}{\lambda}\right\rceil(3n+L-4)+\left\lceil\frac{2\alpha_\rho-3}{\lambda}\right\rceil(n+L-2)$

References

1. Bermond, J.-C., Galtier, J., Klasing, R., Morales, N., Perennes, S.: Hardness and approximation of gathering in static radio networks. In: Proceedings FAWN 2006 (2006)
2. Bonifaci, V., Korteweg, P., Marchetti-Spaccamela, A., Stougie, L.: An Approximation Algorithm for the Wireless Gathering Problem. In: Arge, L., Freivalds, R. (eds.) SWAT 2006. LNCS, vol. 4059, pp. 328–338. Springer, Heidelberg (2006)
3. Chen, X.J., Hu, X.D., Zhu, J.M.: Minimum data aggregation time problem in wireless sensor networks. In: Jia, X., Wu, J., He, Y. (eds.) MSN 2005. LNCS, vol. 3794, pp. 133–142. Springer, Heidelberg (2005)
4. Chen, Z., Qiao, C., Xu, J., Lee, T.: A Constant Approximation Algorithm for Interference Aware Broadcast in Wireless Networks. In: IEEE INFOCOM 2007 (2007)
5. Dessmark, A., Pelc, A.: Tradeoffs between knowledge and time of communication in geometric radio networks. In: Proceedings of the 13th Annual ACM Symposium on Parallel Algorithms and Architectures (SPAA 2001), Crete, Greece, July 2001, pp. 59–66 (2001)
6. Florens, C., McEliece, R.: Packets distribution algorithms for sensor networks. In: IEEE INFOCOM 2003, pp. 1063–1072 (2003)
7. Gandhi, R., Kim, Y.-A., Lee, S., Ryu, J., Wan, P.-J.: Approximation Algorithms for Data Broadcast in Wireless Networks. In: IEEE INFOCOM Mini-conference 2009 (2009)
8. Gandhi, R., Parthasarathy, S., Mishra, A.: Minimizing broadcast latency and redundancy in ad hoc networks. In: Proceedings of the 4th ACM international symposium on Mobile Ad hoc networking and computing (MobiHoc 2003), pp. 222–232 (2003)
9. Groemer, H.: Über die Einlagerung von Kreisen in einen konvexen Bereich. Math. Z. 73, 285–294 (1960)
10. Huang, S.C.-H., Du, H., Park, E.-K.: Minimum-latency gossiping in multi-hop wireless networks. In: ACM Mobihoc 2008 (2008)
11. Huang, C.-H., Wan, P.-J., Deng, J., Han, Y.S.: Broadcast Scheduling in Interference Environment. IEEE Transactions on Mobile Computing 7(11), 1338–1348 (2008)
12. Huang, S.C.-H., Wan, P.-J., Vu, C.T., Li, Y., Yao, F.: Nearly Constant Approximation for Data Aggregation Scheduling in Wireless Sensor Networks. In: IEEE INFOCOM 2007 (2007)
13. Matula, D.W., Beck, L.L.: Smallest-last ordering and clustering and graph coloring algorithms. Journal of the Association of Computing Machinery 30(3), 417–427 (1983)
14. Wan, P.-J., Huang, C.-H., Wang, L., Wan, Z.-Y., Jia, X.: Minimum-Latency Aggregation Scheduling in Multihop Wireless Networks. In: ACM MOBIHOC 2009 (2009)

Traffic-Aware Channel Assignment in Wireless Sensor Networks

Yafeng Wu[1], Matthew Keally[2], Gang Zhou[2], and Weizhen Mao[2]

[1] Computer Science Department, University of Virginia
yw5s@cs.virginia.edu
[2] Computer Science Department, College of William and Mary
{makeal,gzhou,wm}@cs.wm.edu

Abstract. Existing frequency assignment efforts in wireless sensor network research focus on balancing available physical frequencies among neighboring nodes, without paying attention to the fact that different nodes have different traffic volumes. Ignoring the different traffic requirements in different nodes in frequency assignment design leads to poor MAC performance. Therefore, in this paper, we are motivated to propose traffic-aware frequency assignment, which considers nodes' traffic volumes when making frequency decisions. We incorporate our traffic-aware frequency assignment design into an existing multi-channel MAC, and compare the performance with two conventional frequency assignment schemes. Our performance evaluation demonstrates that traffic-aware channel assignment can greatly improve multi-channel MAC performance. Our traffic-aware assignment scheme greatly enhances the packet delivery ratio and system throughput, while reducing channel access delay and energy consumption.

1 Introduction

As an emerging technology, Wireless Sensor Networks (WSNs) have a wide range of potential applications, including environmental monitoring, smart buildings, medical care, and many other industry and military applications. A large number of protocols have been proposed for the MAC, routing and transport layers. However with a single channel, WSNs cannot provide reliable and timely communication with high data rate requirements because of radio collisions and limited bandwidth. For example, in the "Ears on the ground" project [7], the network cannot transmit multiple acoustic streams to the sink. On the other hand, current WSN hardware such as Micaz [3] and Telos [12] which use the CC2420 radio [2], already provide multiple frequencies. So it is imperative to design multi-channel based communication protocols in WSNs to improve network throughput and provide reliable and timely communication services.

Typically, multi-channel protocols consists of two major components, channel assignment and media access control. A good channel assignment method can effectively reduce radio interference among concurrent transmissions, mitigate packet congestion within a single channel, and make media access control easier. It is the key performance factor for multi-channel communication. In the state of the art, many channel assignment schemes are proposed in wireless ad hoc networks and mesh networks, but they cannot be directly applied to sensor networks. This is because nodes in ad hoc

B. Liu et al. (Eds.): WASA 2009, LNCS 5682, pp. 479–488, 2009.

and mesh networks are usually equipped with more powerful radios or even multiple radios, each of which can use one unique channel. Conversely, a sensor node such as Micaz, with only a single half-duplex radio, can only use one channel at one time [18]. Recently, some multi-channel protocols are proposed for WSNs. Most of them offer some *static* solutions to channel allocations, aiming to minimize potential interference among nodes. Since topologies of sensor networks are quite static, such static solutions can be executed in the deployment time, or infrequently during runtime, and they help MAC protocols improve communication performance on average.

In this paper, we focus on channel assignment problems in sensor networks. We believe that existing static approaches for channel assignment are insufficient because of two reasons. First, they try to reduce potential interference with the assumption that all nodes have the same amount of traffic to carry simultaneously. This assumption is not true for most WSNs, where only a fraction of nodes need to transmit packets at any time. Second, even though a specific sensor network is deployed statically, the traffic volume and pattern can vary significantly both across the deployment area and across time. For example, a military intrusion detection sensor network [5] may have a regular and low speed traffic involving a few nodes when no intrusion is occurring, but may experience a large burst of traffic affecting a lot of nodes when enemy tanks are detected. Such traffic variability can change the interference pattern, and hence a multi-channel MAC with static channel assignment will severely suffer in terms of performance.

To improve current channel assignment solutions, we develop and systematically study the notion of *traffic-aware* channel assignment for WSNs. We start by considering a setting where perfect information about current and future traffic is available. Then we propose a new channel assignment scheme which exploits this traffic information to minimize interference occurring with real traffic. We compare this scheme with two typical static channel assignment schemes by simulation, and results show that being *traffic-aware* can substantially improve the performance of channel assignment. This baseline analysis helps establish the potential benefits of traffic-aware channel assignment algorithms.

In the future, we are going to study how to efficiently deal with the traffic variability during system runtime. Some questions are: how to predict the future traffic? When traffic varies and the prediction fails, how can we change channel assignment dynamically? Of course, solutions of these questions must not bring too much overhead, and must converge to a stable assignment in limited time.

2 Related Work

In general wireless networks, frequency diversity has been studied for years and a significant number of multi-frequency MAC protocols have been proposed. However, the purposed protocols are a poor fit for wireless sensor networks due to the restricted sensornet hardware, its limited bandwidth, and the small WSN MAC layer packet size [18]. For example, some protocols [13] [14] are designed for frequency hopping spread spectrum (FHSS) wireless cards, and one protocol [4] assumes the busy-tone functionality on the hardware. In other protocols [11] [15] [10] [1], the hardware is assumed to have the ability to listen to multiple frequencies at the same time. In addition to hardware restrictions, the network bandwidth in WSNs is very limited and the MAC layer packet size is very small, 30∼50 bytes, compared to 512+ bytes used in general wireless networks. Different from all above solutions, this paper addresses how to use multiple channels efficiently in the context of wireless sensor networks, where each node only has one radio and can only use one channel at one time.

Some multi-channel MAC layer protocols have been proposed to improve network performance in WSNs. These protocols typically assign different channels to two hop neighbors to avoid potential interference, and also propose sophisticated MAC schemes to coordinate channel switching and transmissions among nodes. Simulation results show that they can significantly improve network throughput over MAC protocols using a single channel. Clearly, the most important problem of these protocols is how to assign different channels to nodes. Most protocols use "static" channel assignment, where the channel selection process are executed at the beginning of system deployment, or very infrequently during runtime. For example, MMSN [18] has a frequency assignment component, which provides four available frequency assignment strategies. Users can select any of these methods to evenly assign different channels among two-hop neighbors. TMCP [16] proposes a tree-based channel assignment scheme. The idea of the TMCP protocol is to first partition the whole network into multiple vertex-disjoint subtrees all rooted at the base station and allocate different channels to each subtree, and then forward each flow only along its corresponding subtree. One common problem of these two protocols is that they use no traffic information to assign frequencies. Instead, both protocols assume that traffic is evenly distributed on each node. However, this is often not true in reality, where traffic patterns change significantly during runtime and some nodes or segments of the network may have more traffic than others. With this uneven traffic distribution, frequency assignment schemes of both protocols may fail to provide good performance because they may waste channels on nodes who have no traffic but assign too few channels to nodes who have heavy traffic. Instead, our traffic-aware channel assignment scheme exploits traffic information to achieve better assignment solutions and can dynamically adapt to traffic pattern changes during runtime.

Recently, a multi-channel protocol [9] is proposed which also has the capability of dynamically changing the radio frequency. However, their approach is based on local decision, where each node makes its own decision to switch channels. Our traffic-aware method collects traffic information from two-hop neighbors, and uses a specific algorithm to assign channels among two-hop neighbors which results in more efficient channel usage.

3 Channel Assignment Scheme

In this section, we first explain two typical static channel assignment schemes [18]: even selection and eavesdropping, and then propose a new *traffic-aware* channel assignment approach, which uses traffic information to achieve load balance among channels and effectively reduces runtime system interference. Lastly, we compare our *traffic-aware* channel assignment with the two existing approaches through simulation evaluation.

3.1 Static Channel Assignment

In channel assignment, each node is assigned a physical channel for data reception. The assigned channel is broadcast to its neighbors, so that each node knows what channel to use to transmit unicast packets to each of its neighbors. In order to reduce communication interference and hence reduce hidden terminal problems [6], static solutions evenly assign available channels to nodes within two communication hops. In WSNs, such static channel assignments are considered to either be done once at the beginning of the system deployment, or it can be done very infrequently for adaptation to system aging. In this subsection, we describe two channel assignment schemes proposed in [18]: even selection and eavesdropping.

Even Selection. In even selection assignment, nodes first exchange their IDs among two communication hops [17], so that each node knows its two-hop neighbors' IDs. To achieve this, each node first beacons its node ID to neighbors, so that each node knows its neighbors' IDs within one communication hop. Then, each node beacons again, broadcasting all neighbors' IDs it has collected during the previous beacon round. Therefore, after two rounds of beacons, all nodes get their neighbors' IDs within two communication hops.

After the two rounds of beacons, nodes begin to choose data receiving frequencies (or channels) in the increasing order of their ID values. If a node has the smallest ID among its two communication hops, it chooses a channel first and it chooses the smallest channel among available channels. The node then beacons its channel choice within two hops. If a node's ID is not the smallest among two hops, it waits for channel decisions from other nodes within two hops that have smaller IDs. When decisions from all those nodes are made and are also received, the node chooses the smallest available (not chosen by any of its two-hop neighbors) channel. If all channels have been chosen by at least one two-hop neighbor, it randomly chooses one of the least chosen channels. After picking a channel, the node broadcasts its choice within two hops. We call this scheme *even selection*, which makes an even allocation of available frequencies to all nodes within any two communication hops.

When the number of frequencies is at least as large as the two-hop node number, *even selection* guarantees to assign different frequencies to different nodes within any two-hop neighborhood. When the number of frequencies is small, *even selection* allows two-hop neighbors evenly share the available frequencies.

Eavesdropping. We observe that although *even selection* results in even sharing of available frequencies among two-hop neighbors, it requires a number of two-hop broadcasts. To reduce the communication overhead, a lightweight eavesdropping scheme is also proposed in [18]. In eavesdropping, each node takes a random backoff before it broadcasts its physical channel decision. Each node also records overheard physical channel choices during the backoff period. After the random backoff, a node randomly chooses one of the least chosen frequencies for data reception. Compared with *even selection*, *eavesdropping* requires less communication overhead, but leads to more potential conflicts since it only collects information within one hop rather than two hops for channel decisions.

3.2 Traffic-Aware Channel Assignment

In this section, we introduce a traffic-aware channel assignment scheme. Here, the term "traffic aware" means that nodes have knowledge about future traffic. More precisely, nodes know their reception data rates of the future. Now, we assume that the traffic data rate does not change, while in the future we intend to discuss dynamic traffic. One practical problem is the dissemination of dymamic traffic information to nodes. One practical way is that at regular intervals, nodes calculate the reception data rate, and use it to determine channel assignment. Also, considering that sensor networks are used to periodically collect environment data in most scenarios, upper layers can pass such application information to the channel assignment component, and then the reception data rate can be inferred from those collection tasks' settings.

Now, every node is assigned a traffic weight, which corresponds to its future reception data rate. The problem is to assign the right channel to each node, aiming to minimize the maximum load of any channels within the two-hop neighborhood of any node. Here, we choose this goal because the more load one channel takes, the more likely radio collisions occur in this channel. Also, the channel load affects the throughput and the latency of communication. We also find that this problem is very similar to the load balancing job scheduling problem, where each channel can be viewed as one machine, and the traffic weight of each node corresponds to the processing time of each job. The difference between these two problems is that in our channel assignment, we require the load balance within any two-hop neighborhood, but the job scheduling problem only asks the load balance for one group of machines. If the diameter of this network is two hops, our traffic-aware channel assignment problem is the exact same problem with the load balancing job scheduling problem. Since the job scheduling problem is NP-hard, it is clear that our traffic-aware channel assignment problem is also NP-hard.

In the light of NP-completeness, there is no polynomial time exact algorithm which can always find the optimal assignment. Next, we propose a greedy traffic-aware channel assignment scheme.

First, nodes exchange their IDs and their traffic weights among two communication hops, so that each node knows its two-hop neighbors' IDs and traffic weights. After nodes collect traffic information of all neighbors within two hops, they make channel decisions in the decreasing order of their traffic weight, with the smallest node ID used as a tie breaker. If a node has the greatest traffic weight among its two communication hops, it chooses the channel with the least load among available channels, and then beacons the channel choice within two hops. After receiving this beacon, nodes update the load of the corresponding channel. If a node's traffic weight is not the greatest one among two hops, it waits for channel decisions from other nodes within two hops that have greater weight. A node also waits for all nodes with equal weight but lower node ID to make decisions first. After decisions from all nodes with greater weight or equal weight but lower node ID are received, a node chooses the channel with the least load. Since nodes choose channels in sequence by decreasing weight with a node ID tiebreaker, our assignment algorithm will always converge for any set of nodes and traffic weights.

This traffic-aware channel assignment scheme uses a similar concept as that of the Longest Processing Time algorithm (LPT) for the job scheduling problem. It is proven that the approximation ratio of the LPT algorithm is $\frac{4}{3} - \frac{1}{m}$, where m is the number of machines. However, we have not yet calculated the approximation ratio for our traffic-aware channel assignment algorithm and leave it to future work. Now, we only know that $\frac{4}{3} - \frac{1}{m}$ is a lower bound for our algorithm. In terms of overhead, our algorithm has similar overhead as the even selection assignment scheme, except adding several bytes in beacon messages to exchange the traffic weight.

4 Performance Evaluation

In this section, we compare the performance of two static channel assignment schemes and the new traffic-aware assignment. For these three approaches, we use the same medium access control method, which is designed in [19]. Also, we assume that every node has perfect knowledge about its future reception data rate.

For this performance evaluation, two groups of experiments are designed. In the first group, different system loads are used, and in the second group of experiments, the number of available channels is varied.

Table 1. Simulation Configuration

TERRAIN	(200m×200m) Square
Node Number	289
Node Placement	Uniform
Application	Many-to-Many CBR Streams
Payload Size	32 Bytes
Routing Layer	GF
MAC Layer	CSMA/MMSN
Radio Layer	RADIO-ACCNOISE
Radio Bandwidth	250 Kbps
Radio Range	20m∼45m

For all the two groups of experiments, four performance metrics are adopted: aggregate MAC throughput, packet delivery ratio, channel access delay, and energy consumption per successfully delivered data byte. The packet delivery ratio is calculated as the ratio of the total number of data packets successfully delivered by the MAC layer over the total number of data packets the network layer requests the MAC to transmit. The aggregate MAC throughput measures the performance gain and is calculated as the total amount of useful data successfully delivered through the MAC layer in the system per unit time. The channel access delay measures the time delay a data packet from the network layer waits for the channel before it gets sent out. The energy consumption per byte is the system wide energy consumed for successfully delivering one byte of user data.

During all the experiments, the Geographic Forwarding (GF) [8] routing protocol is used and the simulation is configured according to the settings in Table 1. For each data value we present in the results, we also give its 90% confidence interval.

4.1 Performance Evaluation with Different System Loads

In the first group of experiments, we explore traffic-aware assignment's performance when different system loads are used, which are generated by different numbers of CBR streams. In the experiments, the node density is set to 38 and the number of available channels is 5.

As Figure 1 shows, for all the system loads we configure from 15 CBR streams to 50 CBR streams, it is observed that traffic-aware assignment always exhibits better performance than static schemes in all performance metrics in all scenarios. For example, as shown in Figure 1, comparing with the best static scheme, traffic-aware scheme achieves on average 13.5% higher aggregate throughput as shown in (b). It is clear that traffic-aware channel assignment effectively reduces radio interference, and by keeping the load balance among channels it mitigates packet congestion within channels and leads to high throughput and lower latency.

Another interesting trend is that when the system load is light or heavy, the traffic-aware assignment outperforms static schemes with a large gap, but when the system load is medium, like 30 streams, the performance of the traffic-aware scheme is very close to static schemes. One possible reason is that with such medium loads, most nodes have similar traffic weights, which also allows static schemes to perform well.

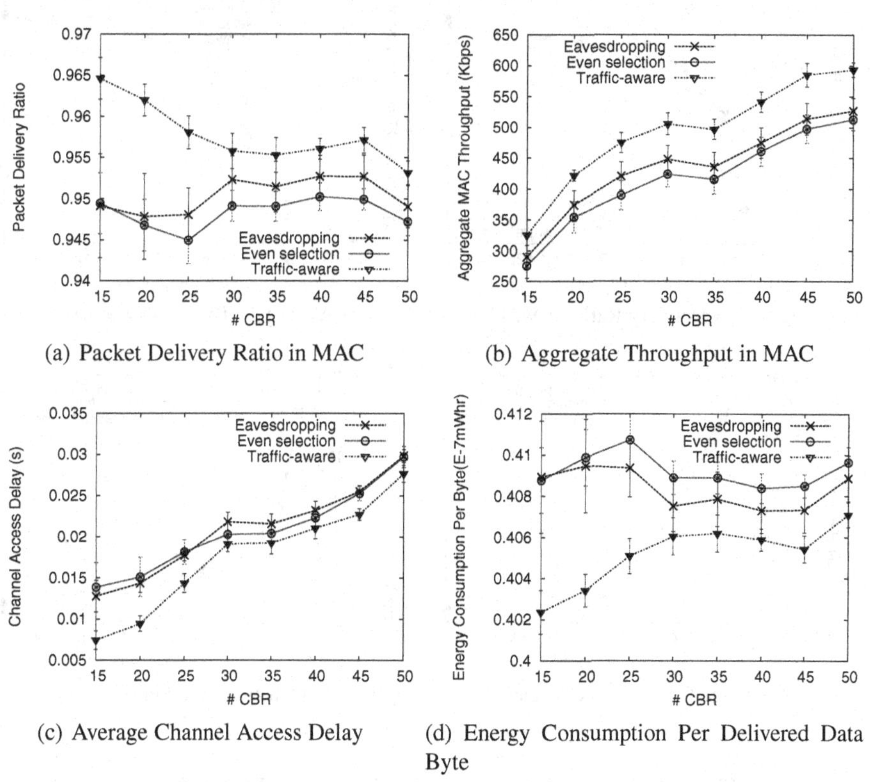

(a) Packet Delivery Ratio in MAC

(b) Aggregate Throughput in MAC

(c) Average Channel Access Delay

(d) Energy Consumption Per Delivered Data Byte

Fig. 1. Performance Evaluation with Different System Loads

4.2 Performance Evaluation with Different Numbers of Channels

In many deployed sensor network systems, the number of available channels may vary. For example, in an indoor scenario, the interference from WiFi networks may decrease the number of available channels that sensor networks can use. So, in the second group of experiments, we evaluate the performance of channel assignment schemes when different numbers of channels are utilized. The number is increased from 1 to 16, and a many-to-many traffic pattern is used that consists of 50 CBR streams.

Once again, the experimental results confirm that traffic-aware assignment always achieves a higher performance than static schemes, which can be observed in Figure 2 (a)∼(d). The corresponding reasons can be found in the first groups of experiments and are not repeated here.

It is shown that when the channel number is small, for example 1 or 2, the performance of all schemes is very close. When we have many channels, such as 16, the performance is also close. On the other side, when the channel number is medium, like 4, 6, 8, the traffic-aware scheme obviously outperforms others. We believe that in practice, one sensor network may co-exist with other sensor networks or WiFi networks, and in most cases, the number of available channels is around such medium values.

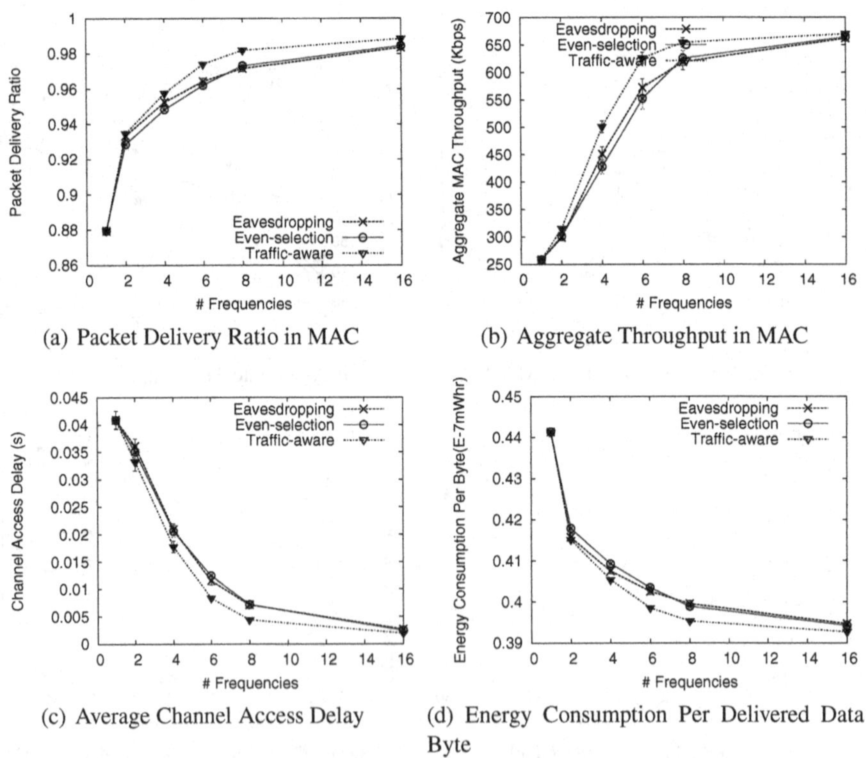

(a) Packet Delivery Ratio in MAC

(b) Aggregate Throughput in MAC

(c) Average Channel Access Delay

(d) Energy Consumption Per Delivered Data Byte

Fig. 2. Performance Evaluation with Different numbers of channels

5 Conclusion

Existing frequency assignment efforts in wireless sensor network research focus on assigning available physical frequencies as evenly as possible to neighboring nodes, ignoring the runtime condition that different nodes have different traffic requirements. Failure to address different traffic volumes during frequency assignment design leads to poor MAC performance, which has been identified and demonstrated in our performance evaluation. In this paper, we propose a traffic-aware frequency assignment design that actually considers different traffic requirements from neighboring nodes while making frequency decisions. The traffic-aware frequency assignment is incorporated into the existing MMSN MAC and compared with two conventional frequency assignment methods: even selection and eavesdropping. Our simulation evaluation demonstrates that the traffic-aware channel assignment greatly improves multi-channel MAC performance: it significantly enhances the the packet delivery ratio and throughput, while at the same time reducing channel access delay and energy consumption.

References

1. Caccaco, M., Zhang, L.Y., Sha, L., Buttazzo, G.: An Implicit Prioritized Access Protocol for Wireless Sensor Networks. In: IEEE RTSS (2002)
2. CC2420 2.4 GHz IEEE 802.15.4 / ZigBee-ready RF Transceiver (2008), `http://www.chipcon.com`
3. XBOW Sensor Motes Specifications (2008), `http://www.xbow.com`
4. Deng, J., Haas, Z.: Dual Busy Tone Multiple Access (DBTMA): A New Medium Access Control for Packet Radio Networks. In: IEEE ICUPC (1998)
5. He, T., Krishnamurthy, S., Luo, L., Yan, T., Stoleru, R., Zhou, G., Cao, Q., Vicaire, P., Stankovic, J.A., Abdelzaher, T.F., Hui, J., Krogh, B.: VigilNet: An Integrated Sensor Network System for Energy-Efficient Surveillance. In: ACM Transactions on Sensor Networks (2006)
6. IEEE 802.11, Wireless LAN Medium Access Control (MAC) and Physical Layer (PHY) Specification, ANSI/IEEE Std. 802.11 (1999)
7. Zhang, J., Zhou, G., Son, S., Stankovic, J.A.: Ears on the Ground: An Acoustic Streaming Service in Wireless Sensor Networks. In: IEEE/ACM IPSN Demo Abstract (2006)
8. Karp, B.: Geographic Routing for Wireless Networks. PhD thesis, Harvard University, Cambridge, MA (2000)
9. Le, H., Henriksson, D., Abdelzaher, T.: A practical multi-channel media access control protocol for wireless sensor networks. In: IPSN (2008)
10. Nasipuri, A., Das, S.R.: Multichannel CSMA with Signal Power-based Channel Selection for Multihop Wireless Networks. In: IEEE Vehicular Technology Conference (2000)
11. Nasipuri, A., Zhuang, J., Das, S.R.: A Multichannel CSMA MAC Protocol for Multihop Wireless Networks. In: IEEE WCNC (1999)
12. Polastre, J., Szewczyk, R., Culler, D.: Telos: Enabling Ultra-Low Power Wireless Research. In: ACM/IEEE IPSN/SPOTS (2005)
13. Tang, Z., Garcia-Luna-Aceves, J.: Hop-Reservation Multiple Access (HRMA) for Ad-Hoc Networks. In: IEEE INFOCOM (1999)
14. Tzamaloukas, A., Garcia-Luna-Aceves, J.J.: Channel-Hopping Multiple Access. In: IEEE ICC (2000)

15. Wu, S.-L., Liu, C.-Y., Tseng, Y.-C., Shen, J.-P.: A New Multi-Channel MAC Protocol with On-Demand Channel Assignment for Multi-Hop Mobile Ad Hoc Networks. In: I-SPAN (2000)
16. Wu, Y., Stankovic, J.A., He, T., Lin, S.: Realistic and efficient multi-channel communications in wireless sensor networks. In: INFOCOM (2008)
17. Zhou, G., He, T., Stankovic, J.A., Abdelzaher, T.F.: Radio Interference Detection in Wireless Sensor Networks. In: IEEE INFOCOM (2005)
18. Zhou, G., Huang, C., Yan, T., He, T., Stankovic, J.A., Abdelzaher, T.F.: MMSN: Multi-Frequency Media Access Control for Wireless Sensor Networks. In: IEEE INFOCOM (2006)
19. Zhou, G., Lu, J., Wan, C.-Y., Yarvis, M.D., Stankovic, J.A.: BodyQoS: Adaptive and Radio-Agnostic QoS for Body Sensor Networks. In: IEEE INFOCOM (2008)

Sniffer Channel Selection for Monitoring Wireless LANs

Yuan Song[1], Xian Chen[1], Yoo-Ah Kim[1], Bing Wang[1], and Guanling Chen[2]

[1] University of Connecticut, Storrs, CT 06269
[2] University of Massachusetts, Lowell, MA, 01854

Abstract. Wireless sniffers are often used to monitor APs in wireless LANs (WLANs) for network management, fault detection, traffic characterization, and optimizing deployment. It is cost effective to deploy single-radio sniffers that can monitor multiple nearby APs. However, since nearby APs often operate on orthogonal channels, a sniffer needs to switch among multiple channels to monitor its nearby APs. In this paper, we formulate and solve two optimization problems on sniffer channel selection. Both problems require that each AP be monitored by at least one sniffer. In addition, one optimization problem requires minimizing the maximum number of channels that a sniffer listens to, and the other requires minimizing the total number of channels that the sniffers listen to. We propose a novel LP-relaxation based algorithm, and two simple greedy heuristics for the above two optimization problems. Through simulation, we demonstrate that all the algorithms are effective in achieving their optimization goals, and the LP-based algorithm outperforms the greedy heuristics.

1 Introduction

Wireless LANs (WLANs) have been widely deployed in enterprise and campus networks. A number of studies use air sniffing as an effective technique for understanding and monitoring WLANs [11,6,1,7,2,8]. In air sniffing, sniffers are placed inside a WLAN, each passively listening to the air waves in its vicinity, and collecting detailed MAC/PHY information. This detailed low-level information provides valuable insights into the behavior of wireless medium and protocols. It is also critical for effective monitoring and management of WLANs.

Large-scale WLAN monitoring through air sniffing, however, faces several challenges. First, it requires a large number of sniffers, which can be costly to deploy and difficult to manage. This problem is compounded by the fact that APs in WLANs can operate on different channels (e.g., 802.11b/g supports 3 orthogonal channels, and 802.11a supports 13 orthogonal channels), while an air sniffer only listens to a single channel at any point of time (multi-radio sniffers are large and expensive to deploy [3]). Therefore, in the worst case, the required number of sniffers can be the same as the number of APs. Secondly, the sniffers generate a large amount of measurement data, which can be expensive to store, transfer and process. For instance, in [2], up to 80 Mbps of traffic is generated for monitoring an academic building, which needs to be transferred and processed at a central server.

B. Liu et al. (Eds.): WASA 2009, LNCS 5682, pp. 489–498, 2009.

To overcome the above challenges in large-scale air sniffing, [3] proposes *channel sampling*, where each sniffer samples the network traffic by visiting multiple channels periodically. Using channel sampling, a sniffer can monitor multiple nearby APs that operate on different channels, and hence less sniffers are needed. Furthermore, the sampling of traffic leads to less amount of measurement data. As shown in [3], channel sampling is useful for a number of applications, including security monitoring, anomaly detection, fault diagnosis, network characterization, and assistance to AP deployment. The study of [3] proposes two sampling strategies, equal-time sampling where a sniffer spends equal amount of time scanning each channel, and proportional sampling where the amount of time that a sniffer spends on a channel is proportional to the amount of traffic on that channel. These two strategies are improved in [4] where the scanning of the sniffers are coordinated to increase the number of unique frames.

In this paper, we address an important problem in channel sampling, namely, how to select the channels for the sniffers. Our study differs from [3,4] in two main aspects. First, we require each sniffer to monitor a *subset* of selected channels so that each AP is monitored by at least one sniffer, while [3,4] require each sniffer to monitor all available channels (regardless of whether the channels are being used or not by the nearby APs). By eliminating the scanning over unused channels, our approach provides more effective traffic sampling[1]. Secondly, we formulate and solve two optimization problems on sniffer channel selection: one minimizes the maximum number of channels that a sniffer listens to, and the other minimizes the total number of channels that the sniffers listen to[2]. The first objective is desirable because when a sniffer monitors less channels, it can spend more time on each of these channels; the second objective is desirable because it may reduce the number of sniffers needed (it may need less sniffers than the first objective, see Section 4). We develop a novel LP-relaxation based algorithm, and two simple greedy heuristic algorithms for the above two optimization problems. Through simulation, we demonstrate that all the algorithms are effective in achieving their optimization goals, and the LP-based algorithm outperforms the greedy heuristics.

The rest of the paper is organized as follows. Section 2 describes the problem setting. Sections 3 and 4 describe our sniffer channel selection algorithms and their evaluation, respectively. Finally, Section 5 concludes the paper.

2 Problem Setting

Consider a WLAN with a set of APs, V. Each AP uses a single radio, and hence a single channel, at any point of time (if an AP uses multiple channels simultaneously, we can regard it as multiple APs, each with a single channel).

[1] One motivation of scanning all the channels in [3,4] is that it can capture rogue APs that operate on unused channels. Rogue APs, however, can be effectively detected using other approaches such as [9,10].

[2] In practice, a network administrator may choose one of these two objectives based on the goals of the WLAN monitoring.

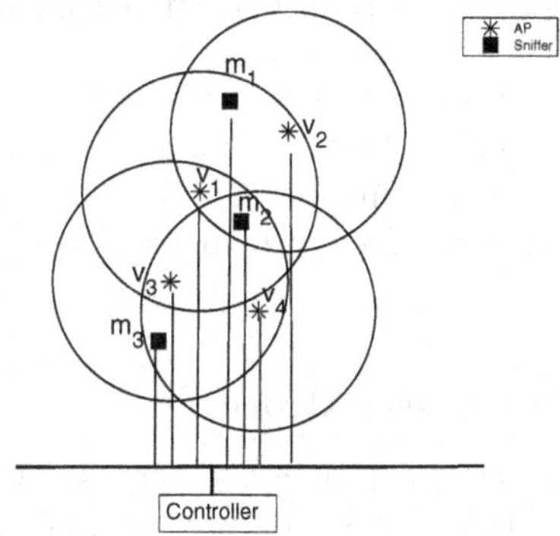

Fig. 1. Problem setting: a central controller controls the channels of the APs and determines the channel assignment for the sniffers

Let C denote the set of channels that the APs operate on. In particular, suppose AP v operates on channel c_v, $c_v \in C$. A set of sniffers, M, is spread out in the WLAN to monitor the APs. Let R_v denote the set of sniffers that are within the transmission range of v (i.e., R_v is the set of sniffers that can overhear the transmission of v when listening to channel c_v), $R_v \subseteq M$. We assume that $|R_v| \geq 1$, i.e., at least one sniffer can monitor v, $\forall v \in V$. Each sniffer has a single radio, and switches among multiple channels to monitor its nearby APs when these APs operate on different channels.

We assume that the WLAN uses a centralized management architecture (as commonly used in commercial products), where a central controller manages the operation of the APs. We assume that the central controller knows the location of the APs, and determines the channel for each AP. Furthermore, it knows the location of the sniffers, and determines the set of channels that each sniffer scans based on the locations of the APs, sniffers, and the channels of the APs. Fig. 1 illustrates the centralized management architecture. In this example, four APs, v_1, v_2, v_3, v_4, and three sniffers, m_1, m_2, m_3, are controlled by the centralized controller. APs v_1 and v_3 operate on channel 1; APs v_2 and v_4 operate on channel 2. Sniffer m_1 is in the transmission ranges of v_1 and v_2; sniffer m_2 is in the transmission ranges of all four APs; sniffer m_3 is in the transmission ranges of v_3 and v_4.

Let $\varphi(v)$ denote the set of sniffers that monitor AP v, referred to as *assignment* to v. Correspondingly, let $C_\varphi(m)$ denote the set of channels that sniffer m monitors. Then $C_\varphi(m) = \{c_v \mid m \in \varphi(v)\}$. We look at two variants of sniffer channel selection. Both variants require that each AP be monitored by at least one sniffer, i.e., $\varphi(v) \neq \emptyset, \forall v \in V$. In addition, the first variant requires minimizing the maximum number of channels that a sniffer listens to, i.e., minimizing $\max_{m \in M} |C_\varphi(m)|$. The second variant requires minimizing the sum of the channels that the sniffers listen to, i.e., minimizing $\sum_{m \in M} |C_\varphi(m)|$. We refer to these two variants as *min-max* and *min-sum sniffer channel selection problems*, respectively.

3 Algorithms for Sniffer Channel Selection

In this section, we develop three algorithms for sniffer channel selection. The first algorithm is based on LP relaxation. The second and third algorithms both use a greedy heuristic, targeting at the min-max and min-sum problem, respectively. We refer to the two greedy heuristics as *Greedy-max* and *Greedy-sum*, respectively.

3.1 LP-Relaxation Based Algorithm

The main idea of this algorithm is as follows. We first formulate the sniffer channel selection problem (the min-max or min-sum problem) as an integer programming (IP) problem, and then solve its corresponding linear programming (LP) problem (by relaxing the integer constraints). After obtaining the optimal solution to the LP problem, we convert it to the integer solution to the original IP problem. More specifically, let $x_{m,c}$ be a 0-1 random variable, $x_{m,c} = 1$ denotes that sniffer m monitors channel c; and $x_{m,c} = 0$ denotes otherwise. Then the min-max sniffer channel selection problem can be formulated as:

$$\text{minimize}: \max_{m \in M} \sum_{c \in C} x_{m,c} \tag{1}$$

$$\text{subject to:} \sum_{m \in R_v} x_{m,c_v} \geq 1, \forall v \in V \tag{2}$$

$$x_{m,c} \in \{0,1\} \tag{3}$$

Similarly, the min-sum problem can be formulated as an IP problem by simply replacing the objective function (1) with

$$\text{minimize}: \sum_{m \in M} \sum_{c \in C} x_{m,c} \tag{4}$$

We relax the integer constraint on $x_{m,c}$, and let $y_{m,c} \in [0,1]$ be the relaxed value of $x_{m,c}$. The original IP problems then become LP problems, which can be solved easily. After solving for $y_{m,c} \in [0,1]$, consider an AP $v \in V$ and the values of y_{m,c_v} for $m \in R_v$ (i.e., the sniffers in the transmission range of v). We round $y_{m,c}$ to obtain x_{m,c_v} as follows. Since an AP only needs to be monitored by one sniffer, we choose one monitor, m', that is closest to 1 among $y_{m,c_v}, \forall m \in R_v$ (i.e., it satisfies $y_{m',c_v} = \max_{m \in R_v} y_{m,c_v}$), and set x_{m',c_v} to 1.

Algorithm 1 summarizes this LP-relaxation based algorithm. Line 1 solves the LP problem (for the min-max or min-sum objective function) to obtain $y_{m,c} \in [0,1], \forall m \in M, \forall c \in C$. Line 2 initializes $x_{m,c}$ to zero, $\forall m \in M, \forall c \in C$. The algorithm then considers all the APs. For an AP $v \in V$, if one monitor, $m \in R_v$, is already assigned to monitor v's channel, c_v, we simply assign m to monitor v; otherwise, we set x_{m',c_v} to 1 where m' satisfies that $y_{m',c_v} = \max_{m \in R_v} y_{m,c_v}$. In the rest of the paper, when this LP-relaxation based algorithm solves the min-max LP problem, we refer to it as *LP-max*; otherwise (i.e., it solves the min-sum LP problem), we refer to it as *LP-sum*.

Algorithm 1. LP-relaxation based sniffer channel assignment

Solve the LP program (objective function (1) for min-max problem; objective function (4) for min-sum problem) to obtain $y_{m,c}, \forall m \in M, \forall c \in C$
$x_{m,c} = 0, \forall m \in M, \forall c \in C.$
$C_\varphi(m) = \emptyset$
for all $v \in V$ **do**
  if $\exists m \in R_v$ s.t. $x_{m,c_v} = 1$ **then**
    $\varphi(v) = \{m\}$
  else
    $m' = \arg\max_{m \in R_v} y_{m,c_v}$
    $x_{m',c_v} = 1$
    $C_{m'} = C_{m'} \cup \{c_v\}$
    $\varphi(v) = \{m'\}$
  end if
end for
Return(φ, C_φ)

We now illustrate this LP-relaxation based algorithm using the example in Fig. 1. Solving the min-max LP problem, we have $y_{m_1,1} = 0, y_{m_1,2} = 1, y_{m_2,1} = 1, y_{m_2,2} = 0, y_{m_3,1} = 0$, and $y_{m_3,2} = 2$. After the LP rounding, we have $C_\varphi(m_1) = \{2\}$, $C_\varphi(m_2) = \{1\}$, and $C_\varphi(m_3) = \{2\}$, leading to a solution of 1 for the min-max problem. Solving the min-sum LP problem, we have $y_{m_1,1} = y_{m_1,2} = 0, y_{m_2,1} = y_{m_2,2} = 1$, and $y_{m_3,1} = y_{m_3,2} = 0$. After the LP rounding, we have $C_\varphi(m_1) = \emptyset$, $C_\varphi(m_2) = \{1,2\}$, and $C_\varphi(m_3) = \emptyset$, leading to a solution of 2 for the min-sum problem.

We now present an approximation-ratio result for the LP-relaxation based algorithm.

Theorem 1. *LP-max is an $O(r)$-approximation algorithm for the min-max sniffer channel selection problem, and LP-sum is an $O(r)$-approximation algorithm for the min-sum problem, where $r = \max_{v \in V} |R_v|$, i.e., r is the maximum number of sniffers that are in the transmission range of an AP.*

Proof. Consider an arbitrary AP, v, and a sniffer $m \in R_v$. Our LP rounding guarantees that $x_{m,c_v} \leq r y_{m,c_v}$. This can be shown by considering the following two cases. When $y_{m,c_v} = \max_{m \in R_v} y_{m,c_v}$, by our LP rounding, $x_{m,c_v} = 1$, and we have $x_{m,c_v} \leq r y_{m,c_v}$ (since $y_{m,c_v} \geq 1/r$). When $y_{m,c_v} \neq \max_{m \in R_v} y_{m,c_v}$, by our LP rounding, $x_{m,c_v} = 0 \leq r y_{m,c_v}$. Since the above AP, v, is chosen arbitrarily, we have

$$\sum_{c \in C} x_{m,c} \leq r \sum_{c \in C} y_{m,c}, \forall m \in M.$$

Let n_m^* represent the optimal solution to the min-max sniffer channel selection problem. We have

$$\max_{m \in M} \sum_{c \in C} x_{m,c} \leq r(\max_{m \in M} \sum_{c \in C} y_{m,c}) \leq r n_m^*. \tag{5}$$

The second inequality above is because the LP provides a lower bound to the original problem. From (5), LP-max is an $O(r)$-approximation algorithm for the min-max sniffer channel selection problem. Similarly, let n_s^* represent the optimal solution to the min-sum problem. We have

$$\sum_{m \in M} \sum_{c \in C} x_{m,c} \leq r\Big(\sum_{m \in M} \sum_{c \in C} y_{m,c}\Big) \leq r n_s^*. \tag{6}$$

Hence LP-sum is an $O(r)$-approximation algorithm for the min-sum problem.

3.2 Greedy-Max Algorithm

Greedy-max heuristic is designed for the min-max objective. Its main idea is as follows. Initially, a sniffer, m, is assigned to monitor an AP, v, as long as m is in the transmission range of v. The algorithm then runs in iterations. In each iteration, it finds the sniffer with the maximum number of channels and removes one channel from this sniffer when feasible (i.e., while still satisfying the monitoring constraints). The iteration stops when none of the sniffers can remove any channel.

Algorithm 2 summarizes this algorithm. Line 1 initializes $\varphi(v)$ to be the set of sniffers that are in the transmission range of v, $\forall v \in V$. Let $V_{m,c}$ denote the set

Algorithm 2. Greedy-max

1: $\varphi(v) = \{m \mid m \in R_v\}, \forall v \in V$
2: $C_\varphi(m) = \emptyset$, $V_{m,c} = \emptyset$, $\forall m \in M, c \in C$
3: **for all** $v \in V$ **do**
4:     **for all** $m \in M$ **do**
5:         **if** $m \in R_v$ **then**
6:             $C_\varphi(m) = C_\varphi(m) \cup \{c_v\}$, $V_{m,c_v} = V_{m,c_v} \cup \{v\}$
7:         **end if**
8:     **end for**
9: **end for**
10: **repeat**
11:     $M' = \emptyset$
12:     **for all** $m \in M$ **do**
13:         **if** $\exists c \in C_\varphi(m)$ s.t. $\forall v \in V_{m,c}, |\varphi(v)| \geq 2$ **then**
14:             $M' = M' \cup m$
15:         **end if**
16:     **end for**
17:     **if** $M' \neq \emptyset$ **then**
18:         Let m be a monitor in M' that monitors the largest number of channels
19:         $C_\varphi(m)' = \{c \mid c \in C_\varphi(m), |\varphi(v)| \geq 2, \forall v \in V_{m,c}\}$
20:         Pick $c \in C_\varphi(m)'$ that has the smallest $|V_{m,c}|$
21:         $C_\varphi(m) = C_\varphi(m) \setminus \{c\}$
22:         $\varphi(v) = \varphi(v) \setminus \{m\}, \forall v \in V_{m,c}$
23:         $V_{m,c} = \emptyset$
24:     **end if**
25: **until** M' is empty
26: Return(φ, C_φ)

of APs that sniffer m monitors on channel c. Lines 2-9 initialize $C_\varphi(m)$ and $V_{m,c}$, $\forall m \in M, c \in C$. In each iteration (lines 11-23), let M' record the set of sniffers that can remove at least one channel. It then picks a sniffer, m, that monitors the maximum number of channels from M'. Afterwards, it finds a channel, c, that can be removed and removes it from $C_\varphi(m)$ (if multiple such channels exist, it chooses to remove the channel with the smallest number of APs, see line 20). Last, line 22 removes m from the assignment of all the APs in $V_{m,c}$ (since m does not monitor channel c any more).

When using this algorithm to solve the example in Fig. 1, we have $C_\varphi(m_1) = \{2\}$, $C_\varphi(m_2) = \{1\}$, $C_\varphi(m_3) = \{2\}$, leading to a solution of 1 for the min-max problem, and a solution of 3 for the min-sum problem.

3.3 Greedy-Sum Algorithm

Greedy-sum heuristic is designed for the min-sum objective. It models the sniffer channel selection problem as a minimum set covering problem: we map each sniffer to $|C|$ *virtual sniffers*, each monitoring one channel in C, then the min-sum problem is equivalent to finding the minimum number of virtual sniffers so that all APs are monitored and the number of virtual sniffers (and hence the sum of the channels used by all the sniffers) is minimized. Many algorithms have been proposed for the minimum set covering problem. Greedy-sum follows a greedy algorithm for minimum set covering problem [5]. It runs in iterations. In each iteration, it picks a sniffer and channel pair that monitors the maximum number of APs. The iteration stops when all the APs are monitored.

Algorithm 3 summarizes this algorithm (we used a similar algorithm for scheduling sniffers to detect rogue APs in [10]). Let $V_{m,c}$ denote the set of APs that sniffer m monitors on channel c. Line 1 initializes $C_\varphi(m)$ to be an empty

Algorithm 3. Greedy-sum

1: $C_\varphi(m) = \emptyset$, $V_{m,c} = \emptyset$, $\forall m \in M, c \in C$
2: **for all** $v \in V$ **do**
3:     **for all** $m \in M$ **do**
4:         **if** $m \in R_v$ **then**
5:             $V_{m,c_v} = V_{m,c_v} \cup \{v\}$
6:         **end if**
7:     **end for**
8: **end for**
9: $V' = V$
10: **repeat**
11:     pick m, c such that $|V_{m,c}| = \max_{m' \in M, c' \in C} |V_{m',c'}|$
12:     $\varphi(v) = \{m\}, \forall v \in V_{m,c}$
13:     $C_\varphi(m) = C_\varphi(m) \cup \{c\}$
14:     $V_{m',c} = V_{m',c} \setminus V_{m,c}, \forall m' \in M$
15:     $V' = V' \setminus V_{m,c}$
16: **until** V' is empty
17: Return(φ, C_φ)

set, and lines 1-8 initialize $V_{m,c}$, $\forall m \in M, c \in C$. Line 9 initializes, V', the set of APs that are not monitored by a sniffer, to V. The algorithm then run in iterations until V' is empty. Using a greedy strategy, line 11 chooses the monitor, m, and the channel, c, such that $|V_{m,c}| = \max_{m' \in M, c' \in C} |V_{m',c'}|$ (if multiple such sniffers exist, we choose the one with the minimum $|C_\varphi(m)|$). Line 12 assigns m to all the APs in $V_{m,c}$; and line 13 adds channel, c, into $C_\varphi(m)$. Afterwards, since the APs in $V_{m,c}$ have already been monitored, line 14 removes $V_{m,c}$ from $V_{m',c}, \forall m' \in M$, and line 15 removes $V_{m,c}$ from V'.

Following the results in [5], the approximation ratio of Greedy-sum is H_d for the min-sum problem, where $H_d = \sum_{i=1}^{d} 1/i$ is the d-th harmonic number, and d is the maximum number of APs that a sniffer can monitor in its neighborhood.

When using this algorithm to solve the example in Fig. 1, we have $C_\varphi(m_1) = \emptyset$, $C_\varphi(m_2) = \{1, 2\}$, $C_\varphi(m_3) = \emptyset$, leading to a solution of 2 for the min-sum problem, and a solution of 2 for the min-max problem.

4 Performance Evaluation

Our performance evaluation uses an empirical dataset that contains both the coordinates and channels for the APs deployed at Dartmouth campus. We consider two 500 m $\times$ 500 m areas in this data set: one has approximately 400 APs, and the other has approximately 200 APs. These APs use both 802.11b/g and 802.11a, and operate on 12 orthogonal 2.4GHz/5GHz channels. The transmission range of each AP is set to 100 m.

To systematically evaluate the performance of our algorithms, for each area we consider, we generate 10,000 topologies by virtually placing sniffers uniformly randomly into the area. The number of sniffers is randomly chosen from 1 to the number of APs. For each topology, we obtain a pair (n_a, n_s), where n_a is the number of APs that can be monitored by at least one sniffer, and n_s is the number of sniffers that can monitor at least one AP (i.e., sniffers that within the transmission range of at least one AP). Therefore n_a and n_s can be smaller than the number of APs and sniffers in the area, respectively). We refer to the ratio, n_s/n_a, as *sniffer density*.

Fig. 2 shows the results for the area with 400 APs (the results for the area with 200 APs are similar). Fig. 2(a) plots the maximum number of channels that a sniffer monitors. The results of the two algorithms that target at this optimization goal (i.e., LP-max and Greedy-max) are plotted in the figure. For comparison, we also plot the results under Greedy-sum. The x-axis of the figure represents sniffer density, i.e., n_s/n_a. The results are aggregated over a bin size of 0.1, i.e., the result under $n_s/n_a = x$ is the average of all the topologies with $n_s/n_a \in (x - 0.1, x]$. We observe that for all three algorithms, as expected, the maximum number of channels used by the sniffers reduces as the sniffer density increases. Furthermore, Greedy-max slightly outperforms LP-max, and both Greedy-max and LP-max outperform Greedy-sum. We also observe a diminishing gain from increasing the density of sniffers: the maximum number of channels decreases dramatically first and then less dramatically afterwards.

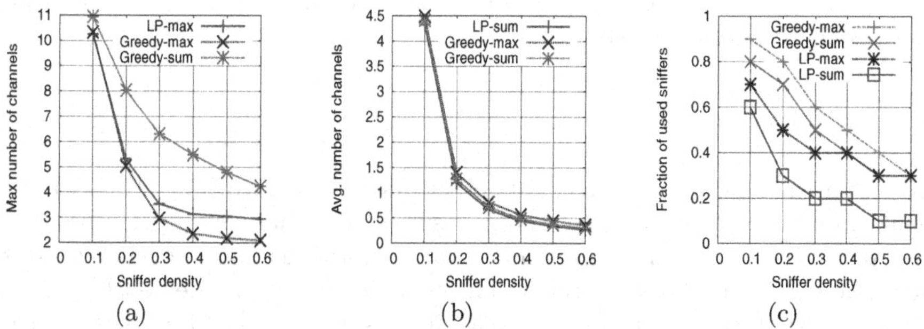

Fig. 2. Results for 400 APs: (a) maximum number of channels that a sniffer monitors, (b) average number of channels that a sniffer monitors, and (c) fraction of sniffers that are used for monitoring

Fig. 2(b) plots the average number of channels that a sniffer monitors. The results of the two algorithms that target at this optimization goal (i.e., LP-sum and Greedy-sum) are plotted in the figure. For comparison, we also plot the results under Greedy-max. We observe that all three algorithms lead to similar performance, and LP-sum slightly outperforms the other two. Again, we observe a diminishing gain from increasing the density of sniffers.

For all the algorithms, the channel assignment solution may not assign a sniffer to monitor any AP (even though the sniffer is in the transmission range of some APs and can be used to monitor these APs). Fig. 2(c) plots the fraction of sniffers that are used (i.e., monitor at least one AP) for various sniffer densities under all the four algorithms. We observe that, for the same sniffer density, the LP-based algorithms require less sniffers than the greedy heuristics: LP-sum requires significantly less sniffers than Greedy-sum, and LP-max requires significantly less sniffers than Greedy-max (particularly for low sniffer densities). We also observe that the min-sum problem tends to require less sniffers than the min-max problem (e.g., the fraction of used sniffers is the lowest under LP-sum, much lower than that under LP-max). This is not very surprising since the channel assignment in the min-max problem needs to be balanced (for the min-max goal), while the min-sum problem does not have this requirement.

Last, combining the results in Figures 2(a),(b), and (c), we conclude that the LP-based algorithms outperform the two greedy heuristics since for both the min-max and min-sum problems, LP-max and LP-sum achieve similar objective values as their greedy counterparts, while using much less sniffers. We also observe that, when deploying sniffers at appropriate positions, the LP-based algorithms only require a small number of sniffers to achieve most of the gains. For instance, for the min-max problem, LP-max leads to a maximum of 3 channels over all sniffers when the number of sniffers is only 12% of the number of APs (this can be seen from Figures 2(a) and (c), which show that when the sniffer density is 0.3, the maximum number of channels is 3, and only 40% of the sniffers are used). For the min-sum problem, LP-sum only requires the number of sniffers to be as low as 6% of the number of APs (this can be seen from Fig. 2(c):

for a sniffer density of 0.1, 0.2, and 0.3, the fraction of used sniffers is around 0.6, 0.3 and 0.2, respectively).

5 Conclusions

In this paper, we studied sniffer channel selection for monitoring WLANs. In particular, we formulated min-max and min-sum sniffer channel selection problems, and proposed a novel LP-relaxation based algorithm, and two simple greedy heuristic algorithms to solve them. Through simulation, we demonstrated that all the algorithms are effective in achieving their optimization goals, and the LP-based algorithm outperforms the greedy heuristics.

Acknowledgement. This work was partially supported by NSF CAREER award 0746841, UConn Faculty Large Grant, and the Science and Technology Directorate of the U.S. Department of Homeland Security under Award NBCH2050002.

References

1. Chandra, R., Padhye, J., Wolman, A., Zill, B.: A location-based management system for enterprise wireless LANs. In: NSDI (2007)
2. Cheng, Y.-C., Bellardo, J., Benko, P., Snoeren, A.C., Voelker, G.M., Savage, S.: Jigsaw: Solving the puzzle of enterprise 802.11 analysis. In: Proc. of ACM SIGCOMM, Pisa, Italy (September 2006)
3. Deshpande, U., Henderson, T., Kotz, D.: Channel sampling strategies for monitoring wireless networks. In: Proc. of the Second Workshop on Wireless Network Measurements, Boston, MA (April 2006)
4. Deshpande, U., McDonald, C., Kotz, D.: Coordinated sampling to improve the efficiency of wireless network monitoring. In: ICON (November 2007)
5. Hochbaum, D.S.: Approximating covering and packing problems: set cover, vertex cover, independent set, and related problems. In: Hochbaum, D.S. (ed.) Approximation algorithms for NP-hard problems, pp. 94–143. PWS Publishing Co., Boston (1996)
6. Jardosh, A.P., Ramachandran, K.N., Almeroth, K.C.: Understanding link-layer behavior in highly congested IEEE 802.11b wireless networks. In: E-WIND (2005)
7. Mahajan, R., Rodrig, M., Wetherall, D., Zahorjan, J.: Analyzing the MAC-level behavior of wireless networks in the wild. In: Proc. of ACM SIGCOMM (2006)
8. Sheth, A., Doerr, C., Grunwald, D., Han, R., Sicker, D.C.: MOJO: A distributed physical layer anomaly detection system for 802.11 WLANs. In: Proc. of ACM MobiSys, pp. 191–204 (2006)
9. Wei, W., Suh, K., Wang, B., Gu, Y., Kurose, J., Towsley, D.: Passive online rogue access point detection using sequential hypothesis testing with TCP ACK-pairs. In: IMC (2007)
10. Yan, B., Chen, G., Wang, J., Yin, H.: Robust detection of unauthorized wireless access points. ACM/Springer Mobile Networks and Applications (in press)
11. Yeo, J., Youssef, M., Agrawala, A.: A framework for wireless LAN monitoring and its applications. In: WiSe (2004)

Uplink Resource Management Design in Multi-access Wireless Networks

Mira Yun[1], Timothy Kim[1], Yu Zhou[1], Amrinder Arora[2], Joseph Gomes[2], and Hyeong-Ah Choi[1]

[1] Dept. of Computer Science, The George Washington University, Washington DC
{mirayun,timothyk,yuzhou,hchoi}@gwu.edu
[2] Dept. of Computer Science, Bowie State University, Bowie MD
{aarora,jgomes}@bowiestate.edu

Abstract. In this paper, we develop a new uplink resource management scheme in heterogeneous networking environments that support multiple radio access technologies (RATs). A common radio resource management (CRRM) model is utilized to handle uplink traffic in multi-access radio networks. To evaluate the effect and performance of CRRM, a simulation study is conducted on scenarios where different scheduling algorithms are applied with and without vertical handoffs through the aid of CRRM.

1 Introduction

Rapid emergence of newer network infrastructure creates a heterogeneous wireless environment where multiple radio access technology co-exist over a single region with different characteristics. In order to support various radio access technologies (RATs) and provide better quality of service (QoS) for users, radio access terminals are being equipped with multiple RATs. One of key issues in such networking environment is how to efficiently utilize the resources of the different RATs while simultaneously providing the desired QoS for users. For service providers, a cost efficient system that balance the load among networks with different RATs is not only desirable but necessary. From the user's perspective, regardless of which networks their devices choose to use, the user experience must satisfy the QoS requirements. It is also critical to give users the freedom of moving across all network providers and regions and changing communication devices while maintaining the continuity of their service.

There are many research and projects that have focussed on how to manage the downlink traffic in multi-access network. However, the new trend in wireless services is shifting from downlink centric services to bidirectional and uplink centric services [1]. Through the popularity of social networking services (e.g. Facebook, YouTube, and Flickr), we are observing the ever increasing amount of user generated content (UGC) also known as user created content (UCC). Due to the rise of uplink traffic via UGC and new services such as video telephony and FTP upload, it is critical for a multi-access network to have an efficient resource management scheme that especially considers high uplink traffic.

B. Liu et al. (Eds.): WASA 2009, LNCS 5682, pp. 499–508, 2009.

In this paper, we develop a common radio resource management (CRRM) model in heterogeneous network environments that support multiple radio access technologies (RATs). Multiple scenarios are devised where different scheduling algorithms are applied with and without vertical handoffs through the aid of CRRM. The scenarios are then simulated on an in-house simulator called MNAS (Multi-Network Access Simulator).

Our paper is organized as follows. In section 2, we present enhanced uplink technologies, covering two most prominent networks available today that handles high amount of uplink traffic: HSUPA and WiMAX. The design of CRRM system that handle efficient management of network resources is presented in Section 3. Performance analysis of CRRM and each scheduling algorithms using a simulator called MNAS (Multi-Network Access Simulator), and its results are presented in Section 4. Finally concluding remarks and future work considerations are presented in Section 5.

2 Resource Management for Uplink Enhancements

Scheduling for uplink services, in contrast to downlink services [2][3], is more complicated due to various reasons. The uplink traffic amount is not known in advance to the central scheduler residing in the base station. Further complicating the scheduling mechanism, base station and mobile stations must work cooperatively in centralized and distributed manners. Moreover, as the transformation of mobile networks from homogeneous closed systems to Internet-connected open networks presents resource management challenges, uplink scheduling and access selection for call admission and vertical handover (handovers to cells using different RATs) have been considered as key management issues [1]. In this section, we briefly review typical uplink enhancement technologies with their well-known scheduling algorithms.

2.1 HSUPA

HSUPA is introduced to improve the capacity of WCDMA uplink in 3GPP Release 6. As the new uplink transport channel, Enhanced-Dedicated Channel (E-DCH) supports fast Node B based uplink scheduling, fast physical layer hybrid ARQ (HARQ) retransmission schemes and, optionally, a shorter transmission time interval (TTI) (2ms) to reduce delays, increase the data rate (up to 5Mbps) and improve the capacity of the uplink [4].

The overall goal of the scheduler is to allocate a large part of the shared resource to users who momentarily require high data rates, while avoiding large interference peaks to keep the operation of the system stable. To access this goal in the uplink direction, tolerance interference or the total received power at Node B is determined by the common resource shared among the mobile stations. This common uplink resource amount depends on data rate used and higher data rate requires larger transmission power and resource consumption. There are researches on the uplink scheduling subject to define an optimum power and

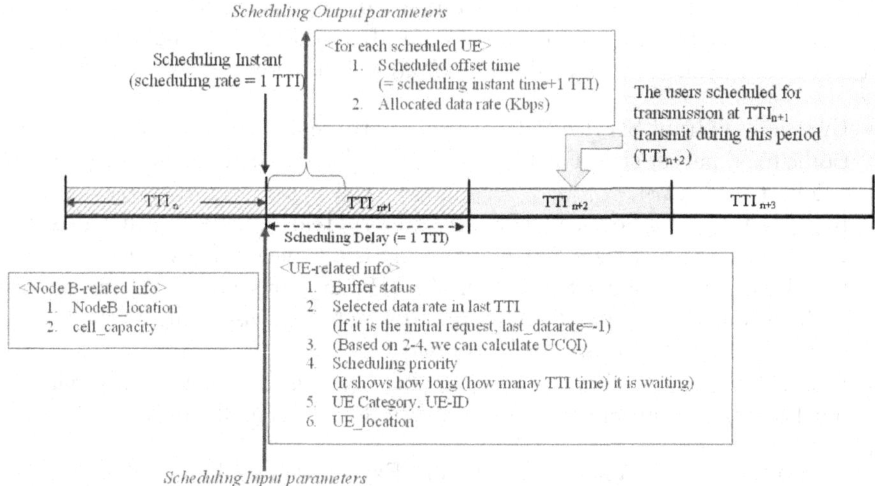

Fig. 1. HSUPA packet scheduler operation

rate allocation scheme that maximizes throughput [5][6]. All proposed solutions assume that the WCDMA system operates with a TDM overlay to perform a simultaneous rate and time scheduling.

Figure 1 illustrates the process of HSUPA packet scheduler (PS). The PS provides scheduled offset time and allocated data rate to each user equipment (UE) on every TTI. All UE requesting to be scheduled provide its buffer status, selected data rate in last TTI and scheduling priority data to the PS and PS allocates appropriate amount of resources to UE based on the cell capacity.

In MNAS, we implemented round robin (RR) and proportional fair (PF) algorithms in HSUPA PS. In RR, PS does not take into consideration the channel-quality but only uses UE's buffer-state data. The buffer-state data contains the delay of the packet at queue head. Before allocating resources for uploads, PS first sorts user equipment (UE) by the delay value in the buffer-state data. Then PS allocates resources based on UE's upload limitation and cell's available capacity in sorted order. If a UE is not scheduled then the delay value will increase, thus increasing its chance of being scheduled in the next round.

The PF algorithm, uses the Uplink Channel Quality Indicator (UCQI) as defined in [5] and average uplink rate to determine the resource allocation to a UE. As the average uplink rate increases, the scheduling priority rate of UE decreases where as the channel quality and the priority rate have direct relationship. This provides fail balance between user fairness and cell throughput.

2.2 WiMAX

WiMAX 802.16 has become the most promising wireless telecommunication technology that can be used for metropolitan area access networks. Though the standard of WiMAX has evolved from the original 802.16 to the latest 802.16e which supports full mobility, some standard details have not been completed yet. The scheduling algorithm is one of them. In WiMAX 802.16-2004, four QoS categories are defined for both downlink and uplink traffic.

- Unsolicited Grant Service (UGS): It supports real-time data traffic with periodic fixed packet size. The typical T1/E1, VoIP without silence suppression belong to this class.
- Real-Time Polling Service (rtPS): It supports real-time data traffic also, but with various packet size. Video streaming is a typical rtPS service.
- Non-Real-Time Polling Service (nrtPS): It supports non real-time service with various packet size, the QoS requirement is not as strong as the former two. FTP and HTTP are nrtPS service.
- Best Effort Service (BE): All the applications that belong to this class do not have QoS requirements. For example, E-mail is a BE service.

In WiMAX 802.16e, a new QoS category Extended Real-Time Polling Service (ertPS) is added, which combines some features from both UGS and rtPS and supports Real-time traffic with variable data rate as well.

Generally, UGS has the highest priority to be scheduled since it is real-time required and the data are loaded periodically with fixed size. The Scheduler provides grants to each SS the assigned symbols and subchannels according to the Maximum Sustained Traffic Rate (MSTR), the Minimum Reserved Traffic Rate (MRTR) and the Maximum Latency. As for rtPS, it also has real-time requirement but with various packet size in fixed interval time. Since rtPS is a polling service, in the uplink scheduling, firstly, the BS calculate the polling interval time for each connection based on the QoS requirements before data transmission. The polls indicated in UL_MAP are broadcasted through the downlink channels to all SSs. After receiving the polls, only those SSs having been polled will be assigned uplink bandwidth which is used for uplink data transmission. Similarly, nrtPS is also real-time required service but has looser QoS requirements than rtPS. Usually nrtPS has a larger polling interval time up to one second. Besides unicast polling which is the same as rtPS, nrtPS is supported by contention-based polling as well. Since BE service doesn't have any QoS requirement, any BE connection will be admitted. BE has the lowest scheduling priority, i.e., BE connection is scheduled only if all other higher services have been scheduled.

The service with lower priority is scheduled only when all services with higher priorities have been scheduled. Within each scheduling service type, we implement RR and PF scheduling algorithms. RR algorithm allocates its resources in the order of mobile stations (MS) IDs. PF uses the ratio between Signal to interference-plus-noise ratio (SINR) value and average uplink rate to determine the allocation ordering. In both algorithms, only those MSs whose queue is not empty and the size of allocation slot is less than the size of the available slot in the frame will be scheduled.

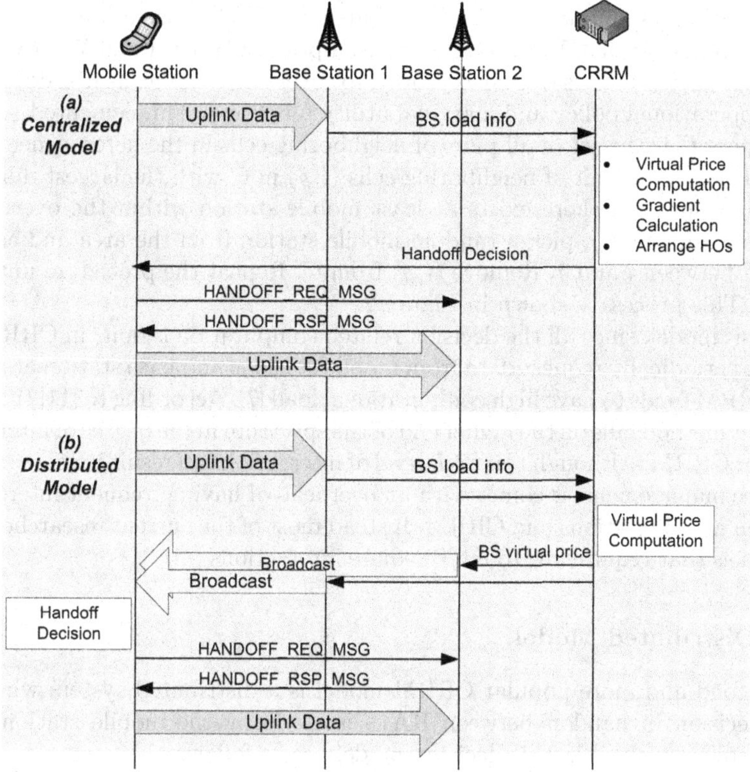

Fig. 2. Uplink CRRM Flow Diagram

3 CRRM System Model

There are many research projects that focus on effects of CRRM on heterogeneous networks with downlink traffic focus. [7] and [8] present a CRRM model based on marginal utility functions. [9] approaches the CRRM issue by minimizing the vertical handoff rate and service cost. [10] introduces a new entity in a multi-access network called Wireless QoS Broker that aids CRRM in QoS management. Most of current research efforts focus on the services that are geared towards downlink traffic. Our system model applies the concept of CRRM in a heterogeneous network environment that are composed of uplink services.

We propose two CRRM system models in making management decision within a multi-access network. First is centralized system where CRRM makes all the handoff decisions for each individual mobile station. Second is distributed system where handoff decisions are made by mobile stations.

3.1 Centralized Model

In centralized model, each base station reports the uplink load information to CRRM. CRRM computes the cost information (virtual price) of each base station, using its uplink load (L_{up}) and capacity (C_{up}) information. MNAS only deals with data traffic. Within it, the virtual price of HSUPA and WiMAX is set as $(L_{up}/C_{up})^2 + 1$. This can be expanded to cover voice traffic, as it is done in [7], where operational policy and marginal utility function are implemented.

Suppose C is the set of all pairs of neighboring cells in the heterogeneous network. Then find a pair of neighboring cells (i, j) in C with the largest difference of virtual prices. If there exists at least mobile station within the overlapping area between i and j, pick a random mobile station from the area and assign a handoff between i and j. Remove (i, j) from C. Repeat the procedure until C is empty. This process is shown in Figure 2.

In this model, since all the decision related computation is done in CRRM and it must periodically request data from mobile stations and base station at a rapid rate CRRM tends to have high computational load [7]. According to [11] this management method falls on the higher end of the spectrum in the degree of interaction scale for CRRM. Although this high level of interaction can result in more efficient resource management, it comes with an overhead of having frequent interactions between mobile stations and CRRM. Instead most of the current researches focus on models that require low to intermediate interactions [11].

3.2 Distributed Model

The second and more popular CRRM model is a distributed system where the final decision in handoff between RATs is made by the mobile stations. The major steps involved in this decision model are as follows.

Virtual Price Computation: First, each base station periodically sends its attribute data over to the CRRM, which then computes the virtual price of each base station based on its load, capacity, or delay data, or combination of them. CRRM can be designed so that virtual price can be a based on the type of service that is being provided by the base stations.

Virtual Price Broadcast: Once the virtual prices has been calculated by the CRRM, those values are broadcasted to all the mobile stations. Period at which these broadcast occur is typically longer than the calculation period of centralized CRRM model

Handoff Decision: Finally mobile stations makes the handoff decisions based on virtual prices that it received. More precisely, handoff is made to the base station with lowest virtual price.

There are two problems that arises when the handoff decisions are made by the each individual mobile stations. One is mass handoff effect where all or most mobile station within a cell decides to switch at once. The other is ping-pong effect. This occurs when a mobile station decides to perform handoff one right after another. To prevent these problematic issues, a ping-pong time is set after a handoff where another handoff is prevented.

4 Performance Analysis

The performance of our CRRM (distributed model) is analyzed by using a C-based simulator called MNAS (Multi-Network Access Simulator) that we developed at GWU. In MNAS we implemented two uplink enhanced networks, HSUPA and WiMAX. For each network, we implemented two well-known scheduling algorithm, RR and PF. Thus the packet scheduler controls each terminal's transmitting time and the rate in the network and our CRRM handles the resource in the different RATs.

In our simulation the network topology consists of nine WCDMA-HSUPA cells and nine WiMAX cells arranged in a grid pattern. The cells are positioned closely so that each cell has overlapping area with its neighboring cells. The cell capacity of each cell type is defined as follows: 2Mbps with 700 meter radius for HSDPA cell; and 8.47Mbps with 500 meter radius for WiMAX. The type of uplink service generated by the mobile stations are described in Table 1. The four types of services, MMS, USB Modem, Video Telephony, and FTP Upload has the usage distribution ratio of 20 : 20 : 30 : 30, respectively. In WiMAX, the services are mapped as BE, nrtPS, rtPS, and nrtPS, respectively. 70 percent of the mobile stations has mobility of 5 meters per second. 1000 mobile stations with both HSUPA and WiMAX capabilities is simulated.

Table 1. Service Type Parameters

Service	Packet Size	Packet Interarrival Time
MMS	lognormal(1.28, 1.66)	N/A
USB Modem	lognormal(1.17, 5.97)	lognormal(2.04, -1.23)
Video Telephony	lognormal(6.1, 0.54)	deterministic(0.1)
FTP Upload	lognormal(14.45, 0.35)	exponential(180)
Service	**Session Duration**	**Session Interarrival Time**
MMS	lognormal(1.54, 0.54)	exponential(50)
USB Modem	lognormal(0.15, 0.003)	exponential(89388)
Video Telephony	lognormal(5.015, 0.06)	exponential(200)
FTP Upload	exponential(300)	exponential(500)

4.1 Scenario 1 – Without CRRM

For the total simulation time of 600 seconds, according to the distributions from Table 1, uplink traffic is generated. CRRM does not make any handoff decisions for this simulation. It uses proportional fair scheduling algorithm.

Figure 3 shows the throughput of each network type when CRRM is not applied. We observe here that amount of throughput on HSUPA and WiMAX is similar. However, when load is observed, HSUPA reaches near 80% in load and WiMAX is at around 10% - Figure 4 (a).

4.2 Scenario 2 – With CRRM

Likewise, according to the distributions from Table 1, uplink traffic is generated for 600 seconds. This time, however, CRRM uses distributed model to allow handoff in mobile devices. It also uses proportional fair scheduling algorithm.

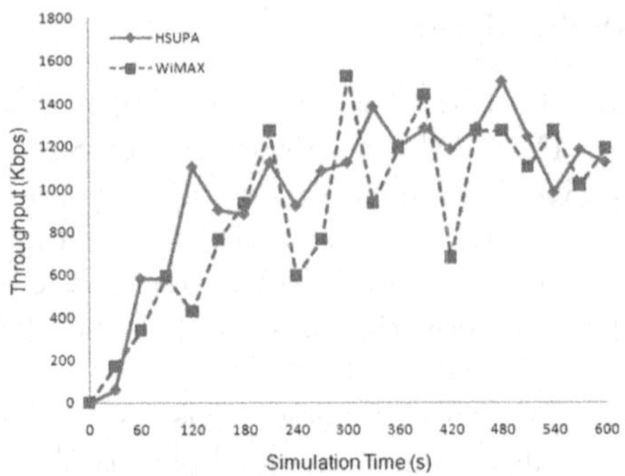

Fig. 3. Throughput without CRRM

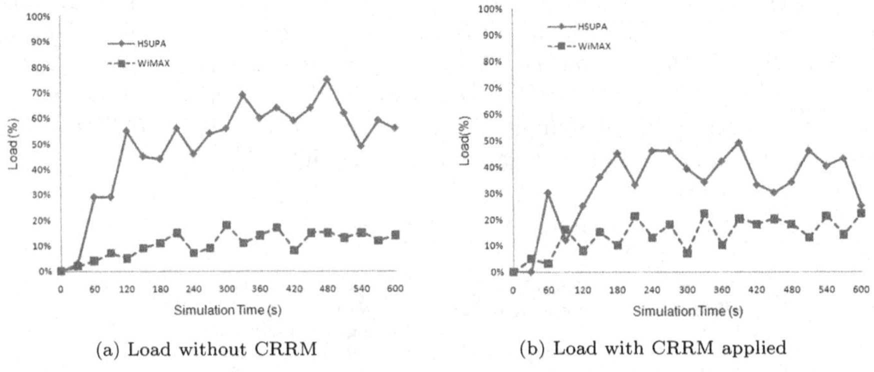

(a) Load without CRRM

(b) Load with CRRM applied

Fig. 4. Simulation Results with and without CRRM

Figure 4 (b) shows the load of each network type when CRRM is applied. We observed that when CRRM is applied, load balancing occurs, effectively dropping HSUPA's average load from 52.74% to 36.19%, while increasing the average load on WiMAX from 12.17% to 15.45%.

Call delay for a mobile station is measured from where a particular packet arrives at the top most position in the transfer buffer to the time when it leaves the buffer. Table 2 and 3 show the average call delay of all the cells in the network. In the case where CRRM is applied, not only network experiences load balancing but call delay gets balanced over the networks.

4.3 Scenario 3 – CRRM with Scheduling Algorithms

Similar to Scenario 1, with CRRM applied, uplink traffic is generated for 600 seconds according to the distributions from Table 1. Instead of using proportional fair, round robin scheduling algorithm is used.

As shown in Table 2 and 3, when CRRM is applied, the network is effected differently depending on the scheduling algorithm used. In the case of RR, it exhibits fair scheduling regardless of the service types nor channel conditions. It performs worse than PF scheduling algorithm which considers the system's average throughput and the current available data rate. Moreover, due the fact that RR does not take in to the consideration the delay data in scheduling, it experiences higher average call delay. Therefore, to achieve efficient resource management scheduling algorithm must be considered along side with CRRM.

Table 2. PF Scheduling Algorithm Simulation Results Without CRRM

	HSUPA	WiMAX
Cell Throughput	1,054,708 bps	1,030,541 bps
Cell Load	52.74%	12.17%
Cell Delay	873 ms	54 ms

Table 3. Scheduling Algorithm Simulation Results With CRRM

	HSUPA (PF)	WiMAX (PF)	HSUPA (RR)	WiMAX (RR)
Cell Throughput	723,807 bps	1,308,216 bps	697,654 bps	1,110,836 bps
Cell Load	36.19%	15.45%	34.88%	13.11%
Cell Delay	232 ms	61 ms	1328 ms	33 ms

5 Conclusion and Future Work

In this paper, we surveyed the current uplink driven wireless network technology and proposed an efficient technique for access selection in multi-access networks. Results obtained through simulations using MNAS showed that distributed CRRM system significantly performs better than when CRRM is not present. Moreover, our simulation result indicates that scheduling algorithm must be taken in to consideration along side with CRRM in order to achieve efficient resource management. It should be interesting to implement and analyze an environment where both uplink and downlink traffic are considered together. We plan to extend our research effort in this direction.

References

1. Yun, M., Rong, Y., Zhou, Y., Choi, H.-A., Kim, J.-H., Sohn, J., Choi, H.-I.: Analysis of Uplink Traffic Characteristics and Impact on Performance in Mobile Data Networks. In: IEEE International Conference on Communications, ICC 2008, May 19-23, pp. 4564–4568 (2008)
2. Gomes, J., Yun, M., Choi, H.-A., Kim, J.-H., Sohn, J.K., Choi, H.I.: Scheduling Algorithms for Policy Driven QoS Support in HSDPA Networks. In: IEEE VTC 2007, Dublin, Ireland, April 22-25 (2007)
3. Hwang, J., Rafaei, M.T., Choi, H.-A., Kim, J.-H., Sohn, J.K., Choi, H.I.: Policy-based QoS-aware Packet Scheduling for CDMA 1xEvDO. In: Proc. of ICC 2007, Glasgow, Scotland, June 24-27 (2007)

4. Holma, H., Toskala, A. (eds.): HSDPA/HSUPA for UMTS: High Speed Radio Access for Mobile Communications. John Wiley & Sons, Chichester (2006)
5. Rosa, C., Outes, J., Sorensen, T.B., Wigard, J., Mogensen, P.E.: Combined time and code division scheduling for enhanced uplink packet access in WCDMA. In: IEEE Vehicular Technology Conference, VTC 2004-Fall, September 26-29, pp. 851–855 (2004)
6. Boche, H., Wiczanowski, M.: Optimal scheduling for high speed uplink packet access - a cross-layer approach. In: IEEE Vehicular Technology Conference, VTC 2004-Spring, May 17-19, vol. 5, pp. 2575–2579 (2004)
7. Jin, F., Choi, H.-A., Kim, J.-H., Sohn, J.K., Choi, H.I.: Common Radio Resource Management for Access Selection in Multi-Access Networks. In: IEEE Radio and Wireless Symposium, Orlando, FL, January 22-24 (2008)
8. Jin, F., Gomes, J., Zhou, Y., Choi, H.-A., Kim, J.-H., Sohn, J.K., Choi, H.I.: Virtual Price Based Policy Enforcement for Access Selection and Vertical Handover in Multi-Access Networks. In: Proc. OPNETWORK 2007, Washington, DC, August 27-31 (2007)
9. Hasib, A., Fapojuwo, A.O.: Analysis of Common Radio Resource Management Scheme for End-to-End QoS Support in Multiservice Heterogeneous Wireless Networks. IEEE Transactions on Vehicular Technology 57(4), 2426–2439 (2008)
10. Ferrus, R., Gelonch, A., Sallent, O., Perez-Romero, J., Nafisi, N., Dohler, M.: A feasible approach for QoS management in coordinated heterogeneous radio access networks. In: 24th IEEE International Performance, Computing, and Communications Conference, IPCCC 2005, April 7-9, pp. 607–614 (2005)
11. Wu, L., Sandrasegaran, K.: A Survey on Common Radio Resource Management. In: The 2nd International Conference on Wireless Broadband and Ultra Wideband Communications, AusWireless 2007, August 27-30, pp. 66–66 (2007)

Throughput Measurement-Based Access Point Selection for Multi-rate Wireless LANs

Yanxiao Zhao[1], Min Song[1], Jun Wang[1], and E.K. Park[2]

[1] Department of Electrical and Computer Engineering, Old Dominion University
[2] Department of Computer Science Electrical Engineering, University of Missouri at Kansas City

Abstract. In this paper, we propose a novel access point (AP) selection algorithm to maximize the system throughput while considering user fairness. The main idea is that when a new-coming user enters an overlapping area of a wireless local area network (WLAN), it first estimates the system throughput as if it were associated with each of the APs involved. Then it chooses the AP that can achieve the highest system throughput. For existing users that locate in the overlapping area, they may also need to change the AP association due to the dynamic nature of traffic load. To enable the fairness among users, each user is guaranteed the minimum transmission opportunity. Another significant contribution of this paper is that we find that load-balancing based approaches could not achieve the maximum throughput for multi-rate WLANs, although load-balancing has been considered as an effective approach to improve the network throughput for single-rate WLANs. In-depth theoretical analysis and extensive simulations are performed to verify the throughput optimization and user fairness.

1 Introduction

With the extensive applications of WLANs and the increasing number of wireless users, network administrators often deploy multiple APs in a WLAN to improve the network capacity. To better take the advantage of this deployment, one problem must be carefully attacked. That is, which AP should be associated with if a user has multiple APs reachable. The traditional AP selection method is signal strength first (SSF) [1], which is known to degrade the system throughput because a significant number of users may be associated with a few APs. Another problem of the signal-strength based methods is the fairness. Users associated with heavy-load APs have less transmission opportunity than other users associated with light-load APs.

To address the throughput issue, many algorithms are developed based on the idea of load balancing. The assumption here is that the system throughput can be maximized as long as the load among the APs are well balanced. While numerical results have suggested considerable improvement on throughput, these algorithms only work for single-rate WLANs. In multi-rate WLANs, a user may generate load varied dramatically to different APs. If the load-balancing approach were used in multi-rate WLANs, it is likely that users are prone to choose APs in which they generate heavier load and thus lead to poor throughput.

B. Liu et al. (Eds.): WASA 2009, LNCS 5682, pp. 509–518, 2009.

Throughput and fairness are both significant metrics to evaluate the network performance. The reality, however, is that they are often contradictory goals. In this paper, we develop a novel AP selection algorithm for multi-rate WLANs. The objective of the algorithm is to maximize the system throughput while taking fairness into account. Our two significant contributions can be summarized as follows.

- A novel AP selection algorithm, named Throughput Measurement-based Selection (TMS) is presented and analyzed. In TMS, a user in the overlapping area selects the AP so that it makes the most increment to the overall system throughput regardless of the throughput or the load of the AP being chosen. Notice that both new-coming users and existing users are carefully handled in our algorithm. To address the fairness issue, we introduce a new concept, called *opportunity fairness*, into the time allocation scheme for users within the same AP.
- A new finding on throughput maximization is presented. Load-balancing has been commonly considered as an effective approach to improve the system throughput for single-rate WLANs. In this paper, however, we prove that the load-balancing approach could not necessarily achieve the maximum throughput for multi-rate WLANs. This is because a user may generate dramatically different load to different APs depending on its transmission rate in multi-rate WLANs.

The rest of paper is organized as follows. In Section 2, we briefly introduce some related work. Section 3 presents the network model and problem statement. In Section 4, we present the detailed design of the Measurement-based Selection (TMS) algorithm. The performance evaluation is presented in Section 5. Concluding remarks are given in Section 6.

2 Related Work

The traditional AP selection method–SSF first drew researcher's attention because it was believed that the uneven load distribution caused the throughput degradation. Consequently, the starting point of most approaches is to distribute the load to all APs as equal as possible. Unfortunately, there is no common definition of the load. In [2, 3], the number of current users of an AP is assumed as the load of an AP. All users are assumed to have the same transmission rate regardless of the distance between a user and an AP in above approaches. However, this is obviously not true for multi-rate WLANs. In our paper, we use a more realistic definition of load by factoring the diversity of transmission rates.

Recently, several other strategies based on load balancing are proposed for multi-rate WLANs. The least load first (LLF) [4] is one of popular heuristic methods. In LLF, a new-coming user selects the AP with the least load, without factoring its own load. Another load balancing technique by controlling the size of WLAN cells is proposed in [5]. This method is similar to cell breathing in cellular networks, which allows APs to adjust their coverage areas by varying the transmission power of beacon frames.

It is acknowledged that fairness measure is another indispensable concern in allocating system sources to multiple users or applications. In [4], an association control is employed to achieve max-min fair bandwidth allocation. They consider load balancing as an efficient to obtain max-min fair bandwidth allocation. A distributed max-min fairness AP selection method extended from LLF (we call it ELLF in this paper) is proposed in [6]. In ELLF, new-coming users select the AP with the least load factoring its own load, to maximize the new users' throughput. Nevertheless, this local throughput optimization of one user is not identical to the overall system throughput maximization. [7] considers proportional fairness in a network of APs. They proposed two approximation algorithms for periodical offline optimization to achieve proportional fairness.

Generally, most of above papers are based on the idea of load balancing to achieve either maximum system throughput or optimal user fairness. While system throughput and user fairness are both significant metrics to evaluate the network performance, in most cases, there is a tradeoff between them. The trade-off relationship of system throughput and fairness with quality of service support is addressed in [8]. An interference-limited wireless network is considered and call admission control is used.

Maximizing network throughput while considering user fairness is one of the critical challenges in WLANs. In our paper, the ultimate objective is to optimize the overall system throughput while maintaining user fairness. To maximize the throughput, we propose a novel Throughput Measurement-based AP Selection algorithm, instead of load balancing. Due to the trade-off between system throughput and user fairness, it is meaningful only when comparing the efficiency of different algorithms based on the same fairness definition. To maintain user fairness, we introduce an opportunity fairness scheme and all methods are performed based on this fairness strategy.

3 Network Model and Problem Statement

3.1 Network Model

Let U denote the set of all users in the entire system and $N_U = |U|$ the number of users. Let A denote the set of all APs and $N_A = |A|$ the number of APs. Each AP is assigned a dedicated non-overlapping channel. We assume each AP has a limited transmission range, and it only serves the users within its range. Only users in the overlapping coverage of multiple available APs are able to be re-associated. Concerning the association model, all the users can only communicate with one AP at any time as in the single-association model. Meanwhile, for the incoming traffic flow, we assume all users are greedy so that they always have traffic to transmit. We define an $N_A \times N_U$ matrix X to denote the associations between users and APs, whose element $x_{a,u}$ is a binary variable, that is: $x_{a,u} = 1$ if the user u associates with AP a and otherwise $x_{a,u} = 0$. And U_a is a set including all users associated with AP a. Transmission rate is a significant parameter in our AP selection algorithm. We introduce an $N_A \times N_U$ matrix R to represent the transmission rate between users and APs, whose element $r_{a,u}$ is the transmission rate of user u to AP a. Another important parameters in our algorithm is load. Here we adopt the definition of load from [4], that is, for user

u, the load $l_{a,u}$ generated on its associated AP a is inversely proportional to its transmission rate $r_{a,u}$. The load of an AP then can be defined as follows:

Definition 1 (*Load of an AP*)**.** The load of AP a, denoted by l_a, is the sum of load induced by all of its associated users, that is,

$$l_a = \sum_{u \in U_a} l_{a,u} = \sum_{u \in U_a} \frac{1}{r_{a,u}}. \quad (1)$$

3.2 Opportunity Fairness

Users associated with the same AP share the same communication channel to AP. Thus an access scheme is needed to allocate the channel access. In order to improve the effective utility of channel and guarantee the fairness among users within the same AP, we introduce a concept named *opportunity fairness* and provide a novel time allocation scheme to multi-rate users. In our scheme, we do not assign equal time to all its users in the same AP. Instead, varied time is allocated to users based on their transmission rates and packet sizes. We define transmission opportunity $O_{a,u}$ for user u connected to AP a as the number of packets transmitted in a time period T. The ideal user fairness means that all users should be allocated an equal opportunity. However, there is a trade-off between system throughput and user fairness. In order to improve the network throughput, faster users should be granted more opportunities. On the other hand, it is important that no users be starved. Thus each user must be allowed to transmit at least one packet in each time period. Here we design a ε-Opportunity Fairness definition as follows:

Definition 2 (*ε-Opportunity Fairness*)**.** User fairness among all the users associated with AP a is defined as the ratio of the maximum transmission opportunity to the minimum transmission opportunity of users, that is, $\varepsilon_a = \frac{\min(O_{a,u})}{\max(O_{a,u})}, \varepsilon_a \in (0, 1]$.

3.3 Problem Statement

Definition 3 (*Throughput*)**.** The throughput of AP a, denoted by θ_a, is the number of packets successfully transmitted in a unit time, that is,

$$\theta_a = \frac{\sum_{u \in U_a} (O_{a,u} \cdot x_{a,u})}{\sum_{u \in U_a} (\frac{O_{a,u} \cdot x_{a,u}}{r_{a,u}})} = \frac{O_a}{L_a}, \quad (2)$$

where O_a represents the total number of packets transmitted in a period time and L_a denotes the time used to transmit all O_a packets. We address that the throughput of an AP is not only determined by its load, but also the transmission opportunity of its associated users. Our objective is to maximize the throughput while maintaining opportunity fairness among users. Therefore, the optimized throughput problem with fairness constraint can be defined as:

$$\max \sum_{a \in A} \theta_a$$

subject to

$$\sum_{a \in A} x_{a,u} = 1, x_{a,u} \in \{0, 1\} \tag{3}$$

$$\frac{\min(O_{a,u})}{\max(O_{a,u})} \geq \varepsilon, \varepsilon \in (0, 1] \tag{4}$$

$$O_{a,u} \geq 1. \tag{5}$$

Constraint (3) represents that each user is associated with only one AP at a time. Constraint (4) represents that the opportunities can not vary dramatically between fast and slow users. Constraint (5) guarantees that no user be starved.

4 Algorithm and Analysis

In this section we present the throughput measurement-based AP selection algorithm to optimize the system throughput. The focus here is the throughput of the entire system rather than of a single AP. We measure the contribution of each user to the overall system throughput. A user selects the AP in which its contribution is maximized. Notice that the chosen AP may not be the one has the highest throughput among all APs. To reduce the computational complexity, the decision is eventually made based on the increment of the system throughput instead of the absolute throughput value. Given the dynamic nature of WLANs, AP associations for both new-coming users and existing users are considered. Therefore, each AP needs to periodically update the information, such as traffic load and the transmission opportunities of associated users.

4.1 For New-Coming Users

We consider the new-coming users that enter the overlapping area of multiple APs. With an attempt to maximize the system throughput, the new-coming user first estimates the system throughput as if it accessed each available AP. It then selects the AP such that the system throughput will be the highest one. Denote the current throughput of each AP by θ_a $(a = 1, 2, ..., N_A)$ and the corresponding system throughput as $\theta = \sum_{a=1}^{N_A} \theta_a$. A new-coming user u enters the system and has several available APs. Suppose that user u chooses AP m, the new system throughput then is:

$$\theta^* = \frac{O_m + O_{m,u}}{L_m + O_{m,u} \cdot l_{m,u}} + \sum_{a=1,a\neq m}^{N_A} \theta_a$$
$$= \begin{cases} \theta + \frac{O_{m,u} \cdot L_m - O_{m,u} \cdot O_m \cdot l_{m,u}}{(L_m + O_{m,u} \cdot l_{m,u}) \cdot L_m} & l_m \neq 0 \\ \theta + \frac{1}{l_{m,u}} & l_m = 0 \end{cases}.$$

Denote $D_{m,u}$ as:

$$D_{m,u} = \begin{cases} \frac{O_{m,u} \cdot L_m - O_{m,u} \cdot O_m \cdot l_{m,u}}{(L_m + O_{m,u} \cdot l_{m,u}) \cdot L_m} & l_m \neq 0 \\ \frac{1}{l_{m,u}} & l_m = 0 \end{cases}. \tag{6}$$

The new throughput θ^* can be represented as: $\theta^* = \theta + D_{m,u}$.

Comparing θ with θ^*, new-coming user u makes a contribution $D_{m,u}$ to the overall system throughput. Notice that $D_{m,u}$ may be a negative value. We call $D_{m,u}$ the contribution to the system throughput when it attempts to associate with AP m. The contribution of the same user to different APs may vary significantly, depending on the factors such as rates, the throughput of current AP, and the transmission opportunity of the chosen AP's users. Therefore, user u should choose the AP with the maximum $D_{m,u}$, which leads to the maximum throughput of the entire system not of the single AP.

It can be seen from (6) that $D_{m,u}$ is a combination of several measurements, such as the load of a new-coming user and the transmission opportunity of the current users. Therefore, this method is more comprehensive to improve the system throughput. On the other hand, it is not necessary to calculate the system throughput estimation when a new-coming user comes, but $D_{m,u}$. All the parameters of $D_{m,u}$ is only from the new-coming user and the AP it attempts to associate with. In this way, the computational complexity can be greatly reduced compared to overall system throughput calculation.

4.2 For Existing Users

Realizing the fact that new-coming users have influence on the existing users and the fact that WLANs environment varies with time, the associations of existing users should be changed dynamically to maximize the system throughput. Suppose that an existing user v in AP j switches to AP k. Before switching, the system throughput is: $\theta = \sum_{a\neq j,k} \theta_a + \theta_j + \theta_k$, where the throughput of AP j and k can be represented as:

$$\theta_j + \theta_k = \begin{cases} \frac{O_j}{L_j} + \frac{O_k}{L_k} & l_k \neq 0 \\ \frac{O_j}{L_j} & l_k = 0 \end{cases}. \tag{7}$$

After switching, the system throughput is changed to: $\theta^* = \sum_{a\neq j,k} \theta_a + \theta_j^* + \theta_k^*$, where the new throughput of AP j and k is:

$$\theta_j^* + \theta_k^* = \frac{O_j - O_{j,v}}{L_j - O_{j,v} \cdot l_{j,v}} + \frac{O_k + O_{k,v}}{L_k + O_{k,v} \cdot l_{k,v}}. \tag{8}$$

$\theta_j^* + \theta_k^*$ in (8) may be larger, smaller or equal to $\theta_j + \theta_k$ in (7). We define their difference as $D_{j,k,v}$:

$$D_{j,k,v} = \theta_j^* + \theta_k^* - (\theta_j + \theta_k), \quad (9)$$

which is also the difference of the system throughput due to the fact that user v switches from AP j to AP k. When $D_{j,k,v} > 0$, the re-association will benefit the system throughput. Hence, we let user v change its association from AP j to AP k. To avoid frequent re-associations, we impose a constraint on the difference, that is, $D_{j,k,v} > \delta, (\delta > 0)$. The proposed AP selection algorithm is summarized in Algorithm 1.

Algorithm 1. Measurement-based AP Selection Algorithm

```
Periodically update the information for each AP
Update matrix X
Update O_{a,u} of each user
Update the current throughput θ_a by (2)

For new-coming users
if u is a new-coming user in the coverage of only one AP then
   Choose this AP for user u
else
   Estimate D_{m,u} by (6) for each available AP m
   Choose the AP with max(D_{m,u})
end if

For existing users
for existing user v(v ∈ U_j) in the overlapping area of more than one AP do
   for each available AP k do
      Find the largest one max(D_{j,k,v}) by (9)
      if max(D_{j,k,v}) > δ then
         User v switch to the AP with max(D_{j,k,v})
      end if
   end for
end for
```

5 Performance Evaluation

In this section, we evaluate the performance of our proposed TMS algorithm in comparison with three other popular methods: Strongest-Signal-First (SSF), Least-Load-First (LLF), and Extension of LLF (ELLF). We assume the transmission rate is determined by the distance between APs and users. Our algorithm is performed iteratively and new users join WLANs one bye one. Two experiments are conducted with different opportunity fairness criteria. In each experiment, all APs are uniformly deployed and all users are deployed randomly. The transmission rate between a user and its APs follow Discrete Poisson distribution with a parameter $\lambda = 10Mbps$.

5.1 1-Opportunity Fairness

In the first experiment, we conduct the performance evaluation based on 1-Opportunity Fairness, that is, $\varepsilon_a = \frac{\min(O_{a,u})}{\max(O_{a,u})} = 1$. The 1-Opportunity Fairness indicates that all the users within a same AP have the equal transmission opportunities, which is the ideal opportunity fairness among users. We compute the system throughput with the users coming based on R. Fig. 1(a) and 1(b) illustrate the system throughput under 10 APs and 15 APs, respectively. Both figures demonstrate that TMS achieves notable system throughput improvement compared with other methods. In Fig. 1(a), the system throughput of TMS is improved about 20% compared to ELLF, 33.3% to SSF, even 125% to LLF. In Fig. 1(b), the advantage of TMS on system throughput is more significant: about 26.7% improved to ELLF, 58.3% to SSF and LLF.

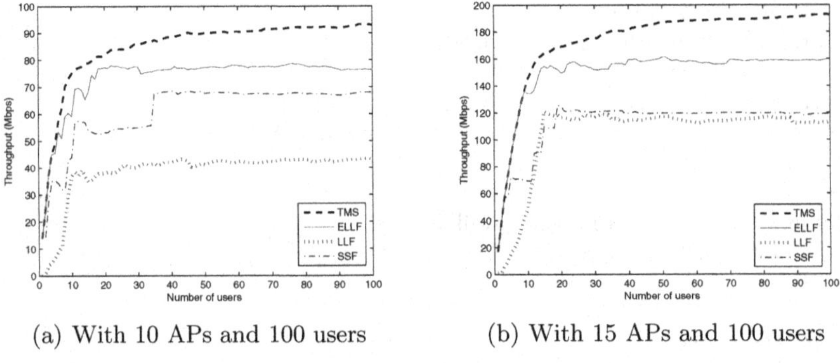

(a) With 10 APs and 100 users (b) With 15 APs and 100 users

Fig. 1. Comparison of the system throughput with different methods: TMS, ELLF, LLF and SSF under 1-Opportunity Fairness

Comparing Fig. 1(a) and Fig. 1(b), with the increasing number of APs, the number of users in the overlapping area of APs are correspondingly increased. At the same time, the increasing number of APs brings more capacity. Both factors contribute to the significant improvement of system throughput. Specifically, the maximum throughput is improved from about 90 Mbps with 10 APs to 180 Mbps with 15 APs. The average of maximum throughput per AP increases about 33.3%.

The load balancing is measured using Jain Index [9] as :$J = (\sum_{a=1}^{N_A} l_a)^2/(N_A \cdot \sum_{a=1}^{N_A} l_a^2)$. Table 1 lists the load balancing degree for 10 and 15 APS with 100 users, respectively. The load balancing of LLF and ELLF outperforms in both cases. This result validates the idea that LLF and ELLF are designed based on load balancing. TMS is relatively low in terms of load balancing. The lower load balancing in TMS is rather reasonable because the idea of TMS is based on the increment of system throughput, rater than load balancing. The results further

Table 1. 1-Opportunity Fairness: Load balancing degree Among APs

Load Balancing	TMS	ELLF	LLF	SSF
Average Jain Index (10 APs and 100 users)	0.5383	0.9015	0.8972	0.4165
Average Jain Index (15 APs and 100 users)	0.5881	0.8471	0.8223	0.2871

prove that load balancing is not the appropriate strategy to achieve optimal system throughput in multi-rate WLANs, on the premise of maintaining the same fairness among users.

5.2 ε-Opportunity Fairness

In the second experiment, we conduct the performance evaluation based on ε-Opportunity Fairness ($\varepsilon \in (0, 1)$). We provide a transmission opportunity design as: $O_{a,u} = \lceil \frac{r_{a,u}}{min(r_{a,u})} \rceil, u \in U_a$. The corresponding user fairness within one AP then can be calculated as: $\varepsilon_a = \frac{\min(O_{a,u})}{\max(O_{a,u})}, u \in U_a$. In this experiment, we use the same deployment of APs and users and transmission rate matrix R as in the first experiment. The only difference is that the user fairness is changed to ε-Opportunity Fairness.

Fig. 2(a) is the counterpart of Fig. 1(a) and Fig. 2(b)is the counterpart of Fig. 1(b) Both Figs. 2(a) and 2(b) once again verify that our proposed algorithm TMS has higher system throughput in ε-Opportunity Fairness situation compared with other methods. In Fig. 2(a), the system throughput of TMS is improved about 17.6% compared to ELLF and 66.7% to LLF. In Fig. 2(b), the system throughput of TMS is improved about 14.3% to ELLF, 60% to SSF and LLF.

Next, we compare the system throughput on 1-Opportunity Fairness and ε-Opportunity Fairness. Observing Fig. 1(a) with Fig. 2(a), and Fig. 1(b)with Fig. 2(b), the system throughput of ε-Opportunity Fairness ($\varepsilon < 1$) is apparently improved about 10% compared with the corresponding system throughput in 1-Opportunity Fairness situation ($\varepsilon = 1$). The reason of the system

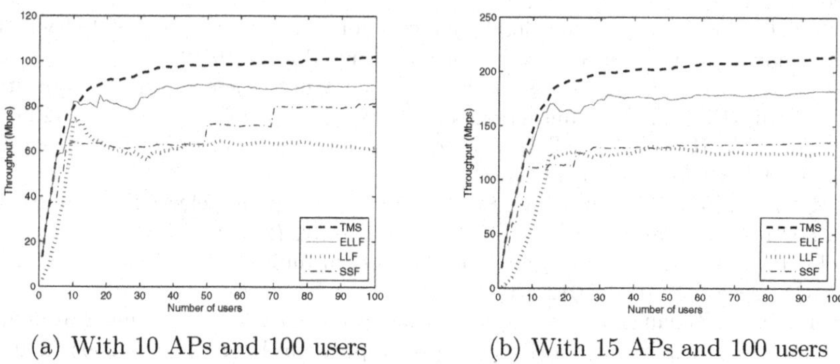

(a) With 10 APs and 100 users (b) With 15 APs and 100 users

Fig. 2. Comparison of the system throughput with different methods: TMS, ELLF, LLF and SSF under ε-Opportunity Fairness

Table 2. ε-Opportunity Fairness: Load Balancing Degree Among APs

Load Balancing	TMS	ELLF	LLF	SSF
Average Jain Index (10 APs and 100 users)	0.4188	0.9012	0.9071	0.4712
Average Jain Index (15 APs and 100 users)	0.3077	0.8312	0.8501	0.5617

throughput improvement is that faster users have more transmission opportunities in ε-Opportunity Fairness compared with the transmission opportunities in 1-Opportunity Fairness.

Table 2 lists the average Jain Index which represents the load balancing degree among APs in ε-Opportunity Fairness. The same conclusion with 1-Opportunity Fairness can be derived: the load balancing of LLF and ELLF are better in both Tables. TMS is relatively low in terms of load balancing among APs. Through numerical experimentations on the relationship between system throughput and load balancing, it shows that a higher throughput may come along with a lower load balancing. However, there is no sufficient evidence to prove that this is of inherent. So we can not conclude that there is an inverse proportional correlation between the system throughput and load balancing degree in multi-rate WLANs.

6 Conclusions

In this paper, we have presented a novel AP selection algorithm to obtain high system throughput while maintaining opportunity fairness among users. Extensive simulations with both 1-Opportunity Fairness and ε-Opportunity Fairness demonstrate that our proposed algorithm significantly improves the system throughput, as compared with three other popular schemes while maintaining the same fairness.

References

1. Fukuda, Y., Fujiwara, A., Tsuru, M., Oie, Y.: Analysis of access point selection strategy in wireless lan. In: Vehicular Technology Conference, pp. 2532–2536 (2005)
2. Papaniko, I., Logothetis, M.: A study on dynamic load balance for ieee 802.11b wireless lan. In: COMCON 8 (2001)
3. Sheu, S.T., Wu, C.C.: Dynamic load balance algorithm (dlba) for ieee 802.11 wireless lan. Tamkang Journal of Science and Engineering, 45–52 (1999)
4. Bejerano, Y., Han, S.J.: Fairness and load balancing in wireless lans using association control. In: IEEE/ACM Transactions on Networking (TON), pp. 560–573 (2007)
5. Bejerano, Y., Han, S.J.: Cell breathing techniques for load balancing in wireless lans. In: INFOCOM, pp. 1–13 (2006)
6. Gong, H., Nahm, K., Kim, J.: Distributed fair access point selection for multi-rate ieee 802.11 wlans. In: CCNC, 5th IEEE, pp. 528–532 (2008)
7. Li, L., Pal, M., Yang, Y.: Proportional fairness in multi-rate wireless lans. In: INFOCOM 2008, pp. 1004–1012 (2008)
8. Cheng, H.T., Zhuang, W.: An optimization framework for balancing throughput and fairness in wireless networks with qos support. In: Proc. QShine 2006 (2006)
9. Alfouzan, I., Woodward, M.: Some new load balancing algorithms for single-hop wdm networks, 143–157 (2006)

Latency-Bounded Minimum Influential Node Selection in Social Networks

Feng Zou[1], Zhao Zhang[2], and Weili Wu[1]

[1] Department of Computer Science, University of Texas at Dallas, Richardson, TX, 75080
phenix.zou@student.utdallas.edu, weiliwu@utdallas.edu
[2] College of Mathematics and System Sciences, Xinjiang University, Urumqi, PR China
zhzhao@xju.edu.cn

Abstract. As one of the essential problems in information diffusion process, how to select a set of influential nodes as the starting nodes has been studied by lots of researchers. All the existing solutions focus on how to maximize the influence of the initially selected "influential nodes", paying no attention on how the influential nodes selection could maximize the speed of the diffusion. In this paper, we consider the problem of influential nodes selection regarding to the propagation speed in social network information diffusion. We define a discrete optimization problem, called *Fast Information Propagation Problem.* We show that this problem is NP-hard problem when the time requirement for information propagation is exactly 1-hop. We also propose a *Latency-bounded Minimum Influential Node Selection Algorithm* to solve the problem in this case.

Keywords: Social network, influential nodes selection, information diffusion.

1 Introduction

Social networks, represented as graphs of relationships and interactions within a group of individuals, have served as an important medium for the communication, information disseminating, and influence spreading. A good example is a recently well studied problem in the area of viral marketing: Suppose we would like to market a new product that we hope could be adopted by a large fraction of the members in the network. By initially targeting at a few " influential" members of the network, eg. offering free or cheaper products, we hope a cascade of influence could be triggered at the end.

This dynamic processes for information diffusion and " word-of-mouth" effects have been studied in many fields, including Epidemiology[5,13], Sociology[2,14],

B. Liu et al. (Eds.): WASA 2009, LNCS 5682, pp. 519–526, 2009.

Economics[12] and Computer Science[1,3,4]. Considering the social network as a undirected graph, and each node has two status: active and inactive, the process looks roughly as follows from macroscopical perspective: initially, a certain set of nodes is set to be active; whether at some time point, a node becomes active itself is influenced by its neighbors; its decision may trigger more and more its' neighbors in the graph become active; as time goes by, more and more nodes become active in the graph, until no more nodes could be turned into active. Thus, the essential problem in diffusion is how to select a set of influential nodes as the active starting node.

Initially, this problem was considered in a probabilistic model of interaction [4,15]. Heuristics were given for choosing customers with a large overall effect on the network. Most recent work consider the issue of choosing influential sets of individuals as a problem in discrete optimization [10,11]. A combinatorial optimization problem called the *Influence Maximization Problem* [10] is proposed, which could be described as following: extract a set of k nodes to target for initial activation such that it yields the largest expected spread of information for a given integer k. Greedy hill-climbing algorithms are proposed [10,11] for this problem.

However, all of these solutions focus on how to maximize the influence of the initially selected "influential nodes", paying no attention on how the influential nodes selection could maximize the speed of the diffusion. In a time-essential information diffusion scenario in the social network, (eg. disease prevention in Epidemiology), the faster information diffusion could be, obviously the better. Therefore, in this paper, we consider the problem of influential nodes selection regarding to the propagation speed in social network information diffusion. We define a discrete optimization problem, called *Fast Information Propagation Problem.* Given a social network, we intend to extract the minimum size of nodes to target for initial activation such that it could sent information to all the nodes in the given social network and also the time needed for information propagation is bounded. In this paper, we use hop count to describe the time cost for information propagation. We show that this problem is a NP-hard problem when the time requirement for information propagation is exactly 1-hop. We also propose a *Latency-bounded Minimum Influential Node Selection Algorithm* to solve the problem in this case.

The rest of this paper is organized as follows. Section 2 presents the related work of influential node selection. Some existing work is discussed. The detailed description of our problem is given in Section 3 and the NP-hardness for the problem when the time requirement for information propagation is exactly 1-hop is shown in detail in Section 4. Afterwards, *Latency-bounded Minimum Influential Node Selection Algorithm* we proposed is presented in Section 5. Section 6 concludes the whole paper.

2 Related Work

Domingos and Richardson [4,15] are the first to propose a fundamental algorithmic solution for influential nodes selection problem. They use probabilistic model, providing several heuristic solutions including single pass, greedy search and hill-climbing search. Based on the calculation of a so-called *expected lifting in profit* value for each customer i, they choose customers with a large overall effect on the network. They estimate the influence probabilities needed in the calculation using the large database available on the Internet.

Kempe, Kleinberg, and Tardos [10] formalized the problem as a maximum influence problem. In their paper, they proposed a greedy hill-climbing algorithm and experimentally showed on large collaboration networks that for the influence maximization problem in the *IC* and *LT* models, this algorithm significantly outperforms the high-degree and centrality heuristics that are commonly used in the sociology literature. Moreover, a performance guarantee of this greedy algorithm for these diffusion models by using an analysis framework based on submodular functions is proved. The greedy algorithm requires computing the vector $\nabla\sigma(A)$ that consists of all the marginal gains for the influence degree $\sigma(A)$ given a set A of nodes. However, it is an open question to compute influence degrees exactly by an efficient method, and so good estimates were obtained by simulating the random process of each model many times. Therefore, the greedy algorithm needed a large amount of computation.

Kimura, Saito and Nakano[11] proposed a method of efficiently estimating all the marginal gains $\nabla\sigma(A)$ for influence degree $\sigma(A)$ on the basis of bond percolation and graph theory. They applied it into the greedy algorithm for influence maximization problem[10].

From our knowledge, none existing work focuses on fast information propagation in a social network, which is an important problem in time-essential diffusion scenarios. In the following sections, we will present in detail the problem formulation and the solutions we propose for the problem.

3 Fast Information Propagation Problem

As we know, one of the important study areas of social network is how to utilize social networks to help alleviate social problems in the physical world. For example, in a real world, the disease prevention programs are important tools to help combat the disease spreading problem in the real world. To alleviate the main source of the problems, people must be protected as soon as possible, either by injection or medicines, to prevent them from infected by the disease virus caught by their friends. Therefore, how to choose a subset of individuals to be part of the prevention program so that the positive effect could spread through the whole social network as soon as possible becomes the key problem.

In order to solve this kind of problems, given a social network, we define a problem called *Fast Information Propagation Problem*. This problem could be described as follows: extract the minimum size of nodes to target for initial activation such that it could sent information to all the nodes in the given social network and also the time needed for information propagation is bounded.

Take the disease prevention problem as an illustration. We want to identify the minimum set of individuals to take part in the prevention program, so that they could result in a globally positive impact on the entire network within a time-bound so that the disease spreading could be controlled.

In our paper, we will speak of each node as being either ACTIVE or INACTIVE. ACTIVE means it adopts the good influence, INACTIVE means it does not adopt the good influence. We will use hop count to describe the time cost for information propagation and we are interested in the case that the time requirement for information propagation is exactly 1-hop. We make two assumptions in the rest of the paper. There are generally two kinds of fundamental information diffusion models widely used in the literature: the *independent cascade (IC) model*[8,9,10] and the *linear threshold (LT) model*[10,16]. We assume: 1) the diffusion model each node adopts is *LT* model and if more than half neighbors of an individual are active, then this individual will be influenced to be active[17]; Besides, we assume: 2) we focus on *progressive case* in diffusion process where each node could switch from INACTIVE to ACTIVE, but not in the other direction [10].

With these definitions and assumptions, we could better describe our problem in detail as following. Given a undirected graph $G = (V, E)$, we look for the minimum subset $P \subseteq V$ so that for each vertex $v \in V \setminus P$, there are at least $\lceil \frac{d(v)}{2} \rceil$ ACTIVE vertices in its neighborhood belonging to P.

4 NP-Hardness Proof

We prove the NP-hardness of this problem by using the well known NP-complete decision version of Vertex-Cover problem, denoted by VC, as follows: Given a graph $G = (V, E)$ and a positive integer k, determine whether G has a vertex cover of size at most k.

We construct a polynomial-time many-one reduction from VC to the decision version of this problem: Given a graph G and a positive integer h, determine whether there exists a subset P of size at most h such that for every vertex $v \in V \setminus P$, at least a half number of its neighbors belongs to P.

For an instance of VC, a graph $G = (V, E)$ and a positive integer k, we construct a new graph G' as follows: First we create $|V| + |E|$ vertices with $|V|$ vertices $\{v_{11}, ..., v_{1,|V|}\}$ representing the vertices in G and $|E|$ vertices $\{v_{21}, ..., v_{2,|E|}\}$ representing the edges in G. We then add an edge between vertex v_{1i} and v_{2j} if and only if the vertex v_{1i} represents an endpoint of the edge represented by v_{2j}.

Now, we connect each vertex v_{2j} to one subgraph constructed as Figure 1, called $3 - star$, and each vertex v_{1i} to $d(v_i)$ such subgraphs where $d(v_i)$ is the degree of vertex v_i in G, represented by v_{1i}. Note that we have attached totally $3|E|$ 3-stars in G'. Figure 2 and 3 give an detailed illustration of how this construction works.

Setting $h = 3|E| + k$, we will prove that G has a vertex cover of size at most k if and only if G' has a subset P of size at most h, meeting our requirement.

If G has a vertex cover C of size at most k, then we define P consisting of centers of all 3-stars (eg. node x in Figure 1) and all vertices v_{1i} representing

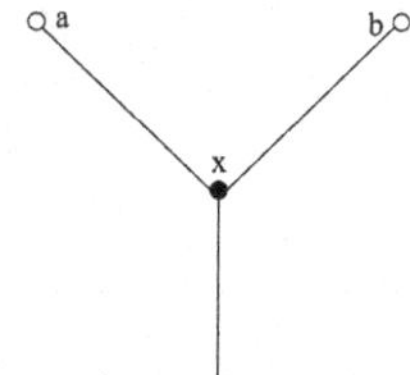

Fig. 1. 3-Star

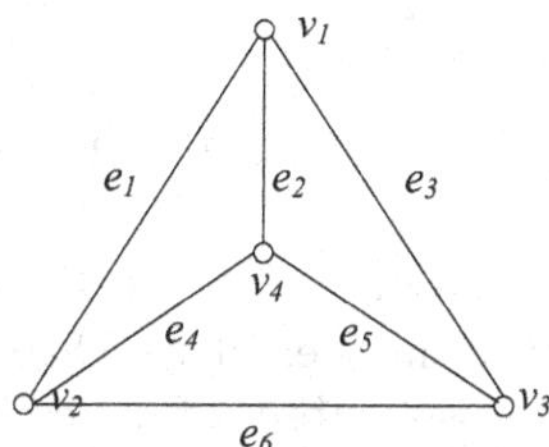

Fig. 2. An Example of Graph G

vertices in C. So, $|C| + 3|E| \leq h$. It is easy to check that every vertex not in P has at least a half number of neighbors in P.

Now, suppose that G' has a subset P of size at most h. Note that P must contain at least one vertex in each 3-star. If we exchange this vertex with the center of the 3-star, then $|P|$ does not increase and the feasibility of P does not change either. Therefore, we may assume that P contains the center of each 3-star. Note that every vertex v_{1i} has at least a half number of its neighbors being 3-star centers and every vertex v_{2j} has degree 3 and has one neighbor being a 3-star center. Therefore, to have P being a feasible solution of our problem, it is sufficient to have that each v_{2j} either belongs to P or has a neighbor v_{1i} in P. In the former case, we may exchange v_{2j} with its neighbor v_{1i}. This does not increase $|P|$ and keeps the feasibility of P. Therefore, we may assume that P does not contain any v_{2j} so that every v_{2j} has a neighbor v_{1i} in P. Since there are totally $3|E|$ 3-star centers, there are at most $h - 3|E|$ v_{1i} in P. Let C be the set of vertices of G, represented by v_{1i} in P. Then C is a vertex cover of size at most k.

5 Latency-Bounded Minimum Influential Node Selection Algorithm

To solve the 1-hop *Fast Information Propagation Problem* described above, we design a *Latency-bounded Minimum Influential Node Selection Algorithm.*

First we define a few terms and definitions used in our description of the algorithm. Recall that each node has two status: ACTIVE and INACTIVE. The

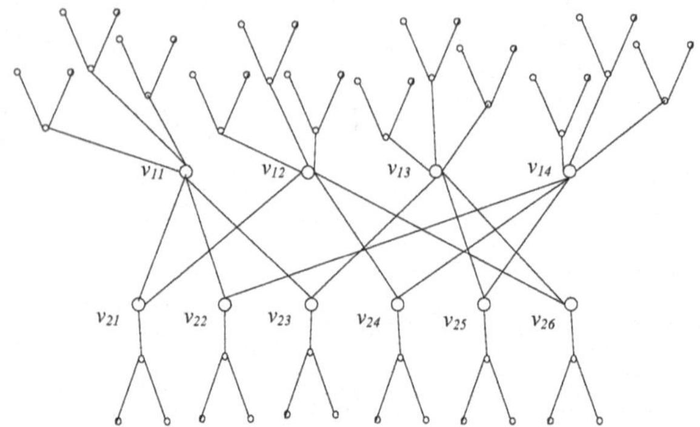

Fig. 3. An Example of Construction of Graph G' with G

active degree of a node is the number of its ACTIVE neighbors. Similarly, the *inactive degree* of a node is the number of its INACTIVE neighbors. A *1-hop dominating set* D of a graph G is a subset of nodes in G such that every vertex not in D has at least one neighbor in D.

The main idea of our algorithm is to select the union of several 1-hop dominating sets as influential nodes to spread out the information to the whole network within 1-hop.

We first introduce the greedy algorithm to find the *1-hop dominating set*, given a graph $G = (V, E)$. This algorithm is quite similar to the FASTGREEDY heuristics introduced in [7]. Difference is that the heuristics introduced in [7] is the solution proposed for finding a set of *locations* dominating *people* in the social network. Our solution is for *people-to-people* dominating relationship.

Algorithm 1. 1-hop Dominating Set

1: INPUT: A undirected graph $G = (V, E)$ with n vertices.
2: OUTPUT: A subset D of V such that any node v not in D has a 1-hop neighbor in D.
3: Set D to be empty.
4: Calculate the degree of each vertex $v \in V$ in graph G, denoted as $d(v)$. Sort them into non-increasing order with $d(v_1) \geq d(v_2) \geq \cdots \geq d(v_n)$.
5: Pick the smallest index i, where for each vertex in the V, it either belongs to the subset $\{v_1, v_2, \ldots, v_i\}$ or has at least one neighbor in the subset.
6: Return the set $D = \{v_1, v_2, \ldots, v_i\}$.

With this algorithm, we could design algorithm 2 as presented in the following to select a subset of latency-bounded influential nodes. Taking a undirected graph with vertex set V, edge set E, algorithm 2 outputs a subset P of V, so that every vertex in $V \setminus P$ has at least $\lceil \frac{d(v)}{2} \rceil$ active neighbors belonging to P.

The algorithm consists of mainly two steps in the while loop. In the first step, using algorithm 1, we find a 1-hop dominating set for the rest of the nodes that are INACTIVE. Secondly, the vertices that could be influenced by the 1-hop

Algorithm 2. Latency-bounded Minimum Influential Node Selection Algorithm

INPUT: A undirected graph $G = (V, E)$.
OUTPUT: A subset P of V such that any node $v \in V \setminus P$ has at least $\lceil \frac{d(v)}{2} \rceil$ 1-hop neighbors in P.
Initialize the status of all nodes in V as INACTIVE, set P to be empty and $V' = V$.
while Not every node $v \in V'$ has at least $\lceil \frac{d(v)}{2} \rceil$ ACTIVE neighbors **do**
    Find a 1-dominating set D that dominates all nodes in V' using algorithm 1.
    Find in the set of 1-hop away vertices of D in V', the subset of vertices T' that could be influenced by D to be ACTIVE according to the $\lceil \frac{d(v)}{2} \rceil$ requirement.
    Set $P = P \bigcup D$
    Let $V' = V' - D - T'$ and set all the status of vertices in $D \bigcup T'$ to be ACTIVE.
end while
Return the set P.

dominating set is calculated. By following these two steps, we could turn each vertex into ACTIVE status according to the requirement of more than half ACTIVE neighbors in iterations.

This *Latency-bounded Minimum Influential Node Selection Algorithm* provides an approximation solution using greedy strategy for the *Fast Information Propagation Problem* when the propagation time is exactly 1-hop.

6 Conclusion

In our paper, we proposed a different discrete optimization problem called *Fast Information Propagation Problem* for influential nodes selection in social networks. Using the hop count as the time cost evaluation criteria, we study the case when the propagation time is exactly 1-hop. The NP-hardness of this problem is proven and a greedy algorithm called *Latency-bounded Minimum Influential Node Selection Algorithm* is proposed for it as well in our paper. For the further research work of the *Fast Information Propagation Problem*, we are interested in the case when the propagation time is k-hop. We will focus on the problem's hardness proof and the algorithm design. Performance evaluations using experiments will be our focus as well in the near future.

References

1. Aspnes, J., Chang, K., Yampolskiy, A.: Inoculation Strategies for Victims of Viruses and the Sum-of- Squares Partition Problem. In: SODA 2005, pp. 43–52 (2005)
2. Berger, E.: Dynamic Monopolies of Constant Size. Journal of Combinatorial Theory B 83(2), 191–200 (2001)
3. Berger, N., Borgs, C., Chayes, J.T., Saberi, A.: On the Spread of Viruses on the Internet. In: SODA 2005, pp. 301–310 (2005)
4. Domingos, P., Richardson, M.: Mining the Network Value of Customers. In: KDD 2001, pp. 57–66 (2001)
5. Dezso, Z., Barabasi, A.-L.: Halting Viruses in Scale-Free Networks. Physical Review E 65 (2002)

6. Du, D.-Z., Ko, K.-I., Hu, X.: Design and Analysis of Approximation Algorithms (unpublished Lecture Notes)
7. Eubank, S., Anil Kumar, V.S., Marathe, M.V., Srinivasan, A., Wang, N.: Structural and algorithmic aspects of massive social networks. In: Proceedings of the fifteenth annual ACM-SIAM symposium on Discrete algorithms (2004)
8. Goldenberg, J., Libai, B., Muller, E.: Talk of the network: A complex systems look at the underlying process of word-of-mouth. Marketing Letters 12, 211–223 (2001)
9. Gruhl, D., Guha, R., Liben-Nowell, D., Tomkins, A.: Information diffusion through blogspace. In: Proceedings of the 7th International World Wide Web Conference, pp. 107–117 (2004)
10. Kempe, D., Kleinberg, J., Tardos, E.: Maximizing the spread of influence through a social network. In: Proceedings of the 9th ACM SIGKDD International Conference on Knowledge Discovery and Data Mining, pp. 137–146 (2003)
11. Kimura, M., Saito, K., Nakano, R.: Extracting influential nodes for information diffusion on a social network. In: Proceedings of the 22nd AAAI Conference on Artificial Intelligence, Vancouver, British Columbia, Canada, pp. 1371–1376 (2007)
12. Morris, S.: Contagion. Review of Economic Studies 67, 57–78 (2000)
13. Pastor-Satorras, R., Vespignani, A.: Epidemics and Immunization in Scale-Free Networks. In: Bornholdt, S., Schuster, H.G. (eds.) Handbook of Graphs and Networks: From the Genome to the Internet, pp. 111–130. Wiley-VCH (2003)
14. Peleg, D.: Local Majority Voting, Small Coalitions and Controlling Monopolies in Graphs: A Review. In: Proceedings of the 3rd Colloquium on Structural Information & Communication Complexity, pp. 170–179 (1996)
15. Richardson, M., Domingos, P.: Mining knowledge-sharing sites for viral marketing. In: Proceedings of the 8th ACM SIGKDD International Conference on Knowledge Discovery and Data Mining, pp. 61–70 (2002)
16. Watts, D.J.: A simple model of global cascades on random networks. Proceedings of National Academy of Science 99, 5766–5771 (2002)
17. Wang, F., Camacho, E., Xu, K.: Positive influence dominating set in online social networks. In: COCOA 2009 (2009)

Design and Implementation of Davis Social Links OSN Kernel

Thomas Tran, Kelcey Chan, Shaozhi Ye, Prantik Bhattacharyya, Ankush Garg, Xiaoming Lu, and S. Felix Wu

Department of Computer Science
University of California, Davis
{ttran,kchan,sye,pbhattacharyya,garg,lu,sfwu}@ucdavis.edu

Abstract. Social network popularity continues to rise as they broaden out to more users. Hidden away within these social networks is a valuable set of data that outlines everyone's relationships. Networks have created APIs such as the Facebook Development Platform and OpenSocial that allow developers to create applications that can leverage user information. However, at the current stage, the social network support for these new applications is fairly limited in its functionality. Most, if not all, of the existing internet applications such as email, BitTorrent, and Skype cannot benefit from the valuable social network among their own users. In this paper, we present an architecture that couples two different communication layers together: the end2end communication layer and the social context layer, under the Davis Social Links (DSL) project. Our proposed architecture attempts to preserve the original application semantics (i.e., we can use Thunderbird or Outlook, unmodified, to read our SMTP emails) and provides the communicating parties (email sender and receivers) a social context for control and management. For instance, the receiver can set trust policy rules based on the social context between the pair, to determine how a particular email in question should be prioritized for delivery to the SMTP layer. Furthermore, as our architecture includes two coupling layers, it is then possible, as an option, to shift some of the services from the original applications into the social context layer. In the context of email, for example, our architecture allows users to choose operations, such as reply, reply-all, and forward, to be realized in either the application layer or the social network layer. And, the realization of these operations under the social network layer offers powerful features unavailable in the original applications. To validate our coupling architecture, we have implemented a DSL kernel prototype as a Facebook application called CyrusDSL (currently about 40 local users) and a simple communication application combined into the DSL kernel but is unaware of Facebook's API.

1 Introduction and Motivation

The rising growth in popularity of online social networks (OSNs) has been phenomenal in the last few years. Millions of people connect with one another and maintain friendships using the available OSNs. As a result, there is a plethora of rich and interesting user data spread across the networks. The user data is not limited to professional and personal information. It also contains status updates, wall posts (e.g. in Facebook),

B. Liu et al. (Eds.): WASA 2009, LNCS 5682, pp. 527–540, 2009.

scraps (e.g. in Orkut), location information, etc. With the growth of OSNs, API's to let developers access this data and build applications have been created.

The scope of applications include social games (e.g. Lexulous, various trivia quizzes), displaying one's musical tastes, etc. However, under our architecture, we can greatly expand the set of applications using social networks by providing digested information gathered and calculated from these OSNs that we believe have never been utilized before. Software classes such as email, search engines, and online telephony can be easily modified to gain the advantages that come the social knowledge in these networks. Furthermore, we present methods with which applications can easily utilize a robust system of trust and reputation inherent to Davis Social Links (DSL) [1].

The graph set present in OSNs due to the interconnection of users is a reflection of the social human network in the digital format. The hypothesis that social networks are small world networks (with property of small diameters) such that everyone can connect to everyone else using a short path length motivates us to exploit the presence of this rich user information set to build communication protocols based on trust and reputation of the users and are robust and secure in nature. In this paper, we present an architecture that attempts to leverage the rich user set represented in the form of social graph to build communication protocols. Our architecture thus attempts to bring the 'social context' in message exchange. The system uses the available OSN API's to build the social graph and facilitate the introduction of social context in the communication layer. So far, a friendship, from the OSN's perspective, has been binary. Two users either are friends, or they are not. However, we hope to present a better model of friendship by realizing that not all friendships are equal. This distinguishes DSL from a normal online social network. It is common for users to trust some friends better than others. Therefore, our DSL architecture captures, analyzes, and presents this information using a robust and easy to use API.

The DSL kernel architecture we have designed and implemented gives standard applications the ability to leverage social network data without requiring the user of the application to access his or her social network site. The only extra step the user needs to handle is authentication to the network. Our architecture also attempts to require little to no modification on pre-existing applications that wish to leverage social network data. Another feature of our architecture is that the application does not break when a social network changes its web layout which is a problem when having a bot crawl web pages for data.

To establish the effectiveness of the architecture, we are currently building an application which uses a Thunderbird or Outlook Express client to send an email using a social path. The social path is computed using the connectivity information imported from an OSN (we currently use Facebook). In this paper, we will delve into how our architecture builds off of DSL to allow software developers unprecedented access to the rich social graphs to add an element of trust and reputation in user-to-user interactions. Furthermore, we will explain how our robust and flexible design allows developers to modify their existing applications with very little effort. By giving some background on DSL in section 2, we can present our architecture in section 3. Next, in section 4, we examine some ways that our architecture can improve on currently existing communication paradigms by examining the modifications we have made to email. We further explain the status of our project and some performance data in section 5. We then compare our work with some related work in section 6 and we conclude our paper in section 7 while also examining some of the current shortcomings and potential research areas opened up by our architecture.

2 Overview of Davis Social Links (DSL)

Since our system utilizes the DSL protocol, it would be useful to first give a quick summary of DSL and how it aims to reduce spam while increasing connectivity amongst its users. To better understand how DSL and our OSN kernel work as well as why we believe it is effective, we will reference an example: Consider the simplest form of communication. Alice wants to send Bob an email. However, Alice does not know Bob's email address nor does she know him well enough to ask him using a different medium. With DSL, she can rely on her network of friends to help find and convey her message to him through a system where he can quantify her trustworthiness. In our example, Alice is friends with Carol, who in turn is friends with Bob. Ignoring the decimal values for each friendship link, refer to the figure below:

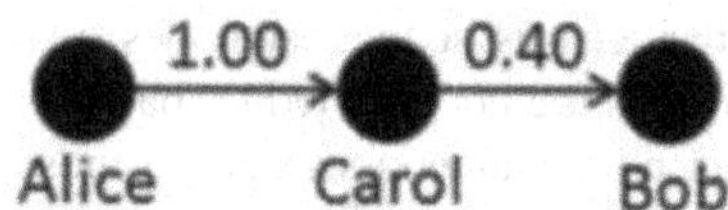

Fig. 1. An example social graph

2.1 Social Routing

We see that in the human society, people can communicate with each other if they can develop a social route amongst themselves. While Alice does not know Bob well, Alice can depend on her friends, namely Carol, to introduce her to Bob. As a result, many of Alice and Bob's initial social interactions are founded on the reputation of their mutual friend. If Alice turns out to be a scammer, then Bob is less likely to trust Carol in the future. On the other hand, if Alice and Bob get along very well, they are both more likely to trust Carol. In the digital world, the current internet model uses routable identities (e.g. email address) as the mechanism for people to interact. Unfortunately, these routable identities are also used by spammers to send unwanted messages with little fear of repercussion. The DSL model of a community based social network model tries to incorporate human behavior of using social routes for message transmission. Here, we use online social networks to define friendship, which can grow stronger or weaker as various users interact with each other. In other words, DSL reaps the benefits of 'social context' existing in OSNs to build communication protocols with reduced spam and higher controllability to message receivers. Each user (or node in the social graph) sets up Profile Attributes ($PAtt$) [1] which are then propagated in the network to allow other people to contact them. Each Profile Attribute k (for node v) is propagated to other users according to the policy associated with it:

$$\forall k \in K_v^{PAtt}, \ \exists Policy(k) = [D, T, C]$$

Keywords received from other nodes are termed as Friendly Attributes ($FAtt$). Only those nodes can contact v with the keyword k which satisfy the above policy i.e., the node must be within D hops, all the links on the social path must have the minimum trust level T and all the nodes on the path must have all the keywords in C in their profile attributes. Thus, the receiver gets a large amount of control on who can contact him/her. The keywords help a node to route messages by deciding the next node in the social path. Previous researches like [2] [3] [4] have also used profile information to route messages or search queries in small world networks. In DSL, the information that nodes use to route messages are based on the keywords that they have. Thus, keywords serve as lose identities for nodes in place of global identifiers. In the following section we discuss the trust model.

2.2 Trust Management

DSL utilizes KarmaNet to manage trust so that bad nodes are removed from the network and good nodes' communication are not affected by bad nodes. In KarmaNet [5], bad nodes are nodes who either send unwanted messages or those who utilizes network resources but do not contribute to the network. Good interaction result will be propagated from destination to source and the nodes on the social route will be rewarded up to the sender. Bad interaction result will cause the social path to be punished from destination to source. If a social link is below a certain threshold, the message sent along that link maybe dropped with probability proportional to trust. In Fig. 1, we show values marking how much each person trusts the previous hop. For example, Carol completely trusts Alice and therefore Alice's trustworthiness, as judged by Carol, is 1.00. On the other hand, Carol is not very well trusted by Bob and her trustworthiness is only 0.40. Note that each person in the relationship may judge the other differently. In this instance, while Carol completely trusts Alice, Alice may not reciprocate. In fact, Carol's trustworthiness, as judged by Alice, may only be 0.30, for example.

KarmaNet is a fully distributed trust management protocol which can be used both in centralized and decentralized system. Therefore we use it for manage the trust of our system.

3 Companion Architecture

The purpose of the architecture is to provide an easy way for many applications to gain meaningful social context. By leveraging this data, applications such as email, Skype, online search, and multiplayer gaming can benefit by adding trust and route discovery to the system. We have purposefully designed our architecture in order to minimize changes to any third party application source code, especially at the client side. For example, we have successfully implemented a DSL-compatible version of email that only requires changing the SMTP server but not the client-side email application. This flexibility allows developers to add DSL functionality without forcing their clients to update anything. In fact, it is possible that the end users may not have to change anything at all. In this section, we will describe the system and how it's architecture facilitates this:

All applications that wish to take advantage of our architecture must have a way to remotely communicate with the architecture. If the application cannot communicate remotely, then a plug-in must be written for it or the source code must be modified and recompiled. Remember, we want to only perform minimal or no changes on pre-existing applications. So our architecture only requires that the user change which SMTP server she will be sending the email too. The SMTP server that the user is sending her email to will be the server that is connected to the underlying architecture, diagramed below, that allows social network data to be used for the application.

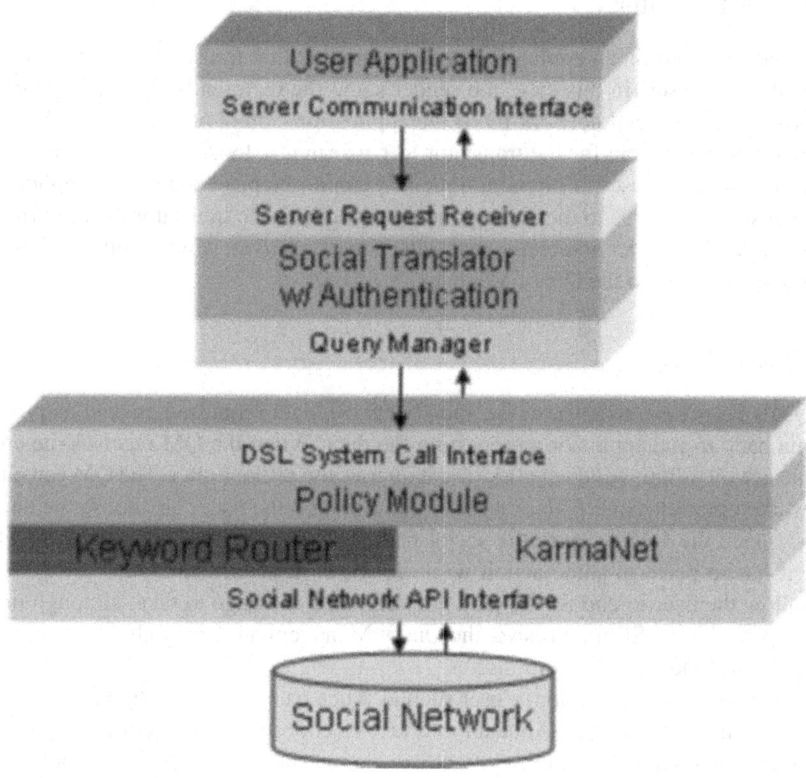

Fig. 2. Davis Social Links Architecture

3.1 Request Receiver

Once a user sends an email, our architecture's request receiver, or the SMTP server in this case, receives the email. The role of the request receiver is essentially to sit and wait for data from the user. The request receiver will typically expect some form of content and the necessary identification which varies between applications. In this case, the request receiver is an SMTP server that waits for the sender and receiver email addresses as well as the email content. Once the request receiver receives data, it then sends the data to the next component of the architecture, the translator.

Returning to our old example, let us say that Alice is using Thunderbird and wants to send an email to Bob along a social path. She first must configure Thunderbird and change the SMTP server address to the address of the SMTP server inside our architecture. This SMTP server is the request receiver of our architecture. Sendmail is setup on the SMTP server to run all email through a milter. This milter is a program that is given every email that Sendmail receives. The milter extracts the source and destination email addresses as well as the content.

3.2 Social Translator

The social translator is an application specific module that translates between the IDs provided by the user (in this case, the sender's and the recipient's email addresses) to the corresponding social network ID. If the application cannot provide a global unique ID, then it is impossible for the translator to perform any lookup. As a result, our architecture cannot be used if global unique IDs cannot be provided by the application. After translating the IDs to the corresponding social IDs, the translator then returns the social IDs for the sender and recipient to our request receiver, which sends the IDs and the message content to the Query Manager.

3.3 Query Manager

The QM's purpose is to retrieve the social network data requested as well as provide the data back to the application requesting the data. When the QM receives the email content as well as the social network IDs, it queries the social router. The QM can either request the optimal social path or a set of paths so that the user can choose the one he prefers. Once the QM receives the social paths between the two users from the DSL layer, it has to perform some action with the social network data. One option would be to allow the user to choose the path he prefers the message to take, although in the interest of making DSL unintrusive, the Query Manager can simply choose a best path according to some preset conditions.

In our email implementation, a user such as Alice can choose a path before actually sending the message. Giving Alice an interface to choose a social path can be accomplished in many ways. We chose to create a web interface via a Facebook application. In this interface, Alice can view all "send pending" message and choose a path to send the email along to Bob. We realize this would be a tedious process to do for each email a user wanted to send. Thus, we have added configurability options. Alice can choose to always send a message through a certain path (for emails sent to Bob after the initial one) thus eliminating the need to deal with the interface every time she wants to send an email to Bob. Once Alice chooses a path, the email will be marked as sent. Alternatively, Alice can simply allow the OSN kernel to choose a path for her.

3.4 Social Router

Given the user's ID and the intended destination ID, the social router will attempt to either find an optimal path between them using the decentralized algorithm [5] or return a set of routes for the user to choose from. If the router is successful, it will return the path(s) along with the likelihood that the message will be delivered successfully (which is a function of the trust between the nodes in the path(s)). If no path from the sender and the recipient can be found, the social router returns an error. Alice, according to her relationships, will discover that the path to Bob through Carol is her best bet on reaching Bob.

Once a social path has been selected, the router will examine each link along the path. If the trust value, τ of any link is less than a preset threshold, then the router will randomly drop the message at that link with probability equal to $1 - \tau$. This is done as punishment to weaker links since social links who's trust value is below the threshold are deemed untrustworthy and may be connected to a malicious user. The social router will then inform the query manager of it's decision and the query manager can then send out the email or drop it accordingly.

If the message is dropped, then the social router will automatically update the trust values along the path, punishing the nodes and the sender. Otherwise, if the message reaches it's destination, then the social router will also update the trust values along the path, rewarding all nodes along the path for delivering the message successfully.

3.5 Policy Module

The policy module is an optional module that can be utilized for path discovery. The policy module allows users to find recipients based on keywords, as discussed in the DSL paper. The user application provides the policy module with a list of keywords along with the sender's ID and the policy module will return a list of potential recipients that also have the keyword along with a few other contraining characteristics.

3.6 The Recipient's Experience

The receiver, Bob, can also use a web interface to choose whether he will accept the email or not. Bob is shown who the sender is (Alice) and which path (including trust values) she chose to send the email along. However, Bob is not shown the content of the email. If Bob rejects the email, then the application makes a request to the DSL layer to penalize the social path. On the other hand, Bob can accept the message. If Bob does so, the email is then sent via SMTP to Bob's inbox where he can open up Thunderbird to view it. Bob also has the same configurability options that Alice did, but for receiving. He can always choose to accept a message from Alice along a certain social path or any path. Bob still has an opportunity to penalize the path after receiving the email to his inbox if the content of the email is considered spam.

4 Extended Features

In addition to creating a social context for messaging, we have redesigned a few key concepts in messaging by incorporating our DSL system to increase controllability of the reply, reply-all, and forwarding functions.

4.1 Reply

Currently, replying to an email simply means that the user sends the original sender an email with the body included for reference. At the system level, there is no clear distinction between a reply and a new email. In our system, we have decided to implement our own reply functionality in order to incorporate social context along with recipient controllability. Due to the nature of keyword routing, the recipient of a message may or may not know what keyword to use in order to send a message back to the original sender. Furthermore, it may be impossible to actually find a social path if the original sender set up his keywords to be restrictive. Returning to the Alice and Bob example, even though Alice can find a path to Bob using keyword K_a, there is no guarentee that Bob can send a message back using the same keyword. In fact, it is possible that there is no such keyword which could allow Bob to communicate to Alice. This seemed to be a crucial feature in communication and we could not consider our architecture to be complete without it. As a result, we have implemented a system-level version of the reply functionality.

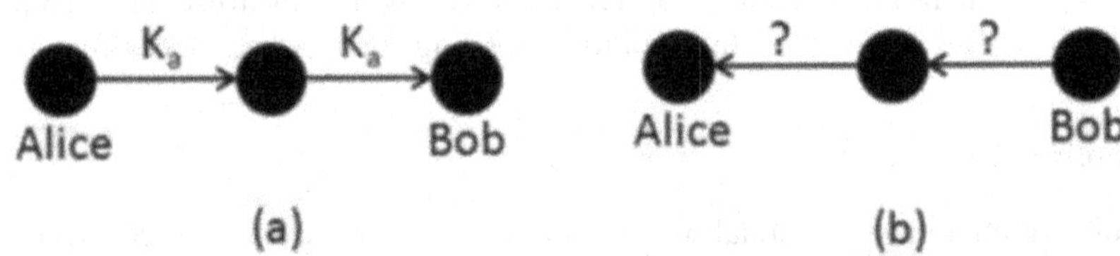

Fig. 3. (a) Alice finds and communicates to Bob using keyword K_a. (b) However, Bob will have trouble responding to Alice if he cannot find a keyword that will return a path to Alice.

When Alice is composing her message, she is given the option of granting reply tokens to her recipient, Bob. Each token allows Bob to reply to Alice once through the social path that Alice used to reach Bob. As a result, Bob does not have to find a social path on his own. After Bob has used up all the reply tokens, if he wishes to contact Alice again, he must find a new social path. By restricting the number of reply tokens granted, Alice can prevent Bob from spamming her.

If, between Alice sending the message and Bob replying, a user along the social path removes himself from DSL, then Bob will simply get a "path not found" error message and will then have to search for a new path.

4.2 Reply-All

Similar to reply, we have implemented reply-all functionality using tokens. When a user (let us use Alice again for this example) wants to send a message to multiple users, she can grant a number of reply-all tokens (in addition to reply-tokens). Note that if Alice grants x tokens, then each recipient will receive x tokens. If Bob is a recipient of her message and wishes to respond back to everyone, he can use up one of his tokens. Bob's message then travels back to Alice, where it is automatically sent by Alice to all of the original recipients. If one of the recipients decides that Bob's message is spam, DSL punishes the social path from this recipient to Alice and also the path from Alice back to Bob.

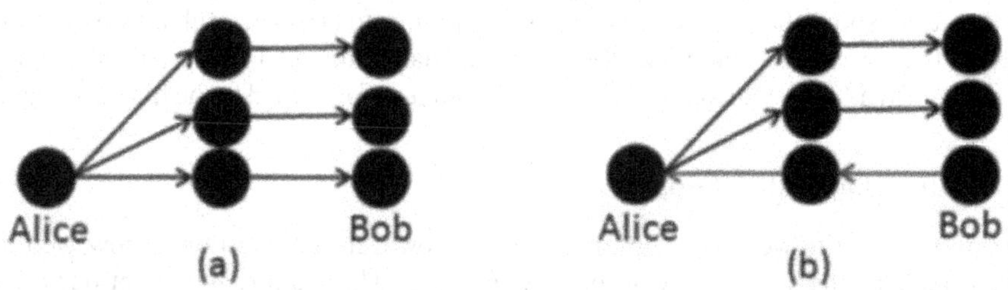

Fig. 4. (a) Alice sends a message to multiple recipients. (b) Bob wishes to reply to all the recipients, which he does so by first sending the message to Alice and having her forward the message to everyone else.

We are currently considering the situation in which one node is part of the path from Alice to Bob along with being part of the path from Alice to some other recipient. If Bob does a reply all, this node will be affected twice. For example, if the recipient marks Bob's message as spam, the node will be punished as the outcome traverses from the recipient to Alice and again when the outcome traverses from Alice to Bob. Similarly, the node can be rewarded twice if the message is marked as being good.

4.3 Forward

Let's assume that Alice and Bob are professors at a university. Alice is going to be giving a presentation on a subject that she thinks Bob's students may be interested in hearing. Alice then sends a message to Bob asking him to forward the message to his students on her behalf. We assume that Alice does not know who all of Bob's students are and therefore are unable to contact them directly. Alice, when composing the email, has the option of granting Bob a forward token, which means that Alice is willing to accept some of the risks that Bob would take by forwarding the message. As a result, if Bob's students decide that the message is spam, Alice would receive some of the punishment, as would Bob. Similarly, if the students really liked the notice about the talk, both Alice and Bob would be rewarded. We have designed a prototype of the forward functionality and we are currently experimenting with how much punishment or reward Alice and Bob should each receive.

One important thing we want Alice to be able to control is the integrity of the message. While Alice most likely trusts Bob, since Alice's reputation can be adversely affected if Bob makes bad changes to the message, we are currently preventing the recipient from modifying the body of the original message before forwarding it. They are, however, allowed to add a new note intended for recipients of the forwarded message.

Another situation that we are currently experimenting with is if Alice knew exactly who the forwarded message's recipient is. For example, let us assume that Alice wishes to send her resume and job application to a hiring manager but she knows that her application would receive more weight if it was forwarded by her friend Eve, who knows the hiring manager very well. We are currently testing out a system where Alice can specify the final recipient (the hiring manager) and Eve will automatically forward the message to the hiring manager. As a result, DSL will find a path from Alice to Eve and then from Eve to the hiring manager.

There are some challenges we need to solve for this to be successful, however. While having the message be automatically forwarded makes things much easier for Eve, Eve is not able to add a personal note before the message is forwarded to the hiring manager.

4.4 Other Application Support

Email works quite well with our architecture. However, the question is how well are other applications supported with our architecture? The main requirement our architecture has for applications is that they must have globally unique IDs within the application's scope. The relationship between the application's IDs and the underlying OSN's IDs is crucial. Without these application IDs, it is nearly impossible to obtain a user's social network information since the kernel cannot translate between the two sets of IDs. In this subsection we will examine how authentication at the application level affects the effectiveness of our OSN kernel architecture.

Another type of communication besides email is Skype[6], which allows users to make telephone calls over the internet. While Skype users do have global unique IDs, they're encrypted and cannot be easily obtained by the user or the architecture. Though it may seem it would be impossible for Skype to work well with the architecture, there is a solution that satisfies the architecture's requirement. The solution involves Skype creating a server that acts as the middleman in the communication between the user and architecture. The user can choose to notify the Skype servers that the user wishes to utilize the architecture which will have Skype decrypt the IDs and send them over to the architecture. This would allow an application ID to social network ID translation. After this, Skype's usage of the architecture can be similar to what we have done with email.

A unique way to utilize the architecture for non-communication purposes would be to associate search words in Google with friends. The idea is that when the user submits a search query, the architecture can find out what friends are associated with particular words in the search terms. The user can simply be presented with what friends are associated with what words in the search terms as a result. On the other hand, an interesting use would be utilizing the friends associated with the search terms to influence Google's search results. How much influence a friend has on the search terms could be fine tuned by the user.

5 Status

Currently, we have adapted email to work with our companion architecture as a proof of concept. To analyze it's performance, we assume that the cost of the sender sending the email to the architecture and the architecture sending the email to the receiver is

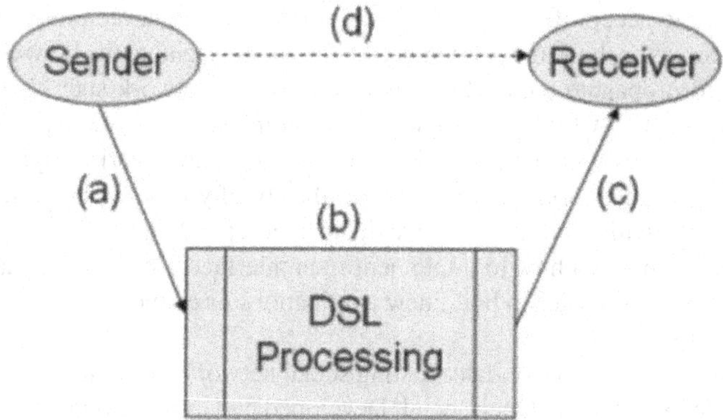

Fig. 5. A high level overview of the architecture. (a) First email sent to DSL. (b) DSL processes the email. (c) DSL sends email to receiver. (d) The original path email follows without DSL.

double the cost of sending email regularly. Thus, we only measure the overhead of the architecture processing. Utilizing the architecture for email can sometimes require human interaction as previously outlined. We chose to measure the scenarios that don't require human interaction. In these scenarios, the emails match some criteria (default path, trust threshold) that allows the emails to simply be sent to the receiver without the need for the receiver or sender to select any options for the message.

The process of sending a message through our system can be broken up into 3 parts. The first part is when the sender sends the email to the supporting architecture. The next part is the architecture applying the required work on the message prior to actually sending out the message to the receiver. The final part is sending the message to the receiver. For this analysis, we assume that the cost of the sender sending the email to the architecture and the architecture sending the email to the receiver is double the cost of sending email regularly. Thus, we only measure the overhead of the architecture processing.

Our tests were ran on a system with an Intel Xeon E5345 (2.33GHz) processor with 8GB of RAM. We measured the overhead that would be presented by the extra architecture processing for 1,000, 10,000, and 100,000 consecutive emails. We ran three tests to confirm that our results could converge to a similar result. Each message was 1000 characters long. Processing each of the 1,000 emails was executed on a single thread and the processing of the next email would only start after the current email finished. The overhead per email in all of those scenarios converges to approximately .00212 seconds. The overhead is quite small in our implementation that still has room for code optimization. We can conclude that the overhead required for our architecture is small enough to warrant the benefits of utilizing the architecture.

6 Related Work

Some work has been done on utilizing social networks in email systems, such as TrustMail [7] and RE [8]. Given a sender and a recipient, TrustMail finds a social path between them and further computes a trust score for the sender, thus the recipient can decide whether to accept the emails from the sender. Different recipients may get different trust scores for the same sender, according to the social paths between them. RE allows users to propagate their whitelists on the social network such that a recipient can decide whether to whitelist a sender based on the social relationship between the recipient and the users who have whitelisted the sender. These work couples their applications with social networks tightly and describes briefly how applications and social networks interact, while in this paper, we dedicate a separate layer for general applications and discuss in detail how to implement such interfaces. We believe that with DSL architecture, it will be easier to build new applications or connect existing applications to social networks.

There is also effort to consolidate existing social networks from industry. Notable examples include OpenID and OpenSocial. Developed by Google along with a number of social networks, OpenSocial provides a set of common APIs for social network applications, which can serve as the communication layer between DSL and existing social networks. OpenSocial, however, does not provide the high level features proposed in DSL such as reputation systems and social routing. Industry may have developed similar ideas as DSL internally, such as some social network projects presented in Microsoft Research TechFest 2009, while to our best knowledge, no details has been published. Presenting DSL architecture here, we wish this paper may initiate further discussions in software system level on how to connect existing social networks to future OSN applications.

7 Conclusion and Future Work

There are three sets of standard applications that we have to accommodate with the architecture. The first is applications that have already been written that dont allow plug-ins to be written for them. These applications are clearly the toughest to satisfy as we have to find ways for them to communicate remotely with a system they were never designed to communicate with. Beyond modifying the source code, we believe there isnt much room for improvement for our architecture to support this set of applications.

On the other hand, the set of applications that support plug-ins can typically be programmed to remotely communicate with any system the programmer desires. Similarly, the third set of applications being applications written from scratch can always be programmed to remotely communicate with any system. Thus, we hope to develop another API layer above the whole architecture presented in this paper to support these two sets of applications. With this API, the architecture is completely hidden from the application as the developer (with sufficient permissions) can read and write data through the API.

Acknowledgements

We would first like to thank Ken Gribble for his tireless help with setting up the milter and configuring it to our specificiations. We would also like to thank Juan Lang, Lerone Banks, and Matthew Spears for their help and guidance on this paper. This research is funded in part by National Science Foundation under CNS-0832202, Intel, and an MURI grant from Army Research Office under the ARSENAL project and we would like to thank them for continued support.

References

1. Banks, L., Bhattacharyya, P., Wu, S.F.: Davis social links: A social network based approach to future internet routing. In: FIST 2009: The Workshop on Trust and Security in the Future Internet (July 2009)
2. Kleinberg, J.: The small-world phenomenon: An algorithm perspective. In: STOC 2000: Proceedings of the 32nd annual ACM symposium on Theory of computing, pp. 163–170. ACM, New York (2000)
3. Milgram, S.: The small world problem. Psychology Today 61, 60–67 (1967)
4. Sandberg, O.: The Structure and Dynamics of Navigable Networks. PhD thesis, Chalmers University (2007)
5. Spear, M., Lang, J., Lu, X., Wu, S.F., Matloff, N.: KarmaNet: Using social behavior to reduce malicious activity in networks (2008), http://www.cs.ucdavis.edu/research/tech-reports/2008/CSE-2008-2.pdf
6. OpenSocial, http://www.skype.com/
7. Golbeck, J., Hendler, J.: Reputation network analysis for email filtering. In: Proceedings of the 1st Conference on Email and Anti-Spam (CEAS) (2004)
8. Garriss, S., Kaminsky, M., Freedman, M.J., Karp, B., Mazieres, D., Yu, H.: Re: Reliable email. In: Proceedings of the 3rd Symposium on Networked Systems Design and Implementation (NSDI), pp. 297–310 (2006)

Appendix: Screenshot of the Application

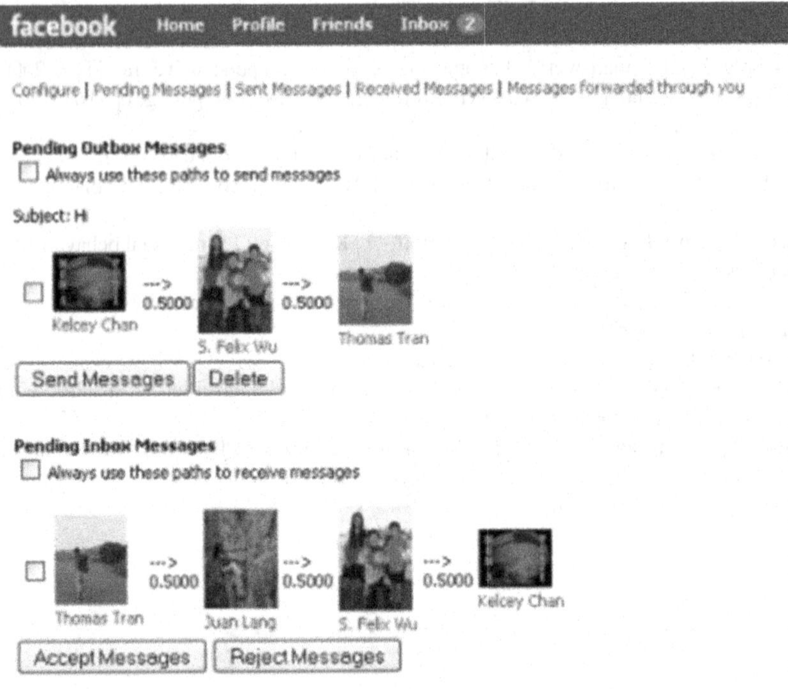

Fig. 6. A user's pending inbox and outbox. Here, the user can manage messages to be sent out along with ones that they are about to receive.

Information Extraction as Link Prediction: Using Curated Citation Networks to Improve Gene Detection

Andrew Arnold and William W. Cohen

Machine Learning Department, Carnegie Mellon University
{aarnold,wcohen}@cs.cmu.edu

Abstract. In this paper we explore the usefulness of various types of publication-related metadata, such as citation networks and curated databases, for the task of identifying genes in academic biomedical publications. Specifically, we examine whether knowing something about which genes an author has previously written about, combined with information about previous coauthors and citations, can help us predict which new genes the author is likely to write about in the future. Framed in this way, the problem becomes one of predicting links between authors and genes in the publication network. We show that this solely social-network based link prediction technique outperforms various baselines, including those relying only on non-social biological information.

1 Introduction and Related Work

Social networks, in the form of bibliographies and citations, have long been an integral part of the scientific process. Most scientists begin their exploration of a new problem with an intense investigation of the relevant literature. In a new or small field, for which the universe of such citations is relatively small, both a broad and deep search is manageable. As the size of the set of related papers grows, however, a researcher's time and attention can easily become overwhelmed. While the Internet has provided scientists with new tools for performing these literature reviews more quickly and precisely, it is usually left up to the user to guide the search themselves. In other words, one has to know what she is looking for. At the same time the space of accessible, and possibly relevant, papers has increased even more swiftly, leaving many valuable publications undiscovered. This is the problem we address in this paper: how to leverage the information contained within these publication networks, along with information concerning the individual publications themselves and a user's history, to help predict which entities the user might be most interested in and thus intelligently guide his search.

Specifically, our application domain is the task of predicting which genes and proteins a biologist is likely to write about in the future (for the rest of the paper we will use the term 'gene' to refer both to the gene and gene product, or protein). We define a *citation network* as a graph in which *publications* and *authors* are represented as nodes, with bi-directional *authorship* edges linking authors and papers, and uni-directional *citation* edges linking papers to other papers (the direction of the edge denoting which paper is doing the citing and which is being cited). We can construct such a network from a given corpus of publications along with their lists of cited works. There exist many so

B. Liu et al. (Eds.): WASA 2009, LNCS 5682, pp. 541–550, 2009.

called *curated* literature databases for biology in which publications are *tagged*, or manually labeled, with the genes with which they are concerned. We can use this metadata to introduce *gene* nodes to our enhanced citation network, which are bi-directionally linked to the papers in which they are tagged. Finally, we exploit a third source of data, namely biological domain expertise in the form of ontologies and databases of facts concerning these genes, to create *association* edges between genes which have been shown to relate to each other in various ways. We call the entire structure an *annotated citation network*.

Although academics have long recognized and investigated the importance of such networks, their investigations have often been focused on historical [1], summary, or explanatory purposes [2,3,4,5]. While other work has been concerned with understanding how influence develops and flows through these networks [6], we instead focus on the problem of link prediction [7, 8]. *Link prediction* is the problem of predicting which nodes in a graph, currently unlinked, "should" be linked to each other, where "should" is defined in some application-specific way. This may be useful to know if a graph is changing over time (as in citation networks when new papers are published), or if certain edges may be hidden from observation (as in detecting insider trading cabals). In our setting, we seek to discover edges between authors and genes, indicating genes about which an author has yet to write, but which he may be interested in.

While there has been extensive work on analyzing and exploiting the structure of networks such as the web and citation networks [9, 10], most of the techniques used for identifying and extracting biological entities directly from publication text [11, 12, 13, 14, 15, 16] and curated databases [17] rely on performing named entity recognition on the text itself [18] and ignore the underlying network structure entirely. While these techniques perform well given a paper to analyze, they are impossible to use when such text is unavailable, as in our link prediction task.

In the following sections, respectively, we discuss the topology of our annotated citation network, along with describing the data sources from which the network was constructed. We then introduce *random walks*, the technique used for calculating the proximity of nodes in our graph, thus suggesting plausible novel links between authors and genes. Finally, we describe an extensive set of ablation studies performed to assess the relative importance of each type of edge, or *relation*, in our model and discuss the results, concluding with a view towards a future model combining network and text information.

2 Data

We are lucky to have access to many sources of good data[1] from which we are able to extract the nodes and edges that make up our annotated citation network[2]:

- PubMed Central (PMC) contains full-text copies of over one million biological papers for which open-access has been granted.

[1] http://pubmedcentral.nih.gov, http://yeastgenome.org, http://geneontology.org

[2] An on-line demo, including the network used for the experiments, can be found at http://yeast.ml.cmu.edu/nies/

- The Saccharomyces Genome Database(SGD) contains various types of information concerning the yeast organism *Saccharomyces cerevisiae*.
- The Gene Ontology (GO) describes the relationships between biological entities across numerous organisms.

Nodes	
Name	**Number**
Paper	44,012
Author	66,977
Gene	5,816

Edges		
Name	**Description**	**Number**
Authorship	Author ↔ Paper	178,233
Mention	Paper ↔ Gene	160,621
Citation	Paper ↔ Paper	42,958
RelatesTo	Gene ↔ Gene	1,604

3 Methods

Now that we have a representation of the data as a graph, we are ready to begin the calculation of our link predictions. The first step is to pick a node, or set of nodes, in the graph to which our predicted links will connect. These are our *query nodes*. We then perform a *random walk* out from the query node, simultaneously following each edge to the adjacent nodes with a probability proportional to the inverse of the total number of adjacent nodes [19]. We repeat this process a number of times, each time spreading our probability of being on any particular node, given we began on the query node. If there are multiple nodes in the query set, we perform our walk simultaneously from each one. After each step in our walk we have a probability distribution over all the nodes of the graph, representing the likelihood of a walker, beginning at the query node(s) and randomly following outbound edges in the way described, of being on that particular node. Under the right conditions, after enough steps this distribution will converge. We can then use this distribution to rank all the nodes, predicting that the nodes most likely to appear in the walk are also the nodes to which the query node(s) should most likely connect. In practice, the same results can be achieved by multiplying the adjacency matrix of the graph by itself. Each such multiplication represents one complete step in the walk.

We can adjust the adjacency matrix (and thus the graph) by selectively hiding, or removing, certain *types* of edges. For instance, if we want to isolate the influence of citations on our walk, we can remove all the citation edges from the graph, perform a walk, and compare the results to a walk performed over the full graph.

Likewise, in order to evaluate our predicted edges, we can hide certain instances of edges, perform a walk, and compare the predicted edges to the actual withheld ones. For example, if we have all of an author's publications and their associated gene mention data for the years 2007 and 2008, we can remove the links between the author and the genes he mentioned in 2008 (along with all other edges gleaned from 2008 data), perform a walk, and then see how many of those withheld gene-mention edges were correctly predicted. Since this evaluation is a comparison between one unranked set (the true edges) and another ranked list (the predicted edges) we can use the standard information retrieval metrics of precision, recall and F1.

4 Experiment and Results

To evaluate our network model, we first divide our data into two sets:

- `Train`, which contains only *authors*, *papers*, *genes* and their respective relations which were published before 2008
- `Validation`, which contains new[3] (*author* $\overset{Mentions}{\rightarrow}$ *genes*) relationships that were first published in 2008.

From this `Train` data we create a series of subgraphs, each emphasizing a different set of relationships between the nodes. These subgraphs are summarized in Figure 1. By selectively removing edges of a certain type from the $FULL$ graph we were able to isolate the effects of these relations on the random walk and, ultimately, the predicted links. Specifically, we classify each graph into one of four groups and later use this categorization to assess the relative contribution of each edge type to the overall link prediction performance.

4.1 Baseline

The baseline graphs are $UNIFORM$, ALL_PAPERS and $AUTHORS$. $UNIFORM$ and ALL_PAPERS do not depend on the *author* node. $UNIFORM$, as its name implies, is simply the chance of predicting a novel gene correctly given that you select a predicted gene uniformly at random from the universe of genes. Since there are 5,816 gene names, and on average each author in our query set writes about 6.7 new genes in 2008, the chance of randomly guessing one of these correctly is $6.7/5816 = .12\%$. Using these values we can extrapolate this model's expected precision, recall and F1. Relatedly, ALL_PAPERS, while also independent of authors, nevertheless takes into account the distribution of genes across papers in the training graph. Thus its predictions are weighted by the number of times a gene was written about in the past. This model provides a more reasonable baseline. $AUTHORS$ considers the distribution of genes over all papers previously published by the author. While this type of model may help recover previously published genes, it may not do as well identifying new genes.

4.2 Social

The social graphs ($RELATED\_PAPERS$, $RELATED\_AUTHORS$, $COAUTHORS$, $FULL\_MINUS\_RELATED\_GENES$ and $CITATIONS$) are constructed of edges that convey information about the social interactions of authors, papers and genes. These include facts about which authors have written together, which papers have cited each other, and which genes have been mentioned in which papers.

[3] We restrict our evaluation to genes about which the author has never previously published (even though an author may publish about them again in 2008), since realistically, these predictions would be of no value to an author who is already familiar with his own previous publications.

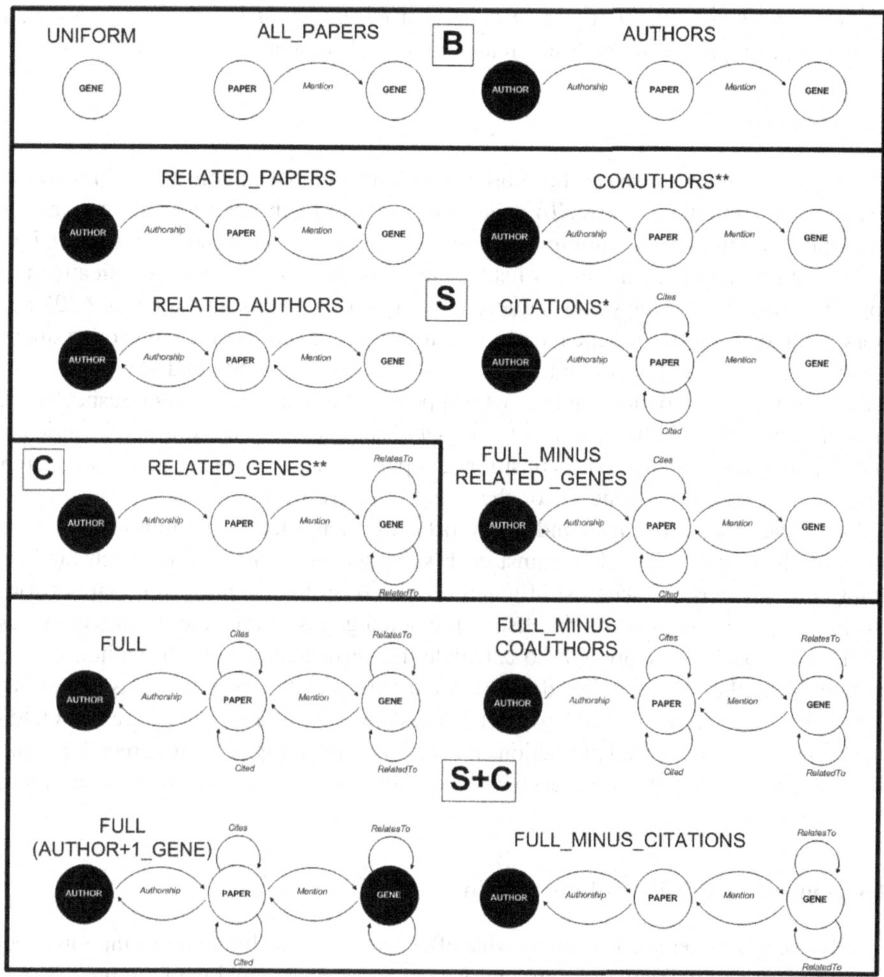

Fig. 1. Subgraphs queried in the experiment, grouped by type: **B** for baselines, **S** for social networks, **C** for networks conveying biological content, and **S+C** for networks making use of both social and biological information. Shaded nodes represent the node(s) used as a query. **For graph $RELATED\_GENES$, which contains the two complimentary uni-directional *Relation* edges, we also performed experiments on the two subgraphs $RELATED\_GENES_{\mathit{RelatesTo}}$ and $RELATED\_GENES_{\mathit{RelatedTo}}$ which each contain only one direction of the *relation* edges. For graph $CITATIONS$, we similarly constructed subgraphs $CITATIONS_{\mathit{Cites}}$ and $CITATIONS_{\mathit{Cited}}$.

4.3 Content

In addition to social edges, some graphs also encode information regarding the biological content of the genes being published. The graph $RELATED\_GENES$ models only this biological content, while $FULL\_MINUS\_COAUTHORS$,

$FULL\_MINUS\_CITATIONS$, $FULL$ and $FULL(AUTHOR + 1\_GENE)$ all contain edges representing both social and biological content.

4.4 Protocol

For our query nodes we select the subset of authors who have publications in both the `Train` and `Validation` set. To make sure we have fresh, relevant publications for these query authors, and to minimize the impact of possible ambiguous name collision, we further restrict the query author list to only those authors who have publications in both 2007 and 2008. This yields a query list, ALLAUTHORS, with a total of 2,322 authors, each to be queried independently, one at a time. We further create two other query author lists, FIRSTAUTHORS and LASTAUTHORS containing 544 and 786 authors respectively, restricted to those authors who appear as the first or last author, respectively, in their publications in the `Validation` set. The purpose of these lists of queries is to determine whether an author's position in a paper's list of authors has any impact in our ability to predict the genes he or she might be interested in.

Given these sets of graphs and query lists, we then query each author in each of our three lists, independently, against each subgraph in Figure 1. Each such (author, graph) query yields a ranked list of genes predicted for that author given that network representation. By comparing this list of predicted genes against the set of true genes from `Validation` we are able to calculate the performance of each (author, graph) pairing. Since the list of predicted genes is sometimes quite long (since it is a distribution over all genes in the walk), we set a threshold and all evaluations are calculated only considering the top 20 predictions made. These resulting precision, recall, F1 and MAP metrics, broken down for each set of author positions, are summarized in Figure 2 respectively.

4.5 Querying with Extra Information

Finally, we were interested in seeing what effect adding some limited information about an author's 2008 publications to our query would have on the quality of our predictions. This might occur, for instance, if we have the text of one of the author's new papers available and are able to perform basic information extraction to find at least one gene. The question is, can we leverage this single, perhaps easy to identify gene, to improve our chances of predicting or identifying other undiscovered new genes? To answer this question, in addition to querying each author in isolation, we also queried, together as a set, each author and the one new gene about which he published most in 2008 (see graph $FULL(AUTHOR + 1\_GENE)$ in Figure1). These results are summarized, along with the others, in Figure 2, again broken down by author position.

4.6 Results

Using Figures 1 and 2 as guides, we turn now to an analysis of the effects different edge types have on our ability to successfully predict new genes[4]. We should first explain

[4] A summery of the claims made and their associated statistical tests are summarized in Table 1.

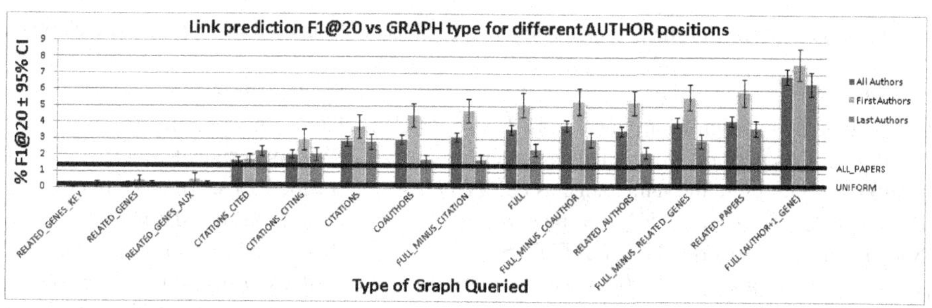

Fig. 2. Mean percent F1 @20 of queries across graph types, broken down by author position, shown with error bars demarking the 95% confidence interval. Baselines $UNIFORM$ and ALL_PAPERS are also displayed.

the absence of results for the $AUTHORS$ graph, and the lines for $UNIFORM$ and ALL_PAPERS in Figure 2. Since these baselines do not depend on the query, they are constant across models and are thus displayed as horizontal lines across the charts in Figure 2. $AUTHORS$ is missing because it is only able to discover genes that have *already* been written about by the query authors in the training graph. Since our evaluation metrics only count the prediction of novel genes, $AUTHORS$'s performance is necessarily zero.

Given these baselines, let us next consider the role of author position on prediction performance. It is apparent from the results that, in almost all settings, querying based on the first author of a paper generates the best results, with querying by last author performing the worst. This seems to suggest that knowing the first author of a paper is more informative than knowing who the last author was in terms of predicting which genes that paper may be concerned with. Depending on the specifics of one's own discipline, this may be surprising. For example, in computer science it is often customary for an advisor, lab director or principal investigator to be listed as the last author. One might assume that the subject of that lab's study would be most highly correlated with this final position author, but the evidence here seems to suggest otherwise. Tellingly, the only case in which the last author *is* most significant is in the $CITATIONS\_CITED$ model. Recall that in this model edges from cited papers to their citing papers are present. These results may suggest that in this model, knowing the last author of the paper actually is more valuable.

Given that in most cases the models queried using first authors performed the best, the columns of Figure 2 have been positioned in order of increasing first author F1 performance, and all subsequent comparisons are made with respect to the first author queries, unless otherwise stated. Thus we notice that those models relying solely on the biological GO information relating genes to one another (**Content** graphs from Figure 1) perform significantly worse than any other model, and are in fact in the same range as the $UNIFORM$ model. Indeed, the $FULL$ model benefits from having the relations removed, as it is outperformed by the $FULL\_MINUS\_RELATED\_GENES$ model.

There are a few possible explanations for why these content-based biological edges might be hurting performance. First, scientists might not be driven to study genes which *have already been demonstrated* to be biologically related to one another. Since we are

Table 1. A summary of the claims made and the statistical tests used to support those claims

Claim	**Statistical test**
Last author is most significant in $CITATIONS\_CITED$	80% confidence intervals
Content graphs perform worse than any other model	Wilcoxon signed rank ($p < .01$)
Content graphs are in the same range as $UNIFORM$	Inside 95% confidence intervals
Removing $RELATED\_GENES$ improves $FULL$	Wilcoxon signed rank ($p < .01$)
Social graphs outperform ALL_PAPERS	Outside 95% confidence intervals
$FULL$ outperforms $CITATIONS$ and $COAUTHORS$	Wilcoxon signed rank ($p < .01$)
$FULL$ benefits from having *coauthor* edges removed	Wilcoxon signed rank ($p < .15$)
$RELATED\_PAPERS$ is best single-author query model	Wilcoxon signed rank ($p < .10$)
$FULL(AUTHOR + 1\_GENE)$ performs best	Paired sign ($p < .02$)

necessarily using biological facts already discovered, we may be behind the wave of new investigation. Second, these new investigations, some of them biologically motivated, might not always turn out conclusively or successfully. This would likewise lead to the genes being studied in this way lying outside the scope of our biological content. Finally, it is possible that our methods for parsing and interpreting the GO information and extracting the relationships between genes may not be capturing the relevant information in the same way a trained biologist might be able to. Relatedly, the ontologies themselves might be designed more for summarizing the current state of knowledge, rather than suggesting promising areas of pursuit.

In contrast, the models exploiting the **social** relationships in $CITATIONS$, $COAUTHORS$, $RELATED\_AUTHORS$ and $RELATED\_PAPERS$ all outperform the ALL_PAPERS baseline. While each of these social edge types is helpful on its own, their full combination is, perhaps counter-intuitively, not the best performing model. Indeed, while $FULL$ outperforms its constituent $CITATIONS$ and $COAUTHORS$ models, it nevertheless benefits slightly from having the *coauthor* edges removed (as in $FULL\_MINUS\_COAUTHOR$). This may be due to competition among the edges for the probability being distributed by our random walk. The more paths there are out of a node, the less likely the walker is to follow any given one. Thus, by removing the (many) coauthorship edges from the $FULL$ graph, we allow the walk to reach a better solution more quickly.

Interestingly, the best performance of the single-author query models is achieved by the relatively simple, pure collaborative filtering $RELATED\_PAPERS$ model [20]. Explained in words, this social model predicts that authors are likely to write about genes that co-occur with an author's previously studied genes in other people's papers. This makes sense since, if other people are writing about the same genes as the author, they are more likely to share other common interests and thus would be the closest examples of what the author may eventually become interested in in the future.

Finally we examine the question of whether having not only a known author to query, but also one of this author's new genes, aids in prediction. The results for the $FULL(AUTHOR + 1\_GENE)$ model[5] seem to indicate that the answer is yes.

[5] During evaluation the queried new gene is added to the set of previously observed genes and thus does not count towards precision or recall.

Adding a single known new gene to our author query of the $FULL$ model improves our prediction performance by almost 50%, and significantly outperforms the best single-author query model, $RELATED\_PAPERS$, as well. This is a promising result, as it suggests that the information contained in our network representation can be combined with other sources of data (gleaned from performing information extraction on papers' text, for example) to achieve even better results than either method alone.

5 Conclusions and Future Work

In this paper we have introduced a new graph-based annotated citation network model to represent various sources of information regarding publications in the biological domain. We have shown that this network representation alone, without any features drawn from text, is able to outperform competitive baselines. Using extensive ablation studies we have investigated the relative impact of each of the different types of information encoded in the network, showing that social knowledge often trumps biological content, and demonstrated a powerful tool for both combining and isolating disparate sources of information. We have further shown that, in the domain of Saccharomyces research from which our corpus was drawn, knowing who the first author of a paper is tends to be more informative than knowing who the last author is (contrary to some conventional wisdom). Finally, we have shown that, despite performing well on its own, our network representation can easily be further enhanced by including in the query set other sources of knowledge about a prediction subject gleaned from separate techniques, such as information extraction and document classification.

We plan to extend this work by incorporating the results of these social network models into standard information extraction techniques. Since the end result of our link prediction algorithm is a distribution over nodes, one simple way to do this would be to use that distribution as a prior for a probabilistic information extraction methods. We also see value in incorporating a temporal dimension to our network. In our current model all edges are walked upon with equal probability, regardless of the temporal distance between the two connected nodes. We might do better by taking this time distance into account: for example, coauthorship on a paper 20 years ago may carry less weight than a collaboration just a few years ago.

References

1. Garfield, E., Sher, I., Torpie, R.: The Use of Citation Data in Writing the History of Science. The Institute for Scientific Information (1964)
2. Erosheva, E., Fienberg, S., Lafferty, J.: Mixed membership models of scientific publications. PNAS 101(21) (2004)
3. Liu, X., Bollen, J., Nelson, M., de Sompel, H.V.: Co-authorship networks in the digital library research community. In: Information Processing and Management (2005)
4. Cardillo, A., Scellato, S., Latora, V.: A topological analysis of scientific coauthorship networks. Physica A: Statistical Mechanics and its Applications (2006)
5. Leicht, E.A., Clarkson, G., Shedden, K., Newman, M.E.J.: Large-scale structure of time evolving citation networks. Eur. Phys. J. B 59, 75–83 (2007)

6. Dietz, L., Bickel, S., Scheffer, T.: Unsupervised prediction of citation influences. In: ICML (2007)
7. Cohn, D., Hofmann, T.: The missing link: A probabilistic model of document content and hypertext connectivity. In: NIPS (2001)
8. Liben-Nowell, D., Kleinberg., J.: The link prediction problem for social networks. In: CIKM (2003)
9. Kleinberg, J.M.: Authoritative sources in a hyperlinked environment. In: JACM (1999)
10. Kleinberg, J.M., Kumar, R., Raghavan, P., Rajagopalan, S., Tomkins, A.S.: The web as a graph: Measurements, models and methods. In: Asano, T., Imai, H., Lee, D.T., Nakano, S.-i., Tokuyama, T. (eds.) COCOON 1999. LNCS, vol. 1627, p. 1. Springer, Heidelberg (1999)
11. Cohen, A.M., Hersh, W.R.: A survey of current work in biomedical text mining. Briefings in Bioinformatics 6, 57–71 (2005)
12. Feldman, R., Regev, Y., Finkelstein-Landau, M., Hurvitz, E., Kogan, B.: Mining the biomedical literature using semantic analysis. Biosilico 1(2), 69–80 (2003)
13. Murphy, R.F., Kou, Z., Hua, J., Joffe, M., Cohen, W.W.: Extracting and structuring subcellular location information from on-line journal articles: The subcellular location image finder. In: KSCE (2004)
14. Franzén, K., Eriksson, G., Olsson, F., Asker, L., Lidén, P., Cöster, J.: Protein names and how to find them. International Journal of Medical Informatics (2002)
15. Bunescu, R., Ge, R., Kate, R., Marcotte, E., Mooney, R., Ramani, A., Wong, Y.: Comparative experiments on learning information extractors for proteins and their interactions. Journal of AI in Medicine (2004)
16. Shi, L., Campagne, F.: Building a protein name dictionary from full text: a machine learning term extraction approach. BMC Bioinformatics 6(88) (2005)
17. Wang, R.C., Tomasic, A., Frederking, R.E., Cohen, W.W.: Learning to extract gene-protein names from weakly-labeled text. In: CMU SCS Technical Report Series (CMU-LTI-08-04) (2006)
18. Collins, M., Singer, Y.: Unsupervised models for named entity classification. In: Joint Conference on Empirical Methods in Natural Language Processing and Very Large Corpora (1999)
19. Cohen, W.W., Minkov, E.: A graph-search framework for associating gene identifiers with documents. BMC Bioinformatics 7(440) (2006)
20. Goldberg, D., Nichols, D., Oki, B.M., Terry, D.: Using collaborative filtering to weave an information tapestry. Communications of the ACM 35(12), 61–70 (1992)

Social Network Privacy via Evolving Access Control

Giovanni Di Crescenzo[1] and Richard J. Lipton[2]

[1] Telcordia Technologies, Piscataway, NJ, USA
giovanni@research.telcordia.com
[2] Georgia Tech, Atlanta, GA, USA
richard.lipton@cc.gatech.edu

Abstract. We study the problem of limiting privacy loss due to data shared in a social network, where the basic underlying assumptions are that users are interested in sharing data and cannot be assumed to constantly follow appropriate privacy policies. Note that if these two assumptions do not hold, social network privacy is theoretically very easy to achieve; for instance, via some form of access control and confidentiality transformation on the data.

In this paper we observe that users-regulated access control has shown to be unsuccessful for practical social network, and propose that social networks deploy an additional layer of server-assisted access control which, even under no action from a user, automatically evolves over time, by restricting access to the user's data. The evolving access control mechanism provides non-trivial quantifiable guarantees for formally specified requirements of utility (i.e., users share as much data as possible to all other users) and privacy (i.e., users expose combinations of sensitive data only with low probability and over a long time). To the best of our knowledge, this is the first research solution attempting to simultaneously maximizes utility and safeguards privacy of users sharing data in social networking websites.

Keywords: Social Networking, Privacy, Utility, Access Control.

1 Introduction

Recent trends in social networks include the rise of businesses that manage social networking websites (e.g., Facebook, MySpace, Twitter) where users can freely post their data (images, text, files, etc.) and share it with their friends, peers, or anyone else having access to the website. As the most popular sites are currently attracting tens of millions of users, consequences of site misuses are being documented on a daily base on major newspapers and media entities. One typical class of misuses is that users happen to share various types of sensitive data (e.g., embarrassing images, politically incorrect opinions, proprietary files), which trigger undesired consequences (e.g., impacting decisions with respect to job hiring and firing [12,13,14], provision of medical or other types of insurance, etc.).

Balancing the users' desire of sharing their data (briefly referred as utility) with the users' needs to keep data private against future undesired consequences (briefly referred as privacy) is recognized as a big problem in practical social networks. (See, e.g., [1,3,6] for more general discussions of trust and privacy issues in popular social networking websites.) Note that theoretically speaking, users could keep privacy at the

B. Liu et al. (Eds.): WASA 2009, LNCS 5682, pp. 551–560, 2009.

expense of utility (i.e., by sharing no data), or could maximize utility at the expense of privacy (i.e., by not restricting access to all shared data), or, perhaps the best theoretical compromise, could balance utility and privacy by constantly implementing an access control policy which provides the desired data privacy at current and future times. The latter approach, if possible at all, is expected to be impractical for at least two reasons: drafting a policy that is guaranteed to keep privacy in the future may be hard in many scenarios (i.e., data seeming innocent today may not be so tomorrow); requiring users of a huge social network to perfectly comply to a probably complex privacy policy may have little success in many scenarios, possibly going against the social network's goals. In fact, even in the case of a perfectly complying single user, this user's privacy can be compromised by other users' behavior [13]. Overall, this discussion implies that user-regulated access control alone may not be an acceptable privacy solution.

Our contribution. In this paper we propose a methodology to counteract privacy loss due to sharing data in social networking websites. Specifically, we suggest that in addition to the above "user-regulated" access control, users of a social network are provided an additional layer of "server-assisted" access control. The latter type of access control specifically targets the two mentioned drawbacks of users-regulated access control by providing probabilistic guarantees about privacy and by not requiring any additional action from the user (thus simultaneously avoiding nuisance to the user as well as damage accidentally created by the same user). In a nutshell, our (intentionally minimalistic) model represents a user's shared database as a collection of data objects with an attribute that can be set to private (when shared only among a restricted set of social network users) or public (when shared among all users) at any one out of a sequence of time periods. In this model, the proposed server-assisted access control paradigm automatically updates the access control policy at each time period, by randomly resetting some of the user's data objects as public or private, possibly depending on past and future attribute settings. In other words, this mechanism, which we briefly call *evolving access control*, specifies how data object privacy attributes are set in the time periods when the user is either inactive or unwilling to deal with the privacy problem. The attributes are not mandated to the user (i.e., a user can turn off this mechanism and implement his/her favorite privacy and/or access control policy) and, when set by the server, quantifiably guarantee formally specified requirements about utility (i.e., users leave as much data as possible with the attribute set to public) and privacy (i.e., users keep combinations of sensitive data with the attribute set to private with high probability). Here, for concreteness, we model sensitive data as an arbitrary subset of the user's data objects, which is unknown to the server and, for greater generality, also unknown to the user. We also present a simple technique as an example of an evolving access control. This technique is probabilistic and based on variants of cover-free families [7,4]. In our example, first we observe that conventional cover-free families do not suffice for our goals (for instance, they do not necessarily maximize utility requirements); and then we propose a variation of a known construction for randomized subset selection (the latter being also analyzed as a cover-free family with certain properties in [5,2]) for which we can prove non-trivial and quantifiable utility and privacy properties.

Previous work. We are not aware of any other research paper trying to propose solutions or paradigms to simultaneously safeguard privacy and maximize utility while sharing data in social networking websites. A few papers have recently contributed general discussions of trust and privacy problems with the use of such sites (see, e.g., [3,6,1] and references therein). Moreover, public press is devoting daily attention to these problems, typically writing about undesired events resulting from weak privacy, but occasionally also writing about quick and practical "common sense" ways to limit privacy loss [12]. A few research papers have recently attempted solutions to different privacy problems in social networks (see, e.g., [8,9,10,11] and references therein). For instance, privacy-preserving criminal investigations were studied in [8], privacy characterizations were studied in [10], privacy in graph-based models were studied in [9], and a game theory mechanism that promotes truthfulness while sharing data was proposed in [11].

2 Evolving Access Control: Definitions and Approach

In this section we present our formal definitions for user databases, along with its associated notions of utility and sensitive subset, and for evolving access control algorithms, along with their associated utility and privacy requirements. In the process, we describe how our overall approach guarantees social network privacy via an evolving access control algorithm.

Social network databases. Social networks allow their users different data formats and different sharing and access policies, possibly depending on the data types. With the following formalism we attempt to capture a simplified yet general model so to later facilitate an easier description and a wider applicability of our ideas.

We consider a server S, running centralized software for the social network, and a user U that is one of the many members of the network. Let $D_1, \ldots, D_n \in \mathcal{D}$ be U's data objects (we can think of them as images, text or computer files), where we refer to $\{D_1, \ldots, D_n\}$ as the *user database*, and to $\mathcal{D}$ as the *data object space*. An *attribute function* maps each data object to a privacy state; formally, define $A : \mathcal{D} \rightarrow \{\mathsf{public}, \mathsf{private}\}$, and denote as $b_1, \ldots, b_n \in \{\mathsf{public}, \mathsf{private}\}$ the values such that $b_j = A(D_j)$, for $j = 1, \ldots, n$. Here, by $b_j = \mathsf{public}$ (resp., $b_j = \mathsf{private}$) we mean that data object D_j is shared with all (resp., only a restricted set of) social network users, where the restricted set is chosen by U.

Social network databases: utility. Clearly, the utility obtained by U in the participation to a social network, may depend on U's specific personality and interests. In agreement with the underlying philosophy of many real-life social networks, we assume that setting $b_j = \mathsf{public}$ provides a higher utility, from U's point of view, than setting $b_j = \mathsf{private}$. Thus, we consider maximizing the number of j's from $\{1, \ldots, n\}$ such that $b_j = \mathsf{public}$ as a way to maximize U's utility in the participation to the social network.

Social network databases: sensitive subset. It seems often the case that a single data object may not be sufficient source of sensitive material, while multiple data objects, when correlated, may be considered so. Attempting a reasonably simple and general model for sensitive data, we assume that the *conjunction* of a number s of data objects may at some time become of sensitive nature. Thus, we denote a *sensitive subset* as

$P \subseteq \{1, \ldots, n\}$, $|P| = s$, with the understanding that U's privacy can be maintained if at least one of the s data objects $\{D_j \mid j \in P\}$ satisfies $A(D_j) = \mathsf{private}$.

Evolving access control. We define an *access control algorithm* as a probabilistic algorithm AC that, on input $D_1, \ldots, D_n \in \mathcal{D}$, and time subinterval i, returns values $b_1, \ldots, b_n$, such that $b_j = A(D_j) \in \{\mathsf{public}, \mathsf{private}\}$, for $j = 1, \ldots, n$, and during time subinterval i. Note that by consistently applying an access control algorithm at each time subinterval so that at least one data object in the sensitive subset has attribute private, user U would solve the privacy problem. However, as already partially discussed in the introduction, we assume that U may either not know which subset of data objects will be sensitive in the future, or may be unavailable to apply the access control algorithm, whenever needed. Consistently with practical access control systems (e.g., occasional password resets), we do assume that U is available to apply the access control algorithm at distant times 0 and T. Thus, we consider a sufficiently large time interval, represented as $[0, T]$, and further divide it into m equal-length subintervals. We augment the above notations of $b_j, A(D_j)$ so to incorporate time dependency: specifically, $b_{i,j} = A(i, D_j)$ denotes the attribute value of data object D_j at the i-th subinterval of $[0, T]$, for $i = 1, \ldots, m$ and $j = 1, \ldots, n$. Moreover, it is assumed that at data object submission time it holds that $b_{0,j} = A(0, D_j) = \mathsf{public}$ for all $j = 1, \ldots, n$.

We then define an *evolving access control algorithm* as a probabilistic algorithm $EvAC$ that, on input $D_1, \ldots, D_n \in \mathcal{D}$, and parameter m, returns values $b_{i,1}, \ldots, b_{i,n}$, such that $b_{i,j} = A(i, D_j) \in \{\mathsf{public}, \mathsf{private}\}$, for $i = 1, \ldots, m$, and $j = 1, \ldots, n$. Our goal in this paper is that of designing evolving access control algorithms with interesting utility and privacy properties, as we now define.

Utility requirement. As already mentioned in the case of user databases, the notion of utility is subjective to the user U and thus, even in the case of access control algorithms, one could define utility of such algorithms in terms of a general function f of $b_{i,1}, \ldots, b_{i,n}$, for $i = 1, \ldots, m$, and $j = 1, \ldots, n$.

Formally, for any function $f : \{0,1\}^{m \times n} \rightarrow [0,1]$, we say that evolving access control algorithm $EvAC$ has *f-utility* y if $f(\{b_{i,1}, \ldots, b_{i,n}\}_{i=1}^m) = y$, where $\{b_{i,1}, \ldots, b_{i,n}\}_{i=1}^m = EvAC(D_1, \ldots, D_n, m)$. We also say that f is the utility function for evolving access control algorithm $EvAC$ (meaning that $EvAC$ can be designed so to optimize f).

More realistically, we would like to define a more specific utility function f that attempts to capture utility for as many social network users as possible. We extend the reasoning done for the case of user databases (i.e., utility increases when so does the number of data values that are publicly accessible) both across the number of documents on a given time subinterval (meaning that utility is higher when at any given time the attribute of a higher number of data values is set to public) and across the number of time subintervals for a given document (meaning that utility is higher when the attribute of any given document is set to public during a higher number of time subintervals). To capture this intuition, we first define notations $\boldsymbol{b}_i = (b_{i,1}, \ldots, b_{i,n})$ and $\boldsymbol{b}_j = (b_{1,j}, \ldots, b_{m,j})$, and then their respective Hamming weights $w(\boldsymbol{b}_i) = \sum_{j=1}^n b_{i,j}$ and $w(\boldsymbol{b}_j) = \sum_{i=1}^n b_{i,j}$. Also, for any integers p, x, let $I_{\geq p}(x)$ denote the *indicator threshold function*, defined as equal to 1 if $x \geq p$ and 0 otherwise. Then, for all integers p, q and monotone increasing functions g, h from $\mathcal{N}$ to $[0, 1]$, we define the utility function

$$f_{p,q;g,h}(\{b_{i,j}\}_{i,j}) = \Pi_{i=1}^{m}(I_{\geq p}(w(\boldsymbol{b}_i)) \cdot g(w(\boldsymbol{b}_i))) \cdot \Pi_{j=1}^{n}(I_{\geq q}(w(\boldsymbol{b}_j)) \cdot h(w(\boldsymbol{b}_j))),$$

and refer to it as the *threshold-based utility function.*

In the rest of the paper we target the goal of designing an evolving access control algorithm that maximizes the threshold-based utility function. Ideally, this is done independently of specific settings for p, q, g, h, for sake of greater generality. Note that if we ignore privacy requirements, the algorithm that always sets $b_{i,j} = \mathsf{public}$ for all i, j, trivially achieves this goal. As it will be even clearer after our formal definition of privacy, this solution does not guarantee any relevant privacy properties.

Privacy requirement. Extending the intuition discussed in the case of user databases, we would like to formalize the fact that an evolving access control algorithm only sets all components of the sensitive vector as public with small probability, during a large number of time subintervals, and possibly during the entire time interval $[0, T]$. In other words, we even allow the adversary trying to violate privacy to collect vectors $\boldsymbol{b}_i$ from the output of the evolving access control algorithm, for several, possibly all, values of i in $\{1, \ldots, m\}$. Even allowing this attack, we still require that the probability that this adversary can reconstruct the sensitive vector is small.

Formally, let $P \subseteq \{1, \ldots, n\}$ be an s-size sensitive subset, and let t be the number of time subintervals subject to the adversary's attack. For any $\epsilon > 0$, we say that evolving access control algorithm $EvAC$ satisfies (t, ϵ)*-privacy* if for any $i_1, \ldots, i_t \in \{1, \ldots, m\}$, the probability that $\vee_{i=i_1}^{i_t}(b_{i,j} = \mathsf{public})$ is true for all $j \in P$ is at most ϵ.

We model the vector P as arbitrary and, for sake of greater generality, unknown to both U and S. (Even if U is theoretically in the best position to say which data is sensitive or not, we make the more practical observation that U may not make the best decision with respect to present or even future times, as often reported in news events.) We do assume that the size s of P is known to the evolving access control algorithm. (Even if this may not be true in general, we note that our example construction really only needs to set s as an upper bound on $|P|$). Finally, we model vector P as chosen independently by algorithm $EvAC$ or its output. (One could certainly formally define an adaptive version of this definition, where P depends on the output returned by $EvAC$, but we choose to ignore this variant in this version of the paper as it seems practically not relevant.)

In the rest of the paper we target the goal of designing an algorithm $EvAC$ that simultaneously maximizes the t and minimizes the ϵ for which $EvAC$ is (t, ϵ)-private. Note that if we ignore utility requirements, the algorithm that always sets $b_{i,j} = \mathsf{private}$ for all i, j, trivially achieves this goal. Thus, our overall target is to achieve good trade-offs of (t, ϵ)-privacy and f-utility.

3 An Example of the Evolving Access Control Paradigm

We present a simple $EvAC$ algorithm based on a variant of a known class of almost cover-free families. We start by an informal description of the intuitions behind this construction, then give a detailed description of the $EvAC$ algorithm, and of its utility and privacy properties, and finally formally state our theorem.

An informal description. The overall idea of this approach is to guarantee that the attribute of at least one of the data objects in the sensitive subset P remains set to private during as many as possible time subintervals, possibly during the entire time interval $[0, T]$. Towards achieving this, cover-free families seem a natural solution tool. Moreover, recall that we would like to further achieve the following three goals, with respect to our privacy and utility parameters: maximize the time needed to carry out the attack to violate privacy, minimize the probability that all data objects are eventually set to public, and maximize an appropriate threshold-based utility function (as a function of the number of data objects set to public). The first goal suggests that we vary the choice of cover-free subset at each one of the m time subintervals of $[0, T]$. The second and third goals suggest that we choose a family with good cover-freeness properties and with maximal size of the cover-free subsets, respectively. We continue by recalling the definition of cover-free families.

Let n, m, k be positive integers, let G be a ground set of size n, and let $F = \{S_1, \ldots, S_k\}$ be a family of subsets of G. We say that subset S_j *does not cover* S_i if it holds that $S_i \not\subseteq S_j$. We say that family F is *m-cover free* over G if each subset in F is not covered by the union of any m other subsets in F.

Several results about cover-free families are known. For instance, it is known [4] that there exists a deterministic algorithm that, for any fixed m, ℓ, constructs a m-cover free, k-size, family F of ℓ-size vectors over a ground set of size n, for $\ell = \lceil n/4m \rceil$ and $n \leq 16m^2(1 + \log(k/2)/\log 3)$. In our case, a black-box application of cover-free families would not solve our problem, for the following three reasons:

1. the subset to be covered (i.e., the sensitive subset) has size s, while the covering subsets (i.e., the set of attribute values for $i = 1, \ldots, m$) have size ℓ, where, in general $\ell \neq s$ (as we attempt to maximize ℓ);
2. the subset to be covered (i.e., the sensitive subset) can be any subset of $\{0, 1\}^n$, which, in general, may not be the case in cover-free sets; and
3. we admit a low, but positive probability that the sensitive subset is not covered, while this is not the case for an arbitrary cover-free family.

Reason 3 is actually particularly interesting as it suggests that we might obtain constructions with better performance than using cover-free families. Reason 1 suggests that perhaps we can use a variation of known cover-free families, and reason 2 restricts the search among these. Indeed our example construction is a minor variant of a simple randomized construction, already used in many different contexts, that is (almost) a cover-free family, as noted in [5].

Detailed description. Our example of an evolving access control algorithm $EvAC$ takes as input data objects $D_1, \ldots, D_n$ and the number m of time periods, and does the following.

First U's data objects $D_1, \ldots, D_n$ are randomly permuted. Intuitively, this guarantees that the distribution of the sensitive subset P is uniform over all s-size subsets from $\{0, 1\}^n$. This fact further simplifies our utility and privacy analysis and helps improving the utility and privacy parameters.

Later, the algorithm computes the attribute values $b_{i,j}$, for $i = 1, \ldots, m$, and $j = 1, \ldots, n$, as follows. For each $i \in \{1, \ldots, m\}$, a number ℓ of distinct values $j_1, \ldots, j_\ell$ are uniformly and independently chosen from $\{0, 1\}^n$, and later $b_{i,j}$ is set equal to public for $j = j_1, \ldots, j_\ell$ or is set equal to private otherwise. Here, ℓ is a parameter, depending on n, m, s, ϵ, that is set (and maximized) in the analysis of the utility property of the scheme. In fact, it is not necessary to know the exact value of s: an upper bound of s would suffice.

Proof of privacy and utility properties. Let $\epsilon > 0$, let n be the number of data objects, m be the number of time subintervals of interval $[0, T]$, $t \leq m$ be the number of attacked time subintervals, s be the length of the sensitive subset, and ℓ be the number of the attribute values set to public in each $\boldsymbol{b}_i$, for $i = 1, \ldots, m$. Assuming that $\epsilon^{1/s} > 1 - (1 - 2/n)^m$, we show that algorithm $EvAC$ achieves (t, ϵ)-privacy and we compute the value ℓ that maximizes the threshold-based utility function for any desired values for the privacy parameters t, ϵ.

Privacy. Note that (t, ϵ)-privacy is achieved when an attacker obtaining any $t \leq m$ vectors $\boldsymbol{b}_i$ obtains a value $b_{ij} = \mathsf{private}$ for at least one value $j \in P$ and all of the t different indices i, denoted as $i_1, \ldots, i_t$. In other words, the sensitive subset P is not covered by the logical OR of the $t \leq m$ vectors $\boldsymbol{b}_i$ containing the truth values "$b_{i,j} = \mathsf{public}$", for $j = 1, \ldots, n$. The probability of this latter event can be written, thanks to the random permutation step in algorithm $EvAC$, as the probability that for each of the s values $j \in P$, it holds that $\vee_{i=i_1}^{i_t} (b_{i,j} = \mathsf{public})$. The probability that $\vee_{i=i_1}^{i_t} (b_{i,j} = \mathsf{public})$ is equal to 1 minus the probability that $\wedge_{i=i_1}^{i_t} (b_{i,j} = \mathsf{private})$. Finally, the probability that $(b_{i,j} = \mathsf{private})$ is equal to $1 - \ell/n$. We obtain that

$$\epsilon = \left(1 - \left(1 - \frac{\ell}{n}\right)^t\right)^s.$$

To illustrate this equality, in Figure 1 we plot ϵ as a function of $\ell \in [1, n]$, for 3 different concrete values setups for $n, t = m, s$. This gives a pictorial idea on how the privacy parameter ϵ decreases in a way that is inversely proportional to the growth of the utility parameter ℓ and the number of attack periods t, and directly proportional to the growth of the number of objects n.

Utility. By definition of the threshold-based utility function, maximizing this latter function requires maximizing both the number of values set to public in $\boldsymbol{b}_i$, for each $i = 1, \ldots, m$, and the number of values set to public in $\boldsymbol{b}_j$, for each $j = 1, \ldots, n$. In the above scheme $EvAC$, both these values are maximized when the parameter ℓ (denoting the number of values set to public in all vectors $\boldsymbol{b}_i$, for $i = 1, \ldots, m$) is maximized. Thus, we compute the maximum value for ℓ given numbers n, s, m, ϵ as parameters. Specifically, starting from $\epsilon > (1 - (1 - \ell/n)^m)^s$, and using algebraic manipulations, we obtain that

$$\ell < n \cdot \left(1 - \left(1 - \epsilon^{1/s}\right)^{1/m}\right).$$

It can be verified that the quantity on the right side is ≥ 2 only if $\epsilon^{1/s} > 1 - (1 - 2/n)^m$, as we previously assumed. To illustrate this equality, in Figure 2 we plot ℓ as a function of $\epsilon \in [0, 1]$, for 3 different concrete values setups for n, m, s. This gives a pictorial idea on how the utility parameter ℓ increases in a way that is inversely proportional to the growth of the privacy parameter ϵ, and directly proportional to the growth of the number of objects n and the number of time periods m.

Formally, the above can be summarized in the following

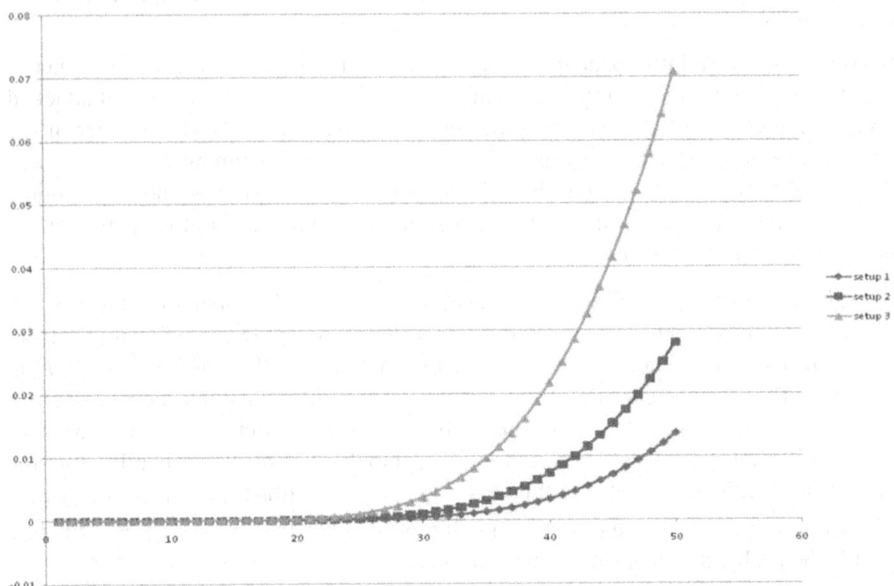

Fig. 1. The value of ϵ as a function of ℓ when $n = 500, t = m = 10, s = 10$ (setup 1), $n = 400, t = m = 9, s = 10$ (setup 2), $n = 300, t = m = 8, s = 10$ (setup 3). The max values of ℓ such that $\epsilon < 0.001$ are 47, 41, and 35, respectively.

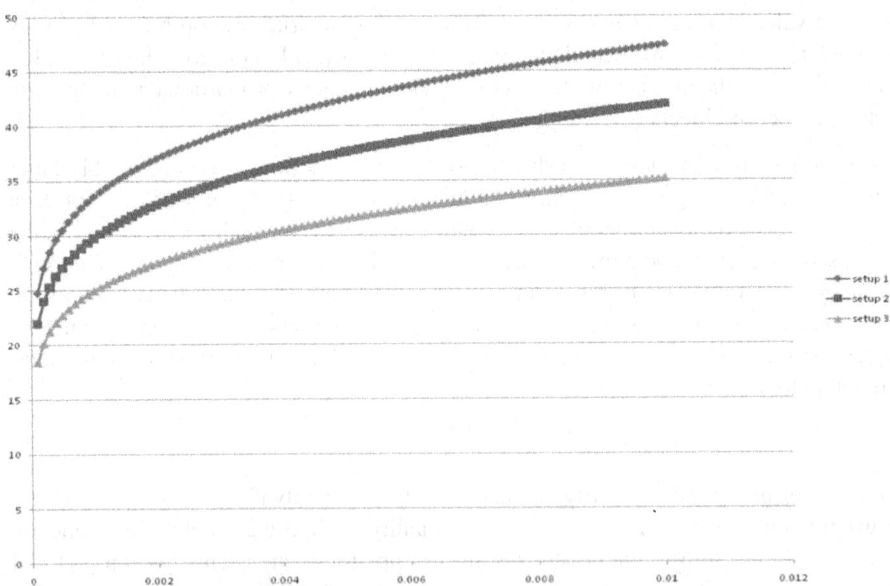

Fig. 2. The value of ℓ as a function of ϵ when $n = 500, m = 10, s = 10$ (setup 1), $n = 400, m = 9, s = 10$ (setup 2), $n = 300, m = 8, s = 10$ (setup 3). The min values of ϵ such that $\ell > 35$ are 0.0014, 0.0032, and 0.0098, respectively.

Theorem 1. Let U have a social network database with n data objects. Over m time periods, the above algorithm $EvAC$ is an evolving access control algorithm that keeps at any given time $\leq \ell$ document attributes set to public and satisfies (t, ϵ)-privacy, for any $t \leq m$, where

$$\epsilon = \left(1 - \left(1 - \frac{\ell}{n}\right)^t\right)^s$$

and s is (an upper bound on) the length of the sensitive subset. Whenever $\epsilon^{1/s} > 1 - (1 - 2/n)^m$, algorithm $EvAC$ satisfies g-utility, where g is the threshold-based utility function and is maximized by the largest value ℓ such that

$$\ell < n \cdot \left(1 - \left(1 - \epsilon^{1/s}\right)^{1/m}\right).$$

Remarks. A few remarks are in place to interpret the contribution from this theorem, with respect to the privacy vs. utility tradeoffs, and on parameter settings.

Non-trivial privacy and utility. Maximizing privacy alone can be obtained by an access control algorithm that sets $b_{i,j}$ = private for all i, j, thus achieving $(m, 0)$-privacy, but minimal utility. Similarly, maximizing utility alone can be obtained by an access control algorithm that sets $b_{i,j}$ = public for all i, j, thus achieving maximal utility for a large class of utility function (including the threshold-based utility function), but does not satisfy $(1, \epsilon)$-privacy, for any $\epsilon < 1$. Instead, our algorithm $EvAC$ achieves interesting privacy vs. utility tradeoffs where, for all $t \leq m$, with respect to privacy, ℓ limits the decrease of ϵ, and, with respect to utility, ϵ limits the increase of ℓ, the precise limitations being given in the theorem.

Parameter settings. The choice of parameter m, together with the duration of each time subinterval, should really depend on the type of social networking website. For instance, if a time period is set to be one month, the choice $m = 10$ (that means: explicitly requiring a user to revisit his access control settings every 10 months) seems quite reasonable for some popular social networking websites.

The choice of the utility function should also depend on the specific social networking website. Thus, instead of defining a single utility function and show numerical results for it, we defined a sufficiently general class of utility functions and proved Theorem 1 assuming one of the functions in the class is used.

In practical events, s may be as small as 1 (e.g., one picture, one comment, one file). In general, a smaller s would force either a smaller choice of the utility parameter ℓ for the same privacy parameters t, ϵ, or less desirable t, ϵ for the same ℓ.

4 Conclusions and Future Work

We proposed a new paradigm to limit privacy loss while participating to online activity at social networking websites: instead of only relying on self-regulated access control, users can elect to choose the option of an additional layer of server-assisted (and time-evolving) access control. We put forward a new model for balancing privacy and utility in social networks, and propose a first solution that achieves non-trivial tradeoffs between these two important and often contradicting goals.

More work needs to be carried out to propose additional solutions according to this paradigm and additional model refinements that increase the paradigm's applicability, including the choice of different utility functions, the extension to more practical and general database structures, and the extension to a higher number of sensitive subsets.

Acknowledgements. We would like to thank Linda Ness for interesting discussions and the committee members for useful comments.

References

1. Boyd, D.: Friendster and Publicly Articulated Social Networks. In: Proc. of the SIGCHI Conf. on Human Factors and Computing Systems (2004)
2. Di Crescenzo, G., Shim, H., Cochinwala, M.: Modeling cryptographic properties of voice and voice-based entity authentication. In: Proc. of ACM CCS 2007 Digital Identity Management Workshop, pp. 53–61 (2007)
3. Dwyer, C., Hiltz, S., Passerini, K.: Trust and privacy concern within social networking sites: A comparison of Facebook and MySpace. In: Proc. of the 13th Americas Conference on Information Systems (2007)
4. Erdos, P., Frankl, P., Furedi, Z.: Families of finite sets in which no set is covered by the union of r others. Israeli Journal of Mathematics 51, 79–89 (1985)
5. Garay, J., Staddon, J., Wool, A.: Long-live Broadcast Encryption. In: Bellare, M. (ed.) CRYPTO 2000. LNCS, vol. 1880, p. 333. Springer, Heidelberg (2000)
6. Gross, R., Acquisti, A.: Information Revelation and Privacy in Online Social Networks (The Facebook case). In: Proc. of the ACM Workshop on Privacy in the Electronic Society (WPES) (2005)
7. Kautz, W., Singleton, R.: Nonrandom binary superimposed codes. IEEE Transactions of Information Theory 10, 363–377 (1964)
8. Kerschbaum, F., Schaad, A.: Privacy-preserving social network analysis for criminal investigations. In: Proc. of the 7th ACM Workshop on Privacy in the Electronic Society. WPES 2008, pp. 9–14. ACM, New York (2008)
9. Korolova, A., Motwani, R., Nabar, S.U., Xu, Y.: Link privacy in social networks. In: Proceeding of the 17th ACM Conference on information and Knowledge Management. CIKM 2008, pp. 289–298. ACM, New York (2008)
10. Krishnamurthy, B., Wills, C.: Characterizing Privacy in Online Social Networks. In: Proc. of ACM WOSN 2008 (2008)
11. Squicciarini, A.C., Shehab, M., Paci, F.: Collective privacy management in social networks. In: Proceedings of the 18th international Conference on World Wide Web. WWW 2009, pp. 521–530. ACM, New York (2009)
12. Nakagawa, T.: How to Avoid Getting Fired by Facebook (September 13, 2007), `http://www.lifehack.org/articles/management/how-to-avoid-getting-fired-by-facebook.html`
13. Stevens, T.: Yet Someone Else Fired for Private Comments on MySpace (May 6, 2009), `http://www.switched.com/2009/05/06/woman-fired-for-private-comments-on-myspace/`
14. Popkin, H.: Twitter Gets you Fired in 140 Characters or Less (March 23, 2009), `http://www.msnbc.msn.com/id/29796962`

Utopia
Providing Trusted Social Network Relationships within an Un-trusted Environment

William Gauvin, Benyuan Liu, Xinwen Fu, and Jie Wang

Department of Computer Science,
University of Massachusetts Lowell
{wgauvin,bliu,xinwenfu,wang}@cs.uml.edu

Abstract. This paper introduces an unobtrusive method and distributed solution set to aid users of *on-line social networking* sites, by creating a *trusted environment* in which every member has the ability to identify each other within their private social network by name, gender, age, location, and the specific usage patterns adopted by the group. Utopia protects members by understanding how the social network is created and the specific aspects of the group that make it unique and identifiable. The main focus of Utopia is the protection of the group, and their privacy within a social network from predators and *spammers* that characteristically do not fit within the well defined usage boundaries of the social network as a whole. The solution set provides defensive, as well as offensive tools to identify these threats. Once identified, client desktop tools are used to prevent these predators from further interaction within the group. In addition, offensive tools are used to determine the origin of the *predator* to allow actions to be taken by automated tools and law enforcement to alleviate the threat.

Keywords: On-line Social Networks, Trusted Environment, Predators, Privacy, Cloud Service.

1 Introduction

Successful social networking websites, such as Facebook, MySpace, and LinkedIn, have experienced an explosion in growth. This growth can be attributed to the ease in which members can find each other and share common interest. The user can typically post photos, send messages, comment on friends profiles, join user groups, and generally interact and build online communities of users who share common interests. The amount and types of information that can be shared in these social networking environments is vast, for example, favorite quotes, music and videos are used to introduce the user to the world. The users network can grow over time as the user connects to more and more users and share more and more information.

Social networking sites unfortunately provide an anonymous avenue for those that seek to prey on the young and naive. There are numerous examples of

B. Liu et al. (Eds.): WASA 2009, LNCS 5682, pp. 561–569, 2009.

unscrupulous activity; examples are, cyberbullying, cyberstalking[1][2][3][4][6][7] and underage solicitation for sex [5]. The National Center for Missing and Exploited Children has identified the following problems inherent within on-line socialization; *Child Pornography, Enticement of Children for Sexual Acts Sex Tourism Involving Children, Extrafamilial Child Sexual Molestation, Unsolicited Obscene Material Sent to a Child, Misleading Domain Names* and *Misleading Words or Digital Images on the Internet.* Many of these categories can directly or indirectly be linked to social networking activity and MySpace specifically[8]. The concern to protect individuals has led to specific agreements between MySpace and government agencies, whose job is to serve and protect the users of MySpace. One of the more detailed works in this area is the "Joint Statement on Key Principles of Social Networking Sites Safety"[9], originating from the Attorney General Martha Coakleys office in Massachusetts and including 49 other Attorney Generals, as well as MySpace. This document provides guidelines and measurements that must be taken to "Provide children with a safer social networking experience", specifically directed towards the "operators of social networking sites"[9]. This paper also advocates the use of online safety tools, as well as design and functionality changes that are geared towards the protection of children. The overall emphasis of the paper is the concept of providing on-line identity authentication tools to include age verification.

Utopia is a systematic approach to address the problems identified above with social networks and provides a means to influence the usage patterns of the individuals within a group. Utopia focuses on the interaction between the owner of a profile and those that publish to that owner's wall, i.e., their friends. Using heuristics gathered from the conception of MySpace to the present; it ascertains local and global usage patterns, and uses these predictable patterns to identify anomalous activity. In addition, these patterns can be applied as behavioral templates to identify both good and bad usage traits. Further characterization is achieved using social *honey-pots*, which emulate an individual buddy of a social network and monitor the activity of the group, with respect to spam or *splogs*. Utopia also addresses privacy concerns by providing a method to encrypt blogs, such that only the members of a group may view the contents, even within a public environment. The goal of Utopia is to facilitate, using unobtrusive techniques, the means to evaluate social network groups of an individual, and ascertain specific characteristics that are deemed unhealthy with respect to the general use of the social networking environment[10]. Once identified, this undesired content is eliminated from the users presence, and is no longer a factor in the overall social network experience.

2 Utopian Approach

The primary goal of Utopia is to provide a means for individual users of online social networking sites and law enforcement to work independently and unobtrusively. The user's MySpace experience must not be negatively impacted by the tools required to protect such individuals and law enforcement must be provided the information required to actively police the social network domain. User level transparency is a major goal of Utopia, it is important to protect, but not interfere with the social network experience. Utopia may be deployed in two environments, they are:

1. A standalone environment
2. A fully distributed environment

In a standalone environment, members of a social network create "Trust-Groups". These groups form ties with each other and share common knowledge about each member of the group. They use a rating system, based on content analysis, that is shared and updated by all members to identify good and bad usage patterns. The ranking system provides a means to associate reputation with a specific publisher, using a global view of the user, as indicated by the behavior and tendencies of the publisher for all members, not just a single individual profile.

The second scenario is a fully distributed environment, in which Trust-Groups are created within the Utopia Social Network *Cloud Service*. The Cloud Service provides a dynamically scalable and virtualized social network environment, which uses software as a service technology to facilitate the assimulation of social network activity into temporal usage patterns which are projected to managed clients. In this environment, members create private social networking groups, as in the standalone environment, but group membership and the usage information is managed and distributed by the cloud service. In addition, the cloud service shares global usage pattern templates with the individual social network group to provide a stronger capability for rating and evaluation.

Figure 1 is an example of both the standalone and distributed environments. In the standalone environment, the group "Family" has ties to each member within an internal home network. They form a private trust group named "Family" and do not participate in the distributed environment offered by the Utopia cloud service. It is important to note that membership is not restricted to computers within the internal network as there are external "Family" members.

The distributed solution set is demonstrated by the group "Team". This group uses the Utopia cloud service to form the group. The membership information is stored using the cloud service and members are added and removed by updates to the Utopia cloud database as required. The database is protected such that only members of a group may obtain the group ranking, usage templates and other characteristics specific to the individual group. Membership within the distributed environment have the added benefit of global usage patterns, policies and tools which may be inherited by the private groups.

The high-level design of Utopia is a set of components which reside on the clients and a cloud service component. The standalone components implement a peer-to-peer network in which clients may distribute membership and ranking information. The implementation of the standalone environment is a sub-set of the distributed cloud service. Users of the tool that are concerned about privacy may restrict the level of information that is reported and prevent unwanted data leakage out side their sphere of influence. Others may choose to

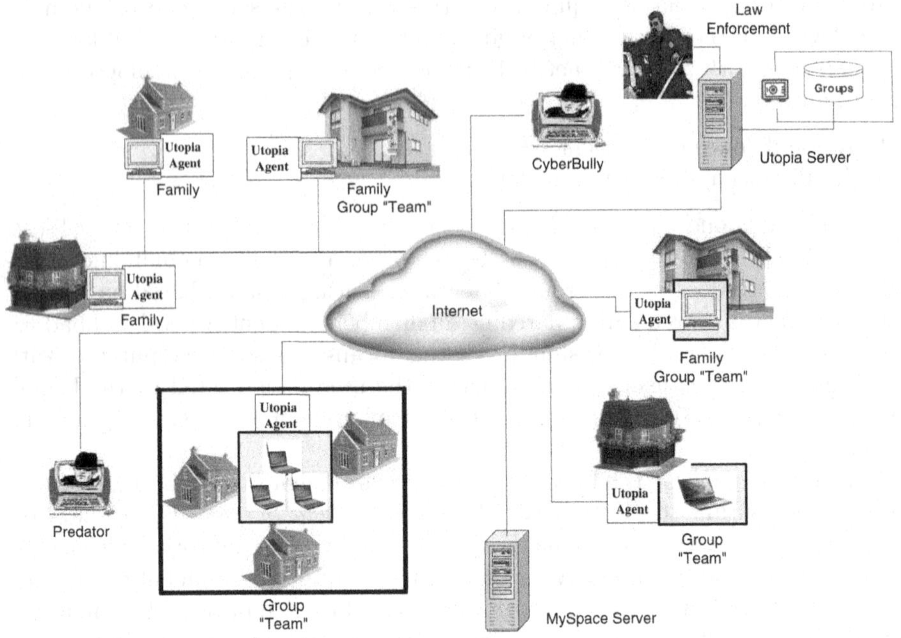

Fig. 1. Utopia High-Level Overview

be highly involved with information sharing of the distributed model and host the group templates in the cloud server; as well as receive updates on predator list and known usage patterns. In addition, both scenarios may report events of questionable origin or material to the cloud service to aid in the collection, identification and assimilation process.

2.1 Utopia Standalone Environment

The strength of Utopia resides in the flexibility of its design to be molded into a solution which meets the specific requirements of the members of the group; with out over burdening the system with unwanted features. In the standalone environment, Utopia provides the means to protect users of social network sites by creating a virtual group, for which group membership is consensual. Members are added to groups using an acceptance model. Each member is analyzed to determine the level of trust and usage reputation. A member's reputation is derived by examining the content being posted by the individual, as well as the hygiene of that content. Members that continually post content associated with splogs (Spam Blogs) and questionable content have a lower rating than those who continually adhere to specific guidelines defined for the group for content publishing. For underage users, the profile guidelines are defined by a guardian.

The goal of the rating system is to teach members the acceptable usage patterns for a specific social network group; a browser plug-in is used to provide "pop-ups" with feedback to the individual to train them on correct usage patterns and suggest better means for providing information. Pop-ups act as a warning mechanism when sensitive information such as phone numbers, addresses or other person information is being published. The overall goal is to train members on the correct methods to use when active within a social networking environment

Once a member's rating goes below a defined watermark, the content posted by that individual and the access to that person's wall is restricted. The Utopia agent consists of a rendering engine, which removes the content of the restricted member by filtering and reformatting the response from the social network server and rendering only "clean" content to the users browser. The mechanism provides a means to protect the user when policies and practices are lacking within the social network provider services.

The general design of the Utopia standalone client services (as well as cloud services) are outlined in figure 2. In this figure, the standalone environment is depicted as Client 1 to Client n with a peer-to-peer communication path (lower orange arrow not within the Internet cloud).

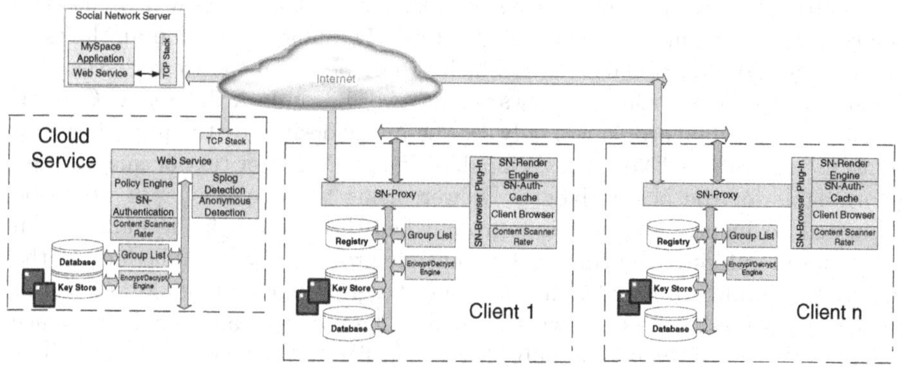

Fig. 2. Utopia Design

The client components consist of the following:

1. A Social Network proxy, which is used to provide a peer-to-peer network for the management of all group associations. The proxy provides an encrypted/authenticated communication channel to distribute rated content to all members within a specific group.
2. A Rendering engine, which modifies or deletes questionable content or total blogs of users which are not members of the group or whose reputation is lower then the weighted value required for viewing. The rendering engine also provides "pop-ups" to suggest better usage patterns to train the user of the tool.
3. An authentication/caching component, which is used by the SN-Proxy to aid in the establishment of communication channels for all groups defined and provide the last measurements, using the cache when clients are not active.

4. A content scanner and rater, which facilitates the means to weigh publishers reputations based on content posted for specific users of the social network group. Included in the content scanner is a honeypot to aid in the local evaluation of splogs and predator friend request.
5. A privacy feature, integrated into the scanner/rendering components.

The result of the standalone solution is a tightly coupled distributed peer-to-peer network which allows all members of the group to participate in globally ranking and propagating reputation of all members of the group. The ranking mechanism is directly reflected in the rendering of the content for each member of the group. In addition, the usage patterns defined for the group are provisioned by a teaching mechanism, which is used to train the individual user of correct on-line behavior, which carries over to all other aspects of their on-line activity.

Utopia accomplishes privacy by using steganographic images posted/hosted on the social network site on a user's profile and the browser plug-in previous defined as a client component in figure 2 that is used to identify these images and translate them to the desired content, rendered by the viewer's browser. A user friendly hosting tool is used to create an image which will be used to embed additional link references and/or text. The image may contain links to other images, or additional content which is only posted if the viewer either is a member of a specific group or knows the password to unlock the image. General viewers of the public profile will only see the image desired by the publisher, this could be the popular "No Image Available" image. No other text or images need be available for the posted blog. A viewer, using the helper plug-in would be evaluated for membership within a group when the image is being pulled down and before rendering; the content for multiple groups may be embedded in the image. Depending on membership, the specific group content would be used to render the content on the viewers browser. The content can include reference links to other photos that the publisher would like to make available as well as text. All would be formatted to be correctly rendered, as if by the hosting site.

Using this method, a person could post an image personalized for their parents, friends and the general public. Figure 3 depicts the use of the Utopia privacy technique for groups *Family*, *Friend* and *Team*. In this figure, an opaque image is rendered on the MySpace server, embedded with private content based on group membership. Non-members only have access to the opaque image. Members of the group *Family* are rendered a picture of the family, with the context string "This is the latest family photo". Members of group *Friend* are rendered a picture of the "friends" and the context string "Remember the dance?". Membership of the group *Team* are rendered a picture of the team with the context string "The rally was great". Membership in multiple groups results in the rendering of multiple individual blogs representing each group.

2.2 Utopia Distributed Environment

The distributed environment uses a globally available server, which contains usage templates and offensive tools used for the detection and assimilation of

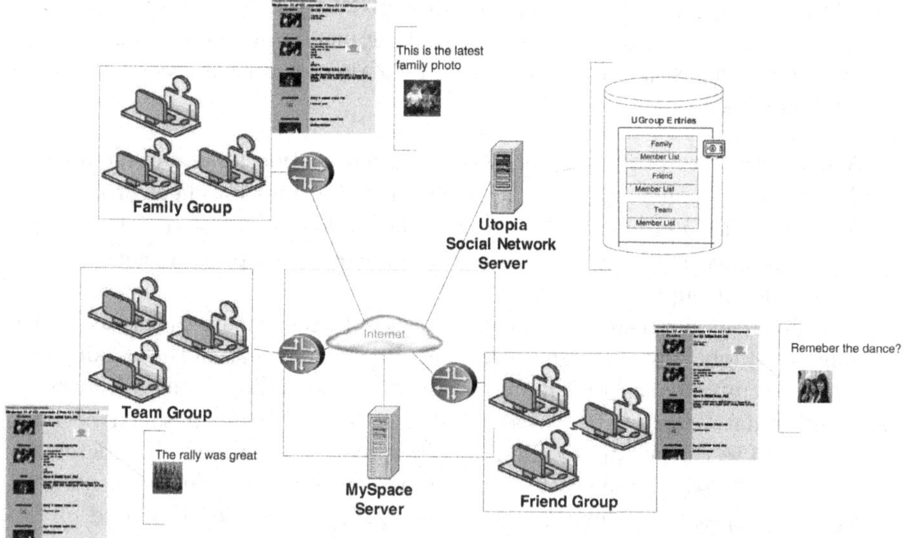

Fig. 3. Utopia Privacy Feature

information to participating clients. It offers a strong solution set to combat cyber-bullying, cyber-stalking and predator identification.

In the distributed environment, the cloud service replaces the localized database in the standalone client solution, as shown in figure 2. Group members use the communication channel to the cloud service (depicted as the green upper arrow in the Internet cload) as the mechanism to receive reputation and usage templates. Clients obtain the usage templates and policies for the specific groups they authenticate into from the cloud service. Client content is transparently altered and rendered based on the policy and results of the reputation database and usage templates.

Clients may be members of many groups; the ranking of which can vary dependent on the policy defined within the client for each specific group. Some variance is allowed between policies, based on trust and the hygiene of the publishers. This allows a flexible and dynamic means for applying policy to "well-behaved" environments that stray slightly from the desired behavior. Client "pop-ups" are used to suggest better usage patterns when this occurs; and may suggest alternative means for rendering the content. It also provides warnings when known anomalies have been detected, such as splogs or predator friend request and outlines key aspects of the content as reference points for future individual observation for detection.

The overall design of both the client and cloud service within the Utopia system is defined in figure 2. The client design does not change drastically from the standalone environment. This provides an easy migration path from standalone to the distributed environment, as well as the converse. As observed above, the client component may use a standalone environment using peer-to-peer techniques or use the cloud service in a client/server environment. In the distributed client/server environment, the client is presented with a rich set of usage templates and a predator database used for ranking member content. This solution provides the strongest protection overall. The major features of the cloud service are the following:

1. A web service to provide client/server communication for group members.
2. A distributed policy engine which contains definitions for client groups.
3. An authentication engine, used during client logon to the social network, the authentication process facilitates the means of mapping clients to their pre-defined groups.
4. A content scanner/rater, used to scan groups defined within the cloud service using the global database and usage patterns. The results of the ranking and pattern templates are distributed to their corresponding client members.
5. A splog detection engine; used to identify spam within a social network and provide the means to filter and remove such content. The detection mechanism uses a honeypot that acts as a member of the social network to receive splogs and sexual solicitations. This information is shared by the rating services when evaluating groups.
6. An anonymous network detection engine, used to determine when unsolicited communication traffic is generated from such a domain. This information is used in the global rating system. The source of the engine takes advantage of the new features added by the social network provider, such as the source address of the image posted to the users profile.
7. A database that manages the user groups, privacy and link service.
8. Encryption/Decryption provisioning; to provide secure channels between the cloud service and its client members.

The virtual service manages groups and the validation of groups using the same means defined above for Trust and Privacy. For privacy, the cloud service provides a virtual link feature, which is used within the steganographic images. These links point to virtual links within the cloud service, and gives the user the ability to change the reference of the virtual links of photos, which is generally desired by many. The rating system includes a crawler, which evaluates various groups to determine hygiene based on publisher identities and content. It facilitates the ability to detect predators that have infiltrated the social network group, spam that taints the content within the group; and behavior recognition software that determines patterns which are disallowed within the group. Its important to note, that clients police themselves through the client side software defined in the standalone section of this document. This information is propagated to the cloud service to trigger cloud service analysis to provide a more detailed evaluation when anomalies exist. Not displayed within the diagram in Figure 2 is the relationship between the rating system and the interaction with the profiles of Registered Sex Offenders identified through the Sentinel SAFE technology, of which Utopia uses to provide a stronger detection mechanisms.

The Utopia web service offers a management console used to configure policies, the notification of events, and generate reports. It is used to give a complete view of activity and provides the means to report scrupulous activity to law enforcement.

3 Total Solution

Utopia provides the means for individual groups to define the policies and usage patterns comfortable for group members. It allows guardians to interject policy based on well defined distributed usage scenarios using unobtrusive methods. Utopia trains members on the correct usage patterns and uses embedded plug-ins to enlighten the users. Privacy considerations are managed by secure content, for which only group members have the access to "unlock". Utopia provisions counter measures to prevent circumvention. These measures prevent users, specifically under-age children, from creating accounts that do not truly represent themselves. Utopia is a total solution that provides the desired level of trust. Member requirements may consists of a private solution, for which the peer-to-peer strategy works well; or, they may desire a rich set of features and participate in "global knowledge" sharing, for which the distributed environment faciliates. Most important, it provides a bridge between information gathered by law enforcement and global techinques and propagates this information to specific individuals where it can best be used to protect and serve its intended audience.

References

1. Cyberbullying (2009), `http://www.cyberbullying.org/`
2. Hinduja, S., Patchin, J.W.: Bullying Beyond the Schoolyard Preventing and Responding to Cyberbullying. Corwin Press (2009)
3. Patchin, J.W., Hinduja, S.: Bullies move beyond the schoolyard: A preliminary look at cyberbullying. Youth Violence and Juvenile Justice 4(2), 148–169 (2006)
4. Hinduja, S., Patchin, J.W.: Cyberbullying: An Exploratory Analysis of Factors Related to Offending and Victimization. Deviant Behavior 29(2), 129–156 (2008)
5. Hinduja, S., Patchin, J.W.: Offline Consequences of Online Victimization: School Violence and Delinquency. Journal of School Violence 6(3), 89–112 (2007)
6. Reuters, Fatal MySpace internet hoax mother is charged (2008), `http://www.news.com.au/heraldsun/story/0,21985,23711115-663,00.html`
7. Lindsay, S.: Boy who posed with guns convicted, Rocky Mountain News (2006), `http://www.rockymountainnews.com/drmn/local/article/0,1299,DRMN_15_4595681,00.html`
8. MySpace exposes sex predators (5/22/2007), `http://www.news.com.au/heraldsun/story/0,21985,21775032-11869,00.html`
9. Commonwealth of Massachusetts, Joint Statement on Key Principles of Social Networking Sites Safety (2008), `http://www.mass.gov/Cago/docs/press/2008_01_14_myspace_agreement_attachment1.pdf`
10. MySpace, ParentCare (2009), `http://www.myspace.com/parentcare`

Discovery and Protection of Sensitive Linkage Information for Online Social Networks Services*

Nan Zhang[1], Min Song[2], Xinwen Fu[3], and Wei Yu[4]

[1] George Washington University
[2] Old Dominion University
[3] University of Massachusetts Lowell
[4] Towson University

Abstract. This paper investigates the problem of suppressing access to sensitive linkage information over data published by users of an online social network service. We unveil the potential threats by inferring linkage information from the user-published data, and suggest a class of data publishing schemes to enable distributed data publication by individual users but hide the sensitive information. Our hope is that this white paper shed lights on the future investigation of privacy-preserving online social network services.

1 Introduction

This paper investigates the problem of suppressing access to sensitive linkage information over data published by users of an online social network service. Online Social Network Services are widely prevalent on the Web. They provide web-based platforms for people to share information with friends who have common interests or activities. There are numerous examples of such services, ranging from online communities connecting users with similar background (e.g., alumni [1], profession [2]), social circles (e.g., friendship [3]), and life styles (e.g., frequent travelers [4]), to collaborative frameworks enabling users to work together in a distributed fashion to achieve certain goals (e.g., scientific research [5]). Here is one running examples that will be used throughout this paper:

Running Example: Linkedin [2]: Every user of LinkedIn publishes a self-describing web page as public information that contains the number of connections she has, but does not contain any information of the connected users [6]. The list of connected users is only visible to a connected user.

As outlined in the above examples, a user of an online social network service usually publishes certain self-describing information to the public, in order to connect with other users. Nonetheless, many users, as well as the operator of an

* This work was supported in part by the National Science Foundation under 0644247, 0845644, 0852673, 0852674, and 0907964. Any opinions, findings, conclusions, and/or recommendations expressed in this material, either expressed or implied, are those of the authors and do not necessarily reflect the views of the sponsor listed above.

B. Liu et al. (Eds.): WASA 2009, LNCS 5682, pp. 570–578, 2009.

online social network service, may also want to impose certain constraints on the published information such that no sensitive information can be inferred from it, while some adversaries inside or outside the social network intend to break such constraints.

In the running example, a user of LinkedIn does not want to disclose her connection with an executive of another company that the user's company is competing against. If such a connection is revealed, the user may be prohibited from participating in secret projects due to risk of competitive disclosure. Notice that every user of LinkedIn may publish aggregates such as the number of connections she has. Thus, a user would like to be guaranteed that no individual linkage could be inferred from the published aggregates.

It is important to note that, unlike many existing work on privacy-preserving data publishing for social networks [7,8] which focuses on the protection of users' identity while publishing the topology of a social network, we investigate online social network services where the identities of individual users are usually available for public access - e.g., most users of Facebook and LinkedIn reveal their real names, professions, and locations on their public profile. **It is the connection between multiple users that need to be discovered or protected.** From honest users' perspective, they want every user to reveal individual data truthfully and efficiently, but hide certain linkage information they do not want to disclose.

To the best of our knowledge, this form of data privacy is novel and unexplored by researchers thus far. Notice that it is not that the sensitivity of linkage information has never been noticed. As a matter of fact, concerns over sensitive linkage [9] information have been raised in recent work. The novelty of our work rests on the traditional belief that such information cannot be revealed via the public interface of an online social network service[1].

In this paper, we address the discovery and protection of sensitive linkage information over online social network services. In particular, we describe change-and-observe, a proof-of-concept attack which compromises sensitive linkage information from the published aggregate data. We also enunciate the key design principles for defending against such attacks. Our vision is that this novel attack will lead to a spectrum of interesting research issues because of the multitude of issues surrounding the design of online social network services - e.g., what information should or should not be published. Our hope is that sensitive-linkage-suppression techniques will become a part of standard online social network service framework in the near future.

The rest of this paper is organized as follows: In Section 2, we introduce background information on social networks and related issues. In Section 3, we demonstrate the feasibility of discovering sensitive information from user published aggregated data, and suggest several techniques to defend against such attacks. Section 4 concludes the paper with a discussion of the future work.

---

[1] Note that the attack discussed in [9] assumes an adversary to be capable of gaining access to (i.e., compromising) multiple user accounts.

2 Background and Problem Statement

2.1 Online Social Network Service

An online social network system consists of a large number of users connected by social relationships or similar background. We call two users as neighbors if they are directly connected, and h-degree friends if the shortest path connecting the two users is of length h. A user of the social network service publishes one or more self-describing web pages that contain certain information about herself and/or her neighbors in the network. There are usually constraints on the which users can access the published information: For example, a user typically publishes different views for public access from those for her neighbors. In Example 1, a user of LinkedIn is willing to reveal her list of neighbors to every neighbor, but may be unwilling to do so for public access. Instead, a user may choose to publish to the public only aggregate information (e.g., location/ profession distribution) about her neighbors and, more broadly, her connected subnetwork.

For each user, how the published information should appear is determined by both the user and the operator of the online social network service. Usually, a user can specify whether to publish certain information, e.g., links to or aggregates of friends, while the service operator controls a universal standard on how such information is published (e.g., the top-k constraint, the precision of published aggregates, and the frequency of updates). Since it is difficult for a normal user to understand the technical perspectives of privacy preservation and data processing, the data publishing strategies we investigate in the paper focus on the standards maintained by the service operator.

2.2 Sensitive Linkage Information

In this paper, we focus on the sensitive linkage information that should be suppressed by an online social network service. A user of an online social network service may consider her connections with other users as sensitive information. In the running example, a user of LinkedIn would not willingly reveal the fact that she has a neighbor who is an executive of another competing company. In general, a user may want to prevent a set of her neighbors from being learned by anyone other than her immediate neighbors. It is important to note the difference between the sensitive linkage information here and the sensitive information protected in the traditional studies of privacy-preserving data publishing for social networks [7,8]. In previous work, the connection graph of a social network is given while the identities of nodes are hidden and should be protected. In our framework, the identity of each user is known (through published profiles), but her connections with other users become sensitive and need to be suppressed.

Given a set of sensitive links, to quantify the success of privacy intrusion or the requirements of privacy, we need to define the notion of compromise. Similar to the privacy models for individual tuples [10], we can define the exact and partial compromise of sensitive links. An exact compromise occurs when an adversary can deterministically decide whether the link exists or not. A partial compromise occurs when there is a significant change between an adversary's prior and posterior confidence about the existence of the link. Clearly, the exact disclosure is a special case of partial disclosure. Due to the sensitivity of linkage information, the exact disclosure notion may not always suffice - For example, if a LinkedIn user's company has a significant change of belief on her friendship with a competing company, the implications of such information disclosure may be profoundly adverse to the user.

2.3 Problem Statement

To suppress access to the sensitive linkage information, an online social network service may have to restrict the information disclosed by an individual user. Nonetheless, limitations on individual users' data publishing process lead to reduction of service quality for bona fide users. For example, Linkedin in *Example 1* has been criticized for limiting the display of the number of a user's connections to an approximate range (e.g., 500+). Thus, the design of data publishing techniques for individual users should suppress access to sensitive information while maintaining the service quality for other bona fide users.

Problem Statement: *The objective of an adversary is to discovery sensitive linkage information from data published by users through the web interface of an online social network service. The objective of privacy-preserving distributed data publishing in an online social network service is to (i) suppress access to sensitive linkage information through the web interface, and (ii) minimize the information loss for the data published by individual users.*

3 Discovering and Suppressing Linkage From Published Data

The main objective of many online social network services is to provide a platform for users to reveal their activities (e.g., flickr.com), thoughts (e.g., blogger.com), or even day-to-day life (e.g., twitter.com). Many users tend to publish aggregate information about their social circles within the network. For example, LinkedIn provides tools for a user to publish the histogram of location and profession for 1, 2, and 3-degree friends. Such aggregate information is usually computed from a broad base of users (usually > 10,000), thus seemingly could not reveal any information about the individual linkage.

Nonetheless, our studies find a simple yet effective attacking strategy, which enable the adversary to infer secret linkage information from broad aggregates. In this section, we first demonstrate the feasibility of such an attack, and then suggest several techniques to counteract it.

3.1 Attack of Linkage Privacy

Consider a social network topology as Figure 1, we follow the default settings in Linkedin, where a user's view consists of its 1 and 2-degree friends. Thus, the view of the adversary is {F1, F2, A, B, C, D}. The adversary knows all neighbors of F1 and F2 but no linkage information for A, B, C, and D. Each node publishes

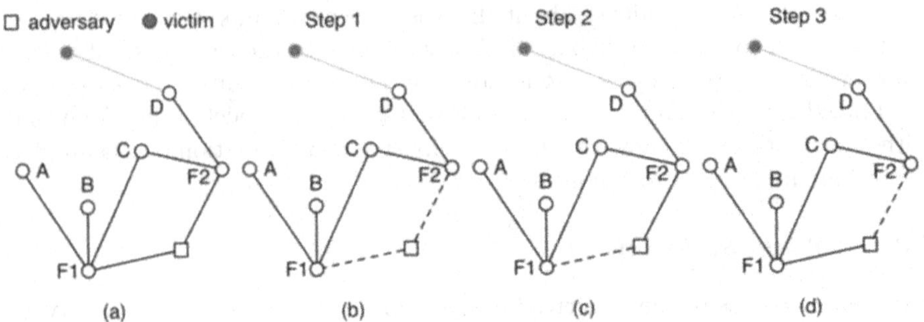

Fig. 1. An Example of Linkage Discovery in a Social Network

the histogram of location and profession of its 1,2, and 3-degree neighbors. The objective of the adversary is to identify the neighbor(s) of the victim node.

Step 1: Consider the first step where an adversary intends to learn whether it is within the victim node's 3-degree friend network. A simple strategy for the adversary is to remove its connections with F1 and F2, and then observe the change of the aggregates published by the victim. Clearly, if the adversarial activities are the only changes made to the social network, then the adversary can infer that it is within the 3-degree network of the victim iff the aggregates published by the victim change.

In practice, however, the aggregates are not updated in real time when the adversary makes the changes. Instead, between consecutive updates of the aggregates (e.g., once a day), many other changes might have been made to the victim's 3-degree network, making the aggregates change regardless of whether the adversary is within its network. In this case, the adversary can still infer whether it belongs to the victim's network by repeatedly performing the *change-and-observe* strategy. Clearly, it cannot repeatedly connect or disconnect with F1/F2, as it may raise suspicion from the neighbors. Nonetheless, the adversary has an alternative strategy for changing its published information, such as location and profession, which may be included in the computation of aggregates by the victim node.

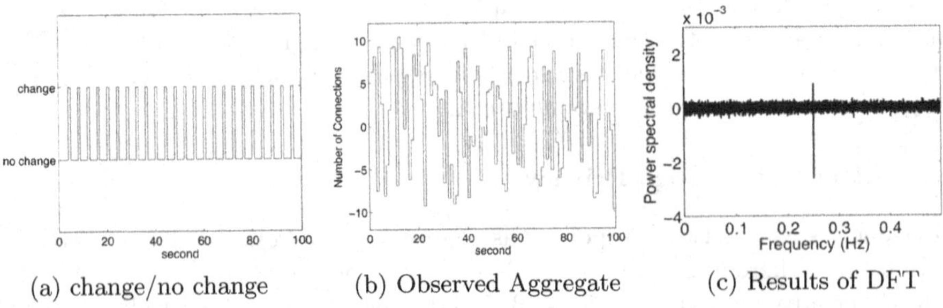

(a) change/no change (b) Observed Aggregate (c) Results of DFT

Fig. 2. An example of repeated change-and-observe attack

In particular, the adversary can randomly construct a Boolean sequence (pattern) of change/no-change operations, and follow this sequence on manipulating its published data (e.g., change on the first day, no change on the second, etc). If the adversary is within the victim node's network, it should be able to match the aggregates published by the victim with the pattern embedded in the adversary's published data, even when the aggregates also reflects changes made by many other users. One can see that the effectiveness of this technique depends on the design of the Boolean pattern. Figure 2 depicts a simple example of such pattern which can be easily identified by discrete Fourier transformation (DFT). In our preliminary work [11], we investigated the design of a class of Boolean patterns that offer a variety of features, including short detection time and invisibility from the victim.

Step 2: As we can see from the example, after the first step, the adversary learns that it is within the 3-degree network of the victim. Recall that the adversary has a list of all of its 1 and 2-degree neighbors. Since the victim is not on the list, at least one of the 2-degree neighbors of the adversary must be directly linked to the victim. In Step 2-3, the adversary aims to compromise such linkage information. In particular, in Step 2, the adversary disconnects with F1, and then uses the repeated change-and-observe attack to determine whether it is still within the 3-degree network of the victim. One can see from Figure 1(c) that if the adversary is still in the victim's network, then the victim must be connected with C or D or both. The reason is that otherwise the victim would have to be connected with A or B, but neither case would make it possible for the adversary to be included in the victim's network.

Step 3: Finally, the adversary reconnects to F1 but disconnects itself from the F2, and then launches the repeated change-and-observe attack to determine whether it is still in the 3-degree network of the victim. One can see from Figure 1(d) that this time the adversary would be excluded from the victim's network. The adversary can then infer that A, B, or C is not directly linked to the victim, because otherwise the adversary would remain in the network. Summarizing the results from Steps 1-3, the adversary can infer that the victim is linked to D, but not to A, B, or C.

We would like to note that, in this example, Steps 1 and 3 are enough to derive the linkage information of the victim node. The only operations required for the adversary is to repeatedly change its location and/or occupation information, and disconnect from F2 at the beginning of Step 3. We include Step 2 in the above discussion nonetheless to demonstrate what linkage information can be inferred from the fact that the adversary remains in the victim's 3-degree network after disconnecting a link.

One can see from the above example that, with our novel repeated change-and-observe attacking scheme, an adversary can infer certain secret linkage information from the published aggregate data. More generally, the repeated change-and-observe attack can be modeled in an information-theoretic manner as data transmission through a noisy communication channel - i.e., the attack can be modeled as the embedding of a binary sequence (pattern) in data provided by the source (adversary) node, and the identification of it in aggregates published by the destination (victim) node, which integrate the data provided by not only the source node but also other nodes in the destination's 3-degree network. If we consider such data integration as a noisy communication channel with the data provided by other nodes in the 3-degree network as noise, then the repeated change-and-observe attack can be considered as the transmission of the binary sequence through such a channel. Clearly, the adversary aims to maximum the channel capacity, so that the minimum number of changes is required on its data, while the victim intends to minimize the channel capacity to prevent an adversary from matching the sequence in the published aggregates. A more comprehensive investigation for the exact inference as well as the analysis of linkage information from a wide variety of published aggregates will be conducted as our on-going study.

3.2 Suppression of Linkage Information

There are two possible methods to suppress sensitive linkage information while allowing the publishing of aggregate information. One is to prevent an adversary from properly identifying the embedded Boolean pattern from the published aggregates. This can be done by the social network service provider or the victim node through limiting the channel capacity. The other method is to detect the repeated change-and-observe attacks, so that an adversary can be prevented from launching them due to fear of being detected.

Manipulation of published aggregate information: A simple method to suppress access to the linkage information is to increase the number of nodes involved in the computation of published aggregates. For example, if the 4-degree network is used, then the adversary needs more changes in order to accurately identify the embedded Boolean pattern. With the information-theoretic model, this method can be understood as increasing the noise in the communication channel, in order to reduce the channel capacity. Similarly, the victim node can also hide the linkage information by directly adding random noise to the published aggregates. The victim node can even manipulate the inserted noise to intentionally mislead the adversary. Another possible method to hide the linkage information is to reduce the frequency of updating the published aggregates such that more changes on the other involved nodes would be reflected in the aggregates, increasing the number of changes required by the adversary.

However, it is also important to note that all these strategies would reduce the utility of the published aggregates, and may affect a user's satisfaction with the social network service. In particular, if a victim node is allowed to manually insert noise into its published aggregates, the integrity of such published information may also a concern for other social network users. For example, the COUNT of neighbors, which is usually a published aggregate, is often used by social network users to determine the trustworthiness of another user. Allowing a user to arbitrarily change such COUNT may degrade the overall usefulness of the social network service. Thus, the tradeoff between the protection of linkage and the utility of published aggregates must be carefully analyzed.

Detection of repeated change-and-observe attacks: This method focuses on the detection of repeated change-and-observe attacks. A simple strategy is to prohibit a user from making frequent changes to the published personal information such as location and profession. Nonetheless, this strategy faces several challenges: First, it affects the usability of the online social network service, as certain published information, such as "favorite song" or "current activity" (as in twitter.com), does require frequent updates from users. Second, this strategy might not be effective against coordinated attacks from colluding adversaries, as the number of changes required for each adversary can be quite low.

Another possible strategy for attack detection is to identify the specific channel coding used by the adversary. However, this method also faces difficulties as certain coding schemes, such as PN code, offers an "invisible" feature which makes it very difficult to be detected without knowledge of the actual (randomly generated) pattern. To address this challenge, we suggest the investigation of detection mechanisms that exploit a specific feature of social networks: the similarity between the activities of a user and its neighbors. Following this principle, our ongoing studies involve anomaly detection techniques in the specialized detection of channel coding schemes.

4 Conclusion

In this paper, we define the novel problem of discovering and protecting sensitive linkage information from data published in online social network services through their public interface. This stands in contrast to most existing work which focuses on protecting the identity of nodes while publishing a snapshot of the social network topology. We demonstrate the feasibility of discovering sensitive linkage information and giving insights into the protection of such sensitive linkage information. As future work, we plan to develop, implement, and deploy a set of linkage discovery and protection tools over a testbed integrated with data from real-world online social network services, in order to evaluate the performance of privacy protection techniques in real-world scenarios.

References

1. Classmates Online, Inc.: (2009), http://www.classmates.com/
2. LinkedIn.: Relationships matter - linkedin (2009), http://www.linkedin.com/
3. Facebook.: Welcome to facebook! – facebook (2009), http://www.facebook.com/
4. Passportstamp Limited (2009), http://www.passportstamp.com/
5. SciSpace.net: Social networking for collaboration (2009), http://www.scispace.net/
6. Nye, D.: Dan nye - linkedin (2009), http://www.linkedin.com/in/danielnye
7. Hay, M., Miklau, G., Jensen, D., Towsley, D.F., Weis, P.: Resisting structural re-identification in anonymized social networks. In: VLDB (2008)

8. Zhou, B., Pei, J.: Preserving privacy in social networks against neighborhood attacks. In: ICDE (2008)
9. Korolova, A., Motwani, R., Nabar, S.U., Xu, Y.: Link privacy in social networks. In: CIKM (2008)
10. Nabar, S., Marthi, B., Kenthapadi, K., Mishra, N., Motwani, R.: Towards robustness in query auditing. In: VLDB (2006)
11. Yu, W., Zhang, N., Fu, X., Bettati, R., Zhao, W.: On localization attacks to internet threat monitors: An information-theoretic framework. In: the 38th IEEE/IFIP International Conference on Dependable Systems and Networks (DSN) (2008)

Social-Stratification Probabilistic Routing Algorithm in Delay-Tolerant Network*

Fuad Alnajjar and Tarek Saadawi

The City College of The City University of New York,
Electrical Engineering Department,
138th St. and Convent Ave, NY, NY - 10031
fuad@ccny.cuny.edu,
saadawi@ccny.cuny.edu
http://www-ee.ccny.cuny.edu

Abstract. Routing in mobile ad hoc networks (MANET) is complicated due to the fact that the network graph is episodically connected. In MANET, topology is changing rapidly because of weather, terrain and jamming. A key challenge is to create a mechanism that can provide good delivery performance and low end-to-end delay in an intermittent network graph where nodes may move freely. Delay-Tolerant Networking (DTN) architecture is designed to provide communication in intermittently connected networks, by moving messages towards destination via "store, carry and forward" technique that supports multi-routing algorithms to acquire best path towards destination. In this paper, we propose the use of probabilistic routing in DTN architecture using the concept of social-stratification network. We use the Opportunistic Network Environment (ONE) simulator as a simulation tool to compare the proposed Social- stratification Probabilistic Routing Algorithm (SPRA) with the common DTN-based protocols. Our results show that SPRA outperforms the other protocols.

Keywords: DTN, MANET, Probabilistic routing protocol, Social network.

1 Introduction

1.1 Delay-Tolerant Network (DTN)

Delay Tolerant Networking (DTN) is an end-to-end network architecture designed to provide communication in and/or through highly stressed networking environments. Stressed networking environments include those with intermittent

* This work is based on research sponsored by the Air Force Research Laboratory under agreement FA8750-09-1-0158. The US Government is authorized to reproduce and distribute reprints for Governmental purposes notwithstanding any copyright notation thereon.

B. Liu et al. (Eds.): WASA 2009, LNCS 5682, pp. 579–591, 2009.

connectivity, large and/or variable delays, and high bit error rates. The DTN Research Group (DTNRG) leads the field in DTN research. Members of the DT-NRG created the Bundle Protocol (BP) to implement the DTN architecture. The key capabilities of the bundle protocols include custody-based reliability, ability to cope with intermittent connectivity, ability to take advantage of scheduled and opportunistic connectivity, and late binding of names to addresses [1], [2] and [3]. As an effort to standardize communications for the Interplanetary Internet (IPN), the Delay-Tolerant Networking architecture and protocols were proposed. ('DTN architecture and protocols were proposed as an effort to standardize communications for the IPN'). As work progressed, researchers observed that military networks running tactical protocols, and remote networks where network resources are scarce and data mules might be used to transport data. These networks all had similarities in that they experienced several of these features: asymmetric communication, noisy links, long delays, and intermittent connectivity. As a result, the network community is developing a body of research for which funding has been established by both NASA and DARPA.

The network architecture and protocol design process involves analysis and implementation of the protocols, validation of their behaviors and performance evaluation [8], [9]. A Mobile Ad hoc Network (MANET) is a dynamic wireless network with or without fixed infrastructure. Nodes may move freely and arrange themselves randomly. The contacts between nodes in the network do not occur very frequently. As a result, the network graph is rarely, if ever, connected and message delivery must be delay-tolerant.

Traditional MANET routing protocols such as DSR, AODV and OLSR requires that the network graph is fully connected and fail to route messages if there is not a complete route from source to destination at the time of sending. For this reason traditional ad hoc routing protocols cannot be used in environments with intermittent connectivity [3]. To defeat this issue, node mobility is exploited to physically carry messages between disconnected parts of the network. Schemes like these designs are occasionally referred to as Mobility Assisted Routing (MAR) that employs the store, carry and-forward model.

Mobility-assisted routing comprises each node separately making forwarding decisions that occur when two nodes meet. A message gets forwarded to encountered nodes until it reaches its destination. Messages may have to be buffered for a long time by intermediate nodes, and the mobility of those nodes must be utilized to bring messages closer to their destination by exchanging messages between nodes as they encounter [4].

Fig. 1 shows how the mobility of nodes in such circumstances can be employed to ultimately deliver a message to its destination. In this figure, node A has a message (indicated by the node being sky blue) to be delivered to node F, but a path does not exist between nodes A and F. As shown in Fig. 1, the mobility of the nodes let the message be transferred to node B Fig. 1(b), then to node E Fig. 1(c), and finally, when node E moves within range of node F to node F which is its final destination [6],[14].

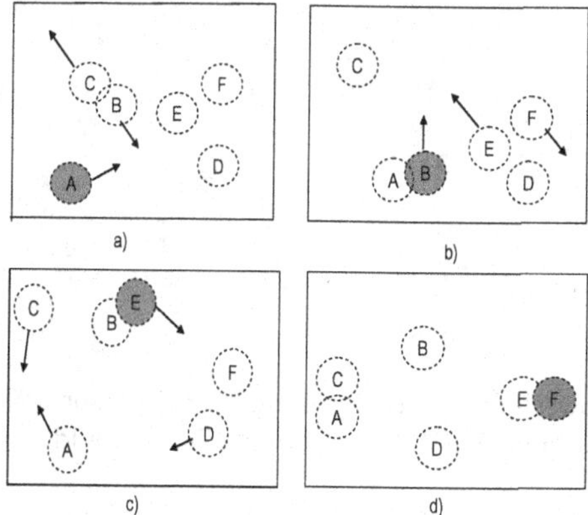

Fig. 1. A message (shown in the figure by the node carrying the message being sky blue) is moved from node A to node F via nodes B and E utilizing the mobility of nodes [6]

1.2 Social Networks

A social network is a social structure formed of nodes that are connected by one or more specific types of interdependency. The nodes in the social network are the people and groups while the links show relationships or flows between the nodes. The notion of social structure in the society is grouped into structurally related groups or sets of roles, with different functions, meanings or purposes [10]. Social stratification in the social structure refers to the idea that society is separated into different levels according to social characteristics such as a race, class, language, gender and religion. Social network analysis presents both a visual and mathematical analysis of human relationship. One example of social structure is the "online social network" which refers to social network websites such as Facebook [11], hi5 [12] and Twitter [13]. When you sign up with any of those social network websites, you will be able to meet new friends, reconnect with people you already know, build up relationships over time, learn from others and share what you know. Furthermore, you can find friends in your hometown or other parts of the world even though there is no prior knowledge of their locations.

Fig. 2 demonstrates the mechanism of how is the online social network works and the mechanism of adding new friends.

In Fig. 2 (a), person A joined a social network and its list of friends is empty. Person A checks the group and sends an invitation to B to become a friend and B accepts the invitation Now, A becomes a member of B's group that contains friends C,D, and E. Now, A is able to contact C, D and E independently as shown in figure 2.b in purple. This process gets repeated until A build up its group that contains B, C, D and E and their subgroups. Fig. 2 (b) shows A and its subgroup (new friends) in purple color.

In online social networks, when you add a highly-social person to your list, it will make the process quick to add and find friends in your hometown or other parts of the world without prior knowledge of their locations. So, we could

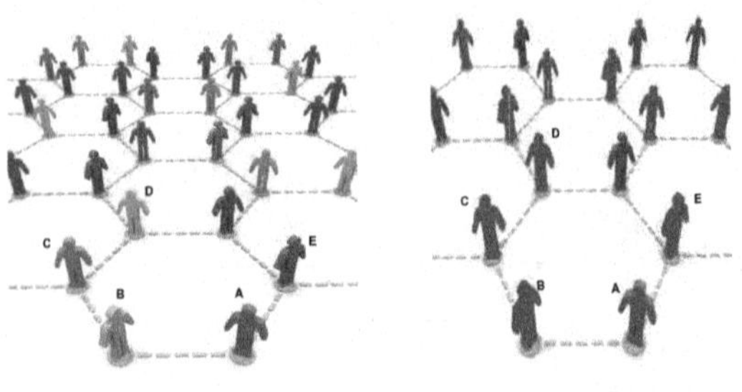

Fig. 2. (a) and (b) show the process of joining a new person (A) to the online social network and becomes a member of B's group and how to add new friends

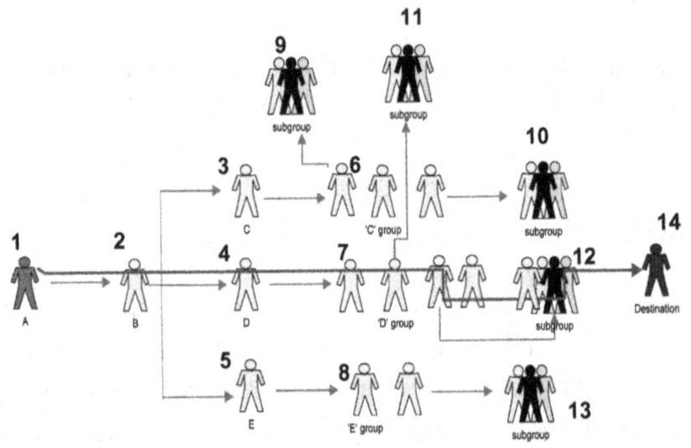

Fig. 3. This figure demonstrates the process of reaching a destination through high socially connected persons

classify people in online social networks based on their social connectivity. This social connectivity called social stratification of each person.

Fig. 3 demonstrate the process of reaching a destination through high socially connected persons. If A wants to send a message to a person to whom no connection is available, the probability to go through D is higher than E since D knows 4 persons whereas E knows only 2 persons.

Table 1 shows that the path through D has a message delivery probability higher than C or E.

Table 1. Mathematical calculation of figure 3 to compute the probabilities to reach destination from A through 3 different paths. The number of possible ways to arrive at the destination is 30.

n=14 The number of subgroup

Path 1 $\Rightarrow$ 1, 2, 3, 6, 10, 14, $\Rightarrow$ through C (3 contacts)
Path 2 $\Rightarrow$ 1, 2, 4, 7, 12, 14, $\Rightarrow$ through D (4 contacts)
Path 3 $\Rightarrow$ 1, 2, 5, 8, 13, 14, $\Rightarrow$ through E (2 contacts)
Path 1 $\Rightarrow$ Probability = 0.2381
Path 2 $\Rightarrow$ Probability = 0.3214
Path 3 $\Rightarrow$ Probability = 0.2143

In this paper we discuss the routing in networks associated with intermittent connection. We present our probabilistic routing algorithm by utilizing the concept of Social-stratification to deliver messages to their destinations. We demonstrate two common DTN based routing protocols, Epidemic and PROPHET routing protocols [5],[6] comparing them to our results. We have used in our simulation the Opportunistic Network Environment simulator ONE-V1.0 [7] This paper is organized as follows: Section 2 describes some related work, Section 3, shows our proposed model. Section 4 shows the simulation setup. Section 5 summarizes the results of the simulations, Section 6 discusses future work and Section 7 our conclusion.

2 Related Work

DTN overcome the problems associated with intermittent connectivity, long or variable delay by using 'store, carry and forward' message switching.[4],[15] Existing DTN-based- Routing protocols are classified by routing protocols that replicate packets and those that forward only a single copy [9]. By moving entire messages (or fragments thereof) in a single transfer, the message-switching procedure provides the nodes in the network with immediate knowledge of the size of messages, and therefore the requirements for intermediate storage space and retransmission bandwidth [3], [4]. In this paper we select two common DTN-based protocols Epidemic Routing protocol and PROPHET routing protocol. We compared our new approach to Epidemic and PROPHET to demonstrate the ability to accomplish good quality performance.

2.1 Epidemic Routing

Vahdat and Becker [5] present a routing protocol for networks associated with intermittent connectivity called Epidemic Routing protocol. Epidemic utilized the theory of epidemic algorithm to ultimately deliver messages to their destination when nodes encounter each other by doing random pair-wise information of messages between the encountered nodes. If bath to destination is not accessible, the node will buffer the messages in index called summary vector. Each node maintains a buffer consisting of messages that it has originated in addition to messages that it is buffering on behalf of other hosts. Once two nodes meet they exchange the summary vectors. If the node finds any unseen messages, it requests them from the encountered node. This mechanism of swapping new messages continues as long as buffer space is available, and messages will spread similar to an epidemic of some diseases inside the network whenever infected node meets susceptible node, a copy is forwarded (flooding), see figure 4. In order to avoid duplicate messages during the exchange process each message has a globally unique message ID. Each message contains source and destination addresses. Also, to lower the utilization of nodes resources, each message has a hop counter to determine the maximum number of hops a message can travel to. Epidemic depends on two factors; buffer size and maximum hop count that those items control the performance of the scheme.

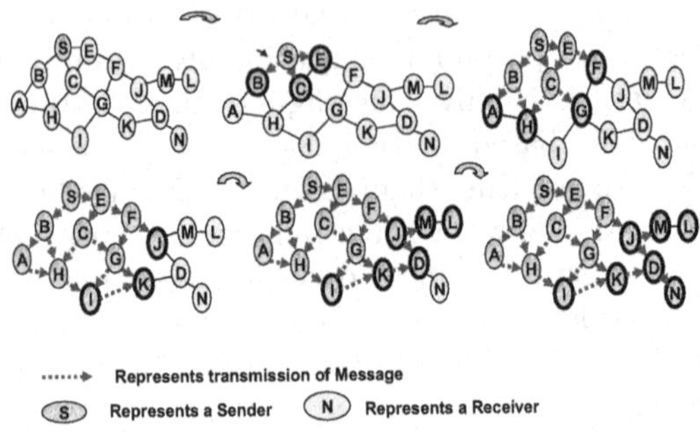

Fig. 4. Epidemic Routing Protocol: Epidemic uses flooding to transfer messages to destination [5]

2.2 PRoPHET Routing

Anders Lindgren and et al [6] present a Probabilistic routing algorithm called PROPHET. It stands for Probabilistic ROuting Protocol using History of Encounters and Transitivity. Authors established a probabilistic metric called delivery predictability at every node a for each known destination b.

$$P_{(a,b)} \in [0, 1] \tag{1}$$

The procedure of PROPHET is like the Epidemic Routing, in which, two nodes exchange summary vectors when they meet. In addition to that, in PROPHET, it contains the delivery predictability information stored at the nodes. This information is used to update the internal delivery predictability vector and then the information in the summary vector is used to decide which messages to request from the other node. The forwarding strategy depends on the delivery predictability of the encountered nodes. If node a meets node b, a carried message destined for node m will be transferred from a to b only if

$$P_{(b,m)} < P_{(a,m)} \tag{2}$$

PROPHET algorithm relies on calculation of delivery predictability to forward messages to the reliable node. The probability is used to decide if one node is more reliable than the other to forward message to the destination node. It includes three parts about the probability. First is to update the probability metric whenever a node is encountered, the node that is frequently encountered having higher delivery predictability than others. Second, if a pair of nodes do not encounter each others during an interval, they are less likely to be good forwarders of messages to each other, thus the delivery predictability values must be reduced. Third, there is a transitive property in delivery predictability. Based on the observation, if node a frequently encounters node b, and node b frequently encounters node c, then node c probably is a good node to forward messages destined for node a.

3 Proposed Work

Delay tolerant networks have been proposed to address data intermittent communication challenges in networks where an instantaneous end-to-end path between a source and destination may not exist, and the links between nodes may be opportunistic, predictably connectable, or periodically-(dis)connected [9].

In this research proposal, we focus on the Delay-Tolerant Mobile Ad Hoc Network to design a probabilistic routing protocol applicable to work in this intermittently connected environment to improve the end-to-end message delivery ratio in a multihop scenario where link availability can be low. We have designed our algorithm to 1) maximize message delivery rate, 2) minimize the total resources consumed in message delivery, 3) minimize the number of hops used in routing and 4) minimize message latency.

In the environment of periodically disconnected, nodes get only episodically connected because of terrain, weather, and jamming that change topology rapidly. As explained in Section 2.1, Epidemic routing protocol solves this issue by epidemically spreading the information through the network and PROPHET routing protocol solves it by applying some knowledge of the mobility of nodes to forward messages based on probabilistic factors [5], [6].

Our improved routing algorithm will overcome the problem of periodically-disconnected network by applying the factor of social stratification of each node for forwarding strategy. We employed the concept of social stratification that used in social network (explained in Section 2.2) to forward messages to encountered nodes. Messages will be transferred towards destination via 'store, carry and forward' technique that is used in DTN based routing protocols. Our new approach is called Social-stratification Probabilistic Routing Algorithm (SPRA).

The operation of SPRA relies on the knowledge of the mobility of nodes to forward messages based on social-stratification probabilistic procedure. We determine the social stratification probabilistic factor of any node based on how many nodes did this node encounter until the moment of meeting a new node. If node a meets node b and the social stratification probabilistic factor of node a is greater than node b, so it means that node a encountered more nodes than node b until the encountering time. In this case, nodes a will not forward any messages to node b. SPRA uses the history of encountered nodes to predict its future suitability to deliver messages to next node toward destination. When two nodes meet, they update the summary vector. Then, they exchange summary vectors which in this case also contains the list of encountered nodes stored at the nodes. This information in the summary vector is used to decide which messages to request from the other node based on the social stratification factor used in the forwarding strategy.

In our approach we applied the concept of social-stratification in social network. When a person called x joins an online social network such as Facebook, hi5, etc... x has the option to join any groups of people or add new friends if we overlook the cases that require a conditional approval for acceptance [10], [11], [12], [13].

If x wants to meet new friends, reconnect with people already known, builds up relationships over time, learns from others and shares what it knows. If x does not know how to start the first step to socialize, it should contact highly social individuals to make the research effortless. Furthermore, individuals with high level of social connections can find friends in x's hometown or other parts of the world even though there is no prior knowledge of their locations.

Our forwarding strategy depends on the social-stratification of nodes in the network. We create a metric called social stratification at every node. This indicates how highly social the node is, which is the number of nodes encountered till that moment. The calculation of messages delivery depends on the social stratification metric. When two nodes meet, the first thing to do is to update the metric (increase the metric by one), then they swap the number of encountered nodes till moment of meeting so that nodes that are often encountered more nodes have a high delivery Probability. Encountered nodes exchange only the number of earlier contacts without any details of those nodes. If they met the same number of nodes in the past they exchange new messages and if one of them encountered more nodes than the other in the past, only the node with low number of earlier contacts will deliver the new messages to the node with high earlier contacts. When a message arrives at a node, there might not be a path to the destination available so the node has to buffer the message. Upon each encounter with another node, a decision must be made on whether or not to transfer that particular message.

Our Mathematical model is based on the probability of an event equals the ratio of its favorable outcomes to the total number of outcomes provided that all outcomes are equally likely. According to the classical definition, the probability P(A) of an event A is determined a priori without actual experimentation: It is given by the ratio

$$P(A) = \frac{N(A)}{N} \quad (3)$$

where N is the number of possible outcomes and NA is the number of outcomes that are favorable to the event A. In SPRA, when node a ,encountered 8 nodes carries messages to deliver to final destinations, meets node b ,encountered 5 nodes, node a will not forward any messages to node b since

$$P(a) = \frac{N_a}{N} > P(b) = \frac{N_b}{N} \quad (4)$$

We will forward messages from a node to another only if the probability of the encountered node is greater than the node that carried messages.

The flow chart in Fig. 5 demonstrates the mechanism of how SPRA is working to deliver messages towards final destination. When node i meets node j they update the summary vector. Then, they exchange the summary vector. Each node will check the social stratification metric of each other. If the social stratification metric of node i is less than node j, node i will transfer any unseen messages to j but not vice versa. Node i will deliver messages to destinations if path to destination available, otherwise, it will store the messages in the buffer and continue mobility till encountering new node. Employing the concept of

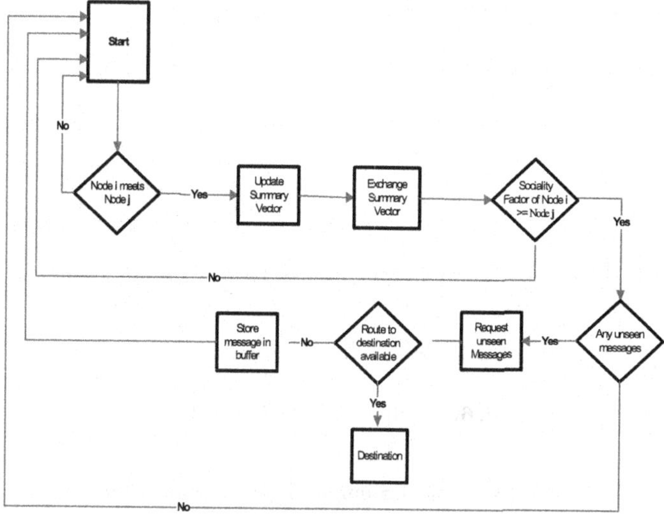

Fig. 5. This diagram shows how the mechanism of message delivery is working in SPRA algorithm

social-stratification factor increases the probability of delivering messages to intermediate nodes and destinations since the probability of delivering messages by highly social-connected nodes is higher than lower social connected nodes.

SPRA utilizes information about the earlier contacts to predict how good nominee a node is to deliver the message to the recipient. In SPRA, messages carried by the node with a higher probability, based on the social stratification condition, only are transferred. Our research results show that SPRA can deliver more messages than PROPHET and Epidemic with lower number of hops.

4 Our Model and Simulation Setup

Ari Keranen and Jorg Ott [7] presented the Opportunistic Network Environment simulator (ONE-V1.0) which provides a powerful tool for generating mobility traces, running DTN messaging simulations with different routing protocols, and visualizing simulations interactively in real-time and results after their completion. We used ONE-V1.0 in our simulation. Figure 6 shows a screenshot of ONE simulator.

For our simulation, we used the simulation setup that used in [7]. Table 2 shows the parameters used in our simulation. We ran our simulation with numbers of nodes starting with 20 nodes till 600 nodes in area of 4500 x 3400 m. We use several different types of speeds of 1.5 m/s (Pedestrians), 15 m/s (cars), 10 m/s (trams). We assume buffer size of 5 Mbyte for each node.

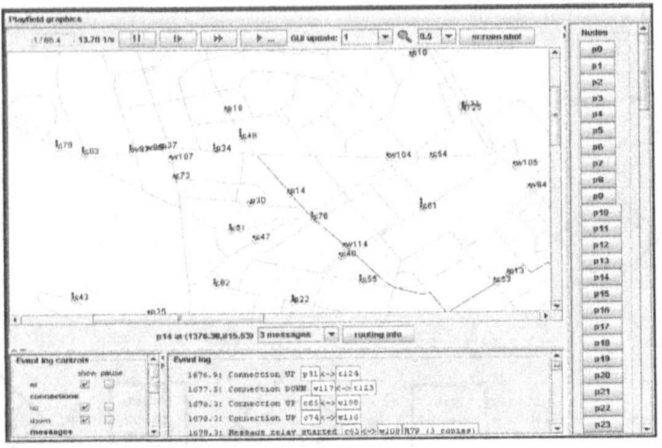

Fig. 6. Simulator ONE Screenshot

Table 2. Critical Simulation setup parameter

Simulation Parameters	Value
Simulation Area (WxH) meter	4500x3400
Simulation duration (hr)	12
Number of nodes	20,35,110,125,215,300,600
Movement Model	Shortest Path Map Based Movement
Message TTL (Minutes)	60
Host speed (m/s)	1.5 -15
Buffer size (Mbyte)	5

5 Results

The results presented in Fig. 7 and Fig. 8 are an average of 10 runs of each scenario by changing number of nodes and buffer size. The buffer size was set to 5 Mbyte in Fig. 7

It is immediately evident from the results given in Fig. 7 (a) that our algorithm, SPRA, outperforms Epidemic and PROPHET in terms of message delivery with increasing number of nodes. This is because SPRA forward messages to highly connected nodes that meet nodes continually that guaranteed the message delivery. Fig. 7 (b) shows that the overhead ratio of SPRA is lower than the other algorithms with increasing number of nodes. Epidemic sends the messages to all nodes that make the overhead ratio number high. Fig. 7 (c) shows that SPRA use less average number of hopcounts to reach destination than Epidemic and PROPHET. SPRA send messages to only highly connected nodes that will reduce the average hopcount number. Fig. 7 (d) shows that Epidemic performs better than SPRA and PROPHET in terms of latency with increasing number of nodes. But SPRA performs similar to Epidemic with middle size network. This is normal in SPRA case since it gives messages to only highly connected nodes which increase the latency. Fig. 7 (e) shows that PROPHET buffers messages

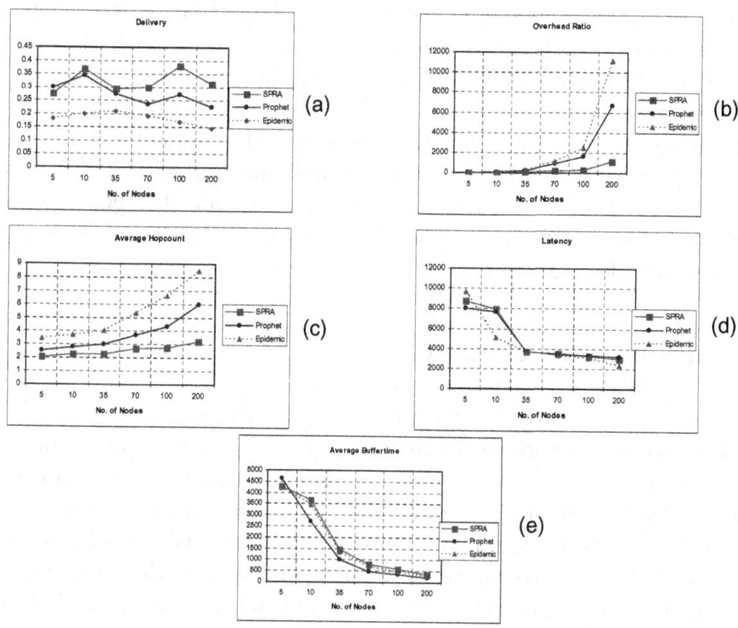

Fig. 7. Results with respect to number of nodes

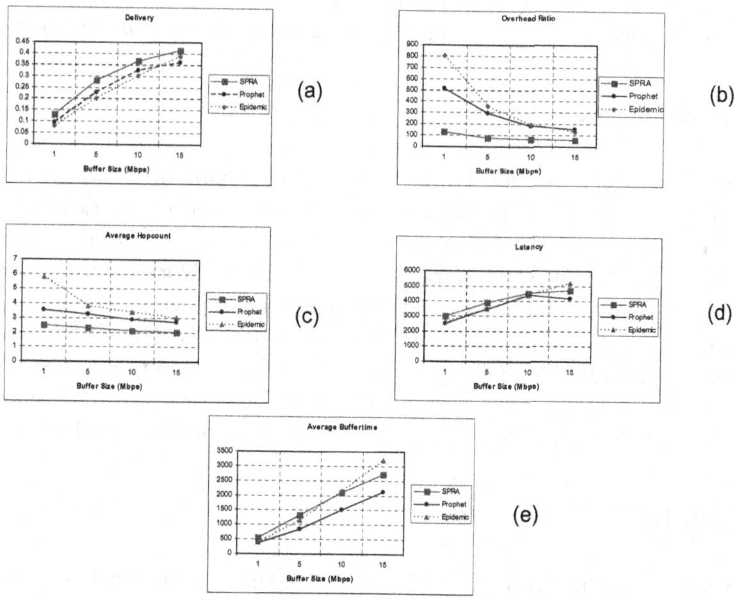

Fig. 8. Results with respect to buffer size

in time less than the others. The last result explains that SPRA needs time to buffer messages since it forward messages to only certain nodes that are highly socially connected and sorting required time for this process.

Fig. 8 show results after we fixed the number of nodes to 40 nodes and changed buffer size from 1 Mbyte to 15 Mbyte. The obtained results are similar to the results obtained in Fig. 7. SPRA outperforms Epidemic and PROPHET in terms of delivery probability, overhead ratio and average number of hopcounts. Whereas Epidemic performs better in terms of latency and PROPHET presents better performance in buffer time.

6 Discussion and Conclusions

In this paper, we have presented our recent results of the novel DTN-based probabilistic routing approach to achieve reliable communication in networks associated with intermittent connectivity. The challenge was to find a routing algorithm that can deal with dynamic environment causing networks to split and merge, considering nodes mobility. The new approach utilizes a DTN technique with the concept of the social network to facilitate smooth information transfer between the heterogeneous nodes in Mobile Ad Hoc Network. We designed our approach using a novel Social-stratification Probabilistic Routing Algorithm: SPRA. Simulation results show that SPRA achieved better performance than other common DTN based protocols in terms of delivery rate, overhead ratio and average number of hopcounts over intermittent network. Also, SPRA performance was consistent with changing number of nodes and nodes' buffer sizes.

7 Future Work

We intend to continue on developing the proposed algorithm and provide a detailed analytical as well as simulation-based study. Our future work will complete the research to achieve the followings: 1) implement DTN based routing algorithms such as SPRA in Aerial/terrestrial Airborne Network environment. 2) we will study and analyze the impact of the physical layer parameters on the performance of the DTN-based probabilistic routing protocols such as SPRA, epidemic, etc. 3) we will design a cross-layer frame assists information exchanges between different network layers, expedites upper layers' response to quick changes of physical links and outside environment, and helps to optimize link selections.

8 Disclaimer

The views and conclusions contained herein are those of the authors and should not be interpreted as necessarily representing the official policies or endorsement, either expressed or implied, of the Air Force Research Laboratory or the US Government.

References

1. Seguí, J., Jennings, E.: Delay Tolerant Networking - Bundle Protocol Simulation
2. DTNRG website, `http://www.dtnrg.org`
3. Ott, J., Kutscher, D., Dwertmann, C.: Integrating DTN and MANET Routing. In: SIGCOMM 2006 Workshops, Pisa, Italy, September 11-15 (2006)
4. Chuah, M.-C., Yang, P., Davison, B.D., Cheng, L.: Store-and-Forward Performance in a DTN. In: IEEE 63rd Vehicular Technology Conference, 2006. VTC 2006-Spring (2006)
5. Vahdat, A., Becker, D.: Epidemic routing for partially connected ad hoc networks. Technical Report CS-200006, Duke University (April 2000)
6. Lindgren, A., Doria, A., Schelen, O.: Poster: Probabilistic routing in intermittently connected networks. In: Proceedings of The Fourth ACM International Symposium on Mobile Ad Hoc Networking and Computing (MobiHoc 2003) (June 2003)
7. Keranen, A., Ott, J.: Increasing Reality for DTN Protocol Simulations. Technical Report, Helsinki University of Technology, Networking Laboratory (July 2007)
8. Fall, K.: A Delay-Tolerant Network Architecture for Challenged Internets. Intel Research, Berkeley, February 26 (2003)
9. Balasubramanian, A., Neil Levine, B., Venkataramani, A.: DTN Routing as a Resource Allocation Problem. In: SIGCOMM 2007, Kyoto, Japan, August 27-31 (2007)
10. Howard, B.: Analyzing Online Social Networks. Communications of the ACM 51(11) (November 2008)
11. Facebook website, `http://www.facebook.com`
12. Hi5 website, `http://www.hi5.com`
13. Twitter website, `http://www.twitter.com`
14. Leguay, J., Friedman, T., Conan, V.: DTN Routing in a Mobility Pattern Space. In: SIGCOMM 2005 Workshops, Philadelphia, PA, USA, August 22-26 (2005)
15. Li, Q., Rus, D.: Communication in disconnected ad-hoc networks using message relay. Journal of Parallel and Distributed Computing (2003)

Author Index